Intimate Relationships, Marriages, and Families

Intimate Relationships, Marriages, and Families

NINTH EDITION

NICK STINNETT

NANCY STINNETT

MARY KAY DEGENOVA

F. PHILIP RICE

New York   Oxford

Oxford University Press

Oxford University Press is a department of the University of Oxford. It furthers the University's objective of excellence in research, scholarship, and education by publishing worldwide. Oxford is a registered trade mark of Oxford University Press in the UK and certain other countries.

Published in the United States of America by Oxford University Press
198 Madison Avenue, New York, NY 10016, United States of America.

Library of Congress Cataloging-in-Publication Data

Names: Rice, F. Philip, author. | Stinnett, Nick, author. | Stinnett, Nancy
    M., author. | DeGenova, Mary Kay, author.
Title: Intimate relationships, marriages & families.
Other titles: Intimate relationships, marriages, and families
Description: Ninth edition / Nick Stinnett, Nancy Stinnett, Mary Kay
    DeGenova, F. Philip Rice. | New York : Oxford University Press, [2017] |
    Includes bibliographical references and index.
Identifiers: LCCN 2016011465 | ISBN 9780190278571 (pbk.: alk. paper)
Subjects: LCSH: Family life education—United States.
Classification: LCC HQ10.5.U6 R53 2017 | DDC 372.37/4—dc23 LC record available at
https://lccn.loc.gov/2016011465

9 8 7 6 5 4 3 2 1

Printed by R.R. Donnelley, United States of America

Brief Contents

Preface   xx

About the Authors   xxv

CHAPTER 1   Intimate Relationships, Marriages, and Families in the Twenty-first Century   2

CHAPTER 2   Gender: Identity and Roles   38

CHAPTER 3   Being Single   66

CHAPTER 4   Attraction and Dating   86

CHAPTER 5   Love and Mate Selection   108

CHAPTER 6   Qualities of a Successful Marriage   144

CHAPTER 7   Marital Relationships over the Family Life Cycle   168

CHAPTER 8   Work, Family Roles, and Material Resources   194

CHAPTER 9   Power, Decision Making, and Communication   224

CHAPTER 10   Sexual Relationships   248

CHAPTER 11   Family Planning and Parenthood   284

CHAPTER 12   Pregnancy and Childbirth   316

CHAPTER 13   Parent–Child Relationships   340

CHAPTER 14   Parents and Extended Family Relationships   364

CHAPTER 15   Conflict, Family Crises, and Crisis Management   386

CHAPTER 16   The Family and Divorce   422

CHAPTER 17   Coming Together: Remarriage and Stepparenting   454

Glossary   479

References   487

Image Credits   534

Index   536

Contents

Preface   xx

About the Authors   xxv

CHAPTER 1 Intimate Relationships, Marriages, and Families in the Twenty-first Century   2

Chapter Outline   3

Learning Objectives   3

What Is a Family?   4

Some Definitions   4

Family Forms   5

   PERSONAL PERSPECTIVE: A LONG 15 INCHES   6

Changes in Family Philosophy and Emphasis   6

From Institution to Companionship   7

From Patriarchy to Democracy   8

Changes in Marriage and Parenthood   9

Marriage Rates   10

Median Age   10

Family Size   11

Working Wives and Mothers   13

One-Parent Families   14

Cohabitation   14

   AT ISSUE TODAY: CHILDREN NOT LIVING WITH MARRIED BIOLOGICAL PARENTS   16

Gay and Lesbian Families   16

Grandparents as Parents   17

Changes in Life Expectancy   18

Changes in Divorce and Remarriage   19

Divorce Rates   19

Remarriage Trends   19

Blended Families   20

Ethnic and Cultural Diversity in Families   20

Increased Ethnic Diversity   20

Hispanic Americans   21

African Americans   21

   CULTURAL PERSPECTIVE: ETHNIC IDENTITY AND ACCULTURATION   22

Asian/Pacific Islander Americans   23

Native Americans   24

Theories to Help Explain Family Behavior   25

Structural-Functional Theory   25

Family Developmental Theory   27

   COPING FEATURE: THE IMPORTANCE OF COPING   28

Symbolic Interaction Theory   28

Systems Theory   29

Social Learning Theory   30

Exchange Theory   30

Conflict Theory   30

Feminist Theory   30

The International Family Strengths Model   31

Critique of Family Theories   32

The Study of Marriage, Families, and Intimate Relationships   32

   FAMILY STRENGTHS PERSPECTIVE: QUALITIES OF STRONG FAMILIES   32

   A QUESTION OF POLICY: GAY AND LESBIAN PARENTING BY ADOPTION   34

Summary   35

Key Terms   36

Questions for Thought   36

For Further Reading   37

CHAPTER 2 Gender: Identity and Roles   38

Chapter Outline   39

Learning Objectives   39

Environmental Influences on Gender 40

Societal Expectations 41

Parental Influences 41

> **AT ISSUE TODAY: WOMEN AND WEIGHT: GENDERED MESSAGES ON MAGAZINE COVERS 42**

The Influence of Popular Press, Television, and Movies 43

School Influences 44

Theories of Gender Role and Identity 44

Social Learning Theory 44

Cognitive Developmental Theory 45

Gender Schema Theory 45

Social Structure/Cultural Theories 46

Evolutionary Theories 46

Biological Theories 47

Traditional Masculine and Feminine Stereotypes 48

Masculinity 48

Femininity 48

Problems with Gender Stereotypes 49

> **PERSONAL PERSPECTIVE: LIFE ON THE BOUNDARIES OF GENDER 50**

Gender Roles and Body Image 51

> **CULTURAL PERSPECTIVE: THE WORD MACHISMO 54**

Race, Class, and Gender 54

Changing Roles of Women and Men 56

Gender Roles in the Family 56

Roles in Marriage 57

> **FAMILY STRENGTHS PERSPECTIVE: DO EVERYDAY THINGS TOGETHER 58**

Housework and Child-Care Roles 58

> **COPING FEATURE: COPING WITH DEPRESSION 59**

Gender, Marriage, and Depression 60

Androgyny 60

> **A QUESTION OF POLICY: TITLE IX 62**

Summary 63

Key Terms 64

Questions for Thought 64

For Further Reading 64

CHAPTER 3 Being Single 66

Chapter Outline 67

Learning Objectives 67

Categories of Singles 69

Voluntary Singles 70

Involuntary Singles 70

Marital Delay 70

> **CULTURAL PERSPECTIVE: AFRICAN AMERICAN SINGLE MOTHERS 71**

Why Some People Remain Single 72

Deliberate Choice 72

Fear of Marriage 72

Lack of Opportunity 72

Circumstances 72

Advantages and Disadvantages of Being Single 72

> **COPING FEATURE: AVOIDING COUNTERPRODUCTIVE STRATEGIES 73**

The Health and Well-Being of Singles 74

Living Arrangements 75

Shared Living Spaces 76

Living with Parents 76

Living Alone 76

Sexual Behavior 76

Teens 76

Adult Heterosexual Activity 77

Same-sex Activity 77

Sexual Orientation 78

Sexual Attraction 78

Selected Health Measures 78

> **AT ISSUE TODAY: FRIENDS WITH BENEFITS 78**

Employment and Income 79

Single Parents 79
Special Issues for Single-Parent Families 80

FAMILY STRENGTHS PERSPECTIVE: TIME TOGETHER: MAKING MEMORIES 81

The Never-Married Adult 82

PERSONAL PERSPECTIVE: SINGLE FATHERHOOD 83

A QUESTION OF POLICY: FUNDING FOR WHICH SEX EDUCATION PROGRAMS? 84

Summary 84

Key Terms 85

Questions for Thought 85

For Further Reading 85

CHAPTER 4 Attraction and Dating 86

Chapter Outline 87

Learning Objectives 87

Attraction 88
Physical Attractiveness 88
Standards of Attractiveness 89
Personality and Social Factors 89
Unconscious Influences 89

The Dating System 89
Courtship in Early America 90
The Emergence of Dating 90
Dating at the End of the Twentieth Century 91
Dating Today 91

Reasons for Dating 92

Finding and Meeting Dates 93
Personal Ads to Online Dating 94

CULTURAL PERSPECTIVE: ARRANGED MARRIAGES 94

Gender Roles in Dating 95

Problems in Dating 96
Honesty and Openness 96
Jealousy and Infidelity 96

FAMILY STRENGTHS PERSPECTIVE: STRENGTHS OF RUSSIAN FAMILIES 97

Getting Too Serious 97

Closeness and Distance in Relationships 97

COPING FEATURE: COPING WITH YOUR OWN JEALOUSY 98

Violence and Sexual Aggression in Dating 99
Gender Differences in Dating Violence 99
Psychological and Emotional Effects of Dating Violence 99
Date Rape 100

AT ISSUE TODAY: DATE RAPE DRUGS 101

Breaking Up a Relationship 102

PERSONAL PERSPECTIVE: LESSONS LEARNED FROM BREAKING UP 103

A QUESTION OF POLICY: SEXUAL ASSAULT ON CAMPUS 104

Summary 105

Key Terms 106

Questions for Thought 106

For Further Reading 106

CHAPTER 5 Love and Mate Selection 108

Chapter Outline 109

Learning Objectives 110

What Is Love? 111

Romantic Love 111
Is Romantic Love a Sound Basis for Marriage? 111

Erotic Love 112
Are Love and Sex the Same? 113
Sex as an Expression of Love 114

Dependent Love 114
Maslow's Theory of Love as Need 115

Friendship Love 116
Loving and Liking 116

Altruistic Love 116
Fromm's View of Altruistic Love 117

Components of Love   117

Research on the Components of Love   117

FAMILY STRENGTHS PERSPECTIVE: COMMITMENT   118

Love and Attachment   119

Changes over Time   120

Theories of Mate Selection   121

Psychodynamic Theories   121

Needs Theories   121

Exchange Theories   122

Developmental Process Theories   122

COPING FEATURE: HAPPINESS   123

Family Background Factors in Mate Selection   126

Socioeconomic Class   126

Education and Intelligence   126

Interracial and Interethnic Marriages   127

Interfaith Marriages   128

Personal Characteristics   129

Individual Traits and Behavior   129

Age Differentials   129

Consensus and Similarity of Attitudes and Values   130

Gender Roles and Personal Habits   130

Nonmarital Cohabitation   131

Patterns of Cohabitation   131

PERSONAL PERSPECTIVE: LIVING TOGETHER   132

The Effect on the Relationship and on Marriage   133

The Transition to Marriage   133

Why People Marry   134

Marital Readiness   134

Marriage and the Law   134

Preparing for Marriage   136

Rites of Passage   137

CULTURAL PERSPECTIVE: CHINESE WEDDING CEREMONIES   138

Engagement   138

The Wedding as a Religious and Civil Rite   138

AT ISSUE TODAY: WEDDING BILL BLUES?   139
A QUESTION OF POLICY: MARRIAGE INCENTIVES   140

Summary   141

Key Terms   142

Questions for Thought   142

For Further Reading   143

CHAPTER 6 Qualities of a Successful Marriage   144

Chapter Outline   145

Learning Objectives   145

Criteria for Evaluating Marital Success   146

Durability   146

Approximation of Ideals   146

Fulfillment of Needs   147

Satisfaction   147

Happy versus Unhappy Marriages   147

COPING FEATURE: HOW WE APPRAISE THE SITUATION   149

Sex and a Happy Marriage   149

CULTURAL PERSPECTIVE: POLYGAMY   150

Twelve Characteristics of Successful Marriages   151

Communication   151

Admiration and Respect   152

Companionship   152

FAMILY STRENGTHS PERSPECTIVE: DIGGING FOR DIAMONDS   152

Spirituality and Values   154

Commitment   154

Affection   156

The Ability to Deal with Crises and Stress   157

Responsibility   158

PERSONAL PERSPECTIVE: FORGIVENESS   159

Unselfishness   159

Empathy and Sensitivity   160

Honesty, Trust, and Fidelity   160

Adaptability, Flexibility, and Tolerance   160

AT ISSUE TODAY: NO TIME FOR LOVE   161

Premarital Predictors of Marital Quality   162

The Newlywed Years as Predictors of Marital Satisfaction   163

Why Some People Regret Their Choice of Mate   163

A QUESTION OF POLICY: COVENANT MARRIAGES   164

Summary   165

Key Terms   166

Questions for Thought   166

For Further Reading   166

CHAPTER 7 Marital Relationships over the Family Life Cycle   168

Chapter Outline   169

Learning Objectives   169

Marriage and Personal Happiness   170

The Family Life Cycle   171

Data on Family Life Cycles   171

Changes in Marital Satisfaction   171

Gay and Lesbian Families   172

Adjustments Early in Marriage   174

Marital Adjustment Tasks   174

COPING FEATURE: HALF FULL OR HALF EMPTY?   175

Problems during Three Early Stages   175

Adjustments to Parenthood   177

Parenthood and Stress   177

Fatherhood and the Life Course   178

CULTURAL PERSPECTIVE: INDIVIDUALISM VERSUS FAMILISM   179

Adjustments During Middle Adulthood   179

Marital Adjustments   180

The Postparental Years   181

Adjustments during Late Adulthood   182

Developmental Tasks   182

FAMILY STRENGTHS PERSPECTIVE: GO WITH THE FLOW   183

Marital Satisfaction   186

Divorce   187

Parent–Adult Child Relationships   187

Widowhood   188

PERSONAL PERSPECTIVE: WIDOWHOOD   188

AT ISSUE TODAY: WHO CARES FOR OLDER PEOPLE?   190

A QUESTION OF POLICY: NATIONALIZED/UNIVERSAL HEALTH CARE   190

Summary   191

Key Terms   193

Questions for Thought   193

For Further Reading   193

CHAPTER 8 Work, Family Roles, and Material Resources   194

Chapter Outline   195

Learning Objectives   195

The American Family Today   196

Work, Stress, and the Family   197

Positive Benefits of Dual-Earner Families   198

Needed: More Time   199

COPING FEATURE: TIME PRESSURE   200

The Parents' Child-Care Role   200

Household Labor   203

AT ISSUE TODAY: THE FAMILY AND MEDICAL LEAVE ACT   203

Marital Adjustment   204

FAMILY STRENGTHS PERSPECTIVE: KEEP THINGS IN PERSPECTIVE   205

Dual-Career Families   205

Material Resources   206

Financial Strains on Families   206

The Gender Wage Gap   209

Families and Debt   211

PERSONAL PERSPECTIVE: HOMELESS   212

Managing Finances   213

Poverty and Family Life 214

Measuring Poverty 214

The Effects of Poverty on Families 215

CULTURAL PERSPECTIVE: RACE OR ECONOMICS? 216

Homelessness 217

The Feminization of Poverty 218

Welfare and the Family 218

The Widening Gap between the Rich and the Poor 220

A QUESTION OF POLICY: EARNED INCOME TAX CREDIT 221

Summary 221

Key Terms 222

Questions for Thought 223

For Further Reading 223

CHAPTER 9 Power, Decision Making, and Communication 224

Chapter Outline 225

Learning Objectives 225

The Meaning of Power 226

Why People Want Power 226

Self-Actualization 226

Social Expectations 226

Family-of-Origin Influences 227

Psychological Need 227

Sources of Power 227

CULTURAL PERSPECTIVE: WEARING A VEIL 228

Cultural Norms 228

Gender Norms 229

Economic Resources 229

Education and Knowledge 230

Personality Differences 230

Communication Ability 230

Emotional Factors 230

Physical Stature and Strength 231

Life Circumstances 231

Children 231

Marital Power Patterns 231

Power Processes 232

COPING FEATURE: THE NEED FOR CONTROL 233

Power Tactics That Help 233

Power Tactics That Can Help or Harm 234

Power Tactics That Harm 234

PERSONAL PERSPECTIVE: HOW DO YOU STOP A PSYCHOLOGICAL GAME? 236

Consequences of Power Struggles 237

Communication 238

Verbal and Nonverbal Communication 238

AT ISSUE TODAY: FACEBOOK, TEXT MESSAGING, AND BEER 239

Barriers to Communication 239

Improving Communication Skills 241

Taking Time 241

Motivation and Concern 242

Empathy 242

Content 242

Self-Disclosure 242

Clarity 243

Listening 243

Feedback 243

Arguing Constructively 243

FAMILY STRENGTHS PERSPECTIVE: LISTEN 244

A QUESTION OF POLICY: THE POWER OF FEDERAL JUDGES 245

Summary 245

Key Terms 246

Questions for Thought 246

For Further Reading 247

CHAPTER 10 Sexual Relationships 248

Chapter Outline 249

Learning Objectives 250

Sexuality 250

Sexual Myths 251

Myth 1: Sexual Satisfaction Increases with Multiple Partners 251

Myth 2: Sexual Satisfaction Is Determined by Frequency of Sexual Intercourse   251

Myth 3: Sex during Menstruation Should Be Avoided   251

Myth 4: Sex during Pregnancy Should Be Avoided   251

Myth 5: Men Are Always Confident about and Ready for Sex   252

Myth 6: Women Are Not Very Interested in Sex   252

Myth 7: A Careful Person Will Never Get Caught in an Extramarital Affair   252

CULTURAL PERSPECTIVE: A CROSS-CULTURAL VIEW OF SEXUAL BEHAVIOR   253

Negative Consequences of Sexual Activity   253

Unplanned Pregnancy   253

Sexually Transmitted Diseases   254

Confusing Sex with Love   254

Staying in a Relationship Longer Than Desirable   254

COPING FEATURE: ATTACHMENT STYLES AND SEXUAL RELATIONSHIPS   255

Emotional Vulnerability   255

Manipulation and Power Games   256

Sexual Response   256

The Masters and Johnson Sexual Response Model   256

The Kaplan Sexual Response Model   257

Gender Differences in Sexual Response   258

Sexual Desire   258

Sexual Arousal   258

Proceeding through Sexual Response Stages at Different Speeds   258

Resolution Stage   258

Orgasm   259

Factors Contributing to a Fulfilling Sexual Relationship   259

Intimacy   259

Commitment   259

Psychological Comfort   260

Good Communication   260

Knowledge of the Sexual Response Cycle   260

Emphasis on the Enjoyment of Each Other Rather Than Performance   260

Good Mental and Physical Health   260

FAMILY STRENGTHS PERSPECTIVE: COMMUNICATION AND SEXUAL RELATIONSHIPS   261

Sexuality and Aging   261

The Female Climacteric   262

Hormone Replacement Therapy for Women   262

The Male Climacteric   262

PERSONAL PERSPECTIVE: AN AFFAIR? CONSIDER THE CONSEQUENCES   263

Hormone Replacement Therapy for Men   263

Getting through the Change-of-Life Period More Successfully   264

Sexual Disorders   264

Sexual Addiction   264

Hypoactive Sexual Desire   265

Vaginismus   266

Female Orgasmic Disorder   266

Male Orgasmic Disorder   267

Dyspareunia   267

Erectile Disorder   267

Premature Ejaculation   269

Alcohol and Drugs   269

Sexually Transmitted Diseases   270

Chlamydia   271

Gonorrhea   271

AT ISSUE TODAY: UNSAFE SEX PRACTICES: WHY SO PREVALENT?   272

Syphilis   273

Human Papillomavirus   274

Herpes   275

Hepatitis   276

Human Immunodeficiency Virus   277

Vaginitis   279

Pediculosis   279

A QUESTION OF POLICY: INTERNET PORNOGRAPHY   280

Summary   280

Key Terms 282
Questions for Thought 282
For Further Reading 282

CHAPTER 11 Family Planning and Parenthood 284

Chapter Outline 285
Learning Objectives 286

The Importance of Family Planning 287

FAMILY STRENGTHS PERSPECTIVE: WHAT IS A STRONG FAMILY? 288

Hormonal Control 288
Oral Contraceptives 289
Other Forms of Hormonal Contraceptives 291

AT ISSUE TODAY: THE ABORTION PILL 292

Vaginal Spermicides 293

Intrauterine Devices 293

Barrier Methods 294
Condoms 294
Diaphragm 295
Cervical Cap 295
Contraceptive Sponge 295

Sterilization 295
Vasectomy 296
Female Sterilization 296

Fertility Awareness 297
Calendar Method 297
Withdrawal 299
Noncoital Stimulation (Outercourse) 300

Choosing a Method of Contraception 300

Abortion 301
Legal Considerations 301
Moral Considerations 302
Social and Realistic Considerations 302

Psychological and Personal Considerations 303

Infertility 303
Causes of Infertility 303

CULTURAL PERSPECTIVE: A PREFERENCE FOR MALES 304
COPING FEATURE: COPING WITH INFERTILITY 305

Infertility and Subjective Well-Being 305
Treatment of Infertility 305
Alternative Means of Conception 306
The Adoption Option 307

PERSONAL PERSPECTIVE: REASONS FOR HAVING CHILDREN 308

The Foster Care Option 309

To Parent or Not to Parent 310
Delayed Parenthood 310
Choosing a Child-Free Marriage 311

A QUESTION OF POLICY: EMBRYOS 312

Summary 313
Key Terms 314
Questions for Thought 314
For Further Reading 315

CHAPTER 12 Pregnancy and Childbirth 316

Chapter Outline 317
Learning Objectives 317

Pregnancy 318
Signs and Symptoms of Pregnancy 318
Tests for Pregnancy 318
Calculating the Expected Date of Birth 319
Emotional Reactions to Pregnancy 319

Prenatal Care 320
Importance of Prenatal Care 320
Nutrition during Pregnancy 321
General Health Care during Pregnancy 321
Environmental Hazards 321
Minor Side Effects of Pregnancy 322

CULTURAL PERSPECTIVE: THE USE OF ULTRASOUNDS 323

Major Complications of Pregnancy   323
Sexual Relations during Pregnancy   325
Mental Health   325

Prenatal Development   326
The Germinal Period   327
The Embryonic Period   327
The Fetal Period   327

Prepared Childbirth   328
AT ISSUE TODAY: OPTIONS FOR DELIVERY   328
The Lamaze Method   329

Labor and Delivery   329
Stages of Labor   330

The Postpartum Period   330
FAMILY STRENGTHS PERSPECTIVE: BONDING WITH BABY   331
Care of the Newborn   331
Parent–Infant Contact and Bonding   331
Rooming-In   332
Postpartum Adjustments   332
Returning to Work   333
COPING FEATURE: BECOMING A PARENT   334
PERSONAL PERSPECTIVE: POSTPARTUM DEPRESSION   335
Sexual Relations after Childbirth   335
A QUESTION OF POLICY: SUBSTANCE ABUSE BY PREGNANT WOMEN   336

Summary   337
Key Terms   337
Questions for Thought   338
For Further Reading   338

CHAPTER 13 Parent–Child Relationships   340

Chapter Outline   341
Learning Objectives   341

Philosophies of Childrearing   342
Parental Differences   342
Value Differences   343
Parent–Child Differences   343
Cultural Differences   344

FAMILY STRENGTHS PERSPECTIVE: BOTHO   345
Life Circumstances   345
CULTURAL PERSPECTIVE: CULTURAL CONFLICT AND ACCULTURATION   346
Differences in Children   347

Stress and Children   348

Fostering Cognitive and Intellectual Growth   349
PERSONAL PERSPECTIVE: SERENDIPITY   349
Parental Contributions   350
Language Development and Cultivation   350
Educational Goals   350

Meeting Emotional Needs   350
Emotional Attachments   351
Autonomy   353
Connectedness   353
Identity   354
AT ISSUE TODAY: FAMILY HAPPINESS AND MATERIAL WEALTH   354

Child Care   355

Social Competence, Socialization, and Discipline   356
Meaning and Goals of Discipline   356
Principles of Discipline   357
COPING FEATURE: THE STRESS OF DISCIPLINE   358
Discipline Styles   359
Corporal Punishment   359
A QUESTION OF POLICY: FAMILY-FRIENDLY POLICIES   360

Summary   361
Key Terms   362
Questions for Thought   362
For Further Reading   363

CHAPTER 14 Parents and Extended Family Relationships   364

Chapter Outline   365
Learning Objectives   365

Parent–Adult Child Relationships   366

When Parents Disapprove of Choice of Partner   366

Children's Identification with Parents   368

Interdependence between Generations   368

CULTURAL PERSPECTIVE: EMERGING ADULTHOOD   370

Parent–Adult Child Relationships and Psychological Functioning   371

Elder Care   371

PERSONAL PERSPECTIVE: MOTHER–DAUGHTER RELATIONSHIPS   372

In-Laws   373

Successful In-Law Relationships   373

The Roots of Conflict   374

FAMILY STRENGTHS PERSPECTIVE: FAMILY REUNION   375

Living with Parents or In-Laws   375

Effects of Co-residence   376

COPING FEATURE: REFRAMING   376

Sources of Stress   377

Grandparents   377

AT ISSUE TODAY: FICTIVE KINSHIP   378

What Grandparents Can Do for Grandchildren   379

Grandparents Who Parent Their Grandchildren   380

Adolescents, Young Adults, and Grandparents   381

What Grandchildren Can Do for Grandparents   382

Adult Sibling Relationships   382

A QUESTION OF POLICY: GRANDPARENTS' RIGHTS   383

Summary   384

Key Terms   385

Questions for Thought   385

For Further Reading   385

CHAPTER 15 Conflict, Family Crises, and Crisis Management   386

Chapter Outline   387

Learning Objectives   388

Conflict and Children   389

The Family Environment   389

Interparent Conflict   389

CULTURAL PERSPECTIVE: THE PLIGHT OF IMMIGRANT FAMILIES   390

Sources of Conflict   390

Personal Sources   391

Physical Sources   391

Interpersonal Sources   391

Situational or Environmental Sources   392

PERSONAL PERSPECTIVE: WHAT WOULD YOU LIKE TO CHANGE ABOUT THE WAY YOU DEAL WITH CONFLICT?   393

Methods of Dealing with Conflict   393

Avoidance   393

Ventilation and Catharsis   394

Constructive and Destructive Conflicts   395

Levels of Marital Conflict Model   396

Family Crises   397

Stage 1: Onset   398

Stage 2: Disorganization   398

Stage 3: Reorganization   398

COPING FEATURE: SEARCH FOR MEANING IN TOUGH TIMES   399

The Crisis of Infidelity   400

Reasons for Infidelity   400

FAMILY STRENGTHS PERSPECTIVE: AFFAIR-PROOFING YOUR MARRIAGE   400

AT ISSUE TODAY: CHEATING IN CYBERSPACE   401

Affairs as Crises for Married People   402

The Crisis of Economic Distress   403

Types of Economic Distress   403

Effects on Individuals and on Family Relationships   403

Coping with Economic Distress   404

The Crisis of Addictions   405

Characteristics of Addiction   405

Reasons for Addiction   405

Effects on the Family   405

Overcoming Addiction: The Addicted Person   406

Overcoming Addiction: The Family and the Addicted Person Working Together   406

The Crisis of Violence and Abuse   408

Factors Related to Violence   410

Child Maltreatment   412

Treatment for Spouse and Child Abuse   415

Detecting Child Maltreatment   415

Elder Abuse   416

The Crisis of Death and Grief   417

A QUESTION OF POLICY: ABUSED AND NEGLECTED CHILDREN   419

Summary   419

Key Terms   421

Questions for Thought   421

For Further Reading   421

CHAPTER 16 The Family and Divorce   422

Chapter Outline   423

Learning Objectives   423

Probability of Divorce: Social and Demographic Factors   424

Marital Age   425

Religion   425

Socioeconomic Status   425

Geographic Area   426

Parental Divorce   426

The Presence of Children   428

Quality of Marriage and Parent–Child Relationships   428

Causes of Marital Breakup   429

Spouses' Perceptions   429

The Marital Disaffection Process   430

The Divorce Decision   431

Alternatives to Divorce   433

Marriage Counseling   433

PERSONAL PERSPECTIVE: GETTING DIVORCED   433

Marriage Enrichment   434

Separation   434

AT ISSUE TODAY: WHY MARRIAGE COUNSELING SOMETIMES DOES NOT SUCCEED   435

No-Fault Divorce and Mediation   436

CULTURAL PERSPECTIVE: ADJUSTMENT TO DIVORCE   437

Adult Adjustments after Divorce   438

Emotional Trauma   438

Societal Attitudes toward Divorce   439

Loneliness and Social Readjustment   439

Adjustments to Custody Arrangements   440

Finances   441

Realignment of Responsibilities and Work Roles   441

Contacts with the Ex-Spouse   442

Kinship Interaction   442

COPING FEATURE: ANGER   442

Children and Divorce   444

Child Custody   444

FAMILY STRENGTHS PERSPECTIVE: FORGIVENESS AND CONFLICT-RESOLUTION SKILLS   444

Child Support   445

Visitation Rights   447

Reactions of Children   447

Adjustments of Children   449

A QUESTION OF POLICY: DIVORCE AND THE SINGLE-MOTHER FAMILY   451

Summary   451

Key Terms   453

Questions for Thought   453

For Further Reading   453

CHAPTER 17 Coming Together: Remarriage and Stepparenting   454

Chapter Outline   455

Learning Objectives   455

Remarriage   456

Divorce or Success in Remarriage?   456

FAMILY STRENGTHS PERSPECTIVE: HAPPY VERSUS UNHAPPY STEPCOUPLES   457

Courtship and Mate Selection in
Remarriage   458
Preparing for Remarriage   458
Facets of Remarriage   459

Challenges of Remarriage   460

Complex Relationships   460
Ambiguous Family Boundaries   460
Ambiguous Cultural Norms   461
Carrying Expectations from One Marriage
to Another   461

**AT ISSUE TODAY: MERGING FAMILIES
AND FINANCES   462**

Finances   463
Relationships with the Ex-Spouse   464
Family Relationships from a Previous
Marriage   464

COPING FEATURE: HUMOR   465

Stepfamilies   466

Stepfathers   468
Stepfamily Turning Points   468

Stepparent–Stepchild Relationships   469

**CULTURAL PERSPECTIVE: STEPFAMILIES IN CULTURAL
CONTEXT   470**

Child Well-Being in Stepfamilies   470
Facilitating Bonds between Stepparents
and Stepchildren   472
Coparents and Parenting Coalitions   473

Stepsibling Relationships   474

PERSONAL PERSPECTIVE: BEING A STEPMOM   475
A QUESTION OF POLICY: STEPFAMILY RIGHTS   476

Summary   476
Key Terms   478
Questions for Thought   478
For Further Reading   478

Glossary   479

References   487

Image Credits   534

Index   536

Boxed Features

At Issue Today

Children Not Living with Married Biological Parents   16

Women and Weight: Gendered Messages on Magazine Covers   42

Friends with Benefits   78

Date Rape Drugs   101

Wedding Bill Blues?   139

No Time for Love   161

Who Cares for Older People?   190

The Family and Medical Leave Act   203

Facebook, Text Messaging, and Beer   239

Unsafe Sex Practices: Why So Prevalent?   272

The Abortion Pill   292

Options for Delivery   328

Family Happiness and Material Wealth   354

Fictive Kinship   378

Cheating in Cyberspace   401

Why Marriage Counseling Sometimes Does Not Succeed   435

Merging Families and Finances   462

Cultural Perspective

Ethnic Identity and Acculturation   22

The Word *Machismo*   54

African American Single Mothers   71

Arranged Marriages   94

Chinese Wedding Ceremonies   138

Polygamy   150

Individualism versus Familism   179

Race or Economics?   216

Wearing a Veil   228

A Cross-Cultural View of Sexual Behavior   253

A Preference for Males   304

The Use of Ultrasounds   323

Cultural Conflict and Acculturation   346

Emerging Adulthood   370

The Plight of Immigrant Families   390

Adjustment to Divorce   437

Stepfamilies in Cultural Context   476

A Question of Policy

Gay and Lesbian Parenting by Adoption   34

Title IX   62

Funding for Which Sex Education Programs?   84

Sexual Assault on Campus   104

Marriage Incentives   140

Covenant Marriages   164

Nationalized/Universal Health Care   190

Earned Income Tax Credit   221

The Power of Federal Judges   245

Internet Pornography   280

Embryos   312

Substance Abuse by Pregnant Women   336

Family-Friendly Policies   360

Grandparents' Rights   383

Abused and Neglected Children   419

Divorce and the Single-Mother Family   451

Stepfamily Rights   476

Personal Perspective

A Long 15 Inches   6

Life on the Boundaries of Gender   50

Single Fatherhood   83

Lessons Learned from Breaking Up   103

Living Together   132

Forgiveness   159

Widowhood   188

Homeless   212

How Do You Stop a Psychological Game?   236

An Affair? Consider the Consequences   263

Reasons for Having Children   308

Postpartum Depression   335

Serendipity   349

Mother–Daughter Relationships   372

What Would You Like to Change about the Way You Deal with Conflict?   393

Getting Divorced   433

Being a Stepmom   475

Family Strengths Perspective

Qualities of Strong Families   32

Do Everyday Things Together   58

Time Together: Making Memories   81

Strengths of Russian Families   97

Commitment   118

Digging for Diamonds   152

Go with the Flow   183

Keep Things in Perspective   205

Listen   244

Communication and Sexual Relationships   261

What Is a Strong Family?   288

Bonding with Baby   331

Botho   345

Family Reunion   375

Affair-Proofing Your Marriage   400

Forgiveness and Conflict-Resolution Skills   444

Happy versus Unhappy Stepcouples   457

Coping Feature

The Importance of Coping   28

Coping with Depression   59

Avoiding Counterproductive Strategies   73

Coping with Your Own Jealousy   99

Happiness   123

How We Appraise the Situation   149

Half Full or Half Empty?   175

Time Pressure   200

The Need for Control   233

Attachment Styles and Sexual Relationships   255

Coping with Infertility   305

Becoming a Parent   334

The Stress of Discipline   358

Reframing   376

Search for Meaning in Tough Times   399

Anger   442

Humor   465

Preface

In the ninth edition of *Intimate Relationships, Marriages, and Families*, various theoretical perspectives (such as symbolic interaction theory, structural functional theory, conflict theory, and developmental theory) are utilized to help understand marriage and family dynamics and to interpret changes taking place in families. Systems theory is integrated throughout the text to illustrate the interdependence of marriage and family members and to provide insights concerning how marriage and family interactions are influenced by culture, law and policy, work, economics, coping and interpersonal skills, and the degree of family strengths.

All people share a fundamental drive to form intimate relationships with other human beings, although these relationships may take a variety of forms. As you go through life, your needs for intimacy constantly change. An infant needs to be fed and cuddled; a school-age child needs to have friends; an adolescent begins exploring sexuality; most adult men and women seek a partner, marry, and have children; and many elderly people need assistance from family in the later years of life.

When people are in relationships, it is almost inevitable that there will be challenges. Few long-term intimate relationships exist without some degree of friction. For most people, it takes considerable effort to create and maintain healthy, fulfilling relationships; for others, it is a constant struggle. And although relationships can be a source of pain, they also can be our biggest source of joy in life, bringing happiness, satisfaction, and even exhilaration. In the end, most people would agree that experiencing intimate and family relationships is the true essence of life and the abiding force that sustains and transforms them. The goal of this textbook—and likely your course overall—is to help you learn to develop the skills to achieve relationships that are warm, close, and enriching.

Each of you has tremendous capacity to grow and change; and the choices in regard to relationships are abundant today. To choose wisely and in ways that are best for you, you need a cognitive understanding of what is involved, what choices you have, and what the consequences of these choices may be. It is here that the information provided by the social and behavioral sciences can help. As a student using this text, you will have the opportunity to learn from thousands of research studies examining many facets of relationships. Objectively studying many different kinds of relationships can help you understand and make better choices in your own relationships and clarify your own personal attitudes and values.

The more you understand about the vast array of relationships and different kinds of challenges they present, the better able you are to be objective and tolerant of others. You will learn from this text that marriage and family patterns are tremendously diverse and that no one way is ideal for everyone. Also, as we study different relationship patterns, we learn that some of our own behavior patterns actually may be more widespread than we would have imagined.

It also is important to understand how your actions as a citizen impact intimate relationships and families on a societal level. When you vote, you elect officials who write laws and policies that determine such things as who can get married or how much funding after-school programs receive. Many public policy issues such as these directly affect families. Each chapter in this book explores a public policy issue and its relationship to families. These issues, like so many family issues, are often controversial. This text adopts neither a liberal nor a conservative view, but it presents different sides of an issue and challenges you to find your own individual values and answers to these important questions.

As you examine relationships over the life course, you will see that they are dynamic. One thing for sure is that change, although it is some people's biggest fear, is inevitable in life. People change, situations change, relationships change. The love you feel today may not be exactly the same as the love you will feel 10 years from now. The person you were in high school changed into the person you are today.

At the same time, there is also continuity to life, and what happens now greatly influences tomorrow. What *happened* in your families when you were children impacts what will happen in your families when you are adults. This book illustrates that there is similarity in the ways humans develop and cope with changes, but there is also diversity. An important aim of this book is to show students what may be expected at a particular life stage, how others have responded, and how those responses have affected the quality of their intimate relationships.

Organization

The text begins with an examination of the trends and changes taking place in marriage and family today and how different theoretical perspectives interpret those changes (Chapter 1). The concepts of gender and gender roles are examined and some of the influences on their development are described in Chapter 2.

Chapters 3 through 5 explore relationships before marriage ranging from singlehood to dating to partner selection. Marriage brings with it a new set of demands for growth and change. Chapter 6 considers first the qualities essential to happy and successful marriages, and Chapter 7 discusses changes in marital relationships over the life cycle. Chapters 8 and 9 explore work and family roles and the effect of economic status and power, decision making, and communication. The nature of sexuality, sexual relationships, sexually transmitted diseases, and sexual disorders are discussed in Chapter 10.

Chapters 11 to 14 focus on parenthood. The decisions involved in parenthood and family planning are discussed in Chapter 11, and Chapter 12 follows from conception through pregnancy and the preparations made by the family for a new baby. Chapter 13 examines parent–child relationships, whereas Chapter 14 considers relationships among members of the extended family, especially aging relatives.

Most families at one time or another experience some conflict or face a period of crisis. The text explores conflict and family crises in Chapter 15, the causes and effects of divorce in Chapter 16, and the special challenges of remarriage and stepparenting in Chapter 17.

New to the Ninth Edition

All chapters were carefully revised and updated to incorporate current research and statistics and newly emerging topics. Careful attention is given to the coverage of cultural diversity, which is not set aside in a separate chapter but integrated throughout the text. Research studies that included a culturally diverse sample are discussed wherever possible.

Recent trends in marriage and families are examined using current U.S. statistics. Among the topics discussed are the following:

- The increase in cohabitation
- Grandparents raising their grandchildren
- Marital delay and lifelong singlehood
- Gay and lesbian families
- Cultural diversity in the United States
- Attachment styles
- Addiction and the effect on families
- Violence in dating relationships
- Internet dating services
- The influence of technology and media on gender roles and families
- The increase in single parenthood
- The increase in interracial, interethnic and interfaith marriages
- Elder care and elder abuse

A careful review of literature that focused on positive aspects of family life and qualities of fulfilling and satisfying intimate relationships was conducted. Among the topics covered are the following:

- Characteristics of strong families
- The importance of couples' rituals and family time
- Qualities of a successful marriage
- Sex and a happy marriage
- The impact of premarital education
- The need for families to have more time together
- Family happiness and material wealth
- Healthy and happy stepfamilies

The ninth edition expands and updates information on the relationship between family life and economics, and it also deals with the increase in the number of families struggling financially. The financial burden of and misconceptions about student loans are new additions. Some of the subjects included are as follows:

- The increase in family and consumer debt
- Student loans
- The shrinking dollar
- Poverty, the working poor, and family life
- The widening gap between rich and poor
- Work, stress, and the family
- Characteristics of dual-earner families
- Household labor
- Financial needs of families
- Homelessness
- The rising cost of health care
- Family-friendly policies in the workplace
- Financial management

New to the eighth edition were the following two features, which have been retained and, where necessary, updated:

Coping Feature is a unique box that provides helpful information in each chapter concerning effective coping strategies and how coping patterns impact relationships. The **Coping Feature** is consistent with one of the text's major premises—that change happens and requires us to cope.

Family Strengths Perspective is also a distinctive perspective throughout the book that provides students with a model for understanding positive functioning in families. It is based on research from thousands of strong families in diverse cultures.

Chapter-by-chapter changes:

Chapter 1

The section "Ethnic and Cultural Diversity in Families" has been updated.

Chapter 2

The Coping Feature "Coping with Depression" has been expanded and updated. Substantially more updated material has been added to the discussion of gender identity and roles.

Chapter 4

The section "Attraction and Dating" has been updated to address date rape on campus and the relationship of this issue to Title IX. In addition, this section includes new material on the brain chemistry of attraction as well as the biological basis for mate selection.

Chapter 5

This chapter includes expanded emphasis and current research on attachment styles.

Chapter 8

A substantially expanded treatment of financial management provides practical suggestions and insights. Three new sections, "Student Loan Debt," "General Debt," and the "Shrinking Dollar," address the economic challenges that contemporary families face.

Chapter 9

Expanded information on communication and material on psychological games are included.

Chapter 10

A discussion on models of sexual response, a discussion of factors contributing to fulfilling sexual relationships, insights into aging and sexuality, information about sexual disorders and sexually transmitted diseases, and a discussion of the effects of alcohol and drugs on sexual response are included. The newly developed second vaccine for human papillomavirus is also discussed.

Chapter 11

Expanded and updated material concerning contraceptive methods is included.

Chapter 12

The section on prenatal care is updated and includes information on teratogens, including new research on the impact of addictive drugs as neonatal abstinence syndrome. The discussion of fetal alcohol syndrome disorders is expanded and updated.

Chapter 13

A new section, "Stress and Children," has been added, and the discussion of discipline styles has been expanded.

Chapter 14

Practical suggestions for improving in-law relationships and an exploration of the issue of grandparents' rights are discussed.

Chapter 15

A levels-of-conflict model provides insights into managing conflict. The "Crisis of Addictions" section is extensive and timely. The topic of overcoming addiction has been expanded into two parts: "Overcoming Addiction: The Addicted Person" and "Overcoming Addiction: The Family and Addicted Person Working Together." In addition, the "Crisis of Violence and Abuse" section is extensively expanded and updated to include discussion of child maltreatment and elder abuse.

Chapter 16

The topic of emotional trauma for adults in response to divorce is expanded. The discussion of children who experience the divorce of their parents has been expanded and reorganized.

Chapter 17

A major section on the challenges of remarriage is thoroughly developed. The section "Divorce or Success in Remarriage?" provides a family strengths perspective for developing success and resilience in remarried families. This reflects a fresh, positive focus on the strengths of remarried families rather than emphasis on their challenges.

Pedagogical Aids

In addition to the changes already mentioned, we include plentiful, current photographs to make the book inviting and relevant for students. Carefully updated tables and figures highlight and amplify the text coverage. Chapter outlines, objectives, marginal definitions, and review sections combine with a comprehensive glossary to help students master the material. And to maintain student interest and spotlight important current issues, we also include a number of innovative features in this edition:

- *A Question of Policy*—This end-of-chapter section, designed to foster debate and develop students' critical thinking abilities, introduces the public or social policy implications of an emerging, often controversial family issue.
- *Cultural Perspectives*—In keeping with the text's emphasis on diversity, these boxes illuminates diversity research and issues—highlighting topics such as cultural conflict and acculturation, racism, family strengths across cultures, and more.
- *Personal Perspective*—In each chapter, a piece titled "Personal Perspective" presents an interview or comments from individuals on a particular topic of discussion. These are designed to help students connect real lives, and possibly their own, to issues.
- *At Issue Today*—Another thought-provoking box type, these focus student attention on some of today's most pressing challenges—date rape drugs, the rising cost of health care, grandparents who parent their grandchildren, and more.
- *Coping Feature*—This unique feature provides helpful information in each of the chapters concerning effective coping strategies. This feature helps students understand that the ways they choose to address problems, deal with stress, and appraise situations have great impact on the quality of their intimate relationships. Change is inevitable; how we cope with it makes all the difference.
- *Family Strengths Perspective*—Throughout the book, this distinctive perspective provides a positive model and insights for understanding the characteristics of strong families and practical, real-life suggestions for implementing them in students' own intimate relationships. This feature is based on many research studies over 4 decades with thousands of families from all over the world.

Supplements

Ensuring Student Success

Oxford University Press offers students and instructors a comprehensive ancillary package for *Intimate Relationships, Marriages, and Families.*

For Students

Companion Website

Intimate Relationships, Marriages, and Families is accompanied by an extensive **companion website** (www.oup.com/us/stinnett), which includes materials to help students with every aspect of the course. For each chapter, you will find:

- Chapter Outlines
- Flashcards and Glossary
- Additional links and further reading
- Self-grading review questions

For Instructors

Oxford University Press is proud to offer a complete and authoritative supplements package for both instructors and students. When you adopt *Intimate Relationships, Marriages, and Families*, you will have access to a truly exemplary set of ancillary materials to enhance teaching and support students' learning.

Ancillary Resource Center (ARC) at www.oup-arc.com is a convenient, instructor-focused single destination for resources to accompany *Intimate Relationships, Marriages, and Families*. Accessed online through individual user accounts, the ARC provides instructors with access to up-to-date ancillaries at any time while guaranteeing the security of grade-significant resources. In addition, it allows OUP to keep instructors informed when new content becomes available.

The ARC for *Intimate Relationships, Marriages, and Families* includes:

- Digital copy of **Instructor's Manual**, which includes:
  - Chapter outlines
  - Learning objectives
  - Key terms and definitions
  - PowerPoint slides
  - Web links
  - In-class activities and project assignments
  - Suggestions for class discussion
- Computerized Test Bank including:
  - Multiple-choice questions
  - True/false questions
- Fill-in-the-blank questions
- Short answer and essay prompts

Acknowledgments

A special acknowledgment goes to the late F. Philip Rice for his years of hard work and commitment to writing this textbook. We thank him for his insight and valuable instruction on marriage and the family, and we are grateful his ideas and writings live on in this text.

This text would not have been possible without the assistance and cooperation of many people. We thank our editor, Sherith Pankratz, and her assistants, Katy Albis and Meredith Keffer, for their support, expertise, and valuable suggestions for improving this edition.

The authors thank the following people who have reviewed and offered guidance and suggestions for the ninth edition:

Anita Glee Bertram, University of Central Oklahoma;

Lillian J. Breckenridge, Oral Roberts University;

Diana Cutchin, Virginia Commonwealth University;

Linda Emerson, College of the Desert;

Carolyn Grasse-Bachman, Penn State University ;

Gladys J. Hildreth, University of North Texas;

Christine Nortz, Florida Gateway College;

Daniel Romesburg, University of Pittsburgh;

Bahira Trask, University of Delaware;

and one anonymous reviewer

About the Authors

NICK STINNETT received his Ph.D. from Florida State University and has taught in the area of family studies at Oklahoma State University, the University of Nebraska, Pepperdine University, and the University of Alabama. Stinnett is a nationally and internationally recognized leader and researcher in the area of family strengths. In addition to his work on *Intimate Relationships, Marriages, and Families*, he is coauthor with Nancy, his wife, and James Walters of *Relationships in Marriage and the Family*. He is also coauthor, with Joe Beam, of *Fantastic Families: 6 Proven Steps to Building a Strong Family*, as well as *Secrets of Strong Families*, which he coauthored with John DeFrain.

NANCY STINNETT has a master's degree from Oklahoma State University. She has taught classes on marriage, parenting, and lifespan human development at the University of Alabama, serving as lead teacher for the university's Infant/Toddler Laboratory for 17 years. Nancy and Nick have coauthored a number of books on marriage and family, including *Magnificent Marriage* (with Donnie Hilliard) and *Loving and Caring—Always and Regardless*. Nick and Nancy have been married since 1968;

they have two sons and seven grandchildren; they live in Northport, Alabama.

MARY KAY DEGENOVA received her Ph.D. in 1992 from Purdue University in child development and family studies. She was an associate professor of family studies at Central Michigan University and the University of New Hampshire and has taught various courses on marriage and the family. Her work on this text is a direct result of her experiences in the classroom and her *experiences* with diversity, including work as a Peace Corps volunteer in West Africa and a Fulbright scholar in Chile. In addition to her work on this text, DeGenova has written *Families in Cultural Context: Strengths and Challenges in Diversity* published by Mayfield. Her principal areas of research and scholarly writing include regrets in later life, women's identity development, family insight through literature and drama, and the development of critical thinking skills through teaching.

F. PHILIP RICE (deceased) was Professor Emeritus at the University of Maine-Orono, where he taught courses in the field of Marriage and Family for many years.

Intimate Relationships, Marriages, and Families

Intimate Relationships, Marriages, and Families in the Twenty-first Century

Learning Objectives

What Is a Family?
- Some Definitions
- Family Forms

PERSONAL PERSPECTIVE: *A Long 15 Inches*

Changes in Family Philosophy and Emphasis
- From Institution to Companionship
- From Patriarchy to Democracy

Changes in Marriage and Parenthood
- Marriage Rates
- Median Age
- Family Size
- Working Wives and Mothers
- One-Parent Families
- Cohabitation

AT ISSUE TODAY: *Children Not Living with Married Biological Parents*
- Gay and Lesbian Families

- Grandparents as Parents
- Changes in Life Expectancy

Changes in Divorce and Remarriage
- Divorce Rates
- Remarriage Trends
- Blended Families

Ethnic and Cultural Diversity in Families
- Increased Ethnic Diversity
- Hispanic Americans
- African Americans

CULTURAL PERSPECTIVE: *Ethnic Identity and Acculturation*
- Asian/Pacific Islander Americans
- Native Americans

Theories to Help Explain Family Behavior
- Structural-Functional Theory
- Family Developmental Theory

COPING FEATURE: *The Importance of Coping*

- Symbolic Interaction Theory
- Systems Theory
- Social Learning Theory
- Exchange Theory
- Conflict Theory
- Feminist Theory
- The International Family Strengths Model
- Critique of Family Theories

The Study of Marriage, Families, and Intimate Relationships

FAMILY STRENGTHS PERSPECTIVE: *Qualities of Strong Families*

A QUESTION OF POLICY: *Gay and Lesbian Parenting by Adoption*

Summary

Key Terms

Questions for Thought

For Further Reading

LEARNING OBJECTIVES

AFTER READING THE CHAPTER, YOU SHOULD BE ABLE TO DO THE FOLLOWING:

- Define *family* and describe various family forms.

- Explain the changes in family philosophy and emphasis: the change from institution to companionship and from patriarchy to democracy.

- Outline the basic trends in marriage rates, median age at first marriage, birth rates and family size, working mothers, one-parent families, cohabitation, and gay and lesbian families.

- Summarize the basic trends in divorce rates, remarriage, and blended families.

- Define *ethnicity* and *culture* and describe the composition of the U.S. population by race.

- Describe Hispanic American, African American, Asian/Pacific Islander American, and Native American families.

- Explain behavior and patterns in families using family theories and models.

- Describe different types of research design and ways in which to analyze data.

Ann lives with her life partner, Sarah, and their adopted daughter, Olivia. They have been together for 21 years; 11 years ago they declared their love and commitment to each other in a public ceremony. After the ceremony, they no longer hid their relationship, began referring to each other as spouses, and noted that other people recognized the significance of their bond. Ann remarks,

> I have some fears about the lack of support from the legal system. We have power of attorney documents and wills that clearly name each other. We have explicitly told our siblings that we want each other to handle legal, medical, and parenting issues as the need arises. But our attorney warned us that all these documents may not be upheld if tested in a court of law. This is a concern for us, and when either one of us goes to the hospital, we bring along all the proper documents.
>
> I am the legal adoptive parent for Olivia, and while the legal documents state that if something happened to me, Sarah would be responsible for her, legally Sarah is treated like someone outside the family. Also I am concerned about the fact that Sarah will not be entitled to my Social Security benefit or pension. Although I would really like for Sarah to stay home with our daughter, I can't make this choice because Sarah needs a job with her own health insurance.
>
> I would like people to know we are not different. We are creating a family. We have jobs and a dog and go on vacation. We drive a mini-van. We need the support of friends and community to keep our relationship healthy.

Families are universal and yet each is unique. In an ever-changing world, families cannot remain static. Thus, families as we know them today differ from those of previous generations—in structure, composition, size, and function. The reasons people marry and their marital expectations have changed. Changes also have occurred in how families are governed, in who supports families, and in how people behave sexually. An analysis of marriage rates and ages, fertility rates, the percentages of working wives and mothers, numbers of one-parent families, cohabitation rates, numbers of gay and lesbian families,

divorce and remarriage rates, and the numbers of blended families reveals some significant trends.

In this chapter we examine some of these changes and trends and their effects on society and the individual. In addition, it is important to consider how these changes have affected us personally.

What Is a Family?

What makes a family? Do its members have to be related by blood? By marriage? Do they have to share the same household? We examine a few of the countless definitions of *family* that have been formulated in recent decades, and then we look at some of the variations in types of families that have been identified by psychologists, sociologists, and anthropologists.

Some Definitions

The U.S. Bureau of the Census (2016) defines a family as a group of two or more people (one of whom is the householder) related by birth, marriage, or adoption and residing together. In the census count, the number of families is equal to the number of family households. However, the count of family members differs from the count of household members because household members include any nonrelatives living in the household. By this definition, the family may consist of two persons who are not necessarily of different genders: two brothers, two female cousins, a mother and daughter, and so on. They may also be of different genders: a husband and wife, a mother and son, a brother and sister, and so on. If the family includes two adults, they may or may not have children. The common characteristics included in this definition are twofold: (1) the individuals must be related by blood or law, and (2) they must live together in one household. Thus, according to the Census Bureau, if adult children move out of their parents' household and establish families of their own, they are no longer considered a part of their parents' family.

Other definitions have been proposed. Winch (1971) defined the family as a group of persons related to each other by blood, marriage, or adoption and whose basic function in society is replacement. But this definition seems to limit family functions to childrearing. Burgess and Locke (1953, 7–8) defined the family as "a group of persons united by ties of marriage, blood, or adoption; constituting a single household; interacting and communicating with each other in their respective social roles (husband and wife, mother and father, son and daughter, brother and sister); and creating and maintaining a common culture." This definition would eliminate those individuals who are cohabiting, although not legally related or married. The definition seems to assume as well that individuals in a family must conform to some sort of prescribed social roles.

None of these definitions seems to cover all types of family situations, particularly nonmarried cohabiting couples and, until recently, gay or lesbian couples who could not marry legally. A more comprehensive definition is used in this book: a **family** is any group of persons united by the ties of marriage, blood, or adoption or any sexually expressive relationship in which (1) the adults cooperate financially for their mutual support, (2) the people are committed to one another in an intimate interpersonal relationship, (3) the members see their individual identities as importantly attached to the group, and (4) the group has an identity of its own.

This definition has a number of advantages. It includes a variety of family structures: for example, the traditional married couple with or without children, single-parent families, or families consisting of blood relatives (such as two widowed sisters or a multigenerational extended family). It also includes persons not related by marriage, blood, or adoption who have a sexual relationship: an unmarried cohabiting couple, for example. Because this definition insists that the persons be committed and in an intimate interpersonal relationship, it eliminates cohabiting couples who live together for practical reasons, without commitment, and those who have only a casual relationship although they may have sex together. The members must see their individual identities as importantly attached to the group, and the group must have an identity of its own.

Family Forms

We can categorize families according to their structure and the relationships among the people in them.

A **voluntarily childless family** is a couple who decide not to have children. (Some people refer to this as a child-free family.)

A **single-parent family** consists of a parent (who may or may not have been married) and one or more children.

A **nuclear family** consists of a father, a mother, and their children. This type of family as a proportion of all families has been declining as the family form has become more diverse.

A **family of origin** is the family into which you are born and in which you are raised. The family consists of you, your parents, and your siblings.

A **family of procreation** is the family you establish if you have children of your own.

An **extended family** consists of you, possibly a partner, any children you might have, and other relatives who live in your household or nearby. It would include grandparents who are helping care for grandchildren, for example.

A **blended, or reconstituted, family** is formed when a widowed or divorced person, with or without children, remarries another person who may or may not have been married before and who may or may not have children. If either the husband or the wife has children from a former marriage or previous relationship, a **stepfamily** is formed.

family Any group of people united by ties of marriage, blood, or adoption or any sexually expressive relationship in which (1) the adults cooperate financially for their mutual support, (2) the people are committed to one another in an intimate interpersonal relationship, (3) the members see their individual identities as importantly attached to the group, and (4) the group has an identity of its own.

voluntarily childless family A couple who decide not to have children.

single-parent family A parent (who may or may not have been married) and one or more children.

nuclear family A father, a mother, and their children.

family of origin The family into which you are born and in which you are raised.

family of procreation The family you establish if you have children of your own.

extended family An individual, possibly a partner, any children the individual might have, and other relatives who live in the household or nearby.

blended, or reconstituted, family A family formed when a widowed or divorced person, with or without children, remarries another person who may or may not have been married before and who may or may not have children.

stepfamily A remarried man and/or woman plus children from a former marriage.

A Long 15 Inches

Will you have success in your intimate relationships? Does that depend on circumstances and luck? Or can you "do" anything to help? This book is based on the following ideas:

1. You can be successful in your intimate relationships.

2. You can learn principles that can help you experience success in your relationships.

3. It is not enough to learn the principles—you must apply them.

The last statement can be a challenge. You can learn about relationships completely enough to make an A in this class and still treat people badly or have an intimate relationship fail. An important question for each of us, then, is, "How do we move the knowledge we have about relationships the 15 inches from our heads (cognitive, unemotional, impersonal realm) to our hearts (affective, emotional, personal realm)?"

Following are some responses students like you gave to that question:

"It takes a conscious decision to put the principles we learn into action. Actions become easier with practice. We also need patience. We didn't learn to walk in a single day!"

"To move from your head to your heart, you have to care about people and put some effort into it."

"I believe that maturing is the main thing that helps me."

"Think before you act about how your action is going to affect the other person and the relationship. It takes some self-control."

"If you practice long enough it becomes natural and stays in your heart."

"Be respectful—no matter how you feel."

A **binuclear family** is an original family divided into two families by divorce. It consists of two nuclear families: (1) the maternal nuclear family headed by the mother and (2) the paternal family headed by the father. The families include whatever children were in the original family and may be headed by a single parent or two parents if former spouses remarry (Ahrons and Rodgers 1987).

A **polygamous family** is a single family unit based on the marriage of one person to two or more mates. If the man has more than one wife, a **polygynous family** is formed. If a woman has more than one husband, a **polyandrous family** is formed. Polyandry is rare, but polygyny is practiced in some African and Asian countries. Both are illegal in the United States.

A **patriarchal family** is one in which the father is head of the household, with authority over other members of the family.

A **matriarchal family** is one in which the mother is head of the household, with authority over other members of the family.

A **gay or lesbian family** consists of a couple of the same sex who are living together and sharing sexual expression and commitment. Some gay or lesbian families include children, usually the offspring of one of the partners.

A **cohabiting family** consists of two people of the opposite sex who are living together and sharing sexual expression and who are committed to their relationship without formal legal marriage.

When talking about the family, then, we must understand the type to which we are referring. With such a wide variety of family forms, we can no longer assume that the word *family* is synonymous with *nuclear family.*

Changes in Family Philosophy and Emphasis

Because the structure and the function of the family have changed over the years, it is important to have a historical perspective to better understand the present and possible future characteristics of the family. Two major changes that have influenced many characteristics of the family have been shifts from institution to companionship and from patriarchy to democracy.

From Institution to Companionship

One of the most important changes in family function has been a shift in emphasis. Traditional views emphasized the role of the family as an institution whose function was to meet the needs of society or the physical needs of society (for example, the bearing and socialization of children to continue the culture) or the physical needs (such as food, shelter, and protection) of family members; this is the **instrumental role** of the family. More modern views of the family tend to emphasize its role in fulfilling emotional and social needs (companionship, belonging, and affection, for example) of family members; this is the **expressive role** of the family. One explanation for this shift is that U.S. society has become highly industrialized.

In an industrial society in which the majority of people live in urban areas, neighbors remain strangers, and it becomes harder for people to find friendship, companionship, and emotional support. Many people are mostly involved in *secondary relationships*—relationships that are superficial and easily replaced. For example, a person may know a little about a coworker in the next cubicle or a friendly server at a favorite café, but true intimacy or friendship is lacking. They may be pleasant people to chat with or to wish "Have a nice weekend," but if they move away, they are soon replaced.

When affectional needs are not met, an individual can feel isolated and alone although he or she is surrounded by millions of people. Erik Erikson (1959) and others have suggested this is because humans long for the profoundly affirming experience of genuine intimacy. Such intimacy is found in *primary relationships*—relationships characterized by breadth and depth of knowledge about someone plus warmth, honesty, and openness. Spouses (or best friends) who know each other's dreams, goals, and fears (as well as favorite color and football team)—and who feel comfortable and safe together—exemplify intimacy. In a highly impersonal society, it becomes more necessary to find

The conventional idea of a family is two parents and one or more children, but in reality, there are many varieties of family structure.

intimacy—belonging and emotional security—in the family itself.

There has been some shift, therefore, in family functions. In the 1800s, people openly admitted to marrying to obtain economic security, to provide

binuclear family An original family divided into two families by divorce.

polygamous family A single family unit based on the marriage of one person to two or more mates.

polygynous family A man married to more than one woman/wife.

polyandrous family A woman married to more than one man/husband.

patriarchal family A family in which the father is head of the household, with authority over other family members.

matriarchal family A family in which the mother is head of the household, with authority over other family members.

gay or lesbian family Two people of the same sex who are living together, having sex, and being mutually committed.

cohabiting family Two people of the opposite sex who are living together and sharing sexual expression and who are committed to their relationship without formal legal marriage.

instrumental role The role of the family in meeting the needs of society or the physical needs of family members.

expressive role The role of the family in meeting the emotional and social needs of family members.

goods and services for one another, to attain social status, to reproduce, and to raise children. Now people marry for love, companionship, and happiness. Rearing healthy, happy children and having economic security are still important goals in marriage, but love, affection, and personal happiness are people's primary expectations in marriage today.

This shift has changed the family itself. When people establish a family for love, companionship, and personal satisfaction but do not find happiness, they may become disappointed or frustrated. Sometimes expectations are charged with so much romantic fantasy that fulfillment is impossible. This is one reason for the high divorce rate; couples often separate because personal needs and expectations are not met.

From Patriarchy to Democracy

Throughout most of our history, the American family was patriarchal. The father was considered head of the household, with authority over and responsibilities for other members of the family. He was the supreme authority in making decisions and settling disputes. He was entitled to the deference and respect of other family members, who were expected to be submissive and obedient.

As head of the household, he owned the property, which was passed to the next generation through the male line. This is known as **patrilineal descent**. The wife and children were expected to reside with the husband and with or near the husband's family, according to his choice. This is **patrilocal residence**. However, as noted earlier, some families are matriarchal, meaning the mother is the head of the household. The terms that refer to female descent and residence are **matrilineal descent** and **matrilocal residence**. This practice was seen in traditional Iroquois society, in which men were expected to move to the female household, and important lines of descent were traced through the female.

Generally, in the 1950s and earlier, one characteristic of the traditional patriarchal family was a clear-cut distinction between the husband's and wife's roles in the family. The husband was the breadwinner and was responsible for clearly defined chores that were considered "man's work," such as making house repairs or mowing the lawn. The wife was responsible for "woman's work,"

The family pictured here was once considered the ideal. The father was traditionally the head of the household, with authority over all the family members.

including housecleaning, cooking, and caring for the children.

With the cultural climate of activism of the civil rights movement in the 1950s and the women's rights movement in the 1960s, the ideals of the patriarchal family were challenged. The patriarchal family was replaced by the democratic family, in which women were treated more as equals and demanded a greater voice in family governance.

This change had several causes. First, with the rise of the feminist movement, women gained some economic power and freedom. The feminist movement in the United States was launched at Seneca Falls, New York, in 1848, with the first women's rights convention. Starting with almost no political leverage and no money and with conventional morality against them, the suffragists won enactment of the Married Women's Property Act in the latter half of the nineteenth century and ratification of the Nineteenth Amendment to the Constitution in 1920, which gave women the right to vote. The Married Women's Property Act recognized the right of married women to hold property and borrow money. As some economic power gradually shifted to women, they gained more power and authority in family governance as well. Property could now be passed on through **bilateral descent** (through both the father and the mother).

Second, in the 1960s and 1970s, increasing educational opportunities for women and the gradual increase in the percentage of married women working outside the home encouraged the adoption of more egalitarian gender roles in the family. As more wives earned an income, more husbands were asked to bear equal responsibility for homemaking and child care. Although sharing responsibilities was the ideal, it was not always followed in practice, and working wives continued to do most of the housework (Blumstein and Schwartz 1983). The general trend, however, is toward a more equal voice in decision making and a more equitable and flexible distribution of family responsibilities (see Chapters 2 and 8 for a detailed discussion). Democratic, egalitarian, dual-career families often prefer a **neolocal residence**—a place where both spouses choose to live—rather than living with either spouse's family.

Third, in the 1960s and 1970s, the demand for equality of sexual expression resulted from the recognition of the sexual needs of women. With such recognition, marriages could be based on the mutual exchange of love and affection. Development of efficient contraceptives also freed women from unwanted childbearing and enabled them to have greater personal and professional choices.

Fourth, the child study movement after World War II catalyzed the development of the child-centered family. No longer was it a matter of what children could do to serve the family; rather, it became a matter of what the family could contribute to the total development of the child. The rights and needs of children as important members of the family were emphasized.

The net result of these and other changes has been the development of a democratic family ideal that emphasizes egalitarian rights and responsibilities in a group concerned with the welfare of all. This ideal has not always been achieved, but family philosophies, forms, and functions continue to change as new needs arise.

After years of protest, in the latter half of the nineteenth century, women won the right to own property and borrow money with the enactment of the Married Women's Property Act. Women who fought for the right to own property may have been arrested for the cause.

Changes in Marriage and Parenthood

As we will see, marriage and parenthood have undergone various changes in recent decades. The marriage rate has gone down, the age at which people marry has gone up, and the number of children per family has declined. Another controversial change is the very definition of marriage.

patrilineal descent Inheritance that is traced through the male line.

patrilocal residence A residential pattern in which a newlywed couple resides with or near the man's family.

matrilineal descent Inheritance that is traced through the female line.

matrilocal residence A residential pattern in which newlyweds reside with or near the woman's family.

bilateral descent Inheritance is passed through both the male and the female line.

neolocal residence A residential pattern in which newlyweds leave their parents' homes and reside in a new location of their choice rather than with either family.

Historically, marriage in the United States has been defined as being united to a person of the opposite sex as husband and wife in a consensual and contractual relationship that is recognized by law. In recent decades, the idea that a legal marriage can exist only between a male and female has been challenged. In 2015, the U.S. Supreme Court ruled that the U.S. Constitution guarantees same-sex couples the right to marry. Furthermore, states cannot prohibit same-sex marriages and must recognize such marriages performed in other states (World Almanac 2016).

Marriage Rates

The marriage rate is the number of persons who marry during the preceding 12 months per 1,000 population. The rate depends on economic and political conditions, as well as on the percentage of persons of marriageable age in the population.

The rate reached a peak of 16.4 per 1,000 population in 1946, just after World War II, and then declined rapidly to 8.5 per 1,000 in 1960. The rate varied at a fairly high level for two decades and then began to fall again in 1980, after most of the baby boom babies had married (see Figure 1.1). Today the rate is 6.8 per 1,000 (National Center for Health Statistics 2016). Some of the decline results from the delaying of first marriages until older ages, the increase in unmarried cohabitation, and a small decrease in the tendency of divorced persons to remarry (Popenoe 2007).

Median Age

One of the dramatic trends in marriage patterns over the decades has been the postponement of marriage to a later age. At the beginning of the twentieth century, the median age at first marriage started a decline that ended in the mid-1950s, reaching a low of 22.5 years for males and 20.1 years for females. Since then, the estimated median age has been rising, with especially rapid increases since 1980. In 2014, the median age was 29.3 for males and 27.0 for females (U.S. Bureau of the Census 2016). Figure 1.2 shows this trend. The gap between males and females has also narrowed over the years, but on average, men are still 2 years older than women the first time they marry.

A higher age at marriage is associated with longer periods of school enrollment. In 2003, 85% of American adults had a high school diploma, compared with 75.2% in 1990, and 27% had earned a bachelor's degree or more in 2000, compared with 21% in 1990 (*Statistical Abstract of the United States* 2012). The delay in marriage is also associated with the decline in negative attitudes toward remaining single, a longer life expectancy, more career options for women, increased opportunities for nonmarital

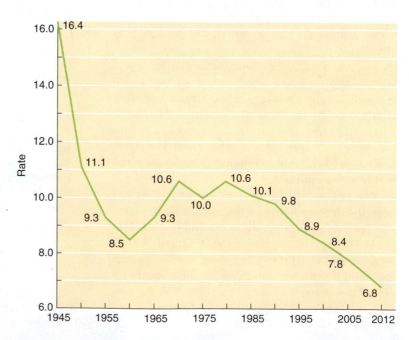

FIGURE 1.1 Marriage Rate per 1,000 Population

Note: From Statistical Abstract of the United States, *2012. U.S. Bureau of the Census. http://www.census.gov.*

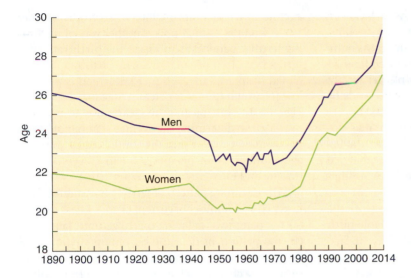

FIGURE 1.2 Median Age at First Marriage, by Sex: 1890–2014

Note: Data from Vital Statistics of the United States, *by U.S. National Center for Health Statistics (U.S. Department of Health and Human Services), annual, 1890–2000; U.S. Bureau of the Census, 2016. http://www.census.gov.*

sexual intercourse, and increased acceptance of non-marital cohabitation.

This trend is significant because those who wait until they are in their middle or late twenties to marry have a greater chance of marital success than do those who marry earlier. In fact, one of the strongest and most consistent predictors of the propensity to divorce is the age at which persons marry. Virtually every study of marital dissolution undertaken since the late 1960s has found both spouses' age at marriage to be statistically significant with respect to the probability of divorce (South 1995). The delay of marriage also has resulted in large numbers of unmarried young adults in the population. In 2010, for example, 88.7% of men and 79.3% of women ages 20 to 24 were never married, and 62.2% of men and 47.8% of women ages 25 to 29 were never married (*Statistical Abstract of the United States* 2012). See Figure 1.3 for a detailed breakdown of marital status for all ages.

Family Size

Over the past 100 years, American family and household sizes have been shrinking. (The U.S. Bureau of the Census measure of family size excludes unrelated people living in the household. Consequently, the family/household numbers differ slightly.) In 1915, the average number of people sharing a home was 4.5; by 1960, the average family size had dropped to 3.65 (3.39 for household size). By 2010, family size had reached 3.14 (2.58 for households) (U.S. Bureau of the Census 2012).

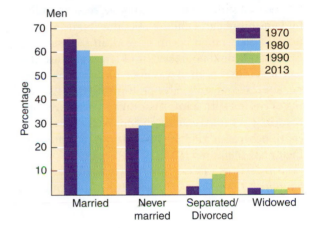

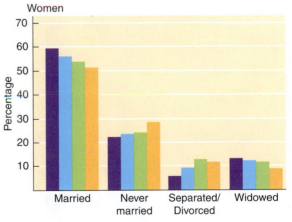

FIGURE 1.3 Marital Status of the Population 15 Years and Older, by Sex: Selected Years, 1970–2013 (in percentages)

Note: From J. Fields (2004), U.S. Bureau of the Census, Current Population Reports, America's Families and Living Arrangements: 2003; *Statistical Abstract of the United States, 2015, U.S. Bureau of Census. http://www.census.gov.*

The decline in family/household size can be attributed to several factors, including changes in fertility, marriage, and divorce patterns. For example, the numbers of single-parent families and child-free families have increased, resulting in fewer people per family. Divorce generally reduces the size of households by separating one household into two smaller ones.

A decline in overall fertility has been a significant factor in families becoming smaller. At the beginning of the twentieth century, the average married woman had five children. At that time, large families were considered not only a blessing but also an economic asset: more hands were available to work the family farm or business. Furthermore, reliable birth control methods were largely unavailable. In fact, federal and state laws made it illegal even to provide information about birth control.

As families moved from farms to cities and became consumers rather than producers, providing for large numbers of children became financially difficult. Also, women began to work in factories and offices and could not take care of large families. Day care for young children was not widely available.

Federal and state laws prohibiting the dispensing of contraception information and methods were gradually repealed. More efficient means of contraception became available; couples were more willing to use them.

The **fertility rate** (number of live births per 1,000 women 15–44 years of age) shows the ongoing decline in fertility since 1960, when it was 118 per 1,000 women, to 62.9 now. Another way of measuring fertility patterns is to assess the **birth rate** (live births per 1,000 population). The birth rate has declined from 23.7 in 1960 to 12.5, which is a record low (National Center for Health Statistics 2016) (see Figure 1.4). Perhaps an even clearer way to measure fertility is to determine the average number of births per woman. Currently, in the United States, the average number of births per woman hovers near 2 (Monte and Ellis 2014; World Bank 2016).

The declining pattern of fertility in America is influenced by a number of current factors. These include (a) the pattern of delaying marriage until later ages; (b) the pattern of delaying becoming parents until later ages (the longer one delays having a first child, the less the chances of having a second or third child); and (c) the economic recession, unemployment, and shrinking middle-class jobs, which have created uncertainty about the future—thus influencing people to have fewer children or to delay parenthood.

The decline in births has affected family composition as well as family size. It has been estimated that 75% of households in the middle 1800s involved children under the age of 18. By 1960, only about half of households did; by 2005, about 32% contained children; and by 2010, approximately 24% contained children under 18 years of age (Popenoe 2007; U.S. Bureau of the Census 2011). This means that adults are less likely to be

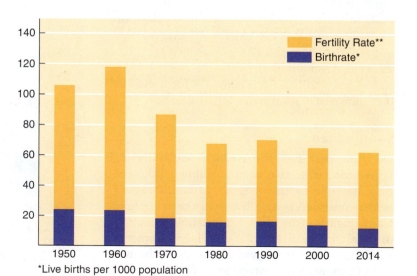

FIGURE 1.4 Birth Rates and Fertility Rates: 1950–2014

Source: National Center for Health Statistics, 2016.

*Live births per 1000 population

**Live births per 1000 women 15–44 years of age

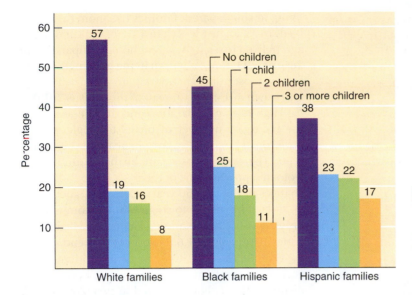

FIGURE 1.5 Percentage Distribution of Families by Number of Own Children under 18 Years Old and by Ethnic Group, 2006

Note: Data from Statistical Abstract of the United States, 2008 *(Table 60), by U.S. Bureau of the Census, 2008, Washington, DC: U.S. Government Printing Office.*

living with children and that neighborhoods are less likely to have children (see Figure 1.5). The welfare, needs, and concerns of children may be receiving less consideration by both family members and the broader culture (Popenoe 2007).

Working Wives and Mothers

Another important change in family living has been the large influx of married women into the workforce. Until the early 1980s, married women with no children under age 18 had higher labor force participation rates than did those with children under age 6. This long-standing pattern began to change during the 1980s and has now reversed. Currently, primarily because of economic necessity, less than half of all mothers are stay-at-home parents. Now, about 61% of mothers with children under the age of 3 are in the labor force, a significant increase from 38% in 1980 (Bureau of Labor Statistics 2014).

Research has revealed some demographic, social, and attitudinal differences between married women who work outside the home and those who do not. Those who do not are more likely to hold traditional attitudes regarding marital roles, mothers' employment outside the home, and sexuality. Married women who are not employed full-time have more children and live in households with less income. Married women who are employed full-time are better educated and have fewer children and more income

than married women who are not employed (Glass 1992; United States Department of Labor 2014).

Women enter the workforce for both economic and noneconomic reasons. The major reason is financial need: factors such as inflation, the high cost of living, and the desire for a higher standard of living pressure families to have two incomes. Employment opportunities for women also have increased. Noneconomic reasons for employment are important as well. Large numbers of women want to work for reasons of personal fulfillment.

In some ways, paid employment has added to women's burdens. Most working wives must meet the usual demands for housework and family care in addition to working outside the home. Although more husbands help with household and parental chores, research indicates that a wife's employment has only a minimal effect on her husband's involvement. Consequently, many employed wives feel that they start the "second shift" when they get home (Cox 2009). In addition, increased employment for mothers has intensified the demand for child care. This trend will be discussed in Chapters 8 and 13.

fertility rate The number of live births per 1,000 women 15–44 years of age.

birth rate The number of live births per 1,000 population.

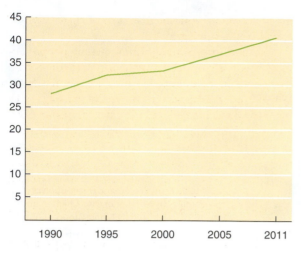

FIGURE 1.6 Percentage of U.S. Births to Unmarried Women, 1990–2013

Source: National Center for Health Statistics, 2016.

One-Parent Families

One major change in families since the 1970s has been the increase in the number of families that consist of a single parent maintaining a household with one or more children. The percentage of families headed by a single parent has increased from 11% in 1970 to 19%; 16% headed by moms and 3% headed by dads (U.S. Bureau of the Census 2016).

Another perspective on this change is to consider that since 1970, the percentage of children

Family life is an important source of life satisfaction for African Americans, especially if the family has a comfortable and steady income.

living in single-parent families has more than doubled. In 1970, just less than 12% of children under age 18 lived in a single-parent home compared with 28% now. Of those children living in a single-parent family, most (more than 80%) are with their mothers (Dawn 2015; U.S. Bureau of the Census 2016).

High rates of separation and divorce as well as the increased number of births to single women have contributed to the large increase in this family type. The large increase in births to unmarried women represents one of the most profound family changes in the past 50 years. Currently, about 41% of all U.S. births are to single women compared to only 28% in 1990 (National Center for Health Statistics 2016). Figure 1.6 illustrates this trend.

Overall, about 30% of American children live in a single-parent family. Black children, however, are disproportionately represented in this family form. Some 56% of black children compared to 22% of white and 31% of Hispanic children under age 18 live in a single-parent family (U.S. Bureau of the Census 2015).

One of the major problem areas associated with the rise in single-parent families is economic because many single-parent households do not have adequate income to support children. Single mothers have a higher rate of unemployment than do married mothers (Bianchi 2011). Financial pressure is one of the most common complaints among single parents, and single-parent families are more likely than two-parent families to live in poverty. For example, nearly 31% of single-mother and 16% of single-father families live in poverty compared with about 7% of married-couple families with children (Dawn 2015; U.S. Bureau of the Census 2016). Research has shown that even when controlling for the effects of education, single fathers are better off economically than single mothers, and white single parents fare better economically than African American single parents (Dawn 2015; Zhan and Pandey 2004). Single-parent families and the impact of economic hardship on a child's development will be discussed in more detail in Chapters 3 and 8.

Cohabitation

One of the most significant changes in family form has been the huge increase in the number of opposite-sex couples who live together and share sexual intimacy without having a legal marriage. As Figure 1.7 shows, the number of cohabiting couples increased from less than 500,000 in 1960 to slightly more than 7 million in 2014. Most cohabitants are young adults; the number of cohabiting couples drops sharply after age 30 (Kreider 2008; U.S. Bureau of the Census 2016).

At first glance it might appear that cohabitation is replacing marriage. Instead, it is more likely that cohabitation has become part of the mate-selection process (Manning, Longmore, and Giordano 2007). Today, between 50% and 60% of opposite-sex couples who plan to marry live together first, up from 10% in 1965 (Guzzo 2009; U.S. Bureau of the Census 2012).

Although cohabitation is convenient and offers an antidote to loneliness, cohabitants tend to have poorer relationship quality—lower levels of happiness and well-being and more depression—than do married couples (Kline et al. 2004; Rhoades et al. 2006). Also, those who cohabited before marriage are more likely to divorce and/or to consider the possibility of divorce, with the divorce rate being highest among serial cohabiters (Jose, O'Leary, and Moyer 2010; D. T. Lichter and Qian 2008). However, cohabiters who report plans to marry their partners are involved in unions that do not differ significantly from marriage.

Furthermore, although many young people believe it is a good idea to live with a person before marrying, numerous studies indicate that living together is not a good way to prepare for marriage or to avoid divorce. Instead, cohabitation increases both the risk of breaking up after marriage and the risks of domestic violence for women and physical and sexual abuse for children. A woman is nine times more likely to be killed by a partner in a cohabiting relationship than by a husband (S. L. Brown and Bulanda 2008; Rhoades et al. 2006; Shackelford and Mouzos 2005).

It is hard to know exactly why cohabitation is not better preparation for marriage. Researchers speculate that overall commitment is less in cohabiting relationships than in marriage and that cohabitation offers less certainty of a lifetime partnership. Lower levels of commitment seem to change the day-to-day dynamics of the relationship. Certainly, cohabiting couples who encounter difficulties or who decide they just do not want to be together may find it easier to end the relationship when commitment is lacking.

It is also possible that it is not the experience of cohabiting that increases marital difficulties and the risk of divorce, but rather the expectations, attitudes, and values of the people who choose cohabitation. Cohabitation is perceived as "different" from marriage—as involving less commitment and relationship quality. Cohabitation may be chosen because it is viewed as practical—a way to share expenses and have a steady sex partner—but with lower expectations of an enduring, satisfying relationship (J. M. Reed 2006).

The increase in cohabitation is a large reason why nonmarital childbearing has increased substantially in the United States. The percentage of live births to unmarried women has increased from 10.7% in 1970 to about 41% today (National Center for Health Statistics 2016; U.S. Bureau of the Census 2008b).

It is estimated that 40% of all children today will spend some time in a cohabiting household. The effect on these children depends a great deal on the quality and harmony of the cohabiting relationship—and on the quality of the relationship that the adults in the household establish with the children. Children need love, affection, security, and guidance in their lives. If the cohabiting relationship supplies these needs, children will

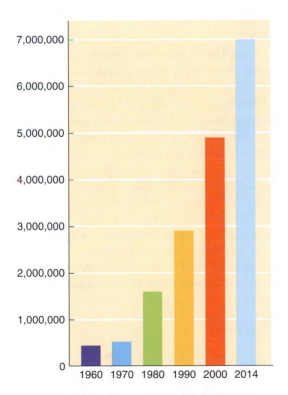

FIGURE 1.7 Number of Unmarried Couples Cohabiting, 1960–2014

Note: Data from U.S. Census Bureau. Households and Families: 2016. http://www.census.gov.

Children Not Living with Married Biological Parents

The increased diversity of family forms in recent decades has raised concerns about the well-being of children growing up in them. Research over the past 20 years supports the idea that, generally speaking, children do best when reared by their two married, biological parents who have a low-conflict relationship (Amato 2005; M. Parke 2003). However, most children reared in other types of family forms grow up without serious problems—thus raising questions about whether the risks are a result of family form and marital status or are caused by other factors such as poverty or the quality of the adults' relationship. Understanding the implications of the findings is complicated by the fact that many children live in more than one family form in the course of childhood and that the risks vary according to family form.

Research findings indicate some specifics:

- Single-parent families have a much higher poverty rate (26%) than two-parent, biological families (5%) or stepfamilies (9%).

- The risk of dropping out of school is lower in two-parent, biological families than in single-parent or stepparent families (11% vs. 28% for whites; 17% vs. 30% for blacks; and 25% vs. 49% for Hispanics).

- Children of unmarried mothers are most at risk for poverty and not completing their education.

- Children of widowed parents fare best of all categories of children of single parents.

- Children living with a parent or parents who cohabit are at great risk for unstable living situations. The average cohabiting relationship lasts 2 years.

- School achievement and behavioral problems are similar among children living with two biological parents—whether married or cohabiting.

- Children in stepfamilies are more likely to have negative behavioral, health, and educational outcomes and to leave home earlier than children living with both married biological parents.

- Children living with same-sex parents tend to have challenges no more difficult than their counterparts reared in heterosexual *divorced* families.

- Children who grow up in married families with high conflict experience lower emotional well-being than those in low-conflict homes.

likely benefit; if it does not, children will be affected negatively (Artis 2007). Children in cohabiting households face a risk five times greater than children in married households that the couple will break up (Manning 2002; Osborne, Manning, and Smock 2007).

In the event of the ending of a cohabiting relationship, property is considered to belong to the person who owned it or bought it; property is not considered to be "common" unless both parties' names appear on a deed or title. Neither is considered to have any responsibility for the financial support of the other (unlike in a divorcing situation where an ex-spouse with financial resources may be

required to pay alimony). When children are involved, the father may have to prove paternity to claim visitation/custody rights with his offspring. And a mother may have to prove paternity of the child to claim child support from a non-custodial father (Find Law 2016).

Gay and Lesbian Families

As stated previously in the chapter, broadening the definition of marriage to include same-sex couples is controversial today. Recent national opinion polls indicate that most (47% to 60%) of the American public supports same-sex marriage (Burke 2015;

McCarthy 2015). Gays and lesbians regard legal marriage as important to them for the same reasons that heterosexuals do.

Same-sex couples who want to be in long-term, committed, and legally recognized relationships have three options. In June 2015, the Supreme Court of the United States ruled that same-sex couples can marry. With this historic decision, same-sex couples now have the right to marry in all states and have all the rights, responsibilities, and benefits of married heterosexual couples (de Vogue and Diamond 2015).

In some states, same-sex couples can enter into a **civil union** that gives them nearly all the same rights and privileges of married couples. These include joint property rights, inheritance rights, visitation in prison/hospitals, and inclusion in insurance and pensions. A couple must obtain a civil union license and have the union certified by a judge or member of the clergy. If the couple breaks up, they must go through family court to obtain a legal dissolution.

In a third option, a number of states as well as some counties and cities recognize **domestic partnerships**. These partnerships allow same-sex couples and certain heterosexual couples (for example, senior cohabitants) to have some of the rights and privileges as married couples—hospital visitation, emergency health care, funeral arrangements, and inheritance without a will. Some major U.S. corporations (including Apple Computer, IBM, and Disney) began to extend employee health insurance benefits to partners of gay and lesbian employees some time ago.

Laws and policies regarding civil unions and domestic partnerships do not include all the rights of marriage and they vary considerably from state to city to company. Nor do civil unions and domestic partnerships carry federal marriage benefits; they may not be recognized by other states. For these reasons and because same-sex marriage is now allowed in all states, the number of same-sex couples choosing civil unions or domestic partnerships likely will decline.

About one-fourth of same-sex couples are rearing children—either children born during a previous heterosexual relationship or born by donor insemination or children who are adopted (Herek 2006). Even so, same-sex parenting is an issue of controversy. Major concerns center around the possible adverse effects of the parents' homosexuality on the children's overall development. Generally, the studies that have been conducted on children who grow up in gay and lesbian families show that the children develop in a positive manner psychologically, intellectually, behaviorally, and emotionally. They have no greater incidence of homosexuality or substance abuse than do children who grow up in a heterosexual family and show no significantly greater retention in school (Manning, Fettro, and Lamidi 2014, Rosenfeld 2010).

In 2002 the American Academy of Pediatrics called for state laws to allow for gays and lesbians to adopt a partner's children. This would allow for children to be covered under health insurance policies and receive survivor benefits. The American Academy of Child and Adolescent Psychiatry has similar views on adoption rights for gay and lesbian parents.

Grandparents as Parents

One notable trend in the evolution of the family in recent decades is the dramatic increase in the number of children (more than 6 million, or 6% of the nation's children) living in households headed by grandparents. This is quite an increase compared to 1970, when 2.2 million (3.2%) children under age 18 lived in their grandparents' homes (U.S. Bureau of the Census 2012). When these households are categorized by the presence of parents, it becomes evident that the greatest increases have occurred in households in which at least one parent is also residing in the home. Since 1970, the number of grandparent-maintained households in which the mother was present more than doubled (Kreider and Fields 2005) (see Figure 1.8). Reasons for this trend include an increase in drug use among parents; higher rates of teen pregnancy, divorce, child abuse, and neglect; and incarceration of parents.

Given the increase in the number of grandparents raising their grandchildren and the impact this arrangement has on both caregiver and child, the government and the community will likely be called on to provide more support (Ellis and

civil union A legally recognized union similar to marriage.

domestic partnership A legal or personal relationship between two people who live together and share a common domestic life but are not joined by marriage or civil union.

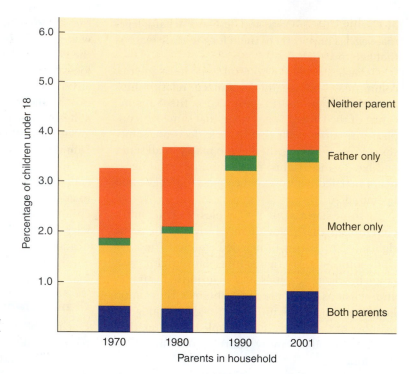

FIGURE 1.8 Grandchildren in Grandparents' Homes by Presence of Parents, 1970–2001

Note: Data from U.S. Bureau of the Census, 1970 and 1980, "Marital Status and Living Arrangements: March 1994" (Table A-6) and "Marital Status and Living Arrangements: March 1997" (Table 4); Kreider and Fields (2005), Living Arrangements of Children: 2001, by U.S. Bureau of the Census, Current Population Reports, *Washington, DC: U.S. Government Printing Office.*

Simmons 2014). Policies and programs intended for traditional and foster families could be extended to grandparent-maintained families as well, and employee benefits for grandparents remaining in the workforce could be extended to their grandchildren, for example.

As life expectancy continues to rise, many Americans will find themselves living well into their nineties.

Changes in Life Expectancy

Although there are racial and gender differences in life expectancy, Americans are living longer than ever before and are healthier in later life. In 1970, life expectancy was 67 years for men and 75 years for women. By 2013 these numbers had increased to 76.4 years for men and 81.2 for women (National Center for Health Statistics 2016). The gap in life expectancy between men and women is narrowing (down from 8 years to 5). Racial differences in life expectancy also continue, with blacks having lower life expectancy than whites by about 3 years for women and 4.5 years for men (National Center for Health Statistics 2016).

The increase in life expectancy is impacting marriages and families. More and more families are caring for their elders during the same years that they are rearing their children. This can strain the financial, emotional, time, and energy resources of family members who are already struggling with the demands of career and children.

The implication of longevity on duration of marriage is also a question to examine. A 25-year-old couple marrying today has good prospects of living long enough to celebrate a golden wedding anniversary—if the marriage can survive. (In 1900, when life expectancy was 47 years, marriages did not have to last as long.) As people grow and change, particularly in a society that is generally tolerant of divorce, many may seek divorce or alternative living arrangements to achieve greater personal fulfillment and happiness.

Changes in Divorce and Remarriage

Another of the dramatic changes in family life over the past four decades has been the increase in the rate of divorce and remarriage, along with the number of stepfamilies. In recent years, rates of divorce and remarriage have declined slightly, but they are still at a relatively high level.

Divorce Rates

An examination of the trends in the proportions of people ever divorced is complicated because that indicator is a function of the proportions both of people getting married and of those getting divorced (Kreider 2005). The U.S. Census defines the divorce rate as the number of people divorced per 1,000 population. Today, the divorce rate is 3.4 per 1,000 individuals (National Center for Health Statistics 2016). Divorce rates increased steadily from 1958 until about 1980, but since then they have declined slightly (see Figure 1.9). Most scholars believe that the divorce rate has stabilized, with about 40% to 50% of new marriages likely to end in divorce. The decline from the all-time high may represent a slight increase in marital stability resulting from the increased age at which people marry for the first time and the higher educational level of those marrying, both of which are associated with greater marital stability (Popenoe 2007; Whitehead and Popenoe 2005).

Other background characteristics of people entering a marriage also have major implications for their risk of divorce. If a person is reasonably well educated with a decent income, comes from an intact family, is religious, and marries after age 25 without having a baby first, the chances of divorce are considerably lower (Popenoe 2007; Whitehead and Popenoe 2005). Divorce will be discussed in detail in Chapter 16.

Remarriage Trends

Many of the people who are divorced or widowed marry again. About 40% of new marriages involve a remarriage for at least one of the persons. Another way of looking at this is that about 23% of married adults have been married before (Livingston 2014).

Remarriage happens fairly quickly. The median number of years between divorce and remarriage is about 3 to 4 years (U.S. Bureau of the Census 2016). Whites remarry more quickly than African Americans and Latinos and men are more likely than women to remarry. Also, among those who do remarry, men generally do so sooner than women (Livingston 2014). Remarriage rates will be discussed in subsequent chapters. However, since the 1960s, the proportion who remarry appears to be declining among younger adults but increasing among seniors (Livingston 2014).

Redivorce rates for remarried persons also show slight signs of decline from previous years and are becoming similar to those of first divorce. Currently, it is estimated that about 67% of second marriages and 75% of third marriages will end in divorce (compared to 40% to 50% of first marriages) (Banschick 2013). For women, the median duration of second marriages that end in divorce is about 8 years, which is the same as for first marriages. The median duration of second marriages for men is slightly longer, at 9 years (Kreider 2005).

FIGURE 1.9 Divorce Rates, 1910–2012

Note: Data from Vital Statistics of the United States, by National Center for Health Statistics (U.S. Department of Health and Human Services), annual, 1910–1998, Washington, DC: U.S. Government Printing Office; National Vital Statistics Reports 49, no. 6, August 22, 2001; National Center for Health Statistics, 2016.

However, the incidence of divorce in the United States remains among the highest in the world. The net effect of a high rate of divorce and remarriage is an increase in reconstituted, or blended, families.

Blended Families

Many American marriages are remarriages for one or both of the spouses. When a parent remarries and brings children from a previous marriage into the new family unit, a blended, or reconstituted, family is formed. If the couple has children together, the blended family may consist of children from her previous marriage, children from his previous marriage, and children born to them since they married each other.

Family relationships in a blended family can become complicated. Each parent faces the challenge of forming relationships with stepchildren, with the children of the new marriage, and perhaps with the spouse's ex-spouse. The children face the challenge of adjusting to stepparents and to stepsiblings, as well as maintaining relationships with natural parents both inside and outside their new family unit. If both of their natural parents remarry, the children must adjust to two stepparents and to any stepsiblings in their newly constituted families. Also, both parents and children may have to form new relationships with other relatives on both sides of the families. In short, many adjustments are required. See Chapter 17 for a detailed discussion of remarriage and stepparenting.

Ethnic and Cultural Diversity in Families

The United States has long been a country with rich diversity of ethnicity and cultures. Because ethnic and cultural backgrounds strongly influence family life, a multicultural perspective is necessary to understand contemporary family relationships.

Increased Ethnic Diversity

Slightly more than 197 million people (64% of the population) are classified as white non-Hispanic; many of their family trees have European roots that date back 200 or more years. Non-Hispanic blacks number 40 million individuals (12% of the

population). Hispanics, whose family roots may be in Mexico, the Spanish-speaking Caribbean, or Central and South America, total about 54 million people (16% of the population). About 16 million people (5% of the population) identify themselves as Asians or Pacific Islanders. Non-Hispanic Native Americans from various tribes number about 2.5 million (1% of the population) (U.S. Bureau of the Census 2015) (see Figure 1.10).

In fact, the United States contains people from virtually all the world's cultures. In a general sense, **ethnicity** can be thought of as the way people define themselves as part of a group through similarities in ancestry and cultural heritage (race, religion, or national origin). **Culture** can be defined as the sum total of ways of living, including the values, beliefs, aesthetic standards, linguistic expressions, patterns of thinking, behavioral norms, and styles of communication that a group of people has developed to ensure its survival in a particular physical and human environment (Hoopes 1979). Ethnicity and culture are not always the same thing because culture can encompass many different ethnicities. For example, American culture is a mixture of the arts, beliefs, customs, and other products of human endeavor and thought created by many different ethnic groups. If people take the time to learn about and benefit from this diversity, the cultural makeup of the nation becomes a significant strength.

The values, beliefs, history, and circumstances of one's ethnic group or ethnic identity result in certain family characteristics (family structure,

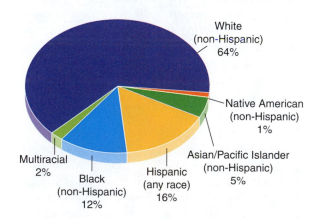

FIGURE 1.10 U.S. Population by Race and Hispanic Origin

Note: Data from "Resident Population by Sex, Race, and Hispanic Origin Status" by U.S. Bureau of the Census, Statistical Abstract of the United States, *2015. http://www.census.gov.*

spousal relationships, power structure, or child-rearing patterns, for example) being different from those of other ethnic groups. Keep in mind, however, that there are a great many similarities across ethnic groups (love of children or values such as honesty, for example) as well as differences within ethnic groups (Asians from Vietnam differ from Asians from China). Research has concentrated on the following ethnic groups: African Americans, Hispanic Americans, Asian/Pacific Islander Americans, and Native Americans.

Hispanic Americans

The Hispanic population is the largest and fastest growing minority group in the United States, currently comprising 16% of the population and expected to grow to 25% of the population by 2050. This is in part a result of high immigration rates and high fertility rates. Traditionally, the Latino family was patriarchal, with the husband/father expected to be dominant as a way of proving his machismo (manhood). Modern Hispanics view machismo in terms of courage, strength, family pride, respect for others, honor, and the proper use of authority (Hamner and Turner 2001; U.S. Bureau of the Census 2015).

Role relationships in marriage are still traditional. The man is the head of the household, but is expected to exercise authority in a fair and dignified manner and to show respect for other family members. Although machismo does often characterize Latin American culture, research of Hispanic families in the United States does not indicate a pattern of male dominance. Egalitarianism is demonstrated to a higher degree than is male dominance—especially as wives enter the workforce (Pinto and Coltrane 2009). Good communication, religion, and children are considered very important to marriage success (Skogrand, Hatch, and Singh 2008).

The fertility rate for Hispanics is the highest of any ethnic group in the United States (National Center for Health Statistics 2015; Popenoe 2007). Parent–child relationships are warm and nurturing; fathers tend to be playful and companionable with their children, but the mother–child relationship is primary. The relationship between children and their parents is typically one of respect. It is common for the younger generation to express great deference to elders (Hamner and Turner 2001).

The family is highly valued, and the needs of the family are emphasized above those of the individual. Individuals find their identity in the family group. The extended family is an important source of strength and help: cousins, aunts, uncles, grandparents, and siblings offer assistance as needed. Approximately 69% of Hispanic children live in intact families, and the divorce rate is lower for this group than for non-Hispanic whites or blacks (National Center for Health Statistics 2012).

African Americans

Black Americans are the second largest racial minority in the United States. The African American population has experienced considerable change over the past 25 years, including the rise of a middle class, the rise of an underclass, and the diminishing of the blue-collar working class. This means that although about one-third of blacks are classified as middle class, another 27.4% live below the poverty level (U.S. Bureau of the Census 2012).

Research on black families in recent years helps present a picture of the diversity within this racial group. Some assumptions from earlier years have also fallen. For example, the common assumption that black families are matriarchal is not always true. In reality, the egalitarian pattern is common in intact families and is the norm in middle-class families (Hamner and Turner 2001; R. L. Taylor 2002).

African American women have a history of having worked outside the home (because of economic need), thus giving them incomes and power in the marital relationship. McAdoo (2007) notes that African American couples expect to work together for the good of the marital unit and share equally in decision making. Contrary to the stereotype of the absent black father, many men are involved in the care of their children—especially in families with financial security.

African American women face several unique challenges in finding spouses. First, there are fewer

ethnicity The way people define themselves as part of a group through similarities in an ancestry and cultural heritage.

culture The sum total of ways of living, including the values, beliefs, aesthetic standards, linguistic expressions, patterns of thinking, behavioral norms, and style of communication a group of people has developed to ensure its survival in a particular physical and human environment.

Ethnic Identity and Acculturation

Minority groups often find it difficult to truly be accepted and to fit into mainstream American culture. This can be the case even for those who have lived in the United States all their lives and have adopted all the mainstream cultural habits. Consider the following quotations from the media regarding Asian Americans:

> *"You know, I'm tired of the Kristi Yamaguchis and the Michelle Kwans! They're not American... when I look at a box of Wheaties, I don't want to see eyes that are slanted and Oriental and almond shaped. I want to see American eyes looking at me."*
>
> —Bill Handel, popular morning DJ for KFI-AM, one of the nation's most listened-to talk radio stations.

> *"American beats Kwan."*
>
> —MSNBC's erroneous headline after figure skater Tara Lipinski beat Michelle Kwan during the 1998 Winter Olympics. Both women are Americans.

Mia Tuan (1999) has explored what she called the "authenticity dilemma" confronting Asian Americans today. She interviewed 95 third-, fourth-, and fifth-generation Chinese and Japanese Americans living in northern and southern California to (1) determine the content, meaning, and salience of ethnicity in their lives; (2) explore the extent to which they felt that ethnicity was an optional rather than imposed facet of their identities; and (3) examine the role played by race in shaping life experiences. The following excerpts are from her interviews:

Q. HOW DO YOU IDENTIFY YOURSELF?

A. That's a really hard question actually. I guess as an Asian-American. I don't consider myself just Japanese, just Chinese. I don't consider myself just American. I don't know. I kinda like terminology like Asian-American and African-American because it's kinda messy.... By blood, I'm Chinese and Japanese. By culture, I don't know if I am so much of either. I don't know.... Mom would always tell me I used to get confused growing up. "How can I be Japanese and Chinese and American?" "Well, you are half Japanese, half Chinese, and all American." (108)

A. I don't think I can be just American just for the fact that I look different from the typical American, white. (Why not just Japanese then?) Because I definitely am Americanized, an American raised in America. And I don't always agree with what Japanese, Japan stands for. (109)

A. Usually I say Chinese American because I realize I'm not Chinese. People from China come over here and like, whoa, they're like a foreign species. And I'm not American because just one look and I'm apart. I used to struggle with this question a lot and to make a long story short, Chinese-American is a hybrid of its own. It's kind of like Afro-Americans. Boy, they're not African and they're not American and it's just its own species and that's the way it is. (116)

A. Like my girlfriend, it's kinda funny because she's of Irish descent, but people would never think that or ask where are you from because they see her as being Caucasian. And if they look at me they would say, "Oh where are you from," because I'm perceived as being Asian first. It's like girl, an Asian girl, and anything that follows after that. For my girlfriend it would be like, she's white, she's of Irish descent but it doesn't really matter. It's like way down the list of whatever. (112)

These statements go to the heart of the dilemma many Asian Americans face: they have learned that others view them as outsiders in American society. Although they are lifelong Americans, they are not perceived as such because they do not fit the image of a "real" American. About half the respondents reported having felt out of place or suddenly conscious of their racial background at some time. Reasons for this reaction included stares, comments, and even threats from others who looked on them as strangers or intruders in a public place. European Americans see it as a matter of personal choice whether to identify along ethnic lines, but the respondents found that not identifying in ethnic or racial terms was problematic in their interactions with non-Asians. Complicating matters for many Asian Americans was that their foreign-born counterparts saw them as "too American" and not knowledgeable enough about Chinese or Japanese ways (Tuan 1999).

Tuan (1999) summarizes:

Today, Asian ethnics exercise a great deal of choice regarding the elements of traditional ethnic culture they wish to incorporate or do away with in their personal lives. They befriend whom they please, date and marry whom they please, choose the careers they please, and pursue further knowledge about their cultural heritage if they please. In this sense, ethnicity has indeed become optional in my respondents' personal lives. But in another very real way, being ethnic remains a societal expectation for them despite how far removed they are from their immigrant roots or how much they differ from their foreign-born counterparts. (123)

black men than women. The problem is compounded for college-educated women because fewer men than women are obtaining college degrees and because women tend not to marry men with less education than themselves.

Whereas the number of one-parent families is growing among all ethnic groups, the number of such families is very high among African Americans. About 56% of black children (compared to 22% of white and 31% of Hispanic children) live in households headed by a single parent—usually the mother (U.S. Bureau of the Census 2015). Reasons for this include a high divorce rate and the rise in the number of births to unmarried women—currently about 41% of all births in the nation and approximately 72% of all live births in the black population (National Center for Health Statistics 2015).

A number of important strengths of black families have been identified by research (McAdoo 2007; D. Olson, DeFrain, and Skogrand 2014; R. L. Taylor 2002). The factors that help these families function successfully include a love of children, caring parenting, a high degree of religious orientation, strong kinship bonds, a favorable attitude toward elderly individuals, strong motivation to achieve, flexible roles, and egalitarian marriages.

Asian/Pacific Islander Americans

The major subgroups of Asian/Pacific Islander Americans, in order of size, are the Chinese, Filipino, Japanese, Vietnamese, and Koreans. Although they show considerable diversity within their group, two aspects of cultural heritage that are shared are that of the Confucian principle of familism and prescribed role relationships within the family (Hamner and Turner 2001; Knox and Schacht 2016). In Asian/Pacific Islander families, the father is the undisputed head of the family with responsibility for the family's economic support and social status. The mother is responsible for the emotional and psychological care of her husband and children. Children show respect to all elders and satisfy their parents (Kelley and Tseng 1992; C. Lin and Liu 1993).

Familism emphasizes the importance of the family group over individual interests. A top priority is placed on loyalty to the family and obedience. Personal desires are subordinated for the good of the group—perhaps helping explain the lower divorce rate and the emphasis on interdependence (Kao, Guthrie, and Loveland-Cherry 2007; Xiong et al. 2005).

Although traditional childrearing methods were authoritarian, the more acculturated parents have become more permissive. They tend to be warm, affectionate, and somewhat indulgent with very young children. Discipline becomes stricter as children get older. Education and high achievement are emphasized (Hamner and Turner 2001).

familism A social pattern in which the interests of the individual are subordinated to the values and demands of the family.

Strengths of Asian/Pacific Islander families include low divorce rates, fewer births to unmarried women, more conservative sexual values, and high levels of education and income (DeNavas-Walt, Proctor, and Lee 2006). The median income of Asian American families is the highest of any racial/ethnic group and about 50% achieve a bachelor's degree or higher—almost double that of all Americans. There is a strong expectation among Asian American parents that their children will get graduate degrees. When compared to other racial/ethnic groups, Asian Americans have the highest proportion who are married and the lowest proportion who are divorced or separated, as well as the lowest proportion who have births outside of marriage (Lauer and Lauer 2011; U.S. Bureau of the Census 2015). In addition, Asian Americans have a solid commitment to the family, including a sense of duty to family and feelings of respect and responsibility for relatives (D. Olson, DeFrain, and Skogrand 2014).

Native Americans

This group includes American Indians as well as Eskimo/Inuit and Aleutians (Knox and Schacht 2016). Native Americans comprise about 1% of the U.S. population and are a diverse group, showing considerable variation among approximately 500 tribal groups. For example, some 200+ languages are reported as well as observable differences in tribal governance, income, religion, and customs (Ogunwole 2006; U.S. Bureau of the Census 2015).

Native American families face a number of challenges. These include achieving higher levels of education, identifying role models, maintaining family traditions, dealing with the conflicting values of the tribe and the broader U.S. culture, facing health challenges such as high rates of alcoholism, and dealing with high poverty rates (Lonczak et al. 2007).

It is difficult to describe a "typical" Native American family because of the diversity within this group. The major source of identity for the individual is the tribe; particular family structure and values vary according to the tribe. For example, some tribes are matriarchal, whereas others are patriarchal. Intermarriage rates are the highest of any racial group. Little stigma is attached to births to unmarried women or to divorce. As women increasingly are employed outside the home, marriages are becoming more egalitarian (McLain 2000).

Family, however, remains the basic unit of Native American society, with extended family ties being strong. *Family* is defined variously in terms of household composition, extended family through distant cousins, and clan membership (several households of relatives).

The extended family is a source of strength and support for Native Americans. For example, children may be reared by relatives living in different households. One distinctive feature of childrearing and socialization is the exposure of children to a wide array of adults with whom they can identify and from whom they can receive nurturance and love. There are important bonding patterns between children and older people; elders are perceived as having great wisdom (Hamner and Turner 2001).

Evidence suggests that Native American children are prepared for independence at earlier ages than are black or white children. Adults rarely hit children and shouting when correcting children is disapproved of. Children are viewed as tribal persons—not merely children. They are included in social activities and encouraged to develop a sense of community, to be responsible, and to meet their share of obligation for community living (Dykeman and Nelson 1995; S. L. Turner et al. 2006).

Certain prominent values serve to guide marriage and family behaviors. Noninterference and self-determination are particularly important. For this reason, any type of intervention by government agencies or social workers is in conflict with deeply held values. Other values and strengths in all the tribal groups include respect for elders, avoidance of personal glory and gain, giving and sharing with multiple generations of relatives, and a love for their land. Native Americans also value collateral relationships in which family involvement, pride, and approval are stressed as opposed to individualism (Hamner and Turner 2001).

In considering Native American and other ethnic groups, we are reminded that it is a mistake for one group to judge another by its own set of values or to believe there is only one ideal family form. The challenge is for people to develop understanding of other groups while maintaining pride in their own. An individual who is proud to be part of a particular cultural group and who is respected by the rest of society can contribute richly to a nation that prides itself on being the world's melting pot.

Theories to Help Explain Family Behavior

As rational creatures, we seek explanations. When a husband and wife divorce, for instance, family and friends look for answers to a variety of questions: What happened? Why are they getting a divorce? What will happen to them and the children after it is all over?

There are dozens of theories related to intimate relationships, marriages, and families. Theories have been formulated to explain why people are attracted to one another, why people fall in love, why people select the partners they do, how gender roles develop, how families make decisions, what causes sexual dysfunctions, how to raise children, and what causes divorce.

Here, we are interested in theories related to the family itself. According to scientific methods, theory building is a process of formulating a problem, collecting data to aid in solving the problem, developing a hypothesis, testing it, and then drawing conclusions, which are stated in the form of a theory. A **theory** is a tentative explanation of facts and data that have been observed (Klein and White 1996).

Psychologists and sociologists have formulated a number of theories about the family. Several important ones have been selected for discussion here: structural-functional theory, family developmental theory, symbolic interaction theory, systems theory, social learning theory, exchange theory, conflict theory, feminist theory, and the International Family Strengths Model. They are certainly not the only theories to help explain family behavior, but they are some of the most often used. Other important theories, such as attachment theory, are discussed in subsequent chapters to help explain certain behaviors or family dynamics.

Structural-Functional Theory

Structural-functional theory looks at the family as a social institution and asks, "How is the family organized, and what functions does it serve in meeting society's needs?" When talking about the family, structural functionalists usually refer to the nuclear family. From this point of view, the family is considered successful to the extent that it fulfills societal expectations and needs.

Family functions have been described in numerous ways. In 1949, Murdock identified four basic functions of the nuclear family: providing a common residence, economic cooperation, reproduction, and sex. Since Murdock's time, the nuclear family has become less common, and some of the functions he identified are not necessarily confined to the family. In an attempt to provide an even more basic definition of the family, sociologists and family theorists have proposed other functions. However, Murdock's four are a good place to start discussing the family's role in society.

COMMON RESIDENCE In recent decades, changes in society have created variations of the function of common residence. In commuter marriages, for example, spouses maintain separate residences for much of the time, seeing each other only on weekends or occasionally during the month. Noncustodial parents and their children share a common residence only some of the time, but they still form a family.

ECONOMIC COOPERATION Economic cooperation is a broad concept that can include a wide range of activities, from cooking, to maintaining a household, to earning an income. It includes the production, allocation, distribution, and management of resources such as money, material goods, food, services, skills, care, time, and space.

Historically, the family was almost self-sufficient. Family members cooperated to grow food and sew clothing, for example. They relied on each other for the care of the infirm or very young.

During and after the Industrial Revolution, many families moved off the family farm and came to depend more on those outside the family for the production of goods and services. As families became consumers rather than producers, earning an income became necessary. Partly because of increasing demands for income, wives also were enlisted in the task of providing a living. Thus, spouses became mutually dependent in fulfilling this task.

The economic functions of the family are still important, but the nuclear family has never been

theory A tentative explanation of facts and data that have been observed.

structural-functional theory A theory that emphasizes the function of the family as a social institution in meeting the needs of society.

Families differ in many ways. In the United States, cultural and ethnic diversity are reflected in differences in family styles and philosophies of childrearing.

able to meet all of them. Some needs have been met by other groups. For example, insurance companies provide health and life insurance, and industries and the Social Security Administration provide pensions for persons who are retired or disabled.

REPRODUCTION Although the reproductive function of the family has always been important, nonmarital reproduction is now common as well. Advances in reproductive technology—in vitro fertilization, for example—have made it possible for fertilization to take place without any sexual contact between a man and a woman.

SEXUAL FUNCTIONS Murdock's (1949) concept of sexuality was synonymous with heterosexual relationships within the family. Obviously, sexual expression, both heterosexual and homosexual, may take place outside a family unit. In the past 40 years, attitudes about nonmarital sexual activity have become much more accepting. Large numbers of single adults are sexually active; many couples cohabit before marriage.

NURTURE AND SOCIALIZATION OF CHILDREN Sociologists have described other family functions. Reiss (1980) insists that the only universal function of the family (nuclear, extended, or otherwise) is the nurturance and socialization of children. Although schools, churches, and groups such as the Girl and Boy Scouts or the YMCA participate in the socialization process, society agrees that family is primarily responsible. Failure to meet this function constitutes legal grounds for charges of child neglect or abuse. Additional information on the socialization of children may be found in Chapter 13.

The structural-functional theory is also relevant to understanding mate selection and marriage success on an individual level. For example, what is your vision for your marriage? What qualities or functions do you want it to possess? Perhaps companionship and sexual fidelity are at the top of your list. If so, you will be more likely to have a successful marriage with someone who shares these values than with someone who does not.

Family Developmental Theory

Family developmental theory includes several basic concepts. The first is that of the family life cycle, which divides the family experience into

Families exist in a variety of forms, but the nuclear family is still much in evidence. Its most enduring function may be the care and guidance of children.

phases, or stages, over the life span and describes changes in family structure and roles during each stage. The traditional family life cycle starts with the new/early marriage (with no children), followed by years devoted to childbearing and childrearing, empty-nest years, retirement, and ends with the death of one's spouse and widowhood. Chapter 7 discusses the family life cycle in more detail.

The second concept is that of developmental tasks, which Duvall (1977) defines as growth responsibilities that arise at certain stages in the life of the family. The successful completion of these tasks leads to immediate satisfaction and approval, as well as to success with later tasks. In contrast, failure leads to unhappiness in the family, disapproval of society, and difficulty with later developmental tasks. Examples of developmental tasks are the need to develop parenting skills when a child is born and the need to make adjustments at the time of retirement. For the family to continue to grow,

family developmental theory A theory that divides the family life cycle into phases, or stages, over the life span and emphasizes the developmental tasks that must be accomplished by family members at each stage as well as the importance of normative order.

The Importance of Coping

Coping is an important life skill. Effective coping contributes to a higher quality of life and to more satisfying relationships. Conflict theory tells us that conflict is inevitable and that there are both constructive and destructive ways of dealing with conflict. How do we cope with conflict? The International Family Strengths Model is based on research that indicates that strong families cope effectively with stress and crises. How do we respond to stress and crises? Symbolic interaction theory maintains that how we perceive behavior and events influences our emotions and relationships. Exchange theory states that we are more likely to be satisfied with a relationship if we perceive that the benefits (the positives) are greater than the costs (the negatives). Do we cope by focusing on the positives in our lives or do we flounder by concentrating on the negatives? Developmental theory proposes different stages in our individual and family lives with unique tasks that we are challenged to master. Do we approach these challenges with rigidity or with flexibility? How do we deal with the transitions in life and the change that is inevitable?

Coping is what we do to deal with problems, stress, change, and crises. Coping is how we respond to transitions, challenges, and hassles. It is about managing our negative emotions and "hanging in there" when it seems there is nothing else to do. Coping is how we choose to perceive an event or a response from another.

We are challenged to cope throughout life, yet we receive little help or formal education in learning successful ways of coping. Good coping skills can be learned and are essential to successful intimate relationships and to good mental health. Because of its great importance, a coping feature—including effective coping strategies—is included throughout this book.

biological requirements, cultural imperatives, and personal aspirations must be satisfied during each stage of the family life cycle.

A third concept that is helpful in developmental theory is that role sequence and normative order—the order in which major transitions take place—are important. For example, a ninth-grade girl who becomes pregnant and then takes on the responsibilities of parenthood faces different and greater challenges than a 25-year-old woman who becomes a mom after she has completed a college education and been married for 2 years. There is evidence that the work → marriage → parenthood sequence is associated with positive mental health and greater happiness (P. B. Jackson 2004).

The developmental theory provides insight concerning some of the problems associated with the recent trend of youth becoming sexually active at younger ages. This theory suggests that a 12-year-old may be physically capable of sexual activity but is not developmentally ready for a sexual relationship, either emotionally or intellectually. This perspective is supported by research indicating that sexual activity at earlier ages is strongly associated with higher risks for teen pregnancies and contracting sexually transmitted diseases (G. F. Kelly 2013).

Symbolic Interaction Theory

Symbolic interaction theory describes the family as a unit of interacting personalities (Winton 1995). It focuses attention on the way that family members interact through symbols: words, gestures, rules, and roles. People are socialized to understand the meaning of various symbols and to use them to communicate messages, feelings, intentions, and actions. Family members interact through symbols, and together they develop roles (such as father, husband, mother, wife, or daughter) and assign roles to others in the family, who "play" the assigned role. Each actor adjusts his or her behavior to what he or she thinks the other person is going to do.

Children derive much of their self-concept, or thoughts and feelings about themselves, from symbolic messages conveyed by their parents. These messages may be expressed in words: "Bill is a naughty boy" or "Joan is very smart." Or they may be expressed in actions, such as withholding or bestowing rewards. From symbolic messages, children learn to play expected roles and follow prescribed behavior.

But meanings are conveyed both ways. That is, children influence the way parents act as well. Parents will respond differently to a child who is rebellious than to a child who is a conformist, for example. The same principles of reciprocal interaction by means of symbols apply to the relationship between spouses and other family members.

Symbolic interaction is important because our actions and feelings are determined not only by what happens to us but also by how we interpret those events. For example, people define family violence differently. One woman may regard a slap by her husband as unacceptable violence and call the police; another woman may view a couple of punches as a loss of temper not worth mentioning.

Symbolic interaction theory is widely used in family therapy to help individuals understand how they perceive one another and how they can modify their perceptions and behavior to develop a more meaningful and harmonious relationship. John Gottman's (2012) research at the University of Washington is a good example of how this theory provides insight into the dynamics of marriage relationships. Gottman observes couples in a laboratory setting as they interact with each other focusing on problem-solving tasks. Based on the couples' patterns of interaction, Gottman has been able to predict with a high degree of accuracy those couples who are most likely to divorce.

Two general types of behavior that are predictive of divorce are high degrees of criticism and expressions of contempt. These research findings are consistent with symbolic interaction theory in that criticism and contempt convey symbolic messages such as "I think you are inadequate" and "I have no respect/regard for you." Interestingly, Gottman identified two specific behaviors that are highly predictive of divorce. One is the facial gesture of rolling the eyes—as if to say, "How could you be so stupid?" The other is the use of expressions such as "Oh!

Come on now!" or "Get serious!" delivered with a derisive voice tone. Both express utter contempt for another person's views or feelings.

Systems Theory

Systems theory emphasizes the interdependence of family members. Family members do not live in isolation; rather, what one does affects all the others. A person with deep-seated anxieties or emotional instability, for example, may upset everyone else in the family. Interdependence may involve not only money, shelter, and food but also love, affection, companionship, socialization, and other nontangible needs.

There may be various subsystems within the total family unit: Three children may constitute one subsystem and their two parents another, for example. A husband and his mother may constitute a subsystem, a mother and her daughter another. Knowing how one subsystem relates to others can be important to understanding the relationships within a particular family. For example, chronic conflict in the husband–wife subsystem may have a negative effect on children in the family. To help the children, a therapist must assist the spouses in dealing with their conflict.

The concept of interdependency of family members has been useful in the treatment of dysfunctional families. Alcoholism, for example, is considered a family illness. A woman who is married to an alcoholic but denies the problem and covers up for him is an "enabler" because she enables him to continue drinking without suffering the full extent of the consequences. Family interactions may become habitual and difficult to change, even when they are dysfunctional. By analyzing the patterns of response and behavior, therapists seek to motivate persons to rethink and restructure the way they relate to each other and to other family members.

symbolic interaction theory A theory that describes the family as a unit of interacting personalities communicating through symbols.

systems theory A theory that emphasizes the interdependence of family members and how those members affect one another.

Social Learning Theory

Social learning theory suggests that parents act as role models for their children; children imitate their parents' behavior, attitudes, and perceptions. For example, exposure of the child to violence in the family of origin is a consistent predictor of later violence against a dating partner, spouse, or children. Also consistent with this idea, young adults' attributions about relationships with their parents (both positive and negative) have been linked to attributions about intimate relationships.

Exchange Theory

Exchange theory is based on the principle that we enter into relationships in which we can maximize the benefits to us and minimize our costs. We form associations that we expect to be rewarding, and we tend to stay away from relationships that bring us pain. At the least, we hope that the rewards from a relationship will be proportional to the costs (Winton 1995).

People seek different things in relationships. For example, people marry for many reasons: love and companionship, sex, procreation, status, power, and financial security. People are usually satisfied with relationships that at least partially fulfill their expectations and that do not exceed the price they expected to pay.

Social exchange theory aids our understanding of why some marriages are successful and others are not. Sometimes relationships can be one sided; one person does most of the giving—for example, the spouse of an alcoholic or an abuser or a chronic complainer—and receives little in return (except misery). Not surprisingly, the costs of remaining in the relationship are greater than the benefits.

The social exchange theory reminds us of the importance of maximizing positive behaviors such as acts of kindness in promoting marriage happiness. It is easy to underestimate the devastation that negative behaviors can cause. In examining marriage success, John Gottman discovered that it takes five positive responses (e.g., expressing appreciation, affection, kindness) to overcome the hurtful impact of one negative response (e.g., expressing criticism, sarcasm, condescension). Those who maintain a 5:1 ratio of positive to negative communications experience greater marital success.

Equity theory is a variation of exchange theory holding that exchanges between people must be fair and balanced so that they mutually give and receive what is needed. People cooperate in finding mutual fulfillment rather than compete for rewards. They can depend on each other and their commitment involves strong motivations to please each other. Exchange theory is applied in more detail in Chapter 5, on love and mate selection, and in Chapter 9, on power, decision making, and communication.

Conflict Theory

Although conflict theory has not achieved the status in contemporary family life literature as have symbolic interaction or systems theory, it is helpful in better understanding marriage and family relationships. **Conflict theory** asserts that it is normal for each person to desire to have a measure of control and power over his or her life. This normal desire is sometimes a source of conflict in relationships because family members have different goals (Knox and Schacht 2016). Not all family decisions are equally beneficial to all family members. A mother's decision to return to college may be good for her personally and professionally, but her husband and children may miss her attention to them.

Competition for resources such as space or time may also be a source of conflict. If the husband works long and late too often, he may find his wife and children unhappy because of it. These examples are consistent with the proposition that conflict and change are a natural part of intimate relationships. An important implication of conflict theory is that family relationships are unsuccessful not because they have conflict (since all close relationships experience conflict) but because conflict has not been resolved constructively—such as through better communication and greater empathy, negotiation, or compromise—and creatively.

Feminist Theory

Feminist theory is often called a perspective rather than a theory because it reflects thinking across the feminist movement and includes a variety of viewpoints that focus on the inequality of power between men and women in society, especially in family life. Although there are many variations within the feminist perspective, at the heart of all of them is the issue of gender roles, particularly traditional gender roles.

Gender is defined as the learned behaviors and characteristics associated with being male or female, and feminist theories examine how gender differences are related to power differences between men and women. Feminist theory argues that family and gender roles have been constructed by society (not derived from biological conditions) to maintain male dominance; these roles exploit, oppress, and devalue women.

Proponents of feminist theories have a common interest in understanding the subordination of women (Osmond and Thorne 1993) and working to change conditions in society that are barriers to opportunities for women (L. Thompson and Walker 1995). Unique to the feminist perspective is the use of knowledge to raise the level of awareness of oppression and to end it. The feminist perspective is concerned with the overall oppression of all groups that are defined on the basis of age, class, race/ethnicity, disability, or sexual orientation (Baber and Allen 1992).

In general, feminists have challenged the definition of family based on traditional roles. They see the family as a dynamic and diverse system whose members are constantly changing, a system that should not confine men or women to prescribed roles. Although men and women may have been socialized to perform particular roles (for example, males as provider and decision maker and females as caregiver and nurturer), feminists maintain that both can play various roles and be quite functional in all of them. This perspective provides couples with flexibility because both men and women can play roles based on their unique skills and interests, as opposed to the roles traditionally assigned based on gender. For example, he can care for home and children while she pursues a career. Or they can both work and share responsibilities for the care of home and children.

Feminists do not object to the idea of women being traditional as long as it is a choice that they make and not a role imposed on them. Women must make their own choices about how to live their lives, and they need access to the same opportunities available to men. And those choices must be supported and valued in the same way as the choices men make in their lives.

Feminist theory is supported by research that indicates that a great imbalance of power in a marriage relationship—as might be expressed in conflict over household responsibilities—is associated with a higher degree of marital dissatisfaction, whereas equality is related to a higher degree of marriage success and happiness (Stinnett and Stinnett 2010; J. Thornton and Lasswell 1997). Feminist perspective also helps us understand the differences in the communication patterns of men and women and the confusion and conflict that can ensue.

The International Family Strengths Model

The International Family Strengths Model has been developed over the past 35 years and is based on research by Nick Stinnett, John DeFrain, David Olson, and their colleagues. This research has involved more than 16,000 strong families in all 50 states and 28 other countries around the world (DeFrain and Asay 2007).

The **International Family Strengths Model** differs from other family theories in that it emphasizes the strengths of families rather than the problems. It does not ignore family difficulties but proposes that family members can use their strengths to meet challenges.

Major premises of this model are that all families have strengths, that strengths can be learned or developed, and that success in family relationships can be promoted by the utilization of family strengths. The International Family Strengths Model proposes that although families are diverse both within and across

social learning theory A theory that suggests that children learn how to behave in relationships by modeling their parents' behaviors and attitudes.

exchange theory The theory that people choose relationships in which they can maximize their benefits and minimize their costs.

equity theory A subcategory of exchange theory holding that people seek a fair and balanced exchange in which the partners can mutually give and receive what is needed.

conflict theory A theory that family conflict is normal and that the task is not to eliminate conflict but to learn to control it so that it becomes constructive.

feminist theory A theory (or perspective) that focuses on male dominance in families and society and examines how gender differences are related to power differentials between men and women.

International Family Strengths Model A model that proposes that all families—from around the world—have basic qualities that make them strong and that can be used to promote success in relationships.

cultures, the qualities that make families robust are remarkably similar. Research has consistently identified six qualities of strong families. These qualities are closely interconnected and all contribute to a sense of positive emotional connection (DeFrain and Asay 2007). See the "Family Strengths Perspective" feature for details of the six qualities.

Critique of Family Theories

No one family theory has a monopoly on the truth. Each time a new theory is introduced, it is described as the key to understanding family phenomena or as the wave of the future. Inevitably, however, each theory falls short of completely explaining family processes. This shortcoming does not detract from the usefulness of theories, but motivates us to look for additional ways to understand the dynamics of intimate relationships.

The Study of Marriage, Families, and Intimate Relationships

The study of intimate and family relationships is multidisciplinary, meaning that family science typically draws from the following disciplines: psychology, sociology, social work, anthropology, human ecology, women's and men's studies, ethnic studies, child development, psychiatry, medicine, law, biology, economics, education, and history. Within each of these disciplines, an individual could focus his or her attention on a particular issue in the study of families. For example, a law student could choose to specialize in family law and, in particular, child custody issues. Those who study intimate relationships and families may be researchers, teachers,

---

FAMILY STRENGTHS PERSPECTIVE

Qualities of Strong Families

The examination of thousands of strong families representing many diverse cultures consistently identified the following as the most important qualities that make families strong:

- *Appreciation and affection.* This strength involves giving sincere compliments, emphasizing the positive qualities of one another, communicating respect, and expressing affection and caring for one another.

- *Communication.* Members of strong families display good communication skills such as being a good listener, sharing feelings, conversing often, avoiding blame or criticalness, and using effective conflict-resolution skills.

- *Commitment.* This foundational trait involves being supportive of one another, being dependable, being honest, having traditions, and

making the family a top priority with regard to the investment of time and energy.

- *Spending time together.* Families need quality time in large quantities to communicate, share good times, and just "hang out" together.

- *Spiritual well-being.* This vital part of promoting strengths in families involves having faith in God; being hopeful; seeing a higher and clearer meaning in life; and possessing values such as kindness, compassion, patience, responsibility, and forgiveness.

- *Effective coping with stress and crises.* Members of strong families face crises and stress with coping and stress-management skills, adaptability, the ability to see some positive in a bad situation, and an awareness of their resources—including those of spiritual well-being, communication, and commitment to one another.

NOTE: DeFrain, J., and Asay, S. (Eds.). (2007). *Strong Families around the World: Strengths-Based Research and Perspectives.* Binghampton, NY: Haworth Press; Stinnett, N., Hilliard, D., and Stinnett, N. (2000). *Magnificent Marriage.* Montgomery, AL: Pillar Press; Stinnett, N., and Stinnett, N. (2005). *Loving and Caring—Always and Regardless.* Northport, AL: Family Vision Press.

family life educators, counselors, therapists, social workers, nurses, or attorneys, to name a few. Although family studies has become its own discipline and department at many universities, it will always be truly multidisciplinary because of the nature of the subject matter.

There are many different types of research designs, methods, and ways to analyze data. It is beyond the scope of this text to discuss research methodology because entire courses and textbooks are devoted to that topic. However, there are some basic methods of studying families that are commonly used, and many research studies use a combination of different formats.

One of the most common methods of research is the questionnaire. Researchers formulate questions or use an already-developed instrument. Some questionnaire formats include multiple choice, open ended, or scale, where participants rate the intensity of their feelings on a numeric range. Another approach to obtain data is through interviewing participants in person or over the phone. Interviews can allow participants to discuss their thoughts and feelings freely and can provide for much richer data than a questionnaire. There are other methods of study, such as case studies, where only a few families or individuals are examined in depth, or observational studies, where behavior is only observed and participants are never questioned or interviewed.

Research designs are based on what the researcher is interested in studying. Some want to examine how families and individuals change over time. In a **longitudinal study**, participants are interviewed or observed over several different periods of time. For example, a longitudinal study could span 20 years and involve interviewing the participants once each year to see how marital satisfaction changes over time. Longitudinal studies can be useful because they can more correctly answer questions involving processes over time. However, longitudinal studies are expensive to conduct because participants must be interviewed more than once, and thus study coordinators must keep track of the participants over time. A less expensive and extensive research design is the **cross-sectional study**. In this design, individuals are selected at various stages of the life course and compared to one another. For example, to study the same question, changes in marital satisfaction over time, a cross-sectional design might draw participants from the newlywed years, those married 10 years, and those married more

Research on families and intimate relationships is an exciting field of science and one that can help individuals develop healthy relationships.

than 20 years for a comparison. The benefit of this approach is that all groups could be studied at the same time. However, it is difficult to determine historical effects, such as the political or economic climate of the time, or to be sure the differences or similarities are not the result of a particular life cycle stage or the unique characteristics of the individuals. Other studies use a combination approach to study a cross-section of families for a shorter period of time (longitudinally), such as 5 years.

Regardless of the type of research method, it is important that the measurement technique has **validity** and **reliability**. When an instrument has validity, or is valid, it is measuring what it is intended to measure. It can be difficult to develop an instrument

longitudinal study A research design with repeated observations of the same individuals at various points in time.

cross-sectional study A research design where individuals are selected at various stages of the life course and compared to one another for similarities or differences.

validity The degree to which the instrument being used is measuring what it is intended to measure.

reliability The degree to which a measurement technique produces similar outcomes when it is repeated.

Gay and Lesbian Parenting by Adoption

Parenting by gays and lesbians is an issue of considerable controversy. The issue is complex because gays and lesbians may—as single parents or as couples—be rearing children in various circumstances: their own biological children from a previous heterosexual relationship, biological children by semen donation or the use of a surrogate mother, or children adopted by one or both of them. Considering the legal, political, and practical environments, parenting and adoption by gays and lesbians is not a matter of "one size fits all." Additionally, this area is charged with emotion (Beitsch 2015). Public polls show opinion in the United States is about equally divided, with 53% to 55% in favor (Craighill 2011).

Proponents argue that a number of gays and lesbians already *are* rearing children (often their own biological children). Research studies over the past 25 years indicate that children reared by same-sex nonadoptive parents seem to fare as well as those reared by heterosexual parents (Manning, Fettro, and Lamidi 2014, Evan B. Donaldson Institute 2008). Much less research has focused on the long-term effects on children adopted by gays or lesbians. However, about 4% of all adopted children in the United States are being raised by gays or lesbians. An additional 14,000 children live in foster families headed by gays or lesbians (Evan B. Donaldson Institute 2008).

Consequently, a number of professional organizations such as the American Academy of Pediatrics and the American Psychological Association support adoption by gays and lesbians as a way of providing permanent homes for some of the 129,000 children waiting for adoptive homes. As an economic bonus, it is estimated that $3.3 to $3.6 billion would be saved nationally each year by adoption of children from foster care.

Laws and policies cannot prevent lesbians and gays from bearing or fathering children. State laws and policies do, however, complicate adoption by these individuals. Adoption by a gay or lesbian *individual* is legal (either directly or implied). Even so, laws in many states are not clear (as when

legality is implied) and are subject to interpretation. Adoptions are typically handled by local courts; judges and clerks accept or deny petitions to adopt based on criteria that vary from one jurisdiction to another.

Laws and policies about adoption by same-sex *couples* are even more complicated. Adoption by a couple can mean the adoption of an unrelated child or the adoption of a partner's biological (or previously adopted) child—termed *second-parent adoption*. In some states, adoption by a same-sex couple is still very difficult—especially if the adoption is of a child from the foster system. Or the law may specify that the adoption has to be done by a *husband and wife*. Other states are more willing to allow second-parent adoptions; about a dozen (including California, Massachusetts, Pennsylvania, and Washington) explicitly allow it.

Opponents of parenting/adoption by gays and lesbians have concerns about long-term outcomes for the children—including gender identity and sexual orientation formation as well as the effects of prejudice because of parental lifestyle. Some research suggests that children fare best when reared by married, biological parents—even if they can do all right in other situations (Amato 2005) while other research suggests that children raised by same-sex couples fare no worse than other children.

Questions to Consider

Should sexual orientation be a consideration in adoption by individuals? Explain.

Should same-sex couples be allowed to adopt an unrelated child? The biological child of a partner? Should such adoptions be limited to former foster children or hard-to-place children (older children, those with special needs, or sibling groups)? Explain.

Some argue that the benefits to a child of living in a permanent home (as opposed to foster care) outweigh any negatives of living with a gay or lesbian parent or parents. What do you think?

that has validity. For example, how do you measure marriage success? Is it by how long the marriage lasts (even if the couple is miserable)? Or is it by the quality of the couple's relationships? Reliability is defined as the degree to which a measurement technique produces similar outcomes when it is repeated; reliability is much easier to ascertain than validity.

No research method or design seems to be without its own shortcomings, and the very nature of the subject matter (family and intimate relationships) can be subjective in nature. Yet, throughout years of research, many studies show similar results although they used different research methods. These results help build our understanding of intimate and family relationships and become a point at which we can build theories about behavior and families. Throughout this text, you will be reading examples and findings from numerous research studies. There are literally hundreds of thousands of research articles on marriage and family relationships that are available through published journals and library databases. An individual can look up a specific topic, such as cohabitation among college students, and find abstracts and references for most of the published research articles about the topic. Family studies is an exciting field of science and one that can help individuals develop healthy relationships.

Summary

1. A family is any group of persons united by the ties of marriage, blood, or adoption or any sexually expressive relationship in which the adults cooperate financially for their mutual support; the people are committed to one another in an intimate interpersonal relationship; the members see their identity as importantly attached to the group; and the group has an identity of its own.

2. Different family forms are determined by their structural arrangement, the persons in them, and their relationship to one another.

3. Modern views of the family emphasize its role in fulfilling personal needs for emotional security and companionship.

4. Although historically the American family was patriarchal, there has been a gradual shift to a more democratic power structure.

5. The marriage rate is the number of persons who marry during the preceding 12 months per 1,000 population.

6. The median age at first marriage is increasing for both men and women, resulting in an increase in unmarried young adults in the population.

7. Declining fertility rates since 1965 have resulted in smaller families.

8. The percentage of married women in the workforce has been increasing steadily. At present, greater percentages of women with either preschool- or grade school–age children are working outside the home than 30 years ago.

9. The number of one-parent families, especially mother–child families, has risen considerably in recent years.

10. Growing numbers of gays and lesbians live in stable couple relationships, such as marriages, civil unions, or domestic partnerships—some with children.

11. Divorce rates increased steadily from 1958 until about 1980, at which time they leveled off and even declined. At the present rate, it is predicted that about 40%–50% of new marriages will end in divorce.

12. About 40% of marriages involve a remarriage for at least one of the partners. The relatively high rates of divorce and remarriage have resulted in a large number of reconstituted, or blended, families.

13. It is important to understand and appreciate the cultures and values of the many ethnic groups that make up the population of the United States.

14. A theory is a tentative explanation of facts and data that have been observed.

15. Psychologists and sociologists have formulated a number of theories about the family. The main theories used in helping explain

families are structural-functional theory, family developmental theory, symbolic interaction theory, systems theory, social learning theory, exchange theory, conflict theory, feminist theory, and the International Family Strengths Model.

16. The study of intimate and family relationships is multidisciplinary, meaning that many disciplines contribute to the field of knowledge.

17. There also are many different types of research designs and ways in which to analyze data. In a longitudinal study, participants are interviewed or observed at several different points over the course of time. In a cross-sectional study, individuals are selected at various stages of the life course and compared to one another.

Key Terms

bilateral descent

binuclear family

birth rate

blended, or reconstituted, family

civil union

cohabiting family

conflict theory

cross-sectional study

culture

domestic partnership

equity theory

ethnicity

exchange theory

expressive role

extended family

familism

family

family developmental theory

family of origin

family of procreation

feminist theory

fertility rate

gay or lesbian family

instrumental role

International Family Strengths Model

longitudinal study

matriarchal family

matrilineal descent

matrilocal residence

neolocal residence

nuclear family

patriarchal family

patrilineal descent

patrilocal residence

polyandrous family

polygamous family

polygynous family

reliability

single-parent family

social learning theory

stepfamily

structural-functional theory

symbolic interaction theory

systems theory

theory

validity

voluntarily childless family

Questions for Thought

1. What is your definition of *family*? How is it similar to or different from the definition used in the text?

2. How well does your family of origin or your present family (if you are married) adhere to instrumental and/or expressive roles?

3. What are the various reasons for current trends in marriage rates, age at first marriage, family size, percentage of working mothers, and one-parent families?

4. The text suggests that family philosophy has changed from an emphasis on institution to an emphasis on companionship. If you were to follow this philosophy, what kind of marriage would you strive to have? Explain.

5. Which family theory makes the most sense to you? How would you use that theory to help explain the behaviors and patterns in your family?

6. What is your ethnic/cultural background? How does it influence your attitudes and behaviors?

For Further Reading

Bengtson, V. (2005). *Sourcebook of family theory and research*. Thousand Oaks, CA: Sage. An overview of contemporary and emerging theories and research methods for studying families.

Cott, N. F. (2000). *Public vows: A history of marriage and the nation*. Cambridge, MA: Harvard University Press. Examines the public and private purposes of marriage throughout history.

For Your Marriage is an initiative of the U.S. Conference of Catholic Bishops. Their website has information on a variety of topics related to marriage, including a look at cohabitation. http://www.foryourmarriage.com.

Hawes, J. M., and Nybakken, E. I. (2001). *Family and society in American history*. Urbana and Chicago: University of Illinois Press. Presents an interdisciplinary perspective on the history of the family.

Management Sciences for Health provides background information to health service providers about various cultural groups, including African, Asian, Native, Arab, Pacific Islander, and Muslim Americans. Look at "An Expanded Look" under "Cultural Groups." Although it is aimed at health-care providers, the information offers insights into the values and practices of various ethnic groups. http://www.msh.org.

Pro Con offers information on 44 controversial topics including gay marriage. http://www.gaymarriage.procon.org.

Williams, H. A. Heather A. Williams discusses "How Slavery Affected African American Families" at the National Humanities Center site. http://nationalhumanitiescenter.org/tserve/freedom.

Gender

Identity and Roles

CHAPTER OUTLINE

Learning Objectives

Environmental Influences on Gender
- Societal Expectations
- Parental Influences

AT ISSUE TODAY: *Women and Weight: Gendered Messages on Magazine Covers*
- The Influence of Popular Press, Television, and Movies
- School Influences

Theories of Gender Role and Identity
- Social Learning Theory
- Cognitive Developmental Theory
- Gender Schema Theory
- Social Structure/Cultural Theories

- Evolutionary Theories
- Biological Theories

Traditional Masculine and Feminine Stereotypes
- Masculinity
- Femininity
- Problems with Gender Stereotypes

PERSONAL PERSPECTIVE: *Life on the Boundaries of Gender*

Gender Roles and Body Image

CULTURAL PERSPECTIVE: *The Word* Machismo

Race, Class, and Gender

Changing Roles of Women and Men

Gender Roles in the Family

- Roles in Marriage

FAMILY STRENGTHS PERSPECTIVE: *Do Everyday Things Together*
- Housework and Child-Care Roles

COPING FEATURE: *Coping with Depression*
- Gender, Marriage, and Depression

Androgyny

A QUESTION OF POLICY: *Title IX*

Summary

Key Terms

Questions for Thought

For Further Reading

LEARNING OBJECTIVES

AFTER READING THE CHAPTER, YOU SHOULD BE ABLE TO DO THE FOLLOWING:

- Define *sex, gender, gender identity,* and *gender role.*

- Explain how concepts of masculinity and femininity vary by society and culture.

- Discuss how the following environmental influences mold masculinity and femininity: societal expectations, parents, television, and school.

- Review different theoretical views about the development of "maleness" and "femaleness."

- Describe masculine and feminine stereotypes and norms and the problems they create.

- Discuss gender-role influences in interpersonal relationships between men and women.

- Discuss differing expectations and attitudes of various ethnic groups; how race, class, and gender are related; gender roles in the family; and the way gender roles affect housework and child care in families.

- Describe how marital quality can be influenced by gender-role expectations.

- Define androgyny and identify its possible advantages and disadvantages.

The family still finds the whole incident amusing. Kate (a college junior) had been dating Scott somewhat seriously when she invited him to come home with her for the weekend to meet her parents. He and she liked each other and had many things in common. However, Scott was a "neat freak" who chided her when her apartment was messy. When he came over for dinner, he wanted dishes to be washed promptly, but rarely offered to help. Kate thought a weekend at her home would help them get to know each other better.

Mom and Dad welcomed Scott and Kate when they arrived on Friday evening. The house was tidy; dinner was home-cooked and good. At dinner, Scott learned a little about the family. Mom worked as a nurse in the ICU; she enjoyed her job and was good at it. Dad, recently retired from the military, was working for an apartment complex and taking some classes at the community college—deciding what he would do as a second career.

On Saturday, Kate showed Scott around town. They returned home to find Mom mowing the lawn. Inside Dad was unloading the dishwasher.

On the way back to their campus, Scott voiced his concerns about their relationship. He knew Kate dreamed of working in genetic research after graduation. Her spouse would have to give some preference to her career because it is limited geographically. He was not sure he could do that. And now that he had met her parents, he knew why she had such strange notions. They were just "very dysfunctional."

Sex describes who we are biologically—male or female. We also manifest **gender**, or personality traits and behavior that characterize us as men (masculine) or women (feminine). Our outward manifestations and expressions of maleness or femaleness are our **gender roles**, which are influenced by cultural expectations of what is considered socially appropriate for males and for females. There is a current trend, however, toward less rigid and more androgynous gender roles.

Our personal, internal sense of maleness or femaleness is our **gender identity**. Most children accept (on a cognitive level) their genetically determined sex as a boy or a girl and then strive to act according to the expectations of society and the group of which they are a part. A few children and adults, however, have difficulty establishing their gender identity. They may experience gender dysphoria, an anxiety or confusion about their gender.

Others have the feeling that their biological sex does not match their gender identity. A high profile

Concepts of masculinity and femininity have undergone considerable change over the centuries. Is this eighteenth-century regency beau similar to the contemporary image of the "true man"?

example is Caitlyn Jenner, formerly Bruce Jenner, a famous Olympic athlete and reality TV star (World Almanac 2016). Such **transgender people** may alter their gender identity occasionally or permanently by cross-dressing or by becoming **transsexuals** with the help of hormones and surgery. In this chapter, we examine the concepts of gender and gender roles and describe some of the influences on their development.

Environmental Influences on Gender

Whereas sex is determined by biological factors, gender identities and gender roles are influenced by the environment. Certain qualities of maleness are defined as and become "masculine" because of society's view of what being male means. Society prescribes how a male ought to look and behave, what type of personality he ought to have, and what roles he should perform. Similarly, we label a woman "feminine" according to culturally determined criteria for femaleness. In this sense, the development of **masculinity** or **femininity** involves an education in what it means to be a man or a woman within the context of the culture in which an individual lives. Gender is as much about a set of beliefs as it is about anatomical differences (Yarber, Sayad, and Strong 2015).

Concepts of masculinity and femininity vary in different societies and cultures. For example, Margaret Mead (1950), in studying three different groups, discovered some interesting variations in conceptions of masculinity and femininity. Arapesh men and women displayed feminine personality traits. Both males and females were trained to be cooperative, unaggressive, and responsive to the needs and demands of others. In contrast, Mundugumor men and women developed masculine traits. They were ruthless and aggressive, with maternal, nurturant aspects of personality at a minimum. In the third group, the Tchambuli, the women were dominant and impersonal, whereas the men were less responsible and more emotionally dependent.

Conceptions of masculinity and femininity have undergone considerable change in the United States. In colonial times, a "true man," especially a gentleman, could wear hose, a powdered wig, and a lace shirt without being considered unmanly. Thus, the judgments made about masculinity or the extent of manliness are subjective, based on the accepted standards of maleness as defined by the culture. These standards vary from culture to culture and from era to era in the same society.

Societal Expectations

Because society plays such an important role in the establishment of the criteria for masculinity and femininity and in the development of maleness or femaleness, it is important to understand how gender identification and gender-role learning take place. Almost as soon as a child is born, society expects him or her to begin thinking and acting like a boy or like a girl, according to its own definitions. For example, a baby girl is dressed in pink ruffles, given dolls and tea sets, and expected to be a polite "little lady." And as she gets older, she likely will help her mother around the house doing traditionally feminine chores. Thus, what society expects the girl to be and do becomes a basic influence in molding her into a woman. She also observes her older sister, her mother, and other females acting like women, and so she begins to identify with them, to imitate them, and to model her behavior after theirs. In short, as soon as a girl is born, she is programmed to behave in acceptable, appropriate ways for a female.

The same process applies to boys: once he is born, a boy is often expected to manifest masculine traits and to do masculine things. He is programmed to become a man. Because programming begins early in life, gender stereotyping appears as early as 2 or 3 years old and peaks at about age 5 (A. Campbell, Shirley, and Candy 2004; Kail and Cavanaugh 2016). As children learn more about men and women (meeting a male nurse or female police officer, for example), their notions about appropriate roles expand.

It is important to understand, however, that in such a diverse society as exists in the United States, social expectations for masculinity and femininity vary by class and race. Later in the chapter a section titled "Race, Class, and Gender" is devoted to the relationship among these three variables. Various other social influences play a role in gender identity and gender-role development. Discussions of three of the most important influences—parents, media, and school—follow.

Parental Influences

One of the ways in which children develop gender identities and gender roles is through identification

---

gender Personality traits and behavior that characterize an individual as masculine or feminine.

gender role A person's outward expression of maleness or femaleness.

gender identity A person's personal, internal sense of maleness or femaleness, which is expressed in personality and behavior.

transgender people People who feel that their biological sex does not match their gender identity.

transsexual A transgender person who seeks to live as a member of the opposite sex with the help of hormones and surgery.

masculinity Personality and behavioral characteristics of a male according to culturally defined standards of maleness.

femininity Personality and behavioral characteristics of a female according to culturally defined standards of femaleness.

Women and Weight: Gendered Messages on Magazine Covers

Media messages regarding bodily appearance differ for men and for women. There has been a strong emphasis on women being slim and beautiful, but that same standard does not apply to men (Juergen 2014). Malkin, Wornian, and Chrisler (1999) analyzed the covers of several issues of 21 popular women's and men's magazines for gendered messages related to bodily appearance. The cover is the primary sales tool of the magazine and must be provocative, hard-hitting, and full of elements that people are interested in ("Make the Cover" 1998). Magazine covers were categorized according to the targeted readership, and each cover was analyzed in terms of visual images and text. The researchers examined 69 covers of women's magazines and 54 covers of men's magazines.

For the 12 magazines most frequently read by women, 54 of the 69 covers (78%) contained some message about bodily appearance, whereas none of the 53 covers of the men's magazines contained such messages. And whereas the majority of the most popular women's magazines focused on how women could improve themselves by changing their appearance, especially by losing weight, the popular men's magazines focused on news,

politics, hobbies, sports, entertainment, activities, and ways to expand knowledge.

When the researchers examined the covers of women's magazines, they found that 94% showed a slender female in excellent shape, whereas only about 3% showed a male on the cover. When they examined the covers of men's magazines, they found that 28% showed a male model or celebrity, whereas almost 50% showed a slim young woman wearing revealing clothing. Apparently, visual images on both men's and women's magazine covers send messages about what women should look like and what men should look for (Malkin et al. 1999).

Perhaps most alarming, noted the researchers, was the position of weight-related messages in relation to other messages on the magazine covers. By their placement of messages, magazines seem to suggest that losing weight or changing the shape of one's body will lead to a better life. For example, messages such as "Get the Body You Want" placed next to "How to Get Your Husband to Really Listen" and "Lose 10 Pounds" placed next to "Ways to Make Your Life Easier, Happier, and Better" imply that by changing their appearance, people will be happier, sexier, and more lovable.

---

with parents and modeling of their behavior. **Parental identification and modeling** is the process by which the child adopts and internalizes parental values, attitudes, behavioral traits, and personality characteristics. Identification begins soon after birth, because of children's early dependency on their parents. This dependency, in turn, normally leads to emotional attachment. Gender identification and gender-role learning take place unconsciously and indirectly in this intimate parent–child relationship. Children learn that mothers are affectionate and nurturing and that fathers are playful and strong. Not only does the child receive different care from each parent, but also he or she observes that each parent behaves, speaks, dresses, and acts differently in relation to the other parent, to other children, and to

persons outside the family. For example, one study found that by the time a child turns 2 years old, subtle messages about gender were apparent in mother–child conversations, even for mothers who expressed gender-egalitarian beliefs (Gelman, Taylor, and Nguyen 2004). Other studies show that even before children reach school age, they have organized patterns of beliefs about gender that affect the way they process social information (Giles and Heyman 2005). Thus, the child learns what it is to be mother/father, wife/husband, and woman/man through parental example, daily contacts, and associations.

How traditional the parents' gender roles are also can affect their children's gender-role attitudes (Sabattini and Leaper 2004; Schmader and Croft 2013). Several studies indicate that young adolescent daughters of mothers who are employed hold less traditional gender-role attitudes than do daughters of women who are not employed (Carine 1998; Schmader and Croft 2013). In addition, the happier the husband is with his wife's employment, the more nontraditional is the daughter. In fact, dads seem to be especially influential in shaping daughters' ideas about gender roles (Schmader and Croft 2013).

The Influence of Popular Press, Television, and Movies

It is difficult to avoid exposure to stereotyped portrayals of men and women because popular media frequently depict men and women acting in a gender-stereotyped manner (Juergen 2014; Yarber, Sayad, and Strong 2010). Despite all the strides made toward equality, research shows only a slight decrease in the stereotypical depiction of women in advertisements (Lindner 2004), and the depiction of women in the hip-hop culture is often described as not only sexist but also misogynistic (Javors 2004). Numerous studies support the stereotypical depiction of gender roles in the media. For example, one study that examined gender roles in daily newspaper comics found women underrepresented, more likely than men to be married and have children, and not as likely as men to have a job. The study also found that when women were employed, they had lower-status jobs than did male characters, more attention was paid to women's appearance, and female characters did more domestic work, such as child care and household chores (Glascock and Preston-Schreck 2004). Another study that examined gender messages in intercollegiate athletics by analyzing National Collegiate Athletic Association media guide covers found that women athletes were less likely to be portrayed as active participants in sports and more likely to be portrayed in passive and traditionally feminine poses (Buysse and Embser-Herbert 2004).

The media's influence on reinforcing gender roles begins as early as our first books and movies. Picture books and movies for young children often portray boys as active leaders and girls as gentle, sweet followers. Men exhibit career skills, whereas women perform tasks in the home. Men are portrayed as hopeless slobs who need a woman to take care of them and as ineffectual parents (D. Anderson and Hamilton 2005; Juergen 2014). This is hardly the message most parents want to send their young children, and yet many are not aware of the bombardment of gender stereotypes reaching their children.

Even self-help books are gender stereotyped. A study of the best-selling self-help books that provided general parenting advice published between 1997 and 2002 found that 82% of the implicit gender messages across all books were stereotypical, and some books actively promoted stereotypically gendered ways of relating, parenting, and being in a family (Krafchick et al. 2005).

Television exerts a significant influence in the socialization process for young and old alike. In most homes, the television is on for more than 7 hours a day—with the average person watching about 3 hours a day. Despite pressure from educators, many children's shows and the accompanying commercials contain considerable gender bias and sexism. Remember, too, that children also watch during prime time.

Although programs from recent decades have increasingly depicted women as employed in a wider range of occupations (Coltrane and Adams 2008), women are still underrepresented by about 2:1 and are less likely to be leading characters (Comstock and Scharrer 2006; Signorielli 1998). In both children's and prime-time shows, males are more likely to be portrayed as aggressive, decisive, powerful, stable, and professionally competent. Women are more often presented as sociable, emotional, warmer, married, and younger. Even strong female characters must also be thoughtful, humble, and gentle to be acceptable (Juergen 2014). A woman on television is most likely in her early thirties; a man is in his late thirties. Men older than 65 are more likely to be cast in younger roles, to be employed, and romantically involved, whereas women older than 65 are cast as elderly (Comstock and Scharrer 2006; Signorielli 1998).

Research supports the impact of such stereotypical presentations of males and females on gender-role formation. Children who are heavy television viewers tend to have stereotypical ideas of gender and to show conformity to culturally accepted gender-role typing (G. Berry 2000; L. M. Ward and Friedman 2006). In adults, television viewing is related to more sexist responses to questions about the nature

parental identification and modeling The process by which the child adopts and internalizes parental values.

Certain qualities of maleness are defined and become "masculine" because of society's view of what being male means.

of men and women and their appropriate roles in society (Signorielli 1998).

School Influences

Gender roles are learned in everyday living, wherever a child goes. Naturally, then, school influences gender development in a variety of ways. As mentioned previously, books may promote gender stereotypes—although publishers have made a concerted effort not to do so. One study of educational psychology textbooks revealed that males were depicted as aggressive significantly more often than females (Yanowitz and Weathers 2004).

Without realizing it, teachers have different ideas about male and female students. For example, math and science are regarded as fields for boys, whereas girls are expected to do better and have more interest in literature. Teachers tend to overrate male students' abilities in math and science, to have higher expectations for them, and to believe math and science are more important to them. Consequently, they encourage children in those directions (Wigfield, Eccles, and Schiefele 2006). Children pick up on these attitudes (Eccles 2007) and internalize them. By high school, many girls say they do not care for math and tend to drop it (D. L. Shea, Lubinski, and Benbow 2001).

In an attempt to diminish the influence of negative stereotypes about choices in science, math, engineering, and technology, Cheryan and colleagues (Cheryan et al. 2014) asked adolescents about their interest in a computer science course. They showed students photos of two classrooms. The classrooms were identical except that one was decorated with stereotypical items (*Star Trek* posters, for example) and the other with neutral items (nature posters). Students were told that the courses required the same amount of homework, covered the same topics, had male teachers, and had a 50:50 boy:girl ratio. Girls expressed more interest in the class with the neutral decorations, whereas decorations made no difference to boys' interest. The researchers concluded that removing negative (geeky and male-oriented) stereotypes can increase recruitment into these fields for girls.

Theories of Gender Role and Identity

Although no one theory adequately explains all aspects of gender roles and identities, various theories do provide helpful ways in which to think about and discuss patterns of behavior. Each theory might hold some of the answers to the mysteries of why females act one way and males another. Common theories used to explain gender roles and identities are the social learning theory, cognitive developmental theory, gender schema theory, social structure/cultural theories, evolutionary theories, and biological theories.

Social Learning Theory

The **social learning theory** emphasizes that boys develop "maleness" and girls "femaleness" through exposure to scores of influences—including parents, television, school, and peers—that teach them what it means to be a man or woman in the culture in which they are brought up. They are encouraged to assume the appropriate gender identity by being rewarded for some behaviors and punished for others. Remember how the boy who played jump rope with the girls was treated? Or the one who cried when he skinned his elbows? Those who live up to societal expectations are accepted as normal; those who do not conform are criticized and pressured to comply.

According to this theory, parental models, particularly those offered by the same-sex parent, are the most influential in shaping gender behavior. Other socializing agents, such as television, teachers, and peers, reinforce children's gender roles. By the first year of life, children begin to be aware of the differences in gender roles, and by the third year, it is evident how girls and boys have been socialized to behave, play, and dress. A great deal of evidence supports social learning theory, but by itself it is insufficient to explain the development of gender roles and gender identity (Lips 1997).

Cognitive Developmental Theory

Cognitive developmental theory suggests that gender, like other things (such as multiplication tables), cannot be learned until a child reaches a certain stage of intellectual development. This theory suggests that between the ages of 3 and 5 children acquire "gender constancy," a fixed concept of gender that cannot be altered by superficial appearance, such as long hair or clothing. Prior to the development of gender constancy, children may confuse gender classifications and believe that classifications can arbitrarily change. For example, a girl who wears a short hairstyle or a baseball cap suddenly becomes a boy.

According to cognitive developmental theory, once children categorize themselves as female or male, they will use this self-categorization to figure out how to behave. In response to positive reinforcement, they will attach higher value to gender-appropriate behaviors than to gender-inappropriate behaviors, which receive negative responses (Leaper and Friedman 2007). As children develop a model for proper gender behavior, they enter a phase of great rigidity. Around the age of 5 or 6, their views of gender roles are oversimplified and inflexible, relying greatly on stereotypes. Boys will refuse even to touch a baby doll, for example. But within a few years, children become secure in their gender identity and so are more comfortable with occasional departures from the stereotypical gender role. She can play trucks with her boy cousins or he can cook in a pretend restaurant.

Whereas social learning theory is based on gender typing, such as sex-appropriate activities or occupations, cognitive developmental theory is based on cognitive aspects, such as knowledge of stereotypes and flexibility in applying them. Although support exists for both theories, neither theory can fully

Because gender roles have become more flexible, females today can now be found in a wide range of professions.

explain the development and maintenance of gender roles and gender identity (Carroll 2010).

Gender Schema Theory

A schema is the framework of logic and ideas someone uses to organize information and make sense of things. We all hold a variety of schemas, such as how an older person should act or what behavior is polite. According to **gender schema theory**, each of us has definite ideas about how males and females should look and behave (Kail and Cavanaugh 2016). For example, there are virtually no pink outfits for baby boys. In addition, girls are often dressed in lace and bows, whereas boys are dressed in

social learning theory A theory emphasizing that boys develop "maleness" and girls develop "femaleness" through exposure to scores of influences—including parents, television, school, and peers—that teach them what it means to be a man or a woman in their culture.

cognitive developmental theory A theory suggesting that gender roles and identities cannot be learned until children reach a certain stage of intellectual development.

gender schema theory A theory suggesting that people have definite ideas about how males and females should look and behave, based on the framework of logic and ideas used to organize information and make sense of it.

clothes imprinted with sports- or tool-related images. From the first days of life, gender schemas influence how males and females are thought of and treated.

Here is an example of a gender schema at work in the mind of a 3-year-old boy.

Kerry enjoys hot tea (lots of milk and a little tea) with his Nana. Recently he watched an advertisement for a pink and purple floral tea set with great interest and remarked, "I need one of those—but for boys."

According to this theory, he has asked himself, "Are floral tea sets for girls or boys?" and concluded, "For girls—therefore not for me (a boy)."

People differ in the degree to which they use their gender schemas to process information about themselves and others, with strongly sex-typed individuals tending to have stronger gender schemas (Bem 1985). Gender schemas are shaped through the socialization of children and the degree to which males and females are treated differently. Thus, gender schema theory builds on both cognitive developmental and social learning theories in suggesting that children both cognitively construct gender categories and learn to respond to environmental cues about gender roles (Yarber, Sayad, and Strong 2015).

Social Structure/Cultural Theories

If we accept that "appropriate" gender behaviors are largely learned, then an important issue is why society supports the perpetuation of these differences. According to **social structure/cultural theories** of gender, most of the differences between male and female gender roles are established because of the status, power, and division of labor in a given society. Researchers have shown that gender differences occur more frequently (and in some cases only) when the sexes are in the typical male dominant/female subordinate relationship and that much so-called feminine behavior is actually powerless behavior (Lips 1991). Cultural theorists argue that if males and females were seen as equally powerful in society, many gender differences would disappear. For example, both women and members of lower-status groups are characterized as more controlled and passive, whereas men and members of higher-status groups are characterized as more direct and opinionated (Henley and Freeman 1995).

These power and status differences are related to the differences in the division of labor between the sexes that still exists. For example, there are still far more male executives and female secretaries than vice versa. However, it is almost impossible to determine whether the division of labor by sex is a cause or a consequence of the status differences between women and men, and most likely the process is a kind of vicious cycle (Lips 1997):

The way work is divided between women and men in our own society practically guarantees that women will have less control over economic resources than men do. Men's greater control over economic resources, achieved through better jobs with higher salaries and through more continuous participation in the paid labor force, creates the expectation that women (and children) will depend on men for support. Under this set of expectations, which is communicated to children long before they understand the economic realities on which it is based, it is little wonder that girls and boys, women and men, tend to make choices that emphasize different aspects of these skills, aspirations, and preferences. These choices lead males and females into different types of work, and the cycle repeats itself. Whatever its source, the division of labor by sex and the parallel male–female difference in control over resources contribute to gender differences in behavior. (55)

However, not all theories about gender differences focus on culture, cognition, or learning, and many people believe it is not nurture but nature that contributes the most to gender differences. Thus, no discussion of theoretical approaches to gender differences would be complete without a discussion of evolution and biology.

Evolutionary Theories

Evolutionary theories are rooted in the concept that human genetics have evolved over time so that men and women are best adapted for their biological functions and reproductive success (Carroll 2010). The prime evolutionary aim is the continuation of the species. Accordingly, genetic heritage is more important than the influence of learning and culture for gender learning.

Proponents believe that male and female genes have adapted over time to meet each sex's reproductive goals—the production of offspring who survive. The inclination of males to fertilize as many eggs as possible arises from the innate drive to guarantee survival of the species. Males with the genetic makeup to be strong, adventurous, rugged, and aggressive are more apt to fertilize more eggs, thus passing along those traits. In contrast, the tendency of females to seek a monogamous partner relates to the biological demands of pregnancy, childbirth, lactation, and caring for the vulnerable offspring for years—all of which require much energy and tend to leave her dependent. Females who are kind, gentle, and affectionate are likely to win the support of males, thus ensuring the care of offspring.

There is little empirical evidence to support evolutionary theories of gender, but they are still the basis for many societal assumptions. No evidence has linked any gender behaviors to a specific gene, and the universality of a trait does not mean that the trait is necessarily genetic rather than learned. If males are biologically predisposed to be aggressive and females to be submissive, it is certainly also true that society reinforces and accentuates these differences.

Biological Theories

Interesting research strongly suggests genetic, hormonal, and neurological ("brain") bases for some of the differences in the behavior of males and females. For example, by about 5 years of age (when the brain reaches adult size), the brains of boys are about 10% larger than those of girls (D. F. Halpern et al. 2007). Other research shows that women's brains are wired to feel and recall emotions more keenly than the brains of men (Canli et al. 2002). Differences in their nervous systems make domination and rough-and-tumble play appealing to boys and intimacy and empathic relationships pleasing to girls (Fabes 1994). This may account for why girls typically prefer to negotiate and cooperate when playing compared to boys being more competitive, aggressive, and rough.

In a similar manner, M. Hines (2004) notes that in no country are violent crime, science, or political and economic power dominated by women—these areas are largely dominated by men. After an extensive review of scholarly literature, she concludes that

differences in the male and female brains are related to differences in male and female behavior, and levels of hormones play a key role in these differences. For example, just as hormones program development of the internal and external genitalia in all mammals, hormones contribute to the development of sex differences in childhood play behaviors. Girls with relatively high levels of testosterone prenatally, for any number of reasons, show relatively high levels of male-typical play in childhood (e.g., a desire to play with vehicles instead of dolls and for rough play with boys). The prenatal hormonal environment also influences sexual orientation and core gender identity, although these influences appear to be less dramatic and less clearly defined than those of childhood play (M. Hines 2004).

Finally, a number of studies suggest that gender identity may be rooted in chromosomes and not easily changed. These studies have involved babies born with ambiguous or missing external genitals. In one study, 27 chromosomally male babies born without penises were raised as girls; 25 still considered themselves boys (Reiner 2000). In another, 14 genetically male babies born with testes (but without normal penises) were surgically assigned to female sex shortly after birth and raised as girls. When they were older (between 5 and 16 years old), 6 declared themselves male, 5 declared definite female identity but had difficulty fitting in with other girls, 2 were living ambiguously, and 1 refused to discuss the issue (Reiner and Gearhart 2004).

Biological theories also fall short of explaining all the differences in males and females. The issue of whether nature or nurture is more important in determining gender roles is a timeless argument most likely never to be resolved. We can think of gender roles on a continuum of scientific views with genetics on one end and environment on the other, with most people's beliefs falling somewhere in between—recognizing that hormonal, cultural, and social factors all play a part in the development of sex-typed behavior.

social structure/cultural theories Theories suggesting that most of the differences between male and female gender roles are established because of the status, power, and division of labor in a given society.

evolutionary theories Theories suggesting that genetic heritage is more important than social learning in the development of gender roles.

Traditional Masculine and Feminine Stereotypes

Many people develop stereotyped concepts of masculinity and femininity. These **gender stereotypes** are assumed differences, norms, attitudes, and expectations about men and women.

Masculinity

According to traditional masculine stereotypes, men were supposed to be all of the following:

Aggressive	Adventurous
Dominant	Courageous
Strong	Independent
Forceful	Ambitious
Self-confident	Direct
Rugged	Logical
Virile	Unemotional
Instrumental	

Traditionally, a masculine man was a provider; he was successful, had status, and was respected. A man was a sturdy rock with an air of toughness, confidence, and self-reliance.

Typically, the assertive male was the initiator in relationships between the sexes, and the woman was expected to follow. He was expected to ask *her* out on a date and to decide where to go and what to do (and to pay). He was expected to court *her* while she demurely but coquettishly responded. He was expected to ask for *her* hand in marriage. The woman who was too bold or forward was regarded as a threat to the traditional relationship. And after marriage, the male continued his dominant role as decision maker and initiator. He was supposed to have the last word over both his wife and his children.

Some people believe that traditional male gender-role socialization, as previously discussed, suppresses men's natural ability for emotional self-awareness and expressivity. This translates to boys growing up to be men who cannot readily sense their feelings and put them into words and who have difficulty with emotional empathy. Consequently, "Men tend to channel their vulnerable emotions (such as fear, sadness, loneliness, feeling unloved) into anger, and to transform their caring feelings (such as fondness, love, attachment) into sexuality" (Levant 2003, 177).

Femininity

What are the traditional concepts of femininity as taught by our society? In the past, women were supposed to be all of the following:

Unaggressive	Nurturing
Submissive	Sentimental
Weak	Softhearted
Sensitive	Dependent
Gentle and tender	Aware of the feelings of others
Kind	Emotional and excitable
Tactful	Somewhat frivolous, fickle, illogical, and talkative
Warm and affectionate	

Concepts of femininity vary, and they change with time. Strenuous, competitive activity, such as this women's hockey game, is no longer automatically assumed to be inconsistent with femininity.

More women than men express a higher level of nurturance. Some anthropologists and psychologists believe the higher degree of nurturance among women is innate, whereas others believe it is learned. Regardless, research indicates that females certainly learn to express nurturing behavior at an early age more than do males (Witt 2010). It is also true that nurturing is a critical factor in emotional well-being and in the socialization of children. A prominent anthropologist, Ashley Montague, concluded that nurturance was vital to the survival of society.

A feminine woman was never aggressive, boisterous, loud, or vulgar in speech or behavior. She was expected to cry on occasion and sometimes to get upset over small events. It was all right for her to like laces, frills, and frivolous things. She was expected to be interested primarily in her home and family.

Along with these stereotyped concepts of femininity, society emphasized gender norms that all women were expected to follow. The primary gender norm was the motherhood mandate. Girls played with dolls because, in most people's minds, doll play prepared girls to become mothers. When they got older, girls were considered more capable of babysitting than boys. When a young woman married, people began to ask when she was going to have a baby. If she delayed too long, friends and family began to worry that something was wrong. If she had the biological capability of having children, she was expected to use it. Then, when baby arrived, the motherhood mandate said that she should be a good mother by devoting a majority of her time to caring for her child (Doyle 1985).

The marriage mandate was second in importance to the motherhood mandate. Women were expected to get married, since it was the rite of passage to the adult world, the way to unlock the shackles of dependency on their parents and best fulfill the motherhood mandate.

As another consequence of stereotypic gender roles, women were taught to please men, regardless of their own needs and desires. Nowhere was this more evident than in intimate relationships. Some women went through years of marriage attending only to their husband's wants. Many were dissatisfied and depressed as a result.

Problems with Gender Stereotypes

One problem with gender stereotypes is that whenever rigid gender standards are applied to all members of one sex, individual personalities can become distorted. Everyone is expected to conform, regardless of individual differences or inclinations. Furthermore, gender identity and gender-role stereotypes place serious limitations on the relationships that people are capable of forming and on career or personal achievements.

Another problem with gender stereotypes is that they lead to different expectations of employment and pay for males and females, even among children. Although the rate of participation in the labor force does not differ for boys and girls, their type of work is segregated by gender early on. Girls are more likely to be employed by family and neighbors to perform "benevolent" jobs, such as babysitting, whereas boys are more likely to do manual work in more formal work settings, such as bagging groceries, mowing lawns, and busing dishes (Desmarais and Curtis 1999). Although boys and girls work the same number of hours per week, girls earn significantly lower hourly wages. This gender inequality in youth employment reflects what is occurring among adult workers. Interestingly, studies show that female college students have lower perceived income entitlement for two main reasons. First, women are socialized to value the social and interpersonal aspects of their work rather than to pursue monetary rewards (Center for American Progress 2015). Second, women learn to downplay their work efforts or contributions when examining whether they are being paid a fair wage and thus tend to compare themselves to other women, who are also underpaid, rather than to men (Desmarais and Curtis 1999).

Findings from the National Opinion Research Center General Social Surveys show that traditional gender-role ideology in both men and women contributes to lower observed earnings for females, independent of the influences of individual characteristics. More traditional women are more likely to choose female-dominated jobs, which have low average earnings, and men with traditional gender views are more likely to think women belong in traditionally female jobs. Sometimes gender bias is manifested in subtle ways and without overt malice. A male boss may know female employees are competent workers, but believe they will put family first (to have babies or care for elders, for example). Consequently, he

gender stereotypes Assumed differences, norms, attitudes, and expectations about men and women.

Life on the Boundaries of Gender

By BETSY LUCAL, *Department of Sociology, Indiana University, South Bend*

What does it mean to live on the boundaries of gender? It means being a woman who answers to "Sir" because it is entirely likely that the speaker is talking to me. It means being a woman who thinks twice about using a public restroom in order to avoid comments like "This is the *ladies'* room!" that make it clear someone thinks I'm in the wrong place. It means facing the possibility that someone will challenge my use of a credit card because they're convinced that a card with a woman's name on it could not possibly belong to me. On the other hand, it also means not being afraid to walk alone at night, feeling safer than most women because I'm fairly certain that a potential attacker would not choose someone who appears to be a (relatively big) man. It means being taken seriously in all-male environments, such as auto parts stores, by people who think I'm one of them, and therefore someone who possesses relevant knowledge, rather than a naive woman.

These are among the consequences I deal with every day of my life as a woman who does not conform to the conventions of femininity. However, despite outward appearances, I am female, and I identify as a woman (that is, I am not transgender—I am not a person whose gender identity is different from my sex). My appearance simply defies the rule that says a person's sex and gender display must match. I am a living illustration of the distinction between sex and gender. I am a female (sex) who is, because of my appearance, regularly mistaken for a man (gender). The fact that this happens shows that gender, contrary to popular belief, is not natural but is instead socially constructed. If gender followed naturally from sex, it would be impossible for a female to display masculinity or for a male to display femininity.

Yet my experiences (and those of other people) show that such a thing *is* possible. They provide a vivid reminder that gender is a set of social characteristics and expectations assigned to men and women, not something biological. Though I possess the physical characteristics of a female, people often see me as a man. This is not surprising, given my large size (six feet tall), short hair, lack of jewelry and makeup, and nonfeminine clothes (no dresses or skirts, simple pants/shorts and shirts). As a member of our society, I understand that these are masculine gender markers—aspects of my appearance that may be taken as evidence that I am a man (and, therefore, also male).

So, why don't I align my gender display with my sex? At first, I did not do this with any purpose in mind. Growing up, I simply appeared in a way that was comfortable to me. The fact that my appearance confused other people and/or made them uncomfortable was just something I learned to live with. But as I gained a sociological understanding of the world, I realized that my life on the boundaries of gender gave me an opportunity to show people how gender is socially constructed, how sex and gender are distinct from one another. Hoping that my life could help break down the inequality that accompanies gender, I not only continued this practice but also began to use it to help people understand the consequences of gender in our society.

As a person who lives on the boundaries of gender, I get to see both the oppression of women and the privilege of men firsthand. Because I am a woman, I face the prospect of earning less money than a man with comparable credentials. As a woman, I must endure the derogatory media images of women that are ubiquitous in our society. On the other hand, I need not worry about the public harassment many women experience as they move through the world. If men think I am also a man, they will not engage in catcalls, sexual remarks, and other verbal harassment. When mistaken for a man, I am treated more respectfully than a woman might be.

Like other social constructions, gender has very real consequences. My experiences show that people are treated differently based on the gender they are perceived to be. My experiences make it clear that gender does matter in our interactions with other people. Life on the boundaries isn't always easy, but it is instructive.

does not consider them for advancement to management levels—thus impacting their earnings negatively. In a similar way, in the 2008 presidential election, the question was raised whether the vice presidential candidate Sarah Palin could balance that job with her family responsibilities. This was not asked about the male candidates.

Traditional gender-role ideology also can impact men's earnings. Employers may view men with sexist views of women as "lacking in openness to diversity" or as open invitations to discrimination lawsuits, which may affect their career success (Firestone, Harris, and Lambert 1999).

Trying to follow traditional male gender roles also can be harmful to men in other ways. Adherence to the traditional male role is associated with higher levels of suicide, substance abuse, health problems, stress, and emotional illness (Good and Mintz 1990). Being openly aggressive, dominant, and unemotional often leads to trouble with friends, family, and society.

Gender Roles and Body Image

Gender roles define not only masculine and feminine behavior but also masculine and feminine ideals of appearance. Trying to live up to these prescribed images can damage self-esteem and even endanger health. For example, more than half of the girls in one study who were unhappy with their bodies were at significantly greater risk for suicide—whether they were overweight or not (Dhaval and Inas 2009).

"Body image" most often refers to positive or negative feelings about specific parts of the body and to overall appearance. How people feel about their body depends on many factors, both external and internal. An individual's body-image attitudes are purely subjective and personal, but some attitudes tend to be common to each gender and based on societal cues.

Today many young girls worry about the shape, size, and muscle tone of their bodies because they are taught that beautiful has a specific look—thin—and that beauty brings success (Juergen 2014; Media Smarts 2015). In contrast to women of a century ago, who controlled their bodies with corsets and girdles, today's young women control their bodies internally, with diet and exercise. Nevertheless, both are overly concerned about outward appearance.

In contemporary society, both males and females, particularly on television and in the movies, are less modest about their bodies and are showing more skin than ever before. This openness is particularly problematic for girls because their bodies, even more than the bodies of boys, are constantly being displayed and appraised. It is not surprising, then, that one half of 9- to 12-year-old girls want to be thinner and had been on a diet (L. Clark and Tiggemann 2006) and half of girls ages 16 to 21 would undergo surgery to improve their appearance (Girl Guiding UK 2009; 2015). It is estimated that although only about 6.5% of high school girls are overweight, approximately 35% of them think they are (Centers for Disease Control and Prevention [CDC] 2001), and adolescent girls who hold stereotyped views of gender roles are dissatisfied with their weight, even when it is in a normal range (Gershon et al. 2004).

This preoccupation with weight and perfectionism stems from our cultural expectations for females, rather than from individual psychopathology. More than two decades ago, Mary Pipher (1994) observed that females measure their bodies against cultural ideals and cannot help but feel inferior against a standard of abnormal thinness, which is unattainable for most females. Furthermore, the widespread use of photo manipulation ("photoshopping"), whereby a model may have ribs, collarbones, or hips erased to make her thinner, sets a standard that is literally impossible to attain (L. Collins 2008; Copeland 2011). Thus, in recent decades, females' dissatisfaction with their bodies has increased along with the incidence of eating disorders. It is not surprising that the number of cosmetic procedures to improve appearance increased from 2.1 million in 1997 to 9 million in 2004 (American Society for Aesthetic Plastic Surgery 2005).

Television, magazines, and other media communicate clear messages about ideal appearance. Several studies have looked at the portrayals of overweight characters from popular television shows and movies and discovered that heavyset men and women

- Had fewer dates or sexual encounters;
- Were made fun of more often;
- Were more likely minorities, older, and unemployed; or
- Were often mean or coarse.

Although only 3 of 100 female characters on television were obese, in real life, 25% to 35% are (Greenberg et al. 2003, Juergen 2014; "More than" 2008).

Although most data collected on gender and body image are female focused, men also are affected by the media's portrayal of them. Boys are not as open about their concerns, but still face an idealized male image of someone who is muscular and not too skinny or too fat (Austin, Haines, and Veugelers 2009; Freeman et al. 2012). Body dissatisfaction among males has been associated with poor psychological adjustment, eating disorders, steroid use, and exercise dependence (Boys and Body Image 2012; Kurtz 2010; M. P. McCabe and Ricciardelli 2004). Although the incidence of anorexia or bulimia in men is less than in women, the UK National Health Service reported a two-thirds increase in hospital admissions of men with eating disorders from 2001 to 2011 (Baghdjian 2011). Male athletes seem especially at risk (Harding 2009).

Steroid use is a growing problem among young men. Steroids are laboratory-made versions of the human hormone testosterone, which aids the growth of muscles, bones, and skin. Men on steroids often do increase their strength and muscle mass, but at the price of interfering with normal body development. Males potentially face premature balding, breast enlargement, and shrunken testicles.

Steroid use is also a difficulty among some young women who use them to build muscle mass and to lose weight—often in conjunction with diet pills, vomiting, and/or laxatives. This type of substance abuse is associated with weight loss tactics as early as middle school (Garry, Morrissey, and Whetstone 2003). As with males, steroid use by women has consequences for healthy development, changes in the menstrual cycle, stunted height, and severe acne. In a national survey of adolescent drug abuse, Leshner (2000) found that nearly 3% of 8th graders and 4% of 12th graders have used steroids.

Toys exert an early and strong influence on children's images of what men and women are like. Although the inappropriate thinness of female dolls has long been noted and criticized, male action figures now also depict inappropriate and sometimes impossible ideals of muscularity. One study of the physiques of G. I. Joe and Star Wars figures showed that the action figures today, as well as pop culture icons like Tarzan, are much more muscular than those of 40 years ago (see Figure 2.1) (Media Smarts 2015; Pope et al. 1999).

Advertisements promote the idea that females' personal happiness is linked to physical appearance rather than good character and positive self-esteem. Although such ads have boosted profits for manufacturers of skin, hair, and diet products, they sap the creativity of girls and threaten their mental and physical health (Copeland 2011). Viewing images of very thin models makes women who are overweight or of normal weight feel bad about themselves. For example, women who viewed typical female model images in magazines had higher levels of anger and depression than did women who viewed only images of objects (Copeland 2011; Pinhas et al. 1999). Viewing images of models had an immediate and negative effect on women's moods, creating feelings of depression, guilt, low self-esteem, and failure. Interestingly, men overestimate the degree of muscularity that is attractive to women, and women overestimate the degree of thinness that is most attractive to men, largely because of the media's portrayal of an ideal body image (Frederick, Fessler, and Haselton 2005).

In our culture, females feel more negatively about their body image than do males. Not surprisingly, a study of 21 popular magazines found that 78% of the covers of women's magazines contained a message regarding appearance, whereas none of the men's magazines did. In addition, 25% of the women's magazine covers contained information on weight loss, perpetuating the idea of slimness as the only attractive ideal. And where the men's magazines focused on entertainment, hobbies, and activities, the women's magazines focused on improving one's life by changing one's appearance (Anjalin, 2015; Malkin et al. 1999).

Although magazine covers do not fully represent the media and their messages, they do reflect cultural standards and shape attitudes regarding gender behavior. Researchers have analyzed the content of *Seventeen* magazine over a number of years to identify patterns in the concerns and interests of the modern teenage girl. Although minor changes have occurred, the magazine's content still conveys the same message that it did when it was first published in 1944: that young women should be concerned with improving their external appearance and pleasing a man (Massoni 2004; Schlenker, Caron, and Halteman 1998). Even today, this publication—a widely distributed teenage magazine—does not address the intellectual issues relevant to young women. Massoni (2004) concludes that *Seventeen*'s overarching message to

FIGURE 2.1 The Evolution of the Physiques of Action Figures and Traditional Heroes

Note: From Time, *April 24, 2000.*

girls about work is that it remains a man's world in which women labor (mostly at being beautiful) as a means to meet or assist more powerful men. Although more women than ever before are pursuing higher education, having careers, and delaying marriage, the content of the publications they read does not seem to reflect the aspirations and levels of achievement of which they are capable.

The Word *Machismo*

The word **machismo** or "macho" referring to Mexican families is frequently misunderstood and construed negatively. Historically, Mexican American families have been considered patriarchal (male dominated). Machismo (the Spanish word for "manhood" that in English connotes masculinity) required that the male head of the household provide for and protect his family; protection included both physical protection against aggressors and protection of the family honor. The woman was thought to be the nurturer and caregiver for the family. In many traditional families, these ideas about gender are largely still in place.

The most recent views of Mexican American families emphasize that machismo is still a persistent feature but that the fathers usually exercise their authority in a dignified and fair manner, showing honor and respect for other family members. The Mexican American family has been characterized as warm and nurturing, with cooperation among family members and egalitarianism in decision making. Role relations range from patriarchal to completely egalitarian, with the most prevalent one being that the husband and wife share in decisions. Although some studies indicate that Mexican American women follow the traditional roles of submission to their spouse's authority, more research rejects the notion that Mexican American women lack power within heterosexual relationships (Gutmann 1996).

A recent study of male Mexican immigrants showed that the men expressed greater concern about their daughters' socioeconomic future and life opportunities than a rigidly ideological concern for maintenance of their daughters' premarital virginity (Gonzalez-Lopez 2004). Although fathers expected their daughters to delay premarital sex, they also promoted an ethic of protection and care that might safeguard a daughter from pregnancy out of wedlock; sexually transmitted diseases; sexual violence; casual sex and promiscuity; and sexual dangers associated with drugs, alcohol use, and gang violence, among other risks. This is seen as a strategy to help their daughters attend and complete college and thus improve their living conditions and socioeconomic future as they survive in an increasingly competitive society. Testimonies of the men from this study challenge stereotypical images of Mexican fathers as "macho," dominant, and authoritarian (Gonzalez-Lopez 2004).

Race, Class, and Gender

Much of what we know about gender is from research on white, middle-class females. There is much less research on males and individuals from different ethnicities and social classes. Making generalizations to other groups based on the lives of white, middle-class women is misleading and results in theoretical and empirical errors (M. Andersen 2005). Today, there are textbooks and courses devoted specifically to the study of the relationship among race, class, and gender. Although the complexity of how these three variables interrelate is beyond the scope of this text, it is important to understand that race, class, and gender influence each other in a complex web of overlapping, intersecting, and interrelating social relationships. Furthermore, gender is manifested differently in its relationship to race, class, and sexuality and is constructed differently in different social locations because of its relational character. Thus, gender can never be studied in isolation from race, class, and related social conditions (M. Andersen 2005).

A fascinating example of this intersection of race, class, and gender is found in the study of adolescent females. According to several studies (L. M. Brown and Gilligan 1992), white girls often struggle against losing their essence: their voice; their self; their beliefs and values; what makes them happy. They begin "losing voice" and "abandoning self" around age 12 in exchange for being perceived as a "perfect" girl: passive, quiet, demure, and attractive to boys—qualities that make up the traditional female gender stereotype. They derive their worth from relationships rather than from their abilities and accomplishments.

Although such gender-role behaviors may be common among middle-class white girls, they are not universal. Consequently, a growing body of research is focused on female gender identity development among urban adolescents from different social classes and ethnic backgrounds. In one sample of 362 girls from five different ethnic groups (Erkut et al. 1996), almost half of the girls cited athletic abilities, rather than relationships, as the main thing that made them feel good about themselves. African American adolescent girls often are described not as losing voice but as being assertive, powerful, resilient, and resistant (Gibbs 1996; J. Ward 1996; Way 1995). Other research supports this idea by showing that African American and Latina girls readily engage in conflict and argue about the rules of a game when they play (Goodwin 1998) and that African American boys and girls often engage in playful arguments when playing together (Aydt and Corsaro 2003; Goodwin 2001). Among African American families, mothers socialize their daughters to be independent, strong, self-confident, self-reliant, and resourceful (P. H. Collins 1987).

Interestingly, in an examination of advertisements in black- and white-oriented magazines depicting women's sexuality, Baker (2005) found that the images of women's sexuality vary depending on the race of the intended audience and the race of the women in the advertisements. Advertisements for white audiences portray women in ways that suggest dependency and submissiveness, whereas advertisements for black audiences portray women as independent and dominant.

Another study exploring the ideas Mexican American girls have about their femininity also showed the importance of culture in understanding how girls negotiate gender roles (Denner and Dunbar 2004). The girls interviewed saw clear differences in the expectations Mexican American adults have for girls and boys. Being a girl was associated with high levels of vulnerability and obligation to the family, which results in external limits on their power. Yet being a girl also presented opportunities to speak up, be strong, and create opportunities for themselves. In general, the girls perceived a high level of power in their lives and relationships. Although they embraced the more traditional expectations associated with becoming a young Mexican American woman, they also asserted their own desires to be seen as strong and

Is cooking the family dinner a gender-typed role? The ability to perform any family task without concern for its gender appropriateness can make it easier for a child, when the time comes, to achieve an egalitarian marriage.

able to protect themselves and their families (Denner and Dunbar 2004).

Body image also seems to differ among ethnic groups. In numerous studies (Chithambo and Huey 2013; Grabe and Hyde 2006; Kronenfeld et al. 2010; K. J. Miller et al. 2000) African Americans reported greater body satisfaction and less overestimation of weight than their white counterparts. African American women also rated themselves as more sexually attractive than did Anglo-American women and had higher self-esteem regarding their weight. Hispanic women rated themselves as less sexually attractive than did African American women but more sexually attractive than did white women. Males in all three groups demonstrated little differences. The differences between the ratings of body satisfaction or attractiveness are small, and the differences are largest in the adolescent and young adult years; girls and older women of all groups are similar in their body satisfaction.

Recent scholarship about male attitudes toward gender roles has documented a variety of standards

machismo Spanish for "manhood"; masculinity.

that define manhood differently across ethnic, class, sexual, and regional boundaries (Shirley and Wallace 2004). Men's attitudes toward female gender roles also vary. The idea that women's roles should be circumscribed by home and family may reflect only a narrow segment of white, middle-class men. For example, generally speaking, African American men are more liberal in their attitudes toward working wives than white men and are far more likely to have lived in a household with a working wife and/or mother (Blee and Tickamyer 1995).

Changing Roles of Women and Men

In the past several decades, major changes in the ways women perceive themselves and their roles in modern society have occurred. Part of the impetus for this rethinking came from the emergence of a national consensus among women that the image of woman as exclusively mother and housekeeper stifled the true feelings and needs of many women. As the need for changes—in attitudes, in legislation, in the workplace, and in the family—became increasingly obvious, some women began efforts to bring about those changes. They have made great strides; however, the work is not finished. For example, many careers previously closed to women are now open, but true equality of wages and representation is lacking. More men are chief executive officers, whereas more women are secretaries; she earns about 80 cents to his dollar—which amounts to $431,360 over a lifetime of work (Center for American Progress 2015; Hegewisch and DuMonthier 2016; Institute for Women's Policy Research 2009; Patten 2015a).

The marriage and motherhood mandates have been relaxed. An unmarried or child-free woman is recognized as having chosen to remain so and to make her own life. As women have gained economic independence, they have less often married or stayed in unhappy marriages simply for economic reasons.

Two major problems facing women today are **role ambiguity** and **role strain**. Strict feminists argue that women can find satisfaction only in salaried work, whereas strict traditionalists insist that only family and motherhood yield true satisfaction. Many women are conflicted about which choice is best and feel guilty regardless of their choice. Some women experience role strain when they combine career, home maintenance, and childrearing. The demands of multiple roles soon overwhelm even the most capable, energetic woman. B. Park (2013) suggests that the role demands of being an "ideal mom" and "ideal worker/professional" do not match up, thus causing women psychological and cognitive distress. In contrast, being an "ideal dad" and an "ideal worker/professional" have more similarities—being a good provider and being decisive, for example.

As role alternatives for women change, men must redefine their roles to adjust to a society in which masculine and feminine roles are less dichotomized. Many men face the dilemma of interacting with women as equal partners, although they are still under the influence of traditions that encourage them to take the initiative and assume a dominant role in a variety of situations.

During this time when the concepts of masculinity and femininity are being broadened, the criteria of dominance, aggressiveness, and accomplishment have become less important in the definition of masculinity. Men have greater freedom to express characteristics traditionally considered feminine—sensitivity, consideration, warmth, and nurturance. It is acceptable for men to communicate their feelings, problems, and concerns to others; they are becoming more emotionally responsive, a factor important to the success of interpersonal relationships. A change significantly affecting family life is that men are assuming greater responsibility in childrearing. As a result, children may enjoy closer relationships with their fathers than they have in the past and both boys and girls will see a wider variety of parental and gender-role models.

Gender Roles in the Family

The awareness and attitudes that men and women hold toward gender differences have a significant influence on many aspects of marital and family dynamics. For example, men and women approach communication, conflict resolution, sexual encounters, stress management, and problem solving differently. See Chapters 9, 10, and 15 for more details.

Changes in gender roles in recent generations have made many situations better for both men and women. And they have made life more complex,

In families in which men help with child care and household responsibilities, working women report considerably less role conflict and stress.

too. Roles once clearly defined are now less distinct; many families struggle with role conflict, strain, and overload. Couples must decide whether to be traditional or modern. How will children be reared? Who will mow the lawn? Decide to buy a new car?

Roles in Marriage

In the marital relationship, some men and women like a more traditional role relationship. One partner may want to be dominant (because of personality or upbringing); another may be more comfortable in a supportive role. When both share this value, the marriage relationship can function well.

Other men and women prefer an **egalitarian marriage**: they want social equality, characterized by mutual respect, shared power, and shared work in their relationship. Neither spouse is dominant; decisions are made jointly. Chores are divided by interest rather than gender. He can cook dinner while she mows the lawn, for example.

The roles that people play also depend partly on the family situation. For example, having a baby typically pushes women into traditional domestic roles, at least for a while. The evidence also supports the idea that the division of labor changes over the family life cycle. Although women shoulder a disproportionate share of the household labor (Bureau of Labor Statistics 2015; Schmader and Croft 2013), the disparity between her share and his appears to be least in the preparental years and in the postparental years (Suitor 1991). Men tend to spend more time performing domestic labor during periods of least occupational involvement—that is, early in their employment career and after retirement (Dorfman and Heckert 1988; Rexroat and Shehan 1987). His contributions to household chores rise when she is employed full-time (Pictman and Blanchard 1996). The division of household chores (as an indication of gender-role performance) is the result not only of ideology, but also of family demands and available resources (time, energy, etc.).

In general, couples who have achieved **gender-role congruence**—that is, agreement on gender-role expectations and performance—report higher marital quality than those who do not. Couples can be strictly traditional or totally egalitarian or some hybrid. The important factor is for them to be in agreement (Stevens, Kiger, and Riley 2001). Couples who focus on mutual support, concern, and thoughtfulness are likely to have good relationships. Contests to determine who is the "boss" or who can get the most while giving the least are disappointing and destructive.

role ambiguity The uncertainty felt when choosing a gender role.

role strain The stress of trying to meet the demands of many roles.

egalitarian marriage A relationship of equality rather than strict role definition; the focus is on shared power and shared work.

gender-role congruence Agreement between partners' gender-role expectations and their performance.

FAMILY STRENGTHS PERSPECTIVE

Do Everyday Things Together

Members of strong families spend lots of time together; it helps communication and the development of family identity. How do families spend time together? Mealtimes and time needed to run a household provide opportunities.

I work late in the afternoon, so I need help getting dinner ready. At first my son protested about having to cook, but I've convinced him that knowing how to cook is a handy thing. Now he's proud of his accomplishments. He often has cookies or a cake ready when I get home.

Our daughter is still too young to handle very hot things or knives, but she sets the table and makes simple salads.

We all get in the kitchen and talk about what went on at school and work while we fix dinner. They're learning other valuable things besides cooking; they're learning they are important in making our family run....

Nearly every Saturday morning we have a clean-up session at the house. We all pitch in to help: Somebody vacuums; somebody dusts; somebody empties trash. We run a couple loads of laundry. It's a real swirl of activity for a couple hours. Then we're done and ready to have fun. Plus the house is tidied up.

Housework and Child-Care Roles

With more than half of all married women employed outside the home, fairness demands a willingness on the part of husbands to assume shared responsibility for housework and child care. Some studies indicate that gender-role stereotypes, especially among college students, may be weakening, but most current research continues to find evidence of traditional gender roles (Cooke 2004; S. N. Davis and Greenstein 2004; Evertsson and Nermo 2004; Schmader and Croft 2013). For example, although the gap between the amount of time women and men spend in family work is shrinking, women are still doing more family work than most men are doing (Fottrell 2015; Schmader and Croft 2013). In addition, women are twice as likely as men to report that family demands negatively affect their job performance. This is largely because women make more adjustments to their workloads, such as refusing overtime or turning down assignments, for the sake of the family (Keene and Reynolds 2005). Overwhelmingly, the evidence suggests that even when women work as many hours outside the home as their spouses, they retain primary responsibility for home care and child care, although men do participate in domestic work more when their partner is employed (Cooke 2004; S. N. Davis and Greenstein 2004; Evertsson and Nermo 2004).

It appears that men do relatively little domestic labor unless both they and their spouse are somewhat egalitarian in their beliefs about gender roles in marriage (T. N. Greenstein 1996). In dual-earner families, fathers are involved and engaged in activities with their children, and this involvement increases as the mother's work hours increase, but all other household chores continue to be gender segregated. Indoor work is predominantly completed by women and outdoor work by men (Gottfried et al. 1999; Kroska 2004).

Marital satisfaction depends partly on partners perceiving themselves and their spouses as each doing a fair share of family work (Stevens, Kiger, and Riley 2001). When women work outside the home and also do most of the work around the house and care for the children, they experience considerable role conflict and strain. It is difficult to combine multiple roles, do all of them well, and still have time to take care of oneself. Sharing domestic work and parenting responsibilities is important, therefore, to individual well-being, to the marital relationship, and to quality parent–child relationships.

In sum, several studies, including ones of single- and dual-earner families and of upper-middle-class families, reveal that women still spend significantly more time doing housework and caring for children than do men (Bureau of Labor Statistics 2015; Cooke 2004; S. N. Davis and Greenstein 2004; Evertsson and Nermo 2004; Kroska 2004; Schmader and Croft 2013). This is the case although women have significantly increased their participation in the paid workforce over the past 30 years (as discussed in Chapters 1 and 8). In most industrialized countries, men's domestic participation in the family is about one-third of women's. For example, in the United States, women on average spend about 19 hours a week in domestic work compared to about 6 hours for men (Evertsson and Nermo 2004). However, it is worth noting that there is a significant gender effect on reporting housework: men tend to overestimate the actual number of hours they spend doing housework and women do not (S. N. Davis and Greenstein 2004; Kamo 2000).

An interesting caveat to the research on the division of household labor is what has been labeled "doing-gender" (Evertsson and Nermo 2004). When

---

COPING FEATURE

Coping with Depression

Everyone feels down or depressed sometimes. Many experience clinical depression that extends over a period of two or more weeks and includes such symptoms as low energy, fatigue, feelings of worthlessness, decreased ability to concentrate, and changes in appetite and sleep. In addition to being uncomfortable for the affected person, depression causes conflict and other problems in relationships. The resulting disharmony in relationships can contribute to more depression—making a vicious cycle (Kleinke 2002).

We can better understand and cope with depression by being aware of some underlying factors of depression, including the following:

- Preoccupation with the negatives in life.
- Insistence on being perfect (and then feeling worthless when perfection is not achieved).
- Self-esteem that is strongly dependent on the approval of others.
- Belief that important life events are externally controlled.
- Lack of social support systems.
- High degree of self-blame, avoidance, wishful thinking, and irritability.

Research indicates certain coping skills are important in reducing or preventing depression. These include the following:

- Seek and use social support systems.
- Use professional counseling and medical help when needed. Cognitive therapy combined with antidepressant medication is associated with higher rates of recovery from major depressive disorders than when medications are used alone (Hollon et al. 2014).
- Use an active problem-solving approach when it is within your control to improve a situation or solve a problem.
- Acknowledge when an unpleasant situation or stressful event is beyond your control.
- Replace negative and irrational appraisals with more positive, rational ones.
- Enhance hopefulness by recognizing your strengths and the positives in your life.
- Set realistic goals that can be reached and reward yourself for your accomplishments.
- Distract yourself when feeling depressed; get busy with other activities.
- Engage in physical activity on a regular basis. Higher frequency of physical activity is associated with fewer depressive symptoms (Pereira, Jeoffrey, and Power 2014).

a husband is economically dependent on a wife and she is seen as the breadwinner of the family, women still report doing a majority of the domestic work. This could be because women want to increase their time spent in gender-typical behavior such as housework to compensate for what they see as "gender deviance" in their family (e.g., breadwinning wife and economically dependent husband) (Evertsson and Nermo 2004). It also could be because women do not want to give up a traditional source of power and control in their lives. The power of making decisions about running a household is valued by both men and women; it is recognized as a source of personal power (M. Williams 2013).

Gender, Marriage, and Depression

Depression is an issue for many families and often involves negative behaviors such as lowered motivation and irritability. The causes of depression are varied, such as a chemical imbalance, personality, or situational factors, but most researchers agree that depression and interpersonal relationships are affected by one another. For example, negative affect in one partner is one of the most consistent predictors of relationship difficulties and, conversely, marital distress can lead to increased negative behaviors, which can lead to clinical depression (P. Papp 2003).

Peggy Papp (2003) observed that men and women become depressed for distinctly different reasons, cope with depressive symptoms differently, and are responded to differently by their spouses. Women's depression is most often related to a disruption in a close personal relationship, whereas men's depression is most often related to a performance failure. There is also a difference in the ability of men and women to recognize and acknowledge depression. In general, women are quicker than men to seek help and better able to connect their depression with certain events or relationships in their lives.

P. Papp's (2003) research also showed that women were nearly always aware of an emotional distance in their marital relationship and thus would reach out for more contact and closeness. When women discussed their underlying feelings, they included statements such as "We never talk to each other" (P. Papp 2003, 213). In contrast, men who were depressed often seemed unaware of their need for intimacy and had difficulty reaching out to a partner for comfort or

more contact. Men rarely connected their depression with any aspect of their relationship. Many men were reluctant to share their feelings, as reflected in comments such as "I've always believed in handling my problems myself" (P. Papp 2003, 213).

When women are depressed, men typically try a problem-solving approach to fix the situation. Depressed women generally experience these efforts as dominating and controlling and would prefer more discussion and sharing of feelings than advice and solutions. When men are depressed, women tend to protect, placate and appease, cater to their moods, shield them from telephone calls, keep the children away, and protect them from their extended families. Although men may rely on this caretaking, they often resent it because it makes them feel dependent and controlled (P. Papp 2003).

Androgyny

What seems to be emerging in today's society is a gradual mixing of gender roles to produce **androgyny**, a gender role that combines both the feminine and the masculine. Androgynous people are not gender typed with respect to roles, although they are distinctly male or female in sex. They match their behavior to the situation, rather than being limited by what is culturally defined as male or female. For example, an androgynous male feels comfortable cuddling and caring for a baby or being a stay-at-home dad who home schools the children; an androgynous female feels comfortable changing the oil in her car or being the sole provider for her husband and children. Androgyny expands the range of acceptable behavior, allowing individuals to cope effectively in a variety of situations.

The mixing of roles is advantageous to both sexes. Both sexes are restricted in their behavior and relationships by narrow gender-typed roles. Both masculine and androgynous people are more independent and less conforming than those identified with femininity, and both feminine and androgynous individuals are more nurturing than those who are traditionally masculine.

Historically, psychologists have taught that mental health depends on a clear-cut separation between male and female roles. However, some studies reveal that androgynous individuals have better

Androgyny expands the range of acceptable behavior. Clothes and hairstyles do not express either maleness or femaleness.

social relationships and are better adjusted than people who have more traditional gender identities. Other studies suggest that more androgynous individuals possess adaptive capabilities and resources, such as creativity, effective coping techniques, emotional integration, communication skills, and a well-defined self-concept with a high level of ego strength (Csikszentmihalyi 2013; Small, Teagno, and Selz 1980).

However, some people do not agree that androgyny should be the model. Rather, they feel that women's and men's biological, emotional, and psychological attributes should be valued equally. By emphasizing nonsexist attitudes in general, one can seek to acknowledge the fundamental difference between men and women and to equally value those differences.

Although researchers may use the categories of masculine, feminine, and androgynous, in reality, our gender self-concept probably changes across the various contexts in which we interact. The gender makeup of the group (that is, same sex or mixed sex) may influence the interactional style of the participants. Or the situation itself may influence the traits exhibited by individuals. For example, around her intimate partner, a woman may exhibit traditional feminine qualities, whereas at work she may exhibit more traditional masculine qualities. An analysis of national data by the National Center on Addiction and Substance Abuse found that girls who want to be one of the boys go drink-for-drink with them (Foster et al. 2003). (This may be problematic for females, who metabolize alcohol more slowly, become intoxicated more quickly, and become alcohol dependent faster than males.)

C. J. Smith, Noll, and Bryant (1999) examined the effect of social context on gender self-concept and found that males are more likely to demonstrate feminine traits when they are with females and to avoid showing feminine characteristics when they are with other males. Females were less likely to change their feminine self-concept across contexts. However, among unfamiliar people, both males and females are more likely to display androgynous characteristics. Overall, we seem to be developing more flexible and interchangeable gender roles.

The concept of our gender role is very much influenced by our environment. What we observe in our own family, in the media, and in school combine to help us develop our own gender identity. Several theories provide ways to think about our behavior in conjunction with gender roles and identity. Sometimes the gender roles promulgated by society cause us to act in unhealthy ways or to be burdened with duties without consideration of the effect. Yet society is changing, and more and more people are moving toward choosing behavior appropriate to the situation regardless of gender roles.

androgyny A blending of male and female characteristics and roles; especially, a lack of gender typing with respect to roles.

TITLE IX

Title IX is a federal law that prohibits discrimination on the basis of sex in federally funded educational institutions. Although most people think of it as just pertaining to sports, the law actually applies to all aspects of education, including admissions, recruitment, counseling, financial assistance, student health, housing, marital and parental student status, harassment, educational programs and activities, employment, and physical education and athletics (M. B. Nelson 2002/2003; Portman 2015).

There is no question that women have not had the same opportunities to participate in sports as men do at the high school and college levels. Although women's participation in high school sports has increased by a factor of 9 and increased in college by 450% (Carpenter and Acosta 2008), some argue that Title IX has not given women truly equal opportunities. For example, men receive $133 million more in athletic scholarships and women's coaches earn 35% less than men's coaches (Nelson 2002/2003).

Opponents of Title IX argue that providing equal access to athletics for women takes away opportunities for men. When funds are low (as is typically true), schools may choose to eliminate men's programs that sometimes are popular and have good participation instead of increasing women's programs. To be in compliance, for example, men's wrestling or cross country may be cut to pay for women's basketball or cross country. Opponents also contend that women are not as interested in sports as men; schools should not have to provide for these sports because they do not reflect the interests of students.

Title IX also aims to protect students from sexual harassment and assault because they interfere with a student's ability to receive an education and, in the case of sexual violence, can be a crime ("Dear Colleague" 2013). Florida State University is under scrutiny for its handling of rape allegations made by a former student, Erica Kinsman, against a quarterback, Jameis Winston, who played after the allegations and won the Heisman Trophy (Portman 2015). Several other universities such as Amherst, Yale, the University of North Carolina–Chapel Hill, Arizona State University, and the University of Colorado have had similar cases.

A 2011 guideline requires institutions to conduct investigations and discipline based on a preponderance-of-evidence basis rather than beyond a reasonable doubt. Critics point to the use of such a standard as potentially damaging to innocent persons. They cite the case of a University of North Dakota student, Caleb Warner, who was suspended for three years based on a report by a complainant who was later charged with filing a false report. Warner's suspension was not removed.

Questions to Consider

Are schools discriminating against men by eliminating some men's sports to create opportunities for women? Give reasons and examples to back up your answer.

Do women want to participate in sports programs as much as men? Is it acceptable to provide fewer opportunities for women because they are less interested, or would more women become interested if more opportunities were presented to them? Discuss.

Are there areas of discrimination other than sports that you are aware of? For example, are women counseled into certain majors (education) and away from others (physics)? Are men?

What is the fair standard for universities to use in handling sexual assault or harassment reports? For example, should the accused person be suspended pending the investigation? Many times the investigation may take months.

Summary

1. Sex refers to one's biological identity, male or female. Gender includes those psychosocial components that characterize one as masculine or feminine. Gender identity is an individual's personal, internal sense of maleness or femaleness that is expressed in personality and behavior. A gender role is the outward expression of one's maleness or femaleness in a social setting.

2. Environmental influences are a major determinant of gender identities and gender roles. Society defines the qualities of maleness and femaleness expected of men and women. Three major influences on children's individual gender identities and roles are parents, television, and school.

3. The social learning theory asserts that concepts of gender roles and appropriate gender behavior are established through exposure to social influences such as parents, teachers, peers, and media.

4. Cognitive developmental theory suggests that children actively seek out cues and learn gender stereotypes at a particular stage of intellectual development, going through phases of rigidity and flexibility concerning gender behavior.

5. Gender schema theory combines elements of both cognitive developmental and social learning theories, suggesting that children have frameworks (schema) of how males and females act and look.

6. Social structure and cultural theories directly relate power, status, and division of labor to concepts of gender identity. The view of women as subordinates in the workplace parallels the gender conception of women as less powerful and in need of support.

7. Evolutionary theories assert that gender roles have been established through genetic evolution based on biological functions of the sexes and reproductive success.

8. Biological theories suggest that some of the differences in male and female behavior are the result of genetic, hormonal, and neurological influences.

9. People develop stereotyped concepts of masculinity and femininity. Traditionally, males were aggressive, dominant, strong, forceful, self-confident, rugged, virile, instrumental, adventurous, courageous, independent, ambitious, direct, logical, and unemotional. To be a man was to be a big wheel, be successful, have status, and be looked up to.

10. Traditionally, females were submissive, weak, sensitive, gentle, tender, kind, tactful, warm and affectionate, sentimental, softhearted, dependent, aware of the feelings of others, emotional and excitable, and somewhat frivolous, fickle, illogical, and talkative. Female gender norms included the marriage and motherhood mandates; that is, women were expected to get married and to have children.

11. The problem with stereotypes is that forcing everyone to conform to the same mold severely limits the development of individual personality and personal achievement. New gender roles encourage women to be more assertive and less passive and men to be less aggressive and more cooperative.

12. Females are socialized to believe that the body is the ultimate expression of the self. Television, magazines, and advertisements influence the way women feel about themselves and create unattainable standards for women to live up to, resulting in an increase in eating disorders and negative self-image.

13. Research on white adolescent girls has shown that, in addition to having increased rates of depression and suicide, they are more vulnerable to eating disorders, substance abuse, and low self-esteem. White girls also tend to "lose voice" and become more passive to fit the traditional gender stereotype. But research focusing on minority adolescent girls suggests that they have greater body satisfaction; specifically, African American girls are more assertive and powerful, rather than losing voice.

14. Recent decades have witnessed major changes in the way women perceive themselves: Marriage and motherhood mandates are relaxed and more mothers are employed. Men have redefined their roles as well, becoming more sensitive, warm, and communicative.

15. Gender-role expectations and attitudes have an effect on marital and family dynamics. Some couples prefer an egalitarian marriage with shared power and work; others prefer a traditional relationship. Congruence between gender-role expectations and behavior is most important in relationship satisfaction.

16. Egalitarian roles have not been achieved fully, although marital satisfaction, individual psychological well-being, and child-care quality are improved when spouses share in family tasks. Women still spend significantly more time than men doing housework and caring for children, even when they work full-time outside the home. This unequal division of labor is a source of resentment and anger for many women.

17. Depression is an issue for many families and often involves negative behaviors such as lowered motivation, self-focus, and irritability. The causes of depression are varied, such as a chemical imbalance or situational factors, but most researchers agree that depression and interpersonal relationships are affected by one another.

18. The present trend is toward androgyny, whereby people are not gender typed with respect to roles. A mixing of roles is advantageous to both sexes. People may actually change gender roles depending on their social context.

Key Terms

androgyny

cognitive developmental theory

egalitarian marriage

evolutionary theories

femininity

gender

gender identity

gender role

gender-role congruence

gender schema theory

gender stereotypes

machismo

masculinity

parental identification and modeling

role ambiguity

role strain

social learning theory of gender identity

social structure/cultural theories

transgender people

transsexual

Questions for Thought

1. What are the traditional conceptions of a masculine person? What effects, both positive and negative, can such conceptions have on a man's life?

2. What are the traditional conceptions of a feminine person? What effects, both positive and negative, can such conceptions have on a woman's life?

3. What roles do you believe men and women should play in marriage and the family? Explain your views.

4. Do you believe the media are becoming more or less influential in children's development of gender roles? Explain.

For Further Reading

Canada's Centre for Digital and Media Literacy gives an in-depth look at how films, the Internet, video games, toys, and advertisements shape our ideas of how we should look. It also has resources for parents and teachers. https://mediasmarts.ca/body-image.

Center for American Progress. *The gender pay gap.* http://www.americanprogress.org/issues/women/news.

Colebrook, C. (2004). *Gender.* New York: Palgrave Macmillan. Examines the variations in the concept of gender over the centuries.

http://www.commonsensemedia.org has information about body image and inaccurate images in the media, such as the use of airbrushing and photoshopping to create impossible appearances.

Gimlin, D. (2002). *Body work: Beauty and self-image in American culture.* Berkeley: University of California Press. Examines the relationship between women's body image and self-image in today's culture.

Hansen, K. (2005). *Not-so-nuclear families: Class, gender, and networks of care.* New Brunswick, NJ: Rutgers University Press. Discusses networks of interdependence in an age of independence in families.

Hunter, A. E., and Forden, C. (2002). *Readings in the psychology of gender: Exploring our differences and commonalities.* Needham Heights, MA: Allyn & Bacon. Focuses on differences and similarities between males and females.

Satow, R. (2002). *Gender and social life.* Needham Heights, MA: Allyn & Bacon. Offers a variety of ideas about how gender structures our feelings about ourselves, expectations of ourselves and others, choices we make, and the opportunities available to us.

Tincknell, E. (2005). *Mediating the family: Gender, culture and representation.* New York: Oxford University Press. Examines the relationship among culture, family, and gender.

U Lifeline Mental Health has resources for college students on a variety of topics. Visit them at http://www.ulifeline.org. Many universities participate in their services, so you may learn what is available on your campus.

Being Single

CHAPTER OUTLINE

Learning Objectives

Categories of Singles
- Voluntary Singles
- Involuntary Singles

Marital Delay

CULTURAL PERSPECTIVE: *African American Single Mothers*

Why Some People Remain Single
- Deliberate Choice
- Fear of Marriage
- Lack of Opportunity
- Circumstances

Advantages and Disadvantages of Being Single

COPING FEATURE: *Avoiding Counterproductive Strategies*

The Health and Well-Being of Singles

Living Arrangements
- Shared Living Spaces
- Living with Parents
- Living Alone

Sexual Behavior
- Teens
- Adult Heterosexual Activity
- Same-Sex Activity
- Sexual Orientation
- Sexual Attraction
- Selected Health Measures

AT ISSUE TODAY: *Friends with Benefits*

Employment and Income

Single Parents
- Special Issues for Single-Parent Families

FAMILY STRENGTHS PERSPECTIVE: *Time Together: Making Memories*

The Never-Married Adult

PERSONAL PERSPECTIVE: *Single Fatherhood*

A QUESTION OF POLICY: *Funding for Which Sex Education Programs?*

Summary

Key Terms

Questions for Thought

For Further Reading

LEARNING OBJECTIVES

AFTER READING THE CHAPTER, YOU SHOULD BE ABLE TO DO THE FOLLOWING:

- Identify in general terms the percentages of people in the U.S. population who are married, single, widowed, and divorced and point out cultural and ethnic differences.

- Explain the reasons for marital delay and the reasons some people remain permanently single.

- Discuss the advantages and disadvantages of being single, including singles' health and well-being.

- Describe the need singles have for companionship, the difference between loneliness and aloneness, and the differences between males and females in relation to companionship issues.

- Discuss the sexual behavior of singles.

- Compare singles with marrieds in terms of employment and level of income.

- Discuss special issues for single-parent families.

- Discuss the life situations of older, never-married adults.

Mary was a senior in high school when her mother died. Her older brother was already away at college so she decided to attend the community college to help her dad and younger brother. In time, she finished a nursing degree and started working in town; her younger brother went off to college. She and Dad had a good life together; she dated some in those years, but no one seemed to work out for her. Dad was protective of Mary and critical of the men she dated; none was quite good enough for her. More time passed and Mary's brothers married and became fathers.

For a long time, Mary assumed her dad would remarry or would become more independent and want to live alone. Instead, when he was diagnosed with diabetes and other minor health problems started, he made it clear that he relied heavily on her care. Eventually, Mary decided she would marry when he died. He lived to just past his 87th birthday. By then Mary was in her sixties.

One of the choices adults make is whether they will marry. In previous generations, adults had less choice: it was widely expected that everyone who could do so would marry, and those who did not faced social disapproval or pity. Today, the number of never-married adults has increased dramatically, reflecting changing social conditions and attitudes.

The U.S. Census shows that slightly more than 32 million Americans live by themselves, some 28% of all households and about 10% of the population (U.S. Bureau of the Census 2016). With the increases in the age at which people first get married, the divorce rate, and longevity, the experience of being single is now one of the most widely shared experiences of adulthood (DePaulo 2001). According to the American Association for Single People, an unmarried majority has emerged in many American cities.

Figures 3.1 and 3.2 illustrate the marital status of the U.S. population, age 18 and older. Overall, 53% are married, 32% are single (never married), 6% are widowed, and 10% are divorced (U.S. Bureau of the Census 2016). The majority of adults were married, and an additional number had been married at one time. Nevertheless, nearly one in three adults had never been married, primarily in the youngest age groups.

When these figures are examined according to ethnic group, we find some variations. Only 39% of blacks were married; nearly 43% had never married. This compares to 59% (24%) of whites, 54% (34%) of Hispanics, and 65.5% (25%) of Asians. The percentage of blacks widowed or divorced is only slightly higher than that for whites. Hispanics have the smallest percentage of widowed (4%) and Asians the smallest percentage of individuals divorced (4.5%).

In this chapter, we examine the facts about being single and the reasons for the increase in those numbers. We examine why some people remain single and some advantages and disadvantages of being single. We discuss the lifestyles and living arrangements of singles, as well as factors such as social life and leisure time, loneliness and friendships, sexual behavior, and employment and income. Finally, we examine the situations of single parents and of older, never-married adults.

Total

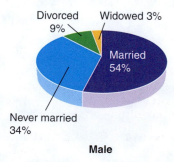

Male

Female

FIGURE 3.1 Marital Status of U.S. Population, Age 18 and Older

Note: Adapted from U.S. Bureau of the Census, 2015. http://www.census.gov.

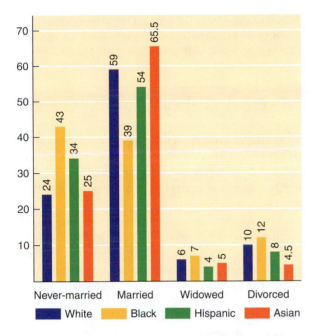

FIGURE 3.2 Marital Status of U.S. Population, Age 18 and Older, by Ethnic Origin, 2012

Note: Adapted from Statistical Abstract of the United States, *2012, by U.S. Bureau of the Census, 2015. http://www.census.gov.*

Categories of Singles

Several sociodemographic variables are related to the likelihood of never marrying—namely, age, race, and gender. First, age is negatively related to the likelihood of never marrying: The older one becomes, the greater the likelihood of remaining single. Approximately 71% of never-married individuals are younger than age 34 (U.S. Bureau of the Census 2012). Although the increase in younger never-marrieds reflects the trend toward delayed marriage, it also could indicate increasing societal acceptance of long-term singlehood. If more people are choosing singlehood as a long-term status, it is reasonable to expect that the social resources and well-being of the never-married now include better social support in and higher satisfaction with their lives (Barrett 1999).

Second, some research suggests that race is related to social support and well-being among the never-married. Nonwhite, never-married individuals have more frequent contact with relatives and are more likely to live with relatives other than their parents than are whites (Raley 1995). Research has shown that white women and men and nonwhite men who have never been married are less satisfied, but no difference is observed between unmarried and married nonwhite women (Mookherjee 1997). As stated, whereas only 24% of whites have never married, 43% of African Americans, 34% of Hispanics, and 25% of Asians have never married (U.S. Bureau of the Census 2015). It is possible that the higher proportion of never-marrieds among nonwhites makes the single status less stigmatizing (Barrett 1999).

Third, some research associates having never married with lower well-being and less social support for men than for women. Among the never-married, women interact more frequently with relatives than do men (Seccombe and Ishii-Kuntz 1991). Studies on psychological health suggest that among the never-married, men have more depression and anxiety and a higher risk of suicide (Kail and Cavanaugh 2016; Papalia, Olds, and Feldman 2009) than women do. Much research supports the idea that never-married women are better off than their male counterparts.

There are various categories of single persons. Stein (1981) developed a typology of single persons based on whether their status is voluntary or involuntary. The results are shown in Table 3.1.

TABLE 3.1   Typology of Singles

	VOLUNTARY	INVOLUNTARY
Temporary	Never-marrieds and previously marrieds who are not opposed to the idea of marriage but are not currently seeking mates	Those who have actively been seeking mates but have not found them
Stable (permanent)	All those (never-marrieds and former-marrieds) who choose to be single	Never-marrieds and former-marrieds who wanted to marry, who have not found a mate, and who have more or less accepted being single

Note: Adapted from Peter Stein, ed., Single Life: Unmarried Adults in Social Context, *pp. 10–12. Copyright © 1981 Peter Stein.*

Voluntary Singles

The category **voluntary temporary singles** includes young people who have never been married and are not currently looking; they are postponing marriage although they are not opposed to the idea of marriage. This category includes cohabiters who will eventually marry each other or someone else as well as divorced or widowed people who need time to be single, although they may eventually want to marry again. It also includes older never-marrieds who are not actively looking but who would marry if the right person came along.

The category **voluntary stable (permanent) singles** includes never-marrieds of all ages who have no intention of marrying, cohabiters who never intend to marry, and formerly married people who never want to marry again. It also includes those who have taken religious vows not to marry.

Involuntary Singles

The category **involuntary temporary singles** includes young adults who have never been married but are actively seeking a mate and divorced or widowed persons who want to remarry soon.

The category **involuntary stable (permanent) singles** includes never-married, widowed, or divorced people who wanted to marry or remarry but who have not found a mate; they have become reconciled to their single state. Involuntary singlehood may involve stress for many single persons in the attempt to view their being single in positive ways (Reynolds, Wetherell, and Taylor 2007).

Marital Delay

Most singles are only temporarily unmarried, since by ages 45 to 54 only 13.6% of males and 10.3% of females have never married (see Figure 3.3). Currently, adults are marrying at older ages than they used to marry.

The reasons for delaying marriage are social, economic, and personal. One particular reason is that societal disapproval of single people has diminished, and it is no longer unacceptable for those in their thirties to be unmarried, especially if they have a flourishing career and an active social life.

The lengthening of the period of education and economic dependency has greatly influenced the delay of marriage. Women who have career aspirations marry later in life than do those who plan to be homemakers. Lower-socioeconomic-status individuals with lower educational and vocational aspirations are more likely to marry at earlier ages.

The sexual revolution with the resulting acceptance of nonmarital sexual intercourse has made sexual expression possible without necessitating marriage. The increased acceptance of nonmarital cohabitation also provides some benefits of marriage without

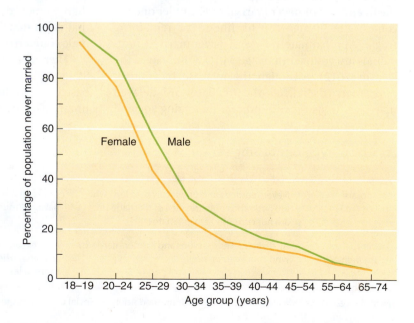

FIGURE 3.3 Never-Married People as a Percentage of Total Population, Age 18 and Older, by Age and Sex, 2007

Note: Adapted from Statistical Abstract of the United States, *by U.S. Bureau of the Census, 2008. http://www.census.gov.*

African American Single Mothers

African Americans are the racial/ethnic group in the United States with the most unmarried people—with 46% of households headed by women, 9% headed by men, and 46% headed by married couples. This means that about 54% of black children live in a single-parent family likely headed by a mother (U.S. Bureau of the Census 2012). Mother-headed, single-parent black families are also disproportionately poor, with 38% (compared to 14% of white) living in poverty (U.S. Bureau of the Census 2005). However, single motherhood is not caused by any deficiency in ideology in relation to the family, nor is it synonymous with the presence of family pathology (R. Hall and Greene 2003). According to R. Hall and Greene (2003), "Similarly, living in female-headed households does not mean that children have no meaningful male role models. Male family members who are blood related or fictive kin provide male role models, as do many biological fathers who, for a variety of reasons, do not live with their children or whose mothers do not publicly reveal that their children's fathers do live with them. Thus, the variety of family constellations in African American families is descriptive but does not explain the presence of pathology" (109).

Single motherhood in the African American community is related to a shortage of black males, especially those who are economically ready for fatherhood and marriage. For example, the ratio of black men to black women over the age of 18 is 1:1.25; for whites, this same ratio is 1:1.05. That is, there are almost 2 million fewer black men than women over the age of 18. In addition, black men and women have rates of unemployment about double that of whites (DeNavas-Walt, Proctor, and Smith 2007).

African Americans place a high value on children. Black parents struggle with building self-esteem in their children to overcome ongoing prejudice. Black mothers have high expectations for their children to be obedient, to be independent, and to control their tempers (Pew Research Center 2007).

It is important to remember that African Americans have strong kinship bonds, so a single mother is not necessarily left to raise her child on her own. Rather, she can rely on the assistance of members of her extended family. It is not uncommon for African Americans to include in their families a wide variety of relationships. Research has shown that regardless of whether there is a biological relationship, African American single mothers define a family as people who share emotional bonds, are willing to help one another in tangible ways, communicate, and enjoy an enduring relationship (McCreary and Dancy 2004).

the commitment—for example, companionship, sex, shared housing, and shared living expenses. As Lauer and Lauer (2011) indicate, fears about commitment and the prevalence of divorce are additional factors that can contribute to a delay in marriage.

The women's movement also has influenced views of marriage. Women are encouraged to seek their own identity, apart from marital identity, and to find career fulfillment and economic self-sufficiency if that is what they desire. Most feminists are not opposed to marriage, but women are encouraged to explore opportunities in addition to

voluntary temporary singles Never-marrieds and previously marrieds who are not opposed to the idea of marriage but are not currently seeking mates.

voluntary stable (permanent) singles Never-marrieds and previously marrieds who choose to be single.

involuntary temporary singles Never-marrieds and previously marrieds who have been actively seeking a mate but have not found one.

involuntary stable (permanent) singles Never-marrieds and previously marrieds who wanted to marry, who have not found a mate, and who have more or less accepted being single.

A growing number of adults are delaying marriage or choosing to stay single throughout their lives.

or as alternatives to family fulfillment. This attitude has led women to postpone marriage as they explore other options.

Why Some People Remain Single

Just as marriage may be delayed for any number of reasons, there are also reasons for never getting married. Research shows that there is an experience of a "transition to singlehood" that corresponds with a cultural timetable for marriage and occurs when an individual identifies more with singlehood than with marriage (Davies 2003). As we have seen, some people remain single because of life circumstances and find singlehood to be the best lifestyle for themselves.

Deliberate Choice

Some people choose to stay single because they enjoy their single lifestyle and have no desire to be married. Some people perceive marriage as incompatible with their careers. Others just prefer to live alone and are much better suited to do so (McGrath 2012). Today, singles' groups do not necessarily focus on matchmaking for lonely hearts. Many singles' groups are organized to support their members' chosen lifestyle and to address the political

issues affecting them (DePaulo 2001). Remember, too, that members of some religious orders take vows of celibacy.

Fear of Marriage

Fear of marriage is a powerful deterrent. Some people are fearful because they were brought up in unhappy homes in which their parents fought all the time or were miserable. Others have been disappointed in love or marriage and are afraid to try again. Emotional involvement may simply be too risky. People who have not witnessed or experienced healthy mutuality and interdependence in relationships may fear dependency or codependency. Others have a profound insecurity about the consequences of caring. As a result, marriage is seen as a source of misery and a trap.

Lack of Opportunity

At the other extreme are people who would prefer to marry but have never had the chance. In particular, women are caught in the "marriage squeeze"; that is, they have difficulty finding eligible male partners (McGrath 2012). Until 1940, the male population in the United States exceeded the female population. Since then, adult women have outnumbered men; this is especially true for African Americans. The older the age group, the greater the discrepancy in numbers.

Circumstances

For many people, remaining unmarried permanently is not a matter of deliberate choice, but a result of circumstances such as family situations (as in the case of Mary), geography, social isolation, or financial condition.

Advantages and Disadvantages of Being Single

People find both advantages and disadvantages in being single. Advantages include the following:

- **Greater opportunities for personal growth and fulfillment.** If singles want to take a course, go to graduate school, or travel, they are freer to do so than are married people, who must consider a spouse's school or career plans and interests. Research shows single individuals spend more time playing musical instruments, singing, acting, dancing, listening to the radio, watching television, socializing with people, going to bars/lounges, and traveling for social activities than married individuals. In sum, married individuals spend significantly less time in leisure activities than do single individuals (Krueger 2014; Y. Lee and Bhargava 2004).

- **Opportunities to enjoy different friendships.** Singles are free to pursue friendships with either men or women, according to their own preferences.

- **Economic independence and self-sufficiency.** As one single person said, "I don't have to depend on a spouse for money. I earn it myself and I can spend it as I want." Singles also are freed from worries about debts incurred by an irresponsible spouse (E. E. Smith 2013).

- **More varied sexual experiences.** Singles are free to seek experiences with more than one partner. Because courtship-type settings involve high hormone levels and brain chemicals associated with feelings of elation, sexual

---

Avoiding Counterproductive Strategies

In response to stress, many of us develop habits that are unhealthy and self-defeating. It is beneficial to recognize these counterproductive coping strategies and to avoid using them. Following are some examples:

- *Blaming.* Looking for someone to blame, either oneself or another, is a common response to problems, conflict, or any kind of stressful situation. For example, "We wouldn't overdraw if he'd be more responsible." Blaming is ineffective because it does not deal with the problem and it produces bad feelings both in the blamer and in the blamed—usually escalating conflict.

- *Alcohol and other drugs.* Some people use alcohol or other drugs to help them forget their current problems or to numb their feelings of fear or hurt. However, substances do nothing to address the causes of stress or pain in one's life and place the person at risk for additional problems. For example, repeated use of marijuana can trigger panic attacks and actually increase the stress response. Even caffeine can increase blood pressure and cortisol levels. Many of the substances used to "self-medicate" such as narcotic pain relievers, antianxiety medications, and alcohol are addictive—which can result in escalating use and eventually financial,

health, legal, and relationship problems (Insel and Roth 2013).

- *Tobacco.* Cigarettes and other tobacco products are used by many individuals to help them feel relaxed and less nervous. Tobacco is highly addictive and smoking is strongly linked to cancer, heart disease, respiratory problems, and impotence.

- *Eating.* Some people eat as a way of reducing stress or feeling better. Naturally, the repeated use of this strategy leads to weight gain, binge eating, and the associated health problems.

- *"Feeding the weeds."* No gardener would actively fertilize and water the weeds. Yet, many do this as a way of coping. Feeding the weeds is demonstrated as being extremely pessimistic and actively searching for reasons why something is not going to work out well. One motivation for using this coping strategy is a fear of failing or being disappointed or losing something or someone highly valued. By using this approach, people may feel that they are protecting themselves from being hurt or disappointed as much as they would if they were hopeful. This is a counterproductive strategy because it sets a self-fulfilling prophecy in motion and creates more negative feelings: Why try? Nothing turns out right anyway.

experiences may be very exciting (E. E. Smith 2013).

- **Freedom to control their own lives.** Singles are free to do what they want without having to consider a spouse's desires; they enjoy more psychological and social autonomy.

- **More opportunities for career change, development, and expansion.** Singles are often not locked into family responsibilities and so can be more mobile and flexible in the climb up the career ladder (Kail and Cavanaugh 2016).

Not all of these advantages apply to all singles. For example, not all singles have opportunities to meet different people, are economically well off, or are free of family responsibilities. Nevertheless, most singles would list at least some of these items as advantages for them.

Disadvantages include the following:

- **Loneliness and lack of companionship.** Research findings consistently identify the absence of a partner or prospective partner as associated with loneliness (Baumbusch 2004; McGrath 2012). Some singles miss having a ready companion to share interests; others worry about growing old alone.

- **Economic hardship.** This is especially true for single women. Single women earn less than single or married men and, because they do not have access to a spouse's income, they have a lower standard of living than do married women (Arnold and Campbell 2013). Also, top positions are more often given to married men than to single men or to women (Linn 2013).

- **Feeling out of place in some social gatherings.** Many social events are organized around couples or families. This is especially the case as people get older (and more of their peers are married). Sometimes singles may be regarded with suspicion or jealousy—as out to take someone else's spouse. Or they may feel stigmatized—lacking or deficient—because of their status (McGrath 2012).

- **Sexual frustration.** Sexual relations with multiple partners may be exciting, but also may be superficial and ultimately not truly intimate (Krueger 2014; E. E. Smith 2013).

- A lack of children or a family in which to bring up children.

The Health and Well-Being of Singles

For years, researchers have been investigating the effects of marriage and singlehood on people's health and sense of well-being. In general, studies indicate that married people live longer and are healthier and happier than single people, indicating marriage may have a beneficial effect on well-being (Grover and Helliwell 2014; A. Hess and Stanton 2012; Insel and Roth 2013; Pew Research Center 2006). Other research supports this idea. Several large surveys and longitudinal studies have indicated that, compared with those who never marry, and especially compared with those who have separated or divorced, married people report being happier and more satisfied with life (DePaulo 2013; Grover and Helliwell 2014; A. Hess and Stanton 2012; D. G. Myers 2000). However, several researchers have noted that the differences in happiness and life satisfaction between marrieds and singles are small. And many suggest that marriage alone does not make the difference; rather, marriage is one of a number of variables that contribute to the quality of life (DePaulo 2013).

The answer to the question of whether singles or marrieds are healthier and happier is, however, complex and difficult to research. For example, the category *singles* includes persons who are never married, divorced, and widowed. Persons who are single because of a divorce they did not want may be dealing with anger and hurt; those divorced after a miserable marriage may be feeling happier and optimistic.

Another difficulty in examining the relationship between marital status and well-being is that the data gathered are correlational—making it unsound to assign cause and effect. For example, some have suggested that it is not that being married makes people happier and healthier, but that people who are healthy and happy are more likely to get married.

Because many variables in addition to marital status determine physical and mental health and life satisfaction or happiness, it might be more accurate to say that certain characteristics of singles tend to encourage physical or mental health and others favor health and well-being in married persons. For example, on the one hand, some surveys indicate that single persons are less likely to gain weight, exercise more, and stress less over chores and money than married persons (MacMillan 2014). These factors would typically be taken as indicators of better health. On the other hand, surgery may be more dangerous for singles; married people recover quicker (A. Hess and Stanton 2012; MacMillan 2014). Other studies indicate that married people have healthier diets and immune systems—factors favoring better health for them (A. Hess and Stanton 2012). They also have a spouse to encourage them to make good health choices.

Just as multiple variables influence physical health and well-being, several factors are involved in life satisfaction, mental health, and/or happiness. Economic circumstances and social support are two such factors. As with physical health, some factors influence in a positive way, whereas others are negative. For example, in a study by C. E. Ross, Mirowsky, and Goldstein (1990), married women with high-prestige jobs had the highest level of well-being. However, having a high-prestige job was the better predictor of well-being. Being single in and of itself was not associated with diminished well-being, but being single and having a low-level job was. Other research indicates that married people typically have economic advantages—such as two incomes and the security of not having to rely only on one's own earnings—that promote a positive outlook (Arnold and Campbell 2013; A. Hess and Stanton 2012; Linn 2013).

In the area of social support, numerous studies show singles having more friends and being more likely to spend time with friends than their married counterparts (Krueger 2014; MacMillan 2014; E. E. Smith 2013). Barrett (1999) found that never-married persons had more interactions with friends, relatives, and neighbors when they were young. However, as they aged, the frequency of interactions increased for the married and previously married. Overall life satisfaction was highest for married persons, followed by never-married persons, and lowest for previously married persons.

A recent international study examined marriage's influence on happiness. The researchers (Grover and Helliwell 2014) noted that persons who are married experience a less-deep dip in life satisfaction during middle age. They suggest that marriage helps to ease the causes of the typical drop in life satisfaction that happens in middle life; marriage provides someone to help meet the challenges. The couples who say "My spouse is also my best

Many single young adults would prefer to be independent but live with their parents for financial reasons.

friend" experience almost twice the well-being effect, leading researchers to conclude that friendship is the factor behind the benefit. Other research supports the benefit to life satisfaction and overall happiness of having a close, intimate (invested) relationship (A. Hess and Stanton 2012).

Living Arrangements

Most singles meet some of their needs for companionship and economic well-being by sharing a residence with friends or family. Singles who are still in school are most likely to live with their parents or with classmates; singles in their late twenties and early thirties are most likely to live with a roommate or by themselves; and older singles are most likely to live alone or with relatives.

Single elderly people often face more serious housing problems than do other singles or elderly people in families. Elderly singles are likely to live in rental housing, where they risk social isolation, and a disproportionate number are poor. In addition to having low fixed incomes, they are likely to lack any asset "cushion" in the form of home equity, and they may have little or no help available if they become disabled. In these circumstances, subsidized housing is an important source of affordable housing for poor, single elderly people.

Shared Living Spaces

Although large numbers of singles live in singles' complexes or apartment buildings, more live with the general population. The majority occupy individual apartments, usually with roommates. The usual pattern is to share an apartment and living expenses with one or more people who provide emotional support and companionship.

Living with Parents

The percentage of young adults (ages 20 to 34) who lived with parents has increased from 17% in 1980 to 24% now (T. Lee 2012). The increase has occurred because of marriage postponement, coupled with high rates of college enrollment, unemployment, divorce, and births to unmarried mothers. Most adults who live with their parents have a plan for achieving independence, such as saving enough money or getting more education. But while they are living at home, their parents still spend a lot of money on their food, clothes, cars, insurance, and other goods and services. Table 3.2 shows the percentage of young adult men and women living at home with parents. Note that greater percentages of men than women of all ages live at home with their parents. Women who are married, separated, or divorced and have children are more likely to live at home with their parents or relatives than are women who do not have any children.

According to a report by Child and Youth Health (2005), young adults generally say that the good things about living at home are support, security, and the company of their parents. They also comment that it is much cheaper so they can save money, and they enjoy services provided by parents such as housework, meals, and laundry. The major reasons for leaving home are to be independent, because of conflict, or to live with a partner. If none of these reasons exists and if there is a reasonable amount of independence and freedom at home, young adults are less likely to leave.

TABLE 3.2 Percentage of Young Adults Living with Their Parents by Age, 1980 and 2012

	18–24 YEARS OF AGE (%)	20–34 YEARS OF AGE (%)
1980	32	17
2012	43	24

Note: From T. Lee (2012). More Young Adults Living with Parents. www.breitbart.com. August 1, 2012.

Living Alone

Figure 3.4 shows the percentage of the population, by age, living alone and includes divorced, separated, and widowed people, as well as the never-married. Greater percentages of males than females in the 15 to 64 age groups live alone. Past age 65, the percentage of females living alone increases. This is because of the greater numbers of older females in the population.

Health status is the most important factor in determining how long aging singles continue to live alone. When a move is necessary, many elderly people go to live with their children. Declining health increases the likelihood of institutionalization.

Sexual Behavior

If we believe the media, all healthy young Americans are having a great deal of sex. The truth is far more complex. Of course, sexual behavior depends on a number of factors such as the availability of a partner, physical and mental health, and age.

The National Survey of Family Growth periodically examines the sexual behavior of young adults by means of interviews with males and females ages 15 to 44 across the United States. The interviewers collect demographic information, but the interviewees enter answers to questions on sexual behavior into a laptop computer to ensure their privacy. Not all of the participants are single but, given the age range, many are; hence the survey gives us reliable national estimates of some basic statistics on certain types of sexual behavior, sexual orientation, and sexual attraction for men and women. The highlights that are presented here are from the survey (Chandra et al. 2011; Mosher, Allen, and Manlove 2005) unless otherwise referenced.

Teens

- Sexual activity is beginning at earlier ages than in the past. For example, slightly more than 6% experience sexual intercourse before age 13, with about 47% of high school students (44% of whites; 61% of blacks; and 49% of Hispanics) reporting having had sexual intercourse. However, only 59% report using condoms during their last sexual intercourse (Centers for Disease Control and Prevention 2015). These statistics reflect sexual behavior patterns that are powerful predictors of the

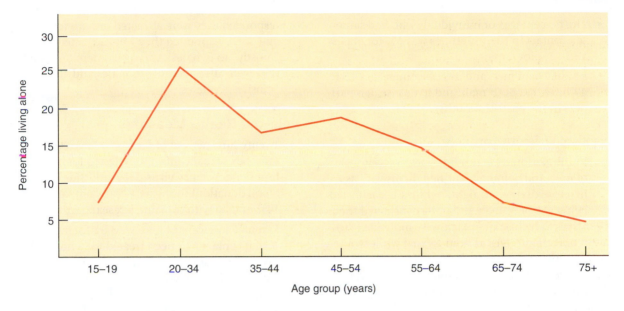

FIGURE 3.4 Percentage of Persons Living Alone by Age, 2010

Note: Data from Statistical Abstract of the United States, *2012, by U.S. Bureau of the Census, 2012. www.census.gov.*

Loneliness is a common problem among single adults. The advantage of the increased freedom of being single is often outweighed by the lack of ready companionship.

likelihood of sexually transmitted diseases (STDs) and teen, unwed pregnancies.

- At ages 15 to 19, about 12% of males and 10% of females had had heterosexual oral sex but not vaginal intercourse. This drops to 3% for both males and females at ages 22 to 24 because most young adults have already had vaginal intercourse.

Adult Heterosexual Activity

- Among adult males ages 25 to 44, 97% have had some form of heterosexual contact. This includes 97% having had vaginal intercourse, 90% having had oral sex, and 44% having had anal sex. Among women ages 25 to 44, 98% have had vaginal intercourse, 89% reported having had oral sex, and 36% reported having had anal sex.

- Males ages 30 to 44 reported having a median number of six female sexual partners in their lifetimes. Among women ages 30 to 44, the median number of male sexual partners in their lifetimes was about four.

- Of persons who identified as being never married and not cohabiting, some 26% to 30% report never having heterosexual contact.

Same-Sex Activity

- Three percent of males ages 15 to 44 have had oral or anal sex with another male in the past 12 months. Four percent of females had a sexual experience with another female in the past 12 months.

- The percentages of individuals who had same-sex contact in their lifetimes was 6% for males and 12% for females.
- About 1% of men and 3% of women ages 15 to 44 have had both male and female sexual partners in the past 12 months.

Sexual Orientation

- In the National Health Interview Survey, 98% of men and women identified themselves as heterosexual or "straight," while 1.6% reported being gay or lesbian and 0.7% considered themselves to be bisexual. Men were more likely to report themselves as homosexual while women were twice as likely to indicate being bisexual. The percentages of men and women indicating they were heterosexual were virtually the same (National Center for Health Statistics 2015).

Sexual Attraction

- Survey participants were asked whether they were sexually attracted to males, to females, or to both. Among men ages 18 to 44, 92%

responded they were attracted only to females, and 3.9% responded they were attracted "mostly" to females. Among women, 86% said they were attracted only to males and 10% "mostly" to males.

Selected Health Measures

- Twenty-nine percent of men who have ever had same-sex sexual contact were tested for human immunodeficiency virus (HIV) (outside of blood donation) in the past year, compared with 14% of men with no same-sex sexual contact.
- Seventeen percent of men who had same-sex sexual contact had been treated for a non-HIV sexually transmitted infection (STI), compared with 7% of those who had never had same-sex sexual contact.
- Among men ages 15 to 44 who had at least one sexual partner in the past 12 months, 39% used a condom during their most recent sex. Among never-married males, this number was 65%, compared with 24% of married males. Among males who had ever had sexual contact

---

Friends with Benefits

Friends with benefits is a term used to describe two friends who have a sexual relationship without being emotionally involved or without any intention of a monogamous, committed relationship. Typically, they consider themselves good friends, but not a girlfriend or boyfriend, and they are engaging in the act of sex for fun. Although friends occasionally having had a sexual relationship is not new, what does seem new is that this has become a part of mainstream culture among young, single individuals, so much so that mainstream magazines and newspapers have written about the phenomenon.

So what has given rise to friends with benefits? Often-cited reasons include lack of time for and interest in an emotionally committed relationship. It can be a no-strings-attached relationship without the possibility of a breakup and someone

getting hurt. It has been described as an efficient means of fulfilling sexual desire in a busy world, and the participants do not need to feign interest in dinner or a movie (Denizet-Lewis 2004). Also, unlike casual sex with a stranger, friends with benefits can give both parties a sense of safety and security.

Many individuals find the entire notion of friends with benefits to be a disturbing one, whereas others find it to be a healthy and natural expression of sexuality. Important questions to consider in examining this phenomenon are: What does healthy sexuality look like in a single person's life? What are the costs and/or benefits to a seemingly emotionally devoid sexual relationship? Who bears the cost and/or reaps the rewards of this type of relationship? Why has it become popular?

with another male, 91% used a condom during their most recent sex, compared with 36% of men who had never had sex with another male.

Employment and Income

One stereotype holds that never-marrieds are richer than marrieds: They have no spouses or children to support, they do not require large, expensive homes, and they can live more cheaply than marrieds. In fact, marrieds typically are better off financially than never-marrieds. It is not surprising that the median income of married householders with both spouses employed is typically greater than that of married households with only one person employed. However, married males consistently make more than their unmarried counterparts. For example, statistics show that married men earn approximately 11% more per hour than men who have never been married, even after controlling for work experience, age, education, and other factors. In addition, economists find that divorced or separated men make about 9% more than do never-married men (Chiodo 2002).

Married women tend to earn less than their single counterparts but fare better when wealth building is considered because of advantages they receive as a result of marital status. For example, a married woman who earns $40,000 a year and files joint income tax returns pays about $1000 less in taxes than a single woman making $40,000. Married women also often receive larger Social Security benefits because the calculations are based on their husbands' typically larger earnings. Health insurance premiums for a family are larger than for an individual but they are not twice as much; consequently health care costs are somewhat less for married individuals. When savings in taxes and healthcare plus gains in Social Security benefits are considered, the married woman who earns $40,000 a year will end up with $484,000 more over her adult years than a single woman earning the same amount (Arnold and Campbell 2013; Linn 2013).

There are a number of theories as to why the salary differences for married men exist. One reason is a practical one. Married people, especially those with families, must earn more money because their needs are greater, and they are more motivated to earn higher incomes. Another theory is that discrimination in the workforce favors married men. Employers may think they are more stable, responsible, mature, and reliable than their unmarried counterparts. Employers also may give preference to married men when it comes to salary raises and promotions because they have a family to support and need the higher pay. Ironically, employers may assume that married women will put their families first—and will be apt to leave to have babies or take care of elderly or sick family members. Consequently, married women may not be offered promotions or opportunities to advance (Linn 2013).

Some economists have considered the possibility that married individuals tend to make more money because the traits that make a person a high wage earner are also the traits that make for a good marriage partner (e.g., honesty, maturity, intelligence, and dependability). Studies even have shown that being physically attractive has a positive effect on wage earning, and we know that individuals look for physical attractiveness when choosing a spouse. It may be that individuals who possess the qualities that make them a good employee also possess the qualities that make them more likely to be married and stay married (Chiodo 2002).

Single Parents

Single parents are becoming increasingly common. The number of single-parent families in the United States grew from 11% of all households in 1970 to 19% of all families now (U.S. Bureau of the Census 2016; Wright 2011). Nearly 28% of children are in families headed by a single parent—most often the mother (U.S. Bureau of the Census 2016). A number of factors are related to the increase: prevalence of divorce, more single women keeping their children as opposed to adoption, technology that allows a woman to become pregnant without a partner (e.g., sperm banks), and more acceptance of single people becoming parents.

Single individuals become parents for the same reasons as do married people. Often it is the desire to nurture another human being and to share life in a full and loving way with a child. Individuals may reach their thirties without a partner but still have a deep yearning to raise a child. Some people are touched by the plight of children with special needs or those who have been abandoned or who live in great poverty whom they could adopt and give a happy home. Also, many children in foster care or institutions would benefit greatly from a home with a loving parent, regardless of marital status.

Although the great majority of single parents are mothers, a growing number of single-parent families are headed by fathers (U.S. Bureau of the Census 2016). Because single men encounter many challenges in trying to adopt, most single-father families are a result of divorce. The increase stems from several societal and legal changes. In the past, fathers often were awarded custody of their children only when the mother was proven unfit. Today, more gender-neutral custody criteria are in place, resulting in more fathers obtaining full or joint custody agreements. In addition, more mothers are choosing to pursue career or personal goals, allowing the fathers custody, or mothers may not want to be full-time parents.

Men adapt to parenting roles well. Many fathers are motivated to fulfill a sense of duty and responsibility, to provide a role model, and to further the bond with their children (Coles 2002). Fathers can provide for social, physical, and emotional needs to the same extent that a mother can (Hamer and Marchioro 2002), and they experience most of the same difficulties in single parenting as do mothers.

One distinction between single mothers and single fathers is that single women can choose to bear children. Although it would have been frowned

upon a couple generations ago, births to unmarried women are no longer unusual. Nearly 41% of births are to single women.

Why are single women choosing to become mothers? One answer is that they want to have children, but no longer feel the "need" to be married to do so. Family sociologists have noted a 30-year trend in American society toward a growing separation of marriage and childbearing. For one thing, women's increased options outside of marriage, including the ability to support themselves (and children), mean that a greater percentage of women do not need a husband's income to afford children.

Women's increased options also include finding satisfaction in life as an independent person—not necessarily part of a couple. Some single mothers do not marry because they put a low priority on marriage. A woman who became a mother by adoption about 5 years after a divorce reflected, "It [marriage] is not something that I care whether it happens or not. I think it is wonderful, being in love and finding someone to live with. But I'm not seeking it out. If it happens, it happens" (Siegel 1995, 203). Others may not marry because of concern that they will not do well in marriage, either because they are not sure how to make marriage work or because they are not interested in doing what they think is necessary for marriage to work. One woman remarked, "I never wanted to be married. In actuality, I always thought I would be, but I have not wanted to be in the real way and am probably not well suited to it" (Siegel 1995, 204).

Special Issues for Single-Parent Families

In many—perhaps most—areas, single parents have the same concerns and challenges as married parents. Children need food and clothes, homework help, and braces. Two-year-olds will have temper tantrums and teens will get body piercings and break curfew. There are, however, several areas in which single parents and married parents experience parenthood differently.

Most single parents face serious role strain trying to perform all the necessary family roles. Imagine working full-time, keeping a house and yard, cooking, doing laundry, paying bills, volunteering at school, driving the kids to soccer practice, and on and on. Not to mention any personal time to relax or for leisure pursuits. To manage role strain, single parents draw from a variety of resources: flextime or work-from-home programs are

One distinction between single mothers and single fathers is that many single women choose to become mothers, whereas most single-father situations are a result of divorce.

used; Grandma helps; the kids have chores; and a neighborhood teen is hired to mow. They also reduce their standards (tolerate more clutter, dust less often, and eat simple meals) and give up personal time. The pressures of so much to do leave most single parents chronically fatigued and overwhelmed. Single parents typically worry about spending enough quality time with their children.

Even if a single parent hires or finds help with practical matters, the daily emotional care of family members is still a challenge. Cases of marital separation may mean dealing with feelings of anger, loss, uncertainty, failure, and loneliness (for both the children and the parent). They often lose their circle of friends and social support at the time of divorce and have the additional burden of rebuilding their social life. Time and energy for socializing are just not there.

Single parents also struggle with finding affordable, quality child care. Care in another person's home (family or home day care) and care in the child's home (by a relative or nanny) are the most common arrangements for children under age 5. Many children are cared for in day-care centers. Most child-care providers have fixed hours (6:00 am to 6:00 pm, for example) that may be difficult for a parent who works shifts and they do not provide sick-child care. And even mediocre care is expensive—about $500 a month or more per child in many areas.

Probably the biggest challenge many single-parent households face is adequate income. This is particularly critical in African American and female-headed homes. Research has shown that even when controlling for the effects of education, single fathers are better off economically than are single mothers, and white single parents fare better economically than do African American single parents (Zhan and Pandey 2004). Even so, single-parent families are three to five times more likely than two-parent families to live in poverty. For example, 31% of single-mother and 16% of single-father families live in poverty compared with about 6% of married-couple families with children (U.S. Bureau of the Census 2015).

Economic hardship can have a negative impact on a child's development. Although disruptions in family structure (through parental separation, divorce, remarriage, or cohabitation) are associated with more problematic parenting and poorer

Time Together: Making Memories

Over the three decades of research on strong families (and remember that research included single-parent families), thousands of people were asked to take a short journey back to childhood. They were asked to close their eyes and remember some of their happiest times. Here are some samples of what they said:

> I remember stories Mom told me when she tucked me into bed—stories about her childhood adventures.

> Having the family together at Christmas was special. The grandparents and all the aunts and uncles and cousins would come. They made us kids eat in the kitchen together. I thought it was so neat then, but it must have been pandemonium.

> Vacation. We'd go fifty miles to my aunt's cabin on the lake. It was very rustic! But we could swim and fish. It was always cool at night so we'd make a campfire and toast marshmallows or roast corn.

> Every Friday night we'd rent movies and make nachos (with all the toppings) for supper.

> On summer evenings we'd go out to listen to the night sounds—crickets and cicadas and sometimes an owl or whip-poor-will. We'd spread a blanket and watch for shooting stars. And catch fireflies.

Now, note that these "happiest memories" involve time together with loved ones. Also note that they were simple things that took little money. Only once (out of thousands of memories) did someone describe a super memory of eating a fancy meal in an expensive restaurant.

outcomes for children, socioeconomic factors do appear to have a stronger impact on the quality of parenting in single-mother households than either family disruption or the absence of a partner (Bronstein et al. 1993).

In female-headed households, the effect of parental absence on the mother is crucial in determining the influence on the children. Many father-absence studies have failed to take into account the mother's changed position following a divorce, a separation, or the death of her spouse. If the mother is upset, if her income is severely limited, if her authority and status in the eyes of the children are significantly reduced, if she must be away from home because she has to work, or if she has inadequate care for her children when she is gone, the children are going to be affected—not because of their father's absence, but because of the subsequent effect his absence has on their mother and their relationship with her.

It is important to remember, too, that father absence is not the opposite of father presence; most fathers, although absent from the child's home, are not absent from the child's life. Fathers, both resident and nonresident, who are responsive and encouraging and who are involved in everyday problem solving, promote well-being and competence in their children whether they are boys or girls (Amato and Gilbreth 1999). In addition, children need the economic contribution of a father. The lack of this contribution can negatively impact the educational level and occupational attainment of children, which is often seen as a difference between two-parent and single-parent families. Overall, the implications of father absence must be viewed in relation to the child's age, the reasons for and duration of the absence, and the quality of the home environment before and after the father's departure.

It is important to remember that not all single-parent families are alike. The characteristics of single parents such as gender, age, ethnicity, and education all influence how a single-parent family functions. Resources such as income and stressors such as residential instability can help determine whether single parents and their children experience positive or negative outcomes in terms of psychological well-being, health, and parent–child relationships (Amato 2000).

The Never-Married Adult

The never-married population has now grown to more than 32% of the population compared to 22% in 1960 (U.S. Bureau of the Census 2016). One difference between older adults who have never married and younger ones is that many younger singles consider their status temporary, whereas older singles are often well adjusted to their situation and have gradually made the transition into the decision to be single (Kail and Cavanaugh 2016). Older singles usually have an active social life and do a variety of things with their friends (Klinenberg 2012; Santrock 2015); their patterns of social support differ from those found in married groups. For example, the never-married are more likely to socialize with friends and neighbors than are married people (Klinenberg 2012). This is consistent with substitution theory, which suggests that the never-married use more remote family members such as nieces and nephews or nonfamily individuals for support compared with the married or the previously married, who turn to spouses or children.

The nonkin relationships that form the social networks of never-marrieds are sometimes referred to as "constructed" ties (Rubinstein et al. 1991). Although these relationships resemble friendships, they involve role sets that are similar to those found in families. For example, one woman described her close friends as her "adopted family" or a friend might be described as "like a sister."

Many older singles value their independence, rarely feel isolated, and are generally happy with their lives.

Single Fatherhood

Brian has been divorced for 5 years and has a 14-year-old son and a 9-year-old daughter. The children live with him from Thursday to Sunday every week. Brian chose that schedule and bought a house near their mother's house to provide constancy and regularity and to minimize disruption in the children's lives.

One big challenge I face as a single parent deals with split supplies (e.g., the shoes and textbooks left at the other house). The kids have to learn to plan ahead or you end up with two or more of everything. You have to pry and push a little to help them develop the skill of planning ahead, such as making lists. Another major difficulty is finances. I'm broke and I know it. It's tough to

find enough money to support my kids. I don't go out because I can't afford it. I would like to be dating but it is expensive to date. The most important thing I have learned by being a single parent is that you have to get to know your children. This is what I try to do each week when they are with me. I try to stop my life and focus on my kids. It gives me an opportunity to be more human. I now volunteer in my kids' classrooms to be a bigger part of their lives. I know the kids watch my daily actions and soak in the reality of how I live. In a joint custody arrangement, you can't control half of the kids' lives, so you just show them and teach them how you will behave as a family when you are together.

Another woman explained (Rubenstein et al. 1991):

Family has had practically no meaning to me. Very little. My friends have been my family. . . . This one friend . . . she said, "You know, Doris, if you ever need me I will come to you." . . . I mean I never had anybody say that.

The differences in dimensions of social support between the never-married and marital groups may be greatest in later life. Compared with marrieds, older never-marrieds are at a disadvantage, in part because of their lower probability of having confidants and their lower levels of interaction and perceived support. Analyses of informal interactions indicate that younger never-marrieds (ages 30 to 45) have more frequent interaction with friends and relatives than do their currently or previously married peers. However, this pattern reverses in two older groups (45 to 60 and 60 and older). It is possible that during middle and later adulthood never-marrieds, in anticipation of health declines in old age, learn to be more self-reliant and independent than do marrieds (Barrett 1999). A possible explanation for the difference between marrieds and never-marrieds in terms of having confidants in later life could involve the potential differences in

the identities of confidants among the groups. For example, never-marrieds are likely to have primary confidants who are significantly older than themselves (such as parents or older siblings), whereas marrieds tend to have similar-age confidants (such as spouses). A factor in the higher proportion of never-marrieds reporting having no confidants in later life may be the loss of close social ties because of death, a phenomenon that occurs somewhat later among married individuals.

Gender differences are significant among singles. A higher frequency of problems are reported by single women. However, single men have a greater incidence of mental health problems, alcoholism, and suicide as well as higher mortality rates (Kail and Cavanaugh 2016).

Overall, however, the happiness of single older adults is dependent on satisfaction with their standard of living and with their level of activity, rather than merely on the extent of their social contacts. Adequate financial resources permit mobility and reciprocation in developing and maintaining friendships. Also, people who are satisfied with their level of activity although they are isolated from family or friends tend to express greater happiness. A life alone does not necessarily mean a lonely one. Most who choose to remain single are content with their lives (Kail and Cavanaugh 2016).

Funding for Which Sex Education Programs?

President Obama's 2010 budget changed the way federal funds are allocated for the teaching of sex education and teen pregnancy-prevention programs. No longer are abstinence-only programs the only ones receiving such monies. Instead, 75% of the funding goes to programs that are "evidence-based and promising" (found by rigorous examination to delay sexual activity, increase contraceptive use, or reduce teen pregnancy). The other 25% goes for the development and testing of "innovative strategies" for preventing teen pregnancy.

Much controversy surrounds which approach to sex education and teen pregnancy prevention is most effective (Paulson 2010). Proponents of *abstinence-only-until-marriage* programs argue theirs is the only certain way to avoid unwanted pregnancies and STDs/STIs. Critics believe this approach is too limited and ignores those (especially older teens) who are already sexually active.

The *safer-sex* approach focuses on teaching about contraception and making condoms available. Critics maintain this approach actually encourages casual sexual activity.

Comprehensive sex education is a more holistic approach emphasizing delaying sexual activity until one is ready (socially and psychologically as well as physically). These programs may discuss abstinence. They also educate about contraceptive methods as a part of protecting oneself from pregnancy and STDs/STIs if sexually active. Critics believe this approach is not strong enough in discouraging sexual permissiveness.

Questions to Consider

What do you think would be an effective approach to preventing teen pregnancy?

What do you think would be an effective approach to preventing the spread of STDs/STIs?

Should federal funds be used to fund sex education and teen pregnancy-prevention programs? If so, which type (abstinence-only, safer-sex, or comprehensive) would you prefer?

What evidence would convince you that a program was effective and promising?

Summary

1. Overall, the great majority of people in the United States marry.

2. Adult singles may be divided into four groups: voluntary temporary singles, voluntary stable (permanent) singles, involuntary temporary singles, and involuntary stable (permanent) singles.

3. Most adults who are single delay marriage rather than remain permanently single. By ages 45 to 54, only 13.6% of men and 10.3% of women have never married.

4. The reasons for marital delay are social, economic, and personal.

5. Reasons people remain single include deliberate choice, fear of marriage, lack of opportunity, and circumstances.

6. There are both advantages and disadvantages to being single. Advantages include greater opportunities for self-development, personal growth, and fulfillment; opportunities to meet different people and enjoy different friendships; economic independence and self-sufficiency; more varied sexual experiences; freedom to control one's own life; and more opportunities for career change, development, and expansion.

7. Disadvantages include loneliness and lack of companionship, economic hardship, feeling out of place in social gatherings organized for couples, sexual frustration, and the absence of children.

8. Overall, studies indicate that married people live longer and are healthier and happier than single people. The divorced, separated, and widowed fare the worst. However, many variables other than marital status influence physical and mental health.

9. There are wide variations in the lifestyles of singles. Singles may share living spaces with friends, live with parents, or live alone.

10. Increasing numbers of singles are returning home to live with parents.

11. Most single adults have had sexual intercourse but confine their sexual experiences to only a few partners during their lifetime. A minority of young adults engage in high-risk sexual behavior.

12. Married people are usually better off financially than are single people.

13. Births to unmarried women have become more common, but births to teenagers have decreased.

14. Issues for single-parent families typically include role strain and adequate finances. Most single parents are concerned about spending enough time with their children because it can be stressful performing and balancing all the necessary family roles.

15. Many older singles are well adjusted to their situation and interact more frequently with friends and less often with relatives than do married people.

Key Terms

involuntary stable (permanent) singles
involuntary temporary singles
voluntary stable (permanent) singles
voluntary temporary singles

Questions for Thought

1. Think of a single person and a married person whom you know. Describe each individual's personality, work life, social life, life goals and values, general outlook, and problems. Then compare and contrast how the two individuals are similar to and different from each other and how their being single or being married influences each.

2. Describe the advantages and disadvantages of being single. If you are not married, would you describe yourself as voluntarily or involuntarily, stable or temporarily single?

3. Under what circumstances should single women and men be allowed to adopt children?

4. What factors should people consider in deciding whether to remain single or get married?

5. Compare singles with marrieds with respect to each of the following:

   a. Loneliness and friendships.

   b. Sexual behavior.

   c. Employment and income.

For Further Reading

Boston Women's Health Book Collective. (2005). *Our bodies, ourselves: A new edition for a new era.* New York: Simon & Schuster. Extensive coverage of health and relationship issues, including singlehood.

Coontz, S. (2005). *Marriage, a history: From obedience to intimacy, or how love conquered marriage.* New York: Viking. Gives a historical perspective on singlehood and marriage.

Lewis, K. G. (2001). *With or without a man: Women taking control of their lives.* Palo Alto, CA: Bull. Explores in depth what issues single women face, how they manage their public and private lives, and what conscious and unconscious views they hold about being single.

Our Bodies Ourselves Resource Center. http://www.Ourbodiesourselves.org has articles aimed at women's health concerns such as body image, relationships and sexuality, and reproductive choices.

OurTime.com and SilverSingles.com are dating and friendship sites for persons who are older (over age 50).

http://singlemothers.org is the official website of the National Organization of Single Mothers, Inc.

Attraction and Dating

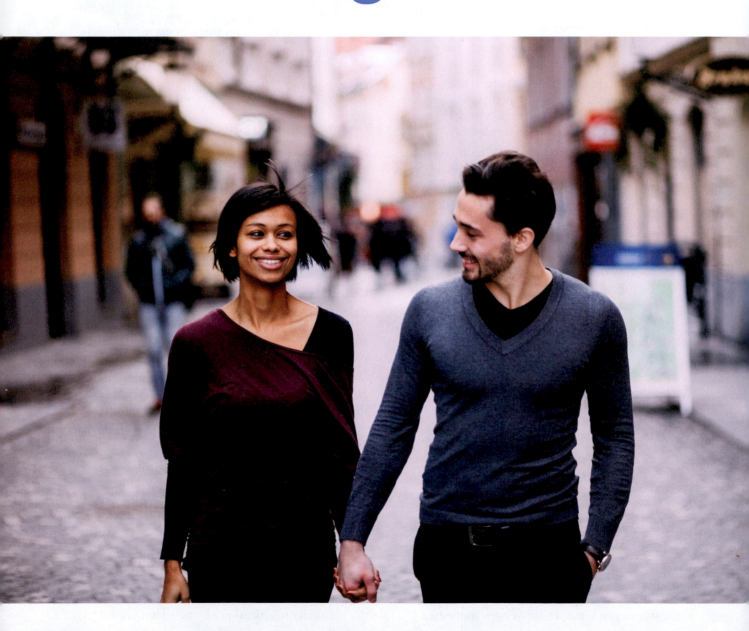

CHAPTER OUTLINE

Learning Objectives

Attraction
- Physical Attractiveness
- Standards of Attractiveness
- Personality and Social Factors
- Unconscious Influences

The Dating System
- Courtship in Early America
- The Emergence of Dating
- Dating at the End of the Twentieth Century
- Dating Today

Reasons for Dating

Finding and Meeting Dates
- Personal Ads to Online Dating

CULTURAL PERSPECTIVE: *Arranged Marriages*

Gender Roles in Dating

Problems in Dating
- Honesty and Openness
- Jealousy and Infidelity

FAMILY STRENGTHS PERSPECTIVE: *Strengths of Russian Families*
- Getting Too Serious
- Closeness and Distance in Relationships

COPING FEATURE: *Coping with Your Own Jealousy*

Violence and Sexual Aggression in Dating
- Gender Differences in Dating Violence
- Psychological and Emotional Effects of Dating Violence
- Date Rape

AT ISSUE TODAY: *Date Rape Drugs*

Breaking Up a Relationship

PERSONAL PERSPECTIVE: *Lessons Learned from Breaking Up*

A QUESTION OF POLICY: *Sexual Assault on Campus*

Summary

Key Terms

Questions for Thought

For Further Reading

LEARNING OBJECTIVES

AFTER READING THE CHAPTER, YOU SHOULD BE ABLE TO DO THE FOLLOWING:

- Discuss and evaluate the factors that contribute to attraction.
- Trace the history of courtship from colonial America to the present day.
- Summarize the reasons for dating.
- Explain how dating can be functional or dysfunctional as a means of partner selection.
- Discuss the ways of finding and meeting dates, including advantages and disadvantages of each.
- Describe the changes in gender roles in dating.
- Relate and explain some of the major problems in dating, such as achieving honesty and openness, jealousy, maintaining extradyadic relationships, and getting too serious.
- Discuss the problem of sexual aggression in dating.
- Discuss the problem of violence in dating.
- Explain how and why relationships end.

SINGLE BLACK FEMALE seeks male companionship, ethnicity unimportant. I'm a very good-looking girl who LOVES to play. I love long walks in the woods, riding in your pickup truck, hunting, camping and fishing trips, cozy winter nights by the fire. Candlelight dinners will have me eating out of your hand. Rub me the right way and watch me respond. I'll be at the front door when you get home from work, wearing only what nature gave me.

Kiss me and I'm yours. Call (XXX) XXX-XXXX and ask for Daisy.

This ad from the *Atlanta Journal–Constitution* is reported to have received numerous calls. Some 15,000 men found themselves talking to the Atlanta Humane Society about an 8-week-old Labrador retriever!

In this chapter, we are concerned with attraction and dating. We explore what attracts us to others and what qualities men and women find attractive in one another. The subject of attraction has fascinated social scientists for years. We now have some of the answers—not all of them, to be sure, but enough to shed considerable light on the subject of interpersonal attraction and its role in relationships. Also, we examine the many issues associated with dating—from systems of dating and reasons for dating, to the process of obtaining dating partners, to problems and violence in dating.

Attraction

One of the most important tasks young adults face is the formation of intimate relationships (Finkel et al. 2012; Regan et al. 2004). Typically this begins with being attracted to someone else.

The most obvious kind of attraction is physical; first impressions often are based on how someone looks. But attraction, especially if the relationship is a lasting one, is also based on the less tangible factors of personality traits and even one's own past experiences and conditioning.

Physical Attractiveness

The most important element in attraction—at least in initial encounters—is physical attractiveness. We are attracted to those with well-proportioned bodies and other physical characteristics that appeal to us

such as shiny hair, a dazzling smile, or being well groomed. One student summed it up as "A nice shape, smile, and smell." Numerous studies concur that physical appearance tops the list of early attractors (D. S. Berry and Miller 2001; Peretti and Abplanalp 2004; Urbaniak and Kilmann 2003). One study of college students revealed that physical attractiveness was more important than relevant sexual history in making judgments about potential risks and probable future sexual activity with the person. This was especially true for males (Agocha and Cooper 1999).

Furthermore, we tend to make judgments about how happy and stable couples are based on our perceptions of their joint attractiveness—called "couple attractiveness." A currently dating couple in which both the man and the woman are physically attractive or in which the woman is more attractive than

The standards of beauty by which Miss America contestants are judged have changed over the years.

the man are perceived as less likely to break up. Our perceptions are correct inasmuch as researchers have noted that both husbands and wives show more constructive, supportive marital behaviors when she is more attractive than he. Both are also more satisfied in the relationship. In contrast, when he is the more attractive member of the duo, he typically demonstrates less constructive, supportive marital behaviors and so does she. And both are more dissatisfied with the relationship (McNulty, Neff, and Karney 2008).

Standards of Attractiveness

Standards of attractiveness are culturally conditioned. In U.S. culture, slender women are considered more attractive than plump ones, tall men more attractive than short ones, and youthful men and women more attractive than the elderly. In contrast, in some cultures, obesity is synonymous with physical beauty.

Furthermore, in U.S. culture, standards of beauty have changed over time. For example, the mean bust–waist–hip measurements of Miss America contest winners in the 1920s were 32–25–35, with no winner having a larger bust than hips. In the 1940s, Hollywood introduced the "sweater girl" Lana Turner and the buxom Jane Russell. Since 1950, the norm has been bust–hip symmetry, with an ideal measurement of 36–24–36.

As the 1950s progressed, the women featured as *Playboy* magazine's "Playmate of the Month" had increasingly larger breasts. This was a period of "mammary madness," with Hollywood and the fashion industry promoting large, cleaved bustlines and tiny waists. Since that time, Playmates have become taller and leaner, but they still have large breasts in proportion to body size. At the same time, the idealized women shown in fashion magazines and on television often are far below normal weight recommendations, bordering on anorexic. For example, the average American woman is 5' 4" tall and weighs 165 pounds; the average for Miss America is 5' 7" and 121 pounds (Copeland 2011; Media Smarts 2015).

Unfortunately, these distorted, unrealistic standards of attractiveness do not make life easier for the average person (Copeland 2011; Media Smarts 2015). It is no wonder that women rate their bodies negatively (Frederick et al. 2007; Markey, Markey, and Birch 2004; Media Smarts 2015). Studies have reported body dissatisfaction greater than 60% for high school girls (Garner 1997) and greater than 80% for college women (Silberstein et al. 1988). Of elementary-school girls who read magazines, 69% say that the pictures influence their concept of an ideal body; 47% say the pictures make them want to lose weight (Martin 2010). A large percentage of young women feel that they are too heavy and resort to drastic diets, purging, or smoking to be thin (Baghdjian 2011; Media Smarts 2015).

Personality and Social Factors

Factors other than physical appearance also are a part of attraction—especially as people contemplate longer-term relationships such as marriage. When seeking mates, we want partners who are nice looking but also healthy, kind, trustworthy, interesting, intelligent, honest, warm, humorous, and personable and who have resources such as education, wealth, and status (Tran, Simpson, and Fletcher 2008). We also are attracted to those who are familiar and similar to ourselves; those who are too different are just not comfortable.

The characteristics that women and men hold as most important differ. Although people have essentially the same "list," women tend to seek mates who first have good personality traits and resources over good looks. For men, it is more important for mates to be nice looking with a good personality over having resources (N. P. Li 2008).

Unconscious Influences

Sometimes people are not aware of why they find another person attractive. Unconscious factors are often at work. If, for example, we experienced love and security with our opposite-sex parent while we were growing up, we may seek to duplicate the relationship and so may be attracted to someone who reminds us of that parent. Or we may be attracted to those who meet our needs and who make us feel good about ourselves. Some people are attracted to those who are helpless, alone, disabled, or dependent; taking care of someone else makes them feel needed, important, and wanted. Other people are attracted to their "ego ideal," to someone who has all the qualities they wish they had.

The Dating System

Cultural beliefs and values influence the social process of how individuals get to know each other prior to marriage, and dating traditions, customs, and practices vary widely across different groups of people (J. Turner and Vasan 2003).

Dating—defined as a courting practice in which two people meet and participate in activities together to get to know each other—is rare in much of the world. For example, it is uncommon in China and India, most areas of Africa and South America, and in some Mediterranean countries, such as Greece, Spain, and Portugal. It is forbidden by many families in Egypt, Saudi Arabia, Iran, Libya, and other Muslim countries.

Dating, as defined previously, is widely practiced in most of Western Europe and is most common in the United States, Great Britain, Canada, Australia, and New Zealand. In these countries, it is now recognized as *the* method by which young men and women get to know one another, learn to get along socially, and select partners by mutual choice.

Dating is a relatively recent phenomenon in the United States; it did not become firmly established until the years after World War I. Before that time, courtship consisted mainly of the young man paying formal visits to the young woman and her family. Dating evolved when marriage started to become an individual rather than a family decision and when love and mutual attraction started to become the basis for marriage.

Courtship in Early America

In the 1700s and 1800s, parents carefully supervised the activities of their children, especially their daughters. Young women did not meet young men casually and indiscriminately. If a man desired the company of a woman, he had to meet her family, be formally introduced, and obtain permission to court her, as well as gain her permission to be courted, before they could "step out." Even then, they were chaperoned or attended social functions in the company of friends or relatives. Parents exerted considerable influence, and even veto power, over whom a son or daughter might see or consider for marriage. Parents were concerned about the social standing, economic status, education, and family background of potential suitors. And if a young man wanted to marry a woman, he had to ask her father's permission for her hand.

The Emergence of Dating

By the late nineteenth and early twentieth centuries, chaperonage and close supervision of courtship had declined. A new pattern of dating emerged whereby young people themselves arranged a time and place to meet. The primary purpose was to have fun and enjoy each other's company. Parents might have sought to maintain some control of dating partners, but the system allowed a high level of freedom from parental supervision.

In the years following World War I, the dating system was still comparatively stylized and formal. The man was expected to take the initiative to ask a woman for a date, plan the activities, pay all the expenses, and exercise his masculine prerogatives as the leader. Over the years, however, the pattern became less structured and more informal, with greater equality between the sexes in initiating and planning dates. Today, couples frequently simply "get together" to do things or to "go out," without going through a specific ritual. "Going together"

In eighteenth-century America, if a man desired the company of a woman, he had to meet her family, be formally introduced, and obtain permission to court her.

has replaced the formal patterns of courtship of previous generations.

The emergence of dating was the result of numerous factors. The most important was the industrial revolution. Thousands of families moved from farms to cities, where young people had increased opportunities for social contact. Working-class women were employed in the mills and factories, where they met male workers. The invention of the telephone made regular contact much easier.

At the same time, the late 1800s saw the rise of free public high schools, where large numbers of physically mature youths were brought together for coeducational schooling (private academies had segregated the sexes). These schools also offered activities for recreation and companionship, which promoted dating.

Increased affluence and leisure time allowed people to devote more time to their own pursuits and social lives. Having a date became a pleasant way to spend an evening. The invention and use of the automobile increased mobility and provided transportation to nightclubs, parties, dances, theaters, and restaurants.

The 1920s also witnessed an early surge in the women's equality movement. The women's movement encouraged women's rights politically, socially, and sexually. A liberated woman was free to take a ride in her boyfriend's car without being under the watchful eye of a chaperone. As a result, dating emerged as an important part of the life of American youths, replacing the previous system of formalized courtship.

Dating at the End of the Twentieth Century

Beginning in the 1960s, advances in the women's movement and the sexual revolution made a significant impact on dating behaviors. For example, college dormitories became coed—providing daily informal contact between the sexes. More women began taking the initiative in arranging a get-together. Attitudes about sexual relationships before marriage became much more accepting; better contraception meant less chance of unwanted pregnancy.

Another major change was the progression of intimacy and commitment from initial meeting to marriage. Earlier generations followed a fairly consistent pattern: casual dating, steady dating, going steady, an understanding (engaged to be engaged),

Coed schooling brings large numbers of adolescents and young adults together.

engagement, and marriage. Some partners in the last decades of the twentieth century did follow the traditional pattern; others dated for a while and then lived together before getting married. There may have been no formal engagement, but marriage developed out of the cohabitation experience. Still other couples dated and then lived together without any intention of marrying—to have a convenient companion and sex partner. In other words, not all couples progressed from dating to formal engagement and then to marriage.

Dating Today

Dating and getting together have undergone many changes since they emerged as a social phenomenon. *Getting together* is a popular term used today by many adolescents to describe the practice of going out with a group of friends rather than going out with one individual on a date. These meetings are usually informal and casual. This change in dating patterns may be a result of the contemporary trend to delay marriage. Many of today's teens will remain single throughout their twenties and engage in casual dating during the 10 or more years before they get married.

dating A courting practice in which two people meet and participate in activities together to get to know each other.

Many researchers who study dating today believe that it is not oriented to marriage, as the dating culture was in the past. Confusion surrounds dating because not only have the rules changed, but also some believe there are no rules anymore. Some researchers raise serious doubts about the fundamental assumption that dating experience helps individuals make a wise choice for a future mate.

One study based on telephone interviews with a nationally representative sample of 1,000 college women found that they were indeed confused about dating on campus (Glenn and Marquardt 2001). The women felt they have two options: hooking up briefly for casual sex or being so seriously involved with a partner that most free time is spent with him. The study found that hookups were common, with about 40% of women having had one hookup and 10% having had more than six. The definition of **hooking up** varies, but generally it means engaging in anything from kissing to having intercourse without emotional involvement. Often partners are almost strangers (37%), have been drinking, get together for a sexual encounter, and do not expect anything more (E. L. Paul, Wenzel, and Harvey 2008). Glenn and Marquardt (2001) found that women are ambivalent about hookups. Some reported feeling hurt and awkward afterward if they had hoped for something more out of a relationship, whereas other women reported feeling strong, desirable, and sexy.

The lack of ritualized dating appears to be no different among noncollege men and women. Popenoe and Whitehead (2000) gathered descriptions of the contemporary dating scene from noncollege men and women who described the dating scene today as a low-commitment culture of "sex without strings and relationships without rings." Young people today want to marry a best friend and "soul mate" who will share and understand their most intimate feelings, needs, and desires. However, despite the strongly held aspiration for marriage and the ideal of a lifelong soul mate, many—especially young women—were not confident that they would achieve this goal. The men and women in this study rarely used the word *love* or the phrase *falling in love*. Instead, they talked about sex and relationships, and they considered sex as being for fun. Most regarded casual sex as part of the dating scene, and only a few took a moral stand against it. Both men and women also agreed that casual sex requires no commitments beyond the sexual encounter itself and no ethical obligation beyond mutual consent. For example, when women and men hook up for sex, they assume that their partner is likely to lie about past sexual history (Popenoe and Whitehead 2000).

Cherlin (1996) believes that this change to more casual sex in dating has resulted in the loss of the ability to slow down the process of becoming intimate and choosing a partner and that many times intimacy just comes too fast. Bryner (2007) also notes that as online daters progress from online contact to face-to-face contact, romance fizzles—perhaps because expectations were too high (based on Internet postings) and reality does not match up. Thus, some social scientists and religious leaders are calling for a return to the rules of courtship. Popenoe and Whitehead (2000) believe that the virtual disappearance of adult participation in, or even awareness of, how today's young people find and marry one another should be seen as a major social problem.

There are some signs of change, however. On the one hand, some people are recognizing that something has been missing over the past decade, and women especially are increasingly fed up with the hookup culture (Kass and Kass 2000; Lambert, Kahn, and Apple 2003). On the other hand, some social demographers see these trends as being persistent and pervasive across advanced Western societies (Popenoe and Whitehead 2000).

Reasons for Dating

Dating fulfills a number of important functions. But if mate selection is no longer one of them, what are they?

First, dating is a form of recreation. Couples go out to relax, enjoy themselves, and have fun. It is a form of entertainment and thereby an end in itself. This is true among high school and college students and senior citizens (Dickson, Hughes, and Walker 2005; Kilborn 2004; Lawson and Leck 2006).

Second, dating provides companionship, friendship, and personal intimacy. Many people have an intense desire to develop close, intimate relationships through dating. Large numbers of people use the Internet or other social media to meet others, hoping for intimate relationships to develop. And, indeed, many relationships start in a virtual world and are transplanted to the face-to-face world (J. Q. Anderson and Rainie 2010; Rosenfeld and Thomas 2012).

Third, dating is a means of socialization. Dating helps people learn social skills, gain confidence and poise, and begin to master the arts of conversation, cooperation, and consideration for others.

Fourth, dating contributes to personality development. One way individuals establish their own identity is in relationship to other people—through successful experiences with others and as a result of positive human associations. One of the reasons young people date is that such associations give them security and feelings of individual worth.

Fifth, dating provides an opportunity to work out gender roles in real-life situations. For example, many women today find that they cannot accept a traditionally passive role; dating helps them discover this and learn what kinds of roles they find fulfilling in close relationships.

Sixth, dating is a means of fulfilling the need for love and affection. No matter how many casual friends people have, they meet their deepest emotional needs for love and affection in close relationships with other individuals. This need for affection is one of the major motives for dating.

Seventh, dating provides an opportunity for sexual experimentation and satisfaction. Dating has become more sex oriented, with large numbers of young people engaging in a variety of sexual behaviors (Glenn and Marquardt 2001; E. L. Paul, Wenzel, and Harvey 2008).

Eighth, dating still is a means of selecting a long-term partner. In our culture, dating is the method for sorting out compatible pairs. The process involves gradually narrowing the field of eligibles from a pool of many to a specific few and eventually to one individual. Whether dating results in the selection of the most compatible partner will depend on the total experience. Not all dating patterns result in wise partner selection, especially if dating partners are chosen on the basis of superficial traits, for example.

Finally, dating prepares individuals for marriage. Dating can not only result in the sorting of compatible pairs, but also become a means of socialization for marriage itself. Through dating, individuals develop a better understanding of each other's behavior and attitudes; the partners learn how to get along and how to discuss and solve problems.

Modern dating couples enjoy a variety of informal activities together.

Finding and Meeting Dates

College provides a large pool of potential dating partners, but single men and women who are not in school—those who are older or divorced, for example—face a challenge in finding dating partners. They may meet through family or friends or work. For example, research suggests that close friends play a critical role in acquiring new dating and sexual partners and in determining the course of dating and sexual relationships (Harper et al. 2004). Some people also try other methods, such as singles bars, personal ads, and dating services.

hooking up Engaging in sexual behavior—from kissing to having intercourse—without emotional involvement.

Personal Ads to Online Dating

Although we tend to think of them as contemporary, personal ads have a history more than 300 years old. In the 1700s, matrimonial agencies used personal ads (in the newly developed newspapers) to help lonely single men find a good wife; these were often a last resort for men and the women who answered them. They were also used by gays and lesbians to find partners (Whipps 2009).

In the early twentieth century, many personal ads had evolved into requests for friends or pen pals—especially during World War I with soldiers who were away from home and lonely. Personal ads again became popular but were viewed as Bohemian or nonconventional in the 1960s as part of the counterculture. As a result, the ads were suspected of having scams or being placed by dangerous individuals (Whipps 2009).

In the mid to late 1990s, with the booming of the Internet, personal ads again became an acceptable way to meet people and form social networks through avenues such as Facebook, Craig's List, e-Harmony, and Match.com. Online dating became a significant social phenomenon (Kreager et al. 2014; Finkel et al. 2012) with thousands of independent dating companies and websites aimed at helping singles meet and get to know one another. The Internet is widely used by millions of American singles; some 37% have tried an online dating site (Gottlieb 2006; Hardey 2004) and an estimated 67% of American households have Internet (Rosenfeld and Thomas 2012).

Dating agencies match people as closely as possible on a number—sometimes hundreds—of characteristics, including geographical area, religion, ethnicity, age, height, body build, education, socioeconomic status, hobbies, interests, and personality traits. Match.com uses the Myers–Briggs temperament test, for example. As the number of people using online dating has grown, sites with specific demographics (niche sites) are becoming more popular as a way of narrowing the search for a potential mate. These include sites such as JDate (Jewish singles), Christian Mingle, Amigos (Latino singles), Black Christian People Meet, and Manhunt (same sex).

Online sites allow singles to upload a profile, photos, and videos. Interested persons get to know each other better through e-mails, webcasts, online chats, telephone chats, and message boards. Many chat online and by phone for several weeks before their first face-to-face meeting. Some couples may use virtual dating as a way of getting to know one another better before a "real-life" meeting. Virtual

---

CULTURAL PERSPECTIVE

Arranged Marriages

Arranged marriages are still common throughout much of the world, such as in Africa, Asia, India, and the Middle East. In an arranged marriage, parents, relatives, or matchmakers have the responsibility of finding suitable spouses for individuals.

At the heart of arranged marriages is the belief that marriage is not about being in love but a serious business economically, politically, and socially. It is not just two people forming a new family, but also two families being merged. Young people cannot be relied on to find a suitable partner in such important matters. They need the wisdom of elders to provide the optimal match for them and for the families. Defenders of arranged marriages claim that love matches start out hot and grow cold, whereas arranged marriages start out cold and grow hot.

How much influence the potential bride and groom have in accepting or rejecting the match made for them varies according to the culture in which arranged marriages take place. In some cultures the parents or a matchmaker may find a suitable partner for a child, but ultimately the daughter or son can refuse to marry the person. Other cultures do not allow for such refusal; children must marry the person selected for them. Sometimes the arrangement for marriage is made between families when children are very young, but the actual wedding does not take place until the children are of marrying age.

dating combines online dating with gaming: couples create avatars who meet in a virtual venue (a romantic tropical island, for example) to explore, play games, and take relationship quizzes. Virtual dating allows a different kind of interaction than chatting.

Meeting someone online or through social media such as Facebook has some advantages. First, it allows singles to interact with many people they would not meet otherwise. Some clients report that they found someone who was a better match (based on personality, hobbies, and interests) than they would have at a singles bar or at work. Individuals who face a "thin market" or small pool of eligibles (middle-age persons, divorced persons with children, gays, or lesbians, for example) are especially likely to meet partners online (Rosenfeld and Thomas 2012).

Others cite the ability to get to know someone before meeting face-to-face as an advantage of meeting online. This gives a minimally threatening context for initiating a relationship—much less threatening than meeting for dinner only to discover it is a mistake by the time the appetizer arrives. Persons who are likely to be poor partners can be omitted from the dating pool before any contact is made (Finkel et al. 2012).

Online meeting also has disadvantages and even perils. First, it is hard to know exactly who is "on the other end." One college-age woman established a romantic online relationship with the man of her dreams only to discover he was 80 years old! Even in less extreme cases, exaggeration may be used to portray oneself in the most favorable way. Men routinely fib about their height (adding a half inch or more) and financial status; women fib about weight (by 5 pounds or more) and attractiveness; photoshopping allows pictures to be altered (O'Sullivan 2008; Media Smarts 2015; Sprecher et al. 2008). Furthermore, having so much information about someone (age, weight, height, career, education, address, likes and dislikes, political and religious beliefs, etc.) gives a false sense of knowing someone. In more serious and dangerous deceptions, con artists may establish relationships with lonely victims to gain access to financial resources and sexual predators may hunt unsuspecting victims online.

Second, online dating provides so many potential partners that a person can feel overwhelmed and as if he or she must speed date to cycle through potential mates quickly—so as not to miss anyone. This contributes to a hypercasual approach for some online daters or to a "shopping mode" when evaluating potential mates (Finkel et al. 2012). Either way, it may help to explain why as online daters get to know more about each other (typically when face-to-face), the romance and excitement often fades quickly. The image portrayed by the Internet contact may build hopes and expectations; when those are not met immediately, the daters "shop" on (Bryner 2007).

A third disadvantage of Internet dating has to do with geography—the perfect match may live hundreds or thousands of miles away or in another country. Geographic closeness still matters to the extent that a face-to-face relationship is the goal. And "online close" is apt to be bigger than your neighborhood or even metropolitan area (Rosenfeld and Thomas 2012). Someone who lives 50 to 100 miles away is much closer than someone on the other coast, but it still will require several hours driving to go to the movies. And if a marriage happens, one or both will have to consider relocating work, maybe schools for children, etc.

Gender Roles in Dating

Male and female roles in the dating process have changed. Traditionally, men initiated, planned, and paid for the date. This arrangement encouraged an unspoken agreement whereby females were expected to reciprocate by allowing expressions of affection and sexual intimacies.

With the advent of the feminist movement, women became aware of the inequalities between the sexes and more intolerant of the power distribution in sexual relationships. Accordingly, they have sought to equalize control within the dating situation by initiating and paying for dates.

Or at least that was how it was assumed gender roles would change. Instead, numerous studies indicate that although both men and women may initiate romantic relationships (ask for that first date), men still take the initiative and the risk of rejection much more often (C. Clark, Shaver, and Abrahams 1999; Mills, Janiszewska, and Zabala 2011). When Mills, Janiszewska, and Zabala (2011) asked heterosexual college undergraduates whether they preferred to ask someone out (on a first date) or be asked out, 83% of men (but only 6% of women) said they preferred to ask. And these students' preferences were reflected in their actual behaviors. When asked how many people they had asked out over the past year, men answered, on average, 4 women; women answered none. On average, the women had been asked out 5 times whereas men had only been asked out once. Kreager et al. (2014) surveyed 13,000 online dating participants and found that men initiate four times as many contacts as women, indicating that both sexes still prefer for the man to make the contact. However, when women do initiate the contact, they are twice as likely to make a connection. This coincides with previous research indicating that women more quickly focus on in-depth qualities of a prospective mate, whereas men focus (at least initially) on physical appearance (Kreager et al. 2014).

Despite decades of increasing sexual equality (in the workplace, for example), women are still more apt to signal interest or receptivity by nonverbal flirting (raised eyebrows, smiles, brief glances, hair flips)—and wait to be asked out for that first date (Mills, Janiszewska, and Zabala 2011). Why? Several researchers (including C. Clark, Shaver, and Abrahams 1999 and Mills, Janiszewska, and Zabala 2011) theorize that it has to do with more than arbitrary social gender roles. Instead, it can better be explained from an evolutionary point of view. The goal from an evolutionary point of view is for human offspring to be reared—so that the species continues. Males and females have different opportunities and constraints when it comes to reproduction. Males look for mates who will be sexually faithful to them because his energies are used in providing and protecting the vulnerable young; he does not want to provide for some other male's offspring. So he prefers females who are not assertive to make those initial advances—as an indication of her potential to be faithful sexually.

Problems in Dating

Some type of dating is usually an important part of the social life of young people. Yet some people have not learned the social skills and developed the self-confidence for a meaningful relationship to develop. Problems surrounding dating usually involve issues of communication and intimacy; maturity and some intimacy skills are required to handle these inevitable problems.

Honesty and Openness

Men and women both look for honesty and openness in relationships. However, because people strive to be on their best behavior while dating, a certain amount of pretense or playacting, called **imaging**, is necessary for them to present themselves in the best possible manner.

In one study (Keenan et al. 1997), researchers surveyed undergraduate students about deception in dating strategies by members of the opposite sex and rated the responses according to financial, commitment, and physical dimensions of deception. The survey revealed that women expect significantly more deception on financial characteristics and on variables related to commitment than men expect from women. However, men do not anticipate significantly more deception from women about physical characteristics than women expect from men. Overall, women expect more deception from men than men expect from women. Women are especially suspicious of claims made by males who are sexually interested in them. These findings support the idea that women, who bear the greater cost for procreation and thus greater corresponding reproductive risk, are more selective and cautious at choosing a partner than are men.

Jealousy and Infidelity

One of the considerations in dating is what types of relationships are acceptable outside the dating dyad. Do they date other people? Do they have sexual relationships with other people? For a heterosexual couple, do they maintain opposite-sex friendships, and what is the level of involvement in these friendships? Jealousy, whether or not it is warranted, is a real problem in many intimate relationships.

Despite general disapproval of **extradyadic involvement** (broadly defined by college students as any emotional or physical intimacy with anyone other than the primary dating partner), nearly all students report having had such an involvement. Dating infidelity typically involves flirtation and passionate kissing; about one half of men and one third of women engage in extradyadic intercourse (McAnulty and Brineman 2007).

In general, men are more distressed by a partner's sexual infidelity, whereas women are more distressed by a partner's emotional infidelity (Shackelford et al. 2004). However, across both genders, sexual infidelity is associated with anger and blame, and emotional

Strengths of Russian Families

The Russian Federation is the largest country in the world. Severe problems experienced by Russian families include financial problems; poverty and unemployment; and the growth of violence, alcoholism, and drug abuse. Despite major problems, there are many strong families in Russia.

According to research by Vladimir Zubkov (2007), the characteristics of strong Russian families are as follows:

- Mutual help and support of family members in problem solving,
- Mutual trust,
- Respect,
- Flexibility in dealing with change,
- More time spent together, and
- Meaningful family traditions.

---

infidelity is associated with hurt feelings (Sabini and Green 2004). One study presented men and women with hypothetical scenarios involving both a sexual and an emotional infidelity and then were asked how jealous, angry, hurt, and disgusted they would be. For both women and men, sexual infidelity elicited greater anger and disgust, but less hurt than emotional infidelity. However, the results suggest that it is women's jealous response to an emotional infidelity that is most different from men's (D. Becker et al. 2004). It appears women are far more jealous over a partner's emotional attachment to someone else. It may be that women find emotional infidelity more threatening to a relationship than sexual infidelity (Buunk and Dijkstra 2004).

Getting Too Serious

Another of the dating problems people face is the situation of one person getting more serious than the other. A university student wrote,

> I am not ready for and have no immediate intentions of getting married. But no matter what we're talking about, my partner always gets around to hinting about marriage. I have two more years of college and then grad school ahead of me.

Sometimes couples make a premature commitment to the relationship. People in new romances tend to expect that their relationship will last, may focus on its present strengths and on their positive feelings, and fail to consider the potential challenges to the relationship. Then one (or sometimes both) of them may have second thoughts. Although it may be difficult, a person who has doubts about a relationship must share those feelings and concerns openly and tactfully with his or her partner.

Closeness and Distance in Relationships

Closeness and distance are both important needs in a dating relationship, and much research has focused on individuals' strategies for balancing autonomy and connection (Feeney 1999; Mikulincer and Shaver 2007b; Nauraine 2011). Although any romantic relationship requires each individual to give up some autonomy to develop a couple identity, giving up too much of one's own identity can be problematic. This contradiction has been called the "me–we pull" because the individual has a desire both to be true to his or her self and to be flexible enough to make the relationship work. Baxter and Montgomery (1997) suggested that romantic partners never fully resolve these issues because the needs for autonomy and distance are constantly changing.

---

imaging The process of playacting to present oneself in the best possible manner.

extradyadic involvement Emotional or physical intimacy outside the dyadic, or couple, relationship.

It is important to remember that every individual is unique and has different needs for distance and closeness in a relationship. In general, men and women differ in their interaction patterns in dating relationships. Researchers have found that women want more closeness in their intimate relationships and push for active discussion of relationship issues, whereas men are more casual and tend to withdraw from such discussions (Christensen and Heavey 1990; Finkel et al. 2012). These differences may be related to gender-role socialization whereby women are taught to be caretakers of relationships and men are taught to be independent and self-reliant. Unfortunately, these patterns tend to cause conflicts with regard to intimacy levels in romantic relationships.

People's attachment styles, which are developed in infancy, also affect their need for closeness and distance in dating relationships. Studies of adult romantic attachment styles have consistently revealed two major dimensions: (1) comfort with closeness and (2) anxiety over relationships. Individuals who are comfortable with closeness (a secure attachment style) prefer a balanced type of relationship characterized by openness and closeness (time spent together and self-disclosure, for example) but also a certain amount of independence (time spent in individual activities) (Feeney 2004; Mikulincer and Shaver 2007b; R. S. Miller 2015).

Individuals who are anxious (in attachment style) typically seek extreme closeness to partners and become overdependent on them (just as they were clingy as infants) (Feeney 2004; Mikulincer and Shaver 2007b; R. S. Miller 2015; Nauraine 2011).

If they don't want to be with you . . . , you wonder what you've done wrong. Or you wonder why; if they don't love you anymore, or if they don't find you attractive anymore, or if they're bored with you, or if it's the end of the road. That's the hardest thing; if S doesn't want to be with me emotionally or doesn't want to be with me, there's nothing to look forward to [sniffling]. There's nothing at all, nothing I can do. It makes me quite miserable, quite alone and quite neglected; ugly, fat, boring, uninteresting; like a nothing. (Feeney 1999, 579)

COPING FEATURE

Coping with Your Own Jealousy

Jealousy is an emotion that everyone experiences to some degree at some time. It can have a destructive effect on one's life and relationships if it is not controlled. Jealousy contributes to irrational appraisals such as the following:

> "She should be available whenever I call her or need her."

> "He should know and meet all my needs."

> "She owes me respect and consideration."

These kinds of irrational appraisals reinforce jealousy. They are unrealistic and put individuals in a no-win situation, evoking negative emotions. The following coping skills can help one deal successfully with jealousy:

- Understanding that roots of jealousy are insecurity and fear of losing something or someone highly desired.

- Concentrating on not feeling sorry for yourself or dwelling on the unfairness of the situation.

- Avoiding blaming others or yourself.

- Remembering that your worth is not controlled by another person.

- Keeping your self-esteem high.

- Making rational appraisals such as "I deeply love him and I want us to be together always, but I do not own him. It is not my right to make unreasonable demands. I cannot make him love me by demanding it."

Avoidant individuals (who learned not to rely much on others as infants) want the most distance in their relationships and so limit closeness, dependence, and affection (Feeney 2004; Mikulincer and Shaver 2007b; R. S. Miller 2015).

> I've never let anybody get really close to me. I think it's just like a self-defense mechanism that I have, to not get hurt. I always keep, you know—there's always a thin distance that I don't let people come near me; not a physical touch, but I think, spiritual. To me this is important, my own space. To have someone invade that space that is special to me, I feel violated. I get angry, I get irritated, I get very irritated. (Feeney 1999, 579)

Violence and Sexual Aggression in Dating

Violence and sexual aggression are, unfortunately, not rare in dating relationships. The exact incidence is difficult to know because researchers use different definitions of abuse (ranging from pushing and slapping to kicking or punching with a fist to use of a weapon for nonsexual violence) and sexual aggression (unwanted sexual attention from verbal coercion to a kiss to forced intercourse); many include stalking (Understanding Teen Dating Violence 2016). Also, many violent or sexually aggressive acts are not reported; a woman may feel that she cannot report an incident because she had been drinking, for example.

It is estimated that about 1.5 million girls experience physical abuse by a dating partner each year (Centers for Disease Control and Prevention 2006); about 10% of boys and 21% of girls experience physical or sexual dating violence (Centers for Disease Control and Prevention 2016; Grunbaum, Kann, and Kinchen 2004). When psychological, emotional, and verbal abuse are included, the number of high school girls and boys who are abused increases to about 30% (A. Davis 2008; Exner-Cortens, Eckenrode, and Rothman 2013). Almost half (43%) of college women experience violent and abusive dating behaviors and 1 in 6 has been sexually abused (Fifth & Pacific Companies 2010; Bureau of Justice Statistics 2016).

Dating violence is common in many other countries as well. One study examined dating violence at 31 universities in 16 different countries (5 in Asia and the Middle East, 2 in Australia and New Zealand, 6 in Europe, 2 in Latin America, and 16 in North America). On average, 29% of the students had physically assaulted a dating partner in the previous 12 months (range = 17% to 45%) and 7% had physically injured a partner (range = 2% to 20%) (Straus 2006).

Gender Differences in Dating Violence

Several research studies challenge the long-held idea that the perpetrators of dating violence are almost always males (Archer 2002; Keen 2006; Straus 2006). In two studies of university students reported by Keen (2006), 29% reported having assaulted a dating partner in the previous year, whereas 54% had been psychologically abusive; 25% had stalked someone. Some 32% of the perpetrators of assault were female compared to 24% who were male. In a large international study, Straus (2006) discovered similar patterns: mutuality in violence (both participated) was the most common pattern, with female only being next, followed by male only.

Questions arise as to how to explain these seemingly contrary findings. What might explain this apparent shift? First, many studies ask only whether persons have committed violence; they do not ask about circumstances. Was she defending herself, for example? Some studies do not differentiate between type of aggression, so if she gets frustrated and pushes him, that is counted the same as if he chokes her. Women tend to use psychological aggression, throw things, slap, kick, or punch; men tend to be more severe—choke, beat up, rape, or murder a partner (Archer 2002; Buss and Duntley 2006; Keen 2006).

This is not to discount that men are also victims of abuse and violence. Both males and females suffer physical and emotional harm as a result of abuse (Kaura and Lohman 2007). It is not surprising, however, that the impact of violence is more serious for women. Most injuries (70%) are suffered by women (Keen 2006).

Psychological and Emotional Effects of Dating Violence

An act of violence is not an isolated incident that does only physical harm—it affects the whole person. Research indicates that adolescents who endure either sexual or physical violence on a date are more likely than other adolescents to engage in subsequent behavior that threatens their health.

Two national studies involving thousands of high school students found that experiences with date violence and rape were associated with binge drinking, marijuana or cocaine use, heavy smoking, multiple sexual partners, unhealthy weight control, and suicidal thoughts or attempts (Exner-Cortens, Eckenrode, and Rothman 2013; Silverman et al. 2001). High school girls exposed to dating violence were four to six times more likely than their peers who were not abused to have been pregnant and eight to nine times more likely to have tried suicide in the previous year (Silverman et al. 2001).

Other studies have yielded similar associations between date violence/rape and eating disorders (such as binging, purging, or fasting) or unhealthy weight control (use of diet pills) (Ackard and Neumark-Sztainer 2002; K. M. Thompson et al. 2001). The link between date violence/rape and suicide is also supported by other studies (Coker, McKeown et al. 2000).

In similar findings, experience with date violence is associated with poorer mental health overall, poorer quality of life, and overall dissatisfaction with life and friends (Ackard and Neumark-Sztainer 2002; Coker 2004). Offman and Matheson (2004) report that women who experience physical or psychological abuse or sexual coercion in dating relationships are more apt to have negative sexual self-perceptions than are nonabused women.

Exner-Cortens and her associates (2013) report consequences of physical or psychological dating violence that last into young adulthood. Their longitudinal study surveyed teens who had been victims of violence as teenagers and then again, five years later, when they were young adults. As teen female victims entered young adulthood, they were more likely to be depressed, to smoke, to have suicidal thoughts, and to be involved in intimate partner violence than their nonabused counterparts. As teen male victims entered young adulthood, they were more likely to be involved in intimate partner violence. This led the researchers to conclude that the long-term effects are more serious for girls/women.

Ackard and Neumark-Sztainer (2002) and Exner-Cortens, Eckenrode, and Rothman (2013) suggest that the negative impact of abusive dating experiences may disrupt normal developmental processes of thought, emotions, and behavior such as the development of stable self-concept and integrated body image. Others caution that teens who are already troubled (who binge drink or have multiple sex partners or are unhappy) may take more risks in dating—such as partners who are also drinking or prone to violence—thus increasing the likelihood of being assaulted.

Date Rape

Date rape is the forcing of involuntary sexual compliance on a person during a voluntary, prearranged date or after a couple meets informally in a social setting. Date rape and other types of sexual aggression are common, with about 65% of males and females having been threatened and about 35% having been attacked (U.S. Bureau of Justice Statistics 2007). Some 15% to 20% of American women report having been raped on a date (*Date rape drugs* 2012; Rickert et al. 2004; Schubot 2001).

Women are told, "Don't go out with a man you don't know. If you do, you're taking a big chance." This is probably sound advice, but one of the purposes of dating is to get to know other people. And no matter how well you know an individual, problems can arise. Date rape can occur in a relationship in which two people have been going out together for a long time. As familiarity grows, a sexually aggressive male may become more insistent and coerce his partner into sexual activity that she finds objectionable.

This coercion may reflect the social learning in our culture: that men are supposed to be the sexual aggressors and overcome the hesitancy of women. Some men believe that when a woman says no she really means yes or that women secretly want to be raped. Furthermore, when the couple has already engaged in sexual activity, she may be judged to have given up her right to say no.

Some men see interactions with women largely in terms of sexual possibilities. They emphasize the value of sex while devaluing (but not hating) women. As a result, they use a wide range of manipulative behaviors—such as making promises, saying things they really do NOT mean, and trying to get their dates to drink too much—to seduce women to meet their own selfish needs for sex.

Several studies indicate that the prevalence of sexual assault on college campuses is higher than that in the general population. The attacks typically

Date Rape Drugs

In recent decades, the use of drugs to facilitate sexual assault (now termed drug-facilitated sexual assault) has attracted much attention. Although a number of drugs could be used, some of the more common are Rohypnol ("Ruffies," "Circles," "R-2"), Xanax (alprazolam), Klonopin (clonazepam), GHB (gamma-hydroxybutyric acid), ketamine ("Cat Valium," "Special K," "Jet"), and Ecstasy (MDMA).

Rohypnol, Xanax, Klonopin, GHB, and ketamine have similar effects on a victim—drowsiness, dizziness, unconsciousness, and no memory of what happened. Nausea, vomiting, coma, and death are also possible. Ecstasy tends to make persons feel "lovey-dovey" and less able to sense danger or resist assault.

Suggestions for protecting against drug-facilitated sexual assault include the following:

- Do not accept drinks from others.
- Open drink containers yourself.
- Watch your drink being made.
- Avoid the punch bowl; it may have extra alcohol.
- Keep your drink with you (even in the bathroom).
- If it smells or tastes funny, pour it out.
- Do not allow someone to urge you to drink more.

- Have a trustworthy friend nearby; watch out for each other.
- If you leave it unattended, pour it out.
- If you feel "drunk" but have not been drinking (or feel like the effects are stronger than usual), get help right away.

If the unthinkable happens and you wake up with no memory of what happened—and think an assault may have happened (clothes torn, bruises, etc.)—some important steps to follow include the following:

- Get medical care right away; call 911 or go to the emergency room.
- Do not urinate, bathe, brush teeth, wash hands, change clothes, or eat or drink before you go. This may eliminate evidence of a rape.
- Do not clean up where the assault happened. A drinking glass or the sheets may have evidence.
- Call the police from the hospital; tell them what you remember. Be honest.
- Ask the hospital to take a urine sample. These drugs leave the system quickly.
- Get counseling and help. Many universities have counseling centers for students. 1-800-656-HOPE is the number for the National Sexual Assault Hotline.

occurred in residences (university or community), were party related, and involved drug or alcohol use—especially binge drinking. A range of types of relationships was reported, from "stranger" to "boyfriend." The men commonly ignored the women's protests and used verbal coercion; physical force was less frequent (Buddie and Testa 2005; *Date rape drugs* 2012). The women were asked how they showed they did not want the sexual involvement. Verbal protests were most common (91%); others resisted physically.

Sometimes verbal or physical force is not used, nor does the victim struggle or protest. Some date rapes happen when the victim is given a date rape drug. These drugs are colorless, odorless, and hard to detect in flavored drinks. Victims become drowsy,

date rape The forcing of involuntary sexual compliance on a person during a voluntary, prearranged date or after a couple meets informally in a social setting.

Many instances of date rape go unreported. Help is becoming more available for women who have experienced abuse, although reluctance to report it continues.

dizzy, unable to resist sex, unconscious, and unable to remember what happened. Weir (2001) reported that one-fourth of the women in one study who had been sexually assaulted said that drugs were a factor. The number would be higher if the use of the oldest date rape drug—alcohol—were counted (Dunn, Bartee, and Perko 2003; E. G. Ryan 2014).

Victims of rape suffer long-term physical and emotional trauma. Long after bruises and physical injuries heal, the psychological damages—depression, fear, posttraumatic stress disorder—may persist. Intimate relationships may be adversely affected (Exner-Cortens, Eckenrode, and Rothman 2013; K. M. Thompson et al. 2001).

Even so, many date rapes are never reported to authorities. People may not realize what incidents qualify as rape; they sometimes feel too ashamed (especially male victims); they may not want to report someone they know. A great many victims do not want to endure the questioning of police and the retelling of the rape at a trial, perhaps to have nothing come of it (National Women's Health Information Center 2008).

Breaking Up a Relationship

A natural and nearly inevitable part of the development of intimate relationships is the ending of some of them. Most people dread the ending of a relationship—even when it is their idea (and even

when the relationship is destructive); we anticipate hurt, loneliness, and uncertainty.

The breakup of some relationships is more painful than others because not all breakups follow the same course. Researchers have developed several theories and models of relationship dissolution. One model, developed by Baxter (1984), proposes that the different paths (trajectories) of dissolving relationships are determined by basic decisions the couple make along the way. These include whether the breakup is wanted by one (two-thirds of the time) or both; whether direct or indirect (most often) methods are used to end the relationship; the sudden (only about one-fourth of the time) or gradual onset of problems; whether exit behaviors are rapid versus gradual (typical); and the presence or absence (most of the time) of repair efforts. Based on this model, in the typical path of a breakup, one member of the couple gradually becomes unhappy with the relationship and makes indirect attempts to end it (acts distant, complains, sees others). Eventually the other member catches on and the couple splits up. Of course, the trajectory of a breakup is different for a couple who experience a sudden problem, decide together to end it, and move on quickly and directly.

Another breakup model is based on social exchange theory. The premise of this model is that a relationship will be dissolved when the rewards of staying in the relationship no longer outweigh the costs. The variables used to make this determination

Lessons Learned from Breaking Up

Some students were asked what they had learned from the ending of a relationship.

I've made a lot of dating mistakes. I've tried approaching relationships in different ways, and I've learned that I need to build a solid friendship (intimacy) as the foundation. I've also learned to show more respect to the person and not be so demanding.

I've been through more relationships than I ever wanted! But you definitely learn a lot. I've learned more about myself and how I handle situations. I have to be able to be myself—to be true to my values and goals; I can't wear a mask. I've also learned how to treat other people: I'm a better listener and more kind.

I also know more about what I want in my future husband (and what I don't!).

I had never given much thought to flirting, pornography, and that kind of stuff as prob lematic. Then I discovered she was "sexting" with some guy she had a crush on in high school. I felt so betrayed—cheated on. I learned how crucial fidelity is and how much it involves.

I've learned that if they lie about little things, they can't be trusted at all.

When a break-up happens, move on. Don't waste time wallowing in grief or guilt. Learn something to make you better in your next relationship. Life WILL go on—with or without you.

---

are people's personal expectations for and feelings about the current relationship and the value they place on the costs and rewards of alternatives to the relationship. Thus, if someone believes that he or she is receiving more from the relationship than any alternatives might offer, the tendency will be toward reconciliation. But if the current relationship seems to offer less than the alternatives, the tendency will be toward dissolution. As one young man explained, "Our relationship got to the point that I was doing everything—or at least it felt that way. I was supposed to call her several times each day just to reassure her I was thinking about her (drama if I didn't). I planned and paid for all our dates. I bought her gifts and romantic surprises like flowers for no special reason. She never so much as made dinner or even baked cookies for me. It was just too one-sided."

Some theories on relationship dissolution describe a sequential process, suggesting phases of a breakup. One such model involves five phases: personal, dyadic, social, grave dressing, and resurrection (Rollie and Duck 2006). In the personal phase, each partner privately assesses his or her satisfaction (or lack of) with the relationship and considers options should it end. During the dyadic phase, the unhappy partner makes his or her feelings known and the couple negotiate, attempt repairs, and confront one another. As each tells friends and family of the impending break and seeks support, the couple moves into the social phase. The grave-dressing phase is characterized by each person's analysis of what went wrong and the construction of his or her "story." In resurrection, ex-partners reenter the social world as unattached persons who have recovered from the breakup.

Another sequential process theory is the cascade model for breaking up (Gottman and Levenson 1992). The elements in this process are the behaviors individuals display when dissolving a close relationship. This process is initiated when one partner begins to complain about and criticize the other partner, resulting in mutual feelings of contempt. As these feelings intensify, first the partner being criticized becomes defensive and then both partners react defensively; eventually, one partner, usually the male, stonewalls, or avoids interaction. These four phases of this cascade model—complaints/criticism, contempt, defensiveness, and stonewalling—have been referred to as the Four Horsemen of the Apocalypse (Gottman 1994).

Breaking up a relationship—and perhaps making someone you care for unhappy or angry—can be uncomfortable. The best way to minimize the pain is through mutual discussion rather than unilateral

Sexual Assault on Campus

Today, most organizations have adopted policies on sexual harassment and assault to protect victims. We focus here on sexual assault that occurs on college campuses, which typically involves students who know each other, as in cases of date rape. In particular, we examine the controversy surrounding universities' policies on sexual assault.

Controversy arises because some universities have adopted a policy of requiring independent corroborating evidence to pursue an investigation into sexual assault. Critics point out that this makes it more difficult for a victim of assault to get a fair hearing and investigation; many times universities will have a hearing (on other issues) based only on complainant and witness testimony. As a result, fewer victims may report their attacks.

Consider the events at Brown University (Kingkade 2015):

In October, 2014, two women who had been at a fraternity party claimed their drinks had been spiked. They had felt the effects immediately and one claimed to have been raped—by a man who was not a fraternity member.

Brown University opened an investigation the next day; hair and urine samples from the two women were sent for testing for date rape drugs. Test results indicated that GHB was present in both women.

Toxicology reports were called into question when the student accused of spiking the drinks (but not the rape) had his own expert review

them. After multiple experts reviewed the results, Brown deemed them inconclusive and dropped the case. The fraternity's four-year disciplinary suspension was reduced to two, but they are not happy. They say they have been falsely accused and punished. The alleged spiker's dad is a large contributor to Brown. Brown apologized for using a lab with a history of problems.

The student accused of committing the rape was found not responsible by Brown because the alleged victim's memory was inconsistent; it could not be determined if the man should have known she was too incapacitated to give consent. She felt she was in a no-win situation: she could not remember because she had been drugged.

Questions to Consider

Does the word of a victim provide enough grounds on which to investigate a rape case? Why or why not?

What laws should be in place to protect those accused of sexual assault? How important is it to protect people from being wrongly accused of sexual assault?

Who should handle date rape or sexual assault incidents on campus? Campus police? Other police? The university?

How do you think a university's policy will affect the incidence of date rape and sexual assault on campus?

---

action, which is the course many are tempted to take. Following are some guidelines to consider when you are thinking of breaking up a relationship.

1. Think clearly about why you want to end the relationship; is it because of an infidelity, dishonesty, lack of intimacy, or no communication, for example?

2. If you want to maintain the relationship but are troubled by unresolved issues, consider counseling to see whether the problems can be resolved.

3. Discuss your feelings and doubts with your partner as truthfully and tactfully as possible, without putting blame on him or her. The other

person deserves to know why you want to end the relationship. Obviously, a gentle approach is easier when the relationship is ending because of a lack of intimacy or having different goals in life. When an infidelity or gross dishonesty is involved, the best approach may be to end the relationship without much discussion.

4. Do not hesitate to bring up the subject of breaking up for fear of hurting the other person. Fear of hurting your partner is no reason to continue an unsatisfactory relationship. In situations where there is mutual dissatisfaction, your partner may feel the same way.

5. Break off cleanly; an on-again, off-again relationship makes the pain worse. Get back together only if you have obtained counseling and/or have resolved your problems.

If your partner has unilaterally decided to break off the relationship, you likely will feel hurt and angry, but you must also get on with your life. The following guidelines may be helpful in this situation:

1. Listen carefully and find out why. Consider what you can learn from the ending of the relationship. Do you need to be a better communicator, more respectful, less manipulative, less "needy," or less jealous?

2. Do not try to force the continuation of a relationship that your partner does not want. Accept your partner's feelings even if you do not feel the same way.

3. Recognize that it takes time to get over some relationships but that time will help the healing process.

This chapter has discussed the ways people get together to form serious relationships. People are first attracted physically, but many other standards are important in considering an intimate partner. Dating is an opportunity to get to know other people and yourself and to experiment and discern what is important to you in a partner. Unfortunately, violence is not uncommon in dating, and it has difficult emotional effects for the victim, including reluctance to report the violence and seek help. Honesty is shown to be the best policy in ongoing dating relationships as well as when a relationship ends.

Summary

1. The most important element in initial attraction is physical attractiveness. Standards of attractiveness are culturally conditioned and change over the years.

2. Personality and social factors are also important in attraction. Personality traits and behavior are significant factors in whether we find others attractive.

3. Sometimes, because of previous conditioning, unconscious factors influence a person's evaluation of the attractiveness of others.

4. Dating as we know it is rare in most of the world. It did not become firmly established in the United States until after World War I. In colonial America, casual meetings were not possible. If a young man wanted to court a woman, he had to meet her family, be formally introduced, and obtain permission to court her.

5. By the late nineteenth and early twentieth centuries, chaperonage and close supervision of courtship had declined. Young people arranged their own get-togethers, and the man was expected to take the leadership role in dating.

6. Dating emerged for a number of reasons: the industrial revolution, the rise of coed public high schools, increased affluence and leisure time, the invention of the automobile, and the women's equality movement.

7. Dating patterns today differ from those of previous generations. Dating has become more casual, there are increased opportunities for informal sexual contacts, and there is

not any set pattern of progression in courtship.

8. Dating fulfills a number of important functions: recreation; companionship, friendship, and personal intimacy; socialization; personality development; the opportunity to try out gender roles; a source of love and affection; the opportunity for sex; mate sorting and selection; and preparation for marriage.

9. People meet prospective dates through family and friends, at parties, at work, in classes, and through other means. Personal ads and online dating have become a significant social phenomenon.

10. Gender roles in dating are changing, with females more frequently asking for dates and planning and paying for them. But men still take the initiative more often.

11. In general, men are more distressed by a dating partner's sexual infidelity, whereas women are more distressed by a partner's emotional infidelity.

12. Closeness and distance are important issues in dating relationships and are related to the attachment styles people develop early in life. Individuals who are secure prefer a balanced type of relationship, characterized by high levels of openness and closeness, and also a degree of autonomy. Individuals who are highly anxious about their relationships typically seek extreme closeness to partners and become overdependent on them. Avoidant individuals want the most distance in their relationships and so limit closeness, dependence, and affection.

13. Date rape is involuntary sexual contact or interaction forced on someone by a dating partner. Many young people and adults do not know how to cope with unwanted sexual aggression. Many date rapes are never reported.

14. Violence in dating tends to progress from verbal aggression to physical aggression unless it is stopped by one of the partners.

15. Breaking up a relationship is always painful. If you are initiating the breakup, the best way to minimize the pain is to discuss your feelings as truthfully and tactfully as possible with the other person. If your partner has initiated the breakup, the best thing to do is to accept his or her feelings and get on with your life.

Key Terms

date rape
dating
extradyadic involvement
hooking up
imaging

Questions for Thought

1. What factors do you believe are most important in attraction between the sexes? In other words, what qualities or characteristics in another person make that person attractive to you?

2. What do you think of the current dating system? How could the system be improved?

3. What are the best ways of meeting new people as potential dates? Explain.

4. What are the principal problems you have experienced in dating? Explain. What could be done about those problems?

5. Research has suggested that one of the principal dating problems people experience is unwanted sexual attention and aggression. Consider this from the point of view of both the offender and the other person. Why does this happen and what can be done to prevent it?

For Further Reading

Fisher, H. E. (2009). *Why him? Why her?* New York: Holt. An investigation into the complex nature of attachment, attraction, personality, and romance.

Johnson, R. M. (2001). *Three faces of love.* DeKalb: Northern Illinois University Press. Explores the meaning of the concept *love*, in all its varied senses, taking as a guide its use both in everyday speech and in the history of theoretical reflections on the subject.

Kansas State University Counseling Services. http://www.ksu.edu/counseling. Information about a variety of topics related to dating on campus including date rape and date rape drugs.

Love and War in Cyberspace. http://www
.counseling.ua.edu/cyberspace. Tips for managing
your online time and avoiding difficulties there.

National Eating Disorders Association. http://
nationaleatingdisorders.org. Information about
eating disorders (anorexia, bulimia, binge eating)
and body image, as well as help, support, recovery,
and help for family members.

Rott, M. P. P. (2001). *Love's revolution: Interracial
marriage.* Philadelphia: Temple University Press.
Breaks common stereotypes and provides insight
as to why people from different racial backgrounds choose to marry one another as it presents the unique successes and failures of mixed
marriages.

http://www.ulifeline.org offers mental health resources for college students online, including
self-assessments for drug/alcohol abuse and anxiety as well as information about a variety of mental
health topics. Many universities participate in
Ulifeline, so you may be able to see exactly what
services are offered on your campus.

5

Love and Mate Selection

Learning Objectives

What Is Love?

Romantic Love

- Is Romantic Love a Sound Basis for Marriage?

Erotic Love

- Are Love and Sex the Same?
- Sex as an Expression of Love

Dependent Love

- Maslow's Theory of Love as Need

Friendship Love

- Loving and Liking

Altruistic Love

- Fromm's View of Altruistic Love

Components of Love

- Research on the Components of Love

FAMILY STRENGTHS PERSPECTIVE: *Commitment*

Love and Attachment

Changes over Time

Theories of Mate Selection

- Psychodynamic Theories
- Needs Theories
- Exchange Theories
- Developmental Process Theories

COPING FEATURE: *Happiness*

Family Background Factors in Mate Selection

- Socioeconomic Class
- Education and Intelligence
- Interracial and Interethnic Marriages
- Interfaith Marriages

Personal Characteristics

- Individual Traits and Behavior
- Age Differentials
- Consensus and Similarity of Attitudes and Values
- Gender Roles and Personal Habits

Nonmarital Cohabitation

- Patterns of Cohabitation

PERSONAL PERSPECTIVE: *Living Together*

- The Effect on the Relationship and on Marriage

The Transition to Marriage

- Why People Marry
- Marital Readiness
- Marriage and the Law
- Preparing for Marriage

Rites of Passage

CULTURAL PERSPECTIVE: *Chinese Wedding Ceremonies*

- Engagement
- The Wedding as a Religious and Civil Rite

AT ISSUE TODAY: *Wedding Bill Blues?*

A QUESTION OF POLICY: *Marriage Incentives*

Summary

Key Terms

Questions for Thought

For Further Reading

LEARNING OBJECTIVES

AFTER READING THE CHAPTER, YOU SHOULD BE ABLE TO DO THE FOLLOWING:

- Define *romantic love*, describe its characteristics, and evaluate it as a sound basis for marriage.

- Discuss the meaning of erotic love and its relationship to sex.

- Describe dependent love and Maslow's theory of love as need.

- Relate how friendship love is important in intimate relationships.

- Describe altruistic love and Fromm's four components of it.

- Define *complete love* and evaluate it as a sound basis for marriage.

- Summarize Sternberg's view of the components of love.

- Describe how love attitudes of men and women are similar and change over time.

- Explain the psychodynamic theories of mate selection: parent image theory and ideal mate theory.

- Describe the traditional exchange theory of mate selection and equity theory.

- Explain the components of the developmental process theory of mate selection.

- Describe how family background factors are related to mate selection.

- Describe how personal characteristics influence mate selection.

- Define *cohabitation*, including the various types, and evaluate its effect on subsequent marriage.

- Discuss marriage as a civil contract and summarize the major legal requirements regulating marriage.

- Discuss the need to prepare for marriage and the roles of education, premarital assessment, and counseling.

- Describe the functions of engagement as a rite of passage and the wedding as a religious and civil rite.

We usually think of love as a feeling—butterflies in your tummy, tingles in your toes, fireworks when you kiss. Of course, those are wonderful feelings! It is great when your spouse's presence makes you feel all aglow. But real life has moments when you disagree and days when the kids drive you crazy. Moods fluctuate; feelings change.

Thus, the word commitment is used to describe a special kind of love—a love steady and sure that is not subject to mood swings or the passage of time or hard times. It is a love that is conscious and unconditional. Commitment love says, "I decide and promise to love you because of who you are, not what you do or how I feel."

In the gardens of Arbor Lodge, the home of J. Sterling Morton, the father of Arbor Day, is a monument with the poem that follows. It sums up commitment love nicely.

> Time flies
>
> Flowers die
>
> New days
>
> New ways
>
> Love stays

In this chapter, we are concerned with the many meanings of love and with the process by which mate selection, nonmarital cohabitation, and the period of transition to marriage can be used to make marriage successful and satisfying. Because the responsibility for mate selection in our culture is an individual one, we must understand the process so that we can make wise choices.

What Is Love?

Love is a central part of our lives. Not only is it the single most prevalent focus of literature, poetry, song, and the popular media, but also most people are highly involved in it (Bergner 2000). Each person defines *love* according to his or her background and experiences. One person may describe love in terms of emotions and strong feelings. Another may describe it as a biological attraction or as a way of treating others. Another may frame love in terms of friendship or concern for someone else. Still another may say that there is no such thing as love, that it is just a delusion.

Although, in a sense, love is what each person thinks it is, this subjective view is not always helpful. It leads to misunderstandings between two people who say they love each other but have entirely different concepts of what they mean. When we talk about love, therefore, we must know what kind of love we mean. The point of view reflected here is that love is not a single concept but has many components such as altruism, commitment, and passion. We will start with five views of love: romantic love, erotic love, dependent love, friendship love, and altruistic love.

Romantic Love

Romantic love has been defined as a profoundly tender or passionate affection for another person. Its chief characteristic is strong emotion, marked by intensity of feelings. A glance, a smile, or a brushing of the hand of one's beloved may arouse powerful feelings of warmth and affection. When the love is mutual, there is a strong sense of exhilaration and well-being.

Romantic lovers desire to be together so that they can enjoy the pleasure of love. When apart, these lovers can become obsessed with thoughts of each other. It is also common for romantic love to result in physiological manifestations: heart palpitations, a quickening pulse, breathlessness, trembling, a tightness in the chest, or halting speech. Loss of love can be so upsetting that the person cannot eat or sleep.

The primary component of romantic love is strong emotion, but current research has indicated that negative emotions, including anxiety and fear, may also be related to increased romantic love. Thus, romantic love appears to be derived from both positive and negative emotions, just as sexual desire may be enhanced by feelings of both intimacy and fear.

Strong sexual attraction and a desire for physical contact are also present in romantic love. In such a state of passion, romantic love is sometimes accompanied by idealization and adoration whereby the lovers focus on those physical traits and qualities of character that embody their ideal of womanhood or manhood. Theodore Reik (1957) theorized that individuals fall in love with people who manifest the characteristics of their ego ideal, and they project these characteristics onto the other person. This is **narcissistic love** in that it really represents love of the self, as reflected in the other person.

But romantic love also can involve altruism and unselfishness, with the lovers filled with generosity and wanting to shower each other with gifts. Their devotion and willingness to sacrifice are often astounding. Along with this desire to give up much for the sake of love comes a renewed feeling of self-confidence that one is beautiful and capable and can do the impossible.

These feelings have been substantiated by others (H. Fisher 2009; Slater 2006; Tennov 1979). When the passion is strong, the relationship eclipses all else. The lovers are in a wildly emotional state, seesawing between bliss and despair. They are obsessed with their loved one: when their loved one responds, they walk on air; when there is no response, they are crushed. Tennov labeled these feelings **limerence**. She reported that people can be this passionately involved with only one person at a time. For a while, at least, the lovers may be completely out of control, and the emotional ups and downs can interfere with their work, study, sleep, and peace of mind.

Is Romantic Love a Sound Basis for Marriage?

An interesting issue regarding romantic love is whether it is a sound basis for marriage. There is no

---

romantic love A profoundly tender or passionate affection for another person, characterized by intense feelings and emotion.

narcissistic love Love of self; selfish, self-centered love.

limerence A term used by Tennov (1979) to describe the intense, wildly emotional highs and lows of being in love.

question that romance plays a significant role in attraction and the decision to marry. Romance brings individuals into serious sexual associations that may eventually lead to marriage. In this sense, romantic love is functional.

However, if romantic love is the only criterion for marriage, love can become problematic. People can fall romantically in love with individuals who are completely unsuitable partners and who will make their lives miserable.

The idealism of romantic love is functional if it approaches reality. Strong et al. (1981) called rational love **conscious love**. They wrote, "When we love someone consciously, we are aware of who that person really is. We do not relate to their image, but to their reality" (201). Romantic love becomes problematic if it blinds us to reality.

In addition, passion, which fuels romantic love, is a function of a rapid increase in intimacy, which cannot be sustained over the lifetime of a marriage (Baumeister and Bratslavsky 1999; Slater 2006). Sharing new experiences, finding out that the other person cares for one deeply, and learning new things about the other person can all increase passion. In contrast, when people reach a point at which they understand each other completely, know all there is to know about each other, and do not share new experiences together, passion fades. Thus, partners in long-term relationships may have to deal with decreased passion even when intimacy and commitment remain high (Baumeister and Bratslavsky 1999; Slater 2006).

Emotional arousal, even from a frightening source, facilitates attraction. Perhaps this is why lovers who meet under dangerous conditions or who risk discovery (as in an affair) experience greater excitement than those who meet under more secure conditions. Perhaps this is why forbidden or secret love can be so intense.

The fear-breeds-passion principle was documented in a classic research study in Vancouver, British Columbia. Dutton and Aron (1974) conducted their experiment on two footbridges that cross the Capilano River. One bridge was a narrow, shaky walkway that swayed in the wind 230 feet above the stream. The other was a solid structure only 10 feet above the water. Near the end of each bridge, an attractive female experimenter approached men who were crossing and asked if they would take part in an experiment on "the effects of exposure to scenic attractions on creative expression." They were asked to write down their associations to a picture she showed them. That the men on the narrow suspension bridge were more sexually aroused than the men on the low, solid bridge was inferred from the amount of sexual imagery in their associations. The men on the suspension bridge also were more likely to call the researcher afterward "to get more information about the study."

Falling in love, along with attraction and sexual arousal, are complex processes that have recently become the subjects of neuroscientific, biochemical investigation (Cacioppo et al. 2012; H. Fisher 2009; Marazzitti and Canale 2004). The relationship between specific changes in the nervous system and various types of emotions is complex. The excitement and arousal of romantic love are a result of increased levels of **dopamine** and **norepinephrine** in the bloodstream. These neurotransmitters are activated by visual cues (by observing an attractive nude or a loved one), and they then bathe the pleasure center of the brain in a sea of chemical messages. Two different but related areas of the brain seem to be involved (at least initially), depending on whether the stimuli are sexual or love (Cacioppo et al. 2012). Orgasms are followed by a release of norepinephrine (energy and exhilaration) plus **oxytocin** and **vasopressin**—the "cuddle chemicals" that make us feel attachment and union with someone.

According to Cacioppo et al. (2012), as sexual feelings are experienced repeatedly, the area of the brain that is activated during sexual activity is the one associated with love. As a result, the more positive excitement a relationship generates, the more likely the participants are to report that they are in love. However, since intense emotional arousal and excitement cannot be sustained, love that is to endure in a marriage must include components other than emotional excitement. This type of love is described as **companionate love**, a love characterized by closeness, warmth, affection, and commitment. When the relationship continues beyond attraction, being around a loved one stimulates the production of **endorphins**—natural painkillers that result in a sense of security and tranquility.

Erotic Love

Erotic love is sensual love. This type of love can be defined as sexual attraction to another person. It is the biological, sensual component of love relationships. What is the relationship between love and sex?

Are Love and Sex the Same?

According to Sigmund Freud, love and sex are really one and the same thing. Freud (1953) defined love as a yearning for a "love object"—for another person who could meet one's own sexual needs. Love, to Freud, was narcissistic in that it was measured by the extent to which the love object could satisfy someone's sexual aims.

Freud emphasized two important elements of the sexual aims of adults. One element is physical and sensual. In both men and women, this element consists of the desire for physical pleasure, such as the release of sexual tension through orgasm.

The second element of sexual aims is psychical; it is the affectionate component—the desire for emotional satisfaction. Freud emphasized that a normal sexual life is ensured when there is a convergence of the affectionate and sensual components. The desire for true affection and for the release of sexual tension are the needs that motivate individuals to seek love objects.

Whereas Freud emphasized that love and sex are the same thing, other writers would say that they are separate entities and that a distinction must be made between them. Sex is a biological function whose aim is the release of physical tension. Love stems from psychic needs and provides affection and emotional satisfaction. Some research indicates only a low correlation between sexual desire and love. This means that many individuals tend to separate the two things—that they can be in love without having sexual desire or they can have sexual desire without being in love (Beck, Bozman, and Qualtrough 1991).

A common manifestation of the separation of love and sex today is casual sex, as discussed in Chapter 3. This type of sex is sex for its own sake, because it is pleasurable and fun, without the necessity of love and commitment. As one student remarked, "What's wrong with just enjoying one another's bodies? Do people have to be in love to do that?" Commonly cited motives for casual sex are sexual desire, spontaneous urges, interest in sexual exploration, and experimentation.

In an opposing viewpoint, Helen Fisher, an anthropologist who has researched the biochemistry of attraction and love extensively, contends that casual sex is "rarely" casual. Sexual interaction such as fondling, kissing, and intercourse stimulate the release of dopamine and norepinephrine—chemicals that cause us to feel passionate love. The oxytocin and vasopressin released after orgasm make us feel attached to a partner (H. Fisher 2009). In other words, sex and love feelings are impossible to separate. This is recognized in other arenas as well. In a recent discussion about the phenomenon of casual sex on campus, a student related that there are unwritten rules such as no kissing and do not hook up with the same person more than three times because people get to having feelings for each other.

Cacioppo et al. (2012) would agree. They conducted a comprehensive meta-analysis of all the functional magnetic resonance imaging studies of the relationship between sexual desire and love. In other words, they looked at these images to see which areas of the brain are activated by sexual stimuli (such as erotic pictures) and which are activated by love stimuli (a picture of a significant other). They discovered that love and sexual desire activate two different but related areas in the brain. However, after repeated sexual experiences, the area activated by love begins to be activated as well: love builds on a neural circuit for emotions and pleasure. Love grows out of and is a more abstract representation of the pleasant sensorimotor experiences that characterize desire (sex).

conscious love Rational, reasoning love.

dopamine A neurotransmitter that functions in the parts of the brain that control emotions and bodily movement.

norepinephrine A hormone secreted by the adrenal glands that has a stimulating effect on blood pressure and acts as a neurotransmitter.

oxytocin A neurotransmitter that produces feelings of attachment and union with someone; a "cuddle chemical."

vasopressin A neurotransmitter that produces feelings of attachment and union with someone; a "cuddle chemical."

companionate love A type of love characterized by warmth, affection, and commitment.

endorphins Chemical neurotransmitters that have a sedative effect on the body and can give a sense of tranquility.

erotic love Sexual, sensuous love.

Is physical attraction more than skin deep? Freud defined love as "a yearning for a 'love object.'" It is possible that, for some, the appearance of one of these men satisfies Freud's definition of a love object, although another might satisfy that definition for someone else.

Sex as an Expression of Love

Many couples cannot separate sex from all other aspects of their relationship, at least in the long term. One woman summed up her feelings:

> I like sex a lot. But it can only supplement a warm, affectionate, mutually respecting, full personhood relationship. It can't be a relationship. It can't prove love. It can't prove anything. I have found sex with people I don't really like, or who I'm not certain will really like me, or with people I don't feel I know well, to be very shallow and uncomfortable and physically unsatisfying. I don't believe you have to be "in love" and married "till death do us part." But mind and body are one organism and all tied up together, and it isn't even physically fun unless the people involved really like each other. (Hite 1981, 48)

In modern Western society, there has been considerable fusion between love and sex. Some adults maintain that love increases the pleasure of sex and that erotic pleasure is reduced when love is at a minimum. Sex can be important as a confirmation of the love relationship; it says to the other person, "I love you." In this view, sex can be both a physical and an emotional expression of deep feeling. But other adults disagree, arguing that it simply is not true that sexual pleasure is less when the partners do not love each other. Whichever view an individual holds, many people want sex with affection, not without it, and insist that love and sex should go together.

Dependent Love

One of the components of a durable love is dependency. **Dependent love** develops when someone's needs are fulfilled by another person. In its simplest form, it works like this: "I have important needs. You fulfill those needs; therefore, I love you." This is the type of love the young child feels for the mother who cares for him or her: "You give me my bottle; you keep me warm; you hold me, cuddle me, and talk to me. That's why I love you."

But it is also the kind of love that develops when the intense psychological needs of adults that have been denied in the past are fulfilled by a lover. For example, a person who has a strong need for approval may be getting that need met through a partner who is full of compliments and praise.

Maslow's Theory of Love as Need

Abraham Maslow (1970, 2000) is one of the chief exponents of love as dependency and need fulfillment. According to Maslow, human needs may be arranged in a hierarchy, ascending from physiological to psychological, as shown in Figure 5.1.

Maslow referred to the first four levels of need as D-needs, or Deficiency-needs, and to the last three levels as B-needs, or Being-needs. He emphasized that the needs at each level must be met before a person can move up to the next level. An individual develops Deficiency-love for a person who meets D-needs and Being-love for the person who fulfills B-needs.

Maslow emphasized that in marriage **D-love** refers to all forms of self-centered love whereby two people love each other because the needs of each are met by the other. It is a sort of bookkeeping arrangement, with the man meeting certain needs of the woman even as she meets certain needs of his and vice versa. Since the focus of attention is on the fulfillment of self and personal needs, D-love may be fragmented. For example, a woman may enjoy her spouse as a sexual partner because he meets her biological and emotional needs but dislike him in some other ways because of his sense of values.

This fragmentation cannot happen in **B-love**, because it is love for the very existence and uniqueness of the other person. The sexual impulse is anchored in the deep love of the qualities of one's mate. With this type of love, neither person feels insecure and threatened because each feels accepted by the other and is comfortable in the other's presence. B-love is not possessive, nor is it motivated by any desire to fulfill some personal need or selfish aim. It is unconditional and offers the kind of relationship in which each person can develop the best that is in him or her.

It is important that need fulfillment be mutual and that partners strive to meet each other's D-needs. This assumes the needs are reasonable and capable of fulfillment. However, difficulty can arise if an individual's D-needs were not met while growing up; he or she may become possessive, domineering, or overly dependent and may manipulate the other person for self-satisfaction. In such a situation, self-actualization and B-love are impossible. There is no room for growth, freedom, and fulfillment because the partner is being used. One woman explained:

> My husband says that if I really loved him, I would want to be together with him all the time. He didn't want me to go to work (we don't have any children), but I did anyhow. He calls me several times during the day. I'd like to go to lunch with the girls once in a while, but he insists on having lunch with me every day. When we're home, he follows me around the house. I can't even go to the bathroom alone. If I don't feel like sex, he pouts, and drinks beer. Sometimes he'll drink the whole weekend because I turned him down (I do so very seldom, however).

In a counseling session, the husband revealed that he had felt rejected and unloved by his mother when he was growing up, that she was never home for him. Unconsciously, he expected his wife to make up for all the love he had missed as a child. His demands were unreasonable, and the more he

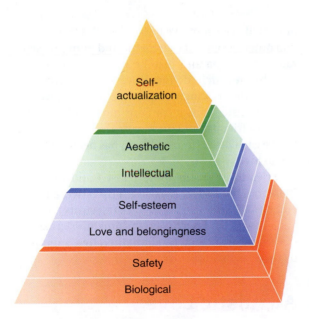

FIGURE 5.1 Maslow's Hierarchy of Needs

Note: From Abraham Maslow, Motivation and Personality, *3rd ed. Copyright © 2000. Reprinted by permission of Pearson Education, Inc., Upper Saddle River, NJ.*

dependent love Love that one develops for someone who fulfills one's needs.

D-love Term used by Maslow for Deficiency-love, which develops when another person meets one's needs.

B-love Term used by Maslow for Being-love, which is love for the very being and uniqueness of another person.

expected, the more she came to resent and shun him (Counseling notes).

If, however, D-needs have been met as one is growing up, the individual does not need to strive for their fulfillment and thus can show an active concern for the life and growth of the loved one. Maslow recognized that there is some mixture of D-love and B-love in every relationship.

People differ regarding their need for emotional closeness and distance in their family relationships. If they experience excessive emotional distance, their anxiety increases because of fears of rejection and abandonment. They then attempt to reduce the anxiety by seeking increased togetherness. However, if people experience excessive togetherness in their family, they may become anxious over perceived threats to their autonomy and independence. Anxiety about excessive closeness prompts them to increase the emotional distance from other family members.

Functional, or healthy, families have ample tolerance for normal variations in closeness and distance, and low levels of anxiety are sufficient to return the family to a balance between closeness and distance. In dysfunctional families, however, minor variations in closeness or distance frequently provoke intense anxiety. Moreover, intense anxiety and persistent reliance on anxiety to regulate closeness and distance result in chronic anxiety within the family (Benson et al. 1993).

Research shows that lovers whose involvement includes friendship maintain more enduring relationships.

Friendship Love

Another important element of love is **friendship love**, similar to what is called companionate love. This implies a type of love between individuals with common concerns. This type of love may exist between good companions because of similar interests; it may arise out of respect for the personality or character of another. Research has shown that the most comprehensive and profound relationships are between two lovers whose involvement includes friendship. Although romance may exist without friendship, love becomes more complete and enduring with it.

Loving and Liking

A website (Answerbag.com) posed the question, "What is the difference between liking someone and loving someone?" and more than 52 people

answered. Yet, some years ago, K. E. Davis (1985) and others proposed that loving and liking are separate phenomena and may be measured separately. But this research defines love only in romantic terms. Other research emphasizes that as love matures over the years, it contains more and more elements of friendship. This means that partners grow to like each other. In fact, liking has been called the key to loving.

Friendship love is more relaxed and less tense than romantic love. It is less possessive and less emotional, and it affords more security without anxiety. In such a secure environment, partners are free to live, work, and go about their lives supported by their friendship.

Altruistic Love

Altruistic love reflects unselfish concern for the well-being of another. It is the investment of someone's psychic energies and abilities in caring for another individual and in seeking what is best for the other person. By nurturing someone else and doing all one can to make that person happy, the individual finds meaning and satisfaction in his or her own life.

Fromm's View of Altruistic Love

Erich Fromm (1956) was one of the chief proponents of altruistic love. He saw love as an activity, not a passive affection; it is a "standing in," not a "falling for." In the most general terms, the active character of love can be described as primarily giving, not receiving. To Fromm, giving did not mean "giving up" something, being deprived, or sacrificing. Rather, it involved giving of oneself— one's joy, interest, understanding, knowledge, humor, even sadness. Thus, we enrich the lives of the people we love.

In addition to the element of giving, Fromm emphasized four basic components of love: care, responsibility, respect, and knowledge. Fromm used the illustration of a woman who says she loves flowers but forgets to water them; it would be difficult to believe she really loves her flowers. As Fromm (1956) put it, "Love is the active concern for the life and growth of that which we love" (22). Where concern is lacking, there is no love. Care and concern also imply responsibility, not as a duty imposed from the outside, but as a voluntary act in which one responds to the needs (primarily psychic) of the other person. Love also depends on respect, which involves not fear and awe, but an awareness of the unique individuality of the other person and a concern that he or she grow and unfold as he or she is. Respect is possible only where freedom and independence are granted. It is the opposite of domination. Finally, love also requires knowledge of the other person to see his or her reality and overcome any irrational, distorted image.

The love that Fromm described is an unselfish, caring, giving love. And, ideally, this type of love should be mutual. If it is not, the relationship will have problems and may not survive.

Components of Love

Western culture emphasizes romantic love as the basis for partner selection. Because it is so highly regarded, it cannot be ignored. When based on reality instead of an idealization of the partner, romantic love provides a functional basis for marriage.

Erotic love is an important part of love. Certainly, sexual attraction is an important factor in relationship building, and sexual satisfaction strengthens the bond between two people. Ordinarily, love and sex are interdependent. A loving relationship becomes a firm foundation for a happy sex life, and a fulfilling sexual relationship reinforces the total love of the partners for each other.

Dependent love is an important basis for a strong relationship when it involves mutual dependency. Integration in the relationship takes place to the extent that each person meets the needs of the other. Difficulty arises if the needs of one person are so excessive that neurotic, possessive dependency becomes the basis for the relationship. Most people need to receive as well as give if they are to remain emotionally healthy. Those who give without receiving become either martyrs or masochists.

Friendship love, based on companionship, is an enduring bond between two people who like each other and enjoy each other's company. It can endure over many years. For most people, friendship alone is not enough for marriage, but it is an important ingredient in loving relationships.

Finally, altruistic love adds genuine concern and care to the total relationship. Behavior, rather than feelings, is the active means by which the individual shows care. As in dependent love, giving and receiving must be mutual. Altruistic love allows the person expressing it to gain satisfaction through caring for another. It allows the receiving person to be cared for and loved for his or her own sake.

Research on the Components of Love

Research findings support the idea that the most complete love has a number of components. Robert Sternberg (1986, 1998, 1999) asked subjects to describe their relationships with lovers, parents, siblings, and friends. Analysis of the results revealed three components of close relationships: intimacy, passion, and decision/commitment to maintain the relationships (see Figure 5.2).

friendship love A love based on common concerns and interests, companionship, and respect for the partner's personality and character.

altruistic love Unselfish concern for the welfare of another.

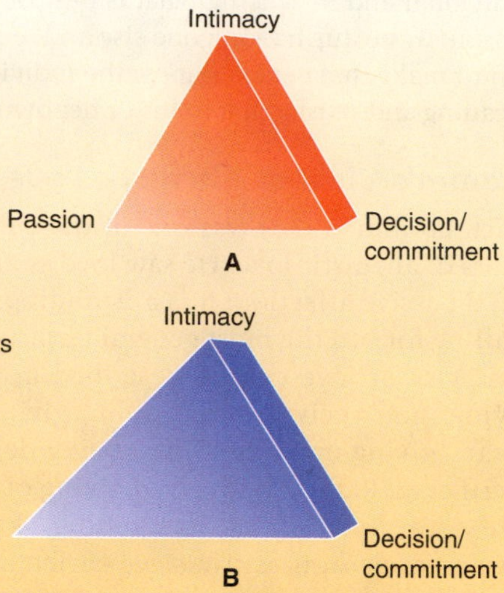

The greater a given component of love, the farther from the center of the triangle. The greater the total love, the greater the area of the triangle. Figure A shows balanced components; Figure B depicts a relationship that has more passion than the other two components.

FIGURE 5.2 The Triangle of Love

Note: From Robert Sternberg, "A triangular theory of love," Psychological Review, 1986, Vol. 93, pp. 119–135. Copyright © 1986 Robert Sternberg. Used with permission.

Intimacy involves sharing feelings and providing emotional support. It usually involves high levels of self-disclosure through the sharing of personal information not ordinarily revealed because of the risk involved. Intimacy gradually increases as the relationship matures and deepens.

The passion component refers to sexuality, attraction, and romance in a relationship.

FAMILY STRENGTHS PERSPECTIVE

Commitment

Commitment is the bedrock on which every enduring family must be built. Commitment means that each family member knows that the others are there and always will be there. As Nick explains,

I like to think of it as being 100 percent for each other. And an incident from my childhood demonstrates this kind of commitment. I was about four years old and we lived on a farm in Alabama. The house was set on a hill several yards from a busy highway. One summer morning my mother told me she was going to walk down to the mailbox, which was located just across the highway, to get the mail. She asked if I wanted to go. I was busy playing and told her no very emphatically. I watched her walk down the driveway. As she approached the mailbox, I changed my mind about going. I began to run very fast. As I ran, I yelled, "I'm coming! I'm coming!" What flashed through

her mind must have been terror as she turned to see me nearing the highway: For she also saw a car—to which I was oblivious—coming at high speed. She knew in that instant that I wouldn't stop and the car wouldn't stop and I would surely be killed. She dropped the mail, raced across the path of the speeding car and scooped me up. We both fell on the shoulder of the highway. The car—which never slowed— barely missed us. My mother narrowly escaped death saving my life.

I've often thought about that incident in the years since. It was one of my favorite stories as a child; I loved to hear it told and retold. As I got older we joked about Mom moving so fast. But as you might guess, even in times when I strongly disagreed with my mother or became irritated by something she had done, I never doubted her 100 percent commitment to me.

The decision/commitment component involves both short- and long-term factors. The short-term factor is the decision, made consciously and unconsciously, to love another person. The long-term factor is the commitment to maintain the love. Sometimes people fall in love but do nothing afterward to maintain it.

Sternberg and Barnes (1988) described eight different combinations of these three components of love:

1. **Absence of intimacy, passion, and commitment**—no love.

2. **Intimacy only**—liking (but no passion or commitment)—friendship.

3. **Passion only**—infatuation (but little intimacy or commitment).

4. **Decision/commitment only**—empty love (with no passion or intimacy).

5. **Intimacy and passion**—romantic love (no commitment).

6. **Intimacy and commitment**—companionate love (without passion).

7. **Passion and commitment**—fatuous love (foolish love, without real intimacy)—love from afar.

8. **Intimacy, passion, and commitment**—consummate love (the most complete love).

Sternberg emphasizes that the most complete love, **consummate love**, results from a combination of all three components. The love relationship is balanced when all three elements are present in relatively equal degrees. People are more likely to be satisfied with their relationship if their love triangles match—that is, if they have fairly equal amounts of the same components of love (Sternberg 1998, 1999; Sternberg and Barnes 1988).

A study that examined the relationship between personality and the three components of love proposed by Sternberg attempted to determine what fundamental personality characteristics were associated with love and whether personality variables were differentially related to intimacy, passion, and commitment (Engel, Olson, and Patrick 2002). The researchers found that conscientiousness was a significant predictor of love for both males and females in close opposite-sex relationships. This study implied that conscientious people tend to be motivated and willing to work at the relationship,

just as they are in jobs and academics. The connection between conscientiousness and the components of love in Sternberg's triangular theory is commitment. Commitment is largely a cognitive decision to engage in a relationship and maintain the relationship over time (Engel, Olson, and Patrick 2002). "Commitment is the extent to which a person is likely to stick with something or someone and persist until the goal underlying the commitment is achieved" (Sternberg 1998, 12). Persons high in conscientiousness are reliable, persistent, and oriented to fulfilling obligations that would likely lead to greater commitment in the relationship (Engel, Olson, and Patrick 2002).

K. E. Davis (1985) described love relationships in terms of three categories that differ somewhat from Sternberg's: passion, caring, and friendship. Each of these, in turn, features a cluster of characteristics. The passion cluster includes fascination with each other, a desire for exclusiveness, and sexual desire. The caring cluster includes giving the utmost of oneself, being a champion and advocate of the partner's interests, and making sure that the partner succeeds. The friendship cluster involves enjoyment, acceptance, trust, respect, mutual assistance, self-disclosure, understanding, and spontaneity.

Moss and Schwebel (1993) described the multidimensional nature of love with a related set of components. They saw intimacy in enduring romantic relationships as depending on the level of commitment and positive affective, cognitive, and physical closeness in a reciprocal (although not necessarily symmetrical) relationship. Their definition specified five components of intimacy: commitment, affective intimacy, cognitive intimacy, physical intimacy, and mutuality.

Love and Attachment

Attachment theory emphasizes the importance of close relationships across the life span (Feeney 2004; Kail and Cavanaugh 2016; Mikulincer and Shaver 2007a) and suggests that early interactions with parents lead to the formation of attachments that reflect

consummate love A term used by Sternberg to describe love as a combination of intimacy, passion, and commitment.

a child's self-worth and expectations about intimate relationships. Three types of attachment styles—secure, anxious/ambivalent, and avoidant—have been applied to romantic relationships. Support for attachment theory is found in research on romantic love. For example, people with lasting relationships tend to be secure, those who fall in love often tend to be anxious/ambivalent, and those doubtful on the existence of romantic love tend to be avoidant (Kinnison 2014).

Longitudinal studies support the proposed relationship between childhood and adolescent/adult attachment styles (G. McCarthy 1999; G. McCarthy and Taylor 1999; Mikulincer and Shaver 2007a). For example, adolescents who were securely attached as infants were more likely to have been socially competent in elementary school and, as adolescents, to have strong friendship groups, be dating, and have closer and more sustained relationships with a dating partner than those who had avoidant or anxious/ambivalent attachment as infants (W. A. Collins et al. 2007).

Attachment styles also have been linked to sexual behavior. One study of college students found that an anxious/ambivalent attachment style was associated with having sex to reduce insecurity and foster intense intimacy. An avoidant style was negatively related to having sex to foster intimacy and positively related to nonromantic goals, such as increasing one's status and prestige among peers. That is, people with an avoidant attachment style reported having sex to impress their peer group, especially if they were having casual, uncommitted sex (Schachner and Shaver 2004).

Other studies have explored the relationship between attachment styles and daily living. W. A. Collins et al. (2007) reported that individuals who were securely attached had more positive daily emotional experiences than those who were insecure or avoidant. Moore and Leung (2002) examined the relationships among romantic attachment styles, romantic attitudes, and well-being among 461 students ages 17 to 21. Those who exhibited secure romantic attachment styles were more likely to be satisfied with their academic progress, less stressed, and less lonely than those in other attachment-style groups. Secure young people, whether in or out of a relationship, were coping best with the academic, social, and daily stress of university life. Researchers believe that the link between romantic attachment style and well-being may be a basic adjustment variable associated with childhood attachment, such as the ability of those with a secure style to obtain social support and/or to have relatively problem-free relationships.

Changes Over Time

Some researchers feel that love changes over time, with romantic love becoming more rational and less emotional. Couples' ideas of love may change over the years, with fewer components of romance and more components of friendship, trust, cooperation, dependability, and acceptance.

Montgomery and Sorell (1997) measured differences in love attitudes across four family life stages: (1) college-age single young adults; (2) young, childless married adults; (3) married adults with children living at home; and (4) married adults with grown children living on their own. Contrary to expectations, the researchers did not find a smooth progression of love attitudes involving the peaking of erotic, romantic love early in life and the rising valuation of friendship in midlife. However, a number of differences were found between young singles and older married adults. Possessive, playful love attitudes were held more strongly by young singles than by any of the married groups, and singles were lowest in altruistic love attitudes. Playful as well as obsessive and possessive attitudes are characteristic of courtship. Marriage, in contrast, may encourage self-giving love and altruism.

In this study, childrearing did not appear to be associated with differences in love attitudes. The older married adults had practical attitudes reflecting generational pressures to form socially and economically viable partnerships. Consistent with previous research, the erotic and altruistic styles of love were associated with high relationship satisfaction for all the groups. Erotic, altruistic, and friendship types of love seemed to have enhanced importance when children were living in the home. Strategies that maintained eroticism were likely to increase a couple's satisfaction with the relationship, no matter the stage of the life cycle. Exclusive commitment to a partner, partner-supportive attitudes, sexual intimacy, and the passionate valuing of the partner and the relationship were most likely to enhance the partners' satisfaction.

In another examination of the changing nature of love, researchers asked younger and older couples to list the qualities that are important for relationship success (Hogan 2013). Older couples responded with the qualities of honesty (being able to confide in one another in a truthful way), communication, companionship, respect, and a positive attitude. Younger couples said love, communication, trust (being able to rely on someone for support and to be faithful), attraction, and compatibility were important. Once again, the developmental stage of younger couples, who are focused on mate selection, helps to explain their inclusion of attraction and compatibility. Older couples, dealing with aging, may put more emphasis on respect and a positive attitude. Older couples more often mentioned religion as important; this may reflect a difference in the importance of religion in the broader culture in older generations.

The findings of both studies suggest that men and women are similar in their love attitudes across adulthood. At all stages, adults value passion, friendship, and self-giving love attitudes. Friendship/companionship love attitudes, honesty, being able to trust, and communication are important for all groups and do not differ by family life stage. We might conclude that passion and friendship/companionship do not occur consecutively in a romantic relationship after all. Rather, they appear to exist concurrently in both dating and married life stage groups (Hogan 2013; Montgomery and Sorell 1997).

Theories of Mate Selection

Selecting a mate is one of the most important decisions we make during our lifetime. We are concerned here with theories of mate selection and their applicability to real life. What factors influence mate selection? How important is family background? What are the possibilities for intermarriage between people of different socioeconomic classes, ethnic groups, and religions? How important is consensus of attitudes and values? How do you know whether you are compatible?

Theories of mate selection attempt to explain the process and dynamics by which people select mates. Some theories have proved more valid than others, and no one theory tells the whole story; but together they provide some explanation of what happens. The major theories discussed here can be divided into four groups: (1) psychodynamic theories, (2) needs theories, (3) exchange theories, and (4) developmental process theories.

Psychodynamic Theories

Psychodynamic theories of mate selection emphasize the influence of childhood experiences and family background on one's choice of mate.

PARENT IMAGE THEORY The **parent image theory** is based on Freud's psychoanalytic concepts of the Oedipus complex and the Electra complex; the theory states that a man will likely marry someone resembling his mother and that a woman will likely marry someone resembling her father. Jedlicka (1984) tested this theory and found that the resemblance between a man's wife and his mother and between a woman's husband and her father occurred more frequently than expected by chance. In general, the data supported the theory of indirect parental influence on mate choice.

IDEAL MATE THEORY The **ideal mate theory** states that people form a fantasy of what an ideal mate should be like, based partly on early childhood experiences. R. Schwartz and Schwartz (1980) wrote,

> Somewhere we "remember" how it felt to have another human being take care of us. We take this memory with us as we mature. Ultimately, it becomes our model, our expectation of a loving relationship. (4)

There is little doubt that many people form fantasies of an ideal mate. Problems arise when people hold unrealistic fantasies that a partner cannot fulfill.

Needs Theories

Needs theories of mate selection are based on the idea that we select a partner who will fill our needs. Various theorists have offered descriptions of how needs influence mate selection. For example, the complementary needs theory, which was originated by Robert Winch (1958), states that people tend to select

parent image theory A theory of mate selection that a person is likely to marry someone resembling his or her parent of the opposite sex.

ideal mate theory A theory that people tend to marry someone who fulfills their fantasy of what an ideal mate should be like, based partly on early childhood experiences.

needs theories Theories of mate selection proposing that we select partners who will fulfill our own needs—both complementary and instrumental.

The ideal mate theory states that people form fantasies of what a mate should be like, but sometimes such fantasy images are not realistic.

mates whose needs are opposite but complementary to their own. According to this theory, a nurturant person would seek out a succorant mate. A dominant person would select a submissive person. Winch later (1967) added a third aspect of complementariness: achievement/vicariousness. The person who has a need to achieve tends to select a person who seeks vicarious recognition through attainment of a spouse.

Since Winch's formulation, subsequent research has provided either no support or only partial support for this theory. In fact, similarity of need may be more functional than complementarity in mate selection.

Exchange Theories

Exchange theories involve a cost–benefit analysis of relationships. These theories are based on the notion that we enter into relationships with those who possess resources (both tangible ones, such as a good income, and intangible ones, such as intelligence or good humor) that we particularly value. If the emotional costs of the relationship begin to outweigh its benefits, we will probably end the relationship.

Traditional exchange theory (discussed in Chapter 1) holds that the basis for a continuing relationship between two partners is that each believes he or she will get at least as much from the relationship as it will cost (Filsinger and Thoma 1988). Each person tries to maximize her or his chances for a rewarding relationship. Sometimes the partners are equal in their abilities to reward each other. Other times, however, those who are motivated primarily to maximize their own benefits may exploit a partner.

An improvement over exchange theory, equity theory (also discussed in Chapter 1), insists on fairness, on the assumption that people should obtain benefits from a relationship in proportion to what they give. The exchanged benefits might not be the same. People desire different things, but they are attracted by a deal that is fair to them. Some people are attracted to others not primarily for what they can get, but for what they can give to a relationship. Judging equity, then, is an individual matter.

Developmental Process Theories

Developmental process theories describe mate selection as a process of filtering and weeding out ineligible and incompatible people until one person is selected. These theories describe various factors that are used in the selection process.

THE FIELD OF ELIGIBLES The first factor in the mate selection process is the field of eligibles. Shortages of potential mates affect not only the likelihood of marriage but also the quality of the spouse in the event of marriage. For example, for women, a favorable marriage market (measured in terms of the relative number of men to women) increases the likelihood of marrying a high-status man rather than a low-status man (measured in terms of education and occupation). At the same time, it decreases the number of eligible women from whom men can choose.

PROPINQUITY Another factor in mate sorting is **propinquity** (Davis-Brown, Salamon, and Surra 1987), or geographic nearness. However, this does not mean simply residential propinquity; institutional propinquity is equally important. In other words, people meet in places of business, schools, social organizations, and churches. Even in a time when many people meet online and can literally meet someone halfway around the world, geographic closeness still matters when a face-to-face relationship (or marriage) is the aim (Rosenfeld and Thomas

Happiness

Happiness is a major life goal for most people. It can be defined as a state of great pleasure or it may be defined as a general satisfaction with life (Waterman 1993). Our happiness is largely influenced by how we cope—which includes how we perceive and appraise experiences, whether we focus on the positives or the negatives in our lives, and whether we have realistic or unrealistic expectations.

Much unhappiness is generated by depending on external events for happiness. Often we think, "I'd be happy if I had more money," or "I'll be happy when I find the right spouse/partner" or "when my partner changes" or "when I get a better job."

Believing that happiness is caused by external events results in people putting happiness on hold until the event happens, which may be infrequent or not at all. Also, although the pleasure of the external event may be intense, it is also usually short lived and may serve to undermine the pleasure that comes from smaller, but more dependable and consistent activities. For example, research indicates that the happiness of people who win the lottery is surprisingly short lived. Why? Apparently the experience of winning so much money is so intense that it diminishes their joy in everyday activities that used to bring pleasure (Kleinke 2002).

We can increase our happiness and life satisfaction by concentrating on what we can do within ourselves to enhance our physical, mental, and emotional health (Insel and Roth 2013; Kleinke 2002). Research indicates that people who practice the following principles report being happier than those who do not:

- Develop optimistic, positive thinking; minimize negative thinking.
- Develop satisfying personal relationships.
- Maintain realistic expectations and rational appraisals of experiences.
- Enjoy the present.
- Enjoy the process rather than obsessing on the final outcome (enjoy planning the party, decorating, and cooking as a part of having a party).
- Be productive at meaningful work.
- Eat nutritious, well-balanced meals.
- Exercise regularly.
- Get adequate sleep and rest.
- Use positive stress-management strategies.
- Value and practice serenity.

2012). It just is not practically possible for most of us to jet to another country to have dinner and go to the movies with someone.

ATTRACTION People are drawn to those whom they find attractive (see Chapter 4). This includes physical attraction and attraction because of specific personality traits. Many mate preferences are thought to be sex linked; in other words, men and women look for different characteristics in potential mates. Women have been shown to look for mates with attributes related to their ability to provide for future offspring, such as intelligence, extroversion, and ambition. Men who possess these characteristics are seen as better providers for offspring. Men, conversely, look for physical signs of health in mates,

most often represented in terms of physical attractiveness. Although individuals have specific and different needs when choosing a mate, many of these sources of attraction fall within this biological framework (Tran, Simpson, and Fletcher 2008).

HOMOGAMY AND HETEROGAMY People tend to choose mates who share personal and social characteristics, such as age, race, ethnicity, education, socioeconomic class, and religion. This propensity to choose a mate similar to oneself is called

propinquity In mate selection, the tendency to choose someone who is geographically near.

homogamy. Choosing a mate different from oneself is called **heterogamy**. Homogamous marriages tend to be more stable than heterogamous marriages, although there are exceptions. Various types of heterogamy and homogamy will be explored in detail in later sections of this chapter.

The major reason that marriages are generally homogamous is that we tend to prefer people who are like us and to feel uncomfortable around those who are different. Another important factor, however, is social pressure toward **endogamy**, or marrying within one's group. People who marry someone who is much older or younger or who belongs to a different ethnic group, religion, or social class may meet with overt or subtle disapproval. Conversely, people are generally prohibited from marrying someone who is too much like them, such as a sibling or a first cousin. This is social pressure for **exogamy**, or marrying outside one's kin group.

COMPATIBILITY The concept of **compatibility** refers to people's capability of living together in harmony. Compatibility may be evaluated according to temperament, attitudes and values, needs, role conceptions and enactment, and personal habits. In the process of mate selection, individuals strive to sort out those with whom they are compatible in many areas.

DESIRED QUALITIES IN A PARTNER Mate selection is influenced by our perceptions of desired qualities for a spouse or partner to possess. The Pew Research Center (2010) conducted a large study in which more

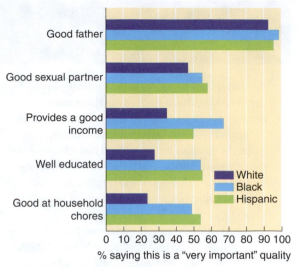

Note: Adapted from Pew Research Center, 2010.

FIGURE 5.4 Perceptions of What Makes a Good Husband/Partner by Race or Ethnicity

than 1,000 adults were asked what qualities make for a good husband/partner and what qualities make for a good wife/partner. It is impressive how similar the perceptions are for the two gender roles, as illustrated in Figure 5.3. The top three qualities for being both a good husband/partner and a good wife/partner are "being a good father/mother," "being caring and compassionate," and "puts his/her family before anything else." The fourth most frequently mentioned quality—represented by a

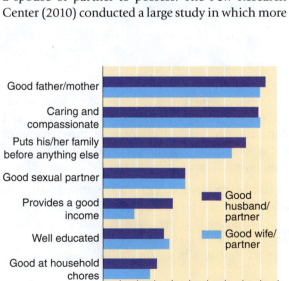

Note: From Pew Research Center, 2010.

FIGURE 5.3 Perceptions of What Makes a Good Husband/Wife

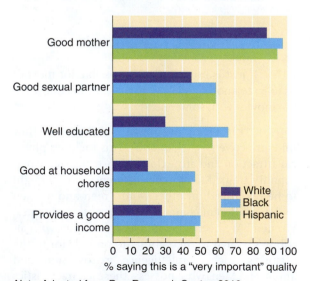

Note: Adapted from Pew Research Center, 2010

FIGURE 5.5 Perceptions of What Makes a Good Wife/Partner by Race or Ethnicity

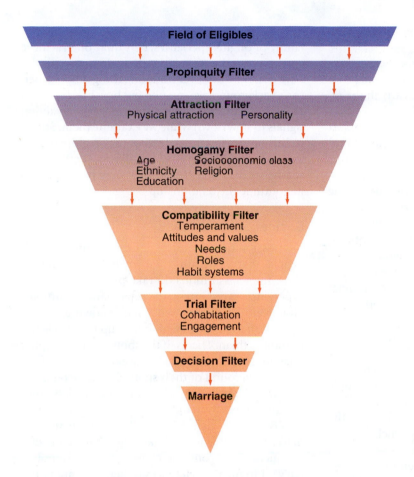

Field of Eligibles

Propinquity Filter

Attraction Filter
Physical attraction   Personality

Homogamy Filter
Age   Socioeconomic class
Ethnicity   Religion
Education

Compatibility Filter
Temperament
Attitudes and values
Needs
Roles
Habit systems

Trial Filter
Cohabitation
Engagement

Decision Filter

Marriage

FIGURE 5.6 The Filtering Process of Mate Selection

substantially lower percentage of responses—is "being a good sexual partner."

The greatest difference in perceptions of what makes a good husband/partner and what makes a good wife/partner is the characteristic of "provides a good income." This quality was reported two times more often as being important for a husband/partner to possess.

The results of the Pew Research Center survey (2010) indicated that men and women closely agree with regard to the most important qualities in a spouse, regardless of whether it is male or female. However, as Figure 5.4 and Figure 5.5 demonstrate, significant differences by race and ethnic background do exist. For example, blacks and Hispanics are about twice as likely to report that it is important for a spouse (either male or female) to "be good at household chores," "be well-educated," and "provide a good income" (particularly for a woman) (Pew Research Center 2010).

THE FILTERING PROCESS Figure 5.6 shows a schematic representation of the **filtering process**. Figure 5.6 is based on numerous theories and research studies. Rather than relying on any one narrow view, the diagram represents a composite of various theories to show the process in detail.

As Figure 5.6 shows, we begin the process of filtering with a wide field of eligibles. This group goes through a series of filters, each of which eliminates ineligibles, so that the numbers are reduced before we pass on to the next filter. Before making a final decision, two people may go through a final trial period through cohabitation, formal engagement,

homogamy The selection of a partner who is similar to oneself.

heterogamy The selection of a partner who is different from oneself.

endogamy Marriage within a particular group.

exogamy Marriage outside of a particular group.

compatibility The capability of living together in harmony.

filtering process A process by which mates are sorted by filtering out ineligibles according to various standards.

or both. If they survive this filtering process, the final filter is the decision to marry.

The order is approximate. Obviously, partners are selected according to propinquity first, and physical attraction plays a significant role early in the relationship, followed by attraction based on other personality traits. Gradually, people begin to sort out homogamous mates according to sociocultural factors: age, ethnicity, education, socioeconomic class, and religion. As the relationship develops, they find out whether they are compatible according to temperament, attitudes and values, needs, role concepts, and personal habits. Some couples place more emphasis on certain factors than on others. Some may explore compatibility without regard for homogamy, but generally, both homogamy and compatibility are important. A testing of the relationship provides further evidence of whether the choice is a wise one.

As you can see, mate selection is a complex process by which people sort out a variety of social, psychological, and personal factors prior to making a final choice. Unfortunately, however, some people are not so thorough. They move from physical attraction to marriage without going through the intervening filters; situational factors, such as pregnancy, may pressure them into a marriage that is unwise. The remainder of this chapter discusses factors in mate selection.

Family Background Factors in Mate Selection

How people are brought up influences how they view marriage, how they want to bring up their children, and what their gender-role preferences are. It influences their personalities, traits, attitudes, values, and feelings. There is probably no area of living that is unrelated to family background.

For these reasons, it is helpful in mate selection to learn about the family background of a potential marriage partner. There is an old saying: "I'm not marrying his or her family." But that is not completely true. We marry a son or daughter, a person who is the product of his or her family experiences. When we marry someone, we marry everything the family has been able to impart to that individual. Knowing something about the family helps us to know the person who grew up in that family.

When both spouses have been exposed to healthy family-of-origin experiences, they more often achieve greater marital satisfaction than do spouses who have not. If we discover troubling things about a person's background, we can find out how he or she feels or has been affected. These problems may be caution signals to slow down while we examine them. Strong feelings about unresolved issues may require professional premarital counseling to see whether they can be worked out. If not, they may be reasons to discontinue the relationship.

Socioeconomic Class

The possibilities of marital satisfaction are greater if people marry within their own socioeconomic class. Interclass unions do take place, but partners experience more stress in heterogamous unions. Moreover, the spouses who marry down are more stressed than the ones who marry up if status is important to them. That is, if the spouses from a higher class are class conscious, they are more aware of the lower background of their spouse; and the relationship with their spouse is less affectionate, less emotionally supportive, and subject to less consensus.

Overall, women are less willing than men to marry someone with low earnings or unstable employment. But economic considerations are not irrelevant to men's preferences either; men are not as willing to marry a woman lacking steady employment. Both men and women with high earnings and education are less willing to marry a person with children or a person with low socioeconomic status. Among African Americans, both men and women report less willingness than their white counterparts to marry someone of low status (Coontz 2005; South 1991). The increasing reliance of families on two incomes might well be altering the field of eligibles. As the tradition of the man as the family's sole source of income disappears, men increasingly are considering the economic characteristics of potential wives in the mate selection process.

Education and Intelligence

Educational homogamy is common in the United States as well as in other nations (Smits and Park 2009). Overall, women with four years of college tend to marry men who are college graduates or who have more education than they do. However, black women are significantly more likely than white women to marry men who are less educated than they are, primarily because the pool of eligible well-educated black males is much smaller (Banks 2011).

Research indicates that educational homogamy is typical in marriage among those who attend college. However, one interesting exception is that those college-goers from the least advantaged socio-economic backgrounds are more likely to marry someone with significantly less education, suggesting the importance of childhood and adolescent cultural influence on mate selection (Musick, Brand, and Davis 2012).

What about the compatibility of spouses who are mixed with respect to education? As a general principle, educationally homogamous marriages tend to be more compatible than educationally heterogamous marriages. College graduates are more likely to marry a partner with a similar level of education and to stay married than others. They also are more likely to have and rear their children within marriage. This is possibly because marriage is a legal status that includes diverse benefits such as social recognition and health insurance that improve the prospects of marriage success (Musick, Brand, and Davis 2012). Among couples with unequal levels of education, the risk of marital disruption is about twice as high if the woman is more educated (Bumpass, Martin, and Sweet 1991). **Hypergamous unions** (woman marries upward) have lower divorce rates than **hypogamous unions** (woman marries downward).

However, educational attainment is not the only important factor. People who lack formal education but who are intelligent may be happily married to those who are well educated. Education and brilliance are not necessarily synonymous. Spouses who are matched according to intelligence levels tend to be more compatible than spouses who differ in intelligence levels.

Interracial and Interethnic Marriages

The great majority of Americans marry within their own racial group. Conflict theorists suggest this is in part because racial competition for resources contributes to people of different races not crossing racial boundaries to marry. Their approach to each other is as competitors rather than potential mates (Lauer and Lauer 2011). However, interracial and interethnic marriages are increasing rapidly. In 1970, about 1% of all marriages were interracial; currently nearly 7% are; and about 12% of new marriages are interracial. This does not count interethnic marriages between Hispanics and non-Hispanics (W. Wang 2012, 2015).

As Figure 5.7 shows, 43% of new interracial or interethnic marriages in 2010 were between whites and Hispanics, followed by whites and Asians (14.5%), and then by whites and blacks (12%) (W. Wang 2012). In 2010, about 28% (twice as many of them were brides) of newlywed Asians married someone of another race or ethnicity compared with 26% of Hispanic newlyweds (about equal numbers of brides and grooms), 17% of black newlyweds (three times more grooms), and 9% of white newlyweds (about an equal number of brides and grooms) (W. Wang 2012).

Marriage brings together two families, not just two individuals. Knowing something about a marriage partner's family experiences can be important to successful marital adjustment.

hypergamous union Marriage in which one spouse marries upward on the social ladder.

hypogamous union Marriage in which one spouse marries downward on the social ladder.

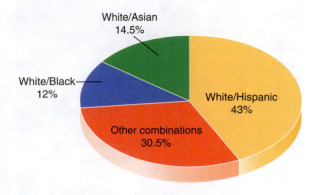

FIGURE 5.7 Percentage of Interracial and Interethnic New Marriages: 2010

Note: Data from American Community Survey 2008–2010. U.S. Bureau of the Census; W. Wang 2012.

Public attitudes about intermarriage have become more positive; 63% say it is "fine" and 43% see intermarriage as a change for the better in society. Even so, barriers to interracial and interethnic dating and marriage still exist. One of the biggest problems for interracial couples rests not with the couple itself, but with the reaction of relatives, friends, and society surrounding the couple. About 11% of people regard intermarriage as a change for the worse in our society (W. Wang 2012). Some families still object to marriage outside of their race or ethnic group. Without the support of family, friends, and society at large, any relationship suffers and is more susceptible to problems. Even interracial adolescent couples sense less societal approval for interracial dating and are less likely to exhibit public displays of affection than are their intraracial counterparts (Vaquera and Kao 2005).

Not surprisingly, the odds of having an interethnic relationship increase significantly if the individual has a relatively ethnically diverse friendship network (Clark-Ibanez and Felmlee 2004). This is already seen in the higher percentages of interracial and interethnic couples in areas such as Alaska, Hawaii, Oklahoma, and California, where racial and ethnic diversity is characteristic of the population (U.S. Bureau of the Census 2012). Hawaii leads the way, with 42% intermarried newlyweds, followed by the western (22%), southern (14%), northeastern (13%), and midwestern states (11%) (W. Wang 2012). As the United States continues to become more diverse, people of different ethnicities will become more familiar with each other at important developmental periods such as adolescence, and thus more interethnic dating will occur.

As a result of interracial unions, larger numbers of children are multiracial. For multiracial children, life can be complex and frustrating in a society that often forces them to identify with a particular race or ethnicity (Dhooper 2003). Understanding where individuals with multiracial backgrounds fit into pre-existing social categories is difficult and controversial (Shih and Sanchez 2005). Many individuals do not want to disown or deny any part of their ethnicity and object to being asked to check a box indicating a clear ethnic choice, as is the case when applying for most schools or jobs. However, many civil rights activists argue against the creation of a separate multiracial category to preserve minority numbers, thus maintaining political power (Rockquemore and Brunsma 2002; Shih and Sanchez 2005). To address this issue, the Census Bureau continues to refine the ways individuals are asked to indicate race.

Interfaith Marriages

Another factor that is considered in choosing a partner is religious preference. There may be strong religious and family pressures to marry within one's own faith, based on the assumption that religiously homogamous marriages are more stable, with less likelihood of dilution of religious principles and greater possibility that the children will grow up with strong religious convictions and well-defined moral standards.

Religious homogamy varies greatly among different religious groups. Jewish persons are most likely to wed someone of their own faith, followed closely by Mormons. Episcopalians are the least likely to be in a religiously homogamous marriage (Sherkat 2004). The more orthodox and conservative the religious group, the greater the pressures exerted to marry within the faith (Sherkat 2004). The degree of religious participation is also important. Increased participation provides more opportunities for interaction with one's field of desirable mates, may influence attitudes toward interfaith date and mate selection, and may also increase the investment in relationships within the religious community (S. K. Marshall and Markstrom-Adams 1995).

Because recent surveys estimate about one-third of marriages are interfaith (L. Fisher 2010), it is important to consider the effect of interfaith marriage on marital happiness and stability. Religious homogamy is associated with higher levels of marital satisfaction and stability. Most studies have identified a moderate negative effect of religious heterogamy on marital stability (S. M. Myers 2006; Sherkat 2004). An exception seems to be Roman Catholics, who overall report similar degrees of happiness whether they are married to other Catholics or to non-Catholics (Lauer and Lauer 2011). The 2001 American Religious Identification Survey found that of all U.S. adults who have had children with someone of another faith, 10% are divorced, compared with 3% of the same faith (Kosmin, Mayer, and Keysar 2001).

With increasing religious diversity in the United States, interfaith marriages include unions not only between and among Christians and Jews, but also between Muslims, Buddhists, Hindus, Pagans, Taoists, and those of other spiritual beliefs. In addition, the religiously faithful and the secularist, the agnostic, and the atheist also intermarry. For many couples, difficulty arises when faced with how to raise their children and what spiritual belief practice, if any, will be taught. It is important for interfaith couples, before getting married, to discuss their expectations for rearing children in a particular spiritual tradition. Also, the pressure from parents and parents-in-law to follow family religious traditions in raising their grandchildren can be intense and can cause considerable stress on a marriage.

Personal Characteristics

When people choose someone with whom to spend the rest of their life, compatibility is essential. In this section, we look at various personal characteristics that contribute to compatibility: traits and behavior, age, attitudes and values, gender-role expectations, and personal habits.

Individual Traits and Behavior

Research on individual traits focuses on physical, personality, and mental health factors. Physical illness puts stress on a relationship, making it less satisfying and less stable. Certain personality traits make it difficult for people to have a happy marriage. Neurotic behavior and mental illness weaken marital stability and quality. Depression has been found to be negatively related to marital quality, and impulsivity has been shown to be negatively related to marital stability. High self-esteem and adequate self-concept are positively related to marital satisfaction. Poor interpersonal skill functioning and unconventionality are related to marital dissatisfaction and instability. Sociability (extraversion) has been found to be positively related to marital stability and quality.

Friends and parents often disapprove of an interracial marriage, creating conflict and hard feelings. However, many interracial marriages are intact after 10 years.

Age Differentials

One consideration in selecting a partner is the age difference between the two people. Overall, the median age differential between spouses in a first marriage is about 2 years. Only 1% of marriages involve an age difference of 20 years or more, and 60% of all married couples are no more than 3 years apart (U.S. Bureau of the Census 2016).

Older individuals are more willing than younger ones to consider a wider age span in mate selection. One study showed that women between the ages of 35 and 50, compared to a group of women between the ages of 20 and 25, preferred men who were younger as an ideal dating partner (Levesque and Caron 2004). However, another research investigation found that when an age gap of 10 years or more existed, those women who were younger than their partners were more committed and satisfied than those women who were older than their partners (Lehmiller and Agnew 2008).

Interestingly, the evidence indicates that those couples who are dissimilar in age have marriage satisfaction as high as those who are similar in age (Lauer and Lauer 2011). Even so, there may be considerations in addition to marital quality when contemplating marriage to someone much older or younger. For example, a young woman married to an older man is likely to be widowed at an early age. For many years it was assumed that marrying a younger spouse extended life expectancy for both men and women. However, Sven Drefahl (2010) surveyed the data with regard to some 2 million Danish couples and discovered that this does seem to be true for men, but not women. Men married to women seven to nine years younger than them enjoyed an 11% reduction in mortality; men who married women older than them experienced lower life expectancy. For a woman, the most benefit to life expectancy is to marry someone about her own age. A larger age gap between her and her husband means lower life expectancy for her, with a younger husband shortening her life more than an older one.

Consensus and Similarity of Attitudes and Values

Marital compatibility is enhanced if spouses develop a high degree of consensus and similar attitudes and values about things that are important to them. Two people can never agree on everything, but ordinarily, the greater the consensus, the easier it is to adjust to each other in marriage. People who share attitudes and values usually feel more comfortable with each other. There is less friction and stress in adjusting to each other.

Consensus develops slowly in a relationship. A dating couple may not even get around to talking about important values until they have been together for some time. The more intimate two people become, the more likely they are to express agreement in a

Declining social barriers between individuals of different ethnic and cultural backgrounds reflect a general decline in prejudice against intergroup marriage.

number of important areas. There may be two reasons for this: (1) being together may create greater understanding and agreement, and (2) those who disagree too much may not progress to the next stage of intimacy. Whichever reason is more valid, value consensus in a couple is related to satisfaction and to progress toward permanence in the relationship.

From this point of view, compatibility may be described partly in terms of the extent of agreement about key issues such as employment, residence, money matters, relationships with parents and in-laws, social life and friends, religion and philosophy of life, sex, manners and living habits, children, and gender roles.

Gender Roles and Personal Habits

Compatibility is based not only on attitudes and values but also on behavior. A couple will have a more pleasant and successful life together if the partners share common expectations about gender roles and if they can tolerate each other's personal habits.

COMPATIBLE ROLE CONCEPTS One measure of compatibility in marriage is the similarity of male and female role expectations. Every man has certain ideas about the roles he should perform as a husband and certain expectations of what roles his spouse should perform. Every woman has certain ideas about the roles she should perform as a wife and certain expectations of what roles her spouse should perform. What two people expect and what they find, however, may differ, as the following examples illustrate:

> **A young husband:** I always wanted a wife who was interested in a home and family. My wife hates to cook and doesn't even want children.

> **A new bride:** In my family, my father always used to help my mother. My husband never lifts a finger to help me. (Counseling notes)

Leigh, Holman, and Burr (1984) found that individuals who had been dating a partner for a year were no more likely to have role compatibility than when they first started dating. They concluded that role compatibility is not important for continuing dating relationships. However, it becomes very important after marriage. People marry with the assumption that a partner will enact the roles they expect, only to find out afterward that he or she has different ideas and expectations.

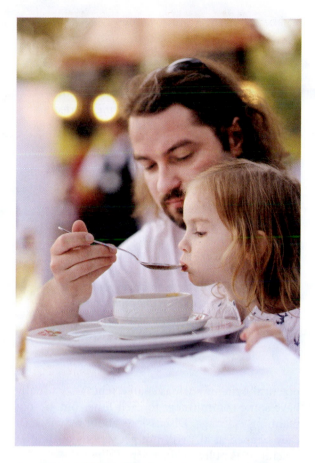

One measure of compatibility in marriage is the similarity of male and female role expectations and the degree to which these are being fulfilled in the relationship. Many partners agree that a male can be a nurturing parent and a woman can have a satisfying professional career.

Eaton and Rose (2011) conducted a review of scholarly articles and popular advice on dating over the past 35 years to see whether gender roles have changed in dating. They discovered that although women have made considerable gains in power and authority in the public sphere, dating roles remain traditional. This has implications in mate selection and future marriage success. The gender roles used to stabilize and structure early relationship interactions may set a trajectory for the future that perpetuates itself. In other words, if they establish a traditional pattern of interacting during courtship, it is likely to continue in marriage. Not revealing one's true role expectations reduces the likelihood of finding a compatible partner.

HABITS Advice columns in newspapers are filled with letters from people complaining about the annoying habits of their spouses. He or she has terrible table manners, is careless about personal cleanliness, smokes, drinks too much, snores, goes to bed too late, will not get up in the morning, leaves dirty dishes scattered all over the house, never replaces the cap on the toothpaste, or has other irritating habits. The writers have either tried to get their partner to change or tried to learn to accept the habit, often without success. Over the years, some of the habits become serious obstacles to marital harmony because personal habits that were annoying before marriage become exasperating in the closer, more continuous shared life of marriage. Most problems can be worked out, however, if people are caring, flexible, and willing to assume responsibility for changing themselves.

Nonmarital Cohabitation

As stated in Chapter 1, cohabitation has become common, with 50% to 60% of new marriages now involving couples who have lived together first (Guzzo 2009; U.S. Bureau of the Census 2012). Today over 7 million couples are cohabiting, most of them younger than age 30 (U.S. Bureau of the Census 2016).

Dating couples tend to end up in cohabiting relationships in one of two broad ways: by "sliding" or "deciding." Sassler (2004) examined this process and discovered that many couples made the transition to cohabiting quickly (within 6 months of dating) and in large measure for reasons of finances, convenience, and housing needs. Wilhelm (2012) describes a similar "natural" progression into cohabiting. In many ways, living together is an advanced stage of dating, preferable to living with roommates, but not so serious as to warrant discussions about marriage or the future (Sassler 2004; Wilhelm 2012).

Other couples who enter cohabitation do so after an active discussion of what living together means to their relationship. They view living together as raising the bar for their relationship; they recognize that cohabitation changes the relationship (Wilhelm 2012).

Patterns of Cohabitation

One important consideration in understanding cohabitation is knowing what the relationship means

Living Together

Wilhelm (2012) describes two situations where students are in cohabiting relationships:

Meghan and her boyfriend have been in a relationship for about three years. They are currently living apart, but spend most nights together. They discussed living together when they both applied for graduate school. Currently, they plan to graduate and move in together. Meghan thinks they will marry and sees cohabitation as a path to greater commitment. She says, "We were both very into the idea. I think we are compatible on pretty much everything, and I don't foresee any big issues."

Seniors Tyler and Nora met when they signed a lease with six of their other friends; they started dating soon after that. They also discussed the implications of living together before moving in. After a year, they feel their relationship is stronger. Nora says, "I think it definitely expedites that process of getting closer, and raises the stakes a little higher for any couple. Sharing a space. . . . It has a profound psychological effect. Rather than giving you the option to leave or bail or retreat into your space, the fact you have the same building to walk into, the same door to pass through, drives you to reconcile, to bring comfort to the other person, because that will serve you too."

to the couple involved. Couples cohabit for numerous reasons; no set pattern or meaning applies to all. Social scientists group cohabiting relationships into a number of basic types (four to seven) based on the nature of the relationship.

Those contemplating cohabitation would be wise to discuss their feelings ahead of time to ascertain the meaning each person associates with the decision to live together. If one partner considers cohabitation tantamount to engagement and the other is participating without love and commitment, hard feelings and emotional pain result.

UTILITARIAN ARRANGEMENT A good number of adults live together for utilitarian reasons. They save money by sharing living quarters and expenses, and they also share the work of housekeeping, laundry, and general maintenance. They may be finishing school or waiting for a divorce to be finalized. Some do not want to get married because they will lose financial benefits: alimony, welfare, pension payments, or tax breaks. In such cases, they may or may not have an intimate relationship. They may be lovers or only friends.

INTIMATE INVOLVEMENT WITH EMOTIONAL COMMITMENT This group includes those who love/like each other, want to have sex together, and want a monogamous relationship. Plus, living together has

practical benefits such as shared rent. They usually have some commitment to each other but are not planning marriage. Discussions about marriage (if they happen at all) will not get serious until after several years of living together.

TRIAL MARRIAGE Some adults live together to test their compatibility and commitment to help them decide whether they are meant for each other and whether they want to be married. The arrangement is considered a "little marriage" to see whether a "big marriage" will last.

PRELUDE TO MARRIAGE A number of adults move in together before they get married. They have already committed themselves to marriage and see no reason to be apart in the meantime (a sort of advanced engagement). They may be waiting to finish a university degree before the wedding, for example. Again, there are practical benefits such as shared expenses. This is the largest group of cohabiting couples.

ALTERNATIVE TO MARRIAGE Couples in this category are cohabiting not as a prelude to marriage but as a substitute for it. These couples do not plan to marry but they do plan to stay together. This includes those who are married to someone else and separated but not divorced and those who have been unhappily married and have become skeptical about the viability of legal marriage. Others have witnessed their friends' unhappy marriages and have concluded that legal marriage is not for them. People have numerous philosophical, legal, and ideological arguments about why they decide not to marry.

The Effect on the Relationship and on Marriage

Because so many contemporary couples cohabit, questions naturally arise as to how cohabiting changes a couple's relationship and whether cohabitation is a good preparation for marriage. The initial thinking was that cohabitation would give a couple chances to test and refine their relationship; it would weed out incompatible couples and prepare others for marriage. However, early studies showed a higher divorce rate among those who cohabited before marriage than among those who had not.

Researchers took a closer look at the dynamics of relationships during cohabitation to try to understand what was going on with relation to cohabitation, the couple's relationship, and marriage success. Rhoades, Stanley, and Markman (2012) conducted a cross-sectional study that revealed a higher degree of commitment among cohabiting couples (than dating couples), but also lower satisfaction, more negative communication, and more physical aggression. They followed with a longitudinal study, gathering data from cohabiting couples at 20-month intervals (six times) (Rhoades, Stanley, and Markman 2012). These couples experienced declines in most indices of relationship quality and in interpersonal commitment; the frequency of sex increased temporarily and constraints to stay together increased.

Later research also failed to support the generalized higher divorce rate for those who cohabited before marriage. It did indicate that the type of cohabitation, including how the couple enters it, is important to the future success of the relationship. "Serial" cohabitants do, indeed, have a higher divorce rate. Popenoe and Whitehead (2002) have reasoned that people who enter several cohabiting relationships have lower levels of commitment and higher levels of autonomy. Once a low-commitment, high-autonomy way of relating is learned (reinforced) by repeated cohabitations, it is hard to unlearn in marriage. Blackwell and Lichter (2000) found that individuals entering a cohabiting relationship were less selective with regard to education level and race of a partner; women were less upwardly selective.

Seligson (2012) argues that socioeconomic class is a factor; lower-income dating couples are more apt to move in together because they cannot afford to live alone—rather than because it is a deliberate, well-thought decision. Other couples who "slide" into cohabitation discover that the dynamics of their relationship change—although they are less satisfied and may have more conflict (than when they were dating), they also accumulate constraints to keep them together (Rhoades, Stanley, and Markman 2012; Wilhelm 2012). In other words, they have a lease together, they have bought furniture, and they have a cat; it truly is not easy to break up.

It is important to remember that many people (about half) enter cohabitation because they decide to—as a prelude to marriage (L. M. Casper and Bianchi 2002). These types of cohabitation are seen as prenuptial and appear not to have negative effects on the future marriage (Rhoades, Stanley, and Markman 2012; Wilhelm 2012).

The Transition to Marriage

How do two people know whether they are ready for marriage? What legal requirements must they fulfill? What can the couple do to prepare for marriage ahead of time? What kinds of marital education, assessment, and counseling might be considered? How can

Nonmarital cohabitation increased rapidly in the 1980s and 1990s, reflecting changes in social norms. One factor associated with the increase in cohabitation may be the increase in the average age at first marriage.

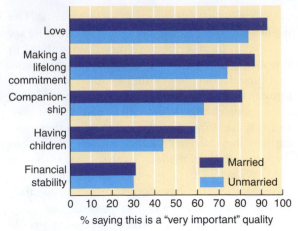

Note: Data from Pew Research Center, 2010.

FIGURE 5.8 Reasons for Getting Married by Marital Status

engagement become a constructive period of preparation? This section attempts to answer these questions.

Why People Marry

In a large study by the Pew Research Center (2010), five major reasons for getting married were cited by both the married and the unmarried. "Love" is the most frequently reported reason for getting married, both among the married and among the unmarried. The other reasons were "making a lifelong commitment," "companionship," "having children," and "financial stability" (see Figure 5.8).

Race and ethnicity also influence the reasons for marriage, as shown in Figure 5.9. Whites and Hispanics are somewhat more likely than blacks to cite

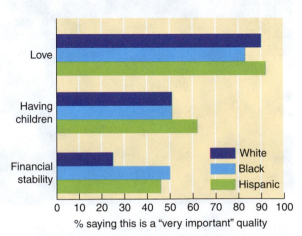

Note: Data from Pew Research Center, 2010.

FIGURE 5.9 Reasons for Marriage by Race and Ethnicity

"love" as a reason to get married. Hispanics are more likely to report that "having children" is a very important reason. Whites are much less likely than blacks or Hispanics to indicate "financial stability" as a very important reason for marriage (Pew Research Center 2010).

Marital Readiness

A number of important factors in the transition to marriage determine marital readiness. Based on research information, the following considerations may be significant.

AGE AT THE TIME OF MARRIAGE People who marry in their teen years often do so because of pregnancy, which may cause them to abandon educational pursuits and accept low-status employment that complicates their marriage considerably. They have the strain of living with low income, a young child, and perhaps unfulfilled dreams.

THE LEVEL OF MATURITY OF THE COUPLE Some people are not mature enough to cope with a marriage relationship because of a lack of communication skills, jealousy, or lack of faithfulness.

MOTIVES FOR GETTING MARRIED Most people marry for love, companionship, and security. But others marry to escape an unpleasant living situation, to heal a damaged ego on the rebound, or because everyone else is. Some people are attracted to and marry people who need to be cared for.

READINESS FOR SEXUAL EXCLUSIVENESS Ordinarily in our society, spouses desire sexual exclusiveness. If someone is not ready for that, he or she is probably not ready for marriage.

EMOTIONAL EMANCIPATION FROM PARENTS People must be ready to give their primary loyalty and affection to a spouse, not to their parents.

LEVEL OF EDUCATION AND VOCATIONAL ASPIRATIONS AND THE DEGREE OF FULFILLMENT In general, the lower a person's educational and vocational aspirations, the earlier in life he or she will marry. Persons with high aspirations wait longer after finishing college to marry and longer after marrying to have children.

Marriage and the Law

All people who marry legally enter into a civil contract. This means that their marriage is not just a personal affair. It is also of social concern, and each state has laws defining people's eligibility to marry and the procedures by which a contract may be established, as well as laws governing the maintenance of the contract once it is made.

Because marital regulation is the responsibility of individual states rather than the federal government, marital laws differ from state to state. However, the following discussion covers most of the major legal requirements regulating getting married. Consult the laws of your state for specifics.

AGE In most states and territories, males and females may marry without parental consent at age 18. The minimum age for marriage with parental consent in most states is 16, although marriage at younger ages is possible in some states with the consent of parents and a judge.

CONSANGUINITY The term **consanguinity** refers to a blood relationship or descent from a common ancestor. Because of the belief in the increased possibility of genetic defects in the offspring of people who share too much of the same genetic makeup, states forbid marriage to one's consanguineous son, daughter, mother, father, grandmother, grandfather, sister, brother, aunt, uncle, niece, or nephew. About half the states forbid marriages of first cousins. Some states also forbid marriages of second cousins or marriage to a grandniece or grandnephew.

AFFINITY The term **affinity** refers to a relationship resulting from marriage. Some states forbid marriage to one's stepparent, stepchild, mother- or father-in-law, son- or daughter-in-law, or aunt- or uncle-in-law. But critics argue that the law has gone overboard in forbidding such marriages, since no biological harm can result from them.

MENTAL DEFICIENCY Because some people who are severely developmentally delayed are not able to meet the responsibilities of marriage, a number of states forbid their marrying. Other states have no clear definition of mental deficiency and so cannot prevent such marriages.

INSANITY Most states prohibit marriages of people who are legally insane because these individuals cannot give their consent. Additionally, such marriages could create severe problems for both family and society.

PROCEDURAL REQUIREMENTS Couples must obtain the legal permission of the state before marrying. This is accomplished through issuance of the marriage

Age and level of maturity at the time of marriage are important factors that determine marital readiness. What other considerations might be significant?

license after the couple have fulfilled certain requirements. For example, licenses are issued to two (not more) people who are free to marry (not already married to someone else). Some states will issue the license the same day the couple applies, but the rest have a waiting period from 24 hours to 5 days. All but about a dozen states also require marriage within a specified period of time (30 days to 1 year) after issuance of the license for the license to be valid.

Some states require a blood test for STDs. A few states require women to be tested for rubella, some states require sickle cell anemia tests, and some give HIV tests or information to marriage license applicants. After obtaining a license, a couple completes the procedural requirements for a legal marriage by having a ceremony. Ceremonies may be civil—in front of a justice of the peace or judge—or religious.

COMMON-LAW MARRIAGES A **common-law marriage** is marriage by mutual consent, without a license or ceremony. The basic requirements to create

consanguinity The state of being related by blood; having descent from a common ancestor.

affinity A relationship formed by marriage without ties of blood.

common-law marriage A marriage by mutual consent, without a license or ceremony, recognized as legal under certain conditions by some states.

Individual counselors or community agencies and organizations may offer classes and workshops in premarital education.

a common-law marriage are that the partners must (1) have legal capacity (of age and with sufficient mental capacity) to marry; (2) intend to marry and have a current agreement to enter a marital relationship; (3) cohabit as spouses; and (4) represent themselves to the world as a married couple (which means, for example, having the mail delivered to "Mr. and Mrs.," filing joint tax returns, or referring to themselves as spouses). With the rising numbers of couples who are opting for cohabitation rather than marriage, it is important to clarify that cohabiting without meeting the requirements just listed will not result in a common-law marriage. Although couples may enter common-law marriages in only about a dozen states and the District of Columbia, they are recognized as valid by other states. There can be difficulties, however, in proving the validity of the marriage in the absence of a recorded marriage license. And a divorce is required to end a valid common-law marriage; there is no "common-law divorce."

VOID OR VOIDABLE MARRIAGES If the legal requirements have not been met, a marriage may be defined as void or voidable. A **void marriage** is never considered valid in the first place, so a court decree is not necessary to set it aside. Marriages may be considered void in cases in which a prior marriage exists (bigamy), the marriage partners are related to each other within certain prohibited degrees, or either party is judged mentally incompetent.

Voidable marriages require an act of annulment to set them aside, after legal action has been instituted by one party. Only one spouse needs to take steps to void the marriage, and action must be brought during the lifetime of both spouses. The most common grounds for voiding a marriage are if either party is under the age of consent, either party is physically incapable of having intercourse, either party consents to the marriage through fraud or duress, or either party lacks the mental capacity to consent to the marriage.

Preparing for Marriage

The need for marriage preparation has long been recognized by professionals. Studies of high school and college students indicate a need for and interest in marriage preparation programs. There also is evidence that numerous marriage education programs are effective (Jakubowski et al. 2004). It seems ironic, then, that couples will spend months planning their wedding but scarcely any time preparing for their marriage. One young man revealed different priorities: "We aren't going to have much of a wedding, but we're going to have a wonderful marriage" (Counseling notes).

The basic theme here is that couples can prepare for marriage in a way that will improve their chances for marital success. The goal of marriage education and enrichment programs is to provide the knowledge and skills to build and sustain happy, healthy relationships (Hawkins et al. 2004).

Much of what we know about marriage and family living was learned as we grew up in our family of origin. This is an important means of learning. But there are other, more formal ways of preparing for marriage.

PREMARITAL EDUCATION Premarital education may include a college-level course in marriage and family living. It may include short courses offered by counselors or by community agencies and organizations such as child and family service agencies, mental health clinics, community counseling centers, women's clubs, service organizations, churches, or schools.

Premarital and marital enrichment programs focus on teaching specific communication skills related to individual and couple functioning. In general, research tends to support the claim that these programs have a positive effect on the participants.

Couples do, in fact, learn the communication skills taught in the programs.

Some clergy and churches require couples to come for instruction before weddings are performed. Such programs are most often designed to interpret the religious meaning of marriage, but they also include discussion of sexual, emotional, economic, social, and familial aspects of marriage.

PREMARITAL ASSESSMENT AND COUNSELING Marriage preparation includes an evaluation of the extent to which the couple is fit and ready for marriage. The most common form of assessment is health assessment: a physical examination and tests for STDs such as HIV, gonorrhea, and herpes. If either partner has a sexually transmitted disease, the other needs to know about it.

Premarital assessment involves more than a health assessment, however. It may profitably include an evaluation of a couple's overall relationship. Such an assessment is difficult for the partners to complete themselves because it is hard for them to be objective. A couple can go to a marriage counselor for the express purpose of exploring important areas of the relationship and determining the level of adjustment and any possible unresolved difficulties. Premarital counseling also helps couples, individually or in groups, address difficulties that have been revealed.

One of the most well-known premarital inventories is called PREPARE/ENRICH (D. H. Olson and Olson 1999; D. H. Olson, Larson, and Olson 2009; L. Williams 2015). PREPARE/ENRICH is designed to identify strengths and weaknesses in several relationship areas, such as realistic expectations, personality issues, communication, conflict resolution, financial management, leisure activities, sexual relationship, children and parenting, family and friends, equalitarian roles, and religious orientation. PREPARE/ENRICH is an online inventory customized to each couple based on several factors such as current status (dating, engaged, married), whether they are previously married or cohabiting, whether they are parents, religious beliefs, and whether they are older than age 55 (D.H. Olson, Larson, and Olson 2009). A facilitator receives a detailed report and gives feedback to the couple, typically in three to six sessions. The couple also receives a handbook with exercises for developing skills and strengthening their relationship (L. Williams 2015).

Validity tests of PREPARE/ENRICH have shown that the inventory can correctly predict in 80% to 85% of cases whether partners will end up divorcing, in 79% of cases whether partners will be happily or unhappily married, and in 78% of cases whether partners will cancel marriage plans (Fowers and Olson 1986; Larsen and Olson 1989; D. H. Olson and Olson 1999).

Another widely used pre-marriage inventory, FOCCUS (Facilitating Open Couple Communication, Understanding, and Study), is used by approximately two-thirds of the Roman Catholic dioceses in the United States as well as by more than 500 Protestant churches of various denominations (L. Williams and Jurich 1995). FOCCUS aims to help couples understand their unique relationship, learn more about themselves, and discuss topics important to lifelong marriage (FOCCUS 2016).

Results indicate that FOCCUS and PREPARE are roughly comparable in terms of their predictive validity. FOCCUS scores during engagement predict a couple's future marital success 4 to 5 years later and indicate with 68% to 74% accuracy (depending on the scoring method used) whether couples will have a high-quality or low-quality marriage. FOCCUS scores are able to identify 75% of the couples who later develop distressed marriages (Jakubowski et al. 2004; Larson et al. 2002). However, no survey is 100% accurate in its ability to predict; this is an important reminder that the purpose of these inventories is to help couples identify strengths and areas of growth in their relationships (L. Williams 2015). (See Jakubowski et al. 2004 for a review of other empirically supported programs.)

Rites of Passage

Rites of passage are ceremonies or rituals by which people pass from one social status to another. In our culture, the rites of passage from a single to a married status include the engagement, the wedding ceremony, and the wedding reception.

void marriage A marriage considered invalid in the first place because it was illegal.

voidable marriage A marriage that can be set aside by annulment under certain prescribed legal circumstances.

rites of passage Ceremonies by which people pass from one social status to another.

Chinese Wedding Ceremonies

All cultures have rituals surrounding weddings. The traditional Chinese wedding ceremony has many rituals that differ from those of the traditional Western wedding. In a traditional Chinese wedding, the color red is important because it symbolizes happiness and prosperity. The color white is associated with death and is not used in traditional families.

Historically, gift giving began about a week before the actual wedding. The family of the groom would go to the house of the bride and give her family gifts placed in red baskets or wrapped in red paper. The baskets were carried by male members of the groom's family and contained various items such as fruit, jewels, linens, and money. The bride opened the gifts with her family and typically returned about half of them to the member of the groom's family who brought them. Three days before the wedding, the bride's family brought gifts in red baskets or red paper to the groom's family. The baskets were carried by females of the bride's family and, again, about half

were returned to the bride's family. Although most of the gifts were for the groom, some contained the bride's personal items such as her clothing and jewelry. By accepting these gifts, the groom's family was welcoming the bride to their family. On her wedding day, when the bride moved into the groom's home, all her personal belongings would already be in place.

Although some ethnic Chinese customs are being combined with Western customs, one wedding ritual that is still practiced and seen as important in Chinese families is a special tea ceremony. On the day of the wedding, the bride and groom serve tea to both sets of parents while kneeling in front of them. This symbolizes paying respect to their parents and asking permission to get married. The couple also serve tea to other older relatives, such as aunts and uncles, as a sign of respect. In return, they are presented with jewelry or money wrapped in red paper as a sign of wishing the couple much happiness and prosperity together.

Engagement

An engagement to be married is an intermediate stage between courtship and marriage after a couple has announced the intention to marry. Engagement may be informal, at least for a while, during which time the two people have an understanding to marry. Marriage may still be too far off to make a formal announcement or the couple may want to further test their relationship. Because many engagements are broken, a couple is probably wise to be certain before making a formal announcement. Some couples move from informal engagement to marriage without ever formalizing the engagement period.

Engagement typically becomes a final testing of compatibility and an opportunity to make additional adjustments. If any problems in the couple's relationship have not been worked out before engagement, this period allows an additional opportunity to address them. The more things are worked out prior to marriage, the fewer adjustments and surprises arise afterward.

The engagement period also involves preparation for marriage itself. A most important part of this period, but one often neglected, is premarital education. A couple may choose to take advantage of premarital assessment and counseling. Marriage preparation may also include practical matters such as housing and banking arrangements.

The Wedding as a Religious and Civil Rite

Most marriages are performed under the auspices of a religious group that treats the wedding as a sacred rite. The Catholic Church considers marriage a sacrament, with special graces bestowed by God through the Church to the couple. The marriage bond is considered sacred and indissoluble. Both Judaism and Protestantism consider marriage a covenant of divine significance, sanctified by God and contracted between the spouses and the religious group with God as an unseen partner. Although lifelong marriage is considered ideal, divorce and remarriage are allowed under certain circumstances.

Any religious rite is rich in meaning and symbolism. Although the rites vary among different religious groups, they have certain things in common. Four parties are represented in the service: the couple, the religious group (clergy), the state (witnesses), and the parents (usually through the father of the bride). Each party to the marriage rite enters into an agreement, or covenant, with the other parties to fulfill his or her obligations so that the marriage will be blessed "according to the ordinances of God and the laws of the state." The religious group, through the clergy, pledges God's grace, love, and blessing. The couple make vows to each other "in the presence of God and these witnesses." The state validates the marriage once the requirements of the law have been fulfilled.

In the wedding rite, the two people indicate their complete willingness to be married; they make certain pledges to each other; they indicate to the clergy their agreement to abide by divine ordinance and civil law. They join hands as a symbol of their

While wedding practices vary among different religious groups, all have certain things in common. Four parties are normally represented in the religious wedding rite: the couple, the religious group, the state (witnesses), and the family.

Wedding Bill Blues?

The planning and purchasing for weddings is a billion-dollar industry. According to a 2012 survey by *Brides* magazine, the average wedding costs $26,989. That breaks down to some $6,500 for rings, $2,000 for the photographer, $1,300 each for her dress and the flowers, $500 for the cake, and $11,600 for the reception (Grossman 2012). Honeymoon not included!

Although about 90% of couples have a wedding budget, nearly one-third go over it. Some 62% of couples contribute to the wedding bills (36% pay the entire bill themselves)—using savings (72%) and credit cards (30%). Why are couples and their families willing to engage in emotional and financial excess to achieve such elaborate weddings?

In their book, *Cinderella Dreams: The Allure of the Lavish Wedding,* Otnes and Pleck (2003) examine the cultural ritual of the big, luxurious wedding and the tie between romantic love and

excessive consumption. They note the pervasiveness of weddings in the cultural landscape—in television shows, films, magazines, toys, and websites all devoted to weddings. Couples fall prey to their own fantasies of "fairytale" enchantment stoked by the media and wedding planners who offer irresistible choices for nearly everything.

The wedding industry is aware that not all couples can spend so lavishly and offers many lower-cost options. Beautiful dresses are available that cost hundreds (not thousands) of dollars, for example. Many couples have cocktails and hors d'oeuvres or a brunch buffet rather than a sit-down dinner. The use of seasonal flowers helps to reduce costs, as does eliminating unnecessary items such as special dance floors, up-lighting, and ice sculptures. Couples can call on talented family members to do flowers, favors, decorations, food, photography, or music.

Marriage Incentives

In the United States today, there is a focus on policy to help promote marriages. The underlying beliefs behind this are that: marriage benefits individuals and society; marriage is an essential part of a society that promotes the interests of children; and policy and education can encourage marriage and two-parent families (Government Mandated 2013; Rector and Marshall 2013). For example, some believe the traditional welfare policy could be construed as having disincentives for marriage. Specifically, in a married-couple family, both parents' earnings are considered in determining the amount of Temporary Assistance for Needy Families or food stamps they receive. But in the same family, if the couple are not married, the man's earnings would not be counted and they would receive a larger award. This led to the idea that some welfare recipients may have chosen to divorce or to remain unmarried to maintain or increase benefits.

In 2003, Congress passed the Personal Responsibility, Work, and Family Promotion Act, which called for equitable treatment of married, two-parent families and awarded grants to states for the promotion of healthy marriages. Funds could be used to support any of the following programs and activities: public advertising campaigns on the value of marriage; education in high schools on the value of marriage, relationship skills, and budgeting; marriage education, including parenting skills, financial management, and conflict resolution; premarital education for engaged couples; marriage enhancement training for married couples; divorce reduction programs that teach relationship skills; marriage mentoring programs that use married couples as role models; and programs to reduce the disincentives to marriage that may be inherent in welfare rules.

Proponents argue that policies that encourage marriage benefit children and reduce poverty. For example, Kickham and Ford (2009) cite a negative effect from marriage initiatives on divorce prevalence. At the same time, they note a positive association between divorce prevalence and childhood poverty.

Opponents of marriage promotion programs argue that they often do not tolerate same-sex or extended kinship family forms. Furthermore, single mothers are stigmatized as poor and single fathers as irresponsible (Government Mandated 2013).

Questions to Consider

What if states offered a monthly payment of $100 to encourage couples to get married or stay married? What might be the consequences of that policy?

To what extent should taxpayers fund marriage initiatives? Are there ways it might reduce tax expenditures in other areas?

Who should decide what information is included in a marriage enhancement program?

Should marriage enhancement programs be offered to anyone or just to low-income families on public assistance? Explain.

new union. Rings are a sign of eternity (having neither beginning nor end) and so symbolize the eternal nature of love. They are also a sign, seal, and reminder of the vows taken. The license is signed and witnessed as evidence that state law has been fulfilled.

Different religious groups have different rules and customs regarding weddings, but more and more clergy of all faiths are giving couples an opportunity to share in some of the decisions and even to help design their own service.

This chapter has discussed ways to define love and some of the components of different types of love. Love leads to selecting a life partner, and there is much research on how people make that choice, from filling subconscious psychological needs, to making sure the bills will always be paid, to working well and living happily together. Although there are many factors that predict which marriages will succeed, there are always indefinable, mysterious ways people connect and stay together against the odds. Many people today choose to live together, in some cases to share expenses or other practical needs and in other cases in preparation for marriage. This chapter considers a variety of factors for determining marriage readiness and discusses the many resources that are available to help people understand their feelings of love and to prepare for marriage.

Summary

1. Love is not a single concept, but has different dimensions. The five dimensions of love discussed here are romantic (emotional), erotic (sensual), dependent (need), friendship (companionship), and altruistic (unselfish).

2. The five elements of love discussed in this chapter are all important in the most complete love.

3. Researchers have identified various components of love. Sternberg described three components—intimacy, passion, and commitment—that he linked together as consummate love. Davis included three categories of love: passion, caring, and friendship. Moss and Schwebel specified five components of intimacy: commitment, affective intimacy, cognitive intimacy, physical intimacy, and mutuality.

4. Psychological intimacy involves two people, with each disclosing, listening, and developing attachment to the other. Intimacy lays the groundwork for growing love; sex alone cannot substitute for intimacy.

5. At all stages of life, adults endorse passion, friendship, and self-giving love as highly important. There are far more similarities than differences between the love attitudes of men and women.

6. Selecting a mate is one of the most important decisions we make during our lifetime. Various theories have been developed to explain the process: psychodynamic theories, needs theories, exchange theories, and developmental process theories.

7. Family background factors are important influences in a person's life and so must be investigated when choosing a mate. Marriages tend to be homogamous with respect to socioeconomic class, education, intelligence, and race.

8. Because of increasing racial, ethnic, and religious diversity in the United States, the numbers of interracial, interethnic, and interfaith marriages are growing. Even so, these marriages have unique challenges.

9. Research on individual traits focuses on physical, personality, and mental health factors. Physical illness puts stress on a relationship, making it less satisfying and less stable. Certain personality traits make it difficult for people to have a happy marriage. Neurotic behavior, mental illness, depression, and impulsivity have been shown to weaken marital stability and quality. High self-esteem and adequate self-concept are positively related to marital satisfaction.

10. Sociocultural and background factors that influence marital quality include age at marriage, education, income, occupation, social class, and ethnicity.

11. Individual personal characteristics that influence the quality of marriage include physical and mental health, self-esteem and self-concept, interpersonal skills, conventionality, and sociability. Age differentials are not a significant factor in marital quality, but marriage at a very young age is.

12. Marital compatibility is enhanced if spouses develop a high degree of consensus and similar attitudes and values about things that are important to them. It is also helpful if the spouses have compatible personal habits and similar gender-role expectations.

13. Danger signals in the choice of a mate include a substance abuse problem, personality and

character flaws, family problems, inability to get along with other people, lack of social skills, a lack of friends, and an unstable job history.

14. Rates of nonmarital cohabitation have increased greatly in recent years.

15. Cohabitation may mean different things to different people. A relationship may be a utilitarian arrangement, an intimate involvement with emotional commitment, a trial marriage, a prelude to marriage, or an alternative to marriage.

16. The transition from singlehood to marriage ordinarily takes place over several years. The transition is more successful if people are ready for marriage.

17. The following considerations may be significant in evaluating partners' marital readiness: age at the time of marriage, level of maturity, motivation for getting married, readiness for sexual exclusiveness, emotional emancipation from parents, and level of educational and vocational aspirations, as well as the degree of their fulfillment.

18. Getting married involves entering into a civil contract. Each state has its own laws regarding marriage. Laws include age requirements as well as restrictions on consanguinity, affinity, and on marrying people who are mentally disabled. Procedural requirements include obtaining a marriage license and having a civil or religious ceremony.

19. Couples can prepare for marriage through marriage education, assessment, and premarital counseling. A number of instruments, usually inventories, have been developed to help couples assess their relationship. Two widely used inventories are PREPARE/ENRICH and FOCCUS.

20. Rites of passage are ceremonies by which people pass from one social status to another.

21. Engagement is an intermediate stage between courtship and marriage. Engagement is a period of final testing of compatibility.

22. The wedding is a religious and civil rite, rich in meaning and significance. Four parties are usually represented: the couple, the religious group, the state, and the parents.

Key Terms

affinity

altruistic love

B-love

common-law marriage

companionate love

compatibility

consanguinity

conscious love

consummate love

dependent love

D-love

dopamine

endogamy

endorphins

erotic love

exogamy

filtering process

friendship love

heterogamy

homogamy

hypergamous union

hypogamous union

ideal mate theory

limerence

narcissistic love

needs theories

norepinephrine

oxytocin

parent image theory

propinquity

rites of passage

romantic love

vasopressin

void marriage

voidable marriage

Questions for Thought

1. Have you ever been romantically in love? Describe the relationship. Would it have been a sound basis for marriage? Why or why not?

2. Describe your views of the relationship between sex and love.

3. Compare friendship love with dependent love. Is one more important than the other in a satisfying marriage? Explain.

4. Describe and evaluate Fromm's view of altruistic love.

5. From your viewpoint, which psychodynamic theory of mate selection seems to be more valid: parent image theory or ideal mate theory? Explain the reasons for your choice.

6. Relate attachment theory to ideal mate theory.

7. Do opposites attract? Do opposites make compatible mates? Explain.

8. What are your views on interracial and interfaith marriages? Explain your views.

9. What things would you want to know and consider before you decided to enter into unmarried cohabitation?

10. How do you know someone is "the one for you?"

For Further Reading

Banks, R. R. (2011). *Is marriage for white people?* New York: Dutton. Provides a look into marriage and the black middle class. Why, despite increasing numbers of interracial marriage, do so many successful black women remain unmarried or marry down rather than marry out?

Interracial marriage challenges. http://www.marriage.about.com/od/interracial.

Johnson, R. M. (2001). *Three faces of love.* Dekalb: Northern Illinois University Press. Explores the meaning of the concept *love*, in all its varied senses, taking as a guide its use both in everyday speech and in the history of theoretical reflections on the subject.

Miller, R. R., and Browning, S. L. (Ed.). (2000). *With this ring: Divorce, intimacy, and cohabitation from a multi-cultural perspective.* Stamford, CT: JAI Press. Examines intimate relationships from both a sociological and a multicultural perspective.

Rott, M. P. P. (2001). *Love's revolution: Interracial marriage.* Philadelphia: Temple University Press. Breaks common stereotypes and provides insight as to why people from different racial backgrounds choose to marry one another as it presents the unique successes and failures found in mixed marriages.

Swidler, A. (2001). *Talk of love: How culture matters.* Chicago: University of Chicago Press. Discusses contemporary ideas about romantic love and the resilient culture of love.

The ten most important questions to ask before you get married. http://www.marriage.about.com/od/engagement/tenquestions. Links to other articles can be found at this site.

Qualities of a Successful Marriage

CHAPTER OUTLINE

Learning Objectives

Criteria for Evaluating Marital Success

- Durability
- Approximation of Ideals
- Fulfillment of Needs
- Satisfaction

Happy versus Unhappy Marriages

COPING FEATURE: *How We Appraise the Situation*

Sex and a Happy Marriage

CULTURAL PERSPECTIVE: *Polygamy*

Twelve Characteristics of Successful Marriages

- Communication
- Admiration and Respect
- Companionship

FAMILY STRENGTHS PERSPECTIVE: *Digging for Diamonds*

- Spirituality and Values
- Commitment
- Affection
- The Ability to Deal with Crises and Stress
- Responsibility

PERSONAL PERSPECTIVE: *Forgiveness*

- Unselfishness
- Empathy and Sensitivity
- Honesty, Trust, and Fidelity
- Adaptability, Flexibility, and Tolerance

AT ISSUE TODAY: *No Time for Love*

Premarital Predictors of Marital Quality

The Newlywed Years as Predictors of Marital Satisfaction

Why Some People Regret Their Choice of Mate

A QUESTION OF POLICY: *Covenant Marriages*

Summary

Key Terms

Questions for Thought

For Further Reading

LEARNING OBJECTIVES

AFTER READING THE CHAPTER, YOU SHOULD BE ABLE TO DO THE FOLLOWING:

- Discuss various criteria of a successful marriage, including durability, approximation of ideals, fulfillment of needs, and satisfaction.

- Identify what makes some marriages happy and others miserable, according to John Gottman.

- Discuss the relationship between sex and a happy marriage and what factors account for sexual satisfaction in a marriage.

- Identify and explain the 12 qualities of successful marriages that are described in the textbook: communication; admiration and respect; companionship; spirituality and values; commitment; affection; the ability to deal with crises and stress; responsibility; unselfishness; empathy and sensitivity; honesty, trust, and fidelity; and adaptability, flexibility, and tolerance.

- Describe potential problems in marriages that often can be seen before the couple actually gets married.

- Discuss how and why the newlywed years are important predictors of marital satisfaction.

- Explain why some people regret their choice of mate.

Sue and Ernest had been married for about 5 years when she began to be concerned that they were growing apart—she at her career, he at his, and little leisure time together. "I realized that we really had no hobbies that we enjoyed together."

She decided that although it was good that they had hobbies they enjoyed separately, they also needed to have something to enjoy together. Otherwise, she was concerned that their marriage was going to fade away. So she took action.

"My hobbies for the most part deal with clothing design and sewing and I did not think Ernest would develop an interest in any of those things," she laughed. If something were going to happen, she would have to take the first step. Sue made the commitment to get involved in Ernest's hobbies—flying and scuba diving.

"I took flying lessons and earned my pilot's license. We enjoy flying and we fly often. It is also safer when we fly now since we are both pilots.

"Scuba diving was much harder. Having my face in the water gives me a panic reaction. At the first lesson—those are in a swimming pool, you know—I had a panic attack and almost drowned! I had to force myself to continue with those lessons; I was so terrified.

"But I stayed with it and earned my certificate. I was so proud of myself. I'm glad I did it. Our son also dives—so we enjoy this as a family."

This book is about relationships: marital relationships, family relationships, and intimate relationships between unmarried persons. We begin here on a positive note by discussing how we can get along with other people and live together in a harmonious, fulfilling way. Living together happily is an art, requiring important qualities of character, a high degree of motivation, and finely tuned personal and social skills.

The focus in this chapter is on the marital relationship. However, most of the principles discussed here can be applied to all intimate relationships and to interpersonal relationships in the larger family unit.

Criteria for Evaluating Marital Success

Before we look at the various characteristics of a successful marriage, we must define a successful marriage. Four criteria of a successful marriage are discussed here—durability, approximation of ideals, fulfillment of needs, and satisfaction. However, it is difficult to define and discuss marital success because the concept is value laden and subjective. For example, he/she might judge the marriage as successful because it is conflict free and has lasted 20 years; she/he might judge the same marriage as not so successful because their relationship is not as close as she/he wants.

Also, much of the early research on marital success and happiness was based on small, nonrepresentative samples such as white, middle-class couples. Culture and family values play a big part in defining both success and happiness in a marriage. For the purpose of discussion, instead of adopting a single criterion, we discuss multiple characteristics of a successful marriage, keeping in mind the subjective nature of this topic.

Durability

What constitutes a successful marriage? One measure that has been used is durability. Many people would say that the marriage that lasts is more successful than the one that is broken. In many cases, marital stability and marital quality do go together. However, duration alone does not indicate the overall quality of the marriage because some people will remain married despite frustration, conflict, and misery. Some spouses have not spoken to each other, except through the children, for decades. For most people, then, marital success involves criteria more important than the number of years a couple stays together.

Approximation of Ideals

Another way of evaluating marital success is the extent to which the marriage approximates a couple's ideals or fulfills their expectations. When asked, "What is your concept of a good marriage?" one student replied,

> A good marriage is one in which two people love one another, get along well, in which they think alike on important issues, share common goals and interests, enjoy each other's company and have fun together, in which they are really good friends, are able to talk to one another to work out problems.

Other students add to this fairly typical reply, describing a good marriage in these terms:

One that allows you to be yourself and to be completely honest with one another.

Fifty–fifty, where partners share everything.

One that allows you freedom to do your own thing and to grow.

One where your partner is your best friend.

Still other students add different characteristics that are important to them. Marital success, in their view, is determined by the extent to which idealistic expectations are fulfilled.

One problem with this way of assessing the success of a marriage is that some people have unrealistic expectations. The standards by which they judge their marriage are impossible to achieve. To be met, expectations must be realistic, not just romantic fantasy.

Fulfillment of Needs

Another measure of marital success is whether the marriage makes a sufficient contribution to individual needs, including the following:

- **PSYCHOLOGICAL NEEDS**—for love, affection, approval, and self-fulfillment.
- **SOCIAL NEEDS**—for friendship, companionship, and new experiences.
- **SEXUAL NEEDS**—for both physical and psychological sexual fulfillment.

This criterion requires the partners to be aware of each other's needs and to be partly able to fulfill them. Note the emphasis here on partial fulfillment. Marriage can never meet every need. Some needs will be met outside of the marriage itself, through one's job, friendships, hobbies, and recreational pursuits, for example. However, a successful marriage makes an acceptable contribution; any marriage that does not has failed in the eyes of most couples.

Two cautions must be added. First, it is helpful if need fulfillment is mutual. When one person does all the giving and the other all the receiving, the giver becomes exhausted. Second, mutual need fulfillment is most possible if needs fall within the limits of realistic expectations. A highly dependent, possessive person, for example, may demand so much love and approval that no one could possibly satisfy those needs. In this case, the marriage might fail, not because of the unwillingness of the giving person but because of the unreasonable demands of the insatiable partner.

Satisfaction

Much of the research on marriage success measures marital satisfaction: the extent to which couples are content and fulfilled in their relationship. According to this view, marital success is defined as the extent to which both partners in the relationship are satisfied that it has met reasonable expectations and mutual needs. This definition recognizes that there are individual differences in expectations and need requirements, so what satisfies one couple might not satisfy another. Marital satisfaction includes marital quality, marital adjustments, and marital happiness (Heyman, Sayers, and Bellack 1994; Koenig 2006). It is important that *both* partners be satisfied. Sometimes one partner is content with a relationship and the other is ready to file for divorce.

There are degrees of success. No marriages live up to *all* expectations and fulfill *all* needs *all* the time. Furthermore, successful couples strive for improvement. Their marriages are in the process of becoming, and few ever feel they have completely arrived. Instead, if they are satisfied with the progress they have made, they judge their effort as successful.

Happy versus Unhappy Marriages

What makes some marriages happy and others miserable? John Gottman has been studying this question for decades and has found the pattern of communication in couples to be important in marital happiness. In happy couples, when one partner makes a positive statement, it is reciprocated in a positive manner; in unhappy couples, partners often have no immediate response to a positive statement. In happy couples, after one partner makes a negative statement, the other offers no immediate response; in unhappy couples, both continue to reciprocate negatively. This **negative affect reciprocity** is a consistent characteristic of distressed couples (Gottman 1998; Gottman and Silver 2012).

negative affect reciprocity A pattern of communication in unhappy couples whereby partners respond negatively to each other's statements.

The number of years a couple stays together is not the most important indicator of marital success. Qualities such as empathy, respect, companionship, and affection are but a few of the characteristics of a successful marriage.

Some messages can be interpreted either positively or negatively. For example, the statement "Stop interrupting me, please" may be an attempt to repair an interaction, but it may also be said with irritation. Gottman believes that in a happy marriage there is a greater probability that the listener will focus on the repair aspect of the message and respond by saying, "Sorry, what were you saying?" In an unhappy marriage, there is a greater probability that the listener will respond only to the irritation in the message and say something like, "I wouldn't have to interrupt if I could get a word in edgewise." In this case, the message does not repair any part of the communication pattern, and the negativity bounces back and forth (Gottman 1998).

Gottman also sees differences in how spouses in happy and unhappy marriages view positive and negative actions of a partner. In a happy marriage, if one partner does something negative, the other partner tends to think that the negativity is fleeting and situational. For example, negative behavior may be attributed to a tough day at work or a bad mood, as opposed to a fixed characteristic of the individual. Thus, the negativity is viewed as temporary and the cause as situational. In an unhappy marriage, however, the same behavior is likely to be interpreted as a sign of inconsideration, selfishness, and indifference and as internal to the partner.

Interestingly, happy couples interpret positive behavior as internal to the partner, whereas unhappy couples are likely to interpret the same positive behavior as a fluke and to believe that it will not last (Gottman 1998).

The "demand–withdraw" (or "pursuer–distancer") pattern is another characteristic of unhappy marriages (Ebrahimi and Kimiaei 2014). With this pattern, it is usually the woman who raises and pursues issues and the man who avoids the discussion and tends to withdraw. Research suggests that in unhappy marriages with high negative affect, men withdraw emotionally and women do not (Gottman and Levenson 1988).

Furthermore, in two longitudinal studies, Gottman (1994) found that it was not anger that led to unhappy marriages and reliably predicted divorce, but four processes that he called "the Four Horsemen of the Apocalypse": criticism, defensiveness, contempt, and stonewalling, or listener withdrawal. Other researchers added belligerence—a behavior that is provocative and designed to escalate conflict ("What can you do if I do go out tonight? What are you gonna do about it? Just try to stop me")—as a likely predictor of divorce. These findings were replicated in a study that found that contempt, belligerence, and defensiveness are common negative behaviors during conflict and lead to unhappy marriages (Gottman et al. 1998).

In a national study of 21,501 married couples, family science researcher David Olson (2000) found that happy and unhappy couples differ in five key areas: (1) how well partners communicate, (2) how flexible they are as a couple, (3) how emotionally close they are, (4) how compatible their personalities are, and (5) how they handle conflict. Happy couples identified those five areas (communication, flexibility, emotional closeness, compatibility, and conflict resolution) as strengths; unhappy ones did not. For example, about 75% of happy couples agreed on the high quality of their communication, whereas only 11% of unhappy couples did. Similarly, 75% of happy couples agreed that they can change and adapt when necessary, whereas only 20% of unhappy couples believed this to be true. Olson believes that spouses must feel they can adapt to change and feel close and connected to have a happy marriage. Other researchers and therapists agree (Koenig 2006; Pamensky 2005).

How We Appraise the Situation

Whenever we are faced with a life challenge, crisis, or conflict, the type of emotions we feel and how we respond to the challenge are greatly influenced by our appraisal of the situation. This principle is emphasized in the cognitive-appraisal model (Lazarus and Folkman 1984; Papalia et al. 2009). The appraisal is our perception or definition of the situation. The appraisal we make might be compared to writing the prologue to a play where we tell the audience what kind of play it is—one of hope and success or one of despair and defeat. Consider the example of a man whose fiancée has broken their engagement. Following are some different appraisals of the situation:

Appraisal	Emotions
I can't live without her. She is all that matters in my life. Why did she break this off? What will I do?	Depression Panic
I've been good to her and invested so much in this relationship. How could she do this to me? She is a real witch.	Anger Hurt
I still love her. This is not what I wanted for us. I miss her, but I will feel better after a while. Maybe there is someone better out there for me	Disappointment Hurt Hope

We have the power to choose an appraisal that will result in more suffering and stress or a more positive, reasonable appraisal that will give us hope—even if it is only a glimmer.

D. Olson also identified five other areas that affect a couple's happiness: (1) the sexual relationship, (2) the choice of leisure activities, (3) the influence of family and friends, (4) the ability to manage finances, and (5) agreement on spiritual beliefs. He advises partners to pay the same sort of attention to the relationship that they did when they were dating and to praise each other for positive things, instead of focusing on what bothers them (D. Olson 2000).

Sex and a Happy Marriage

What is the relationship between sex and a happy marriage? Can people be happily married without a satisfying sex life? Certainly, the positive expression of sexuality contributes to marital satisfaction in particular and to life satisfaction in general. Healthy sexuality is meant to be a blessing, not a problem.

However, what is acceptable to one couple may not be to another. Human beings differ in their sexual needs, preferences, habits, and aims. Some couples want intercourse every day; others would find this frequency unacceptable. If both partners are satisfied with their sex life, it can contribute in a positive way to their overall happiness; but if the partners disagree, or if one or both are frustrated or unhappy with their sex life, it can significantly reduce or even destroy relationship satisfaction.

Questions often asked are "How frequently do couples have intercourse?" and "What is the relationship between frequency and sexual satisfaction?" It is always dangerous to play the numbers game, because any figure mentioned is going to be disappointing to someone. But, as a starter, let's examine what some couples do.

In general, men experience sexual desire somewhat more frequently than do women, although

CULTURAL PERSPECTIVE

Polygamy

A polygamous family is a single family unit based on the marriage of one person to two or more mates. If a man has more than one wife, a polygynous family is formed. If a woman has more than one husband, a polyandrous family is formed. Polyandry is rare. Polygyny, although illegal in the United States, is legal in many parts of Africa, the Middle East, and Asia.

Polygynous families reside in several forms of living arrangements. In some communities, the entire family unit lives in the same household. In other communities, each wife has a separate household and the husband rotates among them. It is also possible that two wives share one household, whereas other wives live separately. As in other living arrangements, family members sometimes get along and sometimes do not.

The religion of Islam permits a man to have up to four wives, but certain conditions must be met for him to take more than one wife. According to Islam, a man must be willing to treat all wives equally and fairly. This means spending equal amounts of time with each wife, as well as equal amounts of money. He must not show preference to one wife over another and must love them all the same. He must also adequately provide food, clothing, and shelter for each wife and her children. These requirements are difficult to follow, both in emotional and in economic terms; many men cannot afford a second wife even if they desire one. Thus, even in those parts of the world where polygamous relationships are permitted and legal, most marital relationships are monogamous.

---

there is a considerable variation among individuals. In studies and surveys over the past three decades, married couples consistently indicate that they are having sex one to three times a week (on average). This is especially true for younger couples and those married less than three years (Bernstein 2013; Fisch 2009; Greenblat 1983; T. W. Smith 1994).

Typically, most couples start out marriage engaging in intercourse more frequently (several times weekly), but then the incidence begins to decline (several times monthly) and they settle into their own individual patterns. However, couples report that affection, love, tenderness, companionship, and physical closeness continue to be strong needs.

Declining health may be an issue for some older men and women with regard to their sexual activity, but for many individuals 60 and older, sexuality remains an important part of their lives. A survey conducted by the American Association of Retired Persons revealed that among 60- to 74-year-olds, 30% of men and 24% of women were having sex at least once per week, and 25% of those 75 years old and older were having sex at least once per week. Although frequency drops with age, more than 60% of men and women who have regular partners have intercourse at least once or twice a month. Older

Americans believe that better health would do more to enhance their sexual pleasure than any other life change, but more than half of men and 85% of women say that their sex lives are unimpaired by illness—even those 75 and older (Jacoby 1999).

Another important consideration is how partners feel about the frequency with which they have intercourse. In cases of marked differences in sexual appetite or fading desire, ignoring the problem only creates tension in the relationship. In a study looking at sexual desire, individuals who were motivated to meet their partner's sexual needs were better able to sustain sexual desire over time (Muise et al. 2013). Researchers called this sexual communal strength, that willingness to engage in sexual activity even when not especially interested. Having sex is viewed as a way to enhance intimacy and feel closer (positive outcomes for the relationship) rather than just to please oneself (Muise et al. 2013). If partners cannot work things out themselves, they may need help from a sex therapist.

Sex has long been intertwined with feelings of intimacy in committed relationships. It involves trust and communication by both partners and, as such, their sexual functioning can directly affect their relationship functioning. Although some research seems to indicate that women place more emphasis on sexual intimacy than men do (with men's focus being on sexual satisfaction), other researchers believe men's emotional need for sex has been underestimated (Bernstein 2013). Sexual interaction provides an opportunity for a man to express feelings of tenderness and closeness through actions (rather than words) and thus is an important emotional outlet for him (Bernstein 2013).

Twelve Characteristics of Successful Marriages

Numerous research studies have sought to describe the qualities of successful marriage. Other chapters in this book discuss family background factors that influence marital success, such as attitudes toward intimacy and sex, gender roles, values, patterns of communication, age, ethnicity, and length of acquaintance. Thus, in this chapter we are concerned with a mixture of personality characteristics of the partners and characteristics of the relationship itself, which together constitute qualities important to marital success. Twelve of these important qualities are described in the following subsections.

Communication

According to numerous studies, good communication is one of the most important requirements in a successful marriage (DeFrain and Asay 2007; Ebrahimi and Kimiaei 2014; Koenig 2006; Mahin et al. 2012; Pamensky 2005; Ruffieux, Nussbeck, and Bodenmann 2014; Stinnett and Stinnett 2005, 2010). Couples who communicate effectively report that they do the following:

We talk about everything.

We talk about our problems and work them out.

We're able to share our feelings.

We each try to listen when the other is talking.

We don't believe in holding things in.

We talk about things and it clears the air.

Talking helps us to understand one another and keeps us close.

When marriages are troubled, it is often because of poor communication. Poor communication results in increasing anger, tension, and frustration at the difficulty in getting others to listen and to understand. One wife commented,

I try to talk to him, but he doesn't seem to care. Finally, I get so upset that I scream and holler at him and start to cry. He just walks away and says to me, "I'm not going to talk to you if you holler at me." There's no way to get through to him. (Counseling notes)

Effective communication involves the ability to exchange ideas, facts, feelings, attitudes, and beliefs so that a message from the sender is accurately heard and interpreted by the receiver and vice versa. However, not all communication is helpful to relationships. Communication can be destructive; saying critical, hurtful things in a cold, unfeeling way may worsen a relationship. One member of a couple who openly shares negative feelings the other cannot handle may increase tension and alienation. Thus, politeness, tact, and consideration are required if communication is to be productive. If an emotionally difficult subject is approached calmly, the level of conflict can be reduced. In happy and strong families, both spouses express fewer negative and more positive emotions in their overall interaction, particularly at the start of a discussion (Gottman 2000b; Schrodt 2009). The issue of

Can this couple talk about anything? Are the two able to share their feelings? Does either one hold back from the other? Answers to such questions about communication in a relationship can tell a lot about how long the relationship is likely to last.

communication is so important that a part of Chapter 9 is devoted to a detailed discussion of it.

Admiration and Respect

One of the most basic human needs is for acceptance and appreciation. The most successful marriages are those in which these needs are partly fulfilled in the relationship. Two people who like each other, who admire and support each other in their respective endeavors, who are proud of each other's achievements, who openly express appreciation of each other, and who build each other's self-esteem are fulfilling their emotional needs and building a satisfying relationship (Stinnett and Stinnett 2005, 2010). Respect in marriage encompasses respect for individual differences and recognition that each is worthy to be loved and each is a unique and important human being (Curran 1983; Koenig 2006).

Partners who are able to meet these needs are usually emotionally secure people themselves. They do not have to criticize or demean another to build themselves up. They like expressing appreciation and giving compliments. Their approval is not conditional, requiring the partner to do certain things before it is granted. Rather, their approval is what psychologists call **noncontingent reinforcement**. It

is **unconditional positive regard**. They do not try to change a spouse but are able to accept him or her as he or she is. If they have complaints, they voice them in private, not in front of other people. They are not threatened by a competent, high-achieving spouse and so avoid destructive competition. They like themselves and each other and express their approval in word and deed.

Companionship

One important reason for getting married is companionship. Successful married couples spend sufficient time together—and it is quality time. The partners enjoy each other's company, share common interests and activities, and have a lot of laughs together. They are interested in each other's hobbies and leisure-time preferences. Furthermore, they try to be interesting companions to each other.

Research indicates that partners who share interests, who do things together, and who share some of the same friends and social groups derive more satisfaction from their relationship than do partners who are not mutually involved (Knox and Schacht 2016). It is important for couples to spend enough quantity of time together to have good quality time together (Glorieux, Minnen, and vanTienoven 2011). This is because it is not only the

---

Digging for Diamonds

Research of several thousand strong families throughout the United States and 26 countries around the world has consistently found one of the important qualities that makes families strong is the expression of appreciation. Appreciation is deeply and fundamentally important to our welfare. Mark Twain said, "I can live for two months on a good compliment" (Stinnett and Stinnett 2005).

Marriage success researcher Dr. John Gottman has found that it takes five compliments or positive responses to undo the damage of one criticism or negative comment. Couples who maintain a ratio of 5:1 positives to negatives are more likely to stay together happily.

Members of strong families recognize and fulfill this need for appreciation by giving sincere compliments and by building one another's self-esteem and confidence. They are adept at recognizing one another's strong points and validating them.

Members of strong families are, in a sense, good diamond hunters. South African diamond hunters sift through thousands of tons of dirt looking for a few tiny diamonds. They know that what they are going to find in all that dirt more than compensates their efforts. Too often in unhappy families people do just the opposite—sweeping aside piles of "diamonds" while eagerly seeking for "dirt" (Stinnett and Stinnett 2005).

amount of time spouses spend together that is related to marital satisfaction, but also the quality of the relationship they enjoy when they are together. Marital satisfaction increases when communication is high and positive during shared time (Stinnett and Stinnett 2005). Research shows that attending to relationships—that is, putting effort into them—is important in maintaining satisfaction (Koenig 2006; Pamensky 2005). Women often attend to relationships by thinking and talking about them, whereas men often attend to relationships by sharing activities and spending time together (Acitelli 2001; Bernstein 2013).

It is unrealistic to expect partners to do everything together or to have all their interests in common, however. Most people want some separateness in their togetherness; they want to be able to do some things with their own friends. Problems arise when partners continue to enjoy most of their social life with friends they knew before marriage rather than spend time together. Some couples drift apart simply because they seldom see each other. Curran (1983) goes so far as to state, "Lack of time together may be the most pervasive enemy the healthy family has." Marital interaction and happiness seem to go together. An acceptable degree of interaction contributes to marital happiness, and marital happiness tends to increase the amount of interaction (Zuo 1992).

Spending enough time together is a major challenge for today's couples and families. This challenge requires active effort, planning, and commitment. Research indicates that having children decreases the amount of time couples spend together. And dual-earner couples spend the least amount of time together (Glorieux, Minnen, and van Tienoven 2011).

Friendship, like companionship, is important in marriage. John Gottman has studied more than 2,000 couples by conducting extensive interviews and videotaping couple interactions. In one study (Gottman 2000b), he found that for women, the vital ingredient in improving sex, romance, and passion in marriage was to increase the sense of friendship. Women need a deep sense of connection to feel passionate, which means that the husband must get to know his wife on a profound level and must express genuine affection toward her. Examples of this type of connection are being able to define a spouse's life dreams; showing respect, affection, and small gestures of appreciation rather than criticizing; and attempting to connect through

Successful married couples share common interests and activities; they enjoy each other's company.

jokes or playful comments. For men, the key to improving sex, romance, and passion was found to be conflict reduction; arguing activated men's "fight or flight" response and left them feeling threatened and not eager for sex.

As with most friendships, having fun together is also a key component of good marriages. It is essential to have fun in a marriage, to make fond memories, to be confident that the marriage will last, and to have a persistent commitment to the relationship (Arp et al. 2000; Koenig 2006; Stinnett and Stinnett 2005, 2010). Fun has been understudied and underestimated in its ability to increase passion and overall satisfaction in a long-term relationship. In addition, research has shown that the pursuit of novel, exciting activities serves to enhance relationship satisfaction in marriage by helping couples grow both individually and relationally (Aron et al. 2000; Stinnett and Stinnett 2005, 2010).

noncontingent reinforcement Unconditional approval of another person.
unconditional positive regard Acceptance of another person as he or she is.

However, P. Schwartz (2000) cautions that the goal of having your spouse be your best friend is difficult to achieve and is not appropriate for everyone. As wonderful as friendship is, most people do not select a partner the same way they select a friend, and marriage does not work the same as friendship does. Most people do not spend nearly as much time with their friends as they do with their spouses, nor do casual friends negotiate such daily challenges as living together, maintaining a sexual relationship, rearing children, and sharing finances.

People also differ on how close a companion they want a spouse to be. When one spouse wants close companionship and the other does not, it can become a source of tension and conflict. David and Vera Mace (1974), pioneers in the marriage enrichment movement in the United States, likened the marriage relationship to the dilemma of two porcupines settling down to sleep on a cold night. If the porcupines get too close, their quills prick each other. If they move too far apart, they get cold. So the porcupines shift back and forth, first together and then apart, until they find a position in which they can be warm with a minimum amount of hurt.

Spirituality and Values

Another factor contributing to successful marriage is shared spirituality, morality, and values (D. Olson, DeFrain, and Skogrand 2014; Koenig 2006; Stinnett

Successful couples commonly share spiritual activities and similar beliefs. Studies find such shared values to be a consistent predictor of marital adjustment, regardless of how liberal or conservative the couple's beliefs are.

and Stinnett 2005, 2010). Successful couples share spiritual activities; they have a high degree of religious orientation and similar beliefs and values that are manifested in religious behavior.

Religious couples indicate that their religion contributes to their marriage in a number of ways. They derive social, emotional, and spiritual support from their faith. In some cases, involvement in a religious community provides friends and activities for the couples to share. Religious faith also encourages marital commitment through the value that is placed on the marital bond and through spiritual support in times of difficulties. Some people point to the increased intimacy that results in sharing something as profound as one's religious faith. Many couples turn to their faith for moral guidance in making decisions, dealing with conflict or anger, and forgiveness (Pamensky 2005; Stinnett et al. 2000; Stinnett and Stinnett 2005, 2010).

Commitment

Successful marriage requires a sincere desire to make the marriage work and the willingness to expend time and effort to ensure that it does (Knox and Schacht 2016). Some couples encounter so many serious problems in their relationship that one wonders how the marriage will ever succeed. But, through extraordinary motivation and determination, they overcome their obstacles, solve their problems, and emerge with a pleasing relationship. Other couples give up after little effort; perhaps they really did not want to be married in the first place, so they never worked at it.

Commitment, rather than satisfaction or investment, is the strongest predictor of relationship persistence (Rusbult et al. 2001). Commitment is regarded as having three components: intention to persist, psychological attachment, and a cognitive orientation to being in the relationship for the long term. Interventions for couples often include components that focus on these cognitive and affective dimensions (Rusbult et al. 2001). Sahlstein and Baxter (2001) made the important point that relationships change over time, often encompassing a number of contradictory elements. Periodically defining levels of commitment and trust in close relationships contributes to marriage maintenance and enhancement.

Marital success is more attainable if the commitment is mutual. One person cannot build a relationship or save a marriage, no matter how much he or she tries. Koenig (2006) points out that a marriage takes work and it takes both people to make it work. People are not going to put forth their best effort if a partner is not equally involved.

One of the important questions is: Commitment to whom and to what? The commitment is really threefold:

1. **The commitment is of the self, to the self.** This involves the desire to grow, to change, and to be a good marriage partner. Rabbi Aryeh Pamensky (2005) describes the purpose of marriage as "a lifetime to constantly provide emotional intimacy to your spouse, thereby uncovering your true self and, ultimately, your unique purpose for being created." Some people who come for marriage counseling want a partner to change, but they are unwilling to change themselves or to assume personal responsibility for making things better. None of us can really change other people, but we can change ourselves. It is not easy, but it can be done.

2. **The commitment is to each other.** When people say "I do" in a marriage ceremony, they make a personal promise or pledge to each other.

3. **The commitment is to the relationship, the marriage, and the family.** Mace and Mace (1980) define commitment as a willingness to support "ongoing growth in their relationship." When children are involved, the commitment goes beyond the couple relationship to include the whole family unit.

Stanley and Markman (1992) make a distinction between personal dedication and constraint commitment. *Personal dedication* refers to the desire of an individual to maintain or improve the quality of a relationship for the joint benefit of the couple. It is evidenced by a desire not only to continue in the relationship but also to improve it, to sacrifice for it, to invest in it, to link personal goals to it, and to benefit the partner as well as oneself. Gordon (2012) describes it as the "want to" part of commitment. She describes personal dedication at work when couples facing great stressors take comfort in the fact that they are together no matter what—"in the same foxhole, side by side, fighting the same battles."

In contrast, *constraint commitment* refers to forces that compel individuals to maintain relationships regardless of their personal dedication to them.

Constraints may arise from either external or internal pressures, and they promote relationship stability by making termination of the relationship more costly economically, socially, personally, and psychologically. For example, constraints would include what a person would lose if the relationship terminated, such as all the time invested in the relationship as well as a house, money, children. Attitudes of family, friends, or a religious organization can also serve as constraints. Gordon (2012) calls this the "have to" part of commitment.

On the one hand, in certain situations (abuse, for example), constraint commitment may work to keep someone in a relationship too long. On the other hand, constraint commitment can keep a couple together long enough to work to make it better, as Gordon (2012) explains:

> I worked with one couple in which the husband had an affair. They worked and worked in therapy to make their relationship better, and the husband tried very hard to make the necessary changes to help his wife trust him and feel safe with him again. They were successful and ended up having a relationship that was better than they ever had experienced. At the end, the wife told us that she only initially stayed because without him, she had no health care and she was a cancer survivor. . . . However, she said she was glad she had to work on the relationship because it gave them both the time and motivation to develop this newer and stronger relationship.

But what happens if there is conflict between commitments? Is the commitment to the family or to one's partner more important? Mae West famously described marriage as an institution but asked, "Who wants to live in an institution?" Indeed, who does, unless it serves the needs of those in it? Some people are able to work out troubled relationships because marriage is sacred to them and they want to preserve the family unit. In so doing, they may find individual and couple fulfillment. For other people, however, commitment to save the marriage may come at great personal cost.

Another basic challenge with commitment is maintaining a sense of autonomy while also experiencing a sense of relatedness to one's partner (Rankin-Esquer et al. 1997). Partners in successful marriages have mastered the art of losing themselves

A. Individuals without union

B. Loss of separate identities in relationship

C. Unity and individualism

FIGURE 6.1 Different Types of Relationships

in their relationship without losing their sense of self. This requires a well-developed identity and high self-esteem. Figure 6.1 depicts three types of relationships. In Figure 6.1A, two people maintain their individual identities but make little effort to achieve oneness as a married couple. In Figure 6.1B, two people lose their separate identities, which become swallowed up in the relationship. In Figure 6.1C, there is sufficient commitment to form a union, but enough separateness for each to maintain a sense of self.

MARITAL RITUALS Most married people need privacy and time to pursue their own interests as individuals. They also need time together as a couple, and they need time to be with their children as a whole family. Keeping a healthy balance is not easy. For example, when children are young, it is easy to become absorbed in taking care of them and thus neglect the marital relationship.

Couple rituals can play a vital role in nurturing a relationship. Families have long engaged in rituals that define who they are and provide a sense of cohesion. Rituals for couples are just as crucial as family rituals and contribute to the success of the

marital relationship. Doherty (2001) defines *marital rituals* as social interactions that are scheduled moments that are mutually decided on, repeated, and coordinated and that have positive emotional significance. These rituals include things such as a loving greeting, a routinely planned "date night," 20 minutes for morning coffee, or an after-dinner walk and conversation. Such marital rituals maintain connection between partners, which in turn helps hold marriages together in times of stress. When couples do not make time for their relationship amid the hectic schedule of everyday life, the marital relationship gets neglected. Marriage needs a commitment of time to maintain its well-being and a mindfully maintained ritual can do that.

Affection

Most married partners expect they will meet each other's need for love and affection. This need varies from couple to couple, depending on the way the partners are socialized. Some people have a higher need for emotional intimacy than others. But most expect their needs to be met in their marriage (Koenig 2006; Pamensky 2005; Stinnett and Stinnett 2005, 2010).

Several related factors are important. Spouses should agree on how to show affection and how often. Some people want a lot of physical contact: hugging, kissing, cuddling, caressing. Others are satisfied with an occasional kiss. Some people are uninhibited in sexual expression and desire playful sex. Others are more restrained. There also may be differences in the desired frequency of intercourse. In successful marriages, couples are able to work out such differences.

Words that express warmth, appreciation, endearment, and approval; that raise low spirits; and that boost damaged egos can be as essential as physical contact and sexual intimacy. Spouses involved in long-term happy marriages often point to each other's admirable qualities, as opposed to their flaws, and appreciate the pleasure they find in their relationship without taking it for granted (Pamensky 2005; Ruffieux, Nussbeck, and Bodenmann 2014; Stinnett and Stinnett 2005, 2010).

Interestingly, although fulfillment of affectional and sexual needs is important to marital success, strong feelings of romantic love are not a requirement. Romantic love is an important factor in emotional attraction and in motivating couples to want to be together. In successful marriages, love continues to grow, but it changes over the years, with fewer components of romance and stronger bonds of attachment and affection.

The Ability to Deal with Crises and Stress

Problems are a normal part of life for all couples, both those who achieve marital success and those who do not. Research indicates that stress can have a negative effect on couples' interactions and that external stressors can lead to lower marital satisfaction through "stress spillover." Interestingly, research evidence also suggests that an existing, habitual pattern of positive couple interactions can serve as a protection against the negative effect of stress depletion (Karney and Neff 2013).

One of the factors that distinguishes couples who achieve marital success from those who do not is that spouses who have successful marriages are able to solve their problems and manage stress in a creative way. One of the characteristics of strong families is that family members turn to one another for strength and assistance. This enhances family unity, cohesiveness, and commitment (Stinnett and Stinnett 2005, 2010).

Successful couples also have a greater tolerance for frustration than do unsuccessful couples. They are more emotionally mature and stable—perhaps in part by nature. Some recent research indicates that some of our emotional reactivity is determined by our genes (Haase et al. 2013). Individuals who inherit two short alleles of the 5-HTTLPR gene (about 17% of the population) tend to be most unhappy when the emotional climate in the marriage is negative or most happy when there are many positive emotions and humor. The other 83%, who get mixed alleles or two long ones, are less bothered by the emotional climate.

Successful couples have also learned healthy, constructive ways of dealing with anger, rather than taking it out on other family members. Similarly, persons who have a positive attitude toward life are more likely to maintain satisfying marriages (Gottman and Silver 2012; Koenig 2006; Karney and Neff 2013), whereas moodiness, abrasiveness, and nervousness are associated with relatively high levels of interpersonal negativity and low levels of marital satisfaction (Caughlin, Huston, and Houts 2000).

Degrees of depression are also a strong predictor of marital quality, and depression both arises from and creates marital dissatisfaction. Persons who are unhappy in their marriage report relatively high levels of depression, and depressed persons and their spouses report stressful, unsatisfying marriages. Depressed persons typically lack energy, appear not to care about anything, lose interest in everything (including sex), and may become irritable. As a result, they lose jobs and stop doing household chores and caring for the children; they may also criticize and complain. The nondepressed partner typically tries to pick up the slack, but eventually becomes exhausted and frustrated, then angry and resentful (Ahrons 2004; Doheny 2009).

Stress comes in a variety of forms and plays a key role in marital satisfaction. Research has shown that the more stressful the environment, the higher the rate of divorce (Cohan and Cole 2002), and exposure to stressful life events is related to an increase in marital aggression (Cano and Vivian 2001). Increases in stress also have been shown to increase negative perceptions of relationship problems (Karney and Neff 2013). An example of a major stress for many families is time management. Many couples spend long hours outside the home in work-related activities. This could include working more, a long commute, or two parents working full-time. These factors increase stress and decrease a couple's coping resources by placing greater demands on them and by introducing new challenges for balancing work and family life.

Story and Bradbury (2004) have outlined two primary paths to reduce the negative effects of stress on marriage. The first is to provide information and skills that enable couples to understand and manage stress. One strategy to deliver this would be courses or training in marriage enrichment and communication skills. Many premarital and marital programs address dealing with common stressors in relationships. It is important to remember that just being aware of stress and its effects on relationship functioning is an important component of any intervention.

The second path outlined is to work toward shaping environments or circumstances to limit the common stressors that families encounter. For example, government could give tax incentives to businesses to provide on-site, affordable, high-quality child care. Or businesses could allow flexible work hours and allow employees to work from home on occasion. For many families, this would reduce the strain of balancing work with child care (Patten 2015b; Story and Bradbury 2004) and hopefully reduce the overall stress in their lives.

Couples and families can enhance their ability to deal more successfully with stress by doing the following:

- Maintaining a pattern of positive interactions and utilizing a resource of family strengths such as commitment, good communication, or appreciation (Karney and Neff 2013; Stinnett and Stinnett 2010).

- Developing productive coping strategies and the ability to appraise situations in a positive, rational, hopeful manner (Insel and Roth 2013; Papalia, Olds, and Feldman 2009).

- Establishing an emotional atmosphere that is positive and healthy (Ruthig, Trisko, and Stewart 2012).

- Developing supportive and empathetic, compassionate relationships (Nicholas et al. 2009).

- Seeking professional help for continuing or recurring depression; this may include medication, individual therapy, and couple therapy (Doheny 2009).

- Utilizing the family strength of spiritual faith and spiritual wellness (D. Olson, DeFrain, and Skogrand 2014; Labbe and Fobes 2010; Stinnett and Stinnett 2010).

Agreement about what must be done in the household and by whom directly contributes to a successful marriage.

- Participating in leisure time activities together and simply having fun as a family (Hornberger, Zabriskie, and Freeman 2010).

Responsibility

Responsibility involves being accountable for one's own behavior. Successful marriage depends on the mutual assumption, sharing, and division of responsibility in the family. Typical complaints brought to marriage counselors include the following:

My partner never does anything around the house. I do everything, inside and outside work both.

My partner is irresponsible in handling money.

My spouse doesn't like to work. He'd rather be out with friends partying and having a good time.

My spouse doesn't ever clean the house. She knows that if she doesn't do it, eventually I'll get it done.

My partner doesn't show any interest in taking care of the children. He feels that because he brings home a paycheck, he can leave everything else to me.

I have to make all the decisions and plans for our social life.

In marriages in which couples report a high degree of satisfaction, two conditions exist in relation to the division of responsibility. First, the partners feel there is an equitable division of labor (Koenig 2006). In situations in which one is working 100 hours a week and the other works little, the working spouse rightfully resents the uneven distribution of responsibility. Women in particular are dissatisfied when they perceive unfairness in the performance of household chores and in the spending of money. Consider this account:

Ed worked hard all his life building up a cleaning business. He was very successful and decided to retire at age 60. He spends his time playing golf at the country club and playing cards at the Elks club. Since the family needs the money and the business needs attention, his wife Edith spends her days managing the company. She resents deeply the fact that she is still working and he isn't.

Forgiveness

Often when conflict occurs, partners may hold grudges and never forgive each other for whatever the conflict was about. They may even bring up old grievances in current conflicts—generating renewed feelings of retaliation or hostility. This snowball effect sparks other ineffective communication methods (sarcasm, name-calling, blaming, etc.) and thus makes the resolution of conflict ever harder.

Research indicates that forgiveness intervenes and offsets this negative, ineffective pattern of conflict resolution. Forgiveness is associated with more successful conflict resolution. This relationship is found to exist longitudinally or over time. As you might expect, forgiveness is associated with marriage satisfaction (Fincham, Beach, and Davila 2007).

Numerous studies reveal than an inequitable division of household and child-care responsibilities causes conflict in families. Women still do the majority of housework, even with increased participation in the workforce and changes in gender roles. The research on household task performance provides little evidence of egalitarianism in marriage when it comes to housework because employed women do far more domestic work than men. For example, research has found that even when spouses work the same number of hours in the workforce, women typically perform considerably more domestic and child-care labor than do men (Bureau of Labor Statistics 2015; Fottrell 2015). This lack of equity is a major source of dissatisfaction for many women. Among dual-earner couples, the division of labor is one of the most important factors affecting women's mental health, and it becomes even more important when children are involved because of the added child-care responsibilities (A. E. Goldberg and Perry-Jenkins 2004). Men's comfort with the current arrangement of women doing more of the household and child-care labor is seen as one of the major impediments in achieving equality (Singleton and Maher 2004).

Second, in successful marriages, gender-role performance matches gender-role expectations. Many couples have set ideas about who should perform what tasks. Thus, if a man expects his wife to perform traditional roles in the family—caring for children, taking care of the home, attending to his needs—but she is more interested in pursuing her career, conflict develops. If the woman expects her spouse to be the primary breadwinner and an all-around handyman at home and he does not live up to her expectations, she may become dissatisfied.

Unselfishness

Ours is an age of individualism in which many try to find happiness through self-gratification and narcissistic **selfism**. Selfism in marriage lessens each partner's responsibility for the success of the relationship. Social exchange theory emphasizes that people seek relationships in which the cost–benefit ratio is satisfactory and fair. From this perspective, decreased investment on the part of one spouse decreases the likelihood that the other will receive sufficient rewards to continue the relationship. The result is marital instability, because relationships continue only when each partner feels he or she is receiving what is deserved and expected.

It is not surprising, therefore, that the most successful marriages are based on a spirit of mutual helpfulness, with each partner unselfishly attending to the needs of the other, as well as to his or her own needs. One woman explained:

> My husband is the most generous, giving man I have ever known. He will give you the shirt off his back. Every day he does so many little things for me. He insists on bringing my coffee in the morning. He helps around the house all the time. He never seems to think about himself. He's too busy thinking about the rest of us.

It is not evident in the quotation, but the woman was just as giving and unselfish as her spouse. They

selfism A personal value system that emphasizes that the way to find happiness is through self-gratification and narcissism.

had a wonderful marriage, primarily because the unselfishness was reciprocal.

Empathy and Sensitivity

Empathy refers to the ability to identify with the feelings, thoughts, and attitudes of another person (Wampler and Powell 1982). It is the vicarious sharing of the experiences of another person. Kagan and Schneider (1987) call this ability **affective sensitivity** and describe its development in five phases:

- **PHASE 1: PERCEPTION.** Developing empathy begins with contact and interaction during which someone perceives the thoughts, feelings, memories, anticipations, and aspirations of another person and the emotional tones associated with them.

- **PHASE 2: EXPERIENCING.** The observer resonates to, or vicariously experiences, the emotions of the other.

- **PHASE 3: AWARENESS.** Awareness is the process of acknowledging to oneself that one has perceived and resonated to the emotions of another individual.

- **PHASE 4: LABELING.** Awareness is acknowledged verbally; the observer speaks of having sensitivity to what another person has experienced.

- **PHASE 5: STATING.** This step requires a person to communicate that he or she has perceived another person's feelings. Communication may be nonverbal, such as touching, or verbal. The purpose of this final phase is to let the other person know that one understands.

It is understandable, then, that empathy is an important ingredient in a successful marriage (Long, Angera, and Carter 1999). An empathetic person is someone who listens, understands, and cares, thus improving communication.

Simpson, Ickes, and Orina (2001) describe empathic accuracy as a relationship maintenance strategy in which one partner accurately identifies the thoughts and feelings of his or her partner. One study examined 48 romantically involved couples who participated in an empathy training program (Long, Angera, and Carter 1999) whose purpose was to increase the expression of empathy among partners. The researchers found not only that couples increased their expression of empathy with a partner but also that the change in empathic expression

was positively related to relationship satisfaction. That is, when individuals improve their abilities to express empathy (and emotional support), the partners' satisfaction with the relationship improves (Koenig 2006; Pamensky 2005).

Honesty, Trust, and Fidelity

The old-fashioned virtues of honesty, trust, and fidelity are important ingredients in contemporary successful marriages. Sincerity, truthfulness, faithfulness, and trust are the ties that bind people together. Partners know they can accept each other's word, believe in each other, and depend on each other to keep promises and to be faithful to commitments that are made. One young woman comments:

> I never have to worry about my husband. When he tells me something I know it's true. He's a very sincere, up-front person. He keeps his word. If he promises the kids something, he never disappoints them. He travels a lot, but I know he's faithful to me. He isn't the kind of man to sneak around. If two people can't believe in one another, or depend on one another, they don't have much of a relationship in my opinion.

When two people first start going out together, one of the things each seeks to discover is whether the other is sincere about the relationship. If one person begins to doubt the honesty and faithfulness of the other, he or she will feel increasingly insecure and vulnerable. In fact, the future of the relationship may be threatened; true intimacy requires honesty. Persons who feel vulnerable in a relationship tend to become guarded and defensive; they do not share openly about themselves. The relationship stays superficial and/or ends. Once trust is broken, developing it again involves a willingness to forgive. When one partner does something that hurts the other but is truly sorry for what has happened, the relationship can be rebuilt only if the person who has been hurt is willing to forgive.

Adaptability, Flexibility, and Tolerance

Spouses whose marriages are successful are usually adaptable and flexible. They recognize that people differ in their attitudes, values, habits, thought processes, and ways of doing things. They recognize that their preferences are not necessarily the only

No Time for Love

Marriage counselors hear couples complaining over and over, "We never spend any time together," or "We don't talk to each other," or "We don't have any interests in common," or "We've drifted apart." These comments come from couples who in the beginning of their marriages said the primary reasons for getting married were companionship and love.

Obviously, something has gone wrong. Usually, one of several things has happened:

- One or both spouses spend most of their time on the job, with little left over for the family.

- One or both spouses have separate friends and spend most of their leisure time with their own friends rather than with joint friends as a couple.

- One or both spouses have individual hobbies and leisure time activities that they pursue separately. If these activities take up most of the leisure time, the couple are separated during leisure hours. One man described his situation: "My wife is a marathon runner. She works out several hours a day and works full-time in addition. It doesn't leave us any time together as a couple." (Counseling notes)

- The spouses spend most of their free time attending movies, concerts, or athletic events, and they spend little time alone together just talking. They are in each other's company, but they are not finding real intimacy based on emotional closeness.

- One or both spouses spend their free time with the children rather than devoting some of it to being together as a couple. One man complained, "Since the baby was born, my wife's whole life has been wrapped up in Sarah. She has no time for me."

- One or both spouses do not enjoy being together. One embarrasses the other (by talking too loud, for example) or they cannot seem to talk without arguing. One man explained, "When we go to another couple's house, my wife totally monopolizes the conversation. She interrupts. She turns the conversation around to something she's interested in. It's very embarrassing." (Counseling notes)

In each of these situations, the couple does not spend enough quality time together. When the partners are together, their activities are not conducive to companionship. Although people in intimate relationships need time for themselves, they also need time for the "we" in the relationship. Planning and scheduling this time in advance, as one often does with other priorities, can help ensure that companionship needs in a marriage will be met. For example, some couples hire a babysitter at regular intervals to go out on a "date." These dates can be set up several weeks in advance to make sure that both partners' schedules are clear, as opposed to being together as a couple only in whatever time is left at the end of the day.

---

viable ones, so they accept individual and group differences. They do not insist that everyone be a carbon copy of themselves.

They recognize as well that life is not static, that situations and circumstances change as we go through life. They are willing and able to adapt to changes in circumstances, understanding that change is inevitable. They grow as their spouses evolve and adjust their expectations of the relationship as necessary.

Adaptability and flexibility require a high degree of emotional maturity. People must be secure enough to let go of old thoughts and habits that are no longer functional or appropriate. But to let go

affective sensitivity Empathy, or the ability to identify with the feelings, thoughts, and attitudes of another person.

requires some confidence that the new will work as well as the old. Flexible people welcome new challenges because they offer a chance to grow and develop. Marcus (1983) wrote,

> One person's capacity to adapt to another requires a degree of security. . . . Instead of feeling threatened by flexibility, they . . . feel proud of their capacity to be flexible. Because marriage requires a series of adaptations, it is of itself a stimulus toward achieving mature adult status. (120)

The most difficult people to deal with are perfectionists, who have one rigid standard by which they judge everyone and everything. Perfectionists have no tolerance for imperfection. They have impossibly high standards for themselves and others and are inflexible in the way they think. Since they believe that they are always right and others are wrong, they insist that any changes in a relationship must be made by someone else. As one man said, "When my wife and I discuss anything, I'm right 99 percent of the time, and she's wrong" (Counseling notes). Such self-important and narrow thinking makes it extremely challenging to work out problems and build a healthy relationship.

Premarital Predictors of Marital Quality

Potential problems in marriage frequently can be seen before the couple actually gets married. What happens in the premarital relationship is often a good predictor of what will happen in a marriage. In an extensive review of more than 60 years of research on premarital predictors of marital quality, Holman et al. (2001) presented the following conclusions: (1) premarital background, beliefs, and behaviors have a continuing influence on marital functioning, even after several years of marriage. (2) Multiple premarital factors such as family of origin, characteristics of the individual, social connections, and couple interactional processes are prominent in influencing later marital quality, either directly or indirectly. (3) Some premarital predictors are more important than others and have a more lasting influence, with family-of-origin background factors (e.g., parent–child relationships) being perhaps the most important.

Of all the family-of-origin issues that could be addressed, the parent–child relationship, the parents' marriage, and the parents' mental health and/or dysfunctional behavior are the most important. Improving these will tend to lead to the most improvement in the probability of adult children's marital success. Thus, the most important things parents can do for the future marital happiness of their children are to maintain a strong marriage; create a pleasant, happy home environment; and be involved in their children's lives. Practitioners must help more parents understand what is happening in their own marriage, in their home, and in their relationship with their children (Holman et al. 2001).

Teaching and intervention should occur before the wedding to improve the likelihood of having a high-quality marriage. Several intervention principles can help practitioners work with couples to this end. Such interventions can help people (1) restructure, come to terms with, or let go of unpleasant issues from the family-of-origin experiences; (2) improve their emotional health and self-esteem and their valuing of marriage and family life; (3) revise negative values, attitudes, and beliefs about marriage; (4) increase social network support, such as the premarital support of the marriage from parents and friends; and (5) improve communication and conflict resolution skills in their relationship and increase perceived similarity and consensus. Intervention strategies such as these will help increase the probability of marital success (Holman et al. 2001).

Gender differences must be taken into account in premarital interventions. For example, family-of-origin factors play a greater role in predicting marital satisfaction six years into marriage for females than for males. A woman's family-of-origin experience has more impact on her husband's marital satisfaction than does his own family-of-origin experience (Holman et al. 2001).

Many more intervention principles and a variety of methods for teaching these principles can be found in the book *Premarital Prediction of Marital Quality or Breakup* (Holman et al. 2001). In addition, examples of some programs and materials that teach about marital preparation have been cataloged by the Coalition of Marriage, Family, and Couples Education. A description of these programs and materials can be found on the Internet at www.smartmarriages.com.

The Newlywed Years as Predictors of Marital Satisfaction

Typically, a couple's feelings about each other going into a marriage are positive and those positive feelings characterize the newlywed years. Yet despite all good intentions, many marriages end in disappointment and bitterness after a few years. So how does such loving affection going into a marriage turn so negative?

To understand this shift, Neff and Karney (2005) examined newlyweds' global relationship evaluations. They found that not all spouses base their overall adoration for their partner on an accurate perception of their partner's specific qualities. Couples may be madly in love, but if they accurately understood their feelings toward specific partner behavior (e.g., being supportive, need for control), their feelings of adoration may not be as high. The authors conclude that love grounded in reality appears to be stronger than love without that accuracy and typically translates to a happier and more successful marriage.

In another examination of this question of why many marriages start off with good feelings and intentions but end in disappointment, Neff and Geers (2013) discovered that newlyweds who were high in *dispositional* optimism did exhibit more positive problem-solving behaviors on days when they had relationship conflict and had fewer declines in marital well-being at the end of a year. However, newlyweds who were high in *relationship-specific* optimism did not demonstrate positive problem-solving behaviors on days when they had relationship conflict and had sharper declines in marital well-being. Their findings suggest the possibility that too much optimism about the relationship may be a vulnerability if it predisposes newlyweds to assume that everything will be OK without any effort on their part.

What happens in the first 2 years of marriage is important in predicting marital satisfaction over the long run. Huston et al. (2001) examined connections between the first 2 years of marriage and marital satisfaction and stability after 13 or more years of marriage. They examined whether newlyweds who were highly affectionate were more likely than other couples to sustain a satisfying marriage

and whether newlyweds who bickered were likely to overcome their initial difficulties or were destined for an unhappy marriage.

In examining these questions among newlywed couples, they found that changes in the marriage over the first 2 years influenced the fate of the marriage after 13 years. For those who stayed married, differences in the intensity of newlyweds' romance, as well as the extent to which they expressed negative feelings toward each other, predicted whether couples were happy later. For those who divorced, intensity of romance and expression of negative feelings toward each other influenced how long the marriage lasted prior to separation. An abatement of love, a decline in overt affection, a lessening of the belief that one's spouse is responsive, and an increase in ambivalence about the relationship distinguished couples headed for divorce from those who established a stable marital bond. The researchers found that most of the differences between couples who stay married, but differed in marital happiness, existed at the outset of marriage rather than developing later (Huston et al. 2001). In a longitudinal study, Ruffieux, Nussbeck, and Bodenmann (2014) also discovered that the best predictor of marital satisfaction and stability 10 years later was relationship satisfaction at the beginning of the study.

Why Some People Regret Their Choice of Mate

There are a number of reasons people regret their choice of a mate. One reason is *they do not really get to know the other person*. People who are in too much of a hurry to get married may not give the relationship enough time to develop. Getting to know another person usually takes several years of being together under varying circumstances. Sometimes, the types of activities a couple share are not conducive to developing rapport and communication. They may participate in a whirl of social activities, spending all their time with other people or going to movies, concerts, or sporting events. The activities are fun, but the relationship remains superficial because of minimal interpersonal interaction.

Some people choose the wrong partner because *they live in a fantasy world*. Their concept of marriage has been gleaned from romantic movies and the

Covenant Marriages

Concern over the high rates of divorce and single-parent families led some to consider ways to help make marriages stronger and divorce less common. As a result, a few states have created what is called a covenant marriage, which binds the couple to stricter legal standards than a traditional marriage would. For example, covenant marriages require couples to have premarital counseling. Divorce under covenant marriage requires proof that there was abuse, abandonment, adultery, addiction, or felony imprisonment. Before a divorce can be granted, couples are required to take reasonable steps to resolve problems such as going to marital counseling or separating for at least 2 years. Already-married couples may at any time change their original marriage to a covenant marriage.

At this time only three states have covenant marriage—Louisiana, Arkansas, and Arizona. Several others have considered it but it did not pass. And only a small number of couples in these states (about 1% or less) opt for covenant marriage.

Proponents believe covenant marriage offers couples an opportunity to demonstrate a stronger commitment to their own marriage. Covenant marriage is optional; therefore, it is not bound on anyone else. There is also an aim of strengthening marriage by having couples give serious consideration to the seriousness of marriage and their readiness for it (required premarital counseling)

and to encourage couples who are experiencing marital difficulties to try to repair their relationship (through counseling) rather than just dissolving it.

Opponents argue that making divorce harder to obtain (by requiring proof of adultery or abuse followed by a lengthy waiting period, for example) does disservice to persons who are caught in an abusive relationship. Requiring "grounds" for divorce also means that lawyers will be involved and divorce will be more expensive and also more adversarial (Stritof 2015; Weisman 2014).

Questions to Consider

What benefits does covenant marriage hold over traditional marriage? What are the disadvantages? Consider the viewpoint of the husband, the wife, and the children.

What reasons might impel a couple to form a legally binding covenant marriage? What reasons might another couple have for deciding against a covenant marriage?

To what extent is covenant marriage a reasonable matter for public policy? Could couples privately commit to this higher standard, as many do, without laws governing it? Explain.

Who benefits the most from a covenant marriage?

Would you consider a covenant marriage for yourself? Why or why not?

---

media; marriage represents an escape from a humdrum existence. Their parents may have a troubled marriage, but it will not happen to them. They overlook the faults of their partner and the problems in their relationship. Love will conquer all, and they will live happily ever after. Their views of marriage are completely unrealistic.

Other people choose the wrong partner because *they look for the wrong qualities in a person.* They emphasize physical characteristics and attractiveness without regard for important personal qualities. They do not stop to think about whether their

partner is a good person. They are also looking for the wrong things in their relationship—perhaps for excitement instead of stability. They are thrilled with new relationships that are emotionally arousing, forgetting that the high level of emotions will subside and that only more permanent qualities will sustain the relationship.

Some people make the wrong choice because *they confuse sex with love.* They enjoy each other sexually whenever they are together. Their relationship focuses on sexual passion, and so they assume they are much in love. But, as explained in Chapter 5, theirs is an incomplete love. Other components, such as friendship and care, are needed to sustain the relationship over a period of time.

Another common reason for marrying the wrong person is *a poor self-image and lack of self-esteem*. Such people cannot believe that anyone desirable would really love them, so they settle for less than they might. They cannot believe they are worthy of love, support, and nurturance, so they accept unhappiness.

Some people *succumb to pressures to marry*. One pressure is from their biological clock. One woman remarked, "I'm 32 years old and I want to have children. I'm marrying Charlie because I'm afraid I might not find someone else in time. I don't really love him, but I can't wait any longer" (Counseling notes). Other people have a now-or-never attitude. They are afraid if they do not get married to this person, they may never have another chance.

Another pressure is that of pregnancy. The number one reason for marrying while still in school is pregnancy. Yet the prognosis of success for the marriage, particularly if the partners are in their teens, is poor. Most such marriages simply do not work out.

Pressure to marry also can come from relatives and friends. When two people have gone together for some time, friends begin to ask, "When are you two going to get married?" Or a cohabiting couple may be pressured by parents to marry.

There are also *unconscious, neurotic needs that people try to fulfill by marrying*. For example, someone who has an unconscious need to feel needed marries someone who is immature, who has problems with alcohol or drug abuse, or who cannot hold a job. In other situations, people feel uncomfortable with successful people, so they marry someone to whom they can feel superior as a means of boosting their own ego. Others boost their ego by choosing a partner they feel will enhance their image in others' eyes—for example, a "trophy wife." Unconscious feelings and needs may draw neurotic people to *play "games."* The partners may fill roles such as rescuer–victim or pursuer–pursued. The people may be drawn to marry their partner in the game or transaction.

Although some people do select the wrong partner or select their partner for the wrong reasons, new behaviors that can result in a happy and successful marriage can be learned when people are committed to the relationship. It is most important that the marriage partners be happy to consider their marriage successful, regardless of whether every objective criterion for a happy marriage is met.

Summary

1. A successful marriage has been defined as one that endures, approximates ideals, fulfills mutual needs, and satisfies both partners.

2. Marital success reflects the extent to which both partners in a relationship are satisfied that it has fulfilled reasonable expectations and mutual needs.

3. In happy marriages, when one partner makes a negative statement, the other partner is likely not to respond immediately, whereas in unhappy marriages, both partners continue to reciprocate negatively.

4. In happy marriages, if one partner does something negative, the other partner tends to think that the negativity is fleeting and situational. In unhappy marriages, however, the same behavior is likely to be interpreted in terms of overall inconsideration, selfishness, and indifference.

5. The "demand–withdraw" pattern is characteristic of unhappy marriages. In this pattern, it is usually the woman who raises and pursues the issues and the man who attempts to avoid the discussion and to withdraw.

6. The presence of criticism, defensiveness, contempt, and stonewalling on the part of one or both partners is characteristic of unhappy marriages.

7. The positive expression of sexuality contributes to marital satisfaction. Typically, most couples start out marriage engaging frequently in intercourse, but then the incidence begins to

decline and they settle into their own individual patterns. If both partners are satisfied with their sex life, it can contribute in a positive way to their overall happiness; but if the partners disagree, or if one or both are frustrated or unhappy with their sex life, it can significantly reduce relationship satisfaction.

8. Twelve characteristics of successful marriage are communication; admiration and respect; companionship; spirituality and common values; commitment; affection; the ability to deal with crises and stress; responsibility; unselfishness; empathy and sensitivity; honesty, trust, and fidelity; and adaptability, flexibility, and tolerance.

9. Potential problems in marriage often can be seen before the couple actually gets married. What happens in the premarital relationship is often a good predictor of what will happen in a marriage.

10. What happens in the first 2 years of marriage is important in predicting marital satisfaction over the long run. An abatement of love, a decline in overt affection, a lessening of the belief that one's spouse is responsive, and an increase in ambivalence about the relationship have been shown to distinguish couples headed for divorce from those who establish a stable marital bond.

11. People regret their choice of partner for a number of reasons: they do not get to know the other person; they live in a fantasy world; they look for the wrong qualities in a person; they confuse sex with love; they have a poor self-image and low self-esteem; they succumb to pressures to marry; or they have unconscious, neurotic needs that they are trying to fulfill by marrying.

Key Terms

affective sensitivity

negative affect reciprocity

noncontingent reinforcement

selfism

unconditional positive regard

Questions for Thought

1. How would you describe a successful marriage, and how is this description different from or similar to the definitions discussed in the textbook?

2. For single students brought up in two-parent families: did your parents have a successful marriage according to your views? Why or why not?

3. For single students brought up in a one-parent family: select a married couple that you know well. Do they have a successful marriage according to your views? Why or why not?

4. For married students: would you define your marriage as successful? Why or why not?

5. Select the four most important qualities for a successful marriage according to your views, discuss them, and tell why you feel they are so important.

For Further Reading

Betchen, S. (2005). *Intrusive partners—Elusive mates: The pursuer–distancer dynamic in couples.* New York: Brunner–Routledge. Explores the traits and tendencies of the pursuer and the distancer in relationships.

Doherty, W., and Carlson, B. (2002). *Putting family first: Successful strategies for reclaiming family life in a hurry-up world.* New York: Holt. Focuses on strategies to help families spend more quality time together.

The website for Focus on the Family, http://www.focusonthefamily.com, offers a Christian perspective on many issues related to marriage and family, such as "American beliefs that weaken marriage."

Golden, L. B. (2000). *Case studies in marriage and family therapy.* Upper Saddle River, NJ: Merrill. Utilizes actual cases to discuss therapy practices for couples and families.

Gottman, J., and Silver, N. (2012). *What makes love last?* New York: Simon & Schuster. Argues that marital stability and satisfaction result from teachable conflict-management skills.

Gray, J. (2000). *Mars and Venus in touch.* New York: HarperCollins. Explores how communication between men and women can increase passion and intimacy in a relationship.

http://www.marriage.about.com has a number of articles about marriage and marriage success, for example: "Building a healthy marriage," "Marriage maintenance," or "Points of conflict."

Noller, P., and Feeney, J. (2002). *Understanding marriage: Developments in the study of couple interaction.* New York: Cambridge University Press. Presents academic research on how and why good marital relationships develop.

Olsen, D., and Stephens, D. (2001). *The couple's survival workbook: What you can do to reconnect with your partner and make your marriage work.* Oakland, CA: New Harbinger. Intends to help individuals change the interactions with their partners.

Marital Relationships over the Family Life Cycle

CHAPTER OUTLINE

Learning Objectives

Marriage and Personal Happiness

The Family Life Cycle
- Data on Family Life Cycles
- Changes in Marital Satisfaction
- Gay and Lesbian Families

Adjustments Early in Marriage
- Marital Adjustment Tasks

COPING FEATURE: *Half Full or Half Empty?*
- Problems during Three Early Stages

Adjustments to Parenthood
- Parenthood and Stress
- Fatherhood and the Life Course

CULTURAL PERSPECTIVE: *Individualism versus Familism*

Adjustments during Middle Adulthood
- Marital Adjustments
- The Postparental Years

Adjustments during Late Adulthood
- Developmental Tasks

FAMILY STRENGTHS PERSPECTIVE: *Go with the Flow*
- Marital Satisfaction

- Divorce
- Parent–Adult Child Relationships

Widowhood

PERSONAL PERSPECTIVE: *Widowhood*

AT ISSUE TODAY: *Who Cares for Older People?*

A QUESTION OF POLICY: *Nationalized/Universal Health Care*

Summary

Key Terms

Questions for Thought

For Further Reading

LEARNING OBJECTIVES

AFTER READING THE CHAPTER, YOU SHOULD BE ABLE TO DO THE FOLLOWING:

- Describe the basic stages of the family life cycle in an intact marriage and in a family in which there is divorce and remarriage.

- Discuss the various trends in marital satisfaction, from the honeymoon stage to late adulthood.

- Summarize the major marital adjustment tasks and problems early in marriage.

- Explain how gay and lesbian families are different from and similar to other types of families.

- Describe the adjustments to parenthood.

- Identify the major adjustments during middle adulthood, including the postparental years.

- Summarize the major adjustments during late adulthood, including divorce.

- Discuss problems of family relationships for elderly and widowed individuals, including alternatives for caring for older people.

"I started my adult life with a bang, you might say. My parents were moderately well-to-do and gave me a good start in my own business. It flourished, I married a wonderful woman, and we had a couple great kids. Everything looked rosy for ten years or so. Then the economy went sour at about the same time I had made some risky investments. One by one, those went down the tubes. In the end, we lost everything—business, house, cars.

"My wife and I sat out by the lake one night and talked until the sun came up. I remember feeling stripped of everything—as if I'd been robbed. 'Why try again?' I asked her. 'We may work and work only to lose it.' We struggled with that one a long time and finally decided we were thinking wrong. We'd been so occupied with making money and the daily 'busy-ness' of life that we'd allowed our faith and people to be crowded out of our lives.

"We decided we needed to enjoy life—because it is a precious gift, to cherish our family and friends, and to help other people. The investments of time and effort we have made in family and friends, in charitable work, and in improving ourselves can never be lost. Things in the heart and mind can never be taken away."

Marriage relationships are constantly changing, developing, and growing. Sometimes relationships are frustrating and troublesome; other times they are rewarding and vital.

The adjustments that people face early in marriage are unique because the relationship is new. The adjustments during middle age relate to the aging process and to children growing up and leaving home. Late adulthood requires establishment of new roles in the family as a couple, as older parents of adult children, and as grandparents. Elderly people must make peace with their past and accept life as they have lived it.

Most people face the prospect of separation from a spouse for some part of their lives. A small percentage of older people divorce; more live out their lives as widows or widowers. Being alone requires special adjustments that couples do not face.

Each phase of life has its own joys and its own problems. Knowing what some of these are helps people pass through each stage more successfully.

Marriage and Personal Happiness

Most married people would agree that the quality of their marriage has a strong effect on their satisfaction with life. An unhappy marriage can decrease happiness in other aspects of life, such as work and friendships. People who are having severe marital problems may not be able to eat properly or to sleep; they may become depressed.

Marital relationships are seldom static. Partners may report a period of harmony during which everything seems fine, only to have everything fall apart to the point of divorce. Even the most stable, loving couples have some ups and downs in their relationship. What is important, however, is the general quality of the relationship over time and the extent to which partners report satisfaction with it.

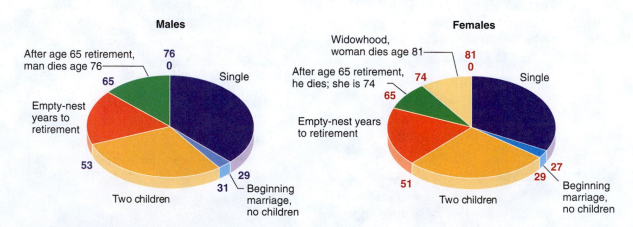

FIGURE 7.1 Family Life Cycle—Intact Marriage

Note: Data from Statistical Abstract of the United States, *2014. U.S. Bureau of the Census. http://www.census.gov.*

The Family Life Cycle

One of the most helpful ways of examining marital relationships over time is in terms of various phases of the family life cycle. The **family life cycle** consists of the phases, or stages, over the life span and seeks to describe changes in family structure and function during each stage. The cycle also can be used to show the challenges, tasks, and problems that people face during each stage, as well as the satisfactions derived. It is important to note that adults continually revise their view of their lives, prompted by individual maturation and the social, cultural, and historical influences that shape their commitments, beliefs, and life pathways (Kail and Cavanaugh 2016).

Data on Family Life Cycles

Figure 7.1 shows the typical traditional family life cycle of spouses in an intact marriage. The ages of the spouses are median ages for the U.S. population. Thus, the man is married at 29 and the woman at 27. They wait 2 years before having the first of two children spaced 2 years apart. The man is 53 and the woman 51 when the youngest child is 20 and leaves home. The empty-nest years until retirement are to age 65 for both. The man dies at age 76, whereas the woman lives to age 81, spending her last years as a widow (U.S. Bureau of the Census 2014).

The family life cycle is different for divorced couples. Figure 7.2 shows separate cycles of spouses who marry, have two children, and divorce; each remarries a spouse with two children. The children reside with their mother after the divorce. Note that the median age of first marriage for couples who divorce is about 2 years younger than that for couples who never divorce. The man is 34 and the woman 32 when they divorce; their children are 3 and 5 years old. He remarries 4 years later, at age 38, to a woman who is 35 with two children 6 and 8 years old who reside with her and her new spouse. The man is 52 when his youngest stepchild is 20 and moves out of the house. He has 13 empty-nest years until he retires at age 65; he dies at age 76.

The woman (32 at the time of the divorce, with children who are 3 and 5) remarries 3 years later. She is 49 when her youngest child is 20 and moves out of the house. She has 16 empty-nest years until she retires at age 65; her husband dies at age 76. She spends the last 8 years of her life as a widow (U.S. Bureau of the Census 2014).

The quality of marriage has a strong effect on personal happiness and life satisfaction. Since the marital relationship is seldom static, most couples will experience periods of both instability and harmony.

As stated previously, the family life cycle is different for everyone, and these graphs do not represent the life cycle of all types of families. However, they do give us a sense of what happens to the majority of people in the United States. Exceptions to the two basic life cycles include those who remarry more than once, those who have much larger families, those who choose not to marry but to cohabit instead, gay and lesbian families, and single-parent families.

Changes in Marital Satisfaction

How does marital satisfaction change over various phases of the family life cycle? The answer depends

family life cycle The phases, or stages, of the family life span, each of which is characterized by changes in family structure, composition, and function.

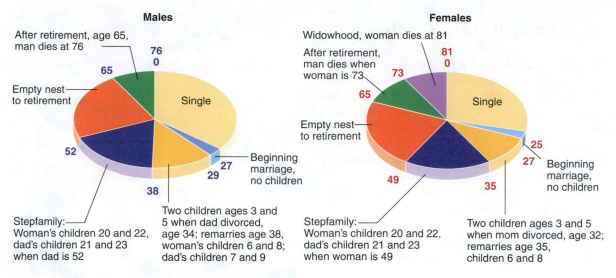

FIGURE 7.2 Family Life Cycle—Marriage, Divorce, Remarriage

Note: Data from Statistical Abstract of the United States, *2014. U.S. Bureau of the Census. http://www.census.gov.*

on the particular family. Family patterns differ. The most helpful model of what happens over long-term marriage has been outlined by Weishaus and Field (1988), who describe six patterns of marital satisfaction in long-term marriages:

1. **Stable/positive.** These partners have stable but not static marriages, maintaining moderately high to high satisfaction and generally positive affection and interaction throughout the years.

2. **Stable/neutral.** These partners never experience emotional closeness but marry for other reasons. They are generally comfortable with each other and are without excessive conflict.

3. **Stable/negative.** These partners experience primarily negative emotions throughout marriage, manifested as hostility or indifference. Lack of positive feeling is apparent. There is little joy, only the feeling that duty has been performed.

4. **Curvilinear.** For these partners, satisfaction is high early in marriage, drops during the middle years, and rises again after the children have left home.

5. **Continuous decline.** These partners experience gradual and more or less continuous eroding of marital satisfaction.

6. **Continuous increase.** These partners derive increasing satisfaction as the years pass.

Gay and Lesbian Families

Most of the research and discussion of gay and lesbian families has focused on how they differ from more traditional family forms. However, they share many similarities with other family types and in many respects are like other families. As Laird (1993) observed,

> They must negotiate their relationships with the larger community and their families of origin, forging social networks and establishing boundaries between themselves and the outside world, as well as negotiating relationships and roles, developing problem-solving strategies, mediating conflicts, and marking boundaries inside the family. They must decide who will do what, when, where, and how in order to meet the particular needs of the family as a whole and of individual family members, whose interests at times may conflict or compete. Like all families, they face possibilities for conflict over divisions of labor, the use of money, space, and time, their sexual and intimate relationships, issues of closeness and distance, dominance and subordination, child-rearing ideologies, and so on. (308)

However, Laird (1993) went on to point out that gay and lesbian families differ from others in at least

Some couples breathe a sigh of relief when the last child leaves home, and many couples report a notable increase in marital satisfaction.

two important ways. First, many of these families are made up of a couple (no children), although one-third of lesbian and one-fifth of gay family households do include children from previous heterosexual relationships, by reproductive assistance such as artificial insemination, or by adoption.

Second, these families are often stigmatized as inappropriate family forms, which presents them with unique challenges. For example, although gay and lesbian single parents face the same issues of finances, time constraints, and dating as most heterosexual single parents, the prospect of forming new long-term relationships is complicated by society's judgment of gay and lesbian families. Gay and lesbian families with children from previous marriages deal with complicated issues similar to those of all stepfamilies. However, there have been instances in which custody or visitation rights were not granted to a parent on the sole basis of his or her sexual orientation. This kind of discrimination will likely decrease as a result of the Supreme Court decision in 2015 allowing same-sex marriage in all states.

Several research studies suggest a third difference: some types of same-sex relationships appear to be more prone to break up than heterosexual marriages. Balsam et al. (2008) reported that same-sex couples without formalization (civil union) had the highest rate of break-up, followed by same-sex couples with civil unions, and well ahead of heterosexual married couples. Lau (2012) reports a similar trend. This sort of upheaval could be a factor in progression through the family life cycle. After controlling for marriage and marriage-like commitments, however, Rosenfeld (2014) found the comparable rates of break-up for same-sex and heterosexual couples.

Some researchers believe that gay and lesbian individuals and families go through other life stages differently because of their sexual orientation and the discrimination they face (R. J. Green 2004; Solomon, Rothblum, and Balsam 2004). For example, forming and maintaining a homosexual identity often entails establishing a greater independence from parental expectations, conventional social norms and gender roles, and social scripts that have traditionally defined relationships and families (Kertzner 2004). The social and cultural climate of the modern lesbian, gay, bisexual, and transgender rights movement, historic shifts in social attitudes toward homosexuality, and the emergence and transformation of the HIV epidemic have shaped the life cycle for many gays and lesbians (Kertzner 2004). Although there are many socially proscribed roles for males/fathers and females/mothers in heterosexual marriage and family, same-sex couples lack clear traditions or guidelines for role and task decision making. This has its benefits in that it allows for tremendous role flexibility. However, it also introduces uncertainty and complexity into role negotiation, and it can be frustrating to continually challenge prevailing notions of family structure and function.

Traditionally, gay and lesbian families were not child centered if one or both partners had not been previously married. This is changing somewhat as more lesbians are opting to have children through donor insemination. The use of a gestational surrogate offers an assisted reproduction option to gays—although it is very expensive. Adoption is difficult because most states have restrictive policies to prevent gays and lesbians from adopting children. Research remains divided as to how children reared in same-sex households fare compared to children reared in heterosexual households (American Psychological Association 2005; MacCallum and Golombok 2004; Marks 2012).

As in all family types, there is tremendous diversity within gay and lesbian families in terms of family patterns, forms, and membership. No two families are ever alike, however similar they may seem superficially. As Kertzner (2004) writes, "Lesbians and gay men are defined by many sources of social identity beyond that of sexual orientation; in addition, homosexuality continues to shape the life passage of many lesbians and gay men in adulthood and provides ongoing sources of meaning in public and private spheres of work, relationships, and beliefs. Furthermore, many adults find freedom from conventional social norms liberating and maintain this conviction throughout the life course" (108). For some adults, the rewards of coming out and being out as a source of meaning in life diminish over time,

Traditionally, lesbian families were not child centered if one or both partners had not been previously married. But this is now changing as many lesbian couples are choosing to become parents through donor insemination.

and they may feel increasingly distant from gay and lesbian social worlds that once gave them a sense of identity and direction in life (Kertzner 2004).

Adjustments Early in Marriage

Most partners discover that marriage does not live up to all of their expectations. As a result, they go through a series of adjustments in which they modify their behavior and relationship to achieve the greatest degree of satisfaction with a minimum of frustration.

Marital adjustment may be defined as the process of modifying, adapting, and altering individual and couple patterns of behavior and interaction to achieve maximum satisfaction in the relationship.

According to this definition, adjustment is not an end in and of itself, but a means to an end: satisfaction in and with the marriage. It is possible for spouses to adjust to each other but still be unhappy and dissatisfied with the relationship. For example, a man who has a high interest in or need for sex may come to accept that his wife does not. This does not mean that either one is satisfied with the situation. Or she adjusts to his bad temper by ignoring outbursts or by "walking on eggshells." Again, they usually have little joy in the adjustment.

Sometimes a particular adjustment may not be exactly what one would like, but it may be successful to the extent that it provides the highest satisfaction possible under the circumstances. Obviously, adjustment is not static—it is not a step taken just once. It is a dynamic, ongoing process that takes place throughout a couple's married life.

Marital Adjustment Tasks

Most couples discover that they must make adjustments to live together harmoniously. The areas of adjustment might be called **marital adjustment tasks**; 12 categories are shown in Table 7.1.

Most couples who enter into a serious relationship are faced with the adjustments listed in Table 7.1. Some couples make many of them before marriage and so have fairly smooth sailing afterward. Other couples make few adjustments ahead of time and so are faced with nearly all of these tasks after marriage—which can be overwhelming. This situation often leads to a period of disillusionment and

Half Full or Half Empty?

One of the most important ways that we can cope more effectively is to change our negative and irrational (unrealistic) appraisals of stressful situations. This requires we first recognize negative appraisals and then replace them with more rational (realistic) and positive ones. In other words, change the way we think.

Albert Ellis, a prominent psychotherapist, states that people make themselves sick and unhappy by their choice of thoughts. Therefore, they can make themselves well and happy in the same way. Ellis offers the insight that people often make negative appraisals because of an underlying belief system that is faulty—irrational and unrealistic. Changing that belief system may be necessary to change our appraisals. Following are some irrational beliefs that get people in trouble, in contrast with their more rational counterparts:

Irrational Beliefs

I must be perfect and competent in all respects.

The people in my life should be perfect and competent in all respects.

I must be loved and approved by all.

My past determines my present and future. I can't change it.

Irrational Appraisals (feelings)

My boss didn't give me that promotion. He hates me and thinks I am incompetent. I have failed.

(insecurity, failure, depression)

My husband forgot my birthday; he didn't even get me a card. He is so thoughtless; obviously he does not care.

(hurt, anger, rejection)

My sister-in-law always makes very rude remarks to me. I am offended and upset. How dare she act like that!

(rejection, anger, helplessness)

More Rational Beliefs

I am not perfect; no one is. This is OK. I can do some things well; I do my best most of the time.

Others are not perfect either; we all make mistakes. Most of them do the best they can, too. They have strengths.

Not everyone will like me. I have friends and family who love me. I am fortunate.

I have made mistakes, but can learn from them. I don't have to repeat them. I have a good future.

More Rational Appraisals (feelings)

I am disappointed, but the promotion went to someone with more experience. I'm a good worker and I'll get one soon.

(disappointment, competence, hopefulness)

My feelings are hurt. He usually remembers; tells me he loves me every day. We all forget stuff.

(hurt, patience, understanding)

She is rude and it hurts my feelings. It is her bad behavior—not mine. I can't make her be nice. I can only control myself—so I will be polite.

(hurt, in-control, higher self-esteem)

---

disenchantment in couples who have not realized what marriage involves.

Problems during Three Early Stages

One longitudinal study investigated the problems of 131 couples during three stages of the early years of their relationship (Storaasli and Markman 1990):

marital adjustment The process of modifying, adapting, and altering individual and couple patterns of behavior and interaction to achieve maximum satisfaction in the relationship.

marital adjustment tasks Areas of concern in marriage in which adjustments must be made.

TABLE 7.1 Marital Adjustment Tasks

Emotional fulfillment and support	**Social life, friends, recreation**
Learning to give and receive affection and love	Learning to visit, entertain as a couple
Developing sensitivity, empathy, closeness	Deciding on type, frequency of social activities as individuals and as a couple
Giving emotional support, building morale, fulfilling ego needs	Selecting, relating to friends
Sexual adjustment	**Family, relatives**
Learning to satisfy, fulfill each other sexually	Establishing relationships with parents, in-laws, relatives
Working out mode, manner, timing of sexual expression	Learning how to deal with families
Finding, using acceptable means of birth control	**Communication**
Personal habits	Learning to disclose and communicate ideas, worries, concerns, needs
Adjusting to each other's personal habits, speech, cleanliness, grooming, manners, eating, sleeping, promptness	Learning to listen to each other and to talk to each other in constructive ways
Reconciling differences in smoking, drinking, drug habits	**Power, decision making**
Eliminating or modifying personal habits that annoy each other	Achieving desired balance of status, power
Adjusting to differences in body rhythms, schedules	Learning to make, execute decisions
Learning to share space, time, belongings, work	Learning cooperation, accommodation, compromise
Gender roles	**Conflict, problem solving**
Establishing spousal roles in and outside the home	Learning to identify conflict causes, circumstances
Working out gender roles in relation to income production, housekeeping, household maintenance, homemaking, child care	Learning to cope with conflict constructively
Agreeing on division of labor	Learning to solve problems
	Learning where, when, how to obtain help if needed
Material concerns, finances	**Morals, values, ideology**
Finding, selecting a residence: geographic area, neighborhood, type of housing	Understanding, adjusting to individual morals, values, ethics, beliefs, philosophies, life goals
Equipping, maintaining a household	Establishing mutual values, goals, philosophies
Earning adequate income, managing money	Accepting each other's religious beliefs, practices
Work, employment, achievement	Making decisions in relation to religious affiliation, participation
Finding, selecting, maintaining employment	
Adjusting to type, place, hours, conditions of employment	
Working out schedules when one or both are working	
Arranging for child care when one or both are working	

(1) before marriage, (2) during the first year of marriage, and (3) after the birth of their first child. Table 7.2 shows the results.

Note that money was the number one problem at all three stages of the relationship. Jealousy was a big problem before marriage but declined thereafter.

Relatives were a problem before marriage and again after the first child was born. Communication and sex became greater problems after marriage and after the first child was born. Relationships with friends, religion, and alcohol and drugs were more of a problem before marriage. Problems having to

TABLE 7.2 Relationship Problems during Three Early Stages

MEAN PROBLEM INTENSITY*					
Before marriage		**First year of marriage**		**After birth of first child**	
Money	48.6	Money	42.3	Money	39.0
Jealousy	25.0	Communication	21.2	Sex	33.5
Relatives	22.7	Sex	19.8	Communication	32.4
Friends	18.5	Relatives	19.7	Relatives	23.9
Communication	17.8	Friends	16.7	Recreation	13.7
Sex	14.2	Children	15.3	Children	12.8
Religion	13.8	Jealousy	13.2	Friends	12.5
Recreation	12.8	Recreation	11.3	Jealousy	9.1
Children	11.8	Alcohol/drugs	8.8	Religion	7.6
Alcohol/drugs	11.8	Religion	6.4	Alcohol/drugs	6.5

*0 indicates no problem; 100 indicates a severe problem.

Note: Data from "Relationship problems in the early stages of marriage," by R. D. Storaasli and H. J. Markman, 1990, Journal of Family Psychology, *4, pp. 80–98.*

do with recreation declined in importance after marriage and then rose after the first child was born.

A survey done by the Center for Marriage and the Family at Creighton University adds support. The newly married (1 to 5 years) couples they surveyed listed money, sex, and time (to be with relatives, friends, children, and for recreation) as their major problems (For Your Marriage 2012).

Adjustments to Parenthood

"First pregnancy," says one psychiatrist, "is a nine-month crisis. Thank God it takes nine months, because a child's coming requires enormous changes in a couple's ways of adjusting to each other" (Maynard 1974, 139). Getting used to living with another adult in a committed relationship is challenging, but adding a third member to the family, an infant who is totally dependent, is a stressful transition in the family life cycle—and one of the most rewarding.

Parenthood and Stress

In recent years, the arrival of a first child is viewed less as a crisis and more as a period of stress and transition. The more stressful a couple's marriage before parenthood, the more likely it is that they will have difficulty adjusting to the first child.

Part of the stress of new parenthood comes because many couples are inadequately prepared for it and because the transition can seem abrupt—although the pregnancy took nine months. As one mother laughed, "We knew where babies came from, but we didn't know what they were like." Many new parents have no experience in caring for infants. Couples who prepare for parenthood by attending infant-care or parenting classes and reading books find greater satisfaction in being a parent than do those who do not prepare. But even those who make an effort to educate themselves can be surprised by the demands of caring for a baby: diapers, night-time feedings, colic, extra laundry, etc.

Stress will vary from child to child depending on each child's temperament and how easy each child is to care for. Some children have sunny dispositions, eat well, and sleep all night. Others are fussy, wake up repeatedly, and get colicky. Children with special needs require enormous amounts of time and energy.

Stress is greater if parents are young and immature. In 2010, some 367,750 babies (slightly more than 9% of all births) were born to teenage mothers

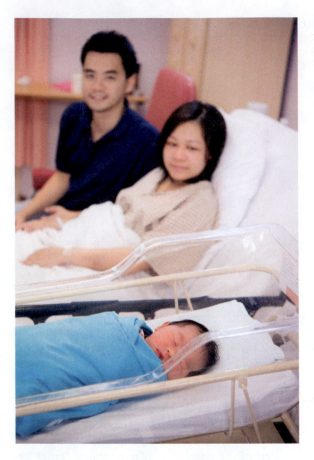

The birth of a first child is a period of transition and stress, but successful adjustments are measures of parenting readiness.

(J. A. Martin et al. 2012). A majority of these parents have not even finished high school—nor will they (Umberson, Pudrovska, and Reczek 2010). It is highly unlikely that many are ready for parenthood.

The economic status of the family also has been found to be a factor in parents' level of distress. It affects both spouses' parenting-related stress and their psychological well-being. Parents who are struggling to make ends meet feel higher levels of stress in providing for and rearing their children than do parents with greater economic resources.

The transition to parenthood ushers in many life changes and adjustments, as well as new responsibilities and routines. Much research has focused on the transition to parenthood and on what concurrent variables in a parent's life are associated with competent parenting. Many variables, including social support from family and spouse, are associated with the degree of warmth and sensitivity a parent exhibits toward an infant. Social support is associated with the adaptation to parenthood and

with positive parent–infant interactions. For example, women who receive support during pregnancy experience more positive mental and physical health outcomes during labor, delivery, and the postpartum period than do women who do not receive support (Berk 2013; Kail and Cavanaugh 2016). Over time, parents adjust to the new routines as they realize they must give up some of their former "preparenting" rituals, routines, and commitments.

Throughout life, social support is important for maintaining healthy relationships in families. For example, children's parents are often the main source for developing a sense of self-worth and for learning effective ways to exercise personal control (Leondari and Kiosseoglou 2002). Research shows that children who receive support from their parents generally report fewer psychological and physical ailments during their childhood than do children who receive less parental support. For example, one study investigating early parental support (B. A. Shaw et al. 2004) found that a lack of parental support during childhood was associated with increased levels of depressive symptoms and chronic conditions in adulthood. Personal control, self-esteem, and family relationships accounted for most of the association between early parental support and adult depressive symptoms, supporting the idea that the mental and psychosocial health of adults may be influenced by conditions dating back to childhood and underscoring the importance of assuming a life-course perspective when studying psychosocial determinants of health (Kail and Cavanaugh 2016; B. A. Shaw et al. 2004).

Fatherhood and the Life Course

Although motherhood and a mother's influence on her child have been researched extensively, fatherhood has gotten considerably less attention from scholars until recent years.

Fatherhood is a profound experience for many men. Men who engage in active parenting develop and mature differently from men who do not (Palkovitz 2002). Palkovitz interviewed 40 fathers from different cultures and parenting situations about their feelings with regard to fathering. Fathers in the sample described the multidimensional and complex nature of fathering as well as the need to achieve balance between work and family life. The most common themes discussed by these men included love; being a provider; being there for their children; and being a model, teacher, and moral guide. The

Individualism versus Familism

Individualism is described as leading one's life with the focus on the pursuit of one's own happiness. Familism, in contrast, emphasizes the needs of the family above the individual. The degree to which a family emphasizes the importance of familism and individualism varies across cultures. For example, in studies that directly compare Mexican American with European American families, the Mexican Americans show stronger levels of obligation, have more frequent social interaction, exchange more support, and are more likely to share living arrangements with elders (E. R. Holmes and Holmes 1995). It is important that individuals be committed to the welfare of the family system as opposed to themselves and that the family remain the center and focus of all endeavors (E. C. Garcia 2001). This familial focus is apparent in such instances as when an older child stays home from school to care for a sick family member. Individuals find their identity and sense of belonging in family groups, and Mexican Americans are much more likely than European Americans to believe that the younger generation should support and provide living accommodations for the older generation if needed (Burr and Mutchler 1999). In addition, Mexican American adolescents possess stronger values and greater expectations regarding their duty to assist, respect, and support than do their European American counterparts (Fuligni et al. 1999).

Chinese Americans also place a great deal of emphasis on intergenerational ties and the extended family being the most important societal unit (S. S. Feldman, Mont-Reynaud, and Rosenthal 1992). Children have a strong sense of duty to parents and of filial responsibility, and parents blame themselves when a young person fails to live up to expectations. A child who misbehaves can bring shame to the family name (Ishii-Kuntz 1997). Thus, an individual's shame can bring loss of face to both himself and his extended family, which is a major concern in many families (Wu 2001). Because of the emphasis Chinese Americans place on family as opposed to the individual, they see education not only for the advancement of the individual, but also for family enhancement as a whole. It is thought that conforming to the group is more important than fulfilling one's own needs and that conformity helps both a family and a society function better (Sue 1997).

---

most prevalent component of what the men considered good fathering was "being there" for their children. They also discussed the role-sharing aspects of parenting and whether they felt they could share the same roles as mothers. Half of the men believed that outside of bearing children and nursing them, there are essentially no differences between what fathers and mothers can do with their children. However, some fathers expressed what they saw as important gender differences with regard to tenderness, emotionality, or gender-role socialization.

The study also found that some men experienced major changes in life course and personality as a direct result of fatherhood. Other men perceived that fathering had less dramatic, but still significant influences on their development. In sum, fathers were able to express significant life-course changes that they attributed directly to fatherhood to a much greater degree than they could to general life-span development changes. For most of the men, the positive aspects of parenting outweighed any negatives such as some significant challenges, hassles, energy demands, resource drains, unmet needs, and fear. Fatherhood gave meaning to their daily routine and anchored their mental, physical, and emotional lives (Palkovitz 2002).

Adjustments during Middle Adulthood

The most notable changes of middle adulthood are physical ones. These changes are very gradual (middle adulthood lasts about 35 years), but wrinkles, graying hair, and balding heads remind us of the aging process. Muscle tone declines, and strength and endurance ebb. Individuals become concerned with the dimensions of their middle-age bodies. Physical exercise is more necessary to keep in shape and to offset the decrease in the body's metabolism, which results in the tendency to put on weight (Kail and Cavanaugh 2016).

Health concerns become increasingly related to life satisfaction. Perhaps for the first time, adults are confronted with their own mortality. Previously, they have counted the years past, but now they begin to count the years ahead. The midlife transformation is precipitated by the awareness that one's years are numbered.

Paradoxically, people are also entering the prime of life in many ways: health is usually still good; careers are established; children are growing. The awareness that time is finite paired with the possibilities that remain may trigger introspection and self-analysis. Middle-age people engage in an existential questioning of self, values, and life itself. They ask, Who am I? What have I done with my life? Where is my life going? What legacy am I leaving for the next generation?

This assessment extends to an examination of responsibilities, career, and marriage. As one middle-age individual put it, "I'm tired of doing what is expected, what I'm supposed to do. I'd like to find out what I want to do, and start thinking of me for a change" (Counseling notes). Financial responsibilities tend to be heavy in middle age. Some men become obsessed with having financial security for retirement. Family income can be an important contributor to feelings of mastery and power over one's life.

Many middle-age people are under considerable stress. This is the time of heaviest responsibilities at work, in the family, and in the community. More than a few middle-age people find themselves caring not only for their children but also for their aging parents. Work and financial strains are typically felt at this time and job burnout may occur. Middle-age men and women often feel stress over the lack of companionship with their spouses, their own work, and the possibility of their young adult children making poor personal and professional choices.

Thus, midlife is a time when personal, practical, and existential issues are all in focus. It can become a time for reexamination, a time to chart new courses in life.

Marital Adjustments

As we have discussed, marital satisfaction tends to be at its lowest ebb when the children are of school age or in their teenage years (and parents are in the middle adult years). If the partners have been busy working and raising children and being active in community affairs, they may have drifted apart, spending less time communicating, playing, and simply being together. It is easy for spouses to get so absorbed with other activities that the marriage suffers. Parents who have "stayed together for the children" now feel freer to dissolve their relationship—and some do.

For others, however, middle age can be a time for revitalizing a tired marriage and for rethinking the relationship. It has been suggested that there are three cycles in most marriages—falling in love, falling out of love, and falling back in love—and that the last cycle is both the most difficult and the most rewarding. If spouses can begin again to express tender feelings of love and affection that they have neglected, they can develop greater intimacy than they have experienced in a long time. Improved communication also can resolve troublesome issues and lead to improved companionship and togetherness.

Middle-age people differ greatly in their ability to make necessary changes during this period of life. Researchers talk about **ego resiliency (ER)**, or the capacity for flexible and resourceful adaptation to stressors. It is an important personality resource that enables individuals to competently negotiate life under changing conditions. Adults entering midlife with high levels of ER are likely to view midlife as an opportunity for change and growth, whereas individuals with lower levels of ER are likely to experience it as a time of stagnation or decline (Kail and Cavanaugh 2016; Klohnen, Vandewater, and Young 1996).

Some middle-age people are called on to assume another role—that of caregiver to an impaired parent or parent-in-law. Some 47% of adults in their forties or fifties have at least one living parent (Parker and Patten 2013). Although elderly people today are less likely to live with their children than they were 40 years ago, grown children, especially daughters or daughters-in-law, still bear primary responsibility for aged parents. Thus, many women are called on to assist elderly relatives in shopping, preparing meals, and so on. The majority of these women assuming the caregiving role also work and face other family responsibilities. The role strain is considerable because they juggle the demands of the competing roles of worker, wife, homemaker, mother, grandmother, and caregiving daughter or daughter-in-law.

Some research indicates two styles of elder care: individualistic or collectivistic. The individualistic style approaches parental caregiving with reluctance and considers it a burden, complaining of inadequate time and relying more on formal support systems. In contrast, in the collectivistic style, parental caregiving is assumed by family members, who emphasize family ties and family cohesiveness (Santrock 2015). Those families who use the collectivistic style, particularly Hispanic Americans and African Americans, report lower levels of caregiver stress, burden, and depression (Kail and Cavanaugh 2016).

There are both rewards and stresses in assuming this caregiver role. Rewards include knowing that the care recipient is well cared for. The caregiver usually receives satisfaction from assuming this role if the care recipient shows affection or appreciation, if the relationship becomes closer and the care recipient's health improves, if he or she is cooperative and not demanding, and if his or her good side comes through despite illness.

But caregiving also creates stresses, especially if the care recipient is critical or complains, is unresponsive or uncooperative, is agitated, is in declining health, asks repetitive questions, or is forgetful. If caregivers do not receive help from family or friends or if considerable extra expenses are involved in the caregiving, these factors become additional sources of stress (Parker and Patten 2013).

Because they are caught between caregiving responsibilities for their children and for their elderly parents, middle-age adults are sometimes called the **sandwich generation**. The responsibilities and demands of caring for both children and aging parents are time-consuming and taxing. About 48% of middle-age adults provide at least some financial support to their grown children (often for school), and about 21% have provided financial help to aging parents. The financial burden comes more from grown children than from elders (Parker and Patten 2013). Related to other issues, middle-age women perceive their adolescent children as more challenging than their elderly parents, whereas middle-age men report the opposite (Kail and Cavanaugh 2016). In a national survey of sandwich-generation adults conducted by Pew Research, they found, perhaps surprisingly, that the change in family responsibilities had little or no effect on caregivers' well-being. Some 31% reported themselves as very happy and an additional 52% say they are pretty happy. More than half (58%) indicate they have enough money to meet their basic needs with some left over; only 11% cannot meet basic needs (Parker and Patten

2013). It could be that there is a selection effect whereby those most able to take on caregiving do so. More persons with incomes greater than $100,000 were involved in the sandwich generation than those with lower incomes (Parker and Patten 2013), for example. Additionally, those individuals who have strong marriages tend to assume multigenerational caregiving responsibilities and are probably generous caregivers in their own marriage. Also, individuals who take on additional care responsibilities may be more proficient at balancing time allocations for family, work, and personal needs. People who take on such responsibilities place a high value on caring for others; consequently, meeting the additional obligations is a source of gratification that offsets any negative effects.

The researchers do not wish to imply that caring for an elderly parent, particularly one who is disabled or in very poor health, does not sometimes adversely affect family caregivers. In general, however, assuming multigenerational responsibilities does not develop into an especially difficult situation for most middle-age adults (Parker and Patten 2013).

The Postparental Years

The term **postparental years** usually refers to the period between the last child leaving home and the parents' retirement. Some writers prefer the term *empty-nest years* because once children are born, one is always a parent (D. Olson, DeFrain, and Skogrand 2014).

In recent times, unmarried children continue living with their parents for a longer period of time than they used to. This corresponds in part to people being older at the time of their first marriage. Moreover, once the children leave, the empty nest may not stay that way; that is, grown children may return to the nest. High divorce rates and financial need have resulted in increasing numbers of adult children returning home to live with their parents. Today's

ego resiliency (ER) The generalized capacity for flexible and resourceful adaptation to stressors.

sandwich generation Middle-age adults caught between caregiving for their children and for their elderly parents.

postparental years The period between the last child leaving home and the parents' retirement; also called the empty-nest years.

When the last child leaves home, the postparental years begin. Although most couples report a notable increase in marital satisfaction, today's empty nest does not always stay empty. What effect might a returning child have on marital satisfaction?

generation of young adults has been referred to as the "boomerang kids" since they may leave home and return several times (D. Olson, DeFrain, and Skogrand 2014; Parker and Patten 2013).

This phenomenon has important ramifications for parents, their adult children, and grandchildren. Many parents do not welcome the permanent return of their adult children and view their stay as a short-term arrangement. The sources of potential conflict include finances; everyday maintenance of self and clothing; the upkeep of house and yard; the use of the family car; and the lifestyle of the child, including sexual expression, drinking, drugs, and friends. Furthermore, although most grandparents love their grandchildren, they may resent having to be the frequent babysitter while the parent goes out to work or play. Sometimes the adult child reverts to the role of dependent child, and the parents return to superordinate roles of earlier times—with a lessening of life satisfaction for all parties involved.

Adjustments during Late Adulthood

Americans over the age of 65 years now comprise close to 15% of the total population (U.S. Bureau of the Census 2015). Late adulthood brings a number of major life changes that affect not only the aging individual but also his or her spouse and other family members. Because late adulthood can extend over a 30-year period and dramatic physiological, psychological, and sociological changes can take place during these years, late adulthood is often divided into three stages. People ages 65 to 74 are sometimes referred to as young-old adults, those 75 to 84 are middle-old adults, and those 85 and older are oldest-old adults. The developmental tasks these three groups face may be quite different. For example, people age 85 and older are more likely than people under 85 to be in poor health; to need assistance in dressing, bathing, eating, and other activities of daily living; and to need home health care (Kail and Cavanaugh 2016).

Late adulthood involves some major transitions: from marriage to widowhood, from living with a family member (spouse or child) to living alone, and from physical independence to physical dependence. The transitions in marital status and household structure are likely to occur around the mid-seventies, usually some years before the onset of any disabilities. The timing of these transitions is significant for long-term survivors. By the time they reach the age when their family could be an important source of assistance, they are unlikely to have a surviving spouse, and a large proportion of them live alone. For example, about 29% of elders live alone; for women older than 75, the number is even higher—47% (U.S. Bureau of the Census 2012).

Developmental Tasks

The major **developmental tasks**, or adjustments, facing elderly people can be grouped into nine categories: (1) staying physically healthy and adjusting to limitations, (2) maintaining adequate income and means of support, (3) adjusting to revised work roles, (4) finding acceptable housing and living conditions, (5) maintaining identity and social status, (6) finding companionship and friendship, (7) learning to use leisure time pleasurably, (8) establishing new roles in the family, and (9) achieving integrity through acceptance of one's life. We will discuss each of these tasks briefly before turning to a more detailed discussion of the marriage and family relationships of the elderly.

STAYING PHYSICALLY HEALTHY AND ADJUSTING TO LIMITATIONS The difficult task of staying healthy as one ages requires good health habits, the practice of preventive medicine, getting enough exercise, and proper nutrition. Many older people fear the loss of their vision, hearing, mobility, and general

Go with the Flow

We had thought of retirement as a reward for years of hard work. All the hoopla leads up to retirement. And then you wake up one morning wondering, "Now what?"

It didn't take Roger long to catch up on sleeping late and watching television sports. Soon he was hanging around watching me do housework. Then he began offering advice, and that was too much for me! I seemed to spend all day puttering around and getting very little done. We both felt aimless.

It took some time, but we worked out a style of living that suits us. For one thing, we follow a general schedule. We're not fanatic clock watchers, but we have breakfast around eight and do house and yard chores until lunchtime. We work together on the chores—Roger especially likes to cook. One day a week we go to town: to the bank, post office, grocery, and such.

Afternoons are varied. I volunteer at the hospital some and take a craft class. Roger has become quite active in county and state politics; he loved working for his favorite candidates during the last elections. In slack times, he enjoys his coin and knife collections.

We visit friends at least one evening a week for cards or board games. We have been able to travel more. We took an extended trip to Australia to visit one of my elderly aunts and my cousins. We hadn't seen them in years and it was wonderful.

We had to structure our time; we had to adapt to more free time and more time together. We changed the way we divided household chores. If we hadn't made those changes, we'd be pretty miserable.

A proverb tells of the mighty oak, so tall and strong, that breaks in the stormy wind, whereas the fragile-looking reeds bend to the ground but do not snap. Strong families are like the reeds—they bend, they change, they adapt, and when the storm is over, they are still intact.

ability to care for themselves. As a consequence, maintaining good health is one of the important predictors of life satisfaction in elderly individuals.

MAINTAINING ADEQUATE INCOME AND MEANS OF SUPPORT Many adults face the problem of inadequate income in the later years: Social Security and retirement benefits are often much less than former paychecks. This financial challenge has become even greater because of a struggling economy and an increase in the age at which people can retire with full benefits. As a result, the percentage of persons age 65 and older participating in the labor force has consistently increased since 1980—reaching a high of over 36% as of 2014 (U.S. Bureau of the Census 2016).

About 10% of people (8% of males and 12% of females) older than 65 live below the poverty level. There are also differences according to ethnicity. Some 19.4% of older African Americans and 19% of older Hispanic Americans live below the poverty level compared to 7.4% of older white people (Cubanski, Casillas, and Damiko 2015; Rhee 2012).

Achieving financial independence in late adulthood requires diligent saving, careful financial management, and often some good luck. In general, people who are financially independent are more satisfied in their daily lives.

ADJUSTING TO REVISED WORK ROLES Retirement typically happens at age 65 to 70. In cases where people choose retirement, plan for it, and are able to retire when they wish, they may not feel stressed by it. This is not the case for those who must delay retirement because they do not have the means to finance it or for those who are forced to retire before they intended because of health limitations. Those most satisfied with retirement are those who have been preparing for it for a number of years. This is an important point, since the quality of the retirement

developmental tasks Growth responsibilities that arise at various stages of life.

experience influences marital satisfaction after retirement (Cullinane and Fitzgerald 2007; Eisenberg 2013; Price 2013).

The major reasons for retiring fall into four broad categories: (1) job stress or dissatisfaction (is not fun anymore); (2) pressure from employer or being laid off or fired; (3) desire to pursue one's own interests or spend more time with family and friends; and (4) circumstances, such as age, health, or health of a loved one (Cullinane and Fitzgerald 2007; Romano 2013). Those who retired to escape job stress found rewards from the reduced stress in retirement. Those who were pressured by their employer to retire were more likely to report a difficult transition, less satisfaction with retirement, and fewer sources of enjoyment in retirement. People who retired to pursue their own interests reported an easier transition to retirement and higher satisfaction with, more sources of enjoyment in, and positive adjustment to retirement. The reaction to retirement of those who retired because of circumstances such as age or health depended on whether they really wanted to retire. Certainly, retirement should be retirement to, not from, something.

Numerous studies have explored a range of contextual factors that influence the effect of retirement on marital quality. The timing of retirement (him first, her first, or both at the same time), goals for retirement, the division of labor within the marriage, social support, health, and marital quality are preretirement factors that affect how retirement influences marital quality. Leaving a high-stress job typically improves marital quality, whereas gender-role reversals, declines in health, or reduced social support associated with the retirement adversely affect marital quality. Furthermore, the effects of retirement vary according to the number of changes that accompany retirement. For example, whereas declines in health reduce retirees' satisfaction, higher perceived income adequacy and retiring because of an early retirement incentive package increase their satisfaction (Cullinane and Fitzgerald 2007; Eisenberg 2013; Price 2013).

These studies suggest that the division of labor within the household, the timing of retirement, and the couple's goals for retirement are the most troubling areas. Given that a substantial number of women are in the labor force and are younger than their spouses, it follows that men typically retire before their spouses do. However, marital quality suffers the most when she continues to work after

Older people dread physical problems that impair mobility and independence. One of the developmental tasks of late adulthood is to stay physically healthy.

he retires. Often she continues her household chores in addition to work, thus leading to resentment and conflict. When she retires before he does, he does not seem affected but she is not satisfied with this arrangement either. The smoothest transition seems to happen when they retire at the same time (Eisenberg 2013; Price 2013).

Research also indicates that the division of household chores in retirement can be important to a couple's happiness. Retired husbands typically do not do an equal share of household chores; their wives (especially if they have worked outside the home) may expect them to pick up a larger share and when this does not happen, they may feel resentment. Other women feel "smothered" or as if their territory has been invaded when their husbands are home all the time—termed the "underfoot syndrome" when he interferes with her household routine (Eisenberg 2013; Price 2013).

The final area that is especially apt to influence marital happiness in retirement involves the goals each has for retirement. Obviously, when partners have different goals, they are more apt to have disagreements than when they share the same plans. For example, if she planned to travel extensively in retirement but he planned to have a mini farm with chickens and a big vegetable garden, negotiation and compromise will be necessary (Eisenberg 2013; Price 2013).

FINDING ACCEPTABLE HOUSING AND LIVING CONDITIONS For some older people, being able to keep their own home is of great importance. It allows them independence and usually more satisfactory relationships with their children.

About 78.5% of people age 65 and older own and maintain their own houses (U.S. Bureau of the Census 2016). Seventy-two percent of men and 46% of women over age 65 live with a spouse; 19% of men and 36% of women live alone; 9% of men and 19% of women have some other living arrangement (with family, assisted living, etc.) (U.S. Department of Health and Human Resources 2014).

MAINTAINING IDENTITY AND SOCIAL STATUS Historically, older individuals had high status and prestige because they possessed the greatest knowledge of skills, traditions, and ceremonies considered essential for group survival. But as our society became more industrialized and modern, elderly people lost their economic advantages and their leadership roles, both in industry and in the extended family. Consequently, they lost status and prestige.

People may lose status as they retire from the workforce because work is often an important factor in an individual's identity and prestige. For example, a former teacher is no longer a teacher—occupationally, he or she is nothing. Those who are able to develop a meaningful identity through avocations, social life, marriage, children, or other activities adjust more easily than those whose identity is inseparable from their occupation (Price 2013).

FINDING COMPANIONSHIP AND FRIENDSHIP Because loneliness is a frequent complaint of older people, they must find meaningful relationships with others. Developing and maintaining friendships with peers seems to be more important to their emotional well-being than does interaction with kin. Some find dating partners to satisfy their need for companionship and emotional fulfillment. One woman stated,

It was a lot harder when my boyfriend, Ted, died than when my husband of forty years passed away. I needed Ted in a way I never needed my husband. Ted and I spent so much time together; he was all I had. And at my age I know it will be hard to find someone else. . . . I would like to date someone like Ted again . . . but, well, let's face it; how many men want a seventy-three-year-old woman? (Bulcroft and O'Connor 1986, 401)

Studies of how friendships change in the later years have found that acquaintances and casual friends become less and less important in old age but that close friends and relatives remain very important. Older adults typically have fewer relationships than do younger or middle-age adults. However, there are indications that the newer cohorts of older adults (the "baby boomers") have more friends and more long-term friends than previous cohorts (Kail and Cavanaugh 2016).

Gender differences that were true in earlier years are continued in the later years. Women are more involved in friendships than are men, whereas men express less desire to make new friends and have less intimate contact with friends (Kail and Cavanaugh 2016). These gender differences were less pronounced at the young-old age and more pronounced at the older stage. The Internet presents opportunities for friendships and dating relationships that some elders have used. Some 25% of online game players, for example, are older than age 50 (Ledbetter and Kuznekoff 2012). Internet users—regardless of age—tend to have more friends than those who do not use it as much (Wang and Wellman 2010).

LEARNING TO USE LEISURE TIME PLEASURABLY Late adulthood offers most people an opportunity to enjoy themselves. As work roles decline, more leisure time is available for preferred pursuits. Life satisfaction in late adulthood is very much dependent on social activity. People need worthwhile, pleasurable activities to help them feel good about themselves and about life in general.

ESTABLISHING NEW ROLES IN THE FAMILY Several events bring about the adjustment of family roles: children marrying and moving away, grandparenthood, retirement, the death of a spouse, or dependence on one's children. These changes require people to take on different roles and responsibilities in the family.

There is some reversal of gender roles in relation to authority in the family as people get older. The man who retires loses some authority in family governance, and the woman often assumes a more dominant role as an authority figure. This is especially true in relation to planning activities for herself and her mate and to assuming a nurturing role that has not been possible since the children left home.

ACHIEVING INTEGRITY THROUGH ACCEPTANCE OF ONE'S LIFE Erikson (1959) stated that the development of ego integrity is the chief psychosocial task of the final stage of life. This includes reviewing one's life, being able to accept the facts of one's life without regret, and being able to face death without great fear. It entails appreciating one's own individuality, accomplishments, and satisfactions, as well as accepting the hardships, failures, and disappointments one has experienced. Ultimately, it means contentment with one's life as it is and has been.

Marital Satisfaction

As the health and longevity of the elderly increase, an increasing proportion of adults older than age 65 are married and living with a spouse. About 72% of men over age 65 were married; some 45% of women ages 65 to 74 were married, with the number dropping as people age. For example, 32% of women over age 75 are married (U.S. Department of Health and Human Services 2014). Far greater numbers of women are widowed than men, as shown in Table 7.3 (U.S. Bureau of the Census 2012).

For many older adults, marriage continues to be a major source of life satisfaction. Marital happiness and satisfaction usually increase during a second honeymoon stage after the children leave home and after retirement. The spouses typically have more time to spend with each other and with adult children

Late adulthood offers an opportunity to pursue leisure activities. Enjoying pleasurable activities is key to life satisfaction for older people.

and grandchildren. Not only do couples have more time, but also the quality of the time is better. Couples in later life tend to argue less and express more affection (Gorchoff, John, and Helson 2008; N. M. Lambert 2011). They depend more on each other for companionship. As one wife remarked, "I feel closer

TABLE 7.3 Marital Status of Older Americans, by Age and Gender, in Percentages, 2010

	MALE			FEMALE		
Marital status	55–64	65–74	75+	55–64	65–74	75+
Never-married	9.1	4.5	3.5	7.1	5.1	3.9
Married	73.9	78	69.8	66.9	55.9	32.3
Widowed	2.5	6.4	21.2	8.1	24.1	56.9
Divorced	14.5	11	5.6	17.8	15	7.0

Note: From Statistical Abstract of the United States, *2012, by U.S. Bureau of the Census. http://www.census.gov.*

to Bill than I have for years. We had forgotten what it meant to have real companionship." Marital satisfaction tends to be high among those whose spouse is also the most important confidant.

Divorce

Divorce at any time of life is a distressing experience. If it comes during late adulthood, it is even more difficult. Both men and women (but especially women) who divorce in later life, compared with those married or widowed, are more disadvantaged materially in terms of income, car ownership, and home ownership (Arber 2004; S. G. Thomas 2012).

Although the overall divorce rate has dropped slightly, divorce among people over age 50 (termed "gray divorce") has doubled since 1990. In 1990, only about 1 in 10 people who divorced was older than 50; that number grew to 1 in 4 in 2009 (S. G. Thomas 2012). The question of why naturally arises. One part of the explanation may be that this cohort is made up of the baby boomers, considered the first to view marriage as largely for self-fulfillment (rather than financial security or fulfillment of roles). Some of these couples may have been waiting for children to leave so that they could also leave an unsatisfactory marriage (Thomas 2012). Slightly more than half of those divorcing after age 50 are in second or third marriages, which quadruples the risk factor for divorce among those who are older than age 65 (Thomas 2012).

Another factor in the increase in gray divorce may be the increase in life expectancy. In earlier generations, people did not live as long, so marriages ended (by death) earlier. Contemporary couples may finish rearing their children and discover that they are not happy in the marriage or do not have much in common anymore, but still can expect to live another 25 to 30 years. They may decide they want to seek happiness in this last chance (Thomas 2012).

As is true for divorce at earlier stages in the family life cycle, gray divorce has serious economic consequences for women. And divorcing fathers are likely to see a decrease in contact with at least one child, compared to stably married dads or to the children's mothers (Thomas 2012).

Parent–Adult Child Relationships

The stereotypical image of parents growing older without contact with their adult children does not coincide with the facts. Most older people are *not* isolated from their children.

Most older people have strong ties to their children and grandchildren. Becoming a grandparent brings about a welcome new status.

Research indicates that older parents and their adult children do, however, evaluate their relationships with each other in different ways. One study, analyzing data from the National Survey of Families and Households, compared the perceptions of intergenerational solidarity among 2,590 adult children and their older parents. The findings indicated disagreement between how adult children and their parents view their relationship. Parents were more likely to report greater relationship quality, whereas children were more likely to report greater contact and exchanges of assistance (A. Shapiro 2004).

Other studies have reported the following important factors in parent–adult child relationships:

- Most adult children want to have good relationships with their parents and their parents want to have good relationships with them (Isay 2008).

- Most parents and their adult children experience at least a little tension or disagreement over a variety of topics such as personality differences, past relationship problems, children's finances, housekeeping habits, and lifestyle. Issues such as basic personality differences and parents providing unsolicited advice tend to cause more problems than other areas (Birditt et al. 2009; Isay 2008).

- Parents and their adult children also view tension differently; parents generally report more intense tension than children do. Tensions may be more upsetting to parents because they have more invested in the relationship (generational stake) and because they are concerned with launching their children into successful adulthood (thus being successful in fulfilling their parental roles) (Birditt et al. 2009).

- Although moderate amounts of intergenerational support are beneficial to older adults, excessive assistance received from adult children actually may do harm by eroding feelings of competence. In the beginning, support from children is much appreciated by older parents, but as time passes, it can begin to depress them and make them feel bad about their situation (Silverstein, Chen, and Heller 1996).

- Birditt et al. (2009) also note ambivalent feelings on the part of adult children. Providing extensive care for parents who are seriously disabled causes extreme stress and hardship for the caregivers. Thus, they may feel irritated or resentful although they also love their parents and want to help them.

Widowhood

Approximately 6% of the U.S. population are widowed, most of whom are middle-age or older adults (U.S. Bureau of the Census 2015). The death of a spouse is one of life's most traumatic events. It is a loss so deeply painful that it is intrinsically linked to the disruption of personal identity. The survivor confronts emotional, economic, and physical problems precipitated by a spouse's death. How one deals with the challenges of widowhood depends on numerous physical, emotional, and spiritual factors (Harris, Lampe, and Chaffin 2004).

The hypothetical couple represented in the family life cycle of an intact marriage (in Figure 7.1) live together for 47 years before he dies. Because life expectancy is longer for her and because he is 2 years older when they marry, she can expect to be a widow for about 7 years (U.S. Bureau of the Census 2015). The greater longevity of women means that the number of widows exceeds that of widowers at all age levels. Table 7.4 shows the ratios at different ages. Partly as a result of these ratios, the remarriage rate for widows is lower than that for widowers. The older a person is when a mate dies, the lower the chances of remarriage.

Older people, especially widows, have a consistently high degree of contact with other family members, including married children. Usually, an elderly woman is closer to her children, especially daughters, than is an elderly man. However, a woman is more likely to depend on them for material aid. The more dependent elderly people become and the more helping roles are reversed, the lower their morale. All research findings stress the importance of peer support in helping widows and widowers adjust and maintain morale.

In addition to the psychological stress of spousal loss and the need to reconstruct a new sense of self, widows must solve some practical, everyday problems of living. The most frequently cited problem is

---

Widowhood

Dorothy was married for 52 years and has been a widow for the past 11 years. She is more than 80 years old and has eight children.

We had 37 perfect years, but when John hit age 55 everything went downhill because of his drinking. He was a different person. Once he retired, he constantly followed me around the house asking what I was doing. It would drive me crazy. Years later, when John got very *sick, I fell in love with him all over again. We spent the last 10 years of his life really celebrating our marriage, remembering, enjoying, and savoring our family. Now, as a widow, I am lonely. I am socially connected and active with many friends and neighbors and enjoy what I am doing, but I'm just waiting for the end and a heavenly reunion with my husband.*

TABLE 7.4   Ratio of Widows to Widowers at Different Ages, 2010

AGE	RATIO OF WIDOWS TO WIDOWERS
45–54	2.8 to 1
55–64	3.5 to 1
65–74	4.3 to 1
75 and older	4.0 to 1

Note: Adapted from Statistical Abstract of the United States, 2012. *U.S. Bureau of the Census. http://www.census.gov.*

Loneliness is the most frequently cited problem of widowhood and is most extreme for widows whose social activities were highly couple oriented.

loneliness. Widowed persons miss their mates as companions and partners in activities. This problem is accentuated if they have a low income and cannot afford many activities outside the home. It can be difficult for widowed individuals to feel welcome in social situations where most people come as couples. Widowed persons who live with a family member or friend or who socialize with family and friends are less likely to be lonely.

A second problem cited by widows is home maintenance and car repair. Younger widows also cite decision making, child rearing, and financial management. Widows in the oldest group mention problems such as ignorance of basic finances, lack of transportation, and fear of crime. The only advantage of widowhood, mentioned by younger women, is increased independence (Utz et al. 2004).

Widowhood can be seen as a dynamic process (Van den Hoonaard 2001) and a period of personal growth. For example, one study found that widowed persons who were highly dependent on their spouses reaped psychological rewards from the recognition that they were capable of managing on their own (Carr 2004). Betty Friedan (1993) wrote in *The Fountain of Age* about her own journey into later life: "It took me all these years to put the missing pieces together, to confront my own age in terms of integrity and generativity, moving into the unknown future with a comfort now, instead of being stuck in the past. I have never felt so free" (638).

Financial problems plague both widows and widowers. In every age category, however, widows have a lower income than widowers and often experience a significant drop in standard of living when a husband dies. Many widows' incomes hover around the poverty line, even with Social Security or a pension.

Approximately 16.5% of the elderly who live alone also live in poverty, compared to 5% of elderly who live in families. The problem is more significant for Hispanic (39%) and black (32%) elderly who live alone (U.S. Department of Health and Human Services 2014).

Finally, widows indicate that another major adjustment is related to role changes. Widowhood, at any age, changes the basic self-identity of a woman. This is especially true of the traditionally oriented woman whose role of wife has been central to her life. Such women must reorient their thinking to find other identities. Specific role changes depend on what roles were emphasized before widowhood.

Families and relationships bring much joy and happiness, but not without adjustments, challenges, and stress. As individuals go through the life-cycle stages, they inevitably will make mistakes, but they also will gain perspective and wisdom.

Who Cares for Older People?

A larger percentage of the U.S. population is now age 65 or older (almost 15%) than at any time since 1900 (U.S. Bureau of the Census 2015). Of people age 65 and older, one in five has self-care or mobility limitations, and one in nine has cognitive/mental limitations. Close to 10% are living in poverty and cannot afford long-term care services. Needs increase substantially as people reach age 85 and older.

Older people often want to live in their own homes as long as possible. Many are able to stay at home by utilizing formal or informal caregivers. A formal caregiver is anyone who provides help through a service agency. An informal caregiver is a spouse, friend, neighbor, or relative who checks on them and provides occasional meals, makes home repairs, cleans their house, or drives them to doctor appointments. Caregivers are typically women and often a daughter or daughter-in-law. As mentioned elsewhere in the chapter, this caregiving work can be a strain on families in middle adulthood.

Federal law provides for Area Agencies on Aging in most states, whereby services are offered for people in their own homes. These include personal care, such as assistance with bathing or dressing, homemaker services, chore services, home-delivered meals, adult day care, case management, assisted transportation, and respite care for the primary caregiver. Medicaid is the major funder of long-term services in the United States and principally serves people with low incomes and minimal assets.

Some older people opt to live in an assisted-living facility that provides support for some meals, transportation, and social activities and, in some cases, the option to transition to a nursing home with a higher level of care when needed. Such a facility, although out of financial reach for some, can be a happy living option that provides independence, support, and a reduced burden on family members.

For some people, nursing home care is required. This is usually the result of serious health problems and insufficient support to remain at home. Although nursing homes are legally mandated to restore and maintain good health and many do achieve that, serious deficiencies in others can make deciding to use a nursing home difficult (Kail and Cavanaugh 2016).

There are no easy answers for the care of older people who are physically limited. Family members must think carefully and explore a variety of options—and, above all, consult the elderly person about his or her preferences.

Nationalized/Universal Health Care

One of the challenges to families of all ages is affording health-care. Although many do not agree on the best way to do it, most agree that the current health-care system in the United States has needed reform. The Affordable Care Act of 2010 addresses the large numbers of uninsured by requiring the purchase of health insurance and preventing insurance companies from denying or limiting coverage. However, there are concerns because premiums have risen substantially—thus burdening individuals and businesses financially. Also, another concern is that because of the higher premiums, more people will have no insurance coverage. This concern is supported by U.S. Census Bureau statistics, which indicate a higher percentage of the population has no health insurance coverage since the passage of the Affordable Care Act than was true in 2000 or 1990 (U.S. Bureau of the Census 2015).

One proposal for dealing with extremely expensive health-care is to provide universal or nationalized (socialized, "free") health-care to everyone. Proponents argue that such a plan would do the following:

- Allow everyone to visit a doctor or clinic when sick—without cost. This reduces situations where people who are unable to pay wait and get worse or visit the emergency room (where they cannot be turned away). Emergency rooms are much more expensive than clinics.

- Encourage preventative care such as immunizations and management of hypertension—thus reducing costs later on.

- Improve the well-being of many, especially working poor and elderly people, as well as children.

- Benefit U.S. companies because they would no longer have to provide employee health insurance. In turn, companies would have resources to expand more jobs and/or pass along the savings to consumers (Longley 2009).

Opponents point out that such a system would do the following:

- Eliminate personal choice—of doctors, for example.

- Create billions (or trillions) of dollars in higher taxes for working people (Carges 2007; *Single-payer* 2009).

- NOT result in equal access to the health-care system. For example, in Canada and the United Kingdom, elderly people have more difficulty obtaining care than do U.S. seniors. Also, those older than a certain age (say, 75) are denied some services such as dialysis (Longley 2009).

- Mean long waits for appointments, at the emergency room, or for surgery.

- Reduce the incentive (in healthcare providers) to provide better care because salaries and expenditures are capped. Working longer hours or developing new technology does not result in financial benefit.

Questions to Consider

Do the benefits of a nationalized system of health-care outweigh the disadvantages?

Some countries have only national health-care; some provide plans (health insurance or private pay); others have a combination. What kind of arrangement do you think works best? Why?

Suggest practical ways to reduce the costs of health-care.

Suggest ways to make health-care more accessible to working poor families (those who earn too much to qualify for Medicaid, but do not have insurance and cannot afford hundreds of dollars for a doctor visit).

Summary

1. The quality of marriage has an important effect on happiness and satisfaction with life, but marriage relationships are seldom static. Their quality varies over time.

2. The family life cycle divides the family experience into phases, or stages, each with its own challenges, tasks, problems, and rewards.

3. Gay and lesbian families share many of the same characteristics of heterosexual families. They differ in more often being a couple (without children). Research regarding children reared in same-sex families indicates that most fare well although there are unique challenges.

4. Marital adjustments may be defined as the process of modifying, adapting, and altering individual and couple patterns of behavior and interaction to achieve maximum satisfaction in the relationship. The goal of adjustment is to achieve the greatest possible degree of marital satisfaction and success.

5. Marital adjustment tasks early in marriage may be grouped in a number of different categories: emotional fulfillment and support; sexual

adjustment; personal habits; gender roles; material concerns; work, employment, and achievement; social life, friends, and recreation; family and relatives; communication; power and decision making; conflict and problem solving; and morals, values, and ideology.

6. Beginning marriage may lead to a period of disillusionment if the spouses do not realize ahead of time what marriage involves.

7. One longitudinal study of marriage satisfaction during three early stages of marriage found that money was the biggest problem. Problems relating to jealousy, friends, religion, and alcohol and drug abuse declined in importance, whereas problems relating to communication and sex increased in importance. Relatives were a greater problem for couples before marriage and after the birth of the first child.

8. Fatherhood is a profound experience for many men. Assuming responsibility for actively parenting a child changes men developmentally, and men who engage in active parenting develop and mature differently from men who do not.

9. Midlife issues include adjusting to physical changes and to the increasing awareness of one's mortality. This leads to a shift in time orientation; to introspection, self-analysis, and self-appraisal; and to basic questions about the purpose of and goals in life.

10. The assessment of self extends to an examination of the responsibilities of one's career and marriage. Midlife can become a time for reexamination and for charting new courses in life.

11. Middle age also can be a time for revitalizing a tired marriage, for rethinking the relationship, and for deciding what things partners want to share.

12. Some middle-age couples must care for aging parents.

13. The postparental years are usually happier for couples, who now have a greater chance to do what they want without the responsibility of children.

14. Sometimes the empty nest does not stay that way. Children move back home for various reasons, resulting in potential conflict.

15. The task of staying physically healthy becomes more difficult as people age. It requires good health habits and the practice of preventive medicine.

16. Many adults face the problem of having inadequate income in their old age. Most people face a significant drop in income when they retire.

17. Retirement is an easier transition when people are able to retire when they want, when they have adequate resources, and when they have positive plans for retirement. Couples seem to be most satisfied when they retire at the same time. People are happier if they retire to, not from, something.

18. Having acceptable housing and living conditions is a problem for many elderly people. Many want their own residence, which allows them independence.

19. Maintaining identity and social status after retirement becomes a problem when people's identities and status were rooted in the work they performed. Older persons must find identity through avocations, social events, marriage, their children, or other activities.

20. Finding companionship and friendship is one important key to life satisfaction in late adulthood.

21. Learning to enjoy leisure time contributes to well-being in late adulthood.

22. Roles in the family change as people get older, but new ones must be established in relation to grown children and grandchildren.

23. The achievement of ego integrity through a life review and acceptance of one's life as it has been is the chief psychosocial task of the last stage of life.

24. Marital happiness and satisfaction usually increase after the children leave home and after retirement.

25. The divorce rate among people older than age 50 has doubled since 1900. The increase may be a result of increased longevity and expectations of marriage as providing personal happiness. When children are launched, people may decide to leave an unhappy marriage to seek satisfaction somewhere else.

26. The image of parents growing out of contact with their adult children does not coincide with the facts. Aging parents and their grown children want to have good relationships. They are troubled by tensions, especially with regard to personality differences and unsolicited advice. Parents tend to perceive the tensions as more serious than the children do. There is also

ambivalence in the adult child and parent relationship. Both parties experience irritation and frustration but also love of and desire for contact.

27. The death of a spouse is one of life's most traumatic events. Because of women's greater longevity and because men are older when they marry, a married woman can expect to live the last 7 years of her life as a widow.

28. Widows face a number of problems, including loneliness, home maintenance and car repairs, finances, and role changes in the family.

29. Widowers are usually not as close to their families as widows are and so have less social support.

30. As longevity increases, the question arises: Who is going to care for people as they get older? The majority of older people care for themselves or for one another. They value their independence and prefer not to live with their children. Socioeconomic resources influence the kind of care that elderly individuals receive. When a spouse is not available, a child (especially a daughter or daughter-in-law) is usually the major source of support.

31. When elderly people become incapable of caring for themselves, alternative living arrangements must be made. If it is necessary for an elderly person to be put in a nursing home, the home ought to be chosen with great care. Family members must consult the elderly person himself or herself and explore a variety of options before committing to any particular type of care.

Key Terms

developmental tasks
ego resiliency (ER)
family life cycle
marital adjustment
marital adjustment tasks
postparental years
sandwich generation

Questions for Thought

1. During which stage of the family life cycle is marital satisfaction usually highest? During which stage is it usually lowest? Explain.

2. From your point of view, which marital adjustments will be most difficult early in marriage? Why?

3. How do the adjustments during middle adulthood compare to those in late adulthood?

4. How do marriage and family relationships change as people become older?

5. What differences can having a baby make in the lives of a couple?

For Further Reading

Carter, E., and McGoldrick, M. (2005). *The expanded family life cycle: Individual, family, and social perspectives.* New York: Pearson Allyn & Bacon. Provides an overview of the expanded individual and family life cycle from a systems perspective.

Day, R., and Lamb, M. (Eds.). (2004). *Conceptualizing and measuring father involvement.* Mahwah, NJ: Erlbaum. Discusses issues of fatherhood and father involvement from an interdisciplinary perspective.

For Your Marriage has information geared to different stages in the family life cycle. http://www.foryourmarriage.org.

Isay, J. (2008). *Walking on eggshells: Navigating the delicate balance between adult children and parents.* New York: Anchor. Shares interviews with 75 families to give insight into the complicated relationship between parents and grown children.

Marks, N., and Ashleman, K. (2005). *Lifecourse influences on women's social relationships at midlife.* Madison: Center for Demography and Ecology, University of Wisconsin–Madison. Discusses issues related to middle-age women and their mental health.

Moore, A., and Stratton, D. (2003). *Resilient widowers: Older men adjusting to a new life.* Amherst, NY: Prometheus Books. Focuses on men coping with the death of a spouse.

Soaring Spirits Loss Foundation offers positive support for anyone suffering the loss of someone they love, with special emphasis on the widowed. They aim to help peers connect in a community of understanding support. Widowed Village and specialty chats are offered at their website, http://www.sslf.org.

Work, Family Roles, and Material Resources

CHAPTER OUTLINE

Learning Objectives

The American Family Today

- Work, Stress, and the Family
- Positive Benefits of Dual-Earner Families
- Needed: More Time

COPING FEATURE: *Time Pressure*

- The Parents' Child-Care Role
- Household Labor

AT ISSUE TODAY: *The Family and Medical Leave Act*

- Marital Adjustment

FAMILY STRENGTHS PERSPECTIVE: *Keep Things in Perspective*

- Dual-Career Families

Material Resources

- Financial Strains on Families
- The Gender Wage Gap
- Families and Debt

PERSONAL PERSPECTIVE: *Homeless*

- Managing Finances

Poverty and Family Life

- Measuring Poverty
- The Effects of Poverty on Families

CULTURAL PERSPECTIVE: *Race or Economics?*

- Homelessness
- The Feminization of Poverty
- Welfare and the Family
- The Widening Gap between the Rich and the Poor

A QUESTION OF POLICY: *Earned Income Tax Credit*

Summary

Key Terms

Questions for Thought

For Further Reading

LEARNING OBJECTIVES

AFTER READING THE CHAPTER, YOU SHOULD BE ABLE TO DO THE FOLLOWING:

- Relate the challenges and stress many American families experience in balancing the demands of work and family life.

- Describe basic facts about the employment and careers of working parents, their search for life satisfaction, their family members' ethics and value systems, the role conflict and strain they experience, and the marital adjustments they face.

- Identify adaptive strategies from successful families for balancing work and family.

- Discuss the financial needs of families, the relationship between money and marital satisfaction, and money management as a source of harmony or discord.

- Describe effects of poverty and homelessness on family life.

- Explain the concept of the feminization of poverty.

- Describe how the welfare program has changed and discuss the advantages and disadvantages of these changes.

"Flashes of insight take only an instant, and I'm thankful for one I had on an airplane one afternoon. I was off on my usual business travel, which took me away from home three or four days a week. I'd left a teenager disappointed because I'd miss her dance recital. My wife felt so swamped that she'd described herself as a 'single parent.' I had a growing sense of alienation from my family; sometimes I missed big chunks of their lives.

"Feeling a bit indignant, I thought, 'Yeah, but they don't mind the money I make. I have work to do. It's important!' Then the flash of insight came.

"What frontier was I crossing? I wasn't curing cancer or bringing world peace. My company markets a soft drink. A soft drink! Granted we sell it all over Ohio and are moving into the Pittsburgh market, but how many gallons of soda would I be willing to trade for my family?

"I didn't quit. I enjoy sales and it's a good job. I make good money. But I did learn to say no to some company demands. And now I plan my travels so that I have more time at home. Sometimes I take my wife or daughter along.

"In a few years I'll retire, and within a few months of that I'll be forgotten in the soft drink market.

"But I'll still be a husband and a father. I'll be that until I die."

In the majority of today's families, both spouses are employed outside the home. Employment has a profound effect on family life, as well as on personal satisfaction. In turn, family life can influence the work environment.

In this chapter, we explore the relationship between work and family living. We are particularly concerned with the effects of employment on family life, when parents are taking on multiple roles: spouse, parent, employee. What are the effects on life satisfaction and marital adjustments, and what might spouses do to increase personal well-being and that of their family?

We also are concerned with material resources and the family: the relationship between money and marital satisfaction, the financial needs of families, the effects of poverty on family life, and some principles of money management.

The American Family Today

Traditionally, most American families had only a single income earner; the man had the responsibility for supporting the family, and the woman had the responsibility for nurturing the family. This is not the case today. The typical American family is now a **dual-earner family**, in which both spouses are involved in the paid labor force (U.S. Bureau of the Census 2016).

Among two-parent families with children, both parents are employed in about 53% of the families, only the father is employed in 19% of the families, and only the mother is employed in about 5% of the families. The labor force participation rate for mothers with children ages 6 to 17 was 76%; for moms with children under 6, it was 65%; and labor force participation for moms of children under 3 was 61% (Bureau of Labor Statistics 2014). This stands in contrast to 1975, when 47% of mothers with children under age 18 were in the labor force (U.S. Bureau of the Census 2008b). Typically, mothers who stay home to care for their children are part of families that are in the top 5% of household incomes and thus can afford to do so economically, or they are in the bottom 25% where the cost of child

The "good provider" role can be rewarding, but it can be stressful if it takes time away from the marital relationship.

care becomes prohibitive to labor force participation. For the majority of American families, it is an economic necessity to have both parents in the workforce.

Work, Stress, and the Family

Maintaining family life through the chores of daily living, such as making meals, providing shelter, and caring for children, is a major stress for families. For many families, work demands can spill over to impact family life in negative ways, such as lack of time together as well as increased stress and conflict.

The shift from male-breadwinner to dual-earner couples and single-parent households has created a precarious balancing act that greatly differs in reality from its portrayal on prime-time television, where work and family rarely come into contact, parents easily manage child care, the living room is always tidy, and everyone is well-groomed. In general, as the strains and demands of work outside the home increase, the work–family conflicts also increase (Patten 2015b; Schulte 2014; Voydanoff 2004). The term **work–family spillover** is defined as the extent to which participation in one domain (e.g., work) impacts participation in another domain (e.g., family).

For example, job stress affects the parents' marriage and their relationship with their children (Amato et al. 2007; Broman 2001; E. J. Hill et al. 2001; Patten 2015b; Voydanoff 2004), and work–family conflict leads to both job and life dissatisfaction. When stressful demands come from both family and work, it is difficult to attain important work and family values (Perrewe and Hochwarter 2001) and employee well-being declines (Amato et al. 2007; Grant-Vallone and Donaldson 2001). Jobs that are particularly stressful for the family include those that are so difficult that one is under constant strain at work and hard to live with at home. Stressful jobs also include those that require periods of separation or that are so time-consuming that one cannot spend any quality time with family. In general, research shows that more working mothers than fathers experience negative work–family spillover (Dilworth 2004).

The stress of balancing both work and family demands also can have negative effects on one's health (Insel and Roth 2013). In a 5-year study involving 292 women who had suffered heart attacks and 292 age-matched healthy women, Orth-Gomer (2001) found that women with work–family stress were four times more likely than those with just family problems to be struck by a first heart attack. Among women who had already suffered heart attacks, those under the most stress at home were 300% more likely than the least stressed to be hospitalized or to die from heart problems. Women coping poorly with conflicts at home were eight times more likely to have recurrent heart problems than those with family troubles but good coping skills.

When people experience stress on the job, a partner is also likely to experience psychological distress. In fact, a partner may experience as much distress over the other person's job as if it were his/her own job. Men with high dual commitments to job and family and who perceive their spouses as very supportive of their work and parenting activities report less role strain than men with less supportive spouses. This reflects the importance of spousal support to marital satisfaction—especially for men (Boerner et al 2014).

Workaholics devote long hours to their jobs with little energy left over for family. The more ambitious the person and the harder he or she works, the less likely he or she is to take the time to develop close family relationships. In other cases, the pressure to work long hours comes from an employer. Satisfying the boss to keep a job must be weighed against fulfilling family obligations, which is a difficult dilemma for most people.

Many people do successfully manage a balance between work and family demands. Supportiveness in the family and supportiveness at work are critical factors in accomplishing that goal (Patten 2015b). For example, the resource of having some control in one's work environment (such as flexibility) has a positive relationship to life satisfaction (Matos and Galinsky 2014); higher life satisfaction reduces the work–family conflict, which in turn increases family satisfaction. Research also indicates that family supportiveness has a significantly positive influence on life satisfaction by reducing work–family conflict, which in turn increases work satisfaction and life satisfaction (Boerner et al. 2014; Rupert et al. 2012).

dual-earner family A family in which both spouses are in the paid labor force.

work–family spillover The extent to which participation in one domain (e.g., work) impacts participation in another domain (e.g., family).

Positive Benefits of Dual-Earner Families

Although it is challenging to juggle the demands of both work and family, many dual-earner families are healthy and thriving (Haddock et al. 2001) and being a dual-earner family has contributed to their well-being. For example, multiple roles can have a beneficial effect for both men and women with regard to mental, physical, and relationship health (Barnett 2004; Barnett and Hyde 2001; McCormack 2007; Patten 2015b; Sotile and Sotile 2004). Both men and women develop a sense of success and accomplishment from balancing work and family. Multiple roles can provide added income, social support, increased self-complexity, varied opportunities to experience success, and expanded frame of reference (Barnett and Hyde 2001). For example, Damaske (2014) found that a number of people report that the workplace is a respite from the stresses, strains, confusion, and demands of daily family life. Fathers who are involved in parenting view the role as central to their psychological and physical well-being. Research shows that strong commitment to one role does not necessarily preclude strong commitment to another role (Barnett and Hyde 2001).

Most parents with children under age 18 are at least somewhat successful in managing work and family and that maternal employment in and of itself appears to have little impact on children. Any impact on the child depends on a number of factors. For example, the benefits or disadvantages of multiple roles depend on the number of roles, the demands of each role, and role quality (Voydanoff 2002). Everyone has limits, and when overloaded individuals reach their upper limits, distress occurs. On the one hand, work that is rewarding can have positive effects in a person's life. On the other hand, work that is not satisfying or that brings with it discrimination or sexual harassment does not contribute to life satisfaction and feelings of success (Barnett and Hyde 2001).

For many parents, working outside the home enhances their lives, especially if they love their jobs and have a spouse and children who help them or if they are able to hire some assistance. Some parents are more relaxed at work than at home and may even go to work to get away from their families. One mother remarked, "I can't wait to get out of the house in the morning. Work is the only place I have any peace and quiet. I'd go absolutely crazy if I had to stay home all day. My children could drive me crazy" (Counseling notes).

Haddock and her colleagues (2001) studied how successful families balance work and family. They found 10 adaptive strategies:

1. **Valuing family:** The highest priority for successful couples was a commitment to family. Couples worked hard at maintaining family time and family rituals, such as bedtime stories every evening and "pizza night" every Friday.

2. **Striving for partnership:** Equality and partnership in the marital relationship were vital to the success of balancing work and family. Important issues of equality and partnership surrounded division of household chores and child care, decision making, respect and appreciation, and support on an interpersonal level.

3. **Deriving meaning from work:** Couples who liked their work and experienced enjoyment from it felt that it brought energy to their lives and helped in the balance of work and family.

4. **Maintaining work boundaries:** Couples who did not allow work to control their lives were better able to balance work and family.

5. **Focusing and producing at work:** Being productive at work helped people put family as a top priority and still feel good about their job performance.

6. **Prioritizing family fun:** Given that many dual-earner families have fewer hours to play, successful families made a point to enjoy playtime together and used it as a way to destress from a busy day on the job.

7. **Taking pride in dual earning:** Most of the successful couples felt that being a dual-earner family was positive for all members of the family. They did not experience guilt for working and felt it was the right choice for them as a family.

8. **Living simply:** Living simply included limiting activities that restrict family time, such as television and children's extracurricular activities, controlling their finances, developing realistic expectations about housework, and finding efficient ways to manage the household.

9. **Making decisions proactively:** Successful couples took control of their lives through decision making rather than allowing the pace of their lives to take control. Their priority to family shaped their decisions.

10. **Valuing time:** Successful couples were aware of the value of time and attempted to maximize their use of time. They were protective and thought about ways to spend meaningful and rewarding time together.

Needed: More Time

The time pressure experienced by contemporary families is greatly influenced by the pattern of dual-income families that has developed over the past 60 years. When compared with single-earner families and families in which neither partner works, dual-earner parents spend less time with their children and less time with each other (Glorieux et al. 2011). These findings are related to other research indicating that when couples have little discretionary time because of work and other responsibilities, both spouses experience an increase in stress and time pressure. The more hours a spouse works, the more energy deficit that spouse has, which in turn causes distress in both spouses (Ten Brummelhuis, Haar, and van der Lippe 2010).

Family scholars have significant concern about the time demands and hectic pace of parents' jobs, which are causing families to become time poor. This can lead to children losing important opportunities to spend time with their families and parents missing chances to connect with their offspring and with each other (Crouter et al. 2004). Data from two national studies on almost 2,000 parents showed that nearly half of the parents reported spending too little time with children, largely because of the hours in paid employment (Milkie et al. 2004).

Considerable disparity exists between how much people would like to work and how much they are working: Most workers indicate they prefer seven-hour work days and four-day work weeks (Gander 2015). Instead, some 42% of full-time workers put in 40 hours a week with some 50% putting in more than that. Part-time workers average 26 hours a week (McGregor 2014).

Long workweeks generally do not reflect employee preferences; some result from demands imposed by the general economy. For example, Mark works full-time for a manufacturing company that caps his hours at 28 per week (to avoid having to offer benefits such as health insurance or retirement). In order to make enough to support his family and to have benefits, he also works as a custodian for the county school system; this job takes about 25 hours a week. For other workers—especially in professions or business, there may be pressure to put in long hours to be seen as committed, productive, and able to advance. It is therefore no surprise that people feel rushed or that many American workers want to work fewer hours.

Much research has documented that long work hours may have negative consequences for families (Crouter et al. 2004; Major, Klein, and Ehrhart 2002; Oscharoff 2011). In a study of 513 employees in a Fortune 500 company, long work hours were associated with increased work–family conflict and psychological distress (Major, Klein, and Ehrhart 2002). People work longer hours when they have strong career identity, have too much to do on the job, perceive that their supervisors expect them to work extra hours as needed, have fewer responsibilities away from work, or they have financial needs.

Regardless of how flexible employees' schedules are or how much responsibility they bear for home and family duties, the more hours a week that people work, the more work interferes with family. Long work hours did not relate to spouses' love or parent-child love, but role overload consistently predicted less-positive family relationships (Crouter et al. 2004; D. Olson, DeFrain, and Skogrand 2014; Oscharoff 2011).

Numerous studies reveal that family time in dual-earner families is rare. Researchers have examined five specific categories of family time: meals, watching television, active leisure, religious activities, and housework. Although most families report at least some time in family meals and about half watch television together, small numbers of families engage in active leisure, religious activities, and housework together. Across 7 days, families spend only about 4 hours, on average, in activities that are shared by all family members. In families with higher levels of family time, parent–child, marital, and sibling relationships are seen as warmer, more loving, and more intimate (Crouter et al. 2004; D. Olson, DeFrain, and Skogrand 2014; Stinnett and Stinnett 2010).

Another barrier to family togetherness is a job schedule that makes it difficult for members to be

Time Pressure

One of the biggest life stressors and a major problem for marriage and family relationships is time pressure (the stress of feeling there is not enough time to do everything one needs or wants to do). How do we deal with time demands in ways that we do not become stressed? Following are some effective coping strategies:

- **Stop trying to do everything.** We often are overwhelmed because we are trying to do too much. Research indicates that members of strong families "reduce the load" by posing these questions for each of their involvements: Is this necessary? Is this truly important? Does this make me happy? When the answer to all three questions is no, that involvement is dropped.

- **Simplify.** Think of ways to make tasks easier and simpler. For example, grill a couple of chickens with your Saturday burgers for leftovers later in the week; double casserole recipes or make a big pot of soup. Shop in a smaller, independent grocery where it is easier and faster to park, find things, and check out. Make flowerbeds lower maintenance by planting perennials or shrubs.

- **Prioritize.** Decide what is most important to do and what will bring the most life satisfaction. For example, what is more important— your health or being the chairperson of four committees?

- **Make a schedule.** This strategy makes it more likely that we will get the things done that we need to accomplish. Also, making a schedule or "to-do" list sometimes makes it clear that it is impossible to do all the tasks— we must prioritize or simplify or reduce the load!

- **Give up perfection.** Remind yourself that it is not necessary to have a perfectly maintained house and yard. Every meal does not have to be a banquet. A compulsion to be perfect often drives a person to create more time pressures by spending more time than necessary on a task and also by creating additional tasks. For example, Suzy wanted to support her children in school so she volunteered to help in the library one afternoon a week. Now she is president of the PTO and on several committees—and at school most days.

---

together. Some couples use nonoverlapping shift work as a way of balancing work and family. Nonoverlapping shift work allows the parents of young children to provide all of the child care themselves and thus save on child-care costs. However, when couples work different shifts, little time is left over for the marital relationship (Foster 2014).

If a couple must work shifts, working the same shift can be important in maintaining a relationship. Divorce is common among couples in which one spouse works nights. Fathers who work nights are six times more likely to divorce than are fathers who work days, and mothers who work nights triple their odds of divorce. Other jobs, such as that of a police officer, are very stressful in and of themselves and require work on weekends and holidays. Some work, such as serving in the armed services and

merchant marines, requires long periods of separation. This can be a source of individual and family stress (Strazdins et al. 2006).

Many couples scale back to have more time for family (E. J. Hill 2006). Some have one full-time and one part-time earner; others give up overtime for family time. Time is a precious commodity; many people recognize that marriage and family relationships, like anything worthwhile, require time and attention to maintain. They are not willing to sacrifice family for a job.

The Parents' Child-Care Role

The decisions that parents make about work and family, especially about how they care for their children, help shape their children's intellectual

Increasing numbers of fathers participate in child care as part of their family responsibilities. A father's involvement in child-rearing benefits his children's academic achievement, social competence, and self-esteem.

development, social behavior, and personalities. In everything they do, from the jobs they choose to the way they allocate household chores, parents provide powerful models of male and female behavior for their children. Parents, inadvertently or intentionally, prepare their children for similar future roles in the workplace and the family.

Today, most fathers are expected to share in the responsibilities of child care, especially in dual-earner families. Several researchers have found that men contribute more to household and child-care responsibilities than they did in the past, but they still do not contribute as much as their wives do (Fottrell 2015; Bureau of Labor Statistics 2015). Some 65% of men are involved in some household activities such as housework, cooking, and lawn care; this compares to 83% of women who are involved. Mothers spend an average of one hour a day on direct child care (bathing or feeding, for example)

to fathers' 23 minutes (Fottrell 2015; Bureau of Labor Statistics 2015).

Both parents benefit from fathers' participation in raising children. Fathers typically become more actively involved caregivers when children move out of infancy (Kail and Cavanaugh 2016; R. D. Parke 2002). Fathers who assume responsibility for child care ease the burden of employed mothers and reduce the maternal stress associated with work overload, anxiety, and a shortage of time for rest and leisure. Fathers who are actively involved in caring for their children enjoy the positive effects of multiple roles, which include enhanced marital relations and closer father–child bonds. Men, like women, who combine different life roles such as parent, worker, and spouse may be better off emotionally than individuals with fewer life roles.

Although fathers are assuming more child-care responsibility, most parents are still challenged to find appropriate child care during the workday. As stated, some parents work shifts that do not overlap to meet child-care demands. Yet such work schedules often are not available and can contribute to marital dissatisfaction. Thus, most couples do not want to work different shifts.

The challenge of child care is even greater for parents who work evenings, early mornings, or weekends; it is difficult to find child-care centers or other formal arrangements that are available during those hours. Parents who are employed at odd hours have fewer choices in caring for their children and may have to select child care they feel is less than adequate.

The availability of different types of child care will be discussed in more detail in Chapter 13. However, regardless of the type of care, most dual-earner families admit they have to budget their time carefully around child-care issues. Most centers have strict hours of operation; dropping off a child early or picking up a child late is not feasible. Nor is there care for sick children. Most employers also have set hours of business. However, some companies have recognized the struggles their employees face with child care and have **flextime** that allows

flextime A company policy that allows employees to choose the most convenient hours for them to work during the day, selected from hours designated by the employer.

workers to choose the hours during the day when they will work.

Research shows that job flexibility is associated with less negative spillover from work to family and is also associated with less stress. Job flexibility is related to improved work–family balance and appears to be beneficial to both individuals and businesses. For example, employees with perceived job flexibility were better able to work longer hours before workload negatively impacted their work–family balance (E. J. Hill 2006; Jang, Zippay, and Park 2012). Employees with flextime have been found to be more satisfied with their jobs and more committed than those without flextime.

A large national survey of American employers indicates that 77% of companies offer flextime; 87% allow workers to take time off to tend to important family needs (take an elderly parent to a doctor's appointment or attend a child's recital, for example); and 63% allow workers to work from home on an occasional basis. However, fewer companies offer job sharing, working from home on a full-time basis, or sabbaticals (E. J. Hill 2006; Matos and Galinsky 2014). Consequently, working parents make time for necessary tasks by giving up personal and leisure time and volunteer or community activities.

One way that some middle-class dual-earner couples cope with the demands of work and family is by "scaling back." That is, the partners place limits on the number of hours they work (working part-time or giving up overtime, for example), reduce expectations for career advancement, decide to have a one-job/one-career marriage, or trade family and job responsibilities over the life course. Women, however, do the most scaling back (Gerson and Jacobs 2007). Twice as many women work part-time (26%) as men (13%) and few families have a stay-at-home dad (about 4%) compared to 19% where mom is not employed (Bureau of Labor Statistics 2014).

Although both parents may agree that having the mother stay home with the children is the most practical plan for child care, there are important consequences to consider. Research shows that compared to their employed counterparts, women who leave the labor force, even for a couple years, have more difficulty with career advancement and salary gains if they decide to return to the labor force. They experience "human capital depreciation" (their skills get rusty) and work networks change to the extent that they cannot make up for the losses (Hymowitz 2013). This must be considered against the fact that large numbers of marriages end in divorce; a stay-at-home mother may face serious financial disadvantage if the couple divorces.

Maternity leave, which allows pregnant women to take a leave of absence from work to have their babies (or to welcome an adopted child), helps eliminate the conflict between having to work and wanting to stay home and care for a newborn. Parental leave allows new fathers the same opportunity. Women who have maternity leave have lower infant mortality rates among their infants. Maternity leave allows women to breastfeed longer; this benefits the babies and can save $55 to $200 a month from the budget. The early months of life are a critically important time for infants to establish secure attachments to their parents and parents to bond with their babies (Kail and Cavanaugh 2016).

The Family and Medical Leave Act (FMLA) of 1993 and individual company maternity-or paternity-leave policies guarantee that some employees can take time (typically 6 to 12 weeks, unpaid) off for the birth or adoption of a child or for a family emergency and return to the job afterward. (See the "At Issue Today" feature for more information about the FMLA.) Currently three states (California, New Jersey, Rhode Island) offer paid maternity leave benefits; these are funded by payroll deductions of about $30 per month (Elliott 2015).

Questions arise as to how long maternity leave should be to provide the most benefits to everyone without penalizing women for being out of the work force. Maternity leave that is short (less than six weeks) is a risk factor for personal and marital distress. However, many women cannot afford to take a more optimal 3 to 6 months of leave when it is unpaid; employers also have concerns about the cost of such leave to them (of holding a woman's job for her—hiring a substitute, etc.). Women who took paid leaves (of 3 to 6 months) were very likely to be working at their pre-leave jobs a year later and they were 40% less likely to be on public assistance than women who took unpaid leaves (Elliott 2015).

Employers in California (one of the states that offers paid leave) report very positive results. Some 91% said that the paid leave had no effect or a positive effect on profitability or performance (Elliott 2015).

Research focusing on the role of social policies in reducing work–family conflict in 27 countries found that in all but 2 countries, women reported higher levels of work–family conflict than did men. This research also indicated that the existence of policies that encourage child-care availability and, to a lesser extent, maternity leave reduces work–family conflict for both men and women (Stier, Lewin-Epstein, and Braun 2012).

Household Labor

Parents who are employed not only have less time to spend with their children but also spend fewer hours on household chores such as meal preparation and cleaning. For example, since 1965, women's involvement in domestic labor (excluding child care and shopping) has declined. Men, by contrast, have increased their housework during that same time. However, although men are doing more than before, they still are doing less than women. For example, 49% of women do housework/cleaning/laundry as compared to 20% of men; 69% of women do food preparation and cleanup compared to 43% of men (Fottrell 2015; Bureau of Labor Statistics 2015).

Women's and men's sense of fairness in family work has been examined, including what might lead them to view their workloads as fair or unfair. The findings showed that women's perceptions of unfairness were greater when they got less pleasure out of doing household and child-care tasks. What mattered most for husbands was how competent they felt at family work and their wives' sense of their competence in performing such work (Grote, Naylor, and Clark 2002; Huston and Holmes 2004).

While women employed full-time may reduce the amount of time they spend on household tasks, they cannot reduce the range of their responsibilities. Some writers refer to employed mothers as "supermoms"—mothers who remain heavily involved with family responsibilities while also meeting the demands of paid employment.

Judith Warner (2005), in her book *Perfect Madness*, describes what she sees as an epidemic of isolated, stressed-out mothers trying to do it all and do it all well. She asks why the most liberated and privileged women America has ever seen drive themselves crazy in the quest to be the perfect mom and to have perfect children. The hectic pace of juggling employment, domestic work, child care, extracurricular activities for children, exercise, social and intimate relationships, and maybe even some time for themselves can be overwhelming. When a mother is not emotionally healthy, the whole family suffers, and in her struggle to do the multitude of tasks well, the overall goal of a healthy family is often sacrificed.

The Family and Medical Leave Act

The Family and Medical Leave Act (FMLA) of 1993 guarantees *some* workers up to 12 weeks of *unpaid* leave per year for the birth or adoption of a child, to provide extended care for a sick family member (spouse, parent, or parent-in-law, for example), or to care for their own serious illness. However, FMLA has not been as effective as it might have been in helping families because of its restrictions. For example:

- Only full-time employees with 1 year of employment are eligible (about 54% of workers meet this criterion).
- "Key" employees—those whose absence causes substantial injury to the business—can be denied leave.
- Small businesses (less than 50 employees) do not have to comply.
- Many families simply cannot go without a paycheck for 1 to 3 months.

Other industrialized nations provide more extensive paid maternity leave. For example, in the United Kingdom parents can take 18 weeks' leave at 90% of their salary. Norwegian parents can take 42 weeks at 100% of their salary or 52 weeks at 80%. And in Bulgaria, mothers can take 45 days prior to the birth of a baby and 2 *years* after—all paid. They may also opt for an additional year of unpaid leave (Graves 2013; Hymowitz 2013; "Parental leave" 2007; U.S. Department of Labor 2007).

Marital Adjustment

Social science has devoted considerable effort to comparing employed and nonemployed women to determine effects on spousal relationships. Some investigators report a positive relationship between women's employment and marital adjustment. In many families, wives' employment has a positive effect on marital quality through increased family income, particularly when her income reduces financial strain. In addition, shared responsibility for supporting the family promotes a more egalitarian ideology among both men and women (Zuo and Tang 2000). Naturally, too, when wives have jobs they enjoy and can work the number of hours they prefer, the effect on marital satisfaction is apt to be positive.

Conversely, when women *must* work more than they want at jobs they do not enjoy, the effect on marital satisfaction is apt to be negative. For example, when husbands are not employed, either is more likely to leave (Sayer et al. 2011).

The effect of women's employment on marital quality also depends on the number of children in the household. As the number of children in the household increases, so do their needs and the demands on the mother's time and energy. Consequently, work–family role strain is heightened for employed mothers; and marital interaction and quality are compromised (Oscharoff 2011).

In mother–stepfather families, the relationship between maternal employment and marital quality is more complicated. When the family is small, the mother's full-time employment is associated with less marital happiness and more marital conflict. This suggests that combining the demands of work and family has negative effects on the marital relationship that outweigh the potential benefits. When family size increases, however, the mother's full-time employment is associated with greater marital happiness and less marital conflict. The mother's contributions to the family income are likely to ease economic strain and increase marital quality.

Although balancing commitments to children, partner, and career can be demanding and difficult, many working mothers would not choose anything less.

If both members of a couple are career-committed individuals, they will face special challenges in trying to balance professional and family roles.

Keep Things in Perspective

You might have seen the poster of a zebra whose haunch and hind leg stripes have come unraveled. As the zebra stands with its stripes curled around its feet like ribbons, the caption notes, "It must be STRESS."

We have all felt like the zebra—as if our stripes are falling off. It could be because traffic is heavy or the baby is teething or a check has bounced. It could even be because of a promotion at work or a new home or planning a big holiday party. Stress comes in many shapes and sizes—and on a daily basis.

Stress is not new, but our understanding of it has changed in recent years. Our ancestor who encountered a bear while foraging for food experienced stress. Adrenaline flooded his body, his blood pressure surged, his heart beat faster. Chemicals that cause the blood to clot faster were secreted. He was ready to run faster or fight better—and if he was clawed by the bear, his blood would clot faster. Those same reactions take place in our bodies today when we are stressed. Unfortunately, our stress rarely requires fight or flight, and so we experience the strong physical and emotional reactions to stress without an effective way of releasing them.

After months or years of such distress, we feel the effects. Medical science has much evidence that the accumulated effects of stress are important factors in heart disease, angina, arrhythmia, hypertension, migraines, ulcers, diabetes, and many other diseases.

The bad news is that stress can kill us; it can diminish the quality of life in our families, and we cannot get away from it. The good news is that we can take action to manage our reactions to it. Strong families have discovered numerous tactics for dealing with stress—including simplifying, prioritizing, and reducing the load. Another tactic is to keep things in perspective. Following are some specific ways to do this:

- Remember that everyone has tough times. Most of the things that happen are not "enemy action"; they are just part of life.

- Recognize that most stressors are insignificant or minor. Some are best overlooked or forgotten. The driver who honks and whizzes past may be late for something very important. The neighbor who does not return your wave may not have seen you without her glasses.

- Have some compassion for others who may have bigger problems. One woman shared,

One day I was feeling really pressed and depressed. We had company coming for dinner, the house was messy, and I resented having to cook and clean all afternoon. As I washed dishes, I suddenly thought of a young woman we knew. She was gravely ill and too weak to get out of bed. We knew she didn't have long to live. What would she give to have this "awful" day of mine?

Dual-Career Families

Earlier in this chapter, *dual-earner family* was defined as a family in which both spouses are involved in the paid labor force. Ordinarily, having a job does not involve as extensive a commitment, as much continuity of employment, or as much responsibility as the pursuit of a career.

The **dual-career family** is a specific subtype of the broader category of dual-earner families. The dual-career family has two career-committed individuals, both of whom are trying to fulfill professional and family roles. But the pursuit of a career requires a high degree of commitment and continuous development.

dual-career family A subtype of the dual-earner family in which there are two career-committed partners, both of whom are trying to fulfill professional roles that require continuous development as well as family roles.

Individuals with careers tend to be heavily invested in their professional identity (Bird and Schnurman-Crook 2004); they usually must work full-time. Individuals pursue careers by undergoing extensive education and preparation and then moving upward from one job level to another. The greater the responsibility and the higher the position achieved, the greater the commitment required of the individual—leaving less time to devote to spouse and child. The dual-career marriage is actually a minority pattern and, from a strictly managerial standpoint, is difficult to achieve.

There are some real satisfactions and benefits in a dual-career marriage, as well as stresses. The financial rewards in a dual-career marriage can be considerable, especially if both spouses are earning salaries as professionals. Other reasons for wanting a career include the needs for creativity, self-expression, achievement, and recognition. Because the stress in balancing both career and family responsibilities can be overwhelming, successful dual-career spouses treat each other as equal partners and share in the responsibility of child care and household tasks.

Material Resources

As stated previously, although some people work for personal fulfillment and satisfaction, financial necessity and the desire to improve the family's standard of living remain the most important motives for working.

Financial Strains on Families

The financial strains of today's families are great. This is more apparent in times when the national economy is struggling, unemployment is high, and mortgages are being foreclosed.

STAGNANT OR DECLINING INCOMES Individuals who compare current salaries to those of 10 to 20 years ago often are perplexed: people seem to be earning more but having less. Why is this? Table 8.1 shows the median family incomes from 1990 to 2014—in actual dollars and also adjusted for inflation. Salaries that appear at first glance to have increased by thousands have, in reality, not done so. Income in America has been under pressure or compromised over the past 30 years. When adjusted for inflation, income has remained basically the same over the past 15 years or declined (U.S. Bureau of the Census 2015).

Throughout the United States, in almost every demographic category, individuals earned less in 2014 than they did in 2007, for example. The greatest income decline has been in households led by people 55 to 64 years of age, who experienced a 9.7% decline. The second largest income decline was among those in the age category of 25 to 34, whose income fell 8.9%. The median income for all households fell by 8% (U.S. Bureau of the Census 2012, 2015).

THE SHRINKING DOLLAR A look at the consumer price index also gives insight into the financial strain on families. The consumer price index is the most

TABLE 8.1   Median Income* of Families by Race and Hispanic Origin, 1990–2013

	ALL	WHITE	BLACK	ASIAN	HISPANIC
1990	$35,400	$36,900	$21,400	$42,400	$23,400
	($48,000)	($54,500)	($31,000)	($66,000)	($37,300)
2000	$50,700	$53,000	$33,700	$62,600	$34,400
	($57,500)	($61,000)	($40,000)	($73,000)	($45,000)
2007	$61,400	$64,400	$40,100	$76,600	$40,600
	($57,500)	($61,000)	($38,500)	($74,000)	($44,000)
2013	$52,000	$58,300	$34,600	$67,100	$41,000
2014	$53,700	$60,300	$35,400	$74,300	$42,500

*Salaries are rounded to hundreds of dollars.
**Parentheses indicate actual salaries adjusted to show value in 2013 dollars.
Note: From the Current population survey *by U.S. Bureau of the Census, 2015. http://www.census.gov.*

TABLE 8.2 Consumer Price Index, 1915–2014

YEAR	CONSUMER PRICE INDEX
1915	$10.10
1930	$16.70
1940	$14.00
1950	$24.10
1960	$29.60
1970	$38.80
1980	$82.40
1990	$130.70
2000	$172.20
2010	$218.10
2014	$236.70

Note: Data from Bureau of Labor Statistics, 2015, http://www.bls.gov/cpi/home.htm.

commonly used measure of inflation. It calculates the price of an arbitrary bundle of goods and services. As you can see in Table 8.2, what cost $29.60 to buy in 1960 costs $236.70 in 2014 (that is eight times as much!). In other words, the purchasing power of the dollar is much less—prices have gone up more than salaries (Bureau of Labor Statistics 2015).

CHILDREN are a major expense for families. The cost of rearing a child born in 2013 to age 18 in a family making between $61,530 and $106,540 is estimated at $245,340—not including college. Family expenditures depend on family income. Costs also vary by the area of the country where the family lives, with the southeastern United States or rural areas being least expensive ($145,000) and the urban northeast being most expensive ($455,000) (U.S. Department of Agriculture 2015). Figure 8.1 shows a breakdown of the average, annual cost of rearing a child in various regions of the United States. Housing is the largest portion of the cost (30%), followed by child care and education (18%) and food (16%). Many parents are surprised at how expensive child care is—sometimes equal to the mortgage payment.

When college costs are added, the total tab goes up considerably. The College Board reported that the annual in-state tuition and fees at four-year public colleges and universities doubled from $4,586 in 2000/2001 to $9,410 in 2015/2016. Annual tuition and fees at private colleges rose from $23,712 to $32,405. Room and board for a year costs another $8,000–11,000 (College Board 2016).

HOUSING still ranks as one of the biggest expenses for families, accounting for 33% to 37% of the budget, just as it did 40 years ago. In some cities, families earning as much as $70,000 a year cannot find decent housing without spending more than half their income. According to the National Association of Realtors (2016), the median sales price of a one-family home was $230,500 in 2015, up from $208,900 in 2014. The average monthly mortgage payment rollercoasted from $690 in 1998 to $1,040 in 2005 and back to $870 in 2015. The percentage of U.S. householders owning their homes declined from 68.6% in 2005 to just over 63% in 2015 (U.S. Bureau of the Census 2016).

Median rent in 2015 was $935 per month. There are indications that more people are experiencing difficulty paying their rent. A national study by New York University and Capitol One (2015) found that more than 50% of the tenants in 11 major cities are paying rent that is unaffordable for them.

HEALTH CARE A major and increasingly critical financial strain for families is health care and health

For the dual-earner family, finding quality child care can be a big problem. Ensuring the availability of quality day care for children is a national concern.

insurance. The health-care expenditure per person is now more than $9,200—three times what it was in 1990 and a 650% increase compared with 1960, when it was $142 per person (Centers for Disease Control and Prevention 2015).

Without insurance coverage, health-care expenses can be a major financial crisis for any family. About 50 million people (16% of the population) are not covered by health insurance. Lack of insurance is much more common among families with low incomes and among noncitizen immigrants (U.S. Bureau of the Census 2015). The unfortunate consequences are that many of these individuals are not receiving health care or they are not seeking treatment until they are much sicker and must make a trip to the emergency room (where they cannot be denied treatment). Treatment in the emergency room costs many times more than a visit to the doctor's office.

UNEMPLOYMENT Currently, in America, some 17 million people are unemployed or underemployed—a major financial stress for families. The unemployment rate has varied from 4% in 2000 to 8.3% in August 2012 to just under 5% in April 2016 (Bureau of Labor Statistics 2012, 2016). Although unemployment affects all socioeconomic, racial, and ethnic groups, blacks, Hispanics, and families headed by single mothers are especially hard hit.

The reported rate of unemployment is probably significantly lower than the true degree of unemployment because it does not count the discouraged people who have not looked for work in more than 12 months. Nor does it distinguish between part-time and full-time employment, and it does not identify "underutilized" employment. Another report by the Bureau of Labor Statistics that does take these issues into consideration estimates the actual unemployment rate to be approximately twice what is reported (Bureau of Labor Statistics 2012).

Unemployment is a crisis for families—an inability to pay bills, a sense of hopelessness and anxiety about the future, a concern about meeting the basic needs (groceries, shelter, clothing, for example) of family members. Extended unemployment means these families probably lose their homes to foreclosure. Many unemployed workers eventually take part-time work or work out of their field or at reduced salaries to have some kind of income. Unemployment requires significant lifestyle changes such as living with relatives, transitioning from a comfortable home to a cramped apartment, or even being homeless.

Individuals who have less adaptability experience more difficulty. Unfortunately, the stress of unemployment often contributes to increased conflict among family members. Factors that help families to deal more successfully with unemployment include a good support system of relatives, friends, church, synagogue, or mosque; a strong commitment to each other; adaptability; having a good problem-solving approach; a strong spiritual faith; and maintaining a sense of hope.

GENERAL DEBT is a chronic, persistent financial strain. Over time, heavy debt can cause family members to feel anxious and overwhelmed; it also can contribute to less hopefulness and increased conflict.

Since the 1950s, families have dramatically wanted more, consumed more, and borrowed more. Buying bigger homes, purchasing luxury cars, eating out more often, spending more on everything from clothes to entertainment to college tuition, and the abuse of credit cards (increasingly used for everyday spending) are all significant factors that have contributed to a soaring debt level for families (Federal Reserve 2015). The total owed by the average U.S. household carrying these types of debt is as follows:

Mortgages	$168,614
Student Loans	$48,172
Auto Loans	$27,141
Credit Cards	$15,762
Any Type Debt	$130,922
(El Issa 2016)	

Total mortgage debt increased as the price of homes soared—until 2008, when the housing bubble burst, leading to massive numbers of foreclosures. As credit (mortgages) became harder to get, sales became fewer and the value of homes fell significantly. As a result, the homeowner equity (an asset to the homeowner) among homes with mortgages has dropped dramatically, from 45% in the early 1980s to 15% (Federal Reserve 2015).

STUDENT LOAN DEBT One area of debt that has not decreased is student loans. Since 2008, student loans have increased to slightly more than $1 trillion. This phenomenal increase in student loan debt is a result of the rising number of young people reaching college age since the mid-1990s, more people entering or returning to college because of unemployment (to train or retrain for a different field), and the dramatic increase in higher-education costs. In response to these conditions, government-sponsored student loans have become common (Federal Reserve Bank of New York 2016).

As might be expected, research based on a large, representative study of over 60,000 college graduates (by Gallup and Purdue University, referred to as the Gallup and Purdue Index) indicated that student debt had a significant impact on well-being and workplace engagement. Those graduates who incurred between $20,000 and $40,000 in student loans were far more likely to have a lower level of well-being based on a number of physical, social, emotional, and financial criteria than did those graduates without any loans to repay (Bruni 2015, 2016).

The average graduate (from a four-year public university) with a bachelor's degree now borrows more than $27,000 and 10% graduate with $40,000 in student loan debt. Graduate students incur $30,000 to $120,000 in debt and approximately half of those who attend professional schools, such as law or medical school, had a student loan debt greater than their annual incomes (College Board 2015; Reiter and Leonard 2013; National Post-Secondary Student Aid Survey 2015).

Although many college students are borrowing thousands of dollars, their parents are also taking out loans to help meet higher-education expenditures. This financial strain is exacerbated when students graduate and cannot find jobs. Furthermore, the consequences of not paying back government-sponsored student loans can be harsh. Typically, student loans are not discharged in a bankruptcy, making them difficult to wipe away, and there is no statute of limitations on collecting them. Substantial collection fees—often far in excess of the original loan amount—can be levied. The government can also garnish wages, seize income tax refunds, and even take federal benefits usually exempt from collection, such as Social Security income, in an attempt to recoup the loan (Reiter and Leonard 2013).

The Health Care and Education Reconciliation Act of 2010, nicknamed the Obama Student Loan Forgiveness Program, offers help for repayment of federal student loans (not private ones). This program allows new borrowers to make payments based on discretionary income and makes them eligible for forgiveness after 20 years (rather than 25). For all borrowers, when the loans come due, the borrower can consolidate his/her loans and select a repayment plan. These include standard repayment (loan amount plus interest over 20–25 years); graduated repayment (monthly payments start out lower than standard and increase every 2 years), income-contingent repayment (payments based on income, family size, loan balance, etc.); income-based repayment (payments based on income and family size); or pay as you earn (payments are 10% of discretionary income). "Forgiveness" also comes in several options: interest forgiveness applies for a portion of the interest only for the first 3 years of income-based repayment; end of term involves forgiveness of any remaining balance of the loan after 20–25 years of payments in the income-contingent, income-based, and pay-as-you-earn plans; public-sector forgiveness qualifies those who work in the public sector after 10 years. Teacher and disability forgiveness is also available (Student Debt Relief 2015).

Although there are no easy strategies for paying back large student loans, other options include seeking a deferment by such avenues as serving in the Peace Corps or the military on active duty and filing bankruptcy. It is highly unlikely that bankruptcy will eliminate student loan debt; however, it can help get rid of other debts, freeing up money to pay back student loans (Reiter and Leonard 2013).

GAS AND RESIDENTIAL HEATING OIL The price of unleaded gasoline ($1.89 in April 2016) has increased significantly since 2000, when it was $1.06 per gallon. This increase has resulted in many families driving less and eliminating family vacation trips because a larger portion of the family paychecks are allocated for gasoline. An increase in the price of gasoline also causes an increase in the price of any goods (such as groceries) that are transported. The increase in the cost of crude oil that sends gasoline prices up also increases the cost of oil to heat residences—meaning that utilities go up even when thermostats are adjusted to less comfortable ranges.

The Gender Wage Gap

The Equal Pay Act in 1963 outlawed wage discrimination based on gender; Title VII of the Civil Rights Act of 1964 was an even broader attempt to

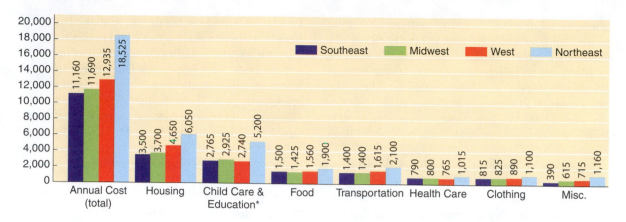

FIGURE 8.1 The Average Annual Costs of Rearing a Child to Age 18 by Region for Families Earning $61,530 to $106,540

correct the inequity. Even so, women consistently earn lower wages than men. For example, the median income for females is about $14,000 less than the median income for males (U.S. Bureau of the Census 2016). Many times women earn less than men, even when employed in the same jobs. Although in some occupations (such as office clerks, nurses, social workers) the gap is narrower or nonexistent, for most occupations (such as retail sales, managers, financial managers) it is still substantial (Hegewisch and DuMonthier 2016;

Hegewisch and Ellis 2015). So why is it that the phenomenon continues?

Some suggest that the wage gap is partly a result of differences in education. But the data show that when education levels are taken into account there is still an inequity in salaries (see Figure 8.2).

Work experience also is cited as a factor in the gender wage gap, but again, the argument is weakened by specific examples in which equal qualifications do not mean equal pay. Studies have shown that even when all the key factors that influence

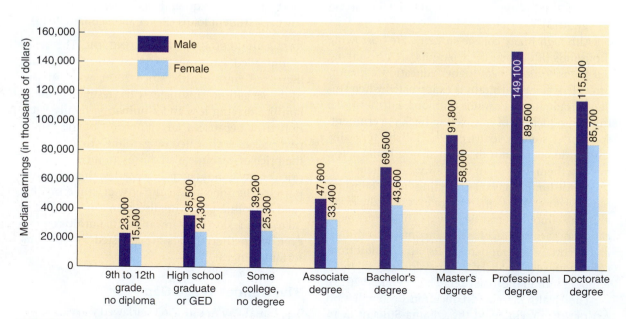

FIGURE 8.2 Median Earnings by Sex and Educational Attainment, Full-Time, Year-Round Workers, Age 18 and Older
Note: From Statistical Abstract of the United States, *2014. U.S. Bureau of the Census. http://www.census.gov.*

earnings are controlled (demographic factors such as marital status, race, and number and age of children, as well as work patterns such as years of work, hours worked, and job tenure), women still earn, on average, only 80% of what men earn (Center for American Progress 2012; O'Brien 2015; Bureau of Labor Statistics 2015).

Evidently, other factors are at least partly responsible for the continued gender wage gap. Three reasons can be attributed to women themselves: (1) they work in lower-paying industries; (2) they do not work as many hours per week as men; and (3) they do not "fight" for their own pay. Whole sections of the economy are traditionally women's jobs and have always been paid less—for example, nursing, secretarial work, and teaching. A sizeable part of the gender pay gap is caused by women's concentration in lower-paying industries and in lower-paying jobs within higher-paying industries. In addition, sometimes the jobs dominated by women in a company are not valued in the same way as men's jobs. Studies have shown that the more women and people of color fill occupations, the less they pay (National Committee on Pay Equity 2005).

Because women typically take on more family responsibilities than men, such as picking the children up from school or day care, they tend to put in less overtime and are less able to travel on business. Some argue that men advance more quickly in companies because of their willingness to work longer hours, particularly if they have a spouse who assumes responsibility for child care. It is also well known among corporate headhunters that women are not always prepared for compensation negotiations and, more often than not, take the offer on the table. That is, they often sell themselves short—and companies know it.

Families and Debt

No matter how much money they make, some people are always in debt. They calculate that if they had a little more each month they would be able to balance their budget, but when that "little more" is obtained, they still cannot make do.

The families that are most in debt are not the poor, but those in the middle-income brackets. The poor less frequently have mortgages, charge accounts, or large installment debts, although they might if they were able to establish credit. Level of income is not the major reason couples go into debt.

The reasons relate more to the lifestyle of the partners and their ability to manage their money wisely.

Couples go into debt for various reasons. One of the main reasons people have gone into debt is because the cost of living (29%) has outpaced income growth (26%) since 2003 (El Issa 2016). Although a 3% difference does not seem like much, it has a cumulative effect—and families slip farther behind each year.

Many people go into debt because of excessive and unwise use of credit. Credit can be helpful: Few couples can afford to pay cash for a home, automobile, or other large purchases. But habitual and unthinking use of credit—as using credit cards to pay for groceries or gasoline—often leads to excessive indebtedness. Americans pay about $6700 in interest each year—a significant debt itself (El Issa 2016).

Some people go into debt because of crisis spending. About 40% of families experience serious unexpected expenses each year. Many do not have the reserves to meet unexpected expenses of $1000 (Bankrate Poll 2016). Unexpected events can throw the family budget off completely and force people to go into debt to meet the emergency. Unemployment is a common crisis; illness is another. Some couples, such as farm couples, have variable incomes; they never know from one year to the next what their earnings will be, so it is hard to plan ahead.

Although a high income makes it easier for a family to weather life's crises, satisfaction with family life also depends on whether people feel that the family's income is adequate.

Homeless

In 2002, the National Conference of Mayors released a report on hunger and homelessness in America's cities. The following are case studies from that report.

Nashville: A single mother with a 2-month-old daughter had lived with friends for several months when her friends were evicted from their apartment. She was without housing, but it was impossible for her to find work without child-care assistance. Without work, she could not afford housing. She came to the Nashville Family Shelter seeking assistance. After only a few weeks of child care and other support services, she obtained full-time employment with a reputable company—with possibilities to advance. She is in search of permanent housing and will leave the shelter soon.

Burlington: The D family moved to Vermont and lined up jobs for him and her and a preschool for their 4-year-old twins. Everything was great for about a month.

Two unrelated medical problems put the D family on the brink of financial ruin. One of the twins was diagnosed with severe ADHD and the parents were advised to remove him from the stresses of preschool. Mom quit her job to stay home with the boys; the family was able to get along on dad's salary. Then, after a large snowfall, mom hurt her back shoveling the sidewalk.

Doctors prescribed bed rest, medications, and physical therapy. Dad had to miss work several times each week so mom could go to physical therapy. The family started falling behind; rent was overdue. Dad lost his job because of excessive absences. Eviction papers were served.

The Committee on Temporary Shelter (COTS) put them up in a hotel for the first week until there was space at COTS. They stayed at COTS with 22 other families for a little more than 2 months before being moved to a newly renovated family shelter that houses 4 families. In time, they moved into Section 8 housing. Dad studies full-time at a community college and works part-time. Mom works part-time at a gift shop while the twins attend kindergarten. All are doing well now and they are pleased to be back on their own.

New Orleans: A woman who is the sole caregiver for her three small grandchildren (mom is in jail) called about help. This family of four was spending each night in a different location. One of the children has a disability and needed other services. The shelter staff met with the grandmother on several occasions. She was reconnected to mental health services and the local homeless health clinic. Transitional housing was obtained to provide the family with stability because this grandmother cares for the children.

Other people go into debt because they buy things carelessly or impulsively. They pay more than is necessary or purchase things they do not really need. One woman reported,

> My husband loves auctions. Whenever he reads about an auction, he always shows up. He loves the crowds and the excitement, but he gets carried away. Once he brought home a cement mermaid. I don't know what he expected to do with it since we don't have a fish pond or swimming pool. It's still down in the family room where he put it. (Counseling notes)

Some people are compulsive buyers. Their buying habits may be an expression of their emotional insecurity; they cannot say no to a salesperson for fear of hurting that person's feelings. Or they buy to gain status and recognition. Another woman reported,

> My husband is a compulsive collector. He spends a fortune on his coin collection, will travel hundreds of miles to see a rare coin, and will outbid everyone else to buy it. He shows his collection to everyone who comes into the house and derives great satisfaction from owning a coin that other collectors have never seen. (Counseling notes)

The habit of living in debt starts early for many couples. As mentioned earlier, some couples start married life with significant student-loan debt. Others have credit card debt—from college or perhaps for a wedding or honeymoon.

Debt is also a problem for older Americans. Many live on little more than their Social Security check, which is often not enough to pay for housing, food, medical bills, and prescription drugs. Although many people who lived through the Great Depression carefully avoided debt, the "new" seniors, ages 50 to 69, who are the earliest baby boomers, are accustomed to living with debt. They are more likely than their elders to use credit cards to cover everyday expenses. Although credit cards can offer a safety net, high interest charges can sink a person farther into debt.

Unfortunately, as financial strain has increased and credit has become more accepted, saving for retirement or a "rainy day" has decreased. Personal saving has decreased from 10% of disposable income in 1980 to just under 5% in 2014, which is about the same as in 1930 (U.S. Bureau of Economic Analysis 2016)—meaning that many families do not have the 2 to 6 months of earnings recommended as an emergency reserve. Few families will get through the year without an emergency such as car breakdown, dental work, or hail damage to the roof. In 2012, slightly more than half of families also felt "behind" in saving for retirement (compared to 38% in 1997) (Princeton Survey Research Associates International 2012).

Managing Finances

There is no right or wrong money management system. The best system is what works for the individual couple. Who actually manages the money is not as important as how well the task is done, shared responsibility, and agreement of the spouses. The person who has the most interest and skill in money management might be the one to exercise the most control, as long as the other person is in agreement. Marital adjustment is smoother when couples adopt a "we" attitude in relation to making financial decisions.

One part of managing finances is to have a financial plan that includes both long-term goals (home ownership, retirement fund, college for the kids) and shorter-term goals (vacation this year,

paying down credit card debt, a second car). The next part of the financial plan is to devise and implement strategies to meet these goals (an individual retirement account and pension fund for retirement, for example; a savings account for a vacation). Any plan must be reviewed and revised periodically: Have goals changed? Is the plan working?

Another part of managing finances in a practical way is to direct the cash flow—to know what your spendable income is and not to exceed it. In other words, live within your means or balance the budget. Indeed, a budget is the way most couples direct their cash flow (see Figure 8.3).

A surprisingly large number of people do not use a budget. The reasons for not using a budget have been identified in a survey of more than 1,000 adults (Choi-Allum 2012). The top four reasons were as follows:

1. "It's not worth my time."
2. "I've tried and it doesn't work."
3. "I don't have time."
4. "I spend all my earnings each month."

Most budgets are planned on a monthly basis and include an accounting of what the income is, as well as a listing of expenditures. Income includes wages, any interest or dividends, and other payments such as child support that is received. Expenses fall into two broad categories: fixed and variable. Fixed expenses are those that are more or less the same from month to month, such as mortgage or rent, insurance premiums, and car and loan payments. Some couples set aside a fixed amount for savings, charity, or investments. Variable expenses include utilities, food, entertainment, medical expenses, and credit card payments.

One purpose of a budget is to avoid overspending. Most couples have an easier time managing cash flow when they know how much money can be spent. For example, if the budget for food is $150 per week, a lavish dinner at an expensive restaurant means macaroni and cheese or beans and franks the rest of the week.

A budget is not meant to be restrictive and can reflect the values and goals of the family members. For example, if supporting the local free medical clinic is important to them, the family may forego expensive recreation to support it.

Income

Wages, salaries _____

Interest, dividends _____

Other (child support, etc.) _____

Total _____

Expenses

Housing _____

Loans (car, furniture, etc.) _____

Insurance premiums (health, life, car) _____

Child support _____

Emergency fund _____

Savings _____

Total fixed _____

Utilities _____

Gas/electric _____

Water/sewer/garbage _____

Cable _____

Phone (land, cell) _____

Internet _____

Car (maintenance, operating) _____

Child care _____

Food _____

Entertainment/recreation _____

Personal (hair, spa, hobbies, gym) _____

Gifts _____

Charitable _____

Work (professional/union dues, uniforms, parking) _____

Medical _____

Credit card payment _____

Total variable _____

FIGURE 8.3 A Sample Budget

Poverty and Family Life

Nearly 47 million Americans, or almost 15% of the population, live in poverty—the highest it has been since 1983. This is an increase of 15 million from 2000 (U.S. Bureau of the Census 2016). About 22% of children and 9% of people age 65 and older live in poverty. The poverty threshold differs by size and makeup of a household and is adjusted annually for inflation. Breaking it down among ethnic groups, the approximate poverty rate for non-Hispanic whites is 13%; for blacks, 26%; for Asian/Pacific Islanders, 11.5%; and for Hispanics, 24% (U.S. Bureau of the Census 2016). For these families, daily life is a struggle merely to pay rent and to buy groceries. Oftentimes, poor families are forced to make choices between buying medicine or groceries or paying the rent.

Measuring Poverty

Whether a family is considered in poverty is determined by two measures. One is the poverty threshold, which is used for gathering statistical information such as what percentage of people live in poverty. The poverty level was originally intended to establish the household income that a family required to afford basic necessities. The first threshold was tied to the spending of the average American family in 1955, starting with the proportion of the budget spent on food. In 1964, the poverty threshold was adjusted because of a rise in food costs, and it has been adjusted for inflation every year since.

Critics of current poverty measures argue that the costs of many necessities have outpaced inflation and that many of the common expenses families incur today were not part of family life in 1955. Although food prices have risen since 1955 at practically the same rate as inflation, food today accounts for barely one-sixth of the average family budget, rather than the one-third of the budget on which the original poverty threshold was based. In the following example, the MIT Living Wage Calculator is used to estimate the costs of meeting basic needs for a family of four, both adults working full-time, raising two children ages 4 and 7, living in a medium-sized town in the midwest:

BASIC NEEDS	MONTHLY COSTS
Housing	$703
Food	$742
Child care	$763
Health care	$560
Transportation	$963
Other	$432
Taxes	$521
Monthly total	**$4,684**
Annual total	**$56,208**

Note that amounts for housing, child care, food, and medical are modest; compare them to estimates for rent and child care given earlier in this chapter.

Poverty guidelines are used to determine whether a family qualifies for certain services such as subsidized housing and child care, Medicaid, and other government assistance such as the Supplemental Nutrition Assistance Program (SNAP—the old "food stamps") or Temporary Assistance for Needy Families (TANF). The basic needs for a family of four far exceed the poverty guideline of $24,300 ($30,380 for Alaska and $27,950 for Hawaii) (Families USA 2016). For example, SNAP electronic benefits transfer may not be used to purchase personal-care items such as shampoo or diapers. Note, too, that this estimate of expenses does not include many items; compare it to the sample budget given in Figure 8.3.

Another factor compounding the plight of families living in poverty is that the minimum wage many of them rely on has lost its value. The minimum wage in 1950 paid about 110% of the amount needed by a family of four with two full-time workers to survive (J. E. Schwarz 1998). When the adults budgeted well, it was even enough to raise a family into the middle class, but by the 1970s, the minimum wage for two full-time workers had fallen to 90% of necessary income, and it now stands at about 60%. Today, the poorest families are also likely to have only one worker (mom) and to have more than two children.

In 2016, the federal minimum wage is $7.25 an hour. If you work full-time (40 hours a week × 52 weeks a year) at this wage, your yearly earnings would be $15,080. For our hypothetical Midwestern family of four to survive with the parents working for minimum wage, each adult would have to work two full-time jobs (77 hours a week—each) (MIT Living Wage Calculator 2016; Nadeau and Glasmeier 2016). Some states set a minimum wage that is higher than the federal minimum; Nebraska's is $8.00 and Washington's is $9.47, for example. This is a bit better but not nearly enough.

In recent years, there has been a campaign to pay people a living wage, rather than a minimum wage. Typically, the living wage is what it would take to bring a family out of poverty. With a living wage, the workers in our hypothetical family would receive $13.50 an hour.

Some companies have responded to pressure to raise their minimum wage to $10 an hour. For example, Walmart now pays workers at least $10 an hour after six months' employment. However, a full-time schedule is only 34 hours a week. If the adults in our hypothetical family both work fulltime at Walmart, they will earn $35,360 a year; this is almost $21,000 short of what they need to meet basic needs (Traub and McElwee 2015). At the same time they are earning $11,000 over the poverty guidelines—and may not qualify for assistance. A number of families fall in this situation of making too much to qualify for assistance, but not making enough to support themselves. They are termed the working poor.

The Effects of Poverty on Families

Poverty may arise because of factors over which those affected have no control: problems in the economy, the changing nature of jobs, political trends and government policies, business practices, and racism and sexism in society. People with a long history of very low income have an especially difficult time coping because many have few available resources and are never able to break the cycle of poverty. For example, people with low incomes in search of jobs often move to metropolitan areas where there are more jobs; however, the cost of living is also high. Our hypothetical family of four would need $63,900 to live in Atlanta or $73,900 in Los Angeles or $98,700 in New York (Picchi 2015). Low-income neighborhoods are often dangerous, offer poorer municipal services, have inferior schools and day-care facilities, and suffer greater physical deterioration (Evans 2004). The task of raising children is made even more difficult when families are forced to reside in dangerous, crime-ridden neighborhoods.

Unfortunately, millions of American children are being raised in poverty, and the number is growing. Twenty-two percent of all children in the United States now live in poverty compared to 16% in 2000 (U.S. Bureau of the Census 2016). Children growing up in poverty experience a wide range of problems and challenges, starting with basics such as food and health care. For example, poor children are six times more likely to live in homes where not everyone has enough food all the time (Children's Defense Fund 2014). Poor children are less likely to have access to good health care; poor children who have a serious health condition fare worse than higher-income children. For example, a poor child with asthma is more likely to be reported as in poor health, to spend more days in bed, and to have more hospital visits than his/her nonpoor counterpart (Children's Defense Fund 2014).

Poverty is associated with poor school performance and higher school dropout rates. For example,

Race or Economics?

As discussed in Chapter 1, tremendous diversity exists within racial groups. Stereotypical thinking often prevents people from recognizing that diversity. One of the most significant differences within any racial group has to do with economics. We illustrate this point by focusing on the African American family as an example of how economic factors influence family patterns and how variations within cultural groups often stem from differences in socioeconomic status. Wilkinson (1997) described four classes among black families: (1) families in poverty, (2) the nonpoor working class, (3) the upwardly mobile middle class, and (4) the established upper class.

All impoverished families have different histories, parenting behaviors, and expectations from those of families in other classes. African American families are disproportionately represented in poverty. Some 26% of African American families were below the poverty level compared to 13% of the white population (U.S. Bureau of the Census 2016). Poor families experience endless complications in trying to meet basic needs, such as finding safe, affordable housing. Proper attention to children's optimal development is difficult when parents are in constant economic distress, and many children of poverty end up on the streets or in the juvenile justice system. In any culture, daily financial and psychological distress can reduce the quality of parenting and research has consistently shown that compared with well-off parents,

parents who experience economic stress display less nurturance and more harshness in their responses to their children (McLoyd and Wilson 1992). Understandably, in families living in poverty because of a lack of education, job market segregation, and struggles with a welfare existence, the parents may be unable to participate in children's schooling or take an active role in community affairs (Wilkinson 1997). Thus, one may perceive a difference in values, exemplified by behavior, between two different racial or ethnic groups. In reality, however, it is not values but economics that account for the difference.

If one controls for socioeconomic status, African American and white families are similar and share similar mainstream values (Fine et al. 1992). Research has shown that black parents teach their children to be honest, to value education, and to act responsibly. Most black children grow up in loving families, being cared for by an extended kin unit and taught values that include having a strong family, cooperation, respect for elderly persons, shared household work and childrearing, practical skills, racial pride, and flexible gender roles (E. J. Hill 2006; Nobles 1988). Proponents of new models to study families suggest that more value be placed on factors such as support, caring, loyalty, religion, and spirituality than on socioeconomic factors to assess family stability (S. L. Barnes 2001; DeFrain and Asay 2007; Stinnett and Stinnett 2010).

only 25% of poor eighth graders were performing at grade level in reading and math compared to 48% of their higher-income classmates. Rates of dropping out of school are four times higher among poor students (Children's Defense Fund 2014).

In addition, children growing up in poverty are exposed to more family turmoil, violence, separation from their families, instability, and chaotic households (Children's Defense Fund 2014; Evans 2004). For these children, emancipation from family can come early and is often psychologically

premature. These youths frequently are not ready to take their place in the adult world, and many turn to peers to replace family ties. In general, poor children experience less social support from their parents, and parents are more authoritarian or inconsistent in discipline and less involved in children's school and daily activities. For example, poor children have fewer books at home, are read to less often, watch more television, visit fewer museums or libraries, and are less likely to have a computer at home than their higher-income counterparts (Children's Defense Fund 2014; Evans 2004; Slack et al. 2004).

As stated, dropout rates from school are high among low-socioeconomic-status youths. Although parents want their children to have more education and a better life than they did, adolescents may feel pressed to get a job to help support the family. This pressure may contribute to some adolescents' decision to drop out of school because low-income families may need children to work to survive. In their review of the research on family labor in low-income households, Dodson and Dickert (2004) report that girls emerge as a substitute for parents and are often a critical source for family caregiving and household management responsibilities. These demands differ from the typical household chores of children because the adult is often absent and the tasks are often complex and time-consuming. Their findings show that there are significant social implications when children are left to do the work of adults. For example, girls lose the opportunity to focus on education and schoolwork, are precluded from extracurricular opportunities, and are inadvertently encouraged to focus on relational roles, caregiving, and household management that can encourage early partner relationship and teenage motherhood. This in turn affects individual and social development as well as future career and income potential (Children's Defense Fund 2014; Dodson and Dickert 2004). Thus, a survival strategy used by low-income families to get by can, inadvertently, perpetuate the cycle of poverty. That is, children who drop out of school have a much higher likelihood of remaining in poverty than individuals with a higher education. In fact, a good education is one of the best routes out of poverty.

Homelessness

Some poor families face the additional challenge of being homeless, living on the streets or in another place not intended for human habitation or in shelters. According to the National Coalition for the Homeless, two trends are largely responsible for the rise in homelessness over the past 20 to 25 years: a shortage of affordable rental housing and a simultaneous increase in poverty. Other factors that contribute to homelessness are addiction, mental illness, and domestic violence.

Accurate statistics on homelessness are difficult to obtain, but in 1990, the Census Bureau began making yearly one-night counts of homeless people. In 1990, there were approximately 229,000; in 2015, the number had grown to 565,000—of which about 25% were children (National Alliance to End Homelessness 2014; E.M. Johnson 2015; Lee, Tyler and Wright 2010). Some 77% of the homeless are in shelters, with families more apt to be in shelters than are individuals. Some 15% of homeless people are chronically so. An estimated 26% are considered mentally ill and 13% are physically disabled. It has also been estimated that one in three homeless children has a psychiatric disorder such as post–traumatic stress disorder and nearly 90% of homeless mothers have been victimized (National Alliance to End Homelessness 2014; Lee, Tyler and Wright 2010). With a lack of affordable housing, families are forced to stay in shelters for a longer period of time. For example, in the mid-1990s in New York, families stayed in a shelter an average of 5 months before moving on to permanent housing. Currently, families stay nearly a year.

Compounding the problem are inadequate income levels and declining wages that put housing out of reach. For example, although many homeless individuals are actually employed, their wage level simply does not allow them to secure housing. When the Fair Market Rent (40th percentile of gross rents

A growing number of poor families are homeless, living on the streets or staying temporarily in homeless shelters.

for typical, nonsubstandard rental units) is considered, families with one full-time minimum-wage earner cannot afford rent in any state. Estimates of what the hourly wage would need to be for families to afford rent range from about $12–$13 for southern and western states (Alabama, Mississippi, New Mexico, South Dakota, Tennessee, and Kentucky, for example) to $20–$26 in the northeast (New York, New Jersey, Maryland, and Connecticut) to a high of $32 for Hawaii (MIT Living Wage Calculator 2016; National Low Income Housing Coalition 2016).

The Feminization of Poverty

The population living in poverty in the United States, as well as around the world, is disproportionately made up of women, irrespective of ethnicity or age, a phenomenon known as the **feminization of poverty** (Chant 2006; M. Chen et al. 2005). Women have higher poverty rates than men for two main reasons: (1) women's economic resources do not approach parity with those of men, and (2) women are more likely than men to be single custodial parents during their working lives and to be unmarried/widowed and living alone in their later years. For these reasons, poverty is more likely to be a chronic problem among female-householder families. Figure 8.4 compares the income levels of households headed by women with those of households headed by married couples.

Spouses who have been able to agree about earning, saving, and spending patterns have overcome one of the biggest obstacles to a harmonious, happy marriage.

Many mother-headed households experience financial hardship because they have only one income, a situation that makes it nearly impossible to "make ends meet." In other situations, the father may either be completely absent or may not keep up with his financial responsibility to his children. The failure of absent fathers to support their children economically has long-term consequences because mothers have fewer material resources to invest in their children. As a result, children may experience poorer nutrition, health care, and educational opportunities.

For single mothers, poverty reduces their chances of completing their education. A good education provides opportunities (such as better-paying jobs) and allows individuals to make informed choices (Vaughn 2010). Education typically enables a woman to reduce her poverty and enhances her children's chances of achieving good educations as well (UNICEF 2007). Single mothers with little education are often under severe economic pressure and are prone to experience negative life events (poor schooling for children, more stress, illness, and crime victimization, for example) (Panchanadeswaran et al. 2007).

Welfare and the Family

When people hear the word *welfare*, they show different reactions. People who are on welfare or who have been on it find it demeaning, but they admit that they are glad of the needed financial assistance. People who have never been on welfare may assume recipients are lazy and do not want to work since they can live off the government.

The important question we will consider here is how the current welfare system affects the family. In 1996, the welfare system in the United States changed dramatically with the passage of the Personal Responsibility and Work Opportunity Reconciliation Act. The bipartisan welfare reform plan requires work in exchange for time-limited assistance. The new TANF program replaced the Aid to Families with Dependent Children and Job Opportunities and Basic Skills Training programs.

TANF brought an end to entitlement to federal assistance, allowing states, territories, and tribes to operate their own assistance programs. The federal government provides block grants to cover the costs of benefits, administrative expenses, and services, but the states determine eligibility and benefit levels. The average monthly benefit per family

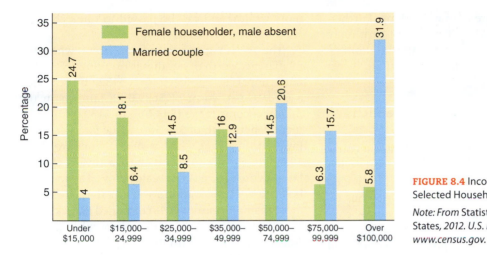

FIGURE 8.4 Income Distribution of Selected Household Types

Note: From Statistical Abstract of the United States, *2012. U.S. Bureau of the Census. http://www.census.gov.*

is approximately $1500; about 1.7 million families receive benefits (Office of Family Assistance, Administration for Children and Families 2016).

States, territories, and tribes are given enormous flexibility, provided that the programs they design accomplish the purposes of TANF, which are (1) to provide assistance to needy families so that children may be cared for in their own homes; (2) to reduce dependency by promoting job preparation, work, and marriage; (3) to prevent out-of-wedlock pregnancies; and (4) to encourage the formation and maintenance of two-parent families. Basic stipulations of TANF include the following: (1) recipients must work after 2 years on assistance; (2) recipients who are not working must participate in community service 2 months after they start receiving benefits; (3) recipients must participate in unsubsidized or subsidized employment, on-the-job training, community service, or vocational training or they must provide child care for individuals participating in community service; and (4) families who have received assistance for 5 cumulative years are ineligible for cash aid.

All states offer basic health services to certain very poor people: individuals who are pregnant, aged, disabled, or blind and families with dependent children. One of these programs is Medicaid. Medicaid eligibility is automatic for almost all cash welfare recipients in the United States. Some states extend Medicaid to others who qualify, such as people with medical expenses that, when subtracted from their income, reach a "medically needy" level. Within federal guidelines, each state determines its own Medicaid eligibility criteria and

the health services to be provided under Medicaid. The cost of providing Medicaid services is jointly shared by the federal government and the states.

The federal Supplemental Security Income program administered by the Social Security Administration provides benefits to individuals who are aged, blind, and disabled. The Supplemental Security Income program provides a minimum income for these persons and establishes uniform national basic eligibility requirements and payment standards. Most states supplement the basic Supplemental Security Income payments.

Although data reported by the U.S. Department of Health and Human Services show some 10 million fewer recipients since 1996, some researchers and welfare reform critics point to failings in the system and distortion in these statistics. A report from the National Poverty Center in 2013 revealed that the number of people in the United States living on less than $2 per person per day (termed "extreme poverty" by the United Nations) increased from 636,000 households in 1996 to 1.65 million households (Edin and Shaefer 2015; Watson 2013). About 3.5 million children live in these households.

Research has shown that even during good economic times, approximately one-third of those no

feminization of poverty Describes the phenomenon in which women represent a disproportionate percentage of the poor.

longer receiving welfare are not working. Furthermore, many who go off welfare do not earn more than they did while receiving aid, thus dooming a significant number of families to continue in extreme poverty.

The Widening Gap between the Rich and the Poor

The United States is often cited as the richest country in the world. But a closer look reveals what scholars have referred to as "two Americas" divided between the rich and everyone else. Numerous reports, cited by the Economic Policy Institute, concluded that the gap between the rich and the poor was greater than ever at the end of the century and continues to grow (Perez 2014).

The gap between the rich and the poor focuses on more than income. Although income and wealth are related (the more you make, the more you can save and invest), wealth focuses on a different measure of financial well-being: how much money and other assets you have accumulated over time. Wealth involves the home, cars, investments, businesses, retirement fund, and stocks that make up a family's "nest egg" for emergencies and hard times. Wealth provides security, bestows social prestige, contributes to political power, can be used to build more wealth, and can be passed to one's children (Cohen 2014; Perez 2014).

The wealth gap becomes apparent when the median net worth of families is examined. Families in the upper-income levels (over $132,000 year) had a median net worth of $639,000; families in the middle-income range ($44,000 to $132,000) had a median net worth of $96,500; while families in the lower-income range had a median net worth of $9,300 (Cohen 2014). Only the top 10% of wealthy families are seeing their wealth grow. The top 0.1% hold 22% of the nation's wealth; they are worth more than the bottom 90% combined (Salles 2014).

Many experts believe that the wealth gap will continue to widen, with the rich getting richer and the poor getting poorer. This belief is based in part on the dynamics that have fueled the gap. One of the foundational causes of the wealth gap is that a concentration of power in a corporate and financial elite has resulted in changes that favor the rich. For example, when the "housing bubble" burst and home values declined, it destroyed much of the wealth (in home equities) of middle and lower income families. In contrast many very large banks and auto manufacturers received federal bail outs (Reich 2015).

The growing wealth gap is a challenging situation to address, and there is disagreement as to how to remedy the problem. One approach is to help families to build assets through actions such as tax-exempt savings programs, expanded earned income credits, a higher minimum wage, and increased access to homeownership. Others believe that changes in the welfare program will help families out of poverty and that the prosperity of the rich has a positive effect on other aspects of the economy (such as job creation) that directly benefit poor and working-class families. However, regardless of political ideology, no one disagrees that living in poverty is detrimental to the health and well-being of families, particularly children.

Families have changed a great deal over the past 40 years in how they provide for their material needs. It is now common to have both parents working outside the home, which is a big change from how previous generations grew up. Although dual incomes make many things possible, many families struggle financially, and although they are employed, they live below or close to the poverty line. For many families, it will likely always be a challenge to balance work demands with family needs.

The population in poverty in the United States is disproportionately composed of women. Programs such as the Supplemental Nutrition Assistance Program and the Women, Infants, and Children program enable many women and children to buy groceries that they would otherwise not be able to afford.

Earned Income Tax Credit

As discussed in the text, many families are struggling economically to provide for their families. In 1975, Congress created the earned income tax credit (EITC) to help families make the transition from welfare to work and to make work more attractive than welfare. The policy was originally intended just for families on welfare but has changed over the years and now includes low-income families. It also applies to working grandparents, foster parents, stepgrandparents, and other relatives caring for children if the children live in the household all year and are cared for as members of the family (P. Friedman 2000). Families use the tax credit to pay for necessities, to repair homes and vehicles that are needed to commute to work, and, in some cases, to help boost their employability and earning power by obtaining additional education or training.

Only families that work are eligible to receive the credit, and the amount of the credit depends on the family's labor market earnings. That is, the size of the credit increases with each additional dollar of earnings, providing an incentive for more work. Working families with children who have annual incomes below $52,000 are encouraged to check at the Internal Revenue website to see if they qualify. Approximately 28 million working families and individuals received the EITC, with an average amount for families with children being $2,400 (IRS 2016). The credit is flat for a range of earnings and is then phased out as earnings increase. The credit can offset taxes for families who make enough to pay taxes or it can provide additional income for those who did not make enough to pay taxes. The idea is that by reducing the tax burden on families, the EITC strengthens their self-sufficiency and provides them with more disposable income.

Questions to Consider

Should low-income families without children be eligible for the EITC? Why or why not?

Should the credit be adjusted to account for family size so that families with more children get more credit? Why or why not?

To what extent is it the role of government to help alleviate economic stress in low-income families? What about in middle-income families?

If a policy provides additional income to families to help make ends meet, should there be any restrictions on how that money is spent? Explain.

Why might a qualified family choose not to take the EITC?

Summary

1. Job stressors negatively affect the emotional health of families.

2. Some types of work are particularly stressful for the family, including work that is difficult, work that requires periods of separation from the family, and work that is too demanding of a person's time.

3. Sometimes the demand to work long hours comes from an employer who has a callous disregard for the employee's mental health and personal life. One of the barriers to family closeness is a job schedule that makes it difficult for family members to be together.

4. Parents provide models of male and female behavior for their children. More fathers are helping with child care, which helps in forming closer father–child bonds, eases the mother's burden, and strengthens the spousal

relationship. In many cases, work hours and schedules affect child-care roles. Dual-earner couples must schedule their time carefully.

5. Excessive demands on their time and the hectic pace of parents' jobs cause families to become time poor. This can lead to children losing important opportunities to spend time with their families and parents missing chances to connect with their offspring and with each other.

6. The number and percentage of mothers in the labor force are increasing. The research on life satisfaction of employed mothers versus that of those who do not work outside the home shows slightly greater satisfaction among those who are employed.

7. Many couples are caught in a quandary between the ethic of equity, defined as a fair division of labor, and the ethic of care, in which couples try to be sensitive to the needs of family members.

8. A specific subtype of the dual-earner family is the dual-career family, in which both spouses' jobs usually require a high degree of commitment and continuous development.

9. Financial necessity and the desire to improve the family's living standard are the most important motives for married women with children to work.

10. Financial strains on modern families can be considerable and include stagnant or declining incomes, a dollar with reduced purchasing power, and high unemployment rates.

11. Children are a major expense for families; it takes about $245,340 to rear a child. This does not include the cost of higher education.

12. Many families have staggering levels of general debt because of mortgages, credit card debt, and other unrestrained spending on cars, vacations, or other items. It is typical for a newly married couple to start married life with student loan indebtedness.

13. Women earn about 80% of what men earn. This gender wage gap cannot be accounted for by differences in education or job qualifications. It seems in large part to be the result of a number of factors, such as women working in lower-paying industries or jobs, women working fewer hours than men, and women not being aggressive in wage negotiations.

14. Money management is also a source of harmony or discord in the family. The best money management system is what works for the individual couple.

15. A budget can be an effective way to direct cash flow—balancing expenses with income. It is one strategy for meeting financial goals.

16. About 15% of families in the United States have incomes below the poverty level.

17. A growing number of poor families are homeless, living on the streets or staying temporarily in homeless shelters.

18. Women have higher poverty rates than men, irrespective of ethnicity and age. The reasons for this feminization of poverty are that women have fewer economic resources, a greater likelihood of being a single custodial parent, and a greater likelihood of living alone in old age.

19. The number of American children in poverty has been growing. Effects of poverty include poor grades, high dropout rates, and greater likelihoods of teenage pregnancy and of remaining in poverty throughout adulthood.

20. Research has shown that even during good economic times, approximately one-third of those no longer receiving welfare are not working and that many who go off welfare do not earn more than they did while receiving aid.

21. Numerous reports concluded that the wealth gap between the rich and the poor was greater than ever at the end of the century and continues to grow.

Key Terms

dual-career family

dual-earner family

feminization of poverty

flextime

work–family spillover

Questions for Thought

1. For men: Would you want your spouse to work outside the home? Explain. For women: Would you like your spouse to stay home raising the children? Explain.

2. For women: Do you intend to work outside the home after you have children? Why or why not?

3. The text mentions that women often settle for offered salaries without any negotiations. Why?

4. What problems do dual-career couples face to which you can relate?

5. If you were in a dual-career marriage and your spouse was offered a job at twice the salary in another part of the country, what would be the attractions of the offer/move and also the drawbacks?

6. What are some strategies for having a happy marriage, children, and a full-time career? Explain.

7. How important are material resources for a happy marriage? Explain.

8. How would you reform welfare?

For Further Reading

Dave Ramsey on Marriage and Money. http://www.success.com/articles/1201-dave-ramsey-on-marriage-and-money.

"Don't blame discrimination for the gender wage gap." Is the gender wage gap caused by discrimination? http://www.bloomberg.com/news/print/2012-08-13.

Ehrenreich, B. (2001). *Nickel and dimed: On (not) getting by in America.* New York: Holt. A journalist assumes the role of a low-wage worker to investigate the lives of low-income women.

Hoffman, S., and Averett, S. (2005). *Women and the economy: Family, work, and pay.* Boston: Pearson Addison–Wesley. Examines the strengths and challenges of women in the workforce and its impact on the family.

MIT Living Wage Calculator. The Living Wage Calculator has information about the cost of living (housing, food, child care, etc.) in every county and many metropolitan areas in all 50 states. Find out if you can afford to live on the beach in Hawaii or the plains of Texas. http://livingwage.mit.edu

Nelson, D. L., and Burke, R. J. (2002). *Gender, work stress, and health.* Washington, DC: American Psychological Association. Provides insights on the issues of gender differences and work stress.

Power, Decision Making, and Communication

CHAPTER OUTLINE

Learning Objectives

The Meaning of Power

Why People Want Power
- Self-Actualization
- Social Expectations
- Family-of-Origin Influences
- Psychological Need

Sources of Power

CULTURAL PERSPECTIVE: *Wearing a Veil*
- Cultural Norms
- Gender Norms
- Economic Resources
- Education and Knowledge
- Personality Differences
- Communication Ability
- Emotional Factors
- Physical Stature and Strength

- Life Circumstances
- Children

Marital Power Patterns

COPING FEATURE: *The Need for Control*

Power Processes
- Power Tactics That Help
- Power Tactics That Can Help or Harm
- Power Tactics That Harm

PERSONAL PERSPECTIVE: *How Do You Stop a Psychological Game?*

Consequences of Power Struggles

Communication
- Verbal and Nonverbal Communication

AT ISSUE TODAY: *Facebook, Text Messaging, and Beer*
- Barriers to Communication

Improving Communication Skills
- Taking Time
- Motivation and Concern
- Empathy
- Content
- Self-Disclosure
- Clarity
- Listening
- Feedback
- Arguing Constructively

FAMILY STRENGTHS PERSPECTIVE: *Listen*

A QUESTION OF POLICY: *The Power of Federal Judges*

Summary

Key Terms

Questions for Thought

For Further Reading

LEARNING OBJECTIVES

AFTER READING THE CHAPTER, YOU SHOULD BE ABLE TO DO THE FOLLOWING:

- Define *power* and *family power*.

- Outline the different units of family power.

- Explain why people want power as it pertains to self-actualization, social expectations, family-of-origin influences, and psychological needs.

- Describe the sources of power in families.

- Describe the four types of marital power patterns: egalitarian, male dominant, female dominant, and anarchic.

- Describe power tactics—that is, the ways power is applied.

- Discuss the consequences of power struggles for individuals and for marital satisfaction and explain why equity is needed.

- Define *psychological games* and describe several common games.

- Define *communication*, both verbal and nonverbal, and tell why it is important in marriage.

- Identify the major barriers to communication: physical and environmental, situational, psychological, cultural, and gender.

- Describe the requirements for improving communication skills: taking time, motivation and concern, empathy, self-disclosure, clarity, listening, feedback, and arguing constructively.

"I know more about my husband and children than anyone else does. I know their fears and vulnerabilities. I have power to hurt them.

"So why don't I pull out all the stops and say those dreadful things that would allow me to 'win'? Because that is too high a price to pay for winning the battle. Generals make that mistake sometimes. My son is a World War II buff, and I've heard him remark several times, 'So-and-so won this battle, but the casualties were terribly high. They won, but it cost too much.'

"I feel it would be a serious violation of the trust we have in each other to use our knowledge, or closeness, as weapons. Even when I get angry, I keep sight of that."

The marital ideology among educated, middle-class people in the United States emphasizes an egalitarian exercise of family power. That is, partners are equal and should share everything 50–50. But exactly what does this mean in relation to making decisions, influencing each other, and governing the family? In fact, this ideology does not often work out in practice. Some people want more power and control than others. Even when partners are equals, they usually do not share all decisions and control.

We are concerned here with patterns of power and with what gives some people power over others. We are concerned as well with the applications of power, the processes of power, and the ways power is applied in intimate relationships. And we are concerned with the outcomes of power as well as the effects of various power patterns on individuals and on marital satisfaction.

One of the most important requirements for a satisfying relationship is the ability to communicate. Because those closest to us cannot read our minds (nor can we read theirs), learning to convey likes, dislikes, hopes, dreams, goals, and desires is an essential part of a relationship with another. Thus, in this chapter, we are also concerned with improving communication skills.

The Meaning of Power

Power disparities underlie most intimate relationships and are typically unsettling. We may not even see power issues in our own relationships because they so completely shape our environment. In perhaps the most popular conceptualization among social scientists, **power** in intimate relationships is defined as the ability to influence one's partner to get what one wants (Anderson, John, and Keltner 2012; Lauer and Lauer 2011). Power may be exercised in social groups and organizations and in all kinds of interpersonal relationships. We are concerned here only with family power. The power exerted by various family members is partly derived from social power that society exerts or delegates. Power within the family can be marital power, parental power, offspring power, sibling power, or kinship power. There also can be combinations of power units, such as father–son, mother–daughter, or mother–son (Hartwell-Walker 2015). We are especially interested in marital power—the power relationship in the marital dyad—and, to a lesser extent, in power exercised by children over parents.

Why People Want Power

Some people always seem to need to be in control, whereas others avoid taking charge. What causes these differences in people's desire for power?

Self-Actualization

Most people want to feel that they have some control over their own lives—that they have the power to change, influence, or direct what happens to them personally. People who are unwilling or unable to use power often lead lives of frustration. They never get to realize their own desires or to carry out their own plans. Indeed, countless seminars are conducted to teach people how to become empowered.

A person who asserts himself or herself eventually will lock horns with someone who has other ideas, and a power struggle may ensue to see whose wishes are carried out. Even people who are not ordinarily combative find that they sometimes must exert power over other people to be able to fulfill themselves. Without some personal power, it is difficult to survive as an independent individual. Even toddlers must learn how to say no (appropriately) and how to influence parents if they are to grow up to be autonomous adults (Hartwell-Walker 2015).

Social Expectations

Often people exert power because that is what they feel they are supposed to do. Each society has institutionalized norms that prescribe domains of authority. This kind of power is referred to as **legitimate power**, or power bestowed by society on men and women as their right according to social prescription. What society prescribes may not always be fair, but it still may exert considerable influence on the behavior of individuals.

Family-of-Origin Influences

Patterns of power often can be traced to experiences in one's family of origin. Children tend to model the behavior of their parents. For example, a son growing up under the influence of a dominant father may have difficulty establishing a more democratic relationship with his spouse. Galvin and Brommel (1986) quoted one man:

> My German father and my Irish mother both exercised power over us in different ways. My father used to beat us whenever we got out of line, and that power move was very obvious. On the other hand, my mother never touched us, but she probably exercised greater power through her use of silence. Whenever we did something she did not approve of, she just stopped talking to us—it was as if we did not exist. Most of the time the silent treatment lasted for a few hours, but sometimes it would last for a few days. I hated the silence worse than the beatings. (135)

The family of origin serves as the first power base from which the child learns to function. Methods used there are often repeated in the child's adult life. Certain types of power applications, such as physical violence and abuse, may be passed from generation to generation. Even techniques of control, such as silence, are learned behavior.

Psychological Need

Sometimes the need for power and the way it is expressed go far beyond ordinary limits. People who have deep-seated feelings of insecurity and inferiority may hide them or compensate for them by becoming autocratic and dictatorial. They cannot let a partner win an argument for fear of feeling weak and ineffective. Their facade of power depends on not letting any cracks develop in their armor.

Three theoretical frameworks often are used to explain the need for power: attachment theory, social control theory, and feminist theory. According to attachment theory, aggression against an attachment figure, at any age, is a control strategy for regaining either emotional or physical closeness to a

person when the bond with that person is perceived to be endangered. Individuals who are insecurely attached to their primary attachment figure are more likely to perceive subjective threats to that bond than are individuals who are securely attached (Bowlby 1977; Hazan and Shaver 1987; Kinnison 2014). This could explain why some people are intensely jealous of a partner's interactions with others and try to limit and control those interactions.

According to social control theory, using power (or violence) as a response to an upsetting behavior by others serves three functions: (1) a means to manage conflict in a relationship, (2) an expression of grievances, and (3) a form of social control. Consistent with this theory, most marital assaults occur in the context of a disagreement. Social control theory can help explain why male batterers sometimes suggest that a partner deserved to be beaten for perceived offenses such as attempts at autonomy, failure to perform household chores, or disrespectful behavior.

According to feminist theory, the patriarchal hierarchy in families allows the use of male–female violence as a way of maintaining male power within the marriage. Consistent with this theory, rates of spousal abuse are lower in societies in which women have economic power within the marriage (D. Olson, DeFrain, and Skogrand 2014) and in which men expect to share power with a spouse (Lauer and Lauer 2011).

Sources of Power

Various efforts have been made to understand power in intimate relationships. What gives spouses power in the marital relationship? Various sources have been identified, including cultural norms, gender norms, economic resources, education and knowledge, personality differences, communication ability, emotional factors, physical stature and strength, and life circumstances. We will examine each of these bases of power as they relate to marriage partners. We

power In intimate relationships, the ability to influence one's partner to get what one wants.

legitimate power Power that is bestowed by society on men and women as their right according to social prescription.

Wearing a Veil

There are many Muslim women in the United States who wear a veil (hijab) when out in public. The veil can cover just the head or the entire body and the meaning and reasons for wearing a veil vary among women and cultures. Some Muslim women veil to express their strongly held convictions about gender differences and the importance of distinguishing men from women. Others wear a veil as a sign of solidarity with other Muslims, as a sign of disapproval for the immodest Western culture, or to protect themselves from the unwanted sexual advances of men. However, the most prominent justification for veiling is that it is believed to be commanded in the Koran and is thus a symbol of devotion to Islam (Read and Bartkowski 2000).

Read and Bartkowski (2000) interviewed Muslim women living in the United States about their motivation for wearing a veil. They found that, aside from their devotion to Islam, many chose to wear a veil because it actually liberated them from men's sexual advances and made possible the pursuit of work outside the home. Many of the women interviewed believed the veil is the great equalizer between men and women because it prevents women from being judged solely on their appearance. They felt liberated from the sexual objectification that so many Western women face at work and could thus work more comfortably alongside men and feel more respected. One of the women interviewed by Read and Bartkowski stated, "Women who wear the hijab are not excluded from society. They are freer to move around in society because of it . . . and if you're in hijab, then someone sees you and treats you accordingly. I feel more free. Especially men, they don't look at your appearance—they appreciate your intellectual abilities. They respect you" (407).

also will briefly look at ways children may exercise power over their parents.

Cultural Norms

The power structure in families varies among cultures. People in some cultures consider males the ultimate authority and power figure in the family and believe that women should be submissive to men. People in other cultures adopt a more egalitarian view; men and women in these cultures have equal opportunity and power in economic and social life.

Culture may instruct families on appropriate and acceptable modes of conduct, but the way in which families interpret and incorporate those modes into their lives varies widely. For example, the Mormon family is traditionally patriarchal, yet the Mormon church teaches that neither the husband nor the wife is more important, and both share in family responsibilities. Fathers are primarily responsible for providing protection and the necessities of life to their families while mothers are primarily responsible for nurturing their children. However, fathers and mothers are equal partners who should help each other fulfill those responsibilities. One woman described this as, ". . . two parts of a whole." Although this is seen as the model patriarchal family structure in the Mormon family, individual families may operate in a variety of ways ("What are Mormon women like?" 2016).

Traditionally, the African American family has been considered matriarchal. But recent research tends to contradict this view. African American marriages tend to be more egalitarian than white marriages, especially among the middle class. However, African American marriages cannot be stereotyped any more than white marriages can. African American couples show variations in power structure within each socioeconomic level, just as white couples do.

Gender Norms

Stereotypical gender roles also influence who has power in a relationship. Gender-role socialization that emphasizes women's passivity, submissiveness, and dependence reinforces patriarchal power structures and reduces women's authority. Traditional gender norms often specified a rigid division of responsibility. The man made financial decisions, whereas the woman cared for the children; he did heavy outdoor chores, whereas she did maintenance inside the house. As more egalitarian gender norms develop and as interest spheres and power domains overlap, more family issues become subject to negotiation and compromise.

P. Smith and Beaujot (1999) examined three groups of men (traditional, intermediate, and liberal) and asked them about the woman's place in the family and whether women prefer to stay at home or be in the workforce. The traditional respondents unanimously thought that women prefer to stay at home, cooking, cleaning, and caring for the children, and that men should be in the workforce and discipline the children. All of the traditional men believed that if a sacrifice was needed in the family, the woman's career should go first because it was secondary to her job as wife and mother. The intermediate group was split on the issue of whether women prefer to stay at home or go to work. This group still held many traditional beliefs,

including the idea that women are more nurturing and therefore should be more responsible for the children and that men should be more responsible for the finances. Most of the liberal respondents believed that women were split between the ideas of staying at home and working outside the home. These men believed that household work, marital power, and important decisions should be shared.

In general, in male-dominated societies, more men than women possess power in the form of resources, social status, respect, positive self-regard, and physical authority. Researchers have found females to be less likely to have access to valued resources (such as high salaries) across the life span. This gender gap is carried over to the intimate relationships between men and women (Gornick 2004).

Economic Resources

According to resource theory, those who control valued resources (such as money and property) needed by other family members hold power over them (S. M. Harvey and Bird 2004). A man who is the primary breadwinner may feel he has a right to dictate family decisions. One man remarked, "It's my money, I earned it; therefore, I have the right to spend it as I please."

Women who are not earning money for the family may not have equal power if their spouses do not allow it or they do not demand it. When the woman is gainfully employed, she usually gains power in decision making in the family.

Tichenor (1999) examined the power differences between traditional families, in which the man made more money than the woman, and status-reversal families, in which the woman earned significantly more than the man. Status-reversal women did receive more help around the house, yet they still were responsible for a larger part of domestic labor than the men in traditional families. In fact, no man in either group who was employed full-time did more than half of the domestic labor. One sentiment common to the status-reversal women was that they were not doing enough around the house although these women earned the bulk of the money—and sometimes all of it. Many of these women spoke with awe of the great job that their partners were doing in raising the children and getting work done around the house. In contrast, none of the men in traditional families spoke this way about a spouse. These findings suggest that power in families has more to do with gender than money. The status-reversal women often tried to downplay the amount of money they earned and emphasized that all money was shared. None of these women claimed that because they made more money they deserved more power.

Education and Knowledge

In a society in which education is valued, a person who has superior education has an important source of power. This type of power is referred to as **expert power**, whereby a person is acknowledged as generally superior in intelligence. The influence of education on power depends partly on the cultural context and partly on the relative difference between the people involved.

Knowledge is also a source of power; the development of new competencies facilitates equality in a relationship (Knudson-Martin and Mahoney 2005). One man commented, "My wife decorates the house. She knows much more about these things than I do." This type of power is referred to as **informational power** because it involves superior knowledge of a specific area.

According to the **theory of primary interest and presumed competence**, the person who is most interested in and involved with a particular choice and who is most qualified to make a specific decision will be more likely to do so. These two aspects, interest and competence, often go together. For example, if the woman will be using the kitchen appliances more than her partner, is more interested

in which ones to buy, and has had more experience in the use of different appliances, presumably she will be the one who will exert the most influence when buying a new refrigerator. If the man does most of the barbecuing, presumably he will take more interest in and exert more influence on choosing what barbecue equipment to buy.

Personality Differences

Personality characteristics also influence power. A considerable age difference between spouses affects power, with the older spouse exerting power over the younger one. Regardless of age, some people are more domineering and forceful than others, exerting considerable influence on all with whom they come in contact.

The degree of power depends partly on how motivated people are to gain strength and control. Some people strive for power to overcome inner feelings of weakness and insecurity. The converse also occurs: those with the greatest relational power also report higher levels of self-esteem (Anderson, John, and Keltner 2012). The two seem to go together. Charming people with a great deal of charisma may be natural leaders whom others follow readily.

Communication Ability

Some people are better talkers than others—as persuasive politicians or salespersons. They have superior verbal skills and are able to explain their ideas clearly and convince others through the power of their words. People described as charismatic typically are eloquent speakers.

With regard to gender differences, women tend to be more skilled in starting conversations, but men tend to take control—especially in disagreements. Generally, men view a disagreement as a time to state a point of view clearly and to defend it. He will say, "That just won't work and here's why." Women typically feel attacked by this assertive approach. Women are more often concerned with the other person's feelings, consequently, they "soften" their comments. "I'm sorry. I don't think I can agree with you," she will say.

Emotional Factors

Partners have an important source of **psychological power**: the ability to bestow or withhold affection. Some spouses use sex as a source of power, withholding it if a partner does not do what they want. For example, he watches football all weekend,

The greater the woman's education and earnings, the more likely she is to share decision-making power with her partner.

every weekend. She is hurt that he puts football ahead of her wishes to spend time with him. She delays going to bed until he is asleep, thus withholding sex.

Of course, love or sex must be valued before it can become a power source. When love dies, so does its power. According to social exchange theory, those with the greatest love and emotional need have the least power. Because they are so dependent, they have the most to lose if the relationship ends. They are so afraid of losing love that they often do everything possible to please a partner (R. S. Miller and Perlman 2009).

Physical Stature and Strength

Coercive power is based on the belief that one spouse can punish the other for noncompliance. One type of coercion is the threat or use of physical violence. One woman commented,

> My husband is a big man, and very strong. When he gets mad I never know what he's going to do. I'm afraid he'll hurt me. He once threw me down the front steps. (Counseling notes)

Life Circumstances

The more limited their alternatives, the less power people have in relationships. If a man feels that his partner cannot leave because she has no one to turn to, no place to go, and no money to support herself, he has more power in the relationship than he would otherwise. The stage in the family life cycle is an important consideration. Women who have dependent children or who are dependent economically have less power over their situation than do employed women who do not have children or whose children are grown.

Circumstances may change power balances, or a crisis may result in a realignment of power in a relationship. Physical incapacitation or illness of one spouse may force an otherwise submissive partner to take a more dominant role. Egalitarian couples, because they are more fluid and flexible, are able to shift and exchange roles to meet the demands of a stressful situation.

Children

Children themselves have sources of power. That is, children exert considerable influence over their parents and other family members. Even the cry of a baby has considerable influence. An older child can render parents powerless if he or she can get them

to disagree (Hartwell-Walker 2015). Parents are wise to be aware of power struggles that can arise in rearing children—especially the ones they cannot "win." For example:

> Claire, 26 months old, and her mother locked in a power struggle over potty training. Mom insisted she sit there until something happened. Claire could sit for a long time—making them late for daycare, delaying bedtime and generally being an annoyance. The more frustrated Mom grew, the more resistant Claire was. Finally Mom said, "OK. Fine. But we're not going to the beach until you use the potty like a big girl!" Claire replied, "I don't care." (The beach was one of Claire's favorite spots.) Big sister was enlisted as a secret helper to remind Claire. In about two weeks Mom heard Claire come out of the bathroom, dancing down the hall, "We're going to the beach! We're going to the beach!"

Marital Power Patterns

Marital power patterns can be divided into four types: egalitarian, male dominant, female dominant, and anarchic. In an egalitarian power pattern, power is distributed equally between the partners. In a male-dominant pattern, the man has more power than the woman; in a female-dominant pattern, the pattern is reversed. In an anarchic power pattern, both partners have power and exercise it in a random manner, disregarding all rules in governing the total family. Male-dominant couples are congruent with a

---

expert power Power that is given because a person is considered superior in knowledge of a particular subject.

informational power Power acquired because of extensive knowledge of a specific area.

theory of primary interest and presumed competence The theory that the person who is most interested in, most involved with, and best qualified to make a particular choice will be more likely to do so.

psychological power The ability to bestow or withhold affection.

coercive power The threat of physical force or other types of punishment to force compliance.

Coercive power is based on the belief that one spouse can punish the other for noncompliance. An economically dependent spouse is more likely to stay in a severely abusive situation.

traditional norm, whereas egalitarian couples are congruent with a more modern norm of balanced power between spouses.

Most research on family power focuses on the distribution of power between spouses and examines the association between power distribution and marital adjustment. Studies of the relationship between power and marriage satisfaction have consistently shown two results: (1) shared power (an egalitarian pattern) is associated with the highest marital satisfaction (Knudson-Martin and Mahoney 2005; Lauer and Lauer 2011), and (2) female-dominant couples are, on the whole, less satisfied than egalitarian or male-dominant couples. Egalitarian couples have a higher level of agreement on the desired distribution of power than couples with hierarchical relationships. Violence occurs least often in marriages in which power is shared (D. Olson, DeFrain, and Skogrand 2014: Payne and Wermeling 2009).

High rates of dissatisfaction have been found in female-dominant relationships. Most spouses in such relationships view dominance by the woman as undesirable. Some argue the level of satisfaction in such marriages is low because the man cannot or will not adequately exercise power, leaving the woman to assume more authority than desired by either spouse and causing dissatisfaction in both. When she confronts his unwillingness and resistance, she may use control tactics or resort to demanding, negative communication, which typically leads to marital dissatisfaction. Interestingly, therapy appears to be more successful for female-dominated couples than for couples with other power patterns (Gray-Little, Baucom, and Hamby 1996).

An association between negative behaviors—such as complaints, hostile comments, and whining—and low marital satisfaction is one of the best-established findings in the literature on marital interaction. There is also a greater incidence of minor violence in both male- and female-dominant marriages than in egalitarian ones. And unhappy partners are more likely to disagree about who has responsibility for what decisions.

Any kind of functional authority pattern may be better than none, however. Anarchic couples exhibit more negative behavior than either male- or female-dominant couples. The lack of decision-making structure is detrimental to marital functioning because there is neither an expressed norm nor an implicit understanding of who will exercise control. Each spouse contests the other's authority. As a result, the anarchic couple is caught up in a struggle to decide who will decide. Each partner tries to be in control while resisting the other's influence. Spouses who are able to negotiate compromises or who are willing to make accommodations to a partner's position tend to have higher levels of marital adjustment than spouses who are habitually confrontational (Gray-Little, Baucom, and Hamby 1996; Rehman et al. 2009).

Power Processes

We have discussed power bases, that is, the sources of power and power patterns. **Power processes** are the ways in which power is applied. A distinction must be made between orchestration power and implementation power. **Orchestration power** is the power to make the important decisions that determine family lifestyles and the major characteristics and features of the family. **Implementation power** sets these decisions in motion. For example, one spouse may decide how much money can be spent on a new appliance, but the other spouse is the one who actually makes the purchase. Conflicts arise when the implementing spouse tries to modify the guidelines and boundaries established by the orchestrating spouse. Thus, power in a

The Need for Control

All of us want to be in charge of our lives; it is natural to feel more comfortable when we do. However, there are times when we have either no or only limited control.

Many with an excessive need for power live in fear that unless they are in command, life will not turn out well; even when they have control, they may be fearful of losing it (Kleinke 2002).

It is important to learn to cope with the need for control. If we have an unbalanced need for control, it will probably cause us to experience anxiety, fear, impatience, and stress. An excessive need for control causes problems and conflict in relationships. It may even contribute to the playing of destructive psychological games, possessiveness, and abusive behavior.

Learning to cope positively with the need for control is a major step toward a more enjoyable, less-stressed life and relationships. Following are some principles that can help (Bourne 1995):

- **Acceptance and trust.** Accept the fact that there are some situations in life where you have no control (or limited control). Trust that things can work out even so. Take comfort in knowing that situations have worked out well in the past—sometimes even better—when you were not in charge. Understand that you will be happier if you are relaxed.

- **Patience.** Patience reduces frustration and usually helps you do a better job at whatever task you are working on. Patience can help you avoid rushing or forcing events in an attempt to manage things.

- **Humor.** Humor helps you not to take yourself so seriously or to take such a desperate attitude toward life. Humor helps maintain a more balanced perspective and can actually help you become somewhat amused at the futility and "silliness" of trying to micromanage every detail of your life.

- **Your own behavior.** Often we get our feelings hurt or become angry because of something another person says or does. It is easy to give other people too much power in determining our happiness and well-being. It is liberating to understand that you can never truly control other people nor are you responsible for their bad behavior. You are responsible only for your behavior; you can control your behavior. Yes, even when events are out of your control, you can still control your response and your appraisal of the situation.

relationship can be associated with control and decision making or with positive relationship qualities such as respect and security (S. M. Harvey and Bird 2004).

Power Tactics That Help

Power tactics are the means that people use to get others to do what they want them to do. Some tactics help build better relationships.

DISCUSSING, EXPLAINING, ASKING, OR TELLING Discussing, explaining, asking, and telling are positive methods of power implementation. Partners who can explain things in a rational, intelligent way or who ask questions directly and clearly are using a gentle, or soft, form of power that is effective.

BARGAINING AND NEGOTIATING Bargaining is the process by which two parties decide what each will give and receive in arriving at a decision. The process involves quid pro quo, which means "something for something." The purpose of bargaining is

power processes The ways in which power is applied.

orchestration power The power to make the important decisions that determine family lifestyle.

implementation power The power that sets decisions in motion.

bargaining The process by which two parties decide what each will give and receive in arriving at a decision.

to reach an agreement or compromise solution to a problem.

Power Tactics That Can Help or Harm

Some power tactics are helpful under some circumstances but harmful in others.

PERSUADING Persuasion is stronger than discussion. Its purpose is to try to convince the other person to believe or do something that he or she is reluctant to do or believe. Sometimes, the person is genuinely convinced and accepts willingly; at other times, the person acquiesces, but against his or her inclinations. Consider this example:

> Bill wanted to go to Hawaii for vacation. Sally was reluctant because of the expense and her anxiety about flying. Bill got all the brochures and for months talked about how wonderful it would be to go to Hawaii. He finally convinced her that Hawaii was *the* place to go. Sally went, but resented Bill's selfishness. (Counseling notes)

BEING NICE Being cooperative, attentive, and considerate may put people in a good mood and make them feel so grateful that they cannot refuse a request. Some spouses are better than others at buttering up a partner. Sincere compliments and consideration are appreciated, but false efforts to win favors are deceitful and create distrust.

Power Tactics That Harm

When power tactics are used to maintain or increase the imbalance of power in a relationship, the consequences are usually undesirable because negative feelings such as insecurity and resentment are generated. The most extreme form of control is cruel and abusive treatment, which may be physical and/or emotional. The man who beats his wife terrorizes her so that he can maintain control over her. He may also convince her that it is her fault that he "loses his temper"—that he would not if only she were more understanding or did not spend so much money, for example. Women can also use abusive power tactics; usually women use emotional maneuvers.

PSYCHOLOGICAL GAMES Most power tactics, however, are more subtle and control through manipulation and deceit. These may range from behaviors such as pleading or crying to sulking or acting helpless or ill. Many of these tactics follow a pattern described as a **psychological game**. A psychological game is defined as a pattern of interaction that superficially appears legitimate, but actually has an ulterior motive. Psychological games are basically dishonest and manipulative. Although some people are not aware they are playing psychological games, their objective is to cover up their true motives and outwit someone into doing something they want.

Psychological games should *not* be considered fun or frivolous. Many are merely annoying and relatively harmless, but others are vicious and destructive. All such games tend to prevent true intimacy and are obstacles to clear communication and successful conflict resolution.

Psychological games are used not only in intimate relationships, but also in business and on the Internet. For example, cybercriminals and scammers exploit people's fears, greed, loneliness, and lust to steal personal and financial information. They fraudulently obtain sensitive data such as usernames, passwords, and account numbers by the use of e-mails that appear to come from nationally recognized credit card companies or banks. Others prey on those who are lonely or lovelorn—promising companions or love for joining their group or buying their product (Gaudin 2007; Sullivan 2010).

SOME COMMON PSYCHOLOGICAL GAMES Psychological games involve pretending, posturing, or "putting on a mask" to achieve a desired goal such as gaining power, building themselves up, or demeaning others. Some examples follow.

Hard to Get. In this common dating game, one person deliberately minimizes his or her availability and interest in the other. For example, a woman gives the appearance that she is not all that interested in a particular man (although she is). She only has "free nights" once a week although he asks more often; she rarely returns his calls. He is supposed to feel that she is sought after—and pursue her even harder.

Prove Your Love for Me. This game has at least two versions. In one, the game player says, "If you love me, you will. . . ." The victim is called on to prove his or her love by a specific act—having sex or giving access to a bank account, for example.

In the other version, a person keeps pushing the limits. Individuals who feel that significant others in their lives have always run out on them may actually test how much stress, bad behavior, or problems a partner will endure. Sadly, there is never enough "proof" and the stress may cause a partner to leave (G. Kelly 2013).

Jealous. A jealous game player demands all the time and attention of the victim, frequently by monitoring his or her activities closely. The victim may be grilled: "Why were you 15 minutes late meeting me? Whom were you with?" "Why didn't you return my calls this morning? What were you doing?" There may be demands that the victim not have conversations with members of the opposite sex—even at social events or with colleagues at work. The player may isolate the victim from family and friends by dominating so much of his or her time and energy.

The player may justify his or her demands as proof of love or commitment; however, the true motive is power and control. The player often fears losing the victim. This may be because other significant people have left; perhaps attachment was disrupted in early life (Kinnison 2014). Whatever the cause, the player decides that people cannot be trusted to stay and so tries to make sure that a partner does not leave by spying and demanding complete devotion. Again, the jealous behavior typically causes stress and conflict.

Corner. In this game, the player reacts to another in such a way that no matter what the victim does, it is wrong. For example, he tells her that she should help more with their finances; she is not being responsible. If she pays bills, it is too soon, too late, or she messed up the checkbook. He scoffs at her suggestions for investments. Needless to say, this game is frustrating to the victim—who is constantly on the defensive.

Sweetheart. This game player indirectly ridicules the victim in public in a manner so subtle that the recipient is probably the only one aware of what happened. The motive for this game is to make the victim feel bad and to make the player feel superior. For example, the husband who resents his wife's earning more money than he does uses a family gathering to express his hostility. In the presence of several others, he tells the story of a woman so wrapped up in her career that she neglected her children (who all met tragic ends, of course). He comments on how sad it is when parents neglect their children, then turns to his wife and says, "Isn't that right, sweetheart?"

Because he appears to be talking about someone else, she cannot disagree or object without seeming completely unreasonable. If she confronts him in private, he can claim he was talking about someone else, "but perhaps she should do something about it if she thinks it applies."

Camouflage. This game is used to avoid confrontation or negative responses; it involves the use of indirect messages, hints, or talking around an issue. For example, she thinks he is getting a bit pudgy and wishes he would trim up. So she talks about the health problems associated with overweight and every neighbor or colleague at work who loses a few pounds—how good they look and how much energy they have. He may catch the hint; chances are he will not.

Wooden Leg. This maneuver is designed to elicit sympathy and as an excuse for failing to be responsible or independent. The game player says, in effect, "Of course I limp. What do you expect of a wooden leg?" The "wooden leg" may be a personality deficiency, a physical challenge, or an unstable past. For example, "Of course I can't keep a job; I'm depressed." Or "Yes, I drink too much; my dad was alcoholic."

It's Your Decision. Sometimes people who wish to escape the responsibility of making a decision place the burden on the shoulders of another with comments such as "It doesn't matter to me" or "Whatever you choose is OK." The problem is that it *does* matter to the player. For example, she insists that any movie he picks is OK, then complains if the theater is crowded or the movie is a disappointment. After all, it was his bad choice—she is not responsible in any way. This game and Corner often go together.

Martyr. The person playing martyr speaks often of all she or he has done for a spouse and/or children—the numerous sacrifices, ruined health, no time for self, and so on. The payoff is to gain admiration and sympathy or to make a spouse (and children) feel guilty—thus making the game player have an easier time getting his or her way.

psychological game A pattern of interaction that appears legitimate but actually has an ulterior motive.

Gaslighting or Crazy Making. The term **gaslighting** comes from the movie *Gaslight*, in which the husband (Charles Boyer) attempts to drive his wife (Ingrid Bergman) insane by a number of means, including causing the gaslights to dim and telling her that she imagines it. Consequently, these terms refer to a variety of maneuvers used to make someone doubt his or her sanity or to send the person "up the wall" to gain power. Many variations are possible, including the following:

- Denying feelings a partner can clearly see. For example, she weeps quietly but says, "Nothing is wrong."

- Denying something that has been discussed and agreed on or insisting on exact wording: "I said I'd mow the yard; I didn't say I'd do it today." (The grass is high; it is sunny and his day off work.)

- Building up hopes and shattering them without an acceptable reason. For example, promising to paint the house when the next payday comes and then refusing—although the budget would bear it easily.

- Attributing vicious motives to another: "Where did you *hide* my socks?" "*Conveniently* forgot to make reservations, didn't you?"

- Ignoring another's wishes. A person who cannot ever be on time and a person who continues a mannerism that annoys after being asked not to do so (repeatedly) are examples.

Scapegoating. **Scapegoating** describes the practice of blaming someone else for every bad or unfortunate thing that happens. The goal is to make someone else feel guilty and allow the player to escape any personal responsibility. For example, he is a mean, cruel husband who bullies her and the children. But when she leaves him, he blames her for separating him from his children.

WHY ARE PSYCHOLOGICAL GAMES USED? The more abusive psychological games target the mental state of others and are designed to cause the victim to feel inadequate or at fault or to doubt his or her judgment or sanity (Stern 2007). The use of psychological games often creates relationship problems, prevents intimacy, and hinders the understanding that most of us desire in our relationships. Game

---

PERSONAL PERSPECTIVE

How Do You Stop a Psychological Game?

Following is a sample of answers given to this question in a survey of college students:

"I've been in a relationship with a mind-gamer before. I played the games back on him and asked him how he liked being treated that way. It didn't stop him, though. He just played meaner games."

"My husband and I had been married for about three years when he got to playing mind games so destructive that it was making me mentally ill. One day, I just broke down and told him, 'I will not live this way any longer or expose our daughter to this kind of life. Stop this or get out!' We started marriage counseling the next week. Two years later we are communicating much more positively. It takes patience and hard work every day."

"It took me awhile to realize it, but my girlfriend likes to play psychological games. I got tired of it and stopped 'dancing with her.' When she starts to manipulate, I just ignore it—as if I wasn't even aware of it. This has helped. She tries to maneuver less now, probably because it doesn't work so well."

"If I realized that I was the one playing the game, I'd do two things to break the habit. First, I'd pop my wrist with a rubber band every time I caught myself about to use a game. Second, I'd pay my friends a dollar each time I said something hurtful and controlling. This way I would learn to be positive and honest or I'd be broke and bruised!"

playing is not an effective way to draw close or to solve conflict, however. So why are psychological games played? Certain common psychological needs and emotions typically underlie their use.

Lack of Trust. When partners do not trust each other, it is difficult to be honest about feelings or desires (Stinnett and Stinnett 2010). For example, he would like to go to the beach, but hesitates to suggest it openly for fear she will not respond favorably. Instead he camouflages, "It is good for people to have a break from the daily grind. You've always enjoyed the beach, haven't you?"

Other times people use games because they do not trust themselves to achieve goals on their own and believe they must rely on others. Yet, because they do not completely trust others, they resort to manipulations. For example, she worries that her grown children will not come to visit unless they feel obligated. So she plays the martyr: "I've sacrificed so much for you. You're all I have and I'm so lonely."

Desire to Avoid Responsibility. Several of the psychological games are designed to allow the player to avoid responsibility for everything from where to have lunch to the consequences of decades of alcoholic behavior. Scapegoating, It's Your Decision, and Wooden Leg are examples.

Fear of Close Relationships. Some individuals are anxious about close relationships because they have been hurt, exploited, or disappointed in a past close relationship and do not want to be hurt again. They protect themselves by keeping others at a distance; they control by keeping others emotionally off balance.

Unfamiliarity with Alternatives. Some people learn to use games as children by observing and imitating the behavior of parents and other adults. Some develop dysfunctional patterns of dealing with people to cope with a difficult environment. It takes courage to alter comfortable ways of behaving and to risk new ways. Consequently, familiar ways may persist even when they are less than desirable.

Although it is true that psychological needs and emotions drive people to play games, it is ironic that game playing really does nothing to meet needs or remove hurts. The lack of trust, the low self-esteem, and the anger still remain.

I suppose we were all searching for someone to teach us the moves we need to win at

life. . . . But a sequence of maneuvers and a system of behavior would never fix what was broken inside. (Strauss 2005, 415)

Consequences of Power Struggles

One of the most important considerations in evaluating patterns of power in the family is the effect that different patterns have on individuals and their relationships. Some people gain control, but at what cost? If they gain the upper hand at the cost of alienating a partner, provoking hostility, or destroying their relationship, what is the point? Some spouses are so intent on winning the battle that they lose the marriage.

Generally, extreme imbalances of power between two people tend to have a negative effect. Lack of power is associated with psychological distress for both men and women. At the other extreme, high levels of power can also be destructive, because power can corrupt. This means that power produces strong psychological changes in power holders, and they start to exploit those they control. They can become self-centered, unfeeling, and abusive. The person dominated becomes an "it" to use rather than a person to cherish.

One of the consequences of power imbalances in relationships is that the person who feels coerced or manipulated becomes frustrated and resentful. A person may accept coercion for a while, but as frustrations increase, the relationship worsens. Couples who habitually deal with decisions on a win-or-lose basis often discover that a victory in a marital conflict is illusory. The victory turns into a loss for both partners when anger and hurt develop between them.

Marital satisfaction is maximized when couples achieve a balance of power that is acceptable to both partners. This balance varies with different couples. Although dominance by one partner works for some couples, an extreme imbalance of power

---

gaslighting The process by which one person destroys the self-confidence, perception, and sense of reality of another person.

scapegoating Blaming someone else for every bad thing that happens.

usually causes dissatisfaction (Knudson-Martin and Mahoney 2005; R. S. Miller and Perlman 2009).

Social science research emphasizes that equitable relations tend to be more stable and satisfying. Women who feel they have power to control the outcome of marital conflicts are more satisfied with their marriages than are women who do not. If women blame a spouse for the conflict and have little control over the situation, they find their marriage unsatisfying. Exchange theorists suggest that satisfaction in marriage hinges on the perception of fairness or equity in exchanges, rather than on the existence of a particular power structure (R. S. Miller and Perlman 2009).

Communication

Marital satisfaction is influenced greatly by good communication, which, practiced regularly, allows a couple to share control of family matters and facilitates positive family interactions. It is a significant factor in creating intimacy.

Common sense says that couples who talk openly and honestly, who are respectful and loving, and who are good listeners are more likely to achieve marital success. Research over the past 30 years verifies that healthy families maintain an accepting, supportive, open, and caring environment in which open and direct communication can thrive (Alayi, AhmadiGatab, and Khamen 2011; Ruffieux, Nussbeck, and Bodenmann 2014; Stinnett and Stinnett 2010).

Communication may be defined as a message one person sends and another receives. It involves both content and process. Content is what is communicated; process is the means by which feelings, attitudes, facts, beliefs, and ideas are transmitted between people. Communication is not limited to words but also occurs through listening, silence, glances, facial expressions, gestures, touch, body stance, and all other non-language symbols and cues used to give and transmit meaning. In short, it may include all the messages sent and received and all the means by which people exchange feelings and meanings as they try to understand and influence one another.

Studies of non-distressed couples and distressed couples with respect to differences in communication skills and marital satisfaction indicate that distressed and non-distressed couples had the same communication skills level; however, the partners in the distressed couples used their skills with more negative intentions and ill will. In other words, it is not always a lack of communication skills that makes a marriage go awry. Rather, it can be the intentions of a partner that cause a marriage to be distressed (Alayi, AhmadiGatab, and Khamen 2011; Stern 2007). Time also may play a role in communication in a relationship. Research shows that the longer a couple is together, the frequency of conflict and arguing increases, whereas remaining calm and keeping opinions to one's self decreases (Stafford et al. 2004).

Verbal and Nonverbal Communication

Nonverbal communication comes in many forms. **Body language** involves physical reactions such as posture, facial expression, eye contact, muscular tension, blushing, movement, panting, tears, sweating, shivering, an increased pulse rate, and a thumping heart. The message "I love you" may be communicated by facial expression (pleasant), touch (gentle and caring), eyes (attentive), speed of speech (slow), tone of voice (soft), and gesture (outstretched arms). The manner of dressing and the use of cosmetics are also forms of communication.

Both verbal and nonverbal communication are strongly associated with good marital adjustment. However, nonverbal communication, the language of signs and signals, is more subject to misinterpretation.

Direct actions are another form of communication; that is why florists remind us, "Say it with flowers." Some nonverbal communication is symbolic communication. A surprise gift can send a message of care and love.

One of the most important uses of words is what has been called the stroking function. This refers to words that soothe; that give recognition, acceptance, and reassurance; and that fulfill emotional needs. Words can heal hurt egos and satisfy deep longings. What person is immune to the words "I think you're a wonderful person" or "Hi, Sweetie" or "I'm so sorry, please forgive me"? Words also are used to solve problems, to convey information, or to reveal emotions. Other important functions of words are to provide companionship and develop intimacy.

Sometimes the verbal and nonverbal messages are contradictory or place the recipient in an impossible situation. A woman may say to her partner,

Facebook, Text Messaging, and Beer

Dramatic changes have occurred in communication among young people since the 1990s. College students, for example, now rely on e-mail, cell phones, text messaging, Twitter, and Facebook pages to communicate on a daily basis. Some research indicates that teens prefer these electronic and computer-mediated ways of communicating to face-to-face communication (Diamanduros, Jenkins, and Downs 2007). In a study of preferences and habits of college students from more than 100 American universities, text messaging and Facebook communications were two of the three most popular activities on campus (beer was the third) (*Student monitor* 2008).

There are a number of benefits to electronic and computer-mediated communication, such as making it easier to stay in touch with family and friends. A student in Alabama can send an e-mail or text to parents in Ohio, to a brother in the military overseas, and to a fiancée at another university and get answers back in minutes rather than days. Some couples indicate electronic communications help them have a more intimate relationship. They feel freer to disclose this way. What are other benefits you can identify?

There are also potential problems with these new methods of communicating. For example, because texting uses abbreviated messages, does it tend, over time, to reduce face-to-face conversation as well as writing skills? Does near-constant communication cause interactions to become superficial and less meaningful? What are other problems that you can think of?

"I'm listening, I'm listening," but she's texting. Or a man may tell his partner "I love you" over and over, but he seldom wants to spend time together and refuses to do little things to help. Or one wants to have a child and says, "But only if you want it, too." What can an unwilling partner do? Be coerced into parenthood or wreck the relationship. Inconsistent words and actions, often referred to as **double-bind communication**, cause stress between partners to increase as anxiety grows (Berry 2011).

Barriers to Communication

Barriers to communication may be grouped under five categories: physical and environmental, situational, psychological, cultural, and gender.

PHYSICAL AND ENVIRONMENTAL BARRIERS There is a close relationship between physical proximity and social interaction. In general, closer physical distances are associated with more intimate relationships. This means that factors such as the size and arrangement of living spaces and the location of furniture in those spaces influence interaction. The closer people sit around a table, the more likely they are to be friendly, talkative, and intimate. Whether couples sleep together in the same bed or in separate bedrooms influences the extent of their interaction.

Physical confinement is associated with accelerated self-disclosure, particularly in intimate areas of exchange. This means that the closer couples are physically, the greater the possibility that intimacy will develop. Of course, there is also the possibility that conflict and tension will arise.

SITUATIONAL BARRIERS Situations also can enhance communication or make it more difficult. If employment separates couples frequently or for long periods of time, the tendency is for communication to break down, with a resultant loss of

---

communication A message one person sends and another receives.

body language Posture, facial expression, eye contact, tense muscles, blushing, panting, tears, sweating, shivering, increased pulse rate, thumping heart, and other bodily reactions that convey feelings and reactions.

double-bind communication Conflicting messages sent when verbal messages and body language do not agree.

intimacy. When a couple lives together with others, lack of privacy becomes a major factor in making intimate communication more difficult. The situational context changes during different periods of marriage and affects communication. For example, men may make great efforts to give emotional support to a spouse during pregnancy; following childbirth, however, they may feel that she does not require the same special support. The closeness reported during pregnancy then declines, resulting in the dissatisfaction that some women feel after childbirth.

PSYCHOLOGICAL BARRIERS The most important barriers to communication are psychological: fear of rejection, ridicule, failure, or alienation and lack of trust between two people. Partners will not share experiences that are unrewarding, threatening, or painful if they are not sure of an empathetic reply.

CULTURAL BARRIERS Culture is that part of ourselves we absorb from our families, neighborhoods, communities, schools, and the broad society in which we grow up. Modern marriages often involve two people who come from vastly different national, racial, socioeconomic, or religious backgrounds. Although thousands of immigrants have proved that it is possible for such marriages to succeed, the couple with dissimilar backgrounds face complex challenges, including divergent attitudes toward sex, family life, roles of men and women, financial responsibility, or childrearing. In some cultures, for example, use of birth control is strictly forbidden.

Each cultural group also has its own set of rules and emphases for everyday conversations,

use of words and expressions, use of praise and criticism, and use of nonverbal communications. For example, a cross-cultural study comparing families from Japan and the United States found significant differences in family communication standards. Americans were twice as likely to express detached, blunt interactions and to minimize interpersonal sensitivity. Japanese families were far more likely to emphasize regular family interaction and obedience to parents. Also, American families significantly more often reported preference for communication that involves a high degree of openness and expression of affection (Matsunaga and Imahori 2009). Several cultural groups deem it acceptable for discussions to be loud and animated, with a great deal of shouting and noisy exchange. In others, issues are discussed quietly, showing self-control and rational thinking. An individual reared in one style may be at a loss when a partner responds in another.

GENDER BARRIERS The communication patterns of men and women have some interesting differences that can interfere with clear communication (see Table 9.1). In conversations, men tend to focus more on activities, facts, and information; women focus more on relationships and interaction (Knox and Schacht 2016). Men more often want to get to the "bottom line" quickly, whereas women prefer to give details and feelings leading up to the bottom line (Stinnett and Stinnett 2010).

In conversations, men are more concerned with making their point, putting their best argument forward, maintaining independence, and avoiding failure. They are more apt to express anger and

TABLE 9.1 Differences in Communication Patterns of Men and Women

MORE MEN THAN WOMEN . . .	MORE WOMEN THAN MEN . . .
Express low self-disclosure	Are skilled in starting and maintaining conversations
Use little nonverbal communication	Are skilled in using and interpreting nonverbal messages
Focus on facts	Focus on feelings and emotions
Prefer to come to major ideas quickly	Prefer to elaborate details
Communicate distant, impersonal messages	Communicate warm, friendly messages
Express anger and contempt	Express sadness and fear
Communicate in a competitive and aggressive manner	Communicate in a nurturing and supportive manner

contempt in interactions (Fitness and Duffield 2004). Women typically interpret this more assertive approach as an attack and react negatively. Women are more sensitive to and aware of the other person's feelings in conversations; their aim is to establish closeness and preserve intimacy (Kim and Aune 1998; Lauer and Lauer 2011).

Women are more skilled in starting and maintaining conversations; they are more open and disclosing (Aylor and Dainton 2004), whereas men are more likely to engage in a silent, non-communicative style of interaction. This difference may be noted when relationship difficulties arise: she is apt to initiate a discussion of the problem, often asking for change; he is apt to withdraw (Holley, Sturm, and Levenson 2010). One woman explained, "My husband just won't argue with me. He just gets up and goes out to his workshop. He makes me furious—why won't he just say something?"

Communication differences in exaggerated form may cause conflict. Couples who have successful, happy marriages make an effort to be sensitive to the communication differences they have and to minimize them. For example, he listens patiently to more details than he really wants to hear getting to the "bottom line," whereas she thoughtfully leaves some of the details out. The willingness to accommodate each other sends powerful messages of respect and commitment.

Improving Communication Skills

The lack of communication skills is associated with lower marriage happiness and higher divorce rates. However, communication skills can be learned and developed. Communication and conflict resolution skills training have been found to be effective in improving marital satisfaction significantly among couples in Western countries as well as in the Middle East (Askan et al. 2012).

Skill in communication has four requirements: (1) a positive feeling between partners who value and care for each other and are motivated to want to develop sympathetic understanding; (2) a willingness to disclose one's own attitudes, feelings, and ideas; (3) an ability to reveal attitudes, feelings, and ideas clearly and accurately; and (4) a reciprocal

Good communication is the key to intimacy and family interaction and is the lifeblood of the marital relationship.

relationship in which disclosure and feedback originate with both partners, who listen carefully and attentively to each other. Successful communicators also know how to argue constructively.

Taking Time

It is a serious problem, but many couples are fragmented by the demands of work, community, children, and personal interests—and their communication deteriorates. They may be completely unaware of what is going on in the hearts and minds of each other, not because they are uncaring, but because they are not together enough to know.

The practice of eating family meals together and the conversation that occurs during the meal offer major benefits. Research investigations show that frequency of family meals is significantly linked to healthier dietary intakes, decreased eating disorders, increased psychological health, lower use of alcohol and drugs, and higher academic success (among children and adolescents). Frequency of family meals is also significantly related to greater family closeness and connectedness for both children and parents (Fruh et al. 2011; Neumark-Sztainer, Wall, and Fulkerson 2012). Unfortunately, since the 1960s, eating family meals together has declined substantially. Work, after-school activities, television viewing, and other activities have fragmented the family and made eating meals together a challenge for many families. However, families who make eating meals together a priority report that it enhances their family strengths (Fruh et al. 2011; Stinnett and Stinnett 2005).

Research consistently reports that happy, successful couples make communication a priority and make time for it. They structure the environment to have time that is sufficient and relaxed for communication—they turn off the television and telephones or take a walk together. Couples and families who establish a daily pattern of taking time to convey interest in and concern for each other as they discuss events of the day report the highest levels of family satisfaction (Burns and Pearson 2011). This principle is foundational: there must be time to gather our thoughts and to express them. There must be someone to take the time to listen—to feelings as well as words (Stinnett and Stinnett 2010).

Motivation and Concern

Communication is most possible when partners show they truly care about each other and when they are motivated to understand each other. It is not only the communication itself that is important but also the spirit behind the message and the partners' feelings for each other. How a message is sent is vital in how the receiver interprets it (Young and Metts 2004). The tone of voice used and the words selected are important as well. Most researchers emphasize the importance of compassion in healthy relationships (Stosny 2004). Being sensitive to others, trying to understand their wishes and feelings, and then responding accordingly is a way to cultivate intimacy. Partners who frequently make positive statements about each other have much higher marital satisfaction than do those who are negative or disparaging in what they say (Schrodt 2009). In addition, supportive communication stimulates reciprocal supportiveness, increasing the degree of marital integration (Karney and Neff 2013).

Empathy

Empathy, the ability to identify with the emotional state of another, is motivated and influenced by a genuine concern for others. Consequently, individuals who are absorbed in their own interests, problems, and needs may not be empathic.

A high degree of empathy makes partners sensitive to each other; empathy helps them see beyond words to inner feelings. Because of their greater understanding, tolerance increases. Empathy inhibits aggression in interpersonal relationships and minimizes antisocial behavior. Defensiveness is reduced (G. Kelly 2013).

Content

It has been said that "people may forget what you say or what you do, but they will never forget how you make them feel." The quality of marriage and family relationships is greatly influenced by how the couple and family members make each other feel, which is determined in large part by the content of the messages communicated to each other.

When couples engage in communication patterns that are primarily criticisms, complaints, contempt, accusations, put-downs, sarcasm, and intimidation, the relationship becomes overloaded with negativity. Over time, the couple begins to have negative feelings about each other, themselves, and their relationship. In contrast, many research studies support that couples who communicate a preponderance of positive messages such as affection, appreciation, respect, and encouragement are much more likely to have a high degree of marriage and family satisfaction (Lauer and Lauer 2011; Matsunaga and Imahori 2009; Stinnett and Stinnett 2010).

Self-Disclosure

Communication depends partly on people's willingness to disclose their real feelings, ideas, and attitudes. People cannot really get to know others unless they are willing to talk about themselves. Some people can be classified as high revealers and others as low revealers. High revealers are more prone to disclose intimate facets of their personalities and to do so earlier in their relationships than are low revealers. They also are able to more accurately assess the intimate attitudes and values of their friends than are low revealers. In general, dyads in which both persons are high revealers are more compatible than are pairs of low revealers or pairs that differ in the level of disclosure.

The time, place, and method of disclosure also affect how much the disclosure really can help the relationship. People who are feeling hostile may be wise not to talk until they can discuss the situation more rationally. There is some evidence to suggest that topic avoidance can be the best strategy at times, depending on the individual's motivation for avoidance (Gable et al. 2004).

Clarity

Although clarity is a communication skill that promotes satisfaction in intimate relationships, people differ in their ability to convey messages clearly and accurately. However, you can learn to say what you mean and to accurately interpret what others say by doing the following:

1. Avoid double-bind messages in which words say one thing and actions and innuendos say another. This includes flippant, kidding remarks that mask your true feelings and opinions: "I didn't really mean that. I was only joking. Don't take everything so seriously."

2. Speak clearly and to the point; avoid vagueness, ambiguity, and indirect approaches.

3. Avoid both exaggeration and understatement.

4. Ask the other person to repeat what was said if there is any doubt about it or if it may have been misinterpreted.

5. Talk about important things when there is a minimum of distraction and when you both can focus your attention completely on what is being said.

Listening

Sending clear messages is an important part of communication, but receiving the message, or listening, is equally important. Family members who do not listen to one another miss a great deal. Furthermore, listening, in and of itself, conveys messages of interest in, respect, and concern for the other person (Stinnett and Stinnett 2010).

It is just as necessary to "listen" to the nonverbal cues as it is to the literal content of the message. Nonverbal signals serve as indicators of a person's emotional state—feelings. In interpretive listening, an individual discerns meanings from cues given by voice tone, pitch, and posture, for example. The statement "I have too much to do" may be a request for understanding and help (stooped shoulders, flat voice tone, slow speech indicating fatigue and discouragement) or a complaint (loud and aggressive tone, upright posture).

Feedback

Feedback involves responding to what the other person has said, as well as disclosing one's own feelings and ideas. This is done by paraphrasing the other person's statement to make sure it is understood, asking clarifying questions, and then giving one's own input or response. Accurate feedback also requires open listening and hearing and giving one's undivided attention to what is said.

Arguing Constructively

Many couples repeatedly argue about the same issues without ever resolving them. At the heart of these quarrels may be matters of closeness and control (Christensen and Jacobson 2000). For many people, these issues define the relationship, affirm their self-image, and determine in large part their satisfaction with the relationship. When issues of control and closeness arise, partners tend to overreact and quarrels erupt.

Christensen and Jacobson (2000) endorsed a concept called "acceptance and commitment therapy" for couples in conflict. According to this therapeutic philosophy, some conflicts simply cannot be resolved. Thus, people must learn to accept a partner, give up trying to change him or her, and instead commit to changing themselves (Serani 2011). Gottman (2000a) reported that many quarrels in relationships are the same fight over and over again and that in these situations partners would do better to stop trying to solve the problem and come to accept both it and each other. Such problems may have their roots in childhood and different family backgrounds or in temperament differences. For example, he may have been raised in an unemotional household, whereas she was raised in one

empathy The ability to identify with the emotional state of another—to feel with him or her.

feedback Response to the message another has sent and disclosure of one's own feelings and ideas.

FAMILY STRENGTHS PERSPECTIVES

Listen

The story is told that one of Abraham Lincoln's most valued advisors was a longtime friend. During times of hard decisions, Lincoln would summon his friend to Washington and the friend would come, riding the train for many hours, to aid his friend, his country, his president.

As they spent time together, Lincoln would speak his concerns, his woes, his burdens, his opinions. And his friend would listen—just listen. No advice or suggestions. No "If I were you, I'd. . . ." After a few days, the friend would return home and Lincoln would arrive at decisions.

Members of strong families know that good communication involves talking and listening.

Listening allows us to understand others—to know what is in their hearts and minds.

Active listeners listen not only to words, but also to facial expressions, body posture, and voice tone. They listen for the feelings behind the words. For example, when he drags in from work, complaining that the boss hates him, and she responds, "Sounds like you're feeling kind of down; let's have some lemonade and you can tell me about it," he is encouraged to keep talking.

On the other hand, if she says, "You think you're the only one who has hard days? Stop complaining. Better be glad you have a job," he likely will not respond or will get angry. Communication is closed down.

---

that was boisterous and filled with laughter. The difference creates conflict in their relationship; he is embarrassed when she is too loud and she wishes he would not always look unhappy. They may both move to the middle, but it is unlikely that one can shift entirely to the other's point of view. Acceptance of a partner's different traits does not mean giving in because of fear or intimidation, but being strongly committed to a more fulfilling and satisfying relationship.

Arguing also is an important part of communication. Since all couples argue from time to time, arguing per se is not a sign of a poor relationship. Christensen and Jacobson (2000) suggested several guidelines for arguing constructively:

1. Develop a "third side" of the argument that incorporates both your own and your partner's view; this can help the two of you see the problem more objectively.

2. See the problem as a difficulty the two of you have, rather than as something your partner does to you.

3. Demonstrate that you have heard your partner by summarizing what he or she has to say; ask your partner to do the same.

4. While arguing, do something positive for your partner with no strings attached.

5. Focus on one problem at a time, not a parade of them.

6. Recognize that your partner's hurtful actions may be a defense mechanism to mask pain.

7. Do not insist that yours is the only way.

8. Remember that the only person you can change is yourself.

9. Rather than arguing the same way every time, do something different, such as sending an e-mail or writing a letter; try going out for coffee or ice cream. Writing it down may help to organize and clarify your thoughts. Being out in public can help prevent you from getting caught up in the argument, escalating it, or raising your voice.

This chapter discussed the invisible factors that hold a relationship together. Power determines how decisions are made and how relationships develop. Effective communication skills can help keep power equitable. The greatest marital satisfaction is found when power and communication are balanced between husband and wife.

The Power of Federal Judges

It may seem out of place to have a discussion of federal judges in a text on intimate relationships. However, most people do not realize the power the U.S. federal judicial system holds and its implications for family life. Rulings by federal judges on thousands of cases each year affect public policy on such things as environmental issues, restrictions on abortion, public schooling, worker and consumer safety, and employment discrimination. For example, federal judges decide whether employees are entitled to receive overtime pay from their employers under the Fair Labor Standards Act and whether they are entitled to take unpaid leave for a serious illness or for the birth or adoption of a child under the Family and Medical Leave Act. Many of the issues presented before federal judges have tremendous implications for families.

Many people today consider the appointment of Supreme Court justices of utmost importance, but in reality all federal court judges are important. These judges are appointed for a life term in the interest of impartiality; not having to worry about being reappointed means that they can rule free from political influences or popular issues. Formerly, judges were appointed primarily according to their ability to objectively uphold the law; today, more emphasis is placed on political ideology (S. B. Goldberg 2003) and appointing judges to advance a party's own political agenda. This has increased controversy regarding lifelong judicial appointments.

Questions to Consider

Should judges be representative of the population at large? For example, should judges be of different races, religions, and genders? Discuss.

What are the consequences of not having a certain interest group represented in the judiciary?

Employment discrimination cases, including sexual harassment, fall under federal law. Consider the example of a woman who feels she was inappropriately touched by a male boss at work. After failing to remedy the situation through company policies and procedures, she files a formal complaint with the Equal Employment Opportunity Commission. Her case is presented to a federal judge. What differences might the background of the judge (e.g., the judge's race, sex, sexual orientation, age, education, income level, or disability) have with regard to the outcome of the case?

Summary

1. *Power* has been defined as the ability of an individual within a social relationship to carry out his or her will, even in the face of resistance by others.

2. People desire power for a variety of reasons: because they want to have control over their life, because society expects them to have it, because they are following the pattern modeled by their parents, or because of a psychological need to compensate for feelings of inferiority and insecurity. Three theoretical frameworks explain the need for power:

attachment theory, social control theory, and feminist theory.

3. Power is based on cultural norms, gender norms, economic resources, education and knowledge, personality differences, communication ability, emotional factors, physical stature and strength, and circumstances. Children as well as adults have sources of power.

4. Marital power patterns can be divided into four types: egalitarian, male dominant, female dominant, and anarchic. Egalitarian power

patterns have been associated with the greatest degree of marital satisfaction and anarchic with the least. Female-dominant power patterns are also associated with marital dissatisfaction.

5. Power processes are the ways power is applied. Orchestration power is the power to make the important decisions that determine family lifestyles. Implementation power sets these decisions in motion.

6. People use various means to get what they want. Some of these tactics help build better relationships; others do not.

7. Helpful power tactics include discussing, explaining, asking, telling, and bargaining and negotiating.

8. Power tactics that harm include a number of psychological games intended to control others through manipulation. These include Corner, Sweetheart, Camouflage, and Jealous.

9. One important consideration is what effect power relationships have on individuals and on marital satisfaction. Generally, extreme imbalances of power between two people tend to have a negative effect. Lack of power is associated with psychological distress for both men and women. At the other extreme, high levels of power can be destructive, resulting in corruption in the power holder and harm to the power subject.

10. Marital satisfaction is maximized when partners achieve a balance of power that is acceptable to them. This balance may vary with different couples as long as they feel that the power relationship they have achieved is fair and equitable.

11. One way for women to gain equity in a relationship is through empowerment: improving their capacities and abilities and recognizing that the feminine traits of sensitivity and caring are sources of strength rather than weakness.

12. Good communication is the key to intimacy, family interaction, and marital satisfaction.

13. *Communication* may be defined as a message one person sends and another receives. It is accomplished through both verbal and nonverbal means. It is one of the most important

requirements for marital satisfaction, but it can be helpful or harmful depending on how it is conducted.

14. Barriers to communication can be grouped into five categories: physical and environmental, situational, psychological, cultural, and gender.

15. Requirements of good communication are taking time, motivation and concern, empathy, willingness to disclose oneself, the ability to transmit messages clearly, listening, the use of feedback, and arguing constructively.

Key Terms

bargaining
body language
coercive power
communication
double-bind communication
empathy
expert power
feedback
gaslighting
implementation power
informational power
legitimate power
orchestration power
power
power processes
psychological game
psychological power
scapegoating
theory of primary interest and presumed competence

Questions for Thought

1. How do you exercise power in your family of origin? How much power do you hold in comparison to other family members?

2. If you are married, what are the major sources of power you have in relation to your spouse?

What are your spouse's sources of power in relation to you?

3. If you are single and dating someone, what are the major sources of power you have in relation to your partner? What are your partner's sources of power in relation to you?

4. What do you view as the most constructive way to exercise power in a family? Discuss.

5. How do you think a couple can best achieve a balance of power?

6. What are some reasons you have observed for people's inability to communicate with others?

7. How would you classify yourself in terms of your degree of self-disclosure in intimate relationships with the following people: your best friend, your mother, your father, and your spouse or a close friend or partner?

For Further Reading

"Communication barriers—Reasons for communication breakdown" and other topics such as feedback, nonverbal communication, and intercultural communication. http://www.managementstudyguide.com/communication_barriers.htm.

http://www.covenantkeepers.org. On this website, a number of topics related to marriage are discussed from a Biblical perspective. These include "What hinders communication in your marriage?" "What causes communication breakdown?" "Developing effective communication," and "How to fight fair."

Haskell, R. (2001). *Deep listening: Uncovering the hidden meanings in everyday conversation.* Cambridge, MA: Perseus. Serves as a method for recognizing, uncovering, and explaining hidden meanings in everyday conversations with friends, family, coworkers, and others.

Olson, D. H. (2000). *Empowering couples: Building on your strengths.* Minneapolis: Life Innovations. Presents guidelines for building practical relationship skills by helping couples identify their strengths.

Orbe, M., and Bruess, C. (2005). *Contemporary issues in interpersonal communication.* Los Angeles: Roxbury. Resource book to help couples work on communication issues.

Payne, K. E. (2001). *Different but equal: Communication between the sexes.* Westport, CT: Praeger. Discusses the changes that have occurred between men and women and how the sexes relate to each other from social, political, and ethical perspectives.

Segrin, C., and Flora, J. (2005). *Family communication.* Mahwah, NJ: Erlbaum. Focuses on patterns of communication in the family.

Sexual Relationships

CHAPTER OUTLINE

Learning Objectives

Sexuality

Sexual Myths

- Myth 1: Sexual Satisfaction Increases with Multiple Partners
- Myth 2: Sexual Satisfaction Is Determined by Frequency of Sexual Intercourse
- Myth 3: Sex during Menstruation Should Be Avoided
- Myth 4: Sex during Pregnancy Should Be Avoided
- Myth 5: Men Are Always Confident about and Ready for Sex
- Myth 6: Women Are Not Very Interested in Sex
- Myth 7: A Careful Person Will Never Get Caught in an Extramarital Affair

CULTURAL PERSPECTIVE: *A Cross-Cultural View of Sexual Behavior*

Negative Consequences of Sexual Activity

- Unplanned Pregnancy
- Sexually Transmitted Diseases
- Confusing Sex with Love
- Staying in a Relationship Longer Than Desirable

COPING FEATURE: *Attachment Styles and Sexual Relationships*

- Emotional Vulnerability
- Manipulation and Power Games

Sexual Response

- The Masters and Johnson Sexual Response Model
- The Kaplan Sexual Response Model

Gender Differences in Sexual Response

- Sexual Desire
- Sexual Arousal
- Proceeding through Sexual Response Stages at Different Speeds
- Resolution Stage
- Orgasm

Factors Contributing to a Fulfilling Sexual Relationship

- Intimacy
- Commitment
- Psychological Comfort
- Good Communication
- Knowledge of the Sexual Response Cycle
- Emphasis on Enjoyment of Each Other Rather Than Performance
- Good Mental and Physical Health

FAMILY STRENGTHS PERSPECTIVE: *Communication and Sexual Relationships*

Sexuality and Aging

- The Female Climacteric
- Hormone Replacement Therapy for Women
- The Male Climacteric

PERSONAL PERSPECTIVE: *An Affair? Consider the Consequences*

- Hormone Replacement Therapy for Men
- Getting through the Change-of-Life Period More Successfully

Sexual Disorders

- Sexual Addiction
- Hypoactive Sexual Desire
- Vaginismus
- Female Orgasmic Disorder
- Male Orgasmic Disorder
- Dyspareunia
- Erectile Disorder
- Premature Ejaculation

Alcohol and Drugs

Sexually Transmitted Diseases

- Chlamydia
- Gonorrhea

AT ISSUE TODAY: *Unsafe Sex Practices: Why So Prevalent?*

- Syphilis
- Human Papillomavirus
- Herpes
- Hepatitis
- Human Immunodeficiency Virus
- Vaginitis
- Pediculosis

A QUESTION OF POLICY: *Internet Pornography*

Summary

Key Terms

Questions for Thought

For Further Reading

LEARNING OBJECTIVES

AFTER READING THE CHAPTER, YOU SHOULD BE ABLE TO DO THE FOLLOWING:

- Explain the holistic nature of sexuality and indicate how sexuality is interrelated with the total person and the total relationship.

- Discuss the myths regarding sexual behavior and relationships.

- Describe potential negative consequences or risks of sexual activity.

- Describe the two sexual response models developed by Masters and Johnson and Kaplan and explain gender differences in sexual response.

- Identify and discuss factors contributing to a fulfilling sexual relationship.

- Discuss sexuality and aging, including the female climacteric and the male climacteric.

- Identify and discuss major sexual disorders.

- Explain the effects on sexual response of alcohol; certain prescribed medications such as antidepressants and high blood pressure medication; and some illegal drugs such as cocaine and marijuana.

- Discuss the major STDs, including symptoms, means of transmission, and effects.

In an interview with Hugh Hefner, the founder of *Playboy*, as he discussed his childhood, he indicated his family rarely showed affection. "Never hugged. Oh, no. There was absolutely no hugging or kissing in my family. There was a point in time when my mother, late in life, apologized to me for not being able to show affection. I said to her, 'Mom, you couldn't have done any better. And because of the things you weren't able to do, it set me on a course that changed my life and the world'" (Bell 2007, 60).

Hefner was denied an essential component of intimacy in his childhood, which is affection. He reacted by going to the other end of the spectrum for the rest of his life (Bell 2007). Interestingly, Hefner typically is seen with not one woman, but surrounded by several beautiful women.

Hefner's story is a powerful example of the holistic nature of sexuality and corroboration that it begins early in life.

Sexuality

The psychotherapist Erich Fromm stated that sexual desire reflects the need for love and union. The need for intimacy is interwoven throughout sexual relationships and is more powerful than the purely physical aspects of sex. It is true that sexual relationships may exist without intimacy; but rarely will a sexual relationship be completely fulfilling without intimacy. The reason that intimacy is so closely linked to a satisfying sexual relationship may be found in the definition of sexuality. Some consider sex only physical and separate from other parts of one's life. In fact, one of the major sources of dissatisfaction in sexual relationships is the attempt to put sex in a "box" and to keep sexuality separate from the rest of one's life. Pornography is an extreme example of this view and portrays a pattern of exploitation of people as sex objects. When sex is viewed and practiced in this manner, intimacy is lost and relationships are shallow and empty. When people are not seen as whole persons, it is easier to exploit them and to ignore emotions.

Sexuality begins at conception, when maleness or femaleness is determined by the chromosomal content of the fertilizing sperm cell. It is paramount to define sexuality in a holistic manner, however. Sexuality involves everything about us that makes us male or female. It obviously includes the physical, but is much more than physical. Our sexuality includes our emotions, social relationships, values, ethics, and spiritual faith. Sexuality also includes our intellect and our decision-making and problem-solving skills. Our good judgment or poor judgment is certainly reflected in our sexual behavior (Stinnett, Hilliard, and Stinnett 2000).

Our sexuality is connected to every other part of our lives. For this reason, an understanding of sexuality requires that it be viewed in a holistic manner—within the context of the total person and the total relationship (Stinnett and Stinnett 2010).

Sexual Myths

Myth 1: Sexual Satisfaction Increases with Multiple Partners

The belief that those who have multiple sex partners experience more sexual satisfaction than do those who are monogamous is prevalent and frequently communicated in movies and television. Although popular opinion may insist that swinging singles with multiple partners are the most satisfied with their sex experience, the research indicates that married couples and those with committed relationships are the most satisfied physically and emotionally with their sexual relationships (J.R. Garcia et al. 2012; Michael et al. 1994; Trudel 2002).

A comprehensive national research study utilizing a large random sample of 3,432 people ages 18 to 59 found that most people, married and single, were faithful to their sexual partners and that physical and emotional satisfaction started to decline when people had more than one sex partner at a time (Michael et al. 1994). Research consistently indicates that satisfaction in a sexual relationship is closely related to a total relationship characterized by commitment, emotional closeness, and good communication (J.R. Garcia et al. 2012; Masters, Johnson, and Kolodny 1995; Ridley et al. 2006; Stinnett and Stinnett 2010). These relationship qualities are less likely to be experienced as the number of sex partners a person has at one time increases.

Myth 2: Sexual Satisfaction Is Determined by Frequency of Sexual Intercourse

The most recent evidence indicates that frequency of sexual interaction should not be construed as an absolute measure of sexual satisfaction. Many couples who have a lower frequency of sexual intercourse report a high degree of satisfaction with their sexual relationships, whereas some couples with a high frequency of sexual interaction report a low degree of satisfaction with their sexual relationships.

Also, as people age, the frequency of sexual interaction decreases but they still tend to be satisfied with their sexual relationships (G. Kelly 2013). These research findings indicate that frequency of sexual interaction does not necessarily determine sexual satisfaction. Instead, they support the holistic nature of sexuality by suggesting that sexual satisfaction is interrelated with the emotional, social, intellectual, and spiritual as well as the physical aspects of the total relationship.

Myth 3: Sex during Menstruation Should Be Avoided

Some women find it somewhat painful to engage in sexual intercourse during menstruation because of reduced vaginal lubrication during this time. The problem often can be eliminated, however, using a sterile water-soluble lubricant.

Menstrual blood is harmless unless the woman has a disease that is transmitted through blood, such as HIV and some kinds of hepatitis. A woman's sexual desire does not usually decrease during the menstrual period. If a couple desire to have sexual intercourse during menstruation, there is ordinarily no reason why they should not do so. In fact, there may be advantages for some couples: (1) intercourse that culminates in orgasm can relieve the discomfort of menstrual cramps for some women, (2) the menstrual period is a time of peak sexual desire for some women, and (3) the possibility of pregnancy is reduced during this time (it is not, however, entirely eliminated).

Myth 4: Sex during Pregnancy Should Be Avoided

Usually, there is little change in most women's sexual interest during the first trimester of pregnancy. Many, however, experience a decrease in sexual desire during the last trimester. For some women, erotic

Sexuality Everything about us that makes us male or female, including emotions, values, ethics, social relationships, and spiritual faith.

feelings are heightened during pregnancy, possibly the result of hormonal changes.

In some cases, limitations on sexual intercourse are necessary during the last month of pregnancy. Physicians believe that strong contractions of the uterus during the orgasmic response may trigger labor contractions if the time of delivery is close. Physicians will recommend abstinence when the pregnancy is at risk because of certain complications such as placenta previa or if there are indications that the amniotic membrane is not intact. The leaking of watery liquid from the vagina is a signal that the amniotic membrane has ruptured. Intercourse at this time increases the danger of infection. A physician should be consulted if pain or bleeding occurs during intercourse or if a couple has questions about the safety or advisability of sexual relations during pregnancy.

Sexuality is connected to every other part of life and, for this reason, is best understood in a holistic manner—within the context of the total person and the total relationship.

Myth 5: Men Are Always Confident about and Ready for Sex

Many men, recognizing that great variability exists among women, are not always confident about how they should approach a specific woman. A man who has a great deal invested psychologically in a woman to whom he is attracted may feel uneasy in how he approaches her because he fears rejection. Generally, men start out slowly, and the rate of progression is dependent on their interpretation of cues provided by the women involved. Many men who appear confident are, in reality, uncomfortable unless they get a great deal of encouragement from a partner.

As a general rule, men are more likely to push for sexual encounters earlier in the relationship than women. Men exhibit considerable variability just as women do. Although some may desire intercourse with every woman they date, others may wish to reserve sexual intercourse for someone they love or for marriage.

Most men do not regard every woman as a potential sex partner. They see little point in having an encounter with someone they do not particularly care about. Mature men consider the consequences of extramarital sexual encounters, and many reject such encounters, believing they are dishonest or immoral.

Myth 6: Women Are Not Very Interested in Sex

Affection plays a greater role among women than men in their readiness for sexual encounters. Men, to a greater extent than women, consider sex desirable in its own right, whereas many women prefer to limit their encounters to a person for whom they feel genuine affection. There are, of course, exceptions. Women are more cautious about sex because they run the risk of pregnancy.

Myth 7: A Careful Person Will Never Get Caught in an Extramarital Affair

People who believe that those who get caught are indiscreet, careless, irresponsible, or unknowledgeable can find themselves in situations they could not have imagined. It is very difficult to be discreet enough to hide an affair from everyone at work. One slip-up is all it takes to get caught in a lie. Physicians regularly treat individuals who are "caught" by an STD. Counselors

A Cross-Cultural View of Sexual Behavior

Research indicates there are many cultural differences in sexual attitudes and behaviors. For example, in the United States, African American males and females are more likely to become sexually active at an earlier age and to have more partners in their lifetimes than other racial and ethnic groups (Fryar et al. 2007). Asian Americans, in contrast, are more likely to become sexually active at a later age than other ethnic groups (Carroll 2015).

The Global Study of Sexual Attitudes and Behaviors investigated sexual behaviors and attitudes of more than 27,000 men and women in 29 countries throughout the world (Laumann et al. 2006). This massive study found that although there are many cultural variations, there are certain predictors of sexual well-being, such as total relationship satisfaction, good mental health, and good physical health that are consistent throughout the various cultures.

A cross-cultural study exploring sexual behavior in 41 countries found that the average age for first intercourse is 17.3 years. The youngest average age (15.6 years) for first intercourse is in Iceland, whereas the oldest average age (19.8 years) is in India (Durex.com 2007).

Another global study examined condom use by 15-year-old adolescents from 24 European and North American countries. The percentages indicating that they had engaged in sexual intercourse ranged from 38% in England to a low of 14% in Croatia. The majority maintained they used condoms during their last sexual intercourse. Condom use in Sweden was the lowest (53%), whereas the highest condom use (90%) was in Greece (Godeau et al. 2008).

---

and attorneys regularly have clients who are individuals who were just a little careless.

Negative Consequences of Sexual Activity

These are risks of sexual activity that are important to consider. The first two discussed here have been highly publicized, whereas other risks have been discussed much less frequently.

Unplanned Pregnancy

A major risk of sexual activity is unplanned pregnancy. About half of all pregnancies and the majority of teen births are unintended and have major emotional, social, family, and financial impacts (Centers for Disease Control and Prevention 2016; Hamilton, Martin, and Ventura 2012). Unplanned or unintended pregnancies may occur among mature married couples or among unmarried teens. Regardless of the circumstances, the consequences are often severe. Mature couples, for example, may be faced with having a baby much later in life than desired—just as older children are near launching.

The financial impact can be substantial regardless of the age of the parents, and many mothers do not receive adequate prenatal care. Negative emotions such as depression and anxiety can be experienced regardless of age or circumstances (Cleland et al. 2006). Unmarried women may feel they are faced with three alternatives: raising the baby in a single-parent home, giving the baby up for adoption, or abortion.

Minority group and socioeconomically disadvantaged youth of any group or ethnicity experience the highest rates of teen pregnancy and childbirth. Together, black and Hispanic youth comprise about 55% of U.S. births to teens (Martin et al. 2015).

Teenagers who become pregnant typically are in a situation of becoming a parent or being married before they are developmentally ready to do so. They are less likely to complete their education, less able to compete successfully in the job market, and more likely to live in poverty (Cleland et al. 2006).

Sexually Transmitted Diseases

STDs have increased dramatically. About 20 million new cases of STDs occur each year in the United States. The medical cost for treating individuals with STDs is about $16 billion annually. The health consequences of STDs are monumental (Centers for Disease Control and Prevention 2016).

Approximately 25% of all infertility is caused by STDs; several thousand individuals become infertile each year as a result (Centers for Disease Control and Prevention 2016; G. Kelly 2013). Some STDs cannot be cured; HIV is eventually fatal and others are fatal if left untreated (Centers for Disease Control and Prevention 2016).

The majority of teenagers do not consider themselves at risk for contracting STDs, yet about 50% of sexually experienced adolescents do not use a condom every time they have sex. For example, over 40% report not using a condom during their last sexual intercourse (Centers for Disease Control and Prevention, 2016). This is particularly significant in that, other than abstinence, condoms are the most effective method for preventing the spread of STDs (Mayo Clinic Staff 2015). They often lack basic knowledge about STDs and many never discuss them with their sexual partners (G. Kelly 2013). In a large, national study of young adult females it was found that sexual networks play an important role in the risk of contracting an STD. The results indicated the most predictive factors for contracting an STD were beginning sexual activity at early ages, having multiple sex partners, lack of or inconsistent use of condoms, and engagement in other high-risk practices such as anal sex or shared needles (intravenous drug use) (Pflieger et al. 2013).

Confusing Sex with Love

A major risk of sex is that many people, particularly adolescents, confuse it with love. During the early stages of a sexual relationship and the early stages of romantic relationships (in general), the brain is stimulated by phenylethylamine, which gives a feeling of euphoria and of being energized. As a result, many individuals conclude they are in love.

Also, the "cuddle chemical," oxytocin, is produced in the brain during cuddling and sexual intercourse. This production creates feelings of sexual satisfaction and attachment, convincing many that they are in a love relationship. Unfortunately, the individuals may be extremely incompatible, know little or nothing about each other, and be in a relationship that lacks caring, commitment, or emotional support (Aron et al. 2005; MacGill 2015; Stinnett and Stinnett 2010).

Many other cultures around the world, particularly in Eastern countries, experience far less confusion between sex and love than we do here in the United States. Love is not considered an excuse for sex in these cultures. Infatuation and sexual passion are not considered legitimate foundations from which to build a long-term intimate relationship such as marriage (G. Kelly 2013).

Staying in a Relationship Longer Than Desirable

Because some people do confuse sex with love, as previously discussed, they may continue in a relationship that is incompatible, dysfunctional, or even abusive. Also, some believe that if they are having sex with someone, it must be love, and this belief makes it difficult for them to see the negative aspects of the relationship.

Even when they do acknowledge the problem in the relationship, they may express a philosophy that "many a tear has to fall, but it is all in the game of love," as communicated in a popular song of the past. This can interfere with the process of mate selection and can result in a person continuing in a bad relationship.

A major risk of sex is that many people confuse it with love.

Attachment Styles and Sexual Relationships

Two coping skills that can benefit your relationships are (1) deciding what you really want in a relationship and (2) becoming aware of what influences are motivating the way you relate to others. The usefulness of these two coping skills can be clearly understood by considering what attachment style you have developed.

The nature of sexual relationships that people form is influenced by the type of attachment style they have adopted: secure, anxious, or avoidant. People tend to use the attachment style they developed with their parents during infancy and childhood.

People who have an anxious style of attachment are more concerned about abandonment. They often are needy in relationships and at the same time are cautious about intimacy and want to keep their distance. Those high in attachment anxiety tend to have passionate but needy sexual relationships that are driven by the great desire to feel accepted by their partners. They often feel a desperation not to displease their partners, which causes them to engage in more high-risk sexual behavior and to do things they really do not want to do to please their partners. Their need for reassurance may make them more inclined to become involved in extramarital affairs (Feeney and Noller 2004; R. S. Miller 2015).

Individuals with an avoidant attachment style tend to avoid intimacy. They lack trust and are uncomfortable with closeness because they expect others to hurt or reject them. Those who use an avoidant style have less frequent sex with their romantic partners and more frequent sex with casual, short-term partners than people with secure attachment styles do. People who have avoidant partners report they wish their sexual relationships were less distant and detached (Brassard, Shaver, and Lussier 2007; Butzer and Campbell 2008).

Individuals who have high levels of either avoidant or anxious styles are less likely than those with a secure attachment style to be open and honest in their communication with their partners. It is not surprising they are less satisfied with their sexual relationships (D. Davis et al. 2006; R. S. Miller 2015).

People with a secure attachment style find it easy to get close to others. They are not often concerned about being abandoned or rejected. They tend to have high self-esteem. They are comfortable with closeness, trust, and interdependency in part because they expect others to be supportive and accepting of them. They tend to appreciate and care for significant others.

Those with the secure attachment style tend to have a higher satisfaction with their sexual relationships in comparison with those with the other attachment styles. They also have the greatest sexual self-confidence and the most positive communication patterns. Also, people with a secure attachment style more strongly commit themselves to faithful, monogamous intimacy (Mikulincer and Shaver 2007a; R. S. Miller 2015).

It is not productive to view one attachment style as good and another as bad, nor should attachment style be considered unchangeable. People can and do change their styles. Awareness of attachment styles helps us better understand what kind of relationships we desire and what type of relationships make us most comfortable. Awareness of attachment styles also helps us understand that sometimes a couple may experience low satisfaction in their relationship because they may have different attachment styles.

Emotional Vulnerability

Entering a sexual relationship creates a situation of emotional vulnerability. There is a risk of being hurt, disappointed, rejected, or manipulated; self-esteem can be damaged. The possibility of emotional hurt is greater if the relationship lacks commitment, caring, and trust. A relationship characterized by mutual respect, responsibility, and commitment enhances the probability of promoting the emotional well-being and fulfillment of the couple.

Manipulation and Power Games

Sex is a common arena for people to attempt to fulfill their power needs. Therefore, power struggles frequently occur in sexual relationships (G. Kelly 2013). Because of the degree of emotional vulnerability, power struggles within sexual relationships can become destructive. The power struggles often involve psychological games. Some examples include the following:

- Being unavailable for sexual interaction because of being too tired or too busy.

- Sabotaging or spoiling a sexual encounter by deliberately creating a conflict about another issue.

- Showing little interest in sex as a way to punish the other person.

- Damaging self-esteem by expressing a lack of satisfaction with sexual encounters and communicating subtle criticisms of the other person's sexual performance.

Engaging in destructive power struggles and psychological games is counterproductive to intimacy. Manipulation destroys trust and satisfaction within sexual relationships.

Sexual Response

There are similarities in the sexual responses of men and women. There are also important differences. Our sexual responses are influenced by many factors, such as quality of the total relationship, mental and physical health, nutrition, fatigue, stress, depression, alcohol, drugs, and medications. The great range of influences on sexual response reflects the holistic nature of sexuality.

The Masters and Johnson Sexual Response Model

The extensive research and observations of Masters and Johnson (Masters, Johnson, and Kolodny 1995) led to the conclusion that the physiological responses to sexual stimulation (called the **Masters and Johnson sexual response model**) are remarkably similar in all people. Although individuals show variations in how

they respond, the sexual response cycle usually has four phases:

1. **Excitement phase.** The first phase can begin with a variety of sexual stimuli. Sexual arousal is multifaceted: Music, daydreams, or a kiss may initiate sexual arousal. This phase is characterized by increased blood pressure and heart rate. Vaginal lubrication appears in the female, and the male achieves an erection. Sexual tensions increase markedly.

2. **Plateau phase.** During the plateau phase, the process begun in the excitement phase (increased heart rate, congestion of the genital blood vessels) intensifies. The plateau phase varies considerably in duration; some couples prolong it by decreasing stimulation momentarily. As a person in the plateau phase reaches the transition to the orgasmic phase, responses are less easily controlled. Many men cannot prevent ejaculation at this point.

3. **Orgasmic phase.** Sexual excitement eventually reaches a peak, and sexual tension built up during the first two phases is released in an orgasm. The orgasmic response involves contractions of the pelvic muscles and tightening of the muscles in the face, feet, and hands for both men and women. Males ejaculate during orgasm; females experience involuntary vaginal contractions. Sometimes an orgasm is intense; sometimes it is mild. It can last a few seconds or several minutes. Fictional descriptions of orgasm generally depict it as a wild, frenzied onslaught of emotional feeling. But as with every other sexual response, each individual has a unique and personal reaction at different times. Many men can reach orgasm within a few minutes of coitus. This is too quick for most women to achieve an orgasm, unless there has been sufficient foreplay. The majority of women, however, can achieve an orgasm within 15 minutes of foreplay and intercourse. For many men this will require careful monitoring of their own behavior.

   The research of Masters and Johnson indicates that with a sufficient amount and type of stimulation, women can experience multiple orgasms; however, fewer than 15% of all women do. This may be because their partners stop sexual stimulation too soon. Second or third orgasms generally are more intense and pleasurable than the first. Sexual therapists often recommend that couples experiment to ascertain whether greater satisfaction is attained if she experiences multiple orgasms.

A few males are capable of renewed intercourse and a second orgasm after only a short time following the initial one. The period of time required to achieve a second orgasm increases as a man grows older. Although the ability to have repeated intercourse decreases as a man ages, this is compensated by the ability to control his orgasms. Increased control makes the sexual experience more pleasurable to both men and women.

4. **Resolution phase.** After the release of sexual tension by orgasm and after the cessation of sexual stimulation, the body returns to its pre-arousal state. This is the resolution phase. Following orgasm, men characteristically experience a **refractory period**, during which re-arousal is impossible. For example, men in their late thirties, on the average, cannot re-stimulate to orgasm for 30 minutes or longer (G. Kelly 2013). As a result, some men prefer an abrupt end to erotic play following orgasm. However, the resolution phase is generally longer for women. Couples must be aware of these physiological differences in males and females and focus on providing pleasure for the other person. The secret is in learning exactly what the other person really likes. One good way for a couple to find out is to share this information with each other verbally.

The Kaplan Sexual Response Model

Another model, referred to as the **Kaplan sexual response model**, is that proposed by Helen Kaplan. Her model involves three stages:

1. **Sexual desire.** This represents the psychological component that precedes the physiological response to arousal. It involves an interplay among mind, emotions, and body (Conaglen and Evans 2006) and reflects the holistic nature of sexuality. Kaplan's model suggests that motivation for sexual activity is influenced not only by desire for physical pleasure but also by such psychological forces as the desire to feel valued by others and by oneself. For many, a feeling of

Sexual desire is psychological and precedes the physical response; it involves an interplay among mind, emotions, and body.

emotional intimacy is a great influence on sexual desire (Basson et al. 2003).

2. **Vasocongestion.** The **vasocongestion** stage involves an increase of blood flow in the pelvic area and building of muscle tension throughout the body. There are also increases in blood pressure, breathing rate, and heart rate.

3. **Reversal of vasocongestion.** Orgasm brings release of vasocongestion and of the muscle tension throughout the body. Gradually, blood pressure, breathing, and heart rate return to normal.

Stages two and three are similar to the stages of Masters and Johnson's model. What distinguishes

---

Masters and Johnson sexual response model Model of human sexual response cycle including the phases of excitement, plateau, orgasm, and resolution.

refractory period A period of time following orgasm when men cannot be re-aroused; stimulation of the penis is unpleasant and orgasm is not physiologically possible.

Kaplan sexual response model Model of human sexual response cycle including the phases of sexual desire, vasocongestion, and reversal of vasocongestion.

vasocongestion The buildup of blood in the pelvic area and penis.

Kaplan's model and makes it useful is the component of desire. By including the component of desire, the psychological and emotional influences on sexual response are recognized.

Gender Differences in Sexual Response

Regardless of whether the Masters and Johnson model or the Kaplan model of sexual response is used, women and men have similar response patterns in that both go through the same stages of sexual response. Differences exist in the way in which they proceed through the stages.

Sexual Desire

One of the greatest differences in the sexual response of men and women is the stage of sexual desire. Research indicates that for men, sexual desire is influenced largely by biological factors such as testosterone level (B. M. King 2013). For most women, sexual desire is determined more by relationship, emotional, psychological, and intimacy needs and less by biological factors (Haning et al. 2007). For example, feeling valued by one's partner, showing value to one's partner, and expressing nurturance to one's partner are important motivations for women's sexual behavior (Basson et al. 2003).

Sexual Arousal

Men tend to become sexually excited quicker than do women and are aware of their sexual arousal sooner than women. For both men and women, the first sign of sexual arousal is a vasocongestion response. For women there is an increase of blood flow in the vaginal walls. The pressure of the increased blood flow causes vaginal lubrication (the vaginal walls secreting drops of fluid). A woman may not be immediately aware that her vagina is lubricating; it may take a few minutes before becoming noticeable. For men, the increased blood flow to the penis results in the penis becoming firm—something he is aware of immediately. Frequently, men mistakenly believe the presence of vaginal lubrication is a sign that a woman is ready to begin intercourse. Vaginal lubrication is simply the first physiological response and does not mean that she is emotionally or even physically ready to begin sexual intercourse (B. M. King 2013).

For men, vasocongestion (blood flow to the penis) leads to erection and indicates arousal. This is often not true for women. Unlike men, the psychological and emotional arousal of women is poorly correlated with their physiological arousal (vasocongestion or vaginal lubrication). Most women are concerned more with psychological and emotional arousal than with physical arousal (Tiefer 2001). For many women the most important factor is the relationship context, commitment, bonding, emotional closeness, and the desire to share physical sexual pleasure for the sake of sharing, more than for satisfying one's individual sexual desire (Basson 2001).

Proceeding through Sexual Response Stages at Different Speeds

Because men become excited more quickly, they may proceed through sexual response stages more quickly than do women. This can result in the man experiencing orgasm while the woman is not yet in the excitement stage. Moving through the sexual response stages at different speeds is one of the most common sexual problems experienced by couples. As sexual therapists such as Masters and Johnson have indicated, the problem is easily solved by increased foreplay and by the man slowing his sexual responses through such strategies as periodic withdrawal of the penis during intercourse. Another effective method is the "squeeze" technique, where the penis is squeezed at the base. This results in the penis nerves being temporarily numbed, which substantially delays the man's orgasm.

Resolution Stage

Another major difference in the sexual response of men and women during the resolution stage is that men experience a refractory period. During the refractory period it is not physiologically possible for the man to achieve another orgasm. Any stimulation of the penis during the refractory period is unpleasant. The length of the refractory period varies from person to person. It tends to be longer as men get older and also gets longer after each successive orgasm (Carroll 2015). Women do not experience such a refractory period after orgasm.

Orgasm

Orgasm is similar for both genders: Women experience rhythmic muscular contractions in the vagina, uterus, and anal sphincter and men experience them in the vasa deferentia, prostate gland, and seminal vesicles.

For men, orgasm occurs in two stages. The first stage is the emission stage, in which the muscular contractions in the vasa deferentia, prostate gland, and seminal vesicles move the sperm and the seminal and prostate fluids into the ejaculatory ducts, creating semen. The sphincter muscles contract and there is a buildup of semen, causing a feeling of urgency that orgasm is about to happen. The second stage of orgasm for men is ejaculation. Muscles at the base of the penis push the semen through the penis.

Women's orgasms, in contrast, often occur in a single stage and without the sense of urgency or inevitability that men experience. Another difference between men and women is that some women are capable of multiple orgasms. Some women have true multiple orgasms—two or more orgasms in a rapid succession—without dropping below the plateau level of sexual arousal. Too much emphasis may be placed on the importance of multiple orgasms, however, since they are not necessary for a fulfilling sexual relationship. Only about 15% of women experience multiple orgasms regularly, and a higher percentage experience them occasionally (B. M. King, 2013).

Men do not experience true multiple orgasms (Masters, Johnson, and Kolodny 1995). Orgasm with ejaculation is always followed by a refractory period, and only when a man's level of sexual arousal is built back to the plateau level can he experience another orgasm. However, men may sometimes experience multiple dry orgasms before having a full wet orgasm (with ejaculation). In such cases, the wet orgasm or ejaculation is followed by a refractory period (B. M. King 2013).

Factors Contributing to a Fulfilling Sexual Relationship

The success of a sexual relationship not only is a matter of physiological factors, but also is integrated with the total interpersonal relationship. Research indicates that a positive total interpersonal relationship characterized by intimacy, commitment, psychological comfort, and good communication contributes to a satisfying sexual relationship.

Intimacy

As the psychotherapist Erich Fromm indicated, sexual desire reflects the need for love and union. This need for intimacy, closeness, and connection is interwoven throughout the sexual relationship. Intimacy is characterized by mutual care, respect, understanding, and responsiveness to each other's needs. It is the foundation for satisfying sexual relationships (Stinnett, Hilliard, and Stinnett 2000; Stinnett and Stinnett 2010).

Commitment

William Masters and Virginia Johnson, on the basis of their research and clinical experience, concluded that commitment is the single most important

A positive total relationship contributes to a fulfilling sexual relationship.

factor contributing to satisfaction in a sexual relationship (Masters, Johnson, and Kolodny 1995). Other research indicates that women who have difficulty experiencing orgasm tend to feel a lack of commitment from others close to them (Stinnett, Hilliard, and Stinnett 2000).

Both men and women tend to be more sexually responsive when they know their partner has a high degree of commitment toward them. Commitment encourages trust and psychological comfort, which in turn generates security that allows couples to give themselves more freely in a sexual relationship. The freedom and safety to give oneself completely and spontaneously to a partner enhances the intimacy of the sexual relationship (Masters, Johnson, and Kolodny 1995; Stinnett, Hilliard, and Stinnett 2000).

Psychological Comfort

Surprisingly, many couples do not feel comfortable with each other. For example, Jeremy and Pat have a strained relationship that is affecting their sex life. Pat is competitive and often uses mind games designed to make Jeremy lose his self-confidence. Jeremy has come to feel increasingly uncomfortable around Pat. He has lost interest in being with her and avoids having sex with her.

Psychological comfort is an important, but largely ignored quality of successful interpersonal relationships. Being uncomfortable with a partner can make it difficult to respond sexually. Two major reasons for lack of psychological comfort in a relationship are distrust and a feeling that commitment is lacking. A couple can increase their psychological comfort together by being emotionally supportive of each other through mutual respect and care. Another way to create psychological comfort is by minimizing threatening behavior such as criticism and ridicule (Stinnett and Stinnett 2010).

Good Communication

Couples with a high level of sexual satisfaction in their relationship tend to have good communication patterns. Simply being able to clearly communicate the type of sexual behavior that pleases and displeases them increases the probability that a couple will experience a satisfying relationship in a broader sense. When the partners talk with each other often and communicate primarily positive messages such as appreciation, their total relationship is strengthened. When they feel they can talk with each other about anything, their psychological comfort is enhanced and they feel greater intimacy.

Knowledge of the Sexual Response Cycle

Possessing basic knowledge of the physiological aspects of the sexual response cycle, as discussed previously, can be helpful in contributing to a good sexual relationship. Many couples experience difficulties and frustration in their sexual encounters simply because they are unaware of the differences in the sexual response cycle of women and men. Such difficulties can usually be easily resolved (Carroll 2015; Masters, Johnson, and Kolodny 1995).

Emphasis on the Enjoyment of Each Other Rather Than Performance

A powerful influence in experiencing a satisfying sexual relationship is for partners to concentrate on simply enjoying sexual interaction with each other. Sexual therapists see many individuals and couples who experience difficulties in sexual responses because they have placed so much emphasis on performance, which creates stress (Masters, Johnson, and Kolodny 1995).

Couples who have a high degree of satisfaction in their sexual relationship do not place much emphasis on performance. They do not think or worry about how they are measuring up or whether they have orgasms, how intense the orgasms are, or how many. Those who do so create tension and anxiety, which tend to remove sexual interaction from its pleasurable context (Stinnett, Hilliard, and Stinnett 2000).

Good Mental and Physical Health

Because sexuality is a holistic concept, our sexual responses are strongly influenced by our mental and physical health (Insel and Roth 2013). Some health problems, for example, involve chronic pain. Chronic pain is stressful both physically and psychologically and may have a negative impact on sexual desire and pleasure (Randolph and Reddy 2006). Diabetes often causes men to have erection difficulties and causes women to experience vaginal dryness and discomfort (G. Kelly 2013). Often, the sex-related difficulties of certain illnesses such as diabetes can be alleviated by medical interventions.

Communication and Sexual Relationships

Good communication is a major characteristic of strong families. It also is a major characteristic of good sexual relationships. Many couples feel awkward talking about sex and so they simply do not talk about it. As a result, each partner may be unaware of the "likes and dislikes" of the other.

The lack of communication can result in misinterpretations of each other's intentions and desires. For example, men frequently misinterpret friendliness from a woman as a sign of sexual interest. Inaccurate judgments of a woman's sexual interest are more common (when alcohol is involved) among men who consider themselves "macho" and who perceive sex as an exploitative contest and who like to dominate women (Jaques-Tiura et al. 2007).

If a couple can have intimate communication in which they can honestly share their sexual preferences with each other, they are more likely to experience a higher degree of satisfaction in their sexual relationship. This intimate communication can also contribute to greater intimacy and satisfaction in the total relationship (M. H. Burleson, Trevathan, and Todd 2007; Byers 2005; R. S. Miller 2015). The higher degree of satisfaction in the total relationship in turn contributes to a better sexual relationship.

The most important way that communication can contribute to a fulfilling sexual relationship is through the content of the messages that are communicated in the total relationship. Communicating messages of appreciation, commitment, respect, acceptance, and supportiveness is associated with a higher degree of satisfaction in the sexual relationship and in the total relationship (Rehman and Holtzworth-Munroe 2007; Stinnett, Hilliard, and Stinnett 2000).

Interestingly, some research indicates that couples who communicate with each other positively (such as expressing appreciation and affection) rated each other to be more physically attractive than those couples who did not communicate such positive messages. The implications of such research are that good positive communication can also enhance physical attractiveness (Albada, Knapp, and Theune 2002).

Of course, the best strategy is to stay in good physical health. Maintaining good physical health through good nutrition, exercise, avoidance of unhealthy habits, and regular dental and medical examinations promotes one's sense of wellness and energy, which in turn enhances sexual responsiveness.

Emotional health involves how we think, how we cope and adapt to change, how we view the future, the dominant emotions we experience, and how we see ourselves. Chronic mental health problems, low self-esteem, lack of trust, and persistent depression leave less energy for relationships and often lead to loss of interest in sex and loss of ability to be sexually responsive (Randolph and Reddy 2006). In contrast, optimism, hope, high self-esteem, ability to trust and share feelings, self-acceptance, and self-control contribute to positive relationships in general and to more satisfying sexual relationships.

Sexuality and Aging

Decreasing hormone production and other physical changes that occur as we age cause changes in sexual functioning. Research consistently indicates that frequency of sexual intercourse steadily declines with age. But the research also indicates that people who are healthy, happy with their lives, and have the availability of a healthy partner usually continue to be sexually active in their later years.

Older people consistently report sexual satisfaction from a broad spectrum of sexual behavior in addition to intercourse, such as caressing, holding, kissing, and other activities that involve both physical and spiritual intimacy. As people age, they often become free of the concerns that interfere with sexual intimacy among many younger people, such

Interest in a sexual relationship does not decline with age.

as the need to "prove" oneself with sex, risk of pregnancy, and obsessions with performance and orgasms. As they age, many people come to value sexual relationships in a more holistic sense. They increasingly view sex as being far more than genital activity (G. Kelly 2013; Lacy 2002).

The Female Climacteric

As women approach midlife, their ovaries gradually cease to function and they enter a long-term process known as the **climacteric** (referred to as the change-of-life period; it also applies to men). As the ovaries stop producing estrogen and progesterone, the drop in hormone levels causes a number of frustrating symptoms, such as irregular/missed menstrual periods; hot flashes; dizziness; heart palpitations; night sweats; loss of bone density; mood changes; painful joints; dry, itchy skin; and decreased vaginal lubrication. It typically takes several months to several years for ovaries to stop functioning completely. During this time (called perimenopause), pregnancy is still possible. When 12 months pass after the last menstrual period, menopause has occurred; this marks the end of the menstrual cycles. The average age for menopause in the United States is 51 (Mayo Clinic Staff 2015).

Some women experience a temporary decrease in sexual desire and responsiveness during menopause (Yarber and Sayad 2013). However, there are usually no major long-lasting changes. The loss of estrogen causes decreased vaginal lubrication, which may make intercourse difficult or uncomfortable. The use of lubricants during intercourse and increased foreplay help minimize this problem (Carroll 2015). Some women feel their sexual responses are greater after menopause; they are no longer concerned about pregnancy.

Hormone Replacement Therapy for Women

To alleviate the symptoms of menopause, women often receive prescribed hormone replacement therapy (HRT) which includes providing estrogen and progesterone supplements. HRT is effective in reducing the severity of the menopause symptoms. The research also indicates that HRT helps reduce hip fractures and the risk of colon cancer (Insel and Roth 2013).

Unfortunately, there are negative effects of HRT. Research has consistently found that HRT increases women's risk of breast cancer, heart attacks, and blood clots (G. Kelly 2013; S. London 2004). In 1997, researchers in a large study recruited approximately 17,000 healthy women. Some were given HRT and some were given a placebo. The study was terminated 3 years before it was scheduled to end because the incidence of heart attacks, blood clots, strokes, and breast cancer increased the longer the women received HRT (Grady et al. 2002).

Many women stopped using HRT after the results were publicized; a substantial reduction in the incidence of breast cancer occurred afterward (G. Kelly 2013). Some physicians now avoid the use of HRT entirely, whereas other physicians believe that women with severe symptoms can benefit from HRT for a short period of time and other medications can be used to help control the risks. Some women have had success using herbs or phytoestrogens (plant estrogens found in soybeans, chickpeas, and flax seeds, for example) to alleviate their symptoms. Herbal supplements can vary significantly in strength and purity; some may also have side effects.

The Male Climacteric

As men age, it is common for the prostate gland (located beneath the urinary bladder) to enlarge, which can cause erectile dysfunction. The enlargement may happen simply because of the aging of the prostate gland or because of a bacterial infection or a malignant tumor (which, if detected early, has a high cure rate). Various medical treatments are

An Affair? Consider the Consequences

Many people become involved in an affair with little or no thought about the probable consequences. Some unrealistically think an affair will have no negative effect on their marriage. Many actually believe no one else will ever know about the affair.

"I have been attracted to two other women during the 35 years that Myra and I have been married," confessed Carl. "I worked with both but at different periods. There was a strong physical attraction. But in both instances there was more: We could talk easily to each other and we had common interests.

"They were both attracted to me," confessed Carl. "I think an affair could have naturally developed in either or both cases."

Carl shared that the critical strategy that was most important in preventing him from slipping into these affairs was that he was able to look ahead and considered the probable consequences. "I thought about what would most likely happen if I started an affair," said Carl.

"I did not like the scenarios that marched before me. I knew it was unrealistic to think that people at work would not find out. I envisioned the gossip and what they would think of me for being unfaithful to my wife. I would definitely lose the respect of my coworkers and the working conditions would become more negative," said Carl. "Someone would tell Myra."

"Then, most of all, I saw the great hurt it would bring to Myra. Did I want to risk losing the great marriage relationship I enjoyed? Would I want her to leave and take the kids away? The answer was no. Too many problems and heartaches would come with having an affair. It was not worth it. I am thankful I had enough sense to realize that."

---

successfully used to shrink prostate tissues. It is desirable for men older than 35 to have regular prostate examinations (G. Kelly 2013).

Men do not have predictable cyclical changes in hormone levels such as the menstrual cycle of women. Also, men do not lose the ability to reproduce as they age. They usually continue to produce sperm cells into very old age. However, the risk of genetic abnormalities in the sperm increases with age. Because there is usually no loss of reproductive capacity, males do not experience anything completely equivalent to menopause.

The major sexual changes that men experience as they age are a decrease in testosterone levels, a decrease in sexual desire, and a decrease in erection capability (Barqawi and Crawford 2006). By age 75, men's testosterone levels frequently decrease by as much as 90%, compared with levels of men younger than 30. For some older men, low levels of testosterone are related to depression (Seidman 2006).

Interestingly, men do experience a pattern of changes and symptoms as they age, which are referred to as the male climacteric, andropause, the male midlife crisis, or "male menopause." The profile of symptoms includes increased anxiety, increased depression, increased body fat (doubles from ages 25 to 75), loss of bone density (not as much as in women), shrinking and weakening of muscles, enlargement of the prostate gland, decrease in testosterone and androgen levels, decrease in sexual desire, and increased erection difficulties (caused by a decrease in hormones, prostate enlargement, and circulation problems).

Hormone Replacement Therapy for Men

Testosterone replacement therapy (TRT) is also prescribed for men experiencing the previously mentioned symptoms associated with andropause. For men with very low levels of testosterone, TRT

---

climacteric The transitional time when fertility ends for women (with menopause) and declines for men (as testosterone declines). Both men and women may experience depression, anxiety, and loss of bone density.

improves sexual interest, enhances erection ability, and may decrease depression (Seidman and Roose 2006).

However, TRT must be prescribed with caution and generally only for men who have lower-than-normal levels of testosterone. Much remains unknown about the long-range effects. There is evidence that TRT increases the risk of blood clots, strokes, cardiovascular disease, and prostate cancer (G. Kelly 2013; B. M. King 2013).

Getting through the Change-of-Life Period More Successfully

As men and women age and experience the climacteric, they are often dealing with other major changes and psychological stresses as well. Changes that add to menopausal stress for women and andropausal stress for men include aging in a youth-oriented culture, sharing the climacteric changes of their partner, dealing with their children leaving home, and experiencing a career plateau in which opportunities are more limited and goals may not have been reached.

Both men and women can more successfully and happily experience aging and the change-of-life period by taking steps such as the following:

- Focusing on deepening intimacy with one's partner and enjoying the mutual support of each other.

- Accepting oneself and remembering one's strengths.

- Understanding that the climacteric is a natural part of human development and that there are positive aspects of this period of life along with the negative.

- Cultivating healthy nutrition.

- Enjoying adequate rest.

- Getting regular exercise.

Sexual Disorders

Sexual Addiction

Sexual addiction is compulsive, "out-of-control" sexual behavior that a person continues to engage in despite severe consequences that cause distress and serious problems such as marriage distress and loss of jobs. Many therapists report an increasing number of clients with sexual addiction; about 40% of pornography addicts divorce (Internet Pornography by the Numbers 2016). It is estimated that this disorder affects millions of people in the United States. Some research suggests that 5% to 6% of the population may be characterized as having a sexual addiction and that it is five times more common among males than females (Dryden-Edwards 2013; F. D. Garcia and Thibaut 2010; B. Hughes 2010).

Although there is debate about how this behavior pattern should fit into the American Psychiatric Association's *Diagnostic and Statistical Manual*, the symptoms of sexual addiction are similar to that of other forms of addiction, including the effects on neural pathways and pleasure centers of the brain. As with other addictions, sexual addiction has distressing consequences in the lives of those who are involved (Giugliano 2012; B. Hughes 2010). For example, sex addicts are at higher risk of contracting STDs such as HIV because of having multiple sex partners (Mayo Clinic Staff 2014; Samenow 2010).

The classic work of Patrick Carnes (Carnes 2001; Carnes and Schneider 2000) has identified 10 signs of sexual addiction that are widely used by therapists. These signs or symptoms are as follows:

- A pattern of out-of-control sexual behavior;

- Severe consequences resulting from sexual behavior;

- Inability to stop despite adverse consequences;

- Persistent pursuit of self-destructive or high-risk behaviors;

- Ongoing desire or effort to limit sexual behavior;

- Sexual obsession or fantasy as a primary coping strategy;

- Increasing amounts of sexual experience because the current level of activity is not sufficient;

- Severe mood changes around sexual activity;

- Inordinate amounts of time spent in obtaining sex, being sexual, recovering from a sexual experience; and

- Important social, occupational, or recreational activities are sacrificed or reduced because of sexual behavior.

Those who are in sexual addiction progress through a four-step addiction cycle (Garcia and Thibaut 2010), which is reported over and over:

1. The *preoccupation* stage in which the person's mind is consumed with thoughts and fantasies about sex.

2. The *ritualization* stage, which involves the addict's routines that lead up to the sexual behavior—the search for a pornographic website or the purchase of new lingerie, for example.

3. *Compulsive sexual behavior*, which the person seems unable to control and which persists despite severe negative consequences.

4. *Despair*, in which the addict experiences feelings of hopelessness and powerlessness. The feeling of despair may lead the addict to engage in more compulsive sexual behavior to try to get some relief from his/her misery (F.D. Garcia and Thibaut 2010; Giugliano 2012).

Sexual addiction brings much conflict and discord to a marriage and frequently results in divorce. It is difficult for the nonaddicted spouse, not only because of the feelings of betrayal and dishonesty, but also because of the extreme mood swings, the inordinate amount of time the addicted person spends away from home in pursuit of the addiction, financial problems because of the addiction, and the increased risk of contracting an STD from the addicted partner (Mayo Clinic Staff 2014; Stinnett and Stinnett 2010).

There is no single cause to explain sexual addiction. Instead, biological, psychological, and social influences are involved (Dryden-Edwards 2013; Mayo Clinic Staff 2014). For example, many sex addicts have experienced traumatic events in childhood. About 80% have experienced sexual abuse as children. A high percentage have experienced abandonment events in childhood, such as the death of a parent or parental divorce. Many sex addicts have attachment issues because they did not have a secure attachment in infancy (Carnes 2001; Samenow 2010).

It is possible for individuals and their families to overcome the pain and frustration of sexual addiction. The most common treatment and support program for sexual addiction is the 12-step program (discussed in Chapter 15). Some of the specific support groups include Sexual Addicts Anonymous, Sex and Love Addicts Anonymous, and Sexaholics Anonymous.

Individual counseling is important to recovery from addiction. Cognitive behavioral therapy is often used to help a person develop effective strategies for controlling his/her behavior; to develop healthier, functional thought patterns; and to understand how dysfunctional thought patterns of the past have led to negative consequences (Dryden-Edwards 2013).

Couple's therapy and/or family therapy can also be productive in strengthening relationships among family members. Another aim is to restore or develop a healthy, satisfying sexual relationship with a spouse or partner. Some clinicians prescribe antidepressant or antianxiety or mood-stabilizer medications for their sex-addicted patients. Naltrexone is used by some clinicians to reduce sexual arousal and compulsive behavior (Dryden-Edwards 2013; Mayo Clinic Staff 2014).

Hypoactive Sexual Desire

Hypoactive (or inhibited) **sexual desire** is defined by the American Psychiatric Association as a persistent or recurrent absence of sexual desire and sexual fantasies. Many sexual therapists report that hypoactive sexual desire is the most common sexual problem of couples who go into sexual therapy. Those with hypoactive sexual desire experience decreased sexual arousal and less self-initiated sexual activity and they also avoid sexual interaction (B. M. King 2013). Maserejian et al. (2012), in a national study of women diagnosed with hypoactive sexual desire disorder, found that approximately half of all the women had lubrication and arousal problems. Being happy in the relationship with a partner was related to fewer lubrication and arousal problems.

Hypoactive sexual desire may be categorized as primary or secondary. *Primary* inhibition of sexual desire may be caused by a variety of factors: a

sexual addiction Compulsive sexual behavior that continues despite severe negative consequences.

hypoactive sexual desire Persistent or recurrent absence of sexual desire; described as *secondary hypoactive sexual desire* when the person has experienced sexual interest but loses it.

homosexual orientation (but in a heterosexual relationship), the inability to be emotional, an upbringing that regards sex as bad or dirty, or sexual abuse. For example, a woman who was sexually abused as a child may have conflicting feelings about sex; she may have conditioned herself to shut off any response when she begins to feel aroused. A man who lacks self-esteem may inhibit sexual feelings because he believes no one would find him attractive. Such individuals stop the sexual arousal process at its earliest stage and avoid the anxiety associated with sexual interaction.

Secondary hypoactive sexual desire occurs when a person who has had sexual interest loses it. For example, a women who has enthusiasm for her sexual relationship with her husband at the beginning of their marriage but is not orgasmic may find her enthusiasm waning after a few years; she may become frustrated and no longer experience sexual desire. A man who is consumed by career and community activities may have no energy for, or interest in, sex. A person who is hurt by a spouse's extramarital relationship may find that his or her sexual desire is replaced by turmoil and anger.

Treatment of hypoactive sexual desire depends on discovering the cause and treating it. For example, hypoactive sexual desire or sexual arousal disorder for both men and women is often caused by a combination of contributing factors, such as depression and anxiety, decreased estrogen or

Sexual disorders or dysfunctions may have physical or emotional causes. Sometimes therapy may be needed to deal with past sexual trauma or other psychological issues.

testosterone, illness such as diabetes, fatigue, stress, effects of drug use (prescription or illegal), alcohol use, and relationship problems (Bitzer, Giraldi and Pfaus 2013).

Vaginismus

Vaginismus is the painful, involuntary contraction of vaginal muscles that makes intercourse exceedingly difficult and sometimes impossible. Vaginismus is usually caused by psychological factors causing anxiety to be associated with sexual activity. For example, it may be a result of past trauma, such as rape. Treatment consists of the gradual dilation of the vaginal orifice, normally through the insertion of progressively larger dilators. Masters and Johnson reported a 100% success rate using this method, with the correction of vaginismus often achieved within 5 days. Other therapists have also reported a success rate approaching 100% (Jeng et al. 2006). Sometimes, counseling may be needed to deal with past sexual trauma or other psychological issues.

Female Orgasmic Disorder

The most common sexual dysfunction among women who seek sexual therapy is orgasmic disorder, which refers to problems in reaching orgasm. **Orgasmic disorder** is defined as personal distress caused by a persistent and ongoing difficulty, delay in, or absence of experiencing orgasm following sufficient stimulation and arousal (Basson et al. 2003).

Female orgasmic disorder can be either primary (lifelong), in which the woman has never had an orgasm; secondary (acquired), in which the woman has been orgasmic in the past, but is having difficulties at the present; or situational, in that she experiences orgasm only in certain situations or under specific conditions. Women typically experience difficulty reaching orgasm because of insufficient stimulation (especially of the clitoris; about half of women require direct clitoral stimulation to reach orgasm) and not enough time in foreplay. Men can mistakenly think there has been enough stimulation and, because they are close to orgasm, assume she is as well (B. M. King 2013).

Sometimes there are physical causes for an inability to achieve orgasm. For example, women who experience orgasmic disorder are frequently found to have clitoral adhesions; many of these women who have their adhesions removed become orgasmic within a few weeks. Other physical causes include thyroid deficiency, adrenal deficiency, pituitary deficiency, spinal cord disease or injury, diabetes, and severe malnutrition and vitamin deficiencies (G. Kelly 2013).

Not all cases of female orgasmic disorder are caused by a lack of sexual stimulation or physical conditions such as clitoral adhesions. Because sexuality is holistic, it involves the emotions and attitudes. For example, primary orgasmic disorder is often associated with guilt, fear, or negative attitudes about sex. Another important influence on orgasmic disorder is the quality of the total relationship. If a woman feels insecure about the relationship or unloved by her partner, she may be less likely to experience orgasm. Women's sexual satisfaction is greatly determined by their happiness in the total relationship and by their degree of emotional involvement with the partner, which are better predictions of women's sexual satisfaction than are the number of orgasms and frequency of sexual interactions (Haning et al. 2007; Carroll 2015).

Male Orgasmic Disorder

Although men experience orgasmic disorder less frequently than do women, national data indicate that about 10% of men report some level of difficulty in reaching orgasm. Male orgasmic disorder is defined as difficulty experiencing orgasm and ejaculation during vaginal intercourse (SX21 2016). It may be either primary (never having experienced orgasm) or secondary (having previously reached orgasm but currently unable to experience orgasm).

Many men with orgasmic disorder are overly concerned with performance, and the resulting anxiety reduces their arousal and ability to reach orgasm. The research of Masters and Johnson indicates that male orgasmic disorder is also associated with fear of getting a woman pregnant or hostility toward a partner.

There are also physical causes of male orgasmic disorder. Among these physical causes are diabetic neuropathy, Parkinson's disease, multiple sclerosis, alcoholism, injury to the nervous system, and use of anti-depressants (especially SSRI's) (SX21 2016).

The treatment of male orgasmic disorder has often been successfully done by what is called the *bridge maneuver*. This treatment helps the man successfully experience orgasm in four separate steps or situations. First, the man masturbates to orgasm while alone, and second, he masturbates to orgasm in the presence of his partner. The third step involves the woman manually stimulating the man to orgasm. After this is consistently successful, the fourth step involves the woman stimulating the man until he is close to orgasm and then inserts his penis into her vagina. The objective and rationale is that if this can be done successfully a number of times, it will help the man overcome his difficulty with ejaculating inside the woman's vagina (B. M. King 2013).

Dyspareunia

Dyspareunia is a sexual disorder that involves persistent pain during sexual intercourse; it can occur with vaginismus. It is experienced only rarely by men. Dyspareunia has both physical and psychological causes. For women, the physical causes include infection of the clitoris or vulva, irritation of the vagina, tumors of the reproductive organs, and vaginal dryness that may be caused by drugs such as antihistamines. Psychological causes include prior trauma such as rape or abuse, negative attitudes about sex, or fear of pregnancy.

Among men, dyspareunia almost always has a physical cause, such as bladder, prostate, or urethral infection or the foreskin of the penis being too tight. The anticipation of pain can become so stressful that it can result in erectile dysfunction in men and can also result in loss of sexual desire and responsiveness in both men and women (Mayo Clinic Staff 2016).

Erectile Disorder

One of the most common sexual dysfunctions in males is **erectile disorder** (ED)—the consistent

---

vaginismus Painful, involuntary contractions of the vaginal muscles that make intercourse exceedingly difficult or impossible.

orgasmic disorder Personal distress caused by a persistent difficulty in, delay in, or absence of experiencing orgasm; causes may be physical or psychological.

dyspareunia Persistent pain during intercourse; may be experienced by both men and women; causes are largely physical, including infection, tight foreskin, or tumors.

erectile disorder A common sexual disorder involving the inability to attain or maintain an erection; causes may be psychological (depression or concern with performance) or physical (disease, medications, alcohol, for example).

inability to attain or maintain an erection. According to current evidence, ED can be either psychological or physiological in nature. Some causes include diabetes, excessive use of alcohol and other recreational drugs, the use of certain prescribed medications, and smoking. In fact, smoking substantially increases the probability of ED (Mayo Clinic Staff 2016).

EDs are categorized as *primary* or *secondary*. *Primary* ED, which is rare, refers to when a man has never achieved an erection. *Secondary* ED refers to when a man has succeeded in intercourse previously but is unable to achieve or maintain an erection at the time. Treatment of secondary ED is highly successful. A physician or therapist can treat low hormone levels with testosterone supplements, for example.

Most men experience occasional erectile difficulty. It may affect men at any age. Among younger men, ED is more closely related to psychological stress, relationship stress, and smoking tobacco. In fact, smoking increases the probability of ED by 50%. As men age, erectile difficulties increase largely because of a reduction in testosterone, increased circulation problems, and prostate gland enlargement. Depression is also linked to ED and men frequently experience an increase in depression in their fifties (Natali et al. 2005; Rowland, Incrocci, and Slob 2005).

There are a number of other physical causes of ED, such as multiple sclerosis, spinal cord injury, arteriosclerosis, diabetes, vascular disease, and endocrine gland disease. Because there frequently are physical causes, a man experiencing erectile problems should have a complete physical exam before beginning treatment. The association between ED and vascular conditions such as hypertension has caused some speculation that ED should be considered a marker for several conditions (Mayo Clinic Staff 2016).

Once physical problems have been ruled out, successful treatment of erectile problems focuses on treating psychological causes. The most common psychological factor causing ED is obsession with performance or performance anxiety. There are numerous other psychological factors that cause erectile problems, such as relationship problems, stress at work, having been sexually abused as a child, or some other type of early traumatic sexual experience. For example, men who were sexually abused by an adult during their childhoods are three times

more likely to experience erectile problems than are other men (B. M. King 2013; Laumann et al. 2006).

Treatment of ED resulting from psychological causes such as performance anxiety often involves therapy with an emphasis on the use of sensate focus exercises. In these exercises, the man and his partner are instructed to use no-demand, mutual-pleasuring techniques. This involves touching and giving pleasure to each other without thinking about intercourse or orgasm. At the beginning of the therapy, the genitals and the breasts are not to be touched. The objective is to learn to be sexual in an undemanding atmosphere, to reduce anxiety, and to learn nonverbal communication skills.

Gradually, the sensate focus exercises include genital and breast stimulation and then finally intercourse. The effectiveness of the sensate focus exercises lies in helping the man and his partner move from the tension and anxiety of being preoccupied with performance to the relaxed pleasure of touching each other in an undemanding situation.

Therapy using sensate focus exercises is effective. Many therapists believe, however, that the highest success rate in the long term is achieved by incorporating sensate focus exercises with in-depth personal and couple counseling, addressing their relationship dynamics. Although Masters and Johnson once maintained that most erectile problems were caused by psychological factors, there is now a growing view that the majority of EDs have a physical basis. As a result, ED is increasingly treated as a medical problem using medical strategies such as surgery, penile implants, and drugs.

This increased medicalization of EDs has led to the use of the oral drugs commonly prescribed today such as Viagra, Levitra, Stendra, and Cialis. They are reported to be highly effective when the cause of the problem is primarily physical. They work by relaxing muscles in the penis and, as a result, allowing arteries to expand and increasing blood flow to the penis. Cialis and Levitra have longer-lasting effects than does Viagra. All four can have similar side effects, such as headaches and blurred vision.

ED, as well as other sexual disorders, is not usually caused by exclusively physical, psychological, or relationship factors, but by a combination of the three interacting with one another. Many men who have erection problems have an underlying physical cause that is compounded by psychological stress and anxiety. Most men who experience ED would likely benefit from therapy and medical treatment (Mayo Clinic Staff 2016).

Premature Ejaculation

An indication of the prevalence of **premature ejaculation** may be seen in the fact that of 448 cases of sexually dysfunctional men treated by Masters and Johnson, 186 were premature ejaculators and approximately one-fifth of all men believe they have climaxed too early at some time. An orgasm is normally considered premature if it occurs within 2 or 3 minutes of intromission and if the timing is frustrating to either partner. Premature ejaculation is considered dysfunctional if the male persistently ejaculates too rapidly for his own or his partner's enjoyment and one or both of them consider it a problem (Grenier and Byers 2001; G. Kelly 2013). In more than 500 cases of premature ejaculation at the Masters and Johnson Institute, only 1 instance was caused by an organic condition. In the vast majority of cases, the difficulty is one of socialization and/or psychological origin (Masters, Johnson, and Kolodny 1995).

Premature ejaculation may be the result of early experiences when males achieve an orgasm within a few minutes after beginning masturbation to rush the pleasure. Within marriage, however, such a pattern is dysfunctional if intromission occurs early within the sexual encounter, since a substantial number of women require 15 minutes or more of sexual stimulation before they attain an orgasm.

Partners can play an important role in helping men who are premature ejaculators by employing the squeeze technique referred to earlier—a technique that involves squeezing the penis just prior to ejaculation. The process involves repeated stops before ejaculation actually occurs and applying firm pressure to reduce the level of excitement. Considerable communication is required between partners. Sexual therapists have reported a great deal of success with this technique.

Many men can prevent premature ejaculation by using a condom; this deceases the sensitivity of the glans, hence slowing sexual excitement and orgasm. Some men can delay ejaculation by thinking nonsexual thoughts.

The start–stop technique is another common method for controlling sexual stimulation and orgasm. When the man perceives he is nearing orgasm, he simply stops movement to relax and to permit the intensity of his excitement to subside. In many cases involving sexual dysfunctions of women, it is recommended that the female be on top to control the level of stimulation; however, in cases of premature ejaculation, it is more advantageous for the male to be on top so that he can better control his movements.

By developing a method of self-monitoring, most couples can extend the period of intromission without ejaculation to accommodate the needs of both. Whatever the difficulty that one incurs in sexual encounters, there is considerable merit in developing the attitude that change can and will occur. The cases that are difficult for sexual therapists to treat are those in which the parties involved become anxious and believe they cannot change.

Although it has traditionally been viewed that premature ejaculation is caused by psychological or relationship factors or by inexperience, there is growing evidence of physical causes as well. For example, some cases of premature ejaculation are caused by certain injuries, illnesses, medications, and withdrawal from specific narcotics. There is increasing evidence that some men have a physiological or neurological predisposition to ejaculate quickly. In such cases, treatment with medications may be most effective.

Although the squeeze technique is still regarded as an effective treatment of premature ejaculation, today other treatments are used depending on the cause. Many therapists believe the most successful treatment is to combine cognitive therapy and sex therapy with a prescribed pharmacological agent that delays ejaculation, when such a medication is needed (T. Barnes and Eardley 2007; B. M. King 2013).

Alcohol and Drugs

Alcohol is often believed to act as an aphrodisiac. Many believe it enhances sexual desire and responsiveness because alcohol has the effect of relaxing and lowering inhibitions, thus increasing confidence in sexual interaction. However, alcohol is in fact a depressant and reduces or inhibits the

premature ejaculation Reaching orgasm too rapidly for his or his partner's enjoyment; easily and successfully treated.

physiological responses of sexual arousal. As the level of alcohol increases, it is more likely to impair the nervous system responses necessary for sexual behavior and to cause sexual dysfunctions, such as ED and a lack of sexual responsiveness (B. M. King 2013).

Some illegal drugs such as cocaine and marijuana are thought by many to enhance sexual pleasure. This belief is greatly influenced by the placebo effect, the user's strong positive expectation that the drug will enhance sexual experience. Cocaine has the effect of stimulating the central nervous system, which may result in a temporary increase in energy and feeling of self-confidence. However, as the use of cocaine continues, it often results in ED and problems experiencing orgasm for both men and women. With chronic use, it reduces sexual pleasure and responsiveness (Yarber and Sayad 2013).

Marijuana increases relaxation and awareness of touch, but it does not increase desire or arousal, nor does it intensify orgasms. Frequent or chronic use of marijuana by men increases the probability of erection problems, reduces testosterone levels, and lowers sperm production. Among both men and women, chronic use reduces sexual responsiveness and pleasure (G. Kelly 2013; B. M. King 2013).

Ecstasy has gained popularity as an aphrodisiac. It is sometimes combined with Viagra and called "sextasy." The combination frequently causes prolonged painful erections and severe headache. Ecstasy causes the release of the brain chemical serotonin and gives a feeling of euphoria.

There are mixed research results concerning the effects of Ecstasy on sexuality. Some indicate an increase in sexual desire, particularly among gay men. However, other studies indicate that Ecstasy decreases sexual desire and responsiveness and increases erection difficulties. Research evidence indicates that Ecstasy causes permanent brain damage in animals and that moderate use in humans results in memory loss (Parrott 2008; Silverberg 2014).

Many have used amphetamines to enhance sexual pleasure. In low doses, this class of drugs, also referred to as "uppers" or "speed," can increase energy. However amphetamine use is related to erectile dysfunction and reduced sexual satisfaction in men. When used chronically, amphetamines can also cause severe paranoia (Venosa 2015).

The opiates include drugs such as oxycontin, morphine, heroin, and methadone, which is a synthetic opiate. Opiates have the effect of reducing libido or sexual desire. Research in which men and women received a spinal infusion of an opiate pain medication reported that 95% of men and 68% of women experienced a serious drop in sex drive (Seay 2014).

Two-thirds of women and over 95% of men who use heroin regularly experience a greatly reduced interest in sex. Heroin causes an increase in the hormone prolactin, which causes a natural decrease in sexual interest. Heroin uses the same brain system that requires activation during orgasm, preventing the delivery of further brain signals (essentially blocking orgasm). People who abuse heroin for extended amounts of time will likely find it impossible to reach orgasm (Seay 2014).

A number of prescribed medications used to treat health conditions other than sexual disorders can have negative effects on sexual functioning. For example, the phenothiazine-derived tranquilizers cause some men not to ejaculate semen at the time of orgasm. Certain antipsychotic drugs can interfere with sexual arousal and orgasmic responses (Knegtering et al. 2006).

Antidepressants such as Prozac, Paxil, Zoloft, and Anafranil can cause a decrease in sexual desire, arousal, or orgasmic experience (Bolton, Sareen, and Reiss 2006). Some high blood pressure medications may inhibit sexual arousal, and certain medications for migraine headaches and antiulcer drugs have been found to contribute to hypoactive sexual desire and arousal problems (G. Kelly 2013).

Sexually Transmitted Diseases

About 20 million new cases of STDs occur each year within the United States, costing the American health-care system about $16 billion in direct medical costs alone. They are most common in young people ages 15 to 24; half of all sexually active young people will contract an STD before age 25. Women contract STDs five times more often than men. The two factors most predictive of contracting STDs are becoming sexually active at a young age and having multiple sex partners (Centers for Disease Control and Prevention 2013, 2016).

Among the major STDs in the United States are human papillomavirus (HPV), chlamydia, genital herpes, gonorrhea, and syphilis. Individuals who contract these diseases have a significantly increased risk of becoming infected with HIV, in part because these STDs may leave open sores that provide HIV easy entry into the body (Centers for Disease Control and Prevention 2013, 2016; Wright 2009).

Approximately 25% of all cases of infertility are caused by STDs (Rodriguez 2015). Approximately 200,000 people die of STDs other than HIV each year in the United States. Those STDs that result in the highest frequency of death are, in order, HIV, syphilis, chlamydia, and gonorrhea (Mishori, McClaskey and WinklerPrins 2012). Because of their potential physical and psychological harm, it is helpful to be aware of them.

Chlamydia

Chlamydia is the most common bacterial STD in the United States with approximately 2.8 million cases of chlamydia each year. It is called the silent STD because about 75% of women and 50% of men show no symptoms until it is a full-blown disease. Symptoms in men include infections of the urinary tract, inflammation of the testicular duct, a burning sensation during urination, discharge from the penis, and itching around the opening of the penis. Women who show symptoms experience vaginal discharge, pain during urination, abdominal pain, bleeding between periods, and pain during intercourse.

Infection of the urinary tract and cervix may result in pelvic inflammatory disease (PID). More than 40% of untreated women develop PID. If untreated, the infection progresses to the fallopian tubes, significantly increasing a woman's risk for infertility (Centers for Disease Control and Prevention 2013, 2016).

PID also increases the chances that a woman will experience an ectopic pregnancy, which is implantation of the fertilized ovum (zygote) in the fallopian tube rather than in the uterus. As the pregnancy continues and the embryo grows, the fallopian tube can rupture, resulting in maternal hemorrhage—and potentially death. Women with chlamydia are also five times more likely to contract HIV (Centers for Disease Control and Prevention 2013).

Chlamydia poses a threat to the eyes of newborns. An inflammation of the eye, conjunctivitis, may be contracted at birth as the baby passes through the birth canal. If it is not treated quickly, blindness can result. This may be the most widespread *preventable*

cause of blindness in the world. Babies can also develop chlamydia pneumonia during the first few months of life (G. Kelly 2013).

Chlamydia trachomatis is the cause of nongonococcal urethritis in about half of cases. It can be effectively treated with tetracycline. Because chlamydia and gonorrhea have similar symptoms, because persons may be infected with both simultaneously, and because some clinics do not have facilities to test for chlamydia, some persons with chlamydia may be treated only for gonorrhea. Unfortunately, chlamydia is not cured by penicillin. It is recommended, therefore, that persons with either gonorrhea or chlamydia be checked for both.

Because of the high occurrence rate of chlamydia today, the CDC recommends yearly screenings for all sexually active women under age 25 and also for women over age 25 who have multiple sex partners (Centers for Disease Control and Prevention 2016). Several lab tests are available to detect chlamydia. Most require a doctor's visit; a few may be ordered online. Urine-based tests have recently become available and are less invasive and easier to use (Carroll 2015; Centers for Disease Control and Prevention 2015; Trigg, Kerndt, and Aynalem 2008).

Gonorrhea

Gonorrhea is one of the oldest and most common bacterial STDs in the United States, with an estimated 800,000 cases each year. The incidence of gonorrhea was in decline a few years ago but is now on the rise again (Centers for Disease Control and Prevention 2013, 2015). Symptoms usually appear within 2 to 6 days. Symptoms in men include yellow or green discharge from the penis, burning sensation during urination, urethral discomfort, and swollen testicles. Fifty percent of women infected with gonorrhea show few or no symptoms until it is a full-blown disease. When symptoms do appear for

chlamydia Common bacterial sexually transmitted disease; women often show no symptoms; may lead to pelvic inflammatory disease if untreated; treated with antibiotics.

gonorrhea Old STD; women often show no symptoms; may lead to infertility in men and women; treated with antibiotics.

Unsafe Sex Practices: Why So Prevalent?

Casual sex has increased, yet safe sex practices are often ignored. One consequence has been a great increase in STDs. For example, the majority of college students (approximately 75%) report having experienced hookups (sexual interactions that are brief in duration and do not involve any expectation of a lasting relationship). The partner may be a friend, an acquaintance who is not well known, or a stranger. Some hookup interactions involve only kissing and heavy petting, but about 50% involve intercourse or oral sex. Condoms are used only about 50% of the time (E. L. Paul et al. 2008).

Similarly, research indicates that even in romantic dating that involves some expectation of a potentially lasting relationship, only about 50% of college students used condoms consistently. A study of 740 women in their thirties and forties who were looking for new partners on dating websites found that they had many long chat-room conversations, negotiated boundaries before agreeing to a face-to-face meeting, and ran background checks. However, their caution did not translate into safe sex practices. Seventy-seven percent of the women did not use condoms when they first had sex with their online partners (R. S. Miller and Perlman 2009; Padgett 2007).

Why do intelligent people often ignore safe sex practices? Why are condoms frequently not used in casual sex encounters or with new romantic partners? Each of the following contributes to unsafe sex practices.

1. *Using the popular hormone-based contraceptives.* Because the pill and other hormone-based methods are highly effective and easy to use, they have become the most preferred contraceptive method in the United States. However, they offer no protection against STDs.

2. *Underestimating the risk.* There is a tendency, especially among younger age groups, to think we are invulnerable and that "it cannot happen to us." However, when we expose ourselves to risk several times, the probability that we will become infected with an STD is greatly increased. For example, if a woman has unprotected sex 10 times with a man infected with HIV, the probability that she will become infected with HIV is 40%. There is also a tendency to underestimate the cumulative risk that a new partner who has been sexually active is infected with an STD. Having multiple partners greatly increases the risk (R. S. Miller and Perlman 2009).

3. *Using poor decision making.* Many unsafe sex practices are the result of poor decision making. For example, when people are drunk they are less likely to use condoms when having sex with someone for the first time (Cooper 2006). Alcohol consumption reduces cognitive processes and normal judgment ability. Also, sexual arousal can interfere with responsible decision making. For example, many people in the heat of sexual arousal view condom use as less desirable. Those who intend to use condoms sometimes change their minds in the intense moments of sexual arousal and later regret their decision (Ariely and Loewenstein 2006; R. S. Miller and Perlman 2009).

4. *Perceiving sex to be more enjoyable without condoms.* One of the major obstacles to safe sex is that many people find sexual interaction to be more enjoyable when condoms are not involved. Some believe their sexual interactions are more emotionally satisfying and intimate without the use of condoms. Men, in particular, are more likely to prefer unprotected sex (G. Smith, Mysak, and Michael 2008). A significant proportion of men and women report having a partner trying to talk them out of using a condom. Interestingly, those who have had more than 10 different sex partners, and therefore are at higher risk for having an STD, are more likely than those with fewer partners to try to persuade their new partners to not use condoms (R. S. Miller and Perlman 2009; Oncale and King 2001).

SEXUALLY TRANSMITTED DISEASES

What can be done in society to promote safer sex practices? Some important recommendations include the following:

1. Reduce casual sex encounters.

2. Reverse the two greatest predictors of contracting STDs: (1) becoming sexually active at a young age and (2) having multiple sex partners.

3. Provide more extensive education that is realistic and includes realistic consequences.

4. Stop viewing condoms as a nuisance and instead view them as part of sexually enjoyable foreplay; for example, a partner could put the condom on in a way that enhances anticipation and excitement (Scott-Sheldon and Johnson 2006).

5. Adopt the view that condom use communicates respect and caring (R. S. Miller and Perlman 2009).

women, they may include yellow or bloody vaginal discharge, burning during urination, and pelvic pain and bleeding associated with intercourse. Individuals who are asymptomatic can have the disease for years and not discover it until considerable damage has been done. Although rare, persons with untreated gonorrhea infections can develop heart valve infections, meningitis, or arthritis (Carroll 2015; Centers for Disease Control and Prevention 2016; Torpy, Lynm, and Golub 2013).

Gonorrhea is treated and cured with antibiotics. However, drug-resistant strains of gonorrhea are making the disease more difficult to treat. If left untreated, there can be serious complications. Untreated gonorrhea in women can lead to PID, which (as with chlamydia) in short time can result in damage to the fallopian tubes and increased risk of infertility and ectopic pregnancy. Untreated gonorrhea in men may lead to epididymitis, causing pain in the testicle ducts and possibly leading to infertility (Centers for Disease Control and Prevention 2013, 2016). An infected woman who gives birth can transmit gonorrhea to her newborn (again, as with chlamydia), with resulting eye infection (risk of blindness) or pneumonia. Most hospital obstetrical units routinely put a few drops of antibacterial agent into the eyes of newborns to kill bacteria.

Syphilis

Syphilis is an ancient bacterial infection that comes from the bacteria *Treponema pallidum.* Many of its symptoms are the same as other STDs and for that reason it is sometimes referred to as "the great pretender." Syphilis is successfully treated and cured with antibiotics. If left untreated, it can result in paralysis, insanity, or death (Mulryan 2013).

Syphilis progresses to three stages if left untreated. The primary stage is characterized by a painless sore called a *chancre.* Most chancres appear within 2 to 6 weeks after contracting syphilis. The chancres usually disappear in 3 to 12 weeks, with or without treatment. The secondary stage is identified by the appearance of a skin rash a few weeks or months after the chancres have disappeared. The rash can appear on the genitals as well as other parts of the body. Syphilis can be transmitted by contact, sexual or nonsexual, with the rash. The rash will disappear even if untreated and may recur over the next few months or years.

If left untreated, syphilis enters the late stage, which involves severe complications such as heart problems, lesions, and damage to the nervous system, eyes, brain, and spinal cord. Late-stage syphilis can eventually lead to paralysis, mental illness, insanity, and death (Centers for Disease Control and Prevention 2016; Mulryan 2013).

Syphilis can be successfully treated with antibiotics; penicillin, tetracycline, or erythromycin are commonly used. In most cases syphilis can no

syphilis Untreated syphilis proceeds through three stages; the last may result in paralysis, insanity, or death; treated with antibiotics; may be transmitted prenatally.

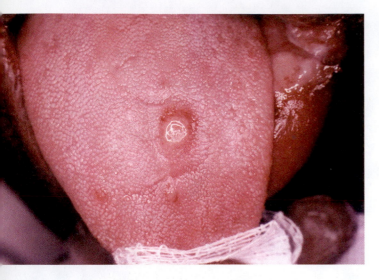

A primary stage symptom of syphilis is a painless chancre that may appear in the mouth or on the genitals or anus.

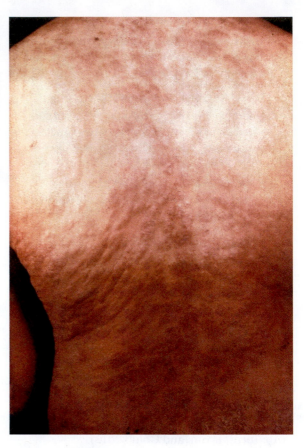

The secondary stage of syphilis is characterized by a rash that neither itches nor hurts. It may appear on the body, including soles of the feet and palms of the hands.

longer be transmitted after 24 hours of starting the antibiotic treatment. However, once the disease has caused internal damage, treatment cannot reverse it.

If a woman is infected with syphilis during pregnancy, she may transmit the disease to the unborn child, causing an increased risk of miscarriage, stillbirth, or mental retardation. If a baby is born with syphilis and is left untreated, it is at risk for blindness, developmental delay, or death (Centers for Disease Control and Prevention 2016).

Human Papillomavirus

Human papillomavirus (HPV) is the most common STD, viral or bacterial, in America. More than 14 million new cases are reported each year in the United States. About 45% percent of women between the ages of 20 and 24 are estimated to be infected with HPV. There are more than 100 different types of HPV infections (Centers for Disease Control and Prevention 2013, 2016; Gostin and DeAngelis 2007).

"Low-risk" HPV (types 6 and 11) can cause genital warts. High-risk HPV (types 16 and 18) can result in abnormal Pap tests and can cause cervical cancer. HPV is the leading cause of cervical cancer; some 90% of cervical cancers are also infected with high-risk HPV. HPV can also cause other types of cancers such as anal, throat, and penile cancers (Carroll 2015; Grce and Davies 2008).

HPV is transmitted through sexual contact, including oral sex, anal sex, or genital-to-genital sex. HPV may also infect the mouth, throat, nose, and anus, contributing to oral and anal cancer. For example, those who have had oral sex with six or more partners have been found to be at higher risk for throat cancer (D'Souza et al. 2007). There have been significant increases in anal HPV among both men and women (D'Hauwers and Tjalma 2008). Research has also found that HPV-associated anal cancer is more common in men who have sex with men than cervical cancer is among women (Chin-Hong et al. 2008).

A great many individuals who are infected with HPV do not have symptoms or health problems from it; about 90% of the time, the body is able to clear itself of HPV within 2 years. However, when the immune system is not successful, HPV infection can cause genital warts or cancer of the cervix, vulva, vagina, penis, throat, or anus (Centers for Disease Control and Prevention 2016).

Genital warts are bumps that appear around the vagina, penis, anus, scrotum, groin, cervix, or thighs. These warts sometimes take the shape of a cauliflower. For some persons the genital warts appear within weeks of becoming infected, whereas for others they appear after several months.

HPV may be detected in Pap testing, but most of the time (80% to 90%) it goes undetected. An HPV DNA test, which can identify 13 of the high-risk types of HPV associated with cervical cancer, was approved by the U.S. Food and Drug Administration in 2003. The HPV DNA test is particularly recommended for women who have more than one sexual partner. Women who are diagnosed with a high-risk type of HPV are advised to have a Pap test and pelvic exams at least once a year (Carroll 2015). Because HPV is not the only cause of cervical cancer, because cervical cancer is more effectively treated in early stages, and because cervical cancer typically has no symptoms until it becomes advanced, it is important for women to get regular screening tests for cervical cancer. Some health-care professionals also recommend regular screening for anal cancer in gay men or HIV-positive individuals.

HPV can be transmitted from a mother to her unborn child. If a baby becomes infected, there is a risk of developing a condition called *respiratory papillomatosis*, development of warts in the throat or voice box (Centers for Disease Control and Prevention 2013).

Three vaccines are available to provide protection from HPV infection. Gardasil prevents infection by four strains of HPV (6, 11, 16, 18) that have been linked to cervical cancer or warts; Gardasil 9 adds additional protection against strains 31, 33, 45, 52, and 58, which are also responsible for cervical cancer (Food and Drug Administration 2014). The vaccines are for females and males and are designed to be administered before the onset of sexual activity, although they can be taken up to 26 years of age if they were not administered at earlier ages. Vaccination is almost 100% effective in preventing the virus infection, but is ineffective with existing HPV infections. Cervarix is similar to Gardasil, but only protects against HPV types 16 and 18—thus against cancers, but not warts (Centers for Disease Control and Prevention 2016).

Questions have been raised about the actual effectiveness of the vaccines and their safety. Opponents of the use of the vaccines point out that the bulk of testing has been done by the drug companies who developed the vaccines and that serious side effects have been underreported (Null and Ashley 2012). Controversy also exists over attempts to institute mandatory HPV vaccinations for girls entering sixth grade in public schools. There is also disagreement over whether boys and men should be encouraged or required to have HPV vaccinations as well (M. Casper and Carpenter 2008; Jordan 2008; Null and Ashley 2012).

Herpes

Herpes is widespread in the United States, with 15.5% of the population already infected with the virus and about 776,000 contracting herpes each year. Herpes infection is two times more prevalent in women than men; herpes is more easily transmitted from men to women than vice versa. The virus herpes simplex causes genital herpes. There are two strains of the virus: herpes simplex virus type 1 (HSV-1) and herpes simplex virus type 2 (HSV-2). HSV-1 commonly causes fever blisters or cold sores around the mouth and it can be spread to the genitals through oral sex. However, HSV 2 is responsible for most forms of genital herpes (Centers for Disease Control and Prevention 2016).

Some people infected with herpes do not show symptoms. When symptoms of genital herpes appear, they are characterized by itching or painful blisters in the genital area, including the cervix, vulva, vagina, scrotum, anus, buttocks, and penis. The first symptoms typically appear within 4 days after infection. Within a few days the blisters open, releasing watery fluid and/or blood. Sores are highly contagious and take about 2 to 4 weeks to heal. After the first episode of genital herpes a person

human papillomavirus Most common sexually transmitted disease; some strains of human papillomavirus cause genital warts; others cause cervical, vulvar, vaginal, and anal cancer.

herpes Widespread viral sexually transmitted disease characterized by painful blisters during outbreaks; medications reduce outbreaks but cannot cure herpes.

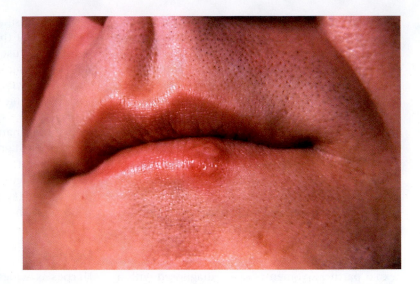

Herpes simplex virus type 1 commonly causes fever blisters or cold sores around the mouth.

typically can expect to have four or five more outbreaks within the year. The outbreaks decrease in frequency over time. The blisters may be accompanied by pain in the thighs or groin, aches, or fever. It is desirable to avoid sexual contact until at least 10 days after the sores have completely healed. The risk of infection does remain even when the blisters or sores are not present (Centers for Disease Control and Prevention 2016).

There are serious complications of herpes in addition to the physical discomfort and psychological distress that may be experienced during the outbreaks. Herpes does increase the risk of HIV infections and makes individuals with HIV more contagious. There is also greater incidence of vulvar and cervical cancer among women who have genital herpes. Therefore, it is advisable for women with genital herpes to have an annual Pap smear and pelvic examination to identify any abnormal cells in the cervix (Centers for Disease Control and Prevention 2016).

Other possible complications of herpes infection occur with pregnancy and childbirth. Herpes during a pregnancy can result in miscarriage or premature birth. If a mother has an active herpes infection at the time of delivery, a cesarean section is used to prevent the baby from becoming infected. Neonatal herpes is a serious and potentially fatal infection (Centers for Disease Control and Prevention 2016).

There is no cure for herpes. However, antiviral drugs are used to relieve symptoms and reduce recurrences. Other suggestions for relieving symptoms are applying an ice pack; using cornstarch or baby powder to absorb the moisture; keeping the affected area clean and dry; and using aspirin or other pain relievers (G. Kelly 2013).

Hepatitis

Hepatitis is a liver infection caused by different viruses. The hepatitis A virus is the most common of the hepatitis viral types. It was previously thought not to be sexually transmitted because it is usually contracted through eating food that contains fecal material. However, it is now known that the hepatitis A virus can be sexually transmitted through oral–anal sexual activity. Washing of genital and anal areas before sex and use of dental dams or condoms can reduce this risk (Centers for Disease Control and Prevention 2016). About 25% of hepatitis A cases are sexually transmitted or contracted through other household contact.

The hepatitis B virus is more likely to be sexually transmitted than the A and C viruses because B is found not only in the blood but also in other body fluids such as semen, vaginal secretions, and saliva. It may also be transmitted through sharing syringes (intravenous drug abuse) or personal items such as toothbrushes and razors with an infected person and through the use of dirty tattooing or piercing tools. Hepatitis B is 50 to 100 times more infectious than HIV and is a major health problem in America, with over 1 million persons having chronic hepatitis B, most of whom are unaware that they are infected and contagious (Centers for Disease Control and Prevention 2016).

The hepatitis C virus is most often contracted by direct contact with contaminated blood. As with hepatitis B, the C virus may be transmitted through dirty instruments used for tattooing or piercing and syringes for intravenous drug abuse. It also can be sexually transmitted. Those who engage in high-risk sexual behavior, such as multiple sex partners, are at greater risk for contracting hepatitis C. Certain sexual practices such as anal sex can increase the chance of becoming infected with hepatitis C because of the increased likelihood of tearing tissue and bleeding. It has now become the most common chronic bloodborne infection in America and there are approximately 200 million infected worldwide (Centers for Disease Control and Prevention 2015).

The symptoms of hepatitis A, B, and C are similar and include joint aches and flulike discomfort, loss of appetite, nausea, vomiting, diarrhea, loss of weight, jaundice (yellowing of skin), dark urine, abdominal pain, itchy skin, and enlargement of the liver. Many people experience mild symptoms or no symptoms at all but still carry the virus and can transmit it to others. Those infected with hepatitis B or C are at risk for developing chronic liver damage, cirrhosis of the liver, and liver cancer (Centers for Disease Control and Prevention 2016).

Although there is no cure for hepatitis A, B, or C, the symptoms can be relieved by certain medications, heavy fluid intake, and bed rest. Most people recover from hepatitis A and B infection. In about 5% of cases in adults, hepatitis B becomes chronic and can be treated with anti-viral medications. Hepatitis C is treated with anti-viral medications with good success, although some hepatitis C becomes chronic. Vaccines are available for preventing hepatitis A and B. No vaccine is available at this time for hepatitis C, although one is in development in the stage of formal preclinical studies (Centers for Disease Control Prevention 2016; Somerville 2012).

Human Immunodeficiency Virus

The World Health Organization (2016) has estimated that at the end of 2014, approximately 37 million people worldwide were living with HIV/AIDS, some 70% of them in sub-Saharan Africa.

AIDS-related deaths in sub-Saharan Africa have decreased since 2010 because free AIDS drug treatment has become widely available in that region. South and Southeast Asia report the second highest rate of HIV/AIDS. An estimated 2 million people were newly infected in 2014; about 46% do not realize they are infected.

The Centers for Disease Control and Prevention (2015) estimate that 1.2 million persons in America are infected with HIV and that as many as 14% may not realize it. The incidence of new infections with HIV has remained relatively stable, but still high, at about 50,000 per year.

The epidemic of HIV infection and AIDS is now into its third decade and continues to receive much worldwide attention. HIV and AIDS have raised economic and political issues (as well as health issues). HIV has changed how people approach their sexual behavior—more concern for safer sex practices, an increase in the use of condoms, less promiscuous behavior, and more monogamous sexual relationships (G. Kelly 2013).

Human immunodeficiency virus (HIV) attacks the immune system and is one of the viruses that can cause **acquired immunodeficiency syndrome** (AIDS), characterized by irreversible damage to the body's immune system and, eventually, death. People with AIDS suffer from combinations of severe weight loss, several types of infection, and various cancers. A person with AIDS usually goes through a long, miserable illness that ends in death 1 to 2 years after the diagnosis. The two diseases most commonly associated with AIDS are a type of cancer (Kaposi's sarcoma) and a rare form of pneumonia (*Pneumocystis jiroveci*), which

hepatitis A liver infection caused by different viruses (A, B, C); all may be transmitted sexually as well as by other ways (sharing dirty needles, for example).

human immunodeficiency virus A sexually transmitted disease caused by a virus that attacks the immune system, eventually resulting in AIDS; HIV is transmitted during sexual contact; in body fluids such as blood, semen, or breast milk; and prenatally.

acquired immunodeficiency syndrome A disease caused by the human immunodeficiency virus and characterized by irreversible damage to the body's immune system and, eventually, death.

accounts for 70% of all AIDS deaths (Knox and Schacht 2016).

Not everyone who has HIV (referred to as HIV+) develops AIDS; however, 50% of those who are HIV+ will develop AIDS within 10 years. Hope for finding a cure was strengthened when in 2013 researchers announced the first "functional cure" of HIV in a toddler in rural Mississippi. A functional cure means standard medical tests no longer detect the virus and the child no longer needs to take medication. The baby girl was born to an HIV+ mother who had received no prenatal care. Doctors administered antiretroviral drugs in the hope of controlling the virus; the baby had tested HIV+, probably from prenatal exposure. The child remained on the antiretroviral drugs for 15 months when her mother stopped them. Doctors were surprised to find her free of HIV and they continued to monitor her. Sadly, HIV and a weakened immune system were discovered during a routine doctor visit at 4 years old (Young and Wilson 2014).

It is important to know that *everyone with HIV is infectious and able to transmit the virus to others.* Tests to determine whether a person has become infected with HIV most often check for the buildup of antibodies in the blood. Because it can take 2 weeks to 3 months for antibodies to develop, these tests are not accurate (false negative) if done too early. In rare cases, it may take 6 months for a person to develop sufficient antibodies (Centers for Disease Control and Prevention 2016).

A recent development in diagnosis, rapid HIV testing, makes results available within 20 minutes instead of 2 weeks. However, rapid HIV testing does not improve the accuracy of the results and does not change the fact that tests are not accurate until the body has sufficient time to build antibodies.

HIV can be transmitted in five ways:

1. **Direct sexual contact.** HIV is found in the body fluids of an infected person—in blood, semen, and vaginal secretions.

2. **Intravenous drug use.** HIV may be transmitted through the sharing of needles and syringes.

3. **Blood transfusions.** Prior to 1985, donor blood was not tested for HIV. Consequently, some people who received blood transfusions before 1985 were infected with HIV. It can still happen but is rare today.

4. **Mother-to-child transmission.** A pregnant woman who is HIV+ has about a 26% chance of transmitting the virus to her unborn child through the placenta, to her baby during birth, or to her infant through breast milk. The chances of transmission of HIV from a mother to her baby drop to about 2% if the mother takes certain medications used to treat HIV during pregnancy and if the baby is delivered by cesarean section (under certain conditions). It further helps to give the medications to the baby for a while following birth and for the mother not to breastfeed her baby. A physician must be consulted because some HIV medications are dangerous to an unborn child (Centers for Disease Control and Prevention 2016).

5. **Organ/tissue transplants and donor semen.** A person who receives a transplant of organs or tissue or receives semen for artificial insemination runs a risk of exposure to HIV if the donors have not been tested for HIV.

In addition, health-care professionals may be exposed to HIV in other ways. HIV is transmitted not only through blood, semen, and vaginal secretions, but also through amniotic fluid surrounding a fetus, the synovial fluid surrounding the joints, and the cerebrospinal fluid surrounding the brain and spinal cord.

By far the most common ways of transmitting HIV are direct sexual contact and intravenous drug use. The greatest proportion of people infected with HIV are, in order of frequency, men who have sex with men, heterosexuals who engage in high-risk sexual behaviors, and intravenous drug users (Centers for Disease Control and Prevention 2016). The major source of HIV infection for men in the United States is homosexual contact. The most common sources of HIV infection among U.S. women are through sharing intravenous drug equipment and heterosexual contact.

Following certain important principles can help prevent contracting or spreading HIV as well as other STDs. These principles include the following:

• Practice sexual abstinence until a long-term committed relationship is involved.

• Practice sexual fidelity (in a long-term monogamous relationship).

- Use contraceptive methods proven to protect against STDs as well as pregnancy, including latex or polyurethane male or female condoms approved by the Food and Drug Administration.

- Avoid anal intercourse with or without a condom since this is the riskiest exposure to semen. Condoms are not well designed for this manner of sexual expression.

- Avoid sexual relations with people who are likely to be HIV+: those who buy or sell sex, for example.

- Do not share needles used to inject drugs.

- Avoid use of alcohol and drugs because they interfere with good judgment.

Although persons who are HIV+ cannot be cured, antiretroviral drugs slow the progress of infection. Because antiretrovirals reduce the amount of HIV in an infected person, they reduce the chance of transmission to others (Centers for Disease Control and Prevention 2015). A number of drugs are also used to treat AIDS-related illnesses; they are expensive, sometimes costing more than $1,000 per month (Knox and Schacht 2016).

Vaginitis

Any inflammation of the vagina is referred to as **vaginitis**. Several kinds of vaginitis are possible and treatment depends on the organism responsible.

1. **Trichomoniasis.** This is caused by a microscopic parasite. The trichomonad can survive for several hours in a moist environment, so infection from public toilets or shared towels is possible. Symptoms of trichomonal infection are an itchy inflammation of the vagina and a frothy, white or yellow vaginal discharge. It is one of the most common causes of vaginal infections, causing approximately 3 million new infections each year. Men may also have trichomonal infections. For men the symptoms include itching and irritation of the penis, a burning sensation after urination or ejaculation, and a discharge from the penis. About 70% of those infected (both men and women) show no symptoms. Even if symptoms are not present, an infected individual is still contagious. The drug for treatment is metronidazole (Centers for Disease Control and Prevention 2013, 2016).

2. **Fungal vaginitis/candidiasis.** The organism responsible for this infection (primarily *Candida albicans*) is present on most people's skin all the time. Candidiasis is commonly referred to as a "yeast infection." Under certain conditions, the number of yeast (a fungus) normally present in the vagina increases rapidly, causing the symptoms of infection: intense vaginal itching and white vaginal discharge. Pregnancy, diabetes, use of oral contraceptives, or use of antibiotics make women more susceptible to yeast infections. Sexual contact is not necessary for a women to develop this disease. Antifungal drugs such as topical ointments or pills taken orally are typically used for candidiasis with 80% to 90% effectiveness (Yarber and Sayad 2013).

3. **Bacterial vaginitis/vaginosis.** A variety of bacterial infections of the vagina are possible, producing symptoms similar to gonorrhea. Women may experience burning after urination, genital itching, and vaginal discharge. Infection may occur without sexual contact.

Pediculosis

Pediculosis is also called body lice. The lice are most often transmitted by close body contact, but can be passed in bedding, towels, or clothing. The symptoms of infection are itching of the head, body, or pubic area. Body lice are removed using an insecticidal cream or shampoo available over the counter (without a prescription) at drug stores. Clothing, bedding, and towels should be laundered in very hot water.

vaginitis Any inflammation of the vagina; may be caused by microscopic parasites, fungal infection, or bacterial infection.

pediculosis Body lice; transmitted by close body contact; cause severe itching.

Internet Pornography

The Internet pornography industry is growing dramatically and is a multi-billion-dollar business. More than 200 new sex sites are added to the Internet daily. The number of online pornography sites has increased 18-fold since 1998 (Carroll 2015; Swartz 2004).

The average age for children to first become exposed to Internet pornography is 11 years. Efforts to protect children from exposure to online pornography are difficult and largely ineffective. Although Internet filters and blocks are available, 70% of children and youth who are 10 to 17 years of age indicate they have viewed pornography online (Delmonico and Griffin 2008).

The easy accessibility, as well as the affordability and anonymity, of the Internet has contributed to the increased consumption of Internet pornography. The leading misuse of the computer in the workplace is Internet pornography. Marriage and family therapists report an increase in clients experiencing Internet pornography addiction, not only among adults but also among children (Internet Pornography by the Numbers 2016).

Those who become involved in compulsive online pornography (those who spend more than 11 hours per week engaging in Internet sexual activities) often experience a decreased satisfaction in their own sexual relationships. In a sense, their real relationships are replaced by digital partners or images. Depression and loneliness are frequently experienced by compulsive online pornography users.

Not surprisingly, this compulsive or addictive behavior contributes to serious problems in marriages, families, and other intimate relationships. Spouses, partners, and children of compulsive Internet pornography users frequently experience negative psychological effects such as loneliness and depression (P. Paul 2005).

Although child pornography is illegal and banned by federal law in all 50 states, the Internet has made the distribution of child pornography more prevalent and easily accessed. Thousands of arrests are made for Internet-related crimes involving child pornography. However, most such crimes go undetected.

Those arrested have access to minor children through a job, involvement in organized youth activities, or living with children. The child pornography that offenders possess includes images of children under ages 3 to 12. The images represent children involved in a range of sexual behaviors including penetration, genital touching, and oral sex (Carroll 2015; Wolak, Finkelhor, and Mitchell 2005).

Questions to Consider

Should Internet pornography be more closely regulated?

What further steps should be taken to protect children from being exposed to Internet pornography?

How can Internet-related child pornography crimes be more effectively prosecuted?

Summary

1. The need for intimacy is interwoven throughout sexual relationships. Our sexuality is connected to every other part of our lives and includes our emotions, social relationships, values, ethics, spiritual faith, our intellect, and our decision-making and problem-solving skills, as well as the biological aspects of being male or female. For this reason, sexuality is best understood in a holistic manner—within the context of the total person and the total relationship.

2. A number of sexual myths exist that promote inaccurate assumptions about sexual behavior. Some myths, such as the belief that sexual satisfaction increases with multiple partners, can negatively impact a sexual relationship and decrease satisfaction.

3. A number of possible negative consequences to sexual behavior must be considered. Some highly publicized risks include unplanned pregnancy or STD. Other less obvious but equally important risks include confusing sex with love or becoming involved in manipulation and power games.

4. Sexual response is influenced by many factors such as quality of the total relationship, mental and physical health, nutrition, fatigue, stress, depression, alcohol, drugs, and medications. The great range of influence on sexual response reflects the holistic nature of sexuality.

5. The Masters and Johnson model and the Kaplan model are the major models of the sexual response cycle. Men and women have similar response patterns in that both go through the same stages of sexual response. Differences exist in the way in which they proceed through the stages. One of the greatest differences between men and women is in the stage of sexual desire.

6. The success of a sexual relationship involves more than the physiological aspect; it is integrated with the total interpersonal relationship. Among the important factors contributing to a satisfying sexual relationship are intimacy, commitment, psychological comfort, good communication, knowledge of the sexual response cycle, emphasis on the enjoyment of each other rather than performance, and good mental and physical health.

7. Changes in hormone production and other physical changes occur as we age; these changes affect sexual functioning. Research consistently indicates that although the frequency of sexual intercourse steadily declines with age, people who are healthy and happy and who have a healthy partner usually continue to be sexually active in their later years.

8. The female climacteric begins well before the last menstrual period and lasts several years. As ovulation gradually stops, the drop in hormone production causes a number of symptoms such as hot flashes, heart palpitations, night sweats, depression, irritability, anxiety, and loss of bone density.

9. Men experience a pattern of changes and symptoms as they age, which are often referred to as "male menopause." The male climacteric (the more accurate term) includes such symptoms as a gradual decrease in testosterone and androgen levels, loss in bone density, anxiety and depression, loss of muscle, enlargement of the prostate, and more erection difficulties.

10. Hormone replacement therapy (HRT) is used to alleviate the symptoms of menopause in women. Testosterone replacement therapy (TRT) is increasingly prescribed to help men who are experiencing uncomfortable symptoms of the male climacteric. However, research consistently indicates that HRT increases women's risk of breast cancer, heart attacks, and blood clots; similarly, TRT increases men's risk of blood clots, stroke, cardiovascular disease, and prostate cancer.

11. Sexual addiction is compulsive sexual behavior that a person continues despite severe negative consequences. Among the consequences are an increased risk for contracting an STD and marital unhappiness. Therapy, participation in a 12-step program, and medication are used to treat sexual addiction.

12. The most common sexual dysfunction among women is orgasmic disorder. Premature ejaculation is believed to be the most common sexual dysfunction in males. There are physical, psychological, and relationship causes of sexual disorders. A high rate of success has been reported in the treatment of most sexual disorders. Among the major treatment methods are therapy, sensate focus exercises, specific physical approaches such as the bridge maneuver, and medications.

13. Alcohol and some illegal drugs such as cocaine or marijuana are thought by many to enhance sexual pleasure. In reality, alcohol is a depressant and reduces (inhibits) the physiological responses of sexual arousal; increased levels of alcohol are likely to cause erectile dysfunction and a lack of sexual responsiveness. Chronic use of cocaine and marijuana reduces sexual pleasure and responsiveness in both men (for example, erection problems) and women.

A number of medications such as antidepressants and some hypertension medications inhibit sexual arousal.

14. About 20 million new cases of STDs occur each year in the United States. Among the major STDs in the United States are chlamydia, genital herpes, gonorrhea, and syphilis. Approximately 25% of all cases of infertility are caused by STDs.

15. Human papillomavirus (HPV) is the most common STD, viral or bacterial, in America. High-risk HPV types (especially 16 and 18) are the leading cause of cervical cancer.

16. Human immunodeficiency virus can be transmitted by direct sexual contact, intravenous drug use (sharing dirty needles), blood transfusions, from mother to child (prenatally, at birth, or through breast milk), and through organ/tissue transplants or donor semen.

Key Terms

acquired immunodeficiency syndrome

chlamydia

climacteric

dyspareunia

erectile disorder

gonorrhea

hepatitis

herpes

human immunodeficiency virus

human papillomavirus

hypoactive sexual desire

Kaplan sexual response model

Masters and Johnson sexual response model

orgasmic disorder

pediculosis

premature ejaculation

refractory period

sexual addiction

sexuality

syphilis

vaginismus

vaginitis

vasocongestion

Questions for Thought

1. What examples can you give of ways that our society (i.e., the media) attempts to "put sex in a box" and treat sexuality as though it is separate from the rest of life?

2. Why is sex often confused with love?

3. If you are male, what would you most like women to know about men and sex (male sexuality)? If you are female, what would you most like men to know about women and sex (female sexuality)?

4. What are four risks (or negative consequences) of sexual activity that you think are most important for young people to understand? What advice would you give to a younger sibling, for example?

5. The prominent sex researchers, William Masters and Virginia Johnson, concluded on the basis of their research and clinical experiences that commitment is the single most important factor contributing to satisfaction in a sexual relationship. Explain possible reasons for this conclusion.

6. Why do you think it is important to have some awareness and knowledge of sexual disorders?

7. What steps do you think must be taken to reduce the high rates of STDs in our society?

For Further Reading

Centers for Disease Control and Prevention. Read more about any of the STDs at the Centers for Disease Control website. http://cdc.gov.

Encyclopedia of Mental Disorders. Learn more about sexual dysfunctions at the Encyclopedia of Mental Disorders website. http://www.minddisorders.com.

Fisher, H. (2009). *Why him? Why her?* New York: Holt. Based on research involving millions of participants, this book explores how personality type is related to desire and attachment. It provides insights into the complex nature of romance and love.

Harrar, S., and DeMaria, R. (2007). *The seven stages of marriage.* Pleasantville, NY: The Reader's Digest

Association. Looks at how marriage evolves through seven stages, each with unique challenges and pleasures.

Meston, C. M., and Buss, D. M. (2009). *Why women have sex.* New York: Holt. Based on a study of more than 1,000 women from diverse backgrounds, this book provides insights into motivations for establishing sexual relationships.

Null, G., and Ashley, N. (2012). *Gardasil: Big Pharma killing us softly.* http://www.vactruth .com/2012/1/25.

Taverner, W. J., and McKee, R. W. (2010). *Taking sides: Clashing views in human sexuality* (11th ed.). New York: McGraw–Hill. A debate-style reader designed to introduce students to controversies in human sexuality.

Family Planning and Parenthood

Learning Objectives

The Importance of Family Planning

FAMILY STRENGTHS PERSPECTIVE: *What Is a Strong Family?*

Hormonal Control

- Oral Contraceptives
- Other Forms of Hormonal Contraceptives

AT ISSUE TODAY: *The Abortion Pill*

Vaginal Spermicides

Intrauterine Devices

Barrier Methods

- Condoms
- Diaphragm
- Cervical Cap
- Contraceptive Sponge

Sterilization

- Vasectomy
- Female Sterilization

Fertility Awareness

- Calendar Method
- Withdrawal
- Noncoital Stimulation (Outercourse)

Choosing a Method of Contraception

Abortion

- Legal Considerations
- Moral Considerations
- Social and Realistic Considerations
- Psychological and Personal Considerations

Infertility

- Causes of Infertility

CULTURAL PERSPECTIVE: *A Preference for Males*

COPING FEATURE: *Coping with Infertility*

- Infertility and Subjective Well-Being

- Treatment of Infertility
- Alternative Means of Conception
- The Adoption Option

PERSONAL PERSPECTIVE: *Reasons for Having Children*

- The Foster Care Option

To Parent or Not to Parent

- Delayed Parenthood
- Choosing a Child-Free Marriage

A QUESTION OF POLICY: *Embryos*

Summary

Key Terms

Questions for Thought

For Further Reading

LEARNING OBJECTIVES

AFTER READING THE CHAPTER, YOU SHOULD BE ABLE TO DO THE FOLLOWING:

- Outline the reasons for family planning.

- Discuss basic facts about oral contraceptives: how they prevent conception; types and administration; effectiveness; advantages and health benefits; risks; and side effects.

- Discuss basic facts about other forms of hormonal contraceptives.

- Relate basic facts about the use of vaginal spermicides as contraceptives.

- Describe the use of intrauterine devices and other mechanical devices or barrier methods: male condom, female condom, diaphragm, cervical cap, and contraceptive sponge.

- Describe the processes of male and female sterilization: vasectomy and tubal ligation.

- Explain methods of birth control without the use of devices, including the calendar method, withdrawal, and noncoital stimulation.

- Summarize the considerations in choosing which method of contraception to use.

- Discuss the legal, moral, social and realistic, and psychological and personal considerations in relation to abortion.

- Summarize the basic facts about infertility: causes; infertility and subjective well-being; treatments; and alternative means of conception.

- Discuss basic issues in relation to adoption and foster care.

- Discuss the basic issues and trends in relation to childlessness, smaller families, and delayed parenthood.

They met at a small college in Oklahoma, fell in love, and decided to marry and make a family—much like countless other couples. Unlike most, they decided (after long and prayerful consideration) NOT to have biological children. Why? Vernita is legally blind because of a hereditary trait; Bob was born with only a left arm. They did not want to pass along any genetic liabilities: they decided to adopt instead.

They finished degrees in education and sociology and when they felt ready for parenthood, applied to adopt. Immediately they ran into barriers. "How will you be able to feed a baby or change a dirty diaper?" agency workers asked Vernita. She answered that washing hands after changing diapers is a good idea—even for people with excellent vision. They were not impressed or amused.

After almost 2 years of delays and diversions, Bob and Vernita were offered a charming little guy with many physical challenges. They reasoned that their personal lives and professional training made them uniquely qualified to be parents to children with special needs. Kris was followed in a few years by Ricky, an African American child who was severely cognitively impaired as a result of strokes during his birth. "Family members, friends, lots of people didn't think we should cross racial lines or take a child so severely challenged," Bob observed.

In time, seven other children joined the family—Kevin and Becky as teens from foster care; Domingo, Kyle, Mark, and Victor from outside the United States; Nik as a newborn. The children are grown now; all have finished high school; some have children of their own; most work or help in the care of the others. The successes and victories of the family have been considerable. Bob and Vernita have been recognized locally and nationally for their service to children.

They have also had difficult and sad times. Mark could not adjust to life in the United States and returned to Thailand when he was old enough: They no longer hear from him. In the summer of 2012, Ricky died unexpectedly during an attack of pancreatitis. They have worked long and hard hours to feed, house, and transport their crew—and to secure medical and social services for their special needs. They have had a deep and abiding conviction that their family planning decision was right. In January 2015, Bob died after a series of health problems; the family grieves but continues strong.

We live in a time when efficient and safe methods of contraception are readily available. Without birth control, couples must resign themselves to having one child after another or to avoid sexual relations after they have the number of children they desire or can afford. Contraception has improved the lives of millions of people because it helps people to plan whether they want to have children, the number of children they want to have, and the time that is best for all concerned. This chapter provides an overview of contraceptive methods. Because abortion is such a polarizing issue today, this chapter examines the different sides of the controversial issue. Some couples will have fertility problems, and the chapter examines infertility treatments and adoption.

The Importance of Family Planning

There are several reasons why individuals use **family planning**—defined as having children by choice and not by chance and having the number of children wanted at the time planned. One reason is health. Births to females who are too young or too old and births that are close together pose health risks for both mothers and children (Kail and Cavanaugh 2016). Numerous studies have established that as women pass age 35, they (and their babies) are at increasing risk for miscarriage, preterm birth, chromosomal abnormalities, gestational diabetes, placenta previa, abruption, and perinatal death (Cleary-Goldman 2005; Tough et al. 2002).

Economics is also a major reason for family planning. As noted in Chapter 8, it costs a middle-class family about $245,340 to raise a child to age 18 and college will cost an additional $80,000 to $150,000 and possibly much more. It does not take much imagination to realize that having a large number of children places a great strain on the family budget.

Timing is an important issue in family planning and a major determinant of childbirth's effect on a family. For example, many teenagers are sexually active but have no desire to become parents at such a young age. In one year in the United States alone, an estimated 1.65 million pregnancies among females ages 15 to 19 were avoided through the use of contraceptives (Kahn, Brindis, and Glei 1999). People typically want to wait to have a child until they finish their education, get married, and/or are situated in their careers. They have a plan for their lives, and the timing of parenthood is part of that plan.

The timing of parenthood affects the way people fill the roles of mothers and fathers. Younger parents have more energy, for example. Older parents may have greater financial and emotional stability. A delay in becoming parents gives a couple time to solidify their marriage before children enter the mix.

Family planning is often necessary for the good of the marriage and the family. The potential negative psychological impact on the mother and father is lessened considerably if parenthood is chosen and welcomed. Having children imposes strains on a marriage; having children early in a relationship adds additional stress. Because both premarital pregnancy and early postmarital pregnancy are associated with a higher-than-average divorce rate, many of these children grow up in a single-parent household.

In recent years, much emphasis has been placed on the humanitarian and ecological importance of family planning. According to the World Population Clock (2016), the world now has 7.4 billion people, and the population in the world's 50 least-developed countries is forecast to double by 2050. Can the world's resources support this many people? More than half of the people in the world already live in poverty. Family planning thus has become an important political issue for many humanitarian groups.

Before we begin our discussion of birth control methods, note that abstinence is the most effective form of birth control. Abstinence means not having

family planning Having children by choice and not by chance; having the number of children wanted at the time planned.

What Is a Strong Family?

First of all, what do we mean by a *family*? Does a family have to include children? Family, of course—and for many people—does include children. Family includes spouses, aunts, cousins, nephews, friends—all those people we acquire by birth or by living. Any definition of family, then, must be broad and designed to be inclusive rather than exclusive. We suggest this definition: *a family is two or more people who are committed to each other and who share resources, decisions, and values.* The definition includes couples who decide to remain child free and devoted to each other, but who dote on their nieces and nephews (or pets); couples who have 1 child or 10 or the traditional 2; singles who have children; families that include a live-in grandma; and families blended from two previous families.

What, then, makes a family *strong* (healthy and happy)? Certainly it is more than the absence of problems. Strong families have troubles just like everyone else. Families in Russia face extreme economic trials; families in Central America live with political unrest. Closer to home, families deal with unemployment, wildfires, hurricanes, and illness. To be a strong family is not to be without challenges. It is much, much more.

Strong families are pleasant, positive places to live because members have learned some beneficial ways of treating one another. Family members can count on one another for support, love, and loyalty.

Members of strong families feel good about themselves as a family unit or team; they have a sense of belonging to one another—a sense of *we*. At the same time, no individual gets smothered; each person is encouraged to develop his or her potential.

Strong families are able to survive the crises that come their way. They unite to meet challenges; they are effective problem solvers. They pull together to get through.

Simply put, a strong family is made up of people (2 or 22) who love and care for one another—always and regardless.

Training programs and community support have helped many teenagers adjust to their roles as new parents.

sexual intercourse with anyone. For most of the past 30 years, the U.S. government has been funding programs to teach "abstinence only" in public schools in an effort to encourage teens to delay becoming sexually active to reduce the teen pregnancy rate and curb the spread of STDs. Considerable criticism has been aimed at abstinence-only programs for not being as effective as more comprehensive sex education programs. Recent legislation requires programs to demonstrate their effectiveness or "show promise" to receive funding.

Hormonal Control

The invention of birth control pills, or oral contraceptives, in the 1960s was a major advancement in contraceptive technology. The pill was more effective than any previous method in preventing pregnancy, and it was a no-mess, no-fuss alternative to condoms and diaphragms. Other forms of hormonal birth control have now been developed and tested and are available to the public.

Oral Contraceptives

Oral contraceptives contain two synthetically produced female sex hormones that are chemically similar to ones a woman already produces in her body to regulate ovulation and the menstrual cycle. The natural hormones are estrogen and progesterone (progestin is the artificially produced equivalent). By manipulating the amount of these two hormones in the woman's bloodstream, birth control pills prevent conception in three ways:

1. Ovulation is prevented in about 90% of menstrual cycles.

2. The cervical mucus remains thick and sticky throughout the month, blocking the entrance to the uterus and making penetration by the sperm difficult.

3. It is also thought that the endometrium, the inner lining of the uterus, is altered so that successful implantation and nourishment of a fertilized ovum are difficult.

TYPES OF ORAL CONTRACEPTIVES There are several types of pills. **Combination pills** contain both estrogen and progestin. The pill should never be taken without a physical examination and a doctor's prescription and guidance. The cost of the pill ranges from $10 to $90 per month depending on insurance, use of generics or name brands, etc. (Bedsider 2016). A visit to the doctor and any tests will be extra.

Most pills are packaged in 21- or 28-pill packets. For the 21-pill packet, 1 pill is taken daily for 3 weeks, followed by a week of no pills. For the 28-pill packet, the 3 weeks of hormone-containing pills are followed by a week of placebos. **Placebos** allow the user to keep the routine of taking a pill every day; some contain iron as a nutritional supplement. A menstrual period/withdrawal bleed happens during the time the woman is not receiving hormones. Two combination pills (Yaz 28 and Loestrin 24Fe) use 24 active days followed by 4 days of placebos. They offer fewer hormone fluctuations than other pills and are used to reduce the severe mood swings and physical symptoms of premenstrual dysphoric disorder. An extended-cycle option (such as Seasonale) uses 84 active pills and 7 placebos; menstrual periods happen every 3 months (WebMD 2016).

Another form of pill (the **mini-pill**) contains only progestin and is taken daily with no break. Women who experience severe side effects with combined pills (high blood pressure and nausea, for example) or who are breastfeeding can usually use progestin-only pills. However, progestin-only pills must be taken at the same time each day to be most effective (Bedsider 2016). If a woman forgets to take a pill, she should consult the instructions on the package or ask her physician. A backup method of contraception may be needed to ensure protection.

Some kinds of oral contraceptives (both combined and progestin only) can be used as **emergency contraceptive pills** (ECPs) to prevent pregnancy following unprotected sexual intercourse. A woman may require emergency contraception because the contraceptive method she was using failed (a condom broke, for example), she neglected to use contraception, or she was sexually assaulted.

In the United States, Plan B One-Step (levonorgestrel), Next Choice, Ella (ulipristal acetate), and several other brands are available as emergency contraceptives. All are taken in one or two doses, 3 to 5 days after unprotected sex; however, they are more effective the sooner they are used. Most brands are available without a prescription to persons older than age 17. A prescription is required for persons under age 17 and for Ella. Some pharmacies sell Plan B One-Step without a prescription or age requirements. The cost is about $60 (Bedsider 2016).

Hormonal ECPs prevent pregnancy by delaying or preventing ovulation or by interfering with fertilization (reducing sperm motility, for example); they do not seem to end an established pregnancy (as does Mifeprex). ECPs make it much less likely (89% less) that conception will happen but they are not effective as routine birth control. And although they are considered safe, they should not be used

oral contraceptives Birth control pills taken orally (by mouth).

combination pills Oral contraceptives containing both estrogen and progestin.

placebo A pill that has no pharmacological effect.

mini-pill An oral contraceptive containing progestin only.

emergency contraceptive pills Oral contraceptives taken after intercourse to prevent unwanted pregnancy.

routinely as birth control. Also, they provide no protection against STDs (WebMD 2016).

ADVANTAGES OF ORAL CONTRACEPTIVES The combination birth control pill is one of the most effective contraceptives, with the typical user's effectiveness rate being 91% (Bedsider 2016). Effectiveness rates are given in two ways that can vary significantly. *Perfect use* rates include only people who use the method consistently and correctly. *Actual* or *typical use* rates include those who use the method incorrectly or inconsistently (forget to take a pill, for example). The perfect-use rate for the pill is 99% (Bedsider 2016; Cornforth 2009; WebMD 2016).

The pill is easy to use and convenient; it does not interfere with spontaneity. The birth control pill is a reversible contraceptive; that is, after a woman stops taking it, her fertility returns. However, some women who stop taking the pill to become pregnant take slightly longer to conceive than do those who have not been on the pill. A minority of women who have been on the pill become more fertile after ceasing to take it, usually because of more regular menstruation and ovulation.

There are also some noncontraceptive health benefits associated with oral contraceptives. The pill's positive effects on the following health problems are well documented:

- **BENIGN BREAST DISEASE.** Oral contraceptives reduce benign breast disease. The longer the pill is used, the lower the incidence of the disease.

- **CYSTS OF THE OVARY.** The combination pills suppress ovarian activity and reduce ovarian cysts.

- **IRON-DEFICIENCY ANEMIA.** Oral contraceptive users suffer approximately 45% less iron-deficiency anemia than do nonusers.

- **PELVIC INFLAMMATORY DISEASE (PID).** Pill users have only half the risk of developing PID. When the pill is used for 1 year or longer, the rate is 70% (Speroff and Darney 2005).

- **ECTOPIC PREGNANCY.** Current users of oral contraceptives have nearly complete protection against this condition.

The pill also seems to offer protection against rheumatoid arthritis, endometriosis, osteoporosis, premenstrual syndrome, and acne (Speroff and Darney 2005). Although the evidence is not conclusive, pill users appear to be only half as likely to develop these conditions. Women who have used oral contraceptives appear to be about half as likely to develop ovarian and endometrial cancer as are women who have never used the pill ("Combined oral contraceptive pills" 2009). The protective effects of the pill against two of the most common cancers in American women appear to be long-lasting (Coker, Harlap, and Fortney 1993; "Combined oral contraceptive pills" 2009).

DISADVANTAGES OF ORAL CONTRACEPTIVES Birth control pills do not protect against STDs, although they do lower the risk of PID. Regular use of condoms is recommended for women taking oral contraceptives unless they are in a monogamous relationship with an uninfected partner.

One of the most serious concerns associated with the birth control pill is that it may cause blood clots, increasing the risk of thrombosis, pulmonary embolism, stroke, and heart attack. Consequently, combined oral contraceptives are not recommended for women with preexisting cardiovascular disease, a family history of blood clots, high cholesterol levels, or severe obesity or for women who are smokers ("Combined oral contraceptive pills" 2009; WebMD 2016).

Many people believe that another drawback of the combination pill is the possible increased risk of breast cancer. However, the current consensus is that the risk is small and that the tumors spread less aggressively than they would in women who were not on the pill ("Combined oral contraceptive pills" 2009). A study of 9,200 women ages 35 to 64 found no increased risk of breast cancer in pill users, with neither race, age, weight, length of time on the pill, nor type of pill used making any difference (Marchbanks et al. 2002). In fact, the increased risk may be caused not by use of the pill but because of the greater likelihood that women taking the pill will also have routine screenings that detect the cancer. However, women who have a family history of breast cancer may wish to discuss alternative contraceptives with their doctor. All women, whether they use oral contraceptives or not, are urged to get annual breast examinations and to perform self-exams monthly.

There is an increase in the risk of cervical cancer among pill users, especially among long-term users who started having sex early and have had multiple sex partners (Cancer Research UK 2006; Hatcher et al. 2011). Again, it is difficult to sort out variables. Women who have been sexually active longer and/or with multiple partners are already at increased risk of contracting an STD. Women who are using only the pill for contraception have no protection from STD infection, including HPV. Two forms of HPV (types 16 and 18) are responsible for large numbers of cervical cancers. Consequently, it is recommended that women consider taking one of the vaccines that protect against the types of HPV linked to cervical cancer and that they have regular Pap tests to detect the early development of cervical cancer.

The effect of taking the pill on sexual drive and frequency of intercourse is variable. For some women the pill alters vaginal secretions and decreases levels of free testosterone, which may decrease sexual drive. However, women who are not having to be concerned about a pregnancy may find sexual interest and interactions enhanced. Some women also feel more comfortable because the pill allows them to make contraception decisions. She does not have to wonder whether he brought a condom or will agree to use one, for example.

Other side effects of the pill, depending on the particular combination of ingredients, can include nausea, weight gain, swollen breasts, headaches, and nervousness. Many of the unpleasant side effects disappear after a woman's metabolism adjusts to the pill or after her doctor alters brands or dosage.

Other Forms of Hormonal Contraceptives

In recent years, scientists have been working to improve hormonal contraception. Since the primary reason for the pill's failure as a contraceptive is failure to take it every day, one of the main focuses of this research has been on methods of safely delivering the hormones in longer-lasting doses.

One method of delivering longer-lasting doses of hormones is by injecting them into the muscle (usually the buttocks or upper arm). Depo-Provera contains high doses of progestin and is effective (94% to 99%) in preventing pregnancy. Each **progestin injection** lasts 3 months.

Side effects of Depo-Provera include changes in the menstrual period (irregular or absent), weight gain, breast tenderness, and depression. Long-term use of Depo-Provera (more than 2 years) may result in loss of bone density; however, it returns when

Depo-Provera is stopped ("Depo-Provera" 2008; WebMD 2016). And there is no increased risk of blood clots or cardiovascular disease with Depo-Provera. Two drawbacks, however, are that the injection does not protect against STDs and must be given by a physician or nurse. The cost is $50 to $120 per injection plus the cost of an office visit and tests (Bedsider 2016). The return of fertility may take several months after Depo-Provera is stopped, but injections should not be skipped or delayed because some women begin ovulating quickly.

Depo-Provera can be used by women with seizure disorders and seems to reduce the risk of cervical cancer and PID ("Injectable" 2007). A major advantage, of course, is that one injection takes care of birth control for 3 months.

Another way of delivering long-lasting doses of hormones is using an implant. **Implants** are matchstick-size rods that release a steady, low dose of progestin. Nexplanon is the brand available in the United States (Bedsider 2016).

Implants can cause the same side effects as other progestin-only contraceptives—irregular menstrual periods and weight gain, for example. A doctor places the implant under the skin of the inner upper arm. Implants are effective (99%) for about 3 years—although they can be removed earlier if desired. The cost for the initial exam, insertion, and the implant itself ranges from $400 to $900; removal costs $100 to $300 (Bedsider 2016). To compare the cost to that of other methods, remember that this is for 3 years; most insurance covers implants.

A **vaginal ring** is a flexible, transparent ring about two inches in diameter that is inserted into the vagina. It contains a combination of estrogen and progestin and releases these continuously at a low dose. A woman must insert a new ring every month; the ring is in place for 3 weeks, with the fourth week ring-free to allow the menstrual period to happen. The ring is about 91% to 99% effective in

progestin injection An injection of progestin to prevent pregnancy.

implant A matchstick-size device that is placed under the skin and releases progestin.

vaginal ring A flexible, transparent ring that is inserted into the vagina and releases a combination of estrogen and progestin continuously at a low dose for 1 month.

preventing pregnancy, but it offers no protection against STDs. Side effects can include vaginal infections and irritation as well as risk factors similar to those of other combined oral contraceptives. An initial exam ($35 to $250) and prescription are required for the ring; each ring costs $30 to $80 (Bedsider 2015).

Introduced in 2001, the **contraceptive patch** is a 1¾-inch adhesive square that is applied to the buttocks, abdomen, or upper body. It releases the hormones estrogen and progestin through the skin. The patch is applied each week for 3 consecutive weeks; the fourth week is patch free to allow a menstrual period. The patch has a 91% to 99% effectiveness rate (possibly less in women who weigh more than 198 pounds), but it does not protect against STDs. The most common side effects are breast tenderness, headache, patch-site irritation, and nausea.

Because patch users are exposed to higher levels of estrogen than are pill users, there may be increased risk of side effects such as stroke, blood clots, and cardiovascular disease. Cost for the patch includes a physician's exam ($35 to $250) and $30 to $80 per month for the patches (Bedsider 2016).

The **intrauterine system** (IUS) is a way of delivering hormones by putting them in a device (such as Mirena, Skyla, or Liletta) that is inserted into the uterus to release small amounts of progestin continuously for 3 to 6 years. When a woman has an IUS, her cervical mucus becomes thicker, which makes it difficult for sperm to enter the uterine cavity. An IUS also suppresses the cyclic growth of the endometrium and, consequently, prevents implantation. The effectiveness of the IUS is similar to that of other intrauterine devices (IUDs). Side effects include bleeding between periods, headaches, breast tenderness, and nausea. These typically occur only during the first months of use. A broader description of IUDs is presented later in this chapter.

AT ISSUE TODAY

The Abortion Pill

After first being approved for use by the French in 1988, the drug formerly known as RU-486 was approved for use in the United States by the Food and Drug Administration (FDA) in 2000. Mifepristone, marketed as Mifeprex, is a drug used for the termination of early pregnancy, defined as 49 days or less from the beginning of the last menstrual period. It has not been approved for use as a "morning-after pill" or as a means to end pregnancy after 49 days.

Mifeprex works by blocking production of the hormone progesterone, which is necessary to maintain a pregnancy. The FDA-approved regimen requires three visits to a doctor's office. During the first visit, she takes three tablets of Mifeprex. Two days later, she visits the doctor to take two pills of a prostaglandin called misoprostol, which helps the uterus expel the embryo. A third visit to the doctor's office or clinic is required 12 days later to confirm that the pregnancy has been terminated.

Nearly all women using Mifeprex experience at least one of its side effects, which include bleeding, cramps, and nausea. Bleeding and spotting usually occur for 9 to 16 days. In July 2005, the FDA issued a public health advisory highlighting the risk of blood infection when using Mifeprex after four cases of death from infection were reported.

Mifeprex can be distributed only through qualified doctors and is not available through pharmacies. To be qualified, doctors must be able to accurately determine the duration of a pregnancy, detect whether it is an ectopic (tubal) pregnancy, and verify that they will be able to provide surgical intervention in case of an incomplete abortion or severe bleeding.

About 5 to 8 women in 100 will experience severe bleeding or an incomplete abortion. Because of the need for doctor visits, exams, ultrasound, and the high cost of the medication itself, use of Mifeprex costs as much as or more than early-term surgical abortion ($300 to $800) (Planned Parenthood 2014; Rx List 2008).

Vaginal Spermicides

Spermicides, or chemicals that kill sperm, come in the form of foam, suppository, cream, jelly, and, most recently, film. They work in two ways: (1) by blocking the entrance to the uterus and (2) by immobilizing the sperm. To be most effective, they must be inserted in the very back of the vagina, over the cervix. Suppositories and films must be inserted at least 10 to 15 minutes before intercourse to become effective. Spermicides lose their effectiveness within about an hour, so they must be reapplied each time intercourse is repeated.

The effectiveness of spermicides varies greatly; it has been estimated that their effectiveness rate is 72% to 82%. Foam can be used alone because it spreads more evenly and blocks the cervix more adequately than other spermicides. Creams and jellies are usually used in conjunction with a diaphragm, cervical cap, or condom.

Vaginal contraceptive film is a newer product; once the transparent 2-inch square is inserted, it dissolves into a gel over the cervix. It is less messy than foams and jellies, which usually create some vaginal discharge, and it seems less irritating for those people who have an allergic reaction to other forms of spermicides.

Spermicides do not protect against HIV and, because they can irritate vaginal tissues, may even increase the risk (Bedsider 2016). Both men and women may experience burning or other adverse reactions to the chemicals, including urinary tract infections in some women. Allergic responses can sometimes be alleviated by switching to another type or brand of spermicide. Spermicides are available without a prescription at a cost of about $1.50 per use.

Intrauterine Devices

An **intrauterine device** (IUD) is made of plastic; it is placed in the uterus to prevent pregnancy. IUDs contain progestin (Mirena, Skyla, and Liletta) or copper (ParaGard); both the "T" shape of the IUD and the progestin/copper inhibit fertilization and also interfere with the implantation of fertilized eggs.

The IUD must be inserted by a physician who loads the IUD in an inserter that resembles a plastic straw and threads it through the cervical canal and into the uterine cavity. The IUD is unwound into a straight line while in the inserter but resumes its former shape when released in the uterus. A thin plastic thread extends from the lower end of the IUD through the cervical canal and into the upper vagina, allowing the woman to check to make sure that the IUD is still in place.

IUDs are commonly used worldwide and were popular in the United States until the 1970s, when there was a high incidence of pelvic infections and infertility and even some deaths among users of a type of IUD called the Dalkon Shield. A number of lawsuits were filed against the manufacturer, and the Dalkon Shield was withdrawn from the market. Other types of IUDs, such as the Lippes Loop and the Copper T, had much better safety records, but because of the widespread publicity about the Dalkon Shield, women became apprehensive about using IUDs.

In 1989, an improved Copper T (380A or ParaGard) was approved for use. It and the Mirena have helped IUDs make a comeback in popularity in the United States. IUDs have an effectiveness rate of better than 99%. Once an IUD is inserted, it requires no attention except periodic checking of the string to make sure it has not been expelled. Mirena must be replaced every 5 or 6 years; Skyla and Liletta every 3 years; ParaGard is effective for 10 to 12 years (Bedsider 2016; Painter 2012).

Most women report discomfort and cramping during and after IUD insertion. Side effects of ParaGard include increased menstrual pain and bleeding. Mirena, in contrast, may decrease these. Skyla is the smallest of the IUDs; Skyla and Liletta are the only ones approved for use in women who have not had children. IUDs carry a slightly increased risk of PID, although some studies suggest the risk

contraceptive patch A patch applied weekly to the buttocks, abdomen, or upper torso that releases hormones to prevent pregnancy.

intrauterine system A contraceptive device that is inserted into the uterus and releases small amounts of progestin continuously for 3 to 6 years.

spermicides Chemicals that are toxic to sperm and are used as a contraceptive in the form of foam, suppository, cream, jelly, or film.

intrauterine device A device that is inserted into the uterus and worn there as a means of preventing pregnancy.

of infection is limited to the first 20 days after insertion (Painter 2012). None protect against STDs. The cost of Mirena, Skyla, Liletta, or ParaGard plus an exam/office visit for insertion and follow-up visits ranges from $500 to $1,000 (Bedsider 2016; Painter 2012).

Barrier Methods

Some of the earliest forms of contraception were barrier methods designed to prevent the meeting of sperm and ovum. The condom was in use as early as the sixteenth century in Italy, primarily to provide protection against syphilis. Reusable diaphragms and cervical caps were in use in Europe in the 1800s (Hatcher et al. 2011).

Although condoms used with vaginal spermicides are more effective than other barrier methods in preventing pregnancy, all barrier methods are less effective than hormonal methods or IUDs. However, they have few adverse side effects and, when used correctly, latex condoms can provide protection against STDs.

Condoms

The **male condom** is usually made of thin, strong latex or, less frequently, of polyurethane or natural membranes. It is placed over the end of the erect penis and then unrolled to enclose the penile shaft. Condoms come in different styles and colors. (Read the label on packages of "novelty" condoms because some of these are NOT intended for pregnancy prevention or STD protection.) Some have a teat on the end to receive the ejaculate. If not, it should be unrolled on the penis so as to leave a half-inch space at the end to receive the semen. Some condoms are packaged singly in fluid, which provides lubrication and allows the penis to be inserted into the vagina easily. If a condom is not lubricated, a contraceptive jelly or cream may be used to aid penetration and to prevent the condom from tearing on insertion. Vaseline, baby oil, and other petroleum- or oil-based products should never be used because they cause the condom to deteriorate.

The typical effectiveness of the male condom by itself is 82%; using a spermicide with the condom increases effectiveness significantly (98%). When failure occurs, it is for one or more of several reasons: (1) the condom has a hole in it, (2) it ruptures, or (3) it slips off. The most common reason for failure of condoms is slipping off the shaft of the penis during either intercourse or withdrawal, allowing the semen to leak out. Side effects of condoms are few. Some people are allergic to latex and must use polyurethane or animal skin. Condoms may decrease sensation for both men and women. Some couples feel condom use interferes with spontaneity in sexual interaction. A new condom must be used for each intercourse. Condoms are widely available without prescription for about $1 to $2 each (Bedsider 2016).

Condoms are sometimes used in addition to other methods of birth control to prevent the spread of STDs. Usage rates are still much too low, however. Findings show that women adopting long-term hormonal contraceptive methods decrease their use of condoms and increase their risk of contracting HIV and other STDs (Cushman et al. 1998). Some 68% of men and 72% of women report they never use condoms; 7% of both report they sometimes use condoms; 25% of men and 21% of women say they always use condoms (Centers for Disease Control and Prevention 2012). When a group of men who are at higher risk for HIV infection (intravenous drug users) were asked about condom use, only 12% responded that they use them consistently with their regular partners and 17% use them consistently with regular and other partners (Kapadia et al. 2007).

Condoms are the most effective contraceptive method for avoiding STDs and reducing the risk of HIV infection. The type and quality of the condom used are important. For example, lambskin condoms, often preferred for their sensitivity, allow the passage of HIV, herpes, and hepatitis viruses through the membrane itself. Syphilis and gonorrhea bacteria are too large to pass through. A latex condom does not allow leakage of small viral organisms unless the condom is torn or improperly used.

A **female or internal condom** is somewhat like a polyurethane plastic bag with a flexible ring at the closed end and another at the open end. The upper ring helps with insertion and keeps the closed end of the condom in place over the cervix; the lower ring keeps the condom from being pushed inside the vagina and also covers part of the vulva, thus protecting a larger genital area from STDs than does the male condom.

Effectiveness rates for the female condom range from 79% alone to 95% with spermicide. As with the male condom, failures are largely caused by breakage, slippage, or spillage. They must also be removed carefully and immediately after sex and a new condom must be used for each intercourse. Some women may experience irritation of the vagina or vulva by the outer ring. The female condom allows women who do not want to use hormonal or other intrusive methods of birth control to exercise control in contraceptive decisions. Female condoms are widely available without prescription for about $2 to $4 each (Bedsider 2016).

Diaphragm

The **diaphragm** is a thick, dome-shaped silicone cup with a flexible ring, designed to cover the cervical opening. It comes in a variety of sizes and most must be fitted to each woman by a physician; a new diaphragm, the Caya, is one-size-fits-all. A snug fit is especially important, since part of the diaphragm's effectiveness as a contraceptive depends on its forming an impenetrable shield over the entrance to the uterus. Otherwise, sperm can get around the edges of the diaphragm and enter the cervix.

To complete the diaphragm's effectiveness, spermicidal cream or jelly is smeared in the cup fitting against the cervix and about the rim to create a protective seal. For additional protection, foam may be inserted into the vagina after the diaphragm is in place and before each act of intercourse. The diaphragm should not be removed until at least 6 hours after intercourse. The typical effectiveness rate for the diaphragm plus spermicide is 88%.

There are few side effects from the diaphragm. Some women report vaginal irritation from the silicone or the spermicides. Other risks include urinary tract and vaginal infections. To reduce the risk of toxic shock syndrome, the diaphragm should not be left in place more than 24 hours or used during vaginal bleeding, including menstruation. The diaphragm does not protect against STDs. Cost of the diaphragm is $15 to $75 plus the exam needed to fit it ($50 to $200). A diaphragm typically lasts for 2 years, but must be refitted after a pregnancy or weight change of 20% (Bedsider 2016).

Cervical Cap

The **cervical cap** (FemCap) is a small cup, shaped rather like a sailor's hat, that fits tightly across the cervix and prevents sperm from entering the uterus. Like the diaphragm, it is used with a spermicide and inserted shortly before intercourse. The cap is approximately as effective (86%) as the diaphragm for

women who have not had children (nulliparous); however, effectiveness for women who have had children (parous) drops to 71%. Side effects and risks are the same as for the diaphragm. The cap requires an exam for fitting and instructions in use ($50 to $200); the cost of the cap is about $60 to $75. The cap typically must be replaced each year (Bedsider 2016).

Contraceptive Sponge

The **contraceptive sponge** is a soft disk of polyurethane foam that contains spermicide. It fits over the cervix to block and absorb semen; it also releases spermicide to increase effectiveness. The sponge is inserted up to 24 hours before sex and left in place for at least 6 hours after sex.

Typical effectiveness rates are 84% for nulliparous women, with a decline to 68% for women who have had children. Side effects include irritation or allergic reaction from the spermicide or sponge material as well as vaginal itching or dryness. Sponges do not provide protection from STDs. Single sponges cost about $5 and are available without prescription (Bedsider 2016).

Sterilization

Slightly more than 10 million women ages 15 to 44 in the United States have chosen **sterilization** as their means of birth control. Sterilization is the

male condom A latex sheath worn over the penis to prevent sperm from being ejaculated into the vagina; also prevents the spread of STDs.

female or internal condom A polyurethane pouch inserted in the vagina to collect sperm, preventing fertilization.

diaphragm A thick, dome-shape, silicone cup that is stretched over a collapsible ring, designed to cover the cervical opening to prevent sperm from entering the uterus.

cervical cap A small, thimble-shape, rubber barrier that fits over the cervix and prevents sperm from entering the uterus.

contraceptive sponge A polyurethane foam disk that contains spermicide and is placed over the cervix to block and absorb semen.

sterilization The process of rendering a person infertile by performing either a vasectomy in the male or tubal ligation in the female.

second leading method of birth control among all women (the contraceptive pill being the first) and is the leading method of birth control in women age 35 and older (Guttmacher Institute 2012). Some female sterilizations now can be performed in a physician's office. More women have been sterilized than men, although the acceptance of vasectomy is increasing.

Vasectomy

Male sterilization, or **vasectomy**, is a simple operation, requiring only 15 to 30 minutes in a doctor's office. A small incision is made in the upper part of the scrotum, and the vasa deferentia (the ducts that carry sperm from the testicles to the penis) are tied, cauterized, or blocked; local anesthesia is used. A new "nonscalpel" method of performing a vasectomy is done by making a very small hole in the scrotum to access the vasa and to block or cauterize them (Planned Parenthood 2014; Vuong 2012). Some bruising and swelling of the scrotum may happen (ice packs help relieve the pain) and infection is a rare complication. Most men resume work in a day or two and sex within a week.

Vasectomy is more than 99% effective. When failure occurs, it is because of (1) a spontaneous rejoining of the severed ends of a vas deferens, (2) a failure on the part of the doctor to tie an accessory vas (some men have three or four), or (3) intercourse without using other contraceptives while there are still residual sperm in the tubes (about 3 months). As a means of fertility control, vasectomy is effective, is less costly ($350 to $1,000) and less complicated than tubal ligation (female sterilization), and has fewer long-term health risks.

There are a number of misconceptions regarding vasectomies. A vasectomy does not involve **castration**, which is the removal of the testicles. With a vasectomy, the man continues to ejaculate semen, but it contains no sperm. His physical ability to have sexual relations is in no way affected; he still has erections, orgasms, and ejaculation as usual. In addition, his voice, body hair, musculature, and beard growth remain unchanged. And he still produces male hormones that are released by the testicles into the bloodstream. Research indicates no adverse health consequences of vasectomy. It appears unlikely to raise men's chances of developing either prostate or testicular cancer (Hatcher et al. 2011; Planned Parenthood 2014).

Vasectomy should be considered permanent, since the chances of rejoining the vasa deferentia through surgery are uncertain. The effectiveness of microsurgery to reverse the vasectomy depends on the type of vasectomy, the skill of the surgeon, and how much time has lapsed since the vasectomy (less than 10 to 15 years is better). About 95% of men have motile sperm in their ejaculate within a year of vasectomy reversal. Pregnancy success rates are another measure of the success of the reversal. Depending on the time between vasectomy and reversal, the difficulty of the surgery, and age of the men's partners, pregnancy rates of 50% to 80% are reported under ideal conditions. Rates drop to 20% to 40% in worse conditions (Planned Parenthood 2014; Woolcott 2014). Some men who decide to have a vasectomy have some of their sperm frozen in a sperm bank.

Female Sterilization

Female sterilization is accomplished by severing or closing the fallopian tubes so that mature egg cells cannot be transported to the uterus and sperm cannot travel up the fallopian tubes to the egg. Since the ovaries and the secretion of female hormones are in no way disturbed, there is no change in a woman's physique, menstrual cycle, sexual interest, or sexual capacity. In many cases, her interest in sex and her sexual responsiveness improve because the fear of unwanted pregnancy has been removed.

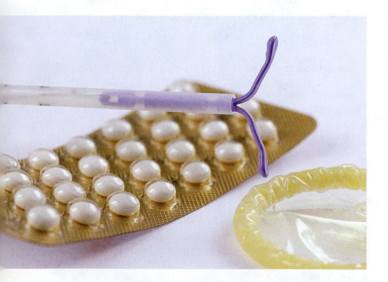

The variety of contraceptives from which to choose is considerable. How does one make the best choice? What are the risks of pregnancy and the health risks associated with each type of contraception?

The most widely used method of **tubal ligation** is **laparoscopy**. With this surgical method, the physician introduces a tubular instrument through a small incision in the abdominal wall and closes the fallopian tubes with tubal rings or clips or through electrocautery. Tubal ligation can also be performed during a cesarean section or through a small incision in the vagina. Side effects include abdominal soreness and pain, reaction to anesthesia, and possible infection. Ligation takes about 30 minutes in a hospital or clinic; most women go home the same day and need only a few days to recover.

Typical effectiveness rates for tubal ligation are greater than 99%. When a pregnancy occurs, it is usually because of an existing, undetected pregnancy at the time of the surgery or the tubes reopening as a result of the body's natural healing process. Younger women have higher failure rates. If a pregnancy occurs, the risk of ectopic pregnancy is greater following tubal ligation (Bedsider 2016; Planned Parenthood 2014). Tubal ligation can be reversed in some cases by microsurgery. Because this is a serious surgery, women who wish to become pregnant after tubal ligation may consider in vitro fertilization instead of reversal.

Sterilization can also be accomplished by blocking the fallopian tubes with inserts (Essure). In this method, a physician accesses the fallopian tubes (via the vagina) and places small, flexible inserts in the tubes. In time (about 3 months), scar tissue grows around the inserts and blocks the tubes. The procedure can be performed in a doctor's office under local anesthetic and requires no incision. Common side effects are mild to moderate pain during the procedure and vaginal bleeding for a few days after. Essure is 97% effective, although another form of birth control must be used until the scar tissue is formed. The cost of sterilization is between $1,500 and $6,000 (Bedsider 2016; Planned Parenthood 2014).

Fertility Awareness

Some people, for religious or philosophical reasons, do not want to use artificial means of birth control. Some advantages of "natural" methods are that they are free and do not require a trip to the drugstore or the doctor's office. However, most are less reliable than other methods of birth control, they provide no protection against STDs, and they require long periods of abstinence (see Table 11.1).

Calendar Method

The **calendar method** of birth control relies on timing coitus so that it occurs only during the time when a woman is least likely to conceive. This means predicting when ovulation occurs and allowing for the viability of ova and sperm. Typically, a woman ovulates 14 days before her next menstrual cycle, with a range of 12 to 16 days being common. Although authorities differ in their estimates, most agree that sperm and ova are viable for at least 48 hours. A woman using the calendar method is asked to keep a record of the number of days in her menstrual cycles for several months. Then she can calculate her most likely fertile times ("Calendar birth control method" 2008). Figure 11.1 illustrates the schedules of the most and least likely times for conception of women with 26- and 31-day cycles and the schedule for a woman whose cycle varies from 26 to 31 days. A woman whose cycles are irregular will have a harder time estimating when ovulation will occur; she is safer to abstain for a longer period. Of course, these are only calculations based on "typical" and "regular." Ovulation can happen at any time in a woman's cycle—even during menstruation.

STANDARD DAYS METHOD The standard days method is a form of calendar method that allows a woman to track her cycle using a special string of 32 beads of various colors (CycleBeads); cost is $14 to $27. On the first day of her menstrual period, she puts a rubber ring attached to the string of beads onto the one red bead. Each day she moves the ring forward one bead. When the ring is on a dark or colored bead, she is less likely to conceive. When the ring is on a white or lighter bead, she should abstain from unprotected sex. CycleBeads now offers

---

vasectomy Male sterilization whereby the vasa deferentia are cut and tied to prevent the sperm from being ejaculated out of the penis.

castration Removal of the testicles.

tubal ligation Female sterilization by severing and/or closing the fallopian tubes so that ova cannot pass down the tube.

laparoscopy Surgical method whereby a tubular instrument is passed through the abdominal wall.

calendar method A method of birth control whereby the couple has intercourse only during those times of the menstrual cycle when the woman is least likely to get pregnant.

TABLE 11.1 Effectiveness Ratings of Contraceptive Methods

METHOD	EFFECTIVENESS RATE (%)*
Sterilization	
Vasectomy	>99
Tubal ligation	>99
Tubal inserts	97
Hormonal methods	
Pill	91
Injectable	94
Implants	99
Vaginal ring	91
Patch	91
Intrauterine system	99
Intrauterine device	>99
Barrier methods	
Male condom	82
Male condom (with spermicide)	98
Female condom	79
Female condom (with spermicide)	95
Diaphragm	88
Cervical cap (nulliparous women**)	86
Cervical cap (parous women**)	71
Contraceptive sponge (nulliparous women**)	84
Contraceptive sponge (parous women**)	68
Fertility awareness	74
Withdrawal	78

* Effectiveness rates are with typical use.
** Nulliparous, women who have not borne children; parous, women who have borne children.

Note: Bedsider 2016; Cornforth 2009; D. Stacey 2009; Planned Parenthood 2014.

iCycleBeads online, which will keep track of which bead she is on and send e-mail updates of fertile days, etc. The cost is $12 per year; iCycleBeads as a Smartphone App costs $3. CycleBeads can be used only by women with regular menstrual cycles of 26 to 32 days (CycleBeads 2016; Planned Parenthood 2014).

Calendar and standard days methods of birth control have typical effectiveness rates of about 74%. CycleBeads claims an effectiveness rate of 95%. Both are free or inexpensive; both require attention to a woman's cycles and extended periods of abstinence (or the use of barrier methods or noncoital sexual interaction) (Planned Parenthood 2014).

BASAL BODY TEMPERATURE METHOD The basal body temperature (BBT) is a person's temperature at the time he or she wakes up. A woman's BBT increases slightly before and during ovulation. A woman using the **basal body temperature method** uses a special thermometer to familiarize herself with her cycle by charting her BBT for 3 months. While using the method, she continues to log each day's BBT and watch for the slight rise. Because sperm can live for 3 days, unprotected intercourse is off limits from the beginning of the menstrual period until the temperature rise indicates ovulation has happened, plus 3 days to allow for the viability of the ovum. Typical effectiveness rate is 74%. Reliability can be disrupted by illness, use of an electric blanket, tobacco and alcohol use, or interrupted sleep cycles (Planned Parenthood 2014).

CERVICAL MUCUS METHOD The **cervical mucus method** relies on changes in the cervix and cervical mucus as indicators of ovulation. A woman using this method observes her cervical secretions each day beginning the day after menstrual bleeding ends. She also checks the position of her cervix. During ovulation the cervix is slightly higher and softer; before or after ovulation it is lower and firmer. Cervical mucus becomes clear, stretchy, and slippery as ovulation happens. The time from the beginning of menstruation and for a few days after—until she observes fertile mucus—is considered safe for unprotected sex. Abstinence should be practiced until mucus decreases in volume and becomes cloudy and sticky or tacky.

The cervical mucus method has a typical effectiveness rate of 74%. It is even less reliable for women who produce little mucus, who have reproductive tract infections, or who use douches or feminine

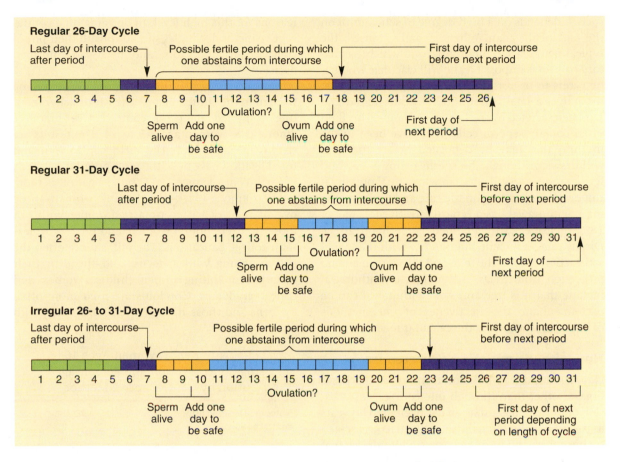

FIGURE 11.1 Fertile and Infertile Periods during a 26-Day, 31-Day, and Irregular (26- to 31-Day) Cycle

hygiene products ("Cervical mucus method" 2008; Planned Parenthood 2014).

SYMPTOTHERMAL METHOD The **symptothermal method** combines several natural family planning methods such as cervical mucus and BBT to more accurately pinpoint ovulation. Calendar method or standard days can be used, too. Using a combination of methods increases effectiveness. However, women with unpredictable cycles, irregular BBT patterns, or reproductive tract infections cannot rely on this method ("Symptothermal method" 2008).

These fertility awareness methods can be helpful as contraceptive techniques, and they can be helpful in conceiving. Physicians often advise couples who are having difficulty conceiving to use a combination of the BBT method and the cervical mucus method. By having intercourse daily when the woman is most likely to be ovulating, a couple can greatly enhance the likelihood of conception.

Withdrawal

Withdrawal (coitus interruptus or the pull-out method) refers to the practice of withdrawing the penis from the vagina before ejaculation occurs. Although this method is better than nothing, its

basal body temperature method A method of fertility awareness based on the rise in basal body temperature that signals ovulation.

cervical mucus method A method of fertility awareness that uses changes in cervical mucus as indicators of ovulation.

symptothermal method Combining several natural family planning methods (basal body temperature plus cervical mucus, for example) to achieve greater accuracy in pinpointing ovulation.

withdrawal Withdrawal of the penis from the vagina prior to ejaculation; used as an attempt at birth control.

success depends on a high degree of self-control on the part of the man. When sexually aroused, the typical man reaches a point beyond which ejaculatory control is impossible; he will ejaculate whether he wants to or not. Also, before orgasm, the male discharges a small amount of lubrication fluid that has been secreted by the Cowper's glands. This fluid often contains sperm cells (that have been in the urethra) that may be deposited before the man withdraws. Although the sperm count is low and fertilization is less likely than with actual orgasm, it can occur. Depending on the care and timing of the man, withdrawal has a typical effectiveness rate of 78% (Bedsider 2016; Planned Parenthood 2014). Disadvantages include interference with the sexual satisfaction of both the man and the woman and no protection from STDs. Advantages of withdrawal include that it is free and safe; withdrawal can be used to enhance the effectiveness of other methods of birth control such as the calendar method.

Noncoital Stimulation (Outercourse)

Couples can use stimulation techniques to achieve orgasm other than through intercourse. Masturbation or mutual masturbation has been used for years as a substitute for intercourse. If the man gets semen on his fingers and introduces sperm into the vaginal canal, however, conception can occur. Interfemoral stimulation is a method whereby the man places his penis between the woman's closed thighs and rubs back and forth along the length of the clitoris. Climax may be reached in this way, but if the male ejaculates near the vaginal opening, there is a possibility the sperm may find their way inside. Oral–genital stimulation is sometimes used, not only as a method of precoital love play but also as a technique of arousal to orgasm. Other couples use fantasy or sex toys for noncoital sexual interaction.

Choosing a Method of Contraception

The ideal contraceptive would be (1) 100% effective; (2) inexpensive; (3) convenient to use, without interfering with lovemaking; and (4) without any risk or adverse side effects. Currently, no one method meets all these criteria. Even with contraceptive use, about 1 in 10 women experience an accidental pregnancy. Inconsistent and incorrect use are the main

reasons for this high level. In deciding on a contraceptive method, couples should consult their physician, weigh all factors, and make an informed decision.

What contraceptive methods are in use among women in the United States? The Guttmacher Institute compiled data on contraceptive practices among U.S. women ages 15 to 44. The results are shown in Table 11.2. The birth control pill and tubal ligation have been the most popular methods of birth control since 1982. Tubal ligation is more popular among black and Hispanic women, those over 35 years of age, ever-married women with 2 or more children, poorer women, and those with less than college educations. The pill is more often the choice among whites, teens, and those in their twenties, cohabiting women, childless women, and college graduates. Condoms are used more often by teens and those in their twenties, women with

TABLE 11.2 Number of Women Ages 15 to 44 Using Contraception and Percentage Distribution by Contraceptive Method

Number of women using contraception	38,214
Contraceptive method	(%)
Female sterilization	27.1
Male sterilization	9.9
Pill	28
Patch or implant	1.1
3-month injectable	3.2
Intrauterine device	5.5
Vaginal ring	2.4
Condom	16.1
Periodic abstinence/calendar rhythm	0.9
Periodic abstinence/natural family planning	0.2
Withdrawal	5.2
Other methods*	0.4

* Includes sponges, cervical cap, female condoms, and other methods.

Note: From Guttmacher Institute (2012). Contraceptive use in the United States. http://www.guttmacher.org.

1 child or none, and those with college educations. About 8% of women use dual methods of birth control—typically condoms with something else (Guttmacher Institute 2012).

Abortion

If contraceptives are not used or a given method fails, then a woman or a couple may be faced with an unplanned pregnancy. One of the alternatives is **abortion**. Abortion raises some difficult questions to which there are no simple answers. Abortion issues may be divided into four categories, which are discussed in the following sections: (1) legal, (2) moral, (3) social and realistic, and (4) psychological and personal.

Legal Considerations

Abortion law is complex in the United States. On January 22, 1973, the U.S. Supreme Court ruled that a state could not inhibit or restrict a woman's right to obtain an abortion during the first trimester of pregnancy (the first 12 weeks) and that the decision to have an abortion was the woman's own in consultation with her doctor (*Doe v. Bolton* 1973; *Roe v. Wade* 1973; Sarvis and Rodman 1974). The major ground for the Court's decision was the woman's right to privacy.

The Court further declared that during the second trimester of pregnancy (weeks 13 to 26)—when abortion is more dangerous—"a state may regulate the abortion procedure to the extent that the regulation relates to the preservation and protection of maternal health" (*Roe v. Wade* 1973). Reasonable regulation might include outlining the qualifications or licensure of the person who performs abortions or the licensing of the facility where the abortion is performed. The Court went on to say that the state's interest in protecting the life of the fetus arises only after viability (after 24 to 28 weeks, when the fetus is potentially capable of living outside the mother's womb). However, the state "may go so far as to proscribe [forbid] abortion during that period except when it is necessary to preserve the life or health of the mother" (J. P. Reed 1975, 205). The reasons the Court rejected the state's interest in protecting human life from the moment of conception were (1) that the "unborn have never been recognized in the law as persons in

the whole sense" and (2) that the rights extended to the unborn, in law, are contingent on live birth, so (3) a state's interest in protecting fetal life cannot override the woman's right to privacy (Sarvis and Rodman 1974).

One heated controversy in abortion law has been over late-term or partial-birth abortions. *Late-term* refers only to the time the abortion takes place, after week 26 and in the third trimester of pregnancy; *partial-birth* refers to the method used in aborting the fetus. Partial-birth abortions are performed in the second and third trimesters of pregnancy, through a procedure known as intact dilation and extraction, which involves inducing a breech delivery with a forceps (Abortion Law Homepage 2000).

In November 2003, former president George W. Bush signed into law a ban on partial-birth and late-term abortions. It permits no exceptions when a woman's health is at risk or a fetus has life-threatening disabilities. Supporters of the law have argued that this procedure is not so much abortion as infanticide, which is illegal. If the partial-birth delivery used in the procedure is indeed a "birth," then a person exists and has constitutional rights. Opponents of the law reject this idea and focus on the fact that other abortion procedures traditionally upheld by the Court can involve the delivery or partial delivery of a live but nonviable fetus that dies as a result of the procedure. They argue that these laws only serve to restrict a woman's right to an abortion (Sykes 2000; Yarber and Sayad 2013).

Another controversy in abortion law has been taking place in Texas. Lawmakers there have passed legislation prohibiting abortion after 20 weeks of gestation; this is because of advances in medicine that have moved the age of viability (the time when a fetus can survive if born) back to 22 weeks. Other provisions in the law require higher standards for the abortion clinics (to surgical standards) and that doctors who perform abortions have admitting privileges at a nearby hospital. Proponents of the law argue that the fetus feels pain at 20 weeks and that the other requirements are safety measures for women. Opponents argue that these are measures to make abortion more expensive and harder to obtain (Fernandez 2013; Lilith Fund 2014).

abortion The expulsion of the fetus. Can be either spontaneous or induced.

In sum, according to current Supreme Court rulings, states can regulate abortion in five ways: (1) ban elective abortions after the fetus is viable, (2) require parental consent or note or a judge's bypass before a minor can obtain an abortion, (3) require informed consent or counseling before an abortion, (4) require certain kinds of record keeping for each state, and (5) require waiting periods, usually 24 to 48 hours, before an abortion.

Moral Considerations

Much of the controversy about abortion has centered on moral issues. For many individuals, abortion is wrong because it represents the murder of a human being. According to this point of view, the soul enters the body at the moment of conception, so the new life is immediately a human.

Opponents of this view argue that to say that a group of human cells, however highly differentiated at the early stages of growth, is a person is to stretch the point. They contend that these cells have neither consciousness nor any distinctly human characteristics and traits. They also point to the teachings of the thirteenth-century theologian and philosopher Thomas Aquinas, who said that there was neither life nor ensoulment until the fetus moved, so abortion was not sinful in the first 16 weeks of pregnancy. Three centuries later, the Catholic Church fixed ensoulment at 40 days after conception, following Aristotle's teaching. Abortion during the first 40 days of pregnancy was not considered sinful until the First Vatican Council in 1869, when it was once more ruled that life begins at the time of conception and that abortion at any time is a grave sin. This view was reaffirmed by the Second Vatican Council in 1965.

Members of the right-to-life movement and others emphasize the right to life of the fetus and say that no individual or state should deprive the fetus of its constitutional and moral right to live. Legally, the Supreme Court has never established that the fetus is a person, enjoying full protection under the Constitution and the Bill of Rights. Right-to-choose proponents emphasize that the moral and legal rights of other parties must also be considered, not just those of the fetus. What about the rights of the mother, the father, and other family members? Should these lives be sacrificed for the sake of the fetus?

The Supreme Court ruling establishes the legal principle that the mother's rights take precedence, at least before viability. The moral dilemmas raised by the abortion issue are not easy to solve.

Social and Realistic Considerations

Those advocating the right to choose emphasize the fact that strict laws against abortion, such as those that permit abortion only when the mother's life is threatened, have never worked. A current example can be found in Ireland, where abortion law is restrictive. The law permits abortion only when a woman's life is threatened (directly or indirectly) by a pregnancy. Nonetheless, thousands of Irish women travel to England, where abortion law is less restrictive, for abortions each year (Francome 1992; McKittrick 2010).

If a woman is determined not to have her baby, she may attempt, however foolishly (and sometimes futilely), to abort her own fetus. Or she may go to an unqualified person and get an illegal abortion that may threaten her life. Various estimates place the number of illegal abortions in the U. S. before 1967 at around 1 million per year, or about 20% of total pregnancies. Maternal death rates from illegal abortions in New York City were about 19 times higher than those from legal abortions.

In reply to these social considerations, right-to-life groups emphasize their fears that without any restriction, except the individual woman and her conscience, an "abortion mentality" develops so that

The Supreme Court has repeatedly been asked to consider when life begins. Who has the right to decide when and if a pregnancy can be terminated? The dilemmas raised by the abortion issue are not easily solved by anyone.

abortions become too commonplace. The majority of abortions today are not for medical reasons, but for personal, social, and economic reasons. About equal numbers of abortions are performed for white women (51%) and black women (41%). Some 57% of abortions are sought by women ages 20–29 years, 16% by women ages 15 to 19, and about 12% are performed for women over 35 years of age (Centers for Disease Control and Prevention 2015; Pazol et al. 2011).

Most thoughtful advocates of abortion agree that it should be only a backup measure, not the primary method of birth control. They urge fuller use of contraceptives among all sexually active people.

Psychological and Personal Considerations

Right-to-life proponents often have emphasized the negative psychological effects on the woman who has had an abortion. But the incidence of psychological aftereffects is a subject of dispute. Both sides support their views. Those advocating the right to choose point out that many women are far more depressed before the abortion is performed than they are afterward. When abortions were illegal, much of the anxiety was over the illegality of the act, so these feelings have been eliminated. Other studies have shown that abortion does not appear to have an adverse effect on women's self-esteem or psychological well-being (APA Task Force 2008).

In contrast, right-to-life proponents point to other studies indicating that some women do suffer psychological scars in the aftermath of an abortion (APA Task Force 2008). For this reason, abortion counseling, which assists the woman in working through her feelings ahead of time (and afterward if needed), is important. For some, abortion provides great relief with little if any disturbance; for others, the experience is upsetting. One key factor seems to be whether the woman wants an abortion (the pregnancy is unwanted) or is reluctant to obtain one (the pregnancy is wanted, but the baby has a serious genetic problem, for example). Another key factor is prior mental health, with women who have existing mental health problems more likely to have difficulties with abortion (APA Task Force 2008). Being refused an abortion and forced to bear an unwanted child can lead to psychological problems such as depression. But a woman who has health problems and has to have an abortion, or who is persuaded to have an abortion against her better judgment, is also likely to have negative psychological reactions. If the decision is the woman's, adverse psychological reactions are minimized.

Infertility

In the United States, **infertility**—the failure to achieve a pregnancy after frequent, unprotected intercourse for a year (or 6 months if she is over 35 years old)—affects an estimated 10% to 15% of couples (Clayton 2004a; Mayo Clinic Staff 2014). Female infertility accounts for about one-third of cases; male infertility is responsible in one-third of cases; and the other third are caused by both individuals (she ovulates irregularly and his sperm count is low, for example) or are unexplained (Mayo Clinic Staff 2014).

Causes of Infertility

Human reproduction is a complex process with many opportunities for disruption. Anything that interferes with ovulation, sperm production, fertilization, implantation, or growth in the uterus can impair fertility. Ovulation disorders—absent or irregular ovulation caused by hormone imbalances or problems in the ovaries—are one cause of female infertility. Other causes of female infertility include damage to the fallopian tubes such as inflammation or scarring as a result of an STD, PID, endometriosis, surgery, or a previous ectopic pregnancy. Blocked fallopian tubes do not allow sperm to reach the ovum or the passage of ova to the uterus. Narrowing or blockage of the cervix can also reduce fertility by preventing sperm from entering. Benign polyps or tumors and scarring in the uterus can disrupt implantation. Some uterine abnormalities—such as with its shape—can cause problems with conceiving or sustaining a pregnancy (Mayo Clinic Staff 2014).

Male fertility involves his being able to produce and deliver healthy sperm into the vagina. Sperm must be properly shaped and able to move (motile) to reach and penetrate an ovum; they must be produced in sufficient number (20 million per milliliter of semen). Consequently, impaired production

infertility Failure to achieve a pregnancy after 1 year (6 months if she is over 35 years old) of frequent, unprotected sexual intercourse.

A Preference for Males

The sex ratio among humans has consistently shown that slightly more males are born than females (the average being about 105 males to 100 females). However, several Asian countries show a significantly higher than average number of male births to female births. The cause of this disparity has been heavily debated, but many people believe the unusually high number of male births is the result of a preference for male children compared to female children. Gender selection of a baby is made possible with technologies such as ultrasound, which reveals the gender of the fetus, followed by selective abortion.

In China, the institution of a one-child policy at the end of the 1970s is believed by many to have caused an increase in female fetus abortions and female infanticide so couples could assure that their one child is a boy (Secondi 2002). Because of the perceived selective abortion problem, the government of China passed a law that bans gender identification before birth unless necessary for medical reasons. However, because the technology for gender identification of the fetus and abortion are both easily accessible, it is a difficult law to enforce. In addition, traditional values make it important to many families to have a male child. For example, in traditional Chinese culture, family membership and economic cooperation, inheritance of property, and lines of authority were defined through males; even today, only a male child can continue the family line and fulfill duties in regard to ancestor worship; aging parents expect to be supported by male offspring; and male labor may be perceived as more valuable for agricultural families (Secondi 2002). These values become more pressing when parents are only allowed one child.

Secondi (2002) examined the determinants of the biased sex ratio in rural China, with a focus on investigating whether the economic status of the parents affects the ratio of sons to daughters. He found that selective abortion and different treatment of boys and girls (e.g., boys getting more to eat) are likely to be the main sources of biased sex ratios and that the unusually high ratio of boys to girls in China can be explained by parental behavior aimed at producing more male offspring than biologically normal. He found that first-born surviving children of lower-income parents were significantly more likely to be boys than girls. The desire to have sons (whether because of preferences or financial considerations) seems equally widespread among rich and poor families, but firstborn girls appear to be a luxury that higher-income parents are able to afford.

The situation of a distorted sex ratio resulting from aborting female fetuses also is a serious problem in India. Although determining the sex of a fetus by sonogram is officially illegal and, if conducted, doctors are banned from reporting the sex of the fetus to the mother, both are common practices and there are no laws against abortion in India. Sex selection can be a lucrative business in India, and there are sonogram mobiles that travel from village to village offering the service easily. It has been estimated that the sex-selection business generates more than $100 million annually. Based on government data collected from 1.1 million Indian families throughout the country, it is estimated that 1 of every 25 female fetuses is aborted, roughly 500,000 per year. This translates to the abortion of roughly 10 million female fetuses over the past 2 decades (Jha et al. 2006).

---

or function of sperm is a leading cause of male infertility. Several conditions can reduce sperm count and motility, including hormonal imbalances and anything that interferes with normal cooling of the testicles, such as varicoceles (swollen veins in the scrotum), an undescended testicle, and frequent use of saunas/hot tubs (a temporary reduction). Abnormal development or inflammation of the testicles, prostate, urethra, or epididymis also may affect sperm production and/or motility. Exposure to chemicals (such as pesticides or lead), radiation or X-rays, and chemotherapy also reduce sperm

Coping with Infertility

Coping with infertility can be physically and emotionally draining. It is impossible to predict what the outcome will be. Testing and treatment and trying to get pregnant involve lots of anxiety, hope, and disappointment. Here are some suggestions for managing (Mayo Clinic Staff, 2014):

- Learn about testing and treatment procedures. This allows you to prepare for each one and to have realistic expectations for outcomes.

- Set limits. Decide which procedures are morally and emotionally acceptable to you as well as financially possible. Some couples might consider hormone treatment a possibility, but the use of a surrogate too extreme, for example. Some treatments cost tens of thousands of dollars, must be repeated, and may not be covered by insurance.

- Consider other options. Decide what you will do if conception does not occur. Using sperm/egg donors, adoption, and remaining childless are all options. Having a "plan B" helps reduce anxiety.

- Get support. Reach out to family and friends or find a support group. Seek professional help.

production, quality, and motility (Mayo Clinic Staff, 2014).

Problems with the delivery of sperm into the vagina include erectile dysfunction, absence of semen (because of spinal cord injury or disease), blockage of the epididymis (part of the testicle that stores sperm) or vasa deferentia, retrograde ejaculation (semen enters the bladder during orgasm rather than emerging through the penis—caused by disease or surgery), and misplaced urinary opening (on the underside of the penis—a congenital condition). Blockage of the epididymis or a vas deferens may result from STDs, injuries, or surgeries that cause scarring (Mayo Clinic Staff, 2014).

A number of other factors may put both men and women at higher risk for infertility. These include age (after the mid-thirties), smoking, overweight or very underweight, and alcohol use (Mayo Clinic Staff, 2014).

Infertility and Subjective Well-Being

Not being able to conceive or carry a child to term is frustrating. Couples facing fertility issues typically feel disappointed and under stress. They may experience anger, depression, guilt, and feelings of being defective or a failure. The relationship may suffer if they blame each other; their sexual interactions may become anxious, focused efforts to conceive (Clayton 2004a; M. C. Miller 2012; Read 2004).

Furthermore, the diagnosis and treatment of infertility involves many visits to physicians and clinics—thus being costly, time-consuming, and stressful. In one study, women described the experience of infertility and treatment as being all-consuming to the point of interfering with leisure time (Parry and Shinew 2004). These women also reported feeling socially isolated. This feeling is not uncommon because some couples keep their situation a secret or because of others' reactions to their problem. It is not helpful to hear, "You just need to relax—take a vacation or have a glass of wine," or "All this new technology stuff isn't normal. You should adopt." Although infertility challenges individuals and couples' well-being, couples who work together also report deepened commitment and intimacy (M. C. Miller 2012; Watkins and Baldo 2004).

Treatment of Infertility

Younger couples (mid-thirties and younger) usually try for a year before seeking help; couples ages 35 to 40 should seek assistance after about 6 months. Persons older than 40 or with a history of certain medical conditions (endometriosis or PID, for example) should seek assistance right away.

Treatment for infertility depends on the cause. Surgical and hormonal treatments are most common. The partners also will probably be instructed in fertility awareness methods (described earlier in the chapter) so that they can have intercourse when there is the greatest likelihood that she is ovulating. If these treatment methods are not successful, the couple may want to consider alternative means of conception that have become available through developments in medical technology.

Alternative Means of Conception

Artificial insemination (AI) **or intrauterine insemination** (IUI) is the injection of sperm into the vagina, cervix, or uterus for the purpose of facilitating conception. AI/IUI may be chosen to resolve problems of low sperm count/motility or problems of sperm delivery such as erectile dysfunction. Sperm may be from the husband (AIH) or from a donor (AID). Injection of sperm into the vagina may be done without a physician's help; do-it-yourself kits are available. Success for AI/IUI ranges from about 5% to 30%, depending on the circumstances and method. A couple using injection into the vagina because of low sperm count would have lower rates, for example, than a couple using donor sperm into the uterus. This is the least invasive of the reproductive technologies and also one of the least expensive—costing about $300 to $900 per try plus tests, fertility medications, and donor fees, if applicable.

In vitro fertilization (IVF) is used when fallopian tubes are blocked or damaged and/or when sperm quality, motility, and/or count are low. Egg and/or sperm donors can be used in situations where her ova or his sperm are not adequate or when they wish to avoid passing along a genetic condition. IVF involves extensive testing as well as surgery to harvest ripe ova. It is also expensive—$10,000 to $15,000 per cycle (attempt); insurance may not cover it.

In vitro fertilization involves removing egg cells from a woman, fertilizing with sperm in the laboratory, growing for 3 or 4 days, and then placing up to four of the subsequent blastocysts (preembryos) in the uterus. Using multiple blastocysts increases the chance of pregnancy. With IVF, there is a 25% to 35% pregnancy rate. Cryopreservation, or the freezing of blastocysts, makes it possible to store any extra blastocysts (preembryos) for later use.

In a **gamete intrafallopian transfer** (GIFT), the eggs (harvested as for IVF) and sperm are inserted directly into the fallopian tube, where conception typically takes place. "GIFT is what nature really does, with a little help from us," says Dr. Ricardo Asch, a professor of gynecology and obstetrics at the University of California at Irvine (Ubell 1990). As a result, GIFT is an acceptable alternative to couples who object to IVF because conception happens outside the body in IVF. GIFT cannot be used in women with most fallopian tube problems. The success rate is 35% to 40% and GIFT costs $15,000 to $20,000 per cycle.

Zygote intrafallopian transfer (ZIFT) is an assisted reproductive procedure that utilizes techniques similar to both IVF and GIFT. Egg cells and sperm are gathered as in both IVF and GIFT; the ova and sperm are then mixed together (as in IVF) and monitored for about 24 hours to ensure that fertilization has occurred. Fertilized egg cells (**zygotes**) are then placed directly into the fallopian tube (as in GIFT). ZIFT offers the advantage over GIFT of making sure fertilization has occurred. It has a success rate of 25–35% and costs $15,000 to $20,000 per cycle.

In cases where the cause of the infertility is related to few or low-quality sperm, a procedure called **intracytoplasmic sperm injection** (ICSI) can be useful. In ICSI, after ova and sperm are gathered, an injection pipette is used to penetrate and deposit one sperm into one egg cell. The fertilized egg cells are then deposited into the uterus. ICSI is used in conjunction with IVF or ZIFT to increase the chances of success. One cycle of ICSI costs $10,000 to $17,000; it has a success rate of about 25% to 30%.

A **surrogate mother** agrees to carry a child for an individual or couple who typically cannot conceive or carry a pregnancy to term. The surrogate mother may be inseminated with the semen of the father-to-be or a sperm donor, thus using her own egg, or may be implanted with a fertilized egg, thus using the egg from another woman. The surrogate mother signs a legal contract agreeing to carry the fetus to term and to give the child to the couple, along with all parental rights.

Couples may locate a surrogate through agencies that match potential surrogates with infertile couples. The cost of using a surrogate is about $80,000 to $120,000 (WebMD 2015).

The ethical, legal, and emotional issues surrounding surrogate parenthood are beyond the scope of this text. Just imagine the complexity of a situation and the issues that may arise when there

This photo shows families attending a 25th anniversary reunion of in vitro fertilization. These babies are living examples of the success of IVF. Louise Brown, front center, was the first person born through in vitro.

are multiple people involved in creating life. The surrogate mother option could include the infertile couple, the egg donor (who may or may not be the surrogate mother or the contracting mother), the sperm donor (who may or may not be the contracting father), and the woman who carries the baby. In this scenario there are five people legally, emotionally, financially, and/or physically involved in the creation of a child. Thus, there often are many unresolved legal questions relating to the rights of the child and to the legitimacy of surrogate agreements.

The Adoption Option

The number of adoptions per year in the United States increased steadily over the decades and reached a peak of 175,000 in 1970. About half of those who petition for adoption are related to the child they wish to adopt; others are stepparents wishing to adopt stepchildren; still others are foster parents who adopt foster children. Persons who decide to adopt generally have two routes: the use of an agency (either public or private) or an independent adoption.

artificial insemination/intrauterine insemination Injection of sperm into the vagina, cervix, or uterus for the purpose of achieving conception.

in vitro fertilization Removing egg cells from a woman, fertilizing with sperm in the laboratory, and then placing the fertilized egg in the uterus.

gamete intrafallopian transfer The process of inserting sperm cells and egg cells directly into the fallopian tube, where fertilization is expected to occur.

zygote intrafallopian transfer Removing egg cells from a woman, mixing with sperm in the laboratory, and placing the fertilized egg cells directly into the fallopian tube.

intracytoplasmic sperm injection The process of injecting a single sperm cell directly into a single egg cell to further enhance the possibility of fertilization.

zygote A fertilized egg cell.

surrogate mother A woman who agrees to be impregnated (by artificial insemination or in vitro fertilization), to carry the fetus to term, and then to give the child to the couple, along with all parental rights.

Reasons for Having Children

The reasons couples give for having children are personal.

My life would not be complete without children. Children help you feel fulfilled. I never felt like an important person until I became a parent.

When you have children, it gives you someone to do things with, to provide companionship, fun, and love.

I think I'd be very lonesome if I and my spouse were all alone.

I don't think you really become a mature adult until you have children. I know I never really grew up until after the kids were born. You learn responsibility and to think of someone besides yourself.

Unless you have children, people think there's something wrong with you. I think it's only natural to be a parent.

I've always wanted someone to love and who loves me.

I think children help to bring you together and to have something in common. It gives you something to work for.

Children are a part of you. When you're gone, they're still here, an extension of you, carrying on your life and family.

I think one of the reasons for marriage is to have children. It's part of finding spiritual fulfillment. (Counseling notes)

The use of an adoption agency can have a number of advantages: agencies are helpful in handling legal matters, acquiring consents, and other details; and agencies offer a variety of services such as counseling to help the adoption be successful. Public agencies are typically funded by the state and consequently are less expensive; they also have a larger pool of children waiting to be adopted; and they may have less stringent criteria for adoptive parents.

Private agencies offer a wide range of services to all the parties involved in the adoption, thus supporting successful adoption; they may also have stricter qualifications (such as age). They are the most likely chance for adoptive parents who want a newborn. Public agencies have more children, but many of them are older or have special needs. Private agencies can be expensive, ranging from $5,000 to $40,000 or more.

In an independent adoption, the adopting parents and the birth mother handle the adoption themselves. Independent adoption also has benefits and hazards. All parties involved may feel they retain more control over the process (no agency is involved) and it can be less expensive and quicker. However, because adoption laws vary from state to state and can be complicated, many independent adoptions involve a lawyer's services. Connecticut,

Delaware, Massachusetts, and North Dakota do not allow independent adoption.

Until the 1970s, adoption in the United States was shrouded in secrecy. Members of the adoption triad (adoptive parents, birth parents, and adopted child) were protected from one another in the belief that all benefited from confidentiality. Birth mothers transferred their parental rights to adoption agencies, which then placed the children with adoptive parents. Biological dads were routinely excluded. Adoptive parents and birth parents never met; adopted children usually were not given the opportunity to meet their birth parents or know anything about them. Called *closed adoptions*, the information in them was often literally sealed (Find Law 2015).

Adoption practices now lie on a continuum of openness (and are termed *open adoption*) that allows for different levels of communication between adoptive parents and birth parents. Increasingly, all parties in the adoption are encouraged to meet and stay in contact. The birth mother may review information about prospective adoptive parents and select ones with whom she feels most comfortable; adoptive parents may be present at the birth; birth parents may continue to visit or receive pictures and updates on the child (Find Law 2015).

Open adoptions offer benefits to all parties in an adoption. Birth parents and adoptive parents have more control in the decisions that are made. Children have access to information about their genetic heritage. Children may also be better able to understand the circumstances of their adoption and may feel less loss or rejection.

There can be negatives, too. Adoptive parents may feel the adoption is never final—that the child will love the birth parents more or want to return to them or that the birth parents will intrude in their lives.

Open adoption can mean different amounts of contact between the parties involved; as a result, it is important for all to be in agreement. Amount of interaction may also change over time. Adoptive parents who agree to birth-parent visits on holidays when a child is young may resent their showing up at school functions or bringing half-siblings into the picture. Birth parents can feel neglected or cut out when the adoptive family moves to another state or when the adolescent child is embarrassed. Negotiating and maintaining boundaries in ways that are comfortable for everyone can be challenging and stressful.

In 2004, close to 23,000 adoptions were from foreign countries, with the largest number being Asian—especially from China. Russia provided almost as many adoptive children, with smaller numbers coming from Africa and South America (Child Trends 2012; Voigt and Brown 2013). By 2011, the number of international adoptions had dropped to about 9,000; the reasons for the decline are complex. In part, political reasons influence adoption regulations imposed by other countries. The Hague Adoption Convention, which the United States joined in 2008, was an attempt to reduce child trafficking and to guarantee that children placed for adoption would have the best possible environment in which to grow up. However, new and strict regulations have slowed the adoption process and made it much more expensive (Voigt and Brown 2013).

Interracial adoptions of minority children in the United States have declined as well. This is in part because of the influence of minority group advocates and social workers who are concerned about identity problems in the children.

The Foster Care Option

For some individuals, foster care is an option for rearing and caring for children. Currently there are about 416,000 children in foster care in the United States in licensed or approved foster homes (AFCARS 2015 Child Trends 2012). Some foster caregivers are related to the children. Children enter foster care for a variety of reasons—most often neglect or abuse by parents, but also because of anything that prevents the parents from caring for them (parental illness or incarceration, for example). Some 108,000 of the children in foster care are waiting to be adopted; for 61,000 of them, parental rights have already been terminated (AFCARS 2015).

One area of concern is the number of African American children in foster care and the lack of African American foster parents to care for them. Twenty-seven percent of children in foster care are black, whereas only 14% of the general population of children are black. This compares to 41% of foster children who are white (53% of general population) and 21% who are Hispanic (24%) (Child Trends 2012). Although African American children can be placed in any family, many child placement agencies feel that for a child to develop a healthy identity, he or she should be placed with a family of a similar racial group. One study comparing role perceptions of African American and white foster parents found that African American foster parents were more likely than their white counterparts to feel responsible for facilitating the relationship between foster children and birth parents, and they were more likely to accept responsibility for their roles of agency partner and emotional developer of the child (Nasuti, York, and Sandell 2004). However, given the numbers of African American children waiting for homes, the importance of race in determining placement is controversial.

Another critical issue for the foster care system is that foster children frequently suffer from developmental delays and severe behavior problems. Caring for children with special needs can be extremely stressful, and many families do not have the emotional or financial resources to handle the challenges of raising a child with special needs. This often leads to repeated displacements that in turn increase the risk for attachment disorders among special-needs children (Child Trends 2012; Gauthier, Fortin, and Jeliu 2004).

One of the most difficult issues surrounding foster care is whether foster children should be adopted quickly by foster parents or whether every attempt should be made to reunite the child with his or her biological parents. This is a particularly difficult issue when a child has developed a significant attachment to his or her foster parents but the biological parents have also worked hard at improving their parenting situation to reclaim their parental rights. For some researchers, the concepts rooted in attachment theory are important in understanding this issue. The critical importance of a child forming secure attachments has led them to believe that a child's best interests lie in preserving their attachment ties; repeatedly breaking those ties can be traumatic for the healthy development of the child (Gauthier, Fortin, and Jeliu 2004). Some families are reluctant to form a close bond with a foster child if the child will eventually be reunited with his or her biological family. The policy section at the end of Chapter 15 discusses this dilemma in more detail.

To Parent or Not to Parent

Couples today can decide when to have children, how many children to have, and even whether to have children. These choices have become possible because of effective means of contraception and changing social norms.

An examination of lifetime birth expectations of all married women ages 18 to 34 revealed that the number of births is 1.9 per woman and that 48% did not expect any future births (J. A. Martin et al. 2012; World Bank 2015). Among those surveyed, 9.3%

In a recent survey, the larger proportion of women who had their first baby after age 30 were highly educated, professional women in dual-career marriages.

expected to have no children at all. Having children is still favored over not having children, although the number of children desired has declined.

Delayed Parenthood

In recent decades, the timing of the birth of the first child has been delayed. In 2014, the mean age for women at first birth was 26 years, compared with 21.4 years in 1970. This is an all-time high for the United States. Birth rates for older women have also increased. Between 1990 and 2012, the birth rate declined among younger age groups of women but the birth rate for women aged 40 to 44 doubled; the rate for women older than 45 was unchanged (J. A. Martin et al. 2012; Mathews and Hamilton 2014). This delay in parenthood may be attributed to delayed marriage, financial considerations, increased pressure for women to get more education and get started in a career, and desire for personal development.

Women who delay childbearing have fewer children and the effect is positive for many families. Partners have time to adjust to marriage before becoming parents. They are usually more emotionally mature, stable, and responsible. Late childbearers are more settled in jobs and careers and more likely to have greater insight, own their own homes, and have more savings. They are usually better able to handle the competing demands of work and parenthood. Thus, a new stage appears to be developing: a transition stage between marriage and parenthood during which partners are free to pursue personal development, to build a stable marriage, and to become financially secure before taking on the responsibility of children.

The trend toward delayed parenthood may or may not be accompanied by increased health risks. Assuming adequate health care during pregnancy, childbirth, and the postpartum period, infants born to women ages 30 to 35 appear to be just as healthy as those born to younger women. However, there does seem to be greater risk of spontaneous abortions, chromosomal abnormalities, and multiple gestations among women older than 30 than among those who are younger. If the mother is 35 or older, the infant is at higher risk for low birth weight and infant death during the first year than if the mother is younger (Kail and Cavanaugh 2016). However, the increased risks are on a continuum— i.e., the risk is only slightly more at 36 than at 35 (Cleary-Goldman 2005).

However, with the infertility treatments that were discussed in this chapter and the trend to delay parenthood, it is important to ask the question, "Is there an age that is too old for individuals to become parents?" Throughout time, men have been siring children and becoming fathers well into their sixties and seventies with seemingly little public concern. This was probably because of the assumption that there was a younger mother involved to care for the child. With physician-assisted fertility treatments, women are now able to have children in their fifties and even sixties, and there is a growing concern about the social and developmental consequences to the child. Of course there is no guarantee of life for anyone, but older parents are naturally at greater risk of dying or being seriously ill before their child reaches adulthood.

Choosing a Child-Free Marriage

Although the vast majority of couples want to have children, childlessness among all women 40 to 44 years old increased from 10% in 1980 to 15% in 2014 (Livingston 2015). Women who were more educated (advanced degrees or professional degrees) continued to have the highest levels of childlessness, although the group of women with advanced degrees was the only group of women that showed a decrease in childlessness—down to 22% from 31% in 1994 (Livingston 2015).

The increase in women choosing to remain child free is often explained by social changes, namely, more access to better contraceptives, more women having careers and participating in the paid workforce, and the adoption of more feminist ideas— but those are not the only reasons. Gillespie (2003) examined why some women choose not to become mothers. She interviewed voluntarily child-free individuals ranging in age from 21 to 50 and found that personal freedom and the ability to develop relationships with other adults were two of the primary attractions to remaining child free, as well as a fundamental rejection of the activities associated with mothering. The participants did not view motherhood as necessarily natural and fulfilling; instead, they saw it in terms of losses they would experience and sacrifices they would make if they had children. Some participants perceived motherhood in terms of a loss of free time, energy, and identity and described the nurturing and caring roles associated with motherhood as unfulfilling. In sum, motherhood included demands, hard work,

responsibilities, and sacrifices to their well-being that they were not prepared to make.

Having children means readjusting one's lifestyle to take into account the children's needs and activities. A mother from Ann Arbor, Michigan, commented, "Suddenly I had to devote myself to the child totally. I was under the illusion that the baby was going to fit into my life, and I found that I had to switch my life and my schedule to fit him" (Counseling notes). It's a simple fact that without children there is no child work and less housework. Childlessness allows partners more freedom to do what they please.

However, choosing to be child free is still negatively stereotyped and seen by some as selfish, unfeminine, and unhealthy. But feminism has helped redefine gender roles and present women with more choices. Gillespie (2003) suggests that "a trend to remain child-free and an articulation of the lack of desire for motherhood create new possibilities to forge a childfree femininity" (134). The decision to have children is an important one. It is helpful if people have seriously considered this question before they marry and choose to marry only if they agree on the matter. Couples who are trying to decide can find resources to help them. Thorough research and discussion of the alternatives about parenthood will increase the likelihood that they are content with their decision.

For many people, one reason for having children is to perpetuate the family. From their older relatives, the children learn family history, values, and traditions to pass on to future generations.

It is helpful if prospective spouses choose each other partially on the basis of their desire to have children or not.

Embryos

Policy issues surrounding abortion and fertility have been at the forefront of political debate for the past 40 years and show no sign of abating. Intensely personal and, in the case of abortion, intensely controversial, these issues revolve around the core of what it means to be human and how we can control the creation of human life. For many people, policies governing abortion and fertility have a huge impact on their lives as individuals and within families.

Abortion and fertility treatment are complicated issues with many different sides. One of the fundamental questions behind the arguments is: When does life begin? On one side is a movement defining the moment of conception as the beginning of life and abortion in all cases as murder. On another side is the belief that the fertilized egg is not yet a life and should not be considered human. Still others believe that regardless of when life begins, it is a woman's choice (and not the government's) to control what happens to her embryo.

The debate becomes even more complicated when we examine current fertility treatments. Many people do not understand that fertility treatments also raise questions regarding the beginning of life. Today, many women seek professional assistance for infertility. A woman may receive a series of hormonal treatments that cause her to produce multiple eggs, which are removed and then fertilized. Typically, multiple eggs are fertilized and placed in the womb in the hope that at least one will result in a pregnancy. If several embryos appear to be viable, the woman may be asked to selectively abort one or more to increase the survival probability of the other(s) as well as to reduce the complications associated with multiple births. If not all embryos are used, they may be frozen for later use. Embryos are typically retained for 5 years and then discarded. The discarded embryos have never been placed in the mother's womb, and their disposal is not viewed as abortion. The public policy question becomes whether these embryos have the same status as the ones in the womb.

Questions to Consider

Does an embryo have a set of rights independent of the mother and deserve the protection of the state? Why or why not?

Is the status of an embryo dependent on how it was formed? That is, does it matter whether an embryo is formed because a woman became pregnant from rape, incest, casual sex, consensual sex within a committed relationship, or was formed by in vitro fertilization? Explain.

What would be an appropriate policy to regulate the use of frozen embryos from fertility clinics?

What rights does a father have with regard to the embryos? What responsibilities?

What happens to frozen embryos if the couple divorces? Who should be given custody of the embryos?

Summary

1. Family planning means having children by choice and not by chance; it means having the number wanted when they are wanted. Family planning is used to protect the health of the mother and children, to reduce the negative psychological impact and stress of parenthood, to maintain the well-being of the marriage and the family and its quality of life, and to avoid contributing to global overpopulation.

2. Oral contraceptives are effective, convenient, and easy to use. They are of several types: combination pills containing estrogen and progestin, the mini-pill (progestin only), and the emergency contraceptive pill.

3. Combination pills have a number of positive health effects: They reduce the risk of benign breast disease, ovarian cysts, iron-deficiency anemia, PID, ectopic pregnancy, rheumatoid arthritis, and endometrial and ovarian cancer.

4. Birth control pills do not protect against STDs.

5. Other hormonal contraceptives include progestin injections or implants, vaginal rings, patches, and IUSs.

6. Contraceptive foam, suppositories, creams, jellies, and film are vaginal spermicides that are used to prevent conception by blocking the entrance to the uterus and by immobilizing and killing the sperm.

7. Mechanical contraceptive devices include the IUD, male and female condoms, the diaphragm, the cervical cap, and the contraceptive sponge.

8. Methods of birth control without devices include various fertility awareness techniques, which rely on limiting intercourse to the so-called safe period of the month, when the woman is less likely to get pregnant (there is really no completely safe period); withdrawal; and various means of noncoital stimulation.

9. Sterilization is the most popular contraceptive method among married women, with the pill second and the condom third.

10. Treatment for infertility will depend on the causes. Surgical and hormonal treatments are most common. The couple also may be instructed in fertility awareness methods to enhance the possibility of conception.

11. Alternative means of conception include AI/IUI (either AIH or AID), IVF, GIFT, ZIFT, ICSI, and surrogate mothers.

12. At one time, adoption was shrouded in secrecy: the adoptive parents and adopted child were prevented from knowing the birth history of the child. Adoption practices now lie on a continuum of openness, allowing for different levels of communication among adoptive parents, birth parents, and child.

13. For many individuals, foster care is an option for caring for children. In fact, there are more children in need of foster homes than there are families who are willing to become foster parents.

14. Couples today can decide when to have children, how many children to have, and even whether to have children.

15. The number of children desired by U.S. families has declined, with most couples wanting no more than two.

16. More women are delaying parenthood so that they can complete their education, get established in their jobs, have more time to adjust to marriage, and have greater opportunity for personal freedom before having their first baby.

17. Women who want to remain childless are more likely to be well educated, urban, less traditional in their gender roles, upwardly mobile, and professional; they also are more likely to marry at a later age than women who want children.

18. There are a number of arguments against having children, such as world overpopulation and restrictions on personal freedom. Without children, there is less work at home, more opportunity for self-fulfillment, less strain on the marriage, less worry and tension, less expense, and fewer obstacles to the pursuit of a career.

Key Terms

abortion

artificial insemination

basal body temperature method

calendar method

castration

cervical cap

cervical mucus method

combination pills

contraceptive patch

contraceptive sponge

diaphragm

emergency contraceptive pills

family planning

female or internal condom

gamete intrafallopian transfer

implant

infertility

intracytoplasmic sperm injection

intrauterine device

intrauterine insemination

intrauterine system

in vitro fertilization

laparoscopy

male condom

mini-pill

oral contraceptives

placebo

progestin injection

spermicides

sterilization

surrogate mother

symptothermal method

tubal ligation

vaginal ring

vasectomy

withdrawal

zygote

zygote intrafallopian transfer

Questions for Thought

1. Do you want to have children? Why or why not? If yes, how many and how spaced?

2. If you were a family planning counselor, what birth control method would you recommend for each of the following and why?

   - A woman who has sexual intercourse only occasionally.

   - A couple who are cohabiting while they finish graduate school; they have no plans to marry. Neither wants children until after careers are established.

   - A married couple in their early thirties; both smoke and have a family history of cardiovascular disease. They have one child and want one more in a few years.

3. Assume you are married and have all the children you want; would you consider sterilization for yourself (vasectomy if you are a man, tubal ligation if you are a woman)? Explain the reasons for your decision.

4. "Octomom" Nadya Suleman made national news by giving birth to octuplets who survived. She caused considerable controversy when it was learned that she already had 6 children for a total of 14—all by IVF. Should there be regulation of the use of assisted reproduction such as age limits for parents, numbers of children, and so on?

5. If you were making legislation regarding abortion, what would you advocate: legal or not? Under what circumstances, if any? Any restrictions such as waiting period before, only until a certain time in the pregnancy, and so forth?

6. Should adopted children have full, ready access to their birth information? Should birth parents' privacy be protected? Why?

7. For you, what is the basic issue, if any, in judging the morality of abortion? Explain.

For Further Reading

http://www.adoption.com has information about adoptions, both domestic and international, as well as resources for adoptees, birth parents, adoption reunions, and foster parenting.

Visit the website of the Centers for Disease Control and Prevention, http://www.cdc.gov/art, for information about assisted reproductive technology, infertility, reproductive health, and preconception care.

Haynes, J., and Miller, J. (Eds.). (2003). *Inconceivable conceptions: Psychological aspects of infertility and reproductive technology.* New York: Brunner Routledge. Considers the experience of infertility from the point of view of professionals working in the field as well as men and women seeking treatment.

McFarlane, D. R. (2000). *The politics of fertility control: Family planning and abortion policies in the American states.* New York: Chatham House. Discusses the political controversy surrounding fertility control and the reasons the debate is so important.

The website for Planned Parenthood, http://www.plannedparenthood.org, has information about birth control, including a chat room for discussions about concerns related to birth control and a "My Method" option to put in some personal information to be advised as to which method of birth control would be best suited for you. Also gives a locator to find a clinic near you.

Shanley, M. L. (2001). Making babies, making families: What matters most in an age of reproductive technologies, surrogacy, adoption, and same sex and unwed parents. Boston: Beacon Press. Focuses on the need for new family laws that reflect the changing nature of the family today.

CHAPTER

12

Pregnancy and Childbirth

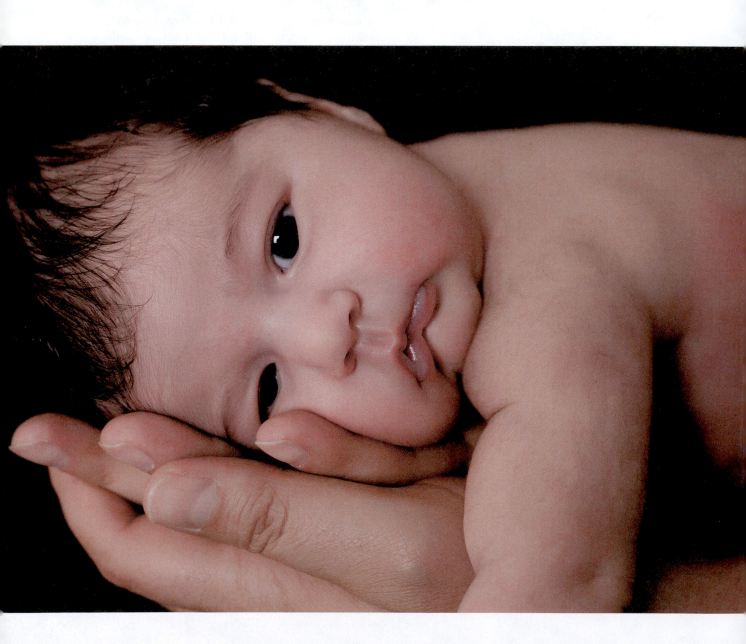

CHAPTER OUTLINE

Learning Objectives

Pregnancy
- Signs and Symptoms of Pregnancy
- Tests for Pregnancy
- Calculating the Expected Date of Birth
- Emotional Reactions to Pregnancy

Prenatal Care
- Importance of Prenatal Care
- Nutrition during Pregnancy
- General Health Care during Pregnancy
- Environmental Hazards
- Minor Side Effects of Pregnancy

CULTURAL PERSPECTIVE: *The Use of Ultrasounds*

- Major Complications of Pregnancy
- Sexual Relations during Pregnancy
- Mental Health

Prenatal Development
- The Germinal Period
- The Embryonic Period
- The Fetal Period

Prepared Childbirth
- The Lamaze Method

AT ISSUE TODAY: *Options for Delivery*

Labor and Delivery
- Stages of Labor

The Postpartum Period

FAMILY STRENGTHS PERSPECTIVE: *Bonding with Baby*
- Care of the Newborn

- Parent–Infant Contact and Bonding
- Rooming-In
- Postpartum Adjustments
- Returning to Work

COPING FEATURE: *Becoming a Parent*

PERSONAL PERSPECTIVE: *Postpartum Depression*
- Sexual Relations after Childbirth

A QUESTION OF POLICY: *Substance Abuse by Pregnant Women*

Summary

Key Terms

Questions for Thought

For Further Reading

LEARNING OBJECTIVES

AFTER READING THE CHAPTER, YOU SHOULD BE ABLE TO DO THE FOLLOWING:

- Describe the signs and symptoms of pregnancy, discuss the use of pregnancy tests, and calculate the due date using Naegele's formula.

- Discuss the emotional reactions to prospective parenthood and pregnancy and the developmental tasks of pregnancy.

- Explain the importance of prenatal care, including the minor side effects and major complications of pregnancy.

- Discuss teratogens, including examples and their effects.

- Identify the stages of prenatal development.

- Discuss prepared childbirth and the Lamaze method of natural childbirth.

- Demonstrate a basic knowledge of the process of labor and options for delivery.

- Discuss the following topics in relation to postpartum care, decisions, and adjustments: care of the newborn, bonding, rooming in, postpartum adjustments, and returning to work.

"Andy was born a robust 8 pounds, 10 ounces, 21 inches long. . . . After a few hours' recuperation following a long and confusing labor and smooth delivery, the nurse brought my first child to me. I held the little stranger in my arms. . . . I stared at him with awestruck concentration and a kind of disbelief. . . . The overwhelming experience of pregnancy and birth was over. I was now a *mother*. Unexpected tears rolled gently down my cheeks. I was indeed a mother, but I didn't feel like one.

"About the third day I began to fall in love with my little stranger, Andy, my son. I began to recognize his gusty cry as he was brought down the long hospital hall to my room. After nursing he would tuck himself against my soft tummy and I could feel his sleepy, full self sink heavily into the outside of my body as if delighting in these brief moments of transition from a cozy womb to a big, airy world. He seemed more and more my boy. The puzzling strangeness, the disappointing distance of those first days were slowly, unmistakably turning into affinity, warmth, and love. With great relief, I began to feel like a mother and to like the feeling very much" (Sherrard 1980, 29).

Most couples want to have children sometime in their lives. But when the time comes, they are faced with important questions: How do they know whether she is pregnant? How can the due date be calculated? What are some typical reactions to pregnancy, and what major adjustments do men and women face? What do they need to know to protect the health of the baby? What are the possible complications of pregnancy? How can they prepare for childbirth? What happens during labor and childbirth itself? What about the use of anesthesia? What about natural childbirth methods? What do couples need to know before and after the baby is born? These are some of the important questions discussed in this chapter.

Pregnancy

Some women suspect they are pregnant before medical tests confirm the fact. They can feel subtle changes in their bodies, and they begin to think about the changes in their lives that a baby will bring. And they wonder how their partners will react to the news.

Signs and Symptoms of Pregnancy

One of the first questions a prospective mother asks is, "How do I know for certain that I'm pregnant?" The signs and symptoms of pregnancy can be divided into three categories. **Presumptive signs** indicate a possibility of pregnancy. Typically, they are the first signs that a woman notices, but they are subjective and may be caused by conditions other than pregnancy. The presumptive signs are (1) cessation of menstruation, (2) morning sickness (nausea and possibly vomiting at any time of day), (3) an increase in the size, tenderness, and fullness of the breasts, along with a darkening of the areolas (the ring around the nipple), (4) frequent urination, and (5) overpowering sleepiness.

Probable signs of pregnancy are more objective than are presumptive signs, since they must be interpreted by a physician. Some of them occur later in pregnancy than the presumptive signs, but they still are not absolute proof. The probable signs include (1) a positive pregnancy test, (2) darkening of vaginal tissues and of cervical mucous membranes (Chadwick's sign), (3) softening of cervical tissue, (4) enlargement of the abdomen and uterus, (5) mapping of the fetal outline manually, (6) intermittent contractions of the uterus, and (7) an increase in the basal body temperature (from 98.6°F to 99.9°F for more than 16 days).

Positive signs of pregnancy are indisputable, since no other condition except pregnancy causes them. There are six of them. The examiner can (1) feel the fetus move, (2) hear the fetal heartbeat, (3) get an electrical tracing of the fetal heart, (4) detect a doubling of human chorionic gonadotropin levels, (5) map the fetal outline by means of ultrasound, and (6) detect the fetal skeleton by X-ray. When any of these signs are discovered, the mother and her physician *know* she is pregnant. (Because of the dangers of radiation to the developing fetus, doctors use X-rays only in rare circumstances.)

Tests for Pregnancy

The sooner a woman knows she is pregnant, the earlier she can begin prenatal care. Since most women want to know as soon as possible whether they are pregnant, pregnancy tests are administered. Modern tests are based on detecting the presence of **human chorionic gonadotropin** (HCG), which is secreted by the placenta. HCG is detectable within days of conception in the blood (2–3 days after implantation) or urine (about 2 weeks after the first missed menstrual period). Tests can be performed by a physician's office; however, a number of home pregnancy tests are available. They are available over the counter (without a prescription), easy to use, relatively inexpensive ($12–$25 for kits with two or three tests), and accurate (95%–99%) when performed correctly. Women are instructed to use first-morning urine and to test at about the time of the first missed menstrual period. A woman who gets a negative result should retest in about a week if a menstrual period does not happen.

Blood tests to detect the presence of HCG are accurate earlier in the pregnancy, but they are also expensive. As a result, blood tests to confirm pregnancy are used in special circumstances such as a suspected ectopic pregnancy or a maternal health condition.

Home pregnancy tests are convenient and relatively inexpensive. Most home pregnancy test kits advise women to see their physician after they have examined the results of the test.

Calculating the Expected Date of Birth

The duration of pregnancy is ordinarily estimated at 280 days, or 40 weeks, from the beginning of the last period. Of course, these are average figures. About 46% of women have their babies either the week before or the week after the calculated date and 80% within a 2-week period before or after the date. Occasionally, pregnancy is prolonged more than 2 weeks beyond the calculated date; usually, an error in calculation is involved.

The expected date of birth (due date) may be calculated using **Naegele's formula** as follows: subtract 3 months from the first day of the last menstrual period and then add 7 days. Thus, if the date of the first day of the last period was November 16, subtracting 3 months gives the date August 16 and adding 7 days gives the birth date as August 23. In other words, a woman ordinarily delivers her baby 9 months and 7 days after the first day of her last menstrual period.

Emotional Reactions to Pregnancy

Becoming a parent is usually one of the most exciting and meaningful experiences in life, but for many

presumptive signs Signs by which a woman presumes she is pregnant. These include cessation of menstruation; morning sickness; an increase in the size, tenderness, and fullness of the breasts; darkening of the areolas; frequent urination; and overpowering sleepiness.

probable signs Signs detected by the examining physician that indicate pregnancy is probable. These include a positive pregnancy test; darkening of vaginal tissues and of cervical mucous membranes; softening of the cervical tissue; enlargement of the abdomen and uterus; mapping of the fetal outline manually; intermittent contractions of the uterus; and an increase in the basal body temperature.

positive signs Signs of pregnancy detected by the physician that indicate positively that the woman is pregnant. These include feeling the fetus move; hearing the fetal heartbeat; getting an electrical tracing of the fetal heart; detecting a doubling of human chorionic gonadotropin levels; mapping the fetal outline by means of ultrasound; and detecting the fetal skeleton by X-ray.

human chorionic gonadotropin A hormone produced by the placenta that, if present in the mother's blood or urine, is an indication of pregnancy.

Naegele's formula A method of calculating the expected date of birth by subtracting 3 months from the first day of the last period and adding 7 days.

individuals it is also a stressful time. Individuals and couples may have to deal with an unplanned, maybe inconvenient or unwanted, pregnancy; the discomfort of physical changes during pregnancy; the stress of a serious complication; and anxiety about childbirth or miscarriage (Geller 2004; Kail and Cavanaugh 2016). How men or women react to prospective parenthood depends on a number of factors. An important one is whether the pregnancy is planned. Do the partners want a child? Do they feel ready to accept the responsibilities? Are the mother and father of appropriate ages? Have they accomplished their preparental goals? Do they have reasonable financial security?

Another important factor is the status of the couple's relationship. Do they have a harmonious and stable relationship? (The more stressful the relationship, the more difficulty the couple will have adjusting to parenthood.) Are they married? If not, how do they feel about raising a child out of wedlock? Does the woman want to be a single or unmarried parent? Will they assist each other in the rearing of the child? Will he accept responsibilities as a father? How will the child affect their relationship? Unpartnered women experience greater psychological risk and more complications during their pregnancies because of inadequate social support.

Pregnancy affects men and women differently. She has to carry the child for 9 months, accompanied by varying degrees of physical discomfort and

How does a woman know when she might be pregnant? What signs may tell her that she is? Signs of pregnancy can be detected, interpreted, and confirmed by a physician.

sometimes by anxiety about childbirth. Many women want to be mothers but hate the period of pregnancy. One woman commented, "I don't like being pregnant. I feel like a big toad. I'm a dancer, used to being slim, and can't believe what I look like from the side. I avoid mirrors" (Boston Women's Health Book Collective 1998, 440). Other women are extremely happy during pregnancy. As one woman noted, "I was excited and delighted. I really got into eating well, caring for myself, getting enough sleep. I liked walking through the streets and having people notice my pregnancy" (Boston Women's Health Book Collective 1998, 440).

Part of the woman's reaction to her pregnancy depends on the reaction of her partner to her and her changing figure. One study emphasized that a woman accepts her pregnancy when it brings her closer to her partner but rejects pregnancy when she feels it distances her from her partner. The woman's reaction to pregnancy is also strongly related to the financial and emotional support and help she receives from her partner.

Prenatal Care

In the United States, some 84% of pregnant women use prenatal care and 9 of every 10 babies are born perfectly healthy. Even so, nearly 4% of expectant mothers receive no care until the last trimester or no care at all (Child Trends 2015; J. A. Martin et al. 2007). And the women most at risk—teenage and unmarried, those in poverty/without insurance, those not wanting the pregnancy or hiding it—are least likely to receive care. An analysis by race indicates that Native American/Alaskan Native women have the highest rates of late/no prenatal care (11%), followed by black (10%), Mexican American (8%), Puerto Rican (6%), white (4%), and Cuban (3.5%) women (Child Trends 2015).

Importance of Prenatal Care

Parents can help ensure successful prenatal development by providing the best possible environment in which the child lives before birth. Time is of the essence with prenatal care because the first 12 weeks are a critical time of tremendous development, when the baby is most vulnerable to the effects of teratogens—agents that can disrupt prenatal development. Consequently, any delay in beginning prenatal care can be serious in impact. Early prenatal care is important for the mother-to-be's health as well. Pregnancy is physically demanding; pregnant women need extra rest and nutrition.

During the initial visits, the physician will take a medical history, perform a complete physical exam, perform various tests, and make recommendations regarding health care during pregnancy, sexual relations, potential minor complications, and danger signs of major complications. Some physicians encourage the father-to-be to come to an early visit. Visits to the doctor will continue through the pregnancy, allowing him or her to monitor the baby's growth and the mom's well-being.

Nutrition During Pregnancy

Because the baby receives all of his or her nutrients and oxygen from the mother's bloodstream via the placenta and umbilical cord, everything the mother consumes affects the fetus. If the mother's diet is nutritionally inadequate, the baby will not receive vital nutrients, and the mother's health will also suffer. For example, women who do not get enough folic acid (a B vitamin) are more at risk to have babies who have spina bifida (which results in spinal cord and nervous system damage). Inadequately nourished fetuses are also at risk for prematurity and low birth weight. As a result, pregnant women need a diet that includes food from each of the five major food groups. Most will also be encouraged to take a vitamin and mineral supplement.

Although a pregnant woman is "eating for two," she does not need to double her food intake. An increase of about 300 calories a day is usually sufficient to meet the needs of prenatal development. Women of normal weight (before the pregnancy) should gain 25 to 35 pounds during pregnancy (the weight of a baby plus amniotic fluid, increased blood volume, increased size of breasts and uterus, etc.). Underweight women should gain 28 to 40 pounds or so; overweight women should gain about 15 pounds (Kail and Cavanaugh 2016).

General Health Care during Pregnancy

Rest and moderate exercise are important to the well-being of a pregnant woman. Pregnant women need more sleep and rest because the energy demands on their bodies are great. Moderate exercise will not harm the embryo/fetus—which is cushioned by the amniotic fluid—and toned muscles will help with labor and delivery. Exercise also typically boosts mood. If she has a medical condition such as diabetes, the mother-to-be will be advised about managing and monitoring it. She will be urged to avoid illnesses and will receive information about alleviating the minor discomforts of pregnancy such as morning sickness and heartburn.

Environmental Hazards

In addition to advice with regard to nutrition, exercise, and general health, prenatal care will include recommendations about environmental hazards to avoid. A number of substances are referred to as **teratogens**, agents that disrupt prenatal development by causing physical or cognitive defects, prematurity, or prenatal death. The baby is most vulnerable to their effects during the first 2 to 3 months of gestation—although later exposure may also be harmful. These include alcohol, nicotine, prescription and over-the-counter medications, illegal drugs, and illnesses.

Drugs may cross the placenta just as nutrients and oxygen do. These include prescription drugs such as the antibiotic tetracycline, hormones such as diethylstilbestrol, anticancer drugs, seizure medications, nonsteroidal anti-inflammatory drugs such as naproxen and ibuprofen (which are also available without a prescription), and the acne medicine Accutane. Because it is difficult to know which drugs are safe to use during pregnancy, the American Academy of Pediatrics Committee on Drugs recommends that a pregnant or breastfeeding woman take *no* medication unless it is essential and after consultation with her physician.

The impact of maternal alcohol consumption during pregnancy is considerable: it is estimated that 1 of every 100 births (about 40,000 each year) yields a child with cognitive and neurological disorders because their mothers drank during pregnancy. These disorders are described by the umbrella term of fetal alcohol spectrum disorders (FASDs).

Approximately 40% to 50% of children born to mothers who drank excessively in pregnancy (two or more drinks per day or in "binges" of four or more drinks at one occasion) have a recognizable set of physical and cognitive difficulties called fetal alcohol syndrome (FAS). Infants with FAS tend to be small physically and do not catch up to normal

teratogens Agents that disrupt prenatal development.

growth; they also show varying degrees of cognitive deficiency. Many have heart defects, facial abnormalities, poor coordination, and behavioral problems. FAS is the leading cause of birth defects in the United States. It is also the primary *preventable* cause of mental retardation (NOFAS 2015; Papalia, Olds, and Feldman 2009).

The children of moderate or social drinkers are at risk to have FASDs that are not as severe as FAS. These are learning (memory, attention), behavioral (impulsive), or physical in nature and are termed partial fetal alcohol syndrome, alcohol-related neurodevelopmental disorder, or neurobehavioral disorder associated with prenatal alcohol exposure. The National Institute on Alcohol Abuse and Alcoholism considers more than two drinks per day a significant risk and as little as two drinks per week may do damage. Women who are pregnant, trying to get pregnant, or think they might be pregnant are advised to avoid *any* alcoholic beverages.

FASDs are completely preventable; they take a terrible financial ($1.5 to $2 million per child) and human toll. Organizations such as the National Organization on Fetal Alcohol Syndrome (NOFAS) are working to eliminate FASDs and to improve the lives of persons living with an FASD. It is a challenge: 51% of women of childbearing age use alcohol and 15% engage in binge drinking. Many of these women are sexually active and, therefore, may be pregnant for several weeks before they even suspect (NOFAS 2015).

The use of tobacco during pregnancy is the most important factor in low-birth-weight babies (less than 5.5 pounds at birth) in developed countries. Smoking also increases the risk for miscarriage, stillbirth, colic, sudden infant death syndrome, and long-term respiratory and cognitive problems (Berk 2013; DiFranza, Aligne, and Weitzman 2004; B. E. Hamilton et al. 2007). A link is also established between smoking during pregnancy and the development of attention deficit hyperactivity disorder—with its inattention, impulsivity, overactivity, and oppositional behaviors (K. Becker et al. 2008; Hudziak and Rettew 2009). Exposure to secondhand smoke is also damaging (Berk 2013; Kail and Cavanaugh 2016).

In a recent survey, pregnant women were asked about the use of e-cigarettes during pregnancy. Although 57% were aware that e-cigarettes do contain nicotine, 40% consider them less harmful than tobacco. In reality, nicotine can be harmful to a developing fetus; e-cigarettes also contain a number of heavy metals (tin, chromium, nickel) that may also be harmful. The use of e-cigarettes is not recommended during pregnancy (E. McCabe and Conley 2015).

Although precise results are difficult to obtain because of legal issues and because women who use illicit drugs also tend to use alcohol and tobacco, studies indicate negative outcomes when women use illegal drugs or misuse prescription drugs during pregnancy. For example, heavy marijuana use is associated with low birth weight and learning difficulties—much like cigarette use. Maternal cocaine use is associated with childhood behavior problems (Bada et al. 2007). Methamphetamine use is related to low birth weight and placental abruption (L. M. Smith et al. 2006; March of Dimes 2015).

The use of any addictive drug—cocaine, heroin, methamphetamine, or methadone, for example—can result in a newborn who is addicted and undergoes withdrawal symptoms, a condition called neonatal abstinence syndrome (NAS). The number of babies with NAS has tripled since 2000. A number of researchers and physicians believe this increase is the result of an epidemic of opioid (narcotic pain killer) drug use by pregnant women—much of it prescribed. When 112,000 women were asked, some 28% said they had a prescription for at least one narcotic during pregnancy (Patrick et al. 2015). About 4% of pregnant women use illegal drugs (March of Dimes 2015) and some misuse or abuse drugs that are prescribed.

Pregnant women are urged to seek prompt treatment for any illness or infection. Although most are not dangerous to the developing baby, a few are devastating and exposure to them should be avoided. These include rubella, toxoplasmosis, and Zika virus. None is serious for an adult, but all are powerful teratogens. Rubella is rare in the U.S. due to immunizations. Toxoplasmosis is from a parasite found in sheep, cattle, pigs, and cats. Consequently, pregnant women should not eat rare meat, should wash vegetables and fruits thoroughly, and should avoid contact with cat feces. Zika virus is carried by mosquitoes; pregnant women should avoid mosquito bites (long sleeves, etc.), They also should not travel to places with Zika virus.

Minor Side Effects of Pregnancy

No pregnancy is without some discomfort. Expectant mothers may experience one or several of the following discomforts to varying degrees and at various times during pregnancy: nausea (morning

The Use of Ultrasounds

There are many cultural variations surrounding pregnancy and childbirth. One study examined the prenatal and childbirth experiences of Japanese couples living in the United States. One striking difference found between Japanese and American couples involved the use of fetal sonograms, or ultrasounds. Japanese women are accustomed to receiving an ultrasound at each prenatal visit to ensure normal fetal development. In Japan, it has become a ritual for the first pictures in a baby photo album to be a series of fetal sonogram pictures. Japanese couples having a baby in the United States expressed concern and anxiety over not having regular sonograms. Ultrasound pictures gave them peace of mind and assurance at each prenatal visit that the baby was developing normally (Yeo, Fetters, and Maeda 2000).

Interestingly, health insurance does not cover the cost of prenatal care or childbirth in Japan, so parents must pay the full cost themselves, including that of every ultrasound examination. However, ultrasounds are relatively inexpensive in Japan, so couples can afford to pay for them. In the United States, health insurance typically covers an ultrasound, but the cost is high, which prevents most Japanese couples in the United States from being able to afford multiple ultrasounds. Japanese parents' need to see the development of their child through multiple ultrasounds, whether to fulfill emotional or cultural needs, often goes unmet in the United States (Yeo, Fetters, and Maeda 2000).

---

sickness), heartburn, flatulence, hemorrhoids, constipation, shortness of breath, backache, leg cramps, uterine contractions, insomnia, minor vaginal discharge, and varicose veins. Because of the many physical and hormonal changes, expectant mothers also often experience fatigue and mood swings.

Major Complications of Pregnancy

Major complications arise only infrequently, but when they do, they present a more serious threat to the health and life of mother and baby than do the minor discomforts already mentioned. For example, pernicious vomiting is prolonged and persistent vomiting. One patient in several hundred suffers from this condition to an extent that hospitalization is required.

Pregnancy-induced hypertension (PIH), also called toxemia or preeclampsia, affects about 7% of pregnant women. It occurs more commonly in first pregnancies, in teens or women older than 40, in women carrying multiple babies, and in women with a family history of PIH. Warning signs of preeclampsia include high blood pressure (especially a sudden rise), unusual swelling of the hands and face in the morning (swollen feet and ankles are common and usually not dangerous), rapid weight gain over 1 or 2 days, and severe headache (American Pregnancy Association 2016).

PIH can prevent the placenta from getting enough blood, causing the developing embryo/fetus to get inadequate oxygen and nutrients. Untreated, it can result in kidney and liver damage to the mother and eventually lead to seizures (eclampsia), coma, and death.

Fortunately, with good prenatal care the outcome is positive for most women with PIH and their babies. Treatment includes careful monitoring, bed rest, and medication. Hospitalization may be needed in some cases; babies are delivered as soon as possible—by cesarean section (c-section) or induced labor (American Pregnancy Association 2016; "Gestational hypertension" 2014).

Spontaneous abortion, or miscarriage, may be indicated by vaginal bleeding. Spontaneous abortion is fairly common, occurring in one of every five or six pregnancies, typically before the 12th week. Early miscarriage may be nature's way of screening out future problems. About 85% of all first-trimester miscarriages are a result of genetic abnormalities of the embryo/fetus. The primary

pregnancy-induced hypertension A dangerous elevation of blood pressure; also called toxemia or preeclampsia.

A woman's reaction to pregnancy is strongly related to the emotional support and help she receives from her partner.

causes of second-trimester miscarriages are maternal factors, including structural problems of the uterus, acute infections, cervical abnormalities, hormonal imbalances, environmental toxins, and undue stress (American Pregnancy Association 2016; "Pregnancy and miscarriage" 2014). Almost all women who have had a miscarriage will be able to go on to have successful pregnancies, and 70% of women who have had two miscarriages will be able to carry subsequent pregnancies to term. Research shows that women who have had a miscarriage are at increased risk for anxiety symptoms immediately following miscarriage and continuing until approximately 4 months after the loss (Geller, Kerns, and Klier 2004).

Abruptio placentae (placental abruption), the premature separation of the placenta from the uterus, happens in about 1% of pregnancies, usually in the last weeks of the pregnancy. Maternal hypertension; multiple fetuses; trauma (auto accident, a fall, for example); and use of alcohol, tobacco, or some illegal drugs are risk factors. Symptoms include vaginal bleeding and abdominal pain (Gaufberg 2008; "Placental abruption" 2014).

In **placenta previa**, the placenta is attached close to or covering the cervix. Painless, bright-red vaginal bleeding that happens near the end of the second or beginning of the third trimester is the main symptom of placenta previa. If the placenta is not completely covering the cervix and bleeding is light, the woman may be sent home on bed rest; a vaginal delivery may even be possible. When bleeding is heavy, hospital bed rest is chosen and a c-section will be planned, ideally after 36 weeks. Severe bleeding during labor—heavy enough to cause maternal death—is the biggest threat to the mom; babies are at risk of having to be delivered prematurely. Fortunately, good prenatal care detects placenta previa early and the outcome is nearly always positive ("Placenta previa" 2014).

Ectopic pregnancy occurs when the fertilized ovum attaches itself and grows somewhere other than the uterus. Most often (98%) it is a **tubal pregnancy**, with the ovum attached to the wall of the fallopian tube. Or the pregnancy may be situated in the ovary, abdomen, or cervix. All such pregnancies must be terminated. Data indicate that the number of such pregnancies has climbed dramatically over the last 40 years. This may be the result of a number of factors: the postponement of childbearing, during which time the fallopian tubes age; previous abortion; PID; STDs; or previous surgery. Any condition that affects the fallopian tubes and impedes transport of the fertilized ovum will contribute to an ectopic pregnancy. Better diagnosis may also explain why it is that even though the rate of ectopic pregnancies has increased, the rate of maternal mortality has decreased equally dramatically (Tenore 2000; Tuland 2015).

Rh incompatibility is determined during an initial prenatal exam by determining the blood types of the pregnant woman and the baby's father. The Rh factor is a protein found in the blood of some people and indicated in the blood type as O$^+$, for example. Persons lacking the Rh factor have negative blood types, such as O$^-$. Because some of a baby's red blood cells cross the placenta and enter the mother's bloodstream during pregnancy and delivery, an Rh-negative mother will develop antibodies to the blood cells of an Rh-positive baby. If she has another Rh-positive baby, the antibodies in her blood will pass through the placenta and destroy some of the baby's red blood cells, possibly causing jaundice, anemia, mental retardation, and even death.

Fortunately, a serum called Rh immunoglobulin (Rhig) can be given to an Rh-negative mother within a few hours of giving birth to an Rh-positive baby to prevent the development of antibodies. Or it may be given at about week 28 of the pregnancy if needed; Rhig should also be given following miscarriage or abortion because these can also trigger the development of antibodies. If tests of the amniotic fluid (amniocentesis) reveal that the fetus already may be affected, intrauterine blood transfusions may be given.

Sexual Relations during Pregnancy

Pregnancy is a major life transition and generally results in a change in sexual activity. Most researchers studying sexuality during pregnancy have reported a decrease in sexual desire and frequency of sexual intercourse from the first to the third trimester, with a sharp decline in the frequency of coitus from the second to the third trimester (Carroll 2015). Although a classic study by Masters and Johnson (1966) found a marked increase in sexual interest in the second trimester and some other studies indicate sexual interactions stay level in the second trimester (LeVay, Baldwin, and Baldwin 2009), in all of the studies, women report a decrease in sexual desire, frequency, and satisfaction throughout pregnancy, but most commonly in the third trimester. Among men, this decrease was common only during the third trimester.

Many reasons have been given for this decline in sexual interest during pregnancy, including chronic exhaustion, the feeling of being less sexually attractive, physical discomfort associated with intercourse, concern for the pregnancy, and fear of causing harm to the fetus by intercourse or orgasm (Carroll 2015; LeVay, Baldwin, and Baldwin 2009). However, in a normal pregnancy the fetus is well protected and couples who wish to do so may continue to enjoy sexual relations until late in the pregnancy, with a few exceptions.

Blowing air into the vagina is regarded as dangerous during pregnancy. Another risk is if the mother acquires an STD; the STD organisms can be transmitted to the fetus during pregnancy or at birth—often with catastrophic results. And there are several medical conditions that may make intercourse unsafe late in pregnancy, including previous miscarriage, threatened miscarriage or premature labor, vaginal bleeding, leakage of amniotic fluid, abnormalities of the placenta (such as placenta previa), and multiple fetuses (American Pregnancy Association 2016; LeVay, Baldwin, and Baldwin 2009).

Mental Health

Research shows that the transition to parenthood is a serious drain on the emotional, physical, and material resources of a substantial number of couples (Pacey 2004; "Pregnancy and baby" 2015). It is normal to experience some stress during pregnancy. However, maintaining good mental health during pregnancy has implications not only for the well-being of the mother, but also for the development, health, and well-being of her unborn child. Studies suggest that psychosocial stress and social support may exert a significant influence on fetal development and birth outcomes (Federenko and Wadhwa 2004; Kail and Cavanaugh 2016). For example, severe mental symptoms during pregnancy have been reported to be associated with an increased rate of complications during pregnancy and delivery, preterm deliveries, low birth weight, a higher rate of postpartum depression, and a long-term impact on the offspring's development (Berk 2013; Halbreich 2004). Women with more resources had fewer low-birth-weight babies and premature births. Factors such as being married, having higher income and education, and giving birth for the first time were associated with lower stress.

Emotional disturbance also may have negative effects on the mother herself. Some research suggests that the harmful effects of stress may be magnified when women are anxious about the pregnancy per se—not just anxious in general (DiPietro et al. 2006). For example, women who suffer from

---

abruptio placentae (placental abruption) The premature separation of the placenta from the uterine wall.

placenta previa A complication of pregnancy in which the placenta grows partly or all the way over the opening to the cervix.

ectopic pregnancy Attachment and growth of the embryo in any location other than inside the uterus.

tubal pregnancy A type of ectopic pregnancy in which attachment and growth of the embryo occur in the fallopian tube.

Rh incompatibility A condition in which the mother has Rh-negative blood and the fetus has Rh-positive blood.

pernicious vomiting during pregnancy have been found to be under considerable emotional stress, usually because of conflict between wanting and not wanting the unborn child.

Pregnancy is not always the euphoric, blissful experience that romantic literature describes. It usually is a happy, healthful time, but it also can be a period of stress and anxiety, especially for the immature or unprepared. That is why preparation for childbirth and for parenthood is so important.

Prenatal Development

Prenatal development takes place during three periods:

1. **The germinal period**—from conception to implantation (attachment to the uterine wall), about 14 days.

2. **The embryonic period**—from 2 weeks to 8 weeks after conception.

3. **The fetal period**—from 8 weeks through the remainder of the pregnancy.

The mother's experience of the pregnancy changes from period to period as the baby grows inside her. All of the major body structures are formed during the first two periods, the time when the baby is most vulnerable to teratogens (see Figure 12.1). By the end of the fourth month, the mother can usually feel fetal movement. The last several months of pregnancy are the most

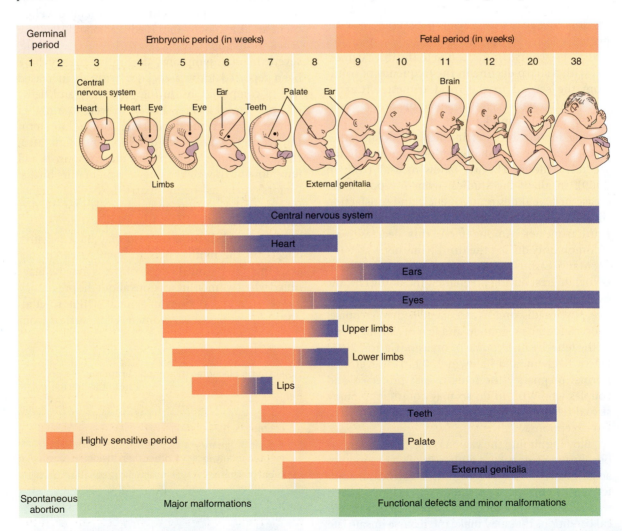

FIGURE 12.1 Sensitive Periods of Development

Note: From Human development: A life-span approach, *by F. P. Rice, 1992, New York: Macmillan.*

uncomfortable for the mother because the growing fetus crowds her internal organs and strains the muscles of her back.

The Germinal Period

As soon as a sperm meets an ovum in the fallopian tube, pierces the cell wall, and mixes its chromosomes with those in the nucleus of the ovum, fertilization happens. The fertilized ovum, called a zygote, is propelled down the fallopian tubes by hair-like cilia and the process of cell division begins. One cell divides into two, two into four, and so on until a hollow ball of cells—a blastocyst—is formed. About 4 to 5 days after fertilization, the blastocyst reaches the uterus and begins to attach to the uterine wall in the process called implantation. Implantation will be completed by approximately 12 to 14 days after fertilization. Occasionally, early in cell division, the zygote separates into two cell clusters that develop into identical twins. The more common fraternal twins develop when two eggs are released and are fertilized by two different sperm cells.

The Embryonic Period

The embryonic period begins at the end of the second week, with the embryo developing from the inner layer of cells of the blastocyst. At 18 days, the embryo is about 2 millimeters long. During its early weeks, the human embryo resembles those of other vertebrate animals, as Figure 12.2 illustrates. The embryo has a tail and traces of gills, both of which soon disappear. The head develops before the rest of the body. Eyes, nose, and ears are not yet visible at 1 month, but a backbone and vertebral canal have formed. Small buds that will develop into legs and arms appear. The heart forms and starts beating, and other body systems begin to take shape. By the end of the embryonic period, the embryo is clearly human; about 95% of body structures and organs are in place in some form. The embryo is still only an inch or so long and weighs less than an ounce.

Hormonal changes in the mother's body begin as soon as the egg is fertilized and may be accompanied by sleepiness, fatigue, and emotional upset. Hormonal changes also cause nausea, or morning sickness, in about two-thirds of pregnant women. Morning sickness usually disappears by the 12th week.

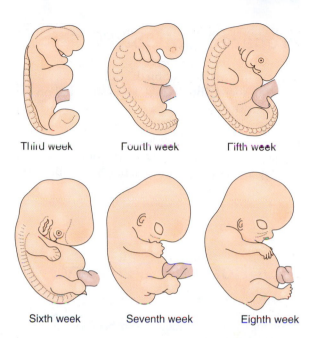

Third week   Fourth week   Fifth week

Sixth week   Seventh week   Eighth week

FIGURE 12.2 Development of Human Embryo from the Third Week to Eighth Week after Conception

Note: From Human development: A life-span approach, *by F. P. Rice, 1992, New York: Macmillan.*

The Fetal Period

From week 9 until birth, the baby-to-be (now called a fetus) grows much larger and body systems begin to work. By about 4 months, the fetus will weigh 4 to 8 ounces and will be large enough for the mom to feel it moving for the first time—called quickening. Also by about 4 months, external genitals will be formed well enough to tell the baby's sex by ultrasound.

The fetus has periods of activity (moves, kicks, turns somersaults) and quiet; sucks his or her thumb and swallows amniotic fluid. The eyes are light sensitive and the fetus can hear his or her mom's heartbeat and digestion and voices. By 22 to 28 weeks of gestation, the fetus will be large enough and will have most systems functioning well enough to have a chance to survive if born early (age of viability). Babies born early are very small and will have difficulty breathing and regulating their body temperature. As a result, they will need medical intervention for weeks. A pregnancy typically lasts 36 to 40 weeks. By then the fetus will weigh 7 to 8 pounds and will be about 20 inches long.

Prepared Childbirth

The term **prepared childbirth**, as used here, means physical, social, intellectual, and emotional preparation for the birth of a baby. Physical preparation involves the mother's taking care of her body to provide the optimal physical environment for the growing fetus and physically conditioning her body so that she is prepared for labor and childbirth.

Prepared childbirth also involves social preparation of the home, partner, and other children so that the proper relationships exist within the family in which the child will be growing up. Prepared childbirth involves intellectual preparation: obtaining full knowledge and understanding of what the process of birth entails and what to expect before, during, and after delivery, including adequate instruction in infant and child care. Finally, prepared childbirth involves psychological and

AT ISSUE TODAY

Options for Delivery

In the early 1900s, about 95% of babies were born at home. Birthing was a family event. By the 1950s, that ratio had been reversed, with 95% of babies being born in hospitals. The switch was at the urging of physicians, who prefer delivery in the sterile, well-equipped, more convenient hospital setting. In the 1970s, the "medicalization" of childbirth began to be criticized. Some expectant parents and some medical practitioners objected to the rigidity, impersonality, and expense of hospital delivery practices. They felt that family members should have the choice of being present during delivery and that women should have more control over the childbirth process. These dissatisfactions led to the development of new options for delivery. In some states, nurse-midwives, rather than physicians, provide prenatal care and assist in or perform routine deliveries. Some hospitals now provide alternatives to sterile and impersonal delivery rooms.

Birthing rooms are lounge-type, informal, cheerful rooms within the hospital itself. Medical equipment is available but unobtrusive. Both labor and delivery take place in the birthing room, attended by the father and medical personnel. The mother is encouraged to keep her baby with her after delivery to facilitate bonding.

Birthing centers offer an alternative to the traditional hospital setting. They are separated from but near a hospital, offering a low-tech, homelike environment with the medical backup of the hospital. They provide complete prenatal and delivery

services and emphasize childbirth as a family-centered event, giving both parents maximum involvement. They also focus on the emotional and social components of childbirth. The parents learn about infant care while still in the center.

Some couples opt for home birth. Supervised by a physician or nurse-midwife, home births are less expensive than hospital deliveries. At home, a woman can labor and give birth in a comfortable environment, surrounded by loved ones. Statistics show that home birth is as safe as hospital birth for low-risk women with adequate prenatal care and a qualified attendant. Typically, the midwife interviews the pregnant woman to determine whether a high-risk situation exists (such as PIH, placental abnormalities, diabetes, blood disorders, **breech birth**, **transverse birth**, or multiple births). If a high-risk situation does exist or is likely, a home birth is not recommended. Occasionally, there will be unexpected complications during home delivery. A midwife is trained to recognize the early stages of complications and to take the appropriate action. Transport to the hospital during the course of the birthing process may be necessary for the health of either the baby or the mother. Some midwives require the mothers to preregister at a nearby hospital in case any complications arise.

Each type of delivery has advantages and disadvantages, which the couple must weigh carefully. The overriding consideration, however, must be the health and well-being of mother and baby.

emotional conditioning to keep fear, anxiety, and tension to a minimum and to make the process as pleasant and comfortable as possible.

Prepared childbirth does not exclude medication during labor and delivery, if the mother desires to use it. In other words, the focus is not only on unmedicated childbirth (often referred to as natural childbirth, when in fact all childbirth is natural), but also on whether the woman, her partner, and her family are prepared for the experience of becoming parents.

The Lamaze Method

One of the most popular childbirth training methods is the **Lamaze method**, which originated in Russia and was introduced to the Western world in 1951 by Fernand Lamaze, a French obstetrician. In the late 1950s, Elisabeth Bing and Marjorie Karmel met and formed ASPO/Lamaze (now Lamaze International) to teach as many women as possible about the Lamaze philosophy (Lamaze International 2013). The important elements of the Lamaze method include the following:

- Learning about birth, including the importance of relaxing uninvolved muscles.
- Exercising to get in good physical condition.
- Learning ways to relax, including controlled breathing, taking a walk, different labor/birth positions, and taking a warm bath. These techniques are useful in pain prevention, which can minimize the need for pain-relieving drugs.
- Offering emotional support to the woman during labor and delivery, primarily by teaching someone how to coach her during the process. The importance of the partners' relationship and communication is emphasized. In this method as well as other prepared childbirth methods, the attendance of the father or another support person in childbirth education classes and during labor and delivery is essential. Research has shown that the presence of a supportive companion or labor coach during labor lessens women's need for obstetric intervention (Lamaze International 2013).

An important feature of the Lamaze method is that the mother is taught that she can be in control during the experience of childbirth (Lamaze International 2013).

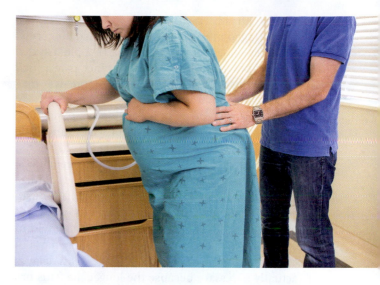

Expectant fathers are encouraged to attend birth preparation classes and to act as coaches during labor and delivery. Fathers who are present at delivery tend to show more interest in their infants and to talk to them more than do fathers who are not present.

Labor and Delivery

Because it is physically demanding, childbirth is also called **labor**. It begins with rhythmic contractions that recur at fixed intervals, usually about 15 minutes apart at first and decreasing to 1- to 3-minute intervals when labor is well under way. In addition, the total length of each muscular contraction increases from less than half a minute to more than a minute. One sign that labor is about to begin

prepared childbirth Physical, social, intellectual, and emotional preparation for the birth of a baby.

breech birth When the buttocks or feet are the first part of the baby to pass through the vagina.

transverse birth When the shoulder and arm of the baby are the first parts seen at the opening of the vagina.

Lamaze method A popular childbirth training method in which the woman has control of the childbirth experience by getting in good physical shape, learning controlled breathing and muscle relaxation techniques, and receiving emotional support from her partner.

labor Rhythmic muscular contractions of the uterus that expel the baby.

or has already begun is the discharge of the blood-tinged mucus plug that has sealed the cervix. The plug passes out of the vagina as a pinkish discharge known as **show**. Its appearance may anticipate the onset of labor by a day or more or it may indicate that dilation has already begun.

Sometimes the first indication of impending labor is the rupture of the **bag of water (amniotic sac)**, followed by a gush or leakage of watery fluid from the vagina. In one-eighth of all pregnancies, especially first pregnancies, the membrane ruptures *before* labor begins. When this happens, labor usually will commence in 6 to 24 hours if the woman is within a few days of term; 80% go into labor within 48 hours. If she is not near term, labor may not commence for 30 to 40 days or longer. This delay is actually necessary because the longer the fetus has to develop completely, the greater the chance of the baby being born healthy. When the membrane ruptures more than 24 hours prior to labor, there is an increase in the risk of infection. It is important at this stage to guard against infection by not taking tub baths, refraining from sexual intercourse, and remaining well rested and hydrated. About half the time, however, the amniotic sac does not rupture until the last hours of labor.

Stages of Labor

The actual process of labor can be divided into three phases. The first stage is the dilation stage, during which the force of the uterine muscles pushing (contractions) on the baby gradually opens the cervix, from one-half centimeter in diameter to 10 centimeters. This phase is longer than the others, typically 12 to 14 hours for a first birth and shorter for subsequent births. There is nothing the mother can do to help except relax as completely as possible to allow the uterine muscles to do their work.

The second stage takes anywhere from a few minutes to 2 to 3 hours. It begins on completion of dilation and ends with the birth of the baby. During this phase of hard contractions, the mother alternately pushes and relaxes to help move the baby through the birth canal. After the baby is delivered and tended to, the obstetrician again turns his or her attention to the mother for the third stage of labor.

The third stage involves the passage of the placenta and membranes. This stage lasts only a few minutes.

Medical complications may require a **cesarean section**, which is direct removal of the fetus by incision of the abdomen and uterine wall. Some medical indications of the need for a cesarean include a small pelvic opening, difficult labor, breech or transverse presentation, placenta previa, heart disease, diabetes, or an STD in the mother.

The Postpartum Period

Just as prospective parents have a number of decisions to make about the delivery of the baby, so new parents have a number of decisions to make about

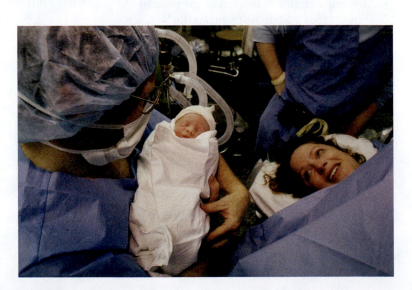

The second stage of labor ends with the birth of the baby. Within the next few minutes, the baby's physical condition will be carefully evaluated.

Bonding with Baby

Parents can take specific actions during pregnancy and after birth that will strengthen the bond between parent and child. During the pregnancy, the mother and father can develop a sense of the fetus as a person and begin to form an emotional bond with that unborn person by actions such as giving the fetus a name (even if it is an affectionate nickname such as "Sweetums"); talking to the fetus; and reading stories, singing, or playing music. Many couples save ultrasound pictures and videos as their first entries in the baby book. Parents who take such actions feel the baby is a part of the family even before the birth.

Following the birth there are certain parental behaviors that are critical to the bonding process. These behaviors include holding, caressing, rocking, kissing, and consistently expressing affection and caring for the baby; talking and singing to the baby; and lovingly comforting and caring for the needs of the baby (such as feeding and changing diapers). When parents communicate affection and caring through physical touch such as cuddling and holding, the brain chemical oxytocin is produced in both the baby and the parents. Oxytocin enhances feelings of attachment and bonding (G. Kelly 2013).

---

the period right after the birth. Different physicians and hospitals have varied policies about the amount of contact between the parents and the newborn and about how long the hospital stay should be. Because caring for a newborn can be exhausting and challenging for new parents, planning ahead for the postpartum period can make the transition easier for both the parents and the infant.

Care of the Newborn

As soon as the baby emerges, the most important task is to get him or her breathing—if he or she does not do so on his or her own. The physician or midwife swabs or suctions the nose and mouth with a rubber bulb to remove any mucus. The **umbilical cord** is clamped in two places—about 3 inches from the baby's abdomen—and cut between the clamps. There are no nerve endings in the cord, so neither the infant nor the mother feels the procedure. Drops of an antibiotic are put in the infant's eyes to prevent infection, since the infant could be blinded by gonorrhea or chlamydia organisms if the mother is infected.

One minute after delivery and again at 5 minutes, the baby is evaluated by a widely used system developed by the pediatrician Virginia Apgar. The **Apgar scale** assigns values for various signs and permits a tentative, rapid diagnosis of the baby's physical condition. The five signs of the baby's condition

that are measured are heart rate, respiratory effort, muscle tone, reflex response (response to breath test and to skin stimulation of the feet), and color. Each sign is given a score of 0, 1, or 2. A total score of 1 to 3 indicates a baby in need of emergency medical care; a score of 4 to 6 means the newborn needs special attention. A score greater than 7 indicates the baby is in good physical condition.

Parent–Infant Contact and Bonding

There is some evidence that parent–infant contact during the early hours and days of life is important for bonding. Studies at Case Western Reserve University in Cleveland confirmed the traditional belief that the emotional bonds between mother and

---

show Blood-tinged mucus plug that is expelled from the cervix.

bag of water (amniotic sac) Sac containing the fluid in which the fetus is suspended.

cesarean section Removal of the fetus by incising the abdominal and uterine walls.

umbilical cord The hollow cord connecting the circulation system of the fetus to the placenta.

Apgar scale A widely used system to evaluate the physical condition of a newborn, named after the originator, Virginia Apgar.

infant are strengthened by intimate contact during the first hours of life. This is referred to as **bonding** (Berk 2013). More discussion of emotional bonding and attachment is found in Chapter 13.

Rooming-In

To avoid separating newborns from their parents, most hospitals are equipped for **rooming-in**, where the baby is cared for most of the time by the mother in her own room. One advantage to rooming-in is that the new father and siblings can share in the baby's care, so that child care is family centered from the beginning. Another advantage is that new mothers can learn much about infant care while still in the hospital, thus reducing the anxiety and even panic that may occur if they are given the total responsibility all at once on their return home. Most mothers and babies return home on the second day after birth.

Postpartum Adjustments

The period following childbirth is one of conflicting feelings. The long period of pregnancy is over, which is a source of relief. If the baby is wanted and healthy, the parents feel considerable happiness. Within several days after delivery, however, a woman may experience various degrees of "baby blues," or postpartum depression. Postpartum depression is often characterized by feelings of sadness, tearfulness, depression, insomnia, irritability,

and fatigue. It may emerge during pregnancy and carry over into many months after the baby is born (Mayo Clinic Staff 2015; O'Hara and Gorman 2004).

Women are vulnerable to mood changes during and after pregnancy because of both biological and psychosocial variables. Biological factors may include genetics, variation in hormonal levels, diminished thyroid activity, and sleep deprivation. The mother may have been under emotional strain while she anticipated her baby's arrival.

Once the tension is over, a letdown occurs, resulting in feelings of exhaustion and depression. Pregnancy and childbirth impose considerable physical strain on her body, which requires a period of rest and recovery. Following childbirth, there is a rapid decline in levels of estrogen and progesterone in the bloodstream, which may have a negative effect on her. Research has found that the best predictor of postpartum depression is the level of depression during pregnancy. For example, chronic stressors such as frequent conflict with support network members, maternal health problems, marital discord, and lack of social support have been linked to postpartum depression (Mayo Clinic Staff 2015; O'Hara and Gorman 2004).

After the birth, the mother feels the strain of wanting to do everything right in caring for the baby. One young mother remarked, "I never imagined that one small baby would require so much

One advantage of rooming-in arrangements is the new father's opportunity to share in the baby's care from the beginning.

extra work. I'm exhausted." If the mother does not have much help from her partner or if her partner continues to make personal demands on her, she may become exhausted from a lack of sleep, from the physical and emotional strain of caring for the baby, from the work around the house, and from caring for other children. She needs help and understanding and a great deal of social support. Conscientious partners who do everything they can to assist also are affected by a lack of sleep, interference with regular work, and the strains imposed on them.

Whereas about half of new mothers experience the baby blues, approximately 15% of postpartum women develop symptoms consistent with major depressive disorder in the first 6 months after delivery (Centers for Disease Control and Prevention 2016), and women who have suffered from postpartum depression before are at greater risk for experiencing it again with another birth (Mayo Clinic 2015; Wisner et al. 2004).

One study compared postpartum depression in 11 different countries and concluded that postnatal depression seems to be a universal condition with similar rates across countries (Oates et al. 2004). However, although the women from different countries shared similar experiences of depression and described it as morbid unhappiness after childbirth, not all women saw the condition as an illness that needed medical intervention.

Nevertheless, postpartum depression is serious for both the mom and the baby because a depressed mom is not as responsive to her baby. She may not cuddle or talk to the baby, resulting in the baby becoming frustrated and angry with his or her discomfort and need for warmth and interaction. If the mom's depression is deep and/or lingers for more than a few weeks, she needs professional help. Interestingly, research indicates that breastfeeding may reduce the risk of postpartum depression (perhaps because it releases hormones that act as antidepressants) (Gagliardi 2005).

Returning to Work

Among the considerations following childbirth are whether the mother or father will return to work and, if so, the timing of that return. Several studies have examined individual, marital, and social factors associated with the length of maternity/ parental leave and its relationship to the transition to parenthood and returning to paid employment. A maternity leave of less than 12 weeks is associated with higher levels of depression, lower parental preoccupations with the infant, less knowledge of infant development, and more marital dissatisfaction (Elliott 2015; R. Feldman, Sussman, and Zigler 2004). Sadly, data from the National Center for Health Statistics indicate that very few women take sufficient time off from work when their babies are born: 16% take 1 to 4 weeks; 50% take 5 weeks; 25% take 9 weeks or more (Aleccia 2013). In another survey of 800 working parents, one in eight women took less than 2 weeks' maternity leave (Aleccia 2013). Fathers take an average of 6.5 days of paternity leave even though longer leaves are related to higher paternal preoccupation with the infant and more marital support.

Mothers adapted better to returning to paid employment when they had shorter work hours, higher marital support, lower depression, and felt their career was central to their lives. In general, shorter parental leave combined with perceived low-quality child care predicted lower parental adjustment to returning to paid employment (Elliott 2015; R. Feldman, Sussman, and Zigler 2004).

Financial considerations play an important role in the timing of women's return to employment after childbirth. In recent years, with the hard economic times (see Chapter 8), women are pressured to return to work because their income is a major source of support for the family—the primary source in about 40% of families (Aleccia 2013). Mom's income is no longer "just icing on the cake." Only three states offer paid parental leave; most families just cannot afford to take three or four months without a paycheck.

Women who are employed in fast-paced and/or competitive jobs may feel they cannot afford to be out of the workplace for long. Being out of work for even a short time puts them behind and at a serious

bonding Development of emotional attachment between the mother and newborn immediately after birth.

rooming-in Method of postpartum care in which the mother and father care for their newborn themselves in an area of the hospital assigned to them.

Becoming a Parent

The transition to parenthood brings many changes and stresses that can cause parents to feel overwhelmed. In fact, the transition to parenthood has been referred to as a developmental crisis because the status quo, as the couple knew it, has changed so much.

When a child is born (or adopted), the parents must adjust to a third person. Their love, affection, and commitment must expand to include the child. There are financial costs plus time and energy pressures. Parents of newborns typically experience sleep deprivation; although newborns sleep 16 to 18 hours, they have cycles of sleeping 2 to 3 hours and waking for an hour or so to eat—around the clock! Parents' lives are understandably more restricted. They no longer can just grab the car keys and go out to the movies or to the grocery store; now they must pack a diaper bag or arrange for a sitter. Everything is more complicated.

Although some parents are overwhelmed by the challenges, many others cope well with these challenges and report increases in their happiness and feelings of being a family. Following are some important considerations that influence how well couples cope with the transition to parenthood:

- *The quality of the couple relationship before the birth of the child.* If the prior couple relationship is distressed or unstable, the probability is greater that the couple will not cope as positively with parenthood. The baby adds another set of stressors.

- *The developmental readiness for parenthood.* People usually cope better with any change if they feel prepared. Successful coping with the transition to parenthood is more likely when the parents have reached adulthood (and are not dealing with the developmental challenges of adolescence such as finishing an education, becoming independent, etc.). A reasonable degree of financial independence, job or career stability, and a measure of emotional maturity will free up adults to spend a significant amount of time nurturing the baby.

- *Coping skills possessed by the parents.* People who have good general coping skills will be able to use them in the transition to parenthood. These skills include patience; flexibility; a high tolerance for inconvenience and clutter; an ability to obtain social support from grandparents, relatives, and friends; and parenting skills gained through parent education classes or materials or from mentors. Another critical coping skill is the ability to make positive and rational appraisals of the situation. This may include reframing or defining the situation differently. The parent who grumbles, "We never have time for ourselves, the house is always a mess, and all we do is change diapers and do laundry" is creating negative emotions and more stress. The more positive and rational appraisal is, "We aren't just a couple anymore—we have this precious baby to make us a family. Our love for each other is enhanced by the baby we share. We can't have as much couple time, but we are having wonderful moments with baby; he smiled at me today when I was changing his diaper. The baby depends on us for everything—it is a huge responsibility, but with huge rewards. We can have couple time when the baby sleeps or the grandparents keep him for the weekend. The baby won't always be in diapers and making so much laundry."

Postpartum Depression

Sarah is a mother of three children and works part-time as a physical therapist. She unexpectedly experienced serious postpartum depression and anxiety after the birth of her third child. She always considered herself in great shape physically and mentally and had always been able to take care of herself and her family. Sarah remarks,

> As I look back now, I did have some depression with my other pregnancies, but it was mild enough for me to function. With the last baby it was over the top. The worst part of the experience for me was how bad I felt and knowing that I didn't feel like myself. I was afraid of what was happening to me, and I couldn't even tell what it was doing to the rest of the family because I was too wrapped up in my emotional, mental, and even physical pain. For a woman who has always been in control, it was a scary feeling not even being able to get the kids dressed. After a weekend

> of crying to my husband, I knew something was seriously wrong. I knew I needed help and called immediately for counseling. I started antidepressants, but I was still nursing the baby. I was so anxious about the antidepressants harming his development in some way that I stopped taking them. I went down even lower after I stopped the medicine so I reluctantly started back up again. I don't want to relapse or ever go back to that depressed state, so I have been on medication for 3 years now. My advice to anyone experiencing postpartum depression is to get treatment early and not to let denial interfere with getting help. I would like people to know that postpartum depression and anxiety are treatable. It takes a good support system and professional help to get through it, but you can get through it. You will get back to feeling like yourself again, even if you think it will never happen.

disadvantage in regard to their careers (Aleccia 2013; Hymowitz 2013).

Access to quality child care also is an important consideration. The decision to return to work requires adequate provision for care of the child while the parent is absent. High-quality child care is difficult to find and can be expensive.

The Family and Medical Leave Act of 1993 enables qualifying parents to take up to 12 weeks off from work without pay and without losing their job. For more information on this act, see the "At Issue Today" feature in Chapter 8.

Sexual Relations after Childbirth

What about sexual interest and activity after childbirth? One study showed that sexual functioning appeared to deteriorate markedly from pre-pregnancy levels (Condon, Boyce, and Corkindale 2004).

In fact, a decrease in sexual activity and interest after pregnancy and childbirth is not surprising: both are physically demanding and accompanied

by hormonal changes that do not usually make people feel sexy. Newborns require huge amounts of care. Everyone is fatigued.

Physicians typically recommend about 4 to 6 weeks for healing of any vaginal or cervical soreness or tears/episiotomy. Women who are breastfeeding have suppressed levels of estrogen and testosterone and elevated levels of prolactin—all of which reduce sexual desire ("Sex after pregnancy" 2012).

Sexual desire and interaction do return; it is helpful if couples can remember that everyone is different. No one timetable fits all cases. It also helps to remember that sexual intercourse is only part of an intimate relationship: spend time together without the baby (or pressure for intercourse), for example.

Although breastfeeding does reduce the chances of conception, couples must make arrangement for some form of birth control. Some hormonal methods are not recommended while breastfeeding or for a period of time right after delivery. Check with a physician ("Sex after pregnancy" 2012).

Substance Abuse by Pregnant Women

For 25 years, policy makers have wrestled with the question of how society should deal with the problem of women's substance abuse during pregnancy. Currently, only Tennessee specifically criminalizes drug use during pregnancy; however, prosecutors have used existing criminal laws in a few instances to attack prenatal substance abuse. For example, the South Carolina Supreme Court upheld a conviction that a woman's substance abuse *late* in pregnancy constitutes criminal child abuse. In 2014, a Tennessee woman was jailed and charged with assault on her unborn child when she told the sheriff she had smoked meth a few days before delivery; both she and the baby tested positive. (Tennessee law allows women to go to drug treatment before the birth of the child, complete it, and have criminal charges dismissed.)

In about 15 states, substance abuse during pregnancy is considered child abuse under current *civil* child-welfare statutes; three states consider it grounds for involuntary commitment to a mental health or substance abuse treatment facility (American College of Obstetricians and Gynecologists 2011/2012). Fourteen states require health-care professionals to report and/or test for suspected prenatal drug use, which can be used as evidence in child-welfare cases.

Many in the medical field and in human development have deep concerns for the babies born to drug-abusing women. The incidence of neonatal abstinence syndrome has tripled since 2000; babies with this syndrome suffer through withdrawal and other complications, spending an average of 23 days in the hospital (compared to 1 or 2 for a typical baby) (Mohney 2014; Patrick 2015; Preidt 2015). The cost for their care is 15 to 16 times that of a typical baby.

Although these policies have been followed in an effort to protect fetal health, they have some shortcomings and some unintended consequences. For the most part, "substance abuse" is confined to illegal drugs. Only a few consider alcohol use. Yet, the use of alcohol or tobacco is strongly supported as detrimental to a developing child (K. Becker et al. 2008; Berk 2013; Hudziak and Rettew 2009).

Opponents of these current policies argue that they actually deter many women from seeking prenatal care because they fear the consequences of their drug use. This is contrary to the welfare of both fetus and mother. And these policies tend to incline the women and fetuses most in need of prenatal care (drug abusing, poor) away from it.

Opponents also argue that current policies treat addiction as a moral failing (needing punishment) rather than as a chronic biological and behavioral disorder that needs medical and behavioral management in the same fashion as diabetes (American College of Obstetricians and Gynecologists 2011/2012). They urge policies to identify and implement strategies to meet the needs of addicted women (such as access to drug rehabilitation) and to reduce the punitive nature of existing policies (Mohney 2014).

Questions to Consider

Should a woman seeking prenatal care be subject to criminal or civil penalties (incarceration, loss of custody, involuntary commitment) because of her misuse of drugs or alcohol?

How does society balance the welfare of the fetus and the mother? Whose welfare takes precedence? How do societal and legal views of the fetus as expressed in relation to abortion figure into this issue? Does a fetus have a right to protection (from exposure to teratogens) as a child would have (from poisons)?

What positive incentives might be offered to reduce the abuse of drugs, alcohol, and tobacco by pregnant women?

Should policies—either punitive or positive—consider tobacco use as well as alcohol and illegal/addictive drugs?

Summary

1. The signs and symptoms of pregnancy can be divided into three categories: presumptive signs, probable signs, and positive signs. Suspicions of pregnancy also can be confirmed by a pregnancy test, the most common of which detect HCG in the urine.

2. The expected birth date can be calculated using Naegele's formula, a short way of counting 280 days from the beginning of the last menstrual period.

3. How men and women react to prospective parenthood and pregnancy depends on a large number of factors, including their desire and readiness to be parents and the status of their relationship. The timing of the pregnancy is extremely important. Part of the woman's reaction to pregnancy depends on the reaction of her mate to her and her changing figure. The developmental tasks of pregnancy for a couple consist of developing an emotional attachment to the fetus; solving practical issues, such as financial and living arrangements; resolving dependency issues in relation to each other; and resolving the relationships with their parents.

4. Women are wise to get good prenatal care as early in the pregnancy as possible. Most women experience only minor discomforts in pregnancy. Major complications such as pernicious vomiting, toxemia, threatened spontaneous abortion, placental abnormalities, ectopic pregnancy, Rh incompatibility, and certain illnesses require expert medical help. Sexual relations usually continue during pregnancy until the later part of the third trimester. The mental health of the mother is also important during pregnancy since her emotional state affects the pregnancy, the childbirth experience, and the emotions of the child.

5. Teratogens are agents that can disrupt prenatal development—resulting in prenatal death, birth defects, low birth weight, or prematurity. They include drugs, alcohol, nicotine, and diseases.

6. Prenatal development takes place during three periods: the germinal period, the embryonic period, and the fetal period.

7. Couples can prepare themselves for childbirth; physical, social, intellectual, and emotional preparations for the baby are necessary. Preparations may include learning about birth, exercising to get in good physical condition, learning relaxation techniques and proper breathing, and preparing the man to give emotional support and help to the woman during labor and delivery. The most popular prepared childbirth method is the Lamaze method.

8. Couples may want to consider all factors before deciding where to give birth, whether in a hospital, at home, or at a birthing center.

9. Labor may be divided into three stages: dilation, childbirth, and passage of the placenta and membranes.

10. Remarkable advances have been made in saving the lives of preterm or small-for-gestational-age babies.

11. Bonding between parent and child is more likely if parents maintain intimate contact with their infant from the time of birth. Rooming-in allows the mother and the father to have this contact and to take care of the baby themselves.

12. Postpartum blues are common. Postpartum depression can be severe enough to need professional treatment.

13. Among the considerations following childbirth are whether the parent will return to work and, if so, the timing of the return.

Key Terms

abruptio placentae (placental abruption)
Apgar scale
bag of water (amniotic sac)
bonding
breech birth

cesarean section

ectopic pregnancy

human chorionic gonadotropin

labor

Lamaze method

Naegele's formula

placenta previa

positive signs

pregnancy-induced hypertension

prepared childbirth

presumptive signs

probable signs

Rh incompatibility

rooming-in

show

teratogens

transverse birth

tubal pregnancy

umbilical cord

Questions for Thought

1. Some physicians and human development professionals suggest preconception care—preparing for pregnancy even before conception. What preconception-care regimen would you prescribe for couples actively trying for a pregnancy?

2. Your friend is about a week overdue for her menstrual period; she feels a bit queasy in the mornings. How can she determine whether she is pregnant? If she is pregnant, when will the baby be due? Her last menstrual period was March 14.

3. What are some major and minor side effects of pregnancy?

4. What would you suggest as ways to encourage women not to smoke (including e-cigarettes), abuse prescription medicines or illegal drugs, or consume alcohol during pregnancy? Would your campaign be different with teens?

5. What ways would you suggest to reach the women most at risk of not receiving or seeking prenatal care?

6. If you or your partner were having a baby, would you consider the Lamaze method of childbirth? Why or why not?

7. What are your views on bottle feeding versus breastfeeding? Explain the reasons for your views.

8. If you or your partner were having a baby, would you consider a home birth? Why or why not?

For Further Reading

Boston Women's Health Book Collective. (2005). *The new our bodies, ourselves.* New York: Touchstone/Simon & Schuster. Represents an updated edition of a classic.

Goldberg, R. (2003). *Ever since I had my baby.* New York: Three Rivers Press. Focuses on understanding, treating, and preventing the most common physical aftereffects of pregnancy and childbirth.

The March of Dimes website at http://www.marchofdimes.org has information about all aspects of pregnancy and prenatal development, including Rh incompatibility, baby blues, colic, vaccines for baby, and prematurity. FAQs answer questions about the safety of flying, spa treatments, and tattoos during pregnancy, among other topics. There are opportunities to volunteer as well.

National Organization on Fetal Alcohol Syndrome. Learn more about fetal alcohol spectrum disorders at the website of the National Organization on Fetal Alcohol Syndrome at http://www.nofas.org.

Stoppard, M. (2005). *Conception, pregnancy and birth.* London: Dorling Kindersley. Provides an overview of what to expect when trying to get pregnant and having a baby.

Parent–Child Relationships

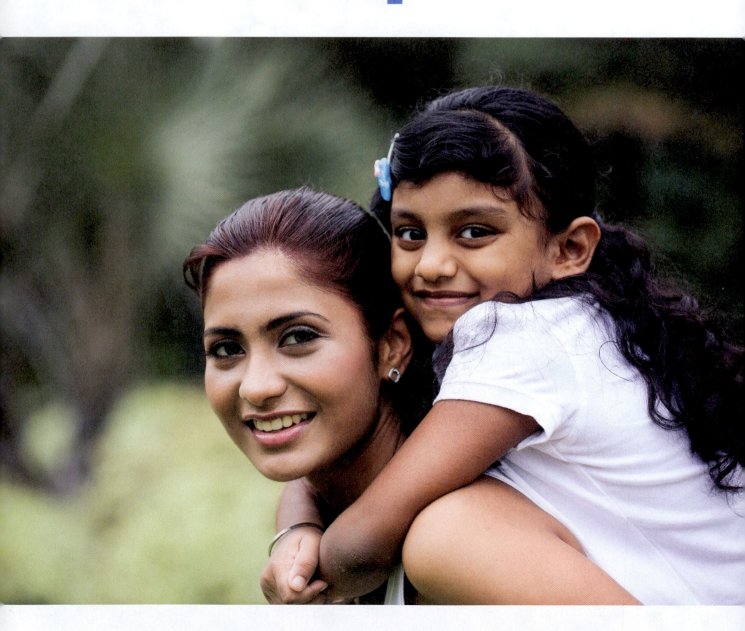

CHAPTER OUTLINE

Learning Objectives

Philosophies of Childrearing

- Parental Differences
- Value Differences
- Parent–Child Differences
- Cultural Differences

FAMILY STRENGTHS PERSPECTIVE: *Botho*

- Life Circumstances

CULTURAL PERSPECTIVE: *Cultural Conflict and Acculturation*

- Differences in Children

Stress and Children

Fostering Cognitive and Intellectual Growth

PERSONAL PERSPECTIVE: *Serendipity*

- Parental Contributions
- Language Development and Cultivation
- Educational Goals

Meeting Emotional Needs

- Emotional Attachments
- Autonomy
- Connectedness
- Identity

AT ISSUE TODAY: *Family Happiness and Material Wealth*

Child Care

Social Competence, Socialization, and Discipline

- Meaning and Goals of Discipline
- Principles of Discipline

COPING FEATURE: *The Stress of Discipline*

- Discipline Styles
- Corporal Punishment

A QUESTION OF POLICY: *Family-Friendly Policies*

Summary

Key Terms

Questions for Thought

For Further Reading

LEARNING OBJECTIVES

AFTER READING THE CHAPTER, YOU SHOULD BE ABLE TO DO THE FOLLOWING:

- Relate how philosophies and emphases in childrearing change over the years and how men and women differ in their views, as do parents and children.

- Describe why cultural and biological differences and life circumstances, as well as differences in children, require varying methods of parenting.

- Discuss parental roles in meeting children's needs and the importance of sharing responsibilities, including paternal involvement in childrearing.

- Identify the basic emotional needs of children.

- Describe some of the basic considerations in fostering children's cognitive and intellectual growth, meeting their emotional needs, and socializing and disciplining them.

Dana is the mother of an 8-year-old boy with cerebral palsy.

"I remember vividly the exact moment the doctors told me my newborn had brain damage and may never learn to walk, talk, or feed himself. All my ideas about what parenting would be like changed at that moment. I never dreamed I would be a mom in this position, and I never wanted to be, and yet it has come with great blessings. One of the greatest is that I never take anything for granted. Anytime my son does anything we never expected him to do we are thrilled. I will never forget when he was 2 years old and took his first step. I was filled with such joy!

"The challenges are trying to accept that he will never be normal and dealing with all the medical problems. Every once in a while, I think about the possibility of having a normal child and what that would be like, and sometimes I am disappointed, but not sad or depressed. I really can't imagine life any other way.

"My biggest worry is about what happens to my son when I can no longer take care of him. I wonder how he will survive—who will take care of him and will there be enough money to meet his needs? Will he be happy?"

Being a parent has many rewards and pleasures. For some people, living childless—even with a loving partner—is unthinkable. They want children as a creative expression of themselves: to love and to be loved by them. They find their own lives enriched by having children.

But parenting is not an easy task. New parents soon learn that taking care of an infant involves long hours of physical labor and many sleepless nights. One mother commented, "No one told me a baby wakes up four or five times a night." Parents also soon realize that they do not have the same freedom of movement and the opportunities to do what they want to do (Claxton and Perry-Jenkins 2008). Parenting is a 24-hour-a-day job, 7 days a week for years and, once begun, is irrevocable. You cannot give the baby back (at least not honorably). Children change everything, so prospective parents are wise to give considerable thought to the responsibilities involved. If they devote themselves to learning how to be the best possible parents, they and their children will better enjoy the experience.

Philosophies of Childrearing

As people become parents, they usually have notions of how they will rear their children. They may believe in a philosophy from a book or discuss ideas with their friends. Childrearing philosophies seem to go in cycles, with one generation reacting to the previous generation's approach. For example, in the middle of the twentieth century, it was common to be strict in discipline and routines. The next generation became more indulgent of their children, putting the child as the center of focus in the home and allowing the child to determine the family's schedule. Some people believe that was too permissive and, for them, the pendulum swings back. Because childrearing practices change over time and because even the "experts" disagree, parents must sort out the advice they receive and decide how to proceed. Furthermore, what parents believe is the best strategy for parenting and how they actually parent are not always the same. Many parents find themselves parenting in ways they never thought they would as a result of child temperament or life circumstances. What is most important is the quality of the parent–child relationship and the overall climate of the family setting, not necessarily the particular philosophy of childrearing that the parents follow.

Parental Differences

Sometimes a child's parents differ in their basic philosophies of childrearing—a situation that can create marital conflict and confusion for the child. Each parent may feel that the way he or she was reared is the right way and that other methods will not be effective. People often pattern their own parenting practices after their parents. Others resolve to raise their children differently from how they were raised.

Mothers and fathers play unique roles in the socialization of their children, and they often parent their children differently. Research shows that, in general, interactions with mothers tend to be more frequent, more directive, more focused on teaching interpersonal behaviors, and intimate, whereas interactions with fathers tend to involve more recreation and problem solving, be more goal oriented, and focus on instrumental behaviors such as independence and assertiveness (Kosterman et al. 2004).

Even though parents may have differing ideas of how to rear children, it is beneficial to them and their children if they can come to an agreement on parenting—get on the same page, so to speak. It increases stress in a family when parents do not agree on how to parent. *Parenting alliance,* defined as the capacity of one parent to acknowledge, respect, and value the parenting roles and tasks of the other parent (Loper et el. 2009), is important for various aspects of family functioning (Harrar and DeMaria 2007). One study investigated spouses' perceptions of their parenting alliance and how it related to other aspects of family life. Interestingly, disagreement on non-child-related topics was a significant predictor of parenting alliance for both husbands and wives, suggesting that conflict in the marital relationship can affect the parenting relationship. Wives who showed signs of depression reported less parenting alliance, suggesting that depressed mothers may have difficulty forming or maintaining a supportive parenting relationship with their spouse. The data also indicated that the wife takes the lead in parenting and sets the tone for both the parental and the marital relationship (Hughes, Gordon, and Gaertner 2004).

Value Differences

Values also play an important role in families and they shape parenting styles. For example, some families parent from a feminist perspective and are devoted to promoting gender equality in their children. This can be seen in how they treat their sons and daughters, as well as how they treat each other. One study examined family values as practiced by feminist parents. In these families, status was not based on sex, race, or even adulthood in the sense that parents were not the unequivocal authority. For example, all families in the study practiced some form of inclusive decision making, taking each member's concerns into account and thereby fostering the empowerment of all members of the family. Because parents routinely involved children in the decision-making process, children expected that their concerns would be given serious attention. The children, who had been encouraged to think for themselves and to be conscious of sexism, racism,

and prejudice, appeared to be able to take this perception further than their parents and heighten their parents' awareness. The older children also expressed a readiness to accept diversity and a willingness to challenge oppression (Mack-Canty and Wright 2004).

The values of feminism clearly shape the parenting practices in these families, whereas other families' parenting practices are shaped by patriarchy and/or children giving authority to parents. For some families, an inclusive form of decision making is not ideal. Rather, they espouse respect for authority and strict obedience without questioning the parents' decisions. Different types of socialization and discipline strategies will be discussed in more detail later in this chapter.

Parent–Child Differences

Several studies have shown that children and parents have overlapping but different perceptions of their relationship and of each other's behavior; that is, children's reports of their parents' behavior may not agree with how the parents perceive themselves. Because thoughts and actions often are based on our definition/perception of a situation, children are also influenced by their *perceptions* of parental attitudes and behaviors as much as by actual parental attitudes. When the perceptions of children and parents are not in agreement, misunderstandings and disagreements result. One of the challenges of childrearing is to communicate so that children and parents can better understand each other.

At no time is this more challenging than in the adolescent years. Although research documents the central role of parents in adolescents' lives (Henricson and Roker 2001), the relationship between parents and teenagers is often characterized by misunderstanding. The developmental period of adolescence, with its numerous physical, social, and emotional transitions, is difficult for most children, but it can be particularly difficult when there truly is a disconnect between parent and child. Although it is natural for a parent to spend less time with an adolescent child who is desiring more autonomy, research shows that when given the opportunity, adolescents are willing and oftentimes eager to talk with their parents.

One study examined what young adolescents would like to ask their parents if given the chance (Richardson 2004). Most adolescents did not cite subjects such as drugs or sex, but identified issues related to knowing themselves and their family better. The largest percentage (44%) of respondents listed questions pertaining to their families, with making sense of their relationship with their parents being the most salient issue for many adolescents. Because parent–child relationships are in a state of flux during early adolescence, the questions that adolescents wanted to ask their parents suggested that they recognized and were trying to make sense of the shifts in their relationships with their parents. This study and numerous others suggest that adolescents are unhappy with conflict and desire closeness with their parents, even as they struggle with autonomy (Ackerman et al. 2013; Richardson 2004; Sacks et al. 2014; Santrock 2014).

In 1971, Bengtson and Kuypers hypothesized that differences in perceptions of closeness between generations reflect the differing developmental perspectives of parents and adult children. They argued that parents, heavily invested in their children, emphasize *continuity* between generations. The adolescent or young adult children, striving for independence, emphasize the *differences*, reflecting their needs for autonomy and individuation. This phenomenon is referred to as *developmental stake*.

Giarrusso, Stallings, and Bengtson (1995) proposed a revision of developmental stake theory, suggesting that the term **intergenerational stake** better represents family perceptions of closeness. In their reconceptualization, the emphasis shifts from a focus on individual development to life course concerns that characterize each generation. Moreover, this reconceptualization extends the focus on young adults and middle-age parents to include middle-age adults and their aging parents. In 2007, Bengston and Oyama described this "problem of generations" as the renegotiation of balance between group continuity (society, values, traditions) and the need for innovation (adaptability) in the face of time-related changes. They argue that although there is a struggle for balance (conflict), there is also solidarity between the generations.

Cultural Differences

There is no doubt about the strong relationship between culture and the way parents and children interact. Culture and parent–child relationships are interdependent (Bornstein 2012; Peterson, Steinmetz, and Wilson 2003): children are exposed to the particular group's shared identity, common ancestry, and common lifestyle that shape unique conceptions of competent parenting and social competence in children. In addition, parents express specific parenting values and priorities based on their commitment to cultural goals (Bornstein 2012; Keller et al. 2004).

An interesting example of cultural differences in childrearing can be found in the practice of consumerism. Some cultures put little emphasis on possession and ownership, or on objects in general, and do not teach children about the pride of ownership. The accumulation of possessions is not the goal in life, nor is achieving a certain level of wealth. Instead, they emphasize family cooperation, sharing, and help. For example, anyone in the family (including nieces, nephews, even cousins) who needs help (shoes for the kids, groceries, rent) has a legitimate claim on family resources. The lessons they teach about respecting the property of others, achievement and success, and consumerism differ from those of parents whose possessions are important to them and who consider their possessions a part of their identity (Gonzalez-Mena 1993). In general, parents raise their children in a manner that allows the children to fit in and survive in their culture (Bornstein 2012).

Several studies have examined the beliefs about childrearing, intelligence, and education among parents from different ethnic backgrounds. Immigrant parents from Asian and Hispanic backgrounds and U.S.-born parents responded to questions about what is most important for children to learn in school and what characterizes an intelligent child. Immigrant parents rated conformity to external standards as more important than development of autonomous behavior. In contrast, U.S.-born parents favored autonomy over conformity and were less concerned about self-control. Immigrant parents indicated that noncognitive characteristics, such as motivation, social skills, and practical school skills, were as important as or more important than cognitive characteristics, such as problem-solving skills, verbal ability, and creative ability. Thus, parents from different cultural backgrounds have different ideas about what it means to be intelligent, what kinds of skills children need to do well in school, and what practices will promote their children's development (Julian, McKenry, and McKelbey 1994; Weale 2014).

FAMILY STRENGTHS PERSPECTIVE

Botho

One aspect of the culture of Botswana that is a strength and protection for families in a stressful and changing society involves childrearing and values that are communicated to the child. This cultural concept is called *Botho*, which emphasizes the importance of mutual respect and empowering one another in relationships. Botho refers to a childrearing goal of helping a child grow into an adult who has a well-rounded character and is disciplined, courteous, and well mannered. This goal is reflected in a saying in Botswana: "Let not our children be without soul." This cultural expression refers to nurturing the total development of children, including the moral aspects of life (Mberengwa 2007).

There are many differences among various cultures. People look different, dress differently, speak differently, eat differently, pray differently, and certainly raise children differently. However, no matter how many differences there may be, beneath the surface there are even more similarities. Stripping away surface differences will uncover a multiplicity of similarities such as people's hopes, aspirations, desire to survive, search for love, and need for family.

Life Circumstances

Not only is family background important in the way parents relate to their children, but also life circumstances affect parent–child relationships. The level of marital satisfaction has a significant effect on parenting practices, as does the level of parental mental health and self-esteem. Parents who experience a great deal of stress in their lives, such as economic stress, often have difficulty being patient and relaxed with their children (Ackerman et al. 2013). In general, lower-social-class individuals tend to have a lower sense of optimism and control over their lives (Chen, Matthews, and Boyce 2002), which can translate to higher rates of irritability, anxiety, and depression (Driscoll and Nagel 2010). One study found that when comparing income levels among mothers, low-income mothers were more likely to become hostile with their young children when the children showed anger, sadness, or fear (Martini, Root, and Jenkins 2004).

Other studies report similar findings. Lower-income parents, perhaps because of the strain of poverty, which straps their energy and resources, tend to use disciplinary methods (such as spanking) that are quick and take less effort. Middle-income

There is a strong relationship between culture and the way parents and children interact. Culture and parent–child relationships are interdependent and cultural differences play an important role in philosophies of childrearing.

parents are more apt to use more democratic discipline such as negotiating or reasoning (Driscoll and Nagel 2010).

Another life circumstance affecting parenting is the age of the parents. When pregnancy occurs in the teen years, it may have long-term negative consequences for a young mother's social, psychological,

intergenerational stake Family members' perceptions of closeness, especially as they relate to life course concerns that characterize each generation.

Cultural Conflict and Acculturation

Cultural pride and values are important to families, but many cultural groups feel that they are faced with a dilemma: whether to integrate in the Anglo-American world or to retain traditional customs and values and live apart. The strain between two cultures can impact parent–child relationships because parents and children may acculturate at different rates and in varying degrees (S. Y. Kim et al. 2009). In one study of Vietnamese immigrant families, most teens perceived their fathers as being less acculturated and as continuing to use authoritarian methods of parenting. Furthermore, the more authoritarian the fathers, the more apt the teens were to have low self-esteem and higher rates of depression (Nguyen 2008).

In a study of reservation and urban American Indian parents and children, Stubben (1998) found that 95% identified that cultural values are very important to their family, but many traditional values are at odds with the dominant culture. Native American culture is oriented to the present; white culture is future oriented, concerned with time and planning ahead. Native Americans see human life as being in harmony with nature; whites seek conquest over nature. Native American life is group oriented and emphasizes cooperation; white society emphasizes individualism and competition (Stubben 2001). Glover (2001) described the traditional Native American values to be generosity, respect for elders, respect for all creation, harmony, and individual freedom; she explained that it is "difficult to separate these values and describe each individually because they are interwoven, interconnected, and related to Native American spirituality and tribalism" (214). In Native American culture, all things are respected and have a spiritual nature, such as children, the earth, and creatures from the land, sea, and sky (Glover 2001). It is important to honor through harmony and balance what is thought to be a sacred connection with the energy of life (Garrett and Wilbur 1999). As everything is intimately connected biologically, spiritually, and emotionally, a person is connected to families, households, and communities (Glover 2001).

Another example of the acculturation dilemma is the comparison of traditional Chinese values with Western urban industrial values. Confucianism has been a major influence on the Chinese family for more than 2,000 years. This philosophy stresses the importance of filial piety, respect and obedience toward parents and older generations, family obligations, harmonious relationships, parental control, and emotional restraint. These concepts, in essence, are the basis of traditional Chinese family life. Confucian beliefs emphasize specific expectations of behavior with regard to age, gender, and birth order. A protocol based on obedience and respect dictates that women defer to men, sons defer to fathers, and younger brothers defer to older ones. Respect follows an upward pattern from young to old and from female to male, with the elderly male being the most revered and having the most power (Wu 2001). This protocol preserves family harmony and minimizes conflict within a family.

Chinese Americans teach children to conform to the wishes of their parents, the elderly, teachers, and people of higher status. Traditional approaches of childrearing feature authoritarian methods: a strict interpretation of good and bad behavior, limitation of social interaction, firm discipline involving physical punishment, expectation of obedience and conformity, and the absence of overt parental praise. Chinese children also are taught emotional restraint and are not typically praised or rewarded by their parents for their good behavior or school performance. Emphasis is placed more on self-discipline than on external control, with the idea being that behavior is based on one's internal morality rather than on fear of being punished or the expectation of reward (Wu 2001). Strictly authoritarian methods such as these may, however, be perceived as unsupportive, resulting in adverse effects on the children, such as depressive symptoms (S. Y. Kim et al. 2009).

Families whose cultural roots are different from the broader culture often struggle to maintain their traditional values while living among other values, and it becomes a difficult balance (Wu 2001). However, Nieto (1996) believes that when people can be part of two different cultures, they afford themselves the advantage of seeing things from different perspectives and becoming comfortable in a variety of situations.

and material well-being and for her child. Teenage fathers often are not involved in the care of their children, particularly when they are not married to the mother. Common obstacles to teenage father involvement are a strained relationship with the child's mother and a disinterest in childrearing. Teen fatherhood is related to a variety of risk factors, such as low educational performance and the associated low occupational achievement, as well as risky sexual behaviors (Mollborn and Lovegrove 2011). Because of immaturity (and the developmental challenges of adolescence) and life circumstances, many teenage parents have a great deal of difficulty meeting their children's total needs (Kail and Cavanaugh 2016).

Regardless of life circumstances, a parent's attitude toward life and its many challenges can be one of the most important influences on the health of the family. Research shows that mothers' use of active coping behaviors predicted more positive parent–child relationship quality, greater child self-regulatory behavior, and fewer perceived behavioral and emotional difficulties in children (Bynum and Brody 2005). It may be that a good attitude in life is the best buffer for the inevitable stresses that occur when parenting.

In sum, the total circumstances of parents' lives influence the quality of parenting. It starts early because the quality of family relationships in the parents' families of origin has both direct and indirect influences on their psychological and physical health. These, in turn, influence the parents' relationships with their own children (Ackerman et al. 2013). With such varying personalities and life experiences in the United States, it is understandable that people will have diverse views about how to parent and also differing abilities to do so effectively.

Differences in Children

Biological influences play a much larger role in childrearing practices than is sometimes recognized. For example, there are biological bases for intelligence and personality. For this reason, no one method of childrearing can be considered best for all children. Children are individuals; what works for one may not work for another. Some children want close relationships with parents, for example, whereas others do not. Some children are more difficult to raise than others because they are very active, emotionally volatile, hard to soothe, or oppositional. Children who are temperamentally easy (quiet, cheerful, cooperative, calm) to raise have a positive effect on healthy family functioning (Kiff, Lengua, and Zalewski 2011).

Although all children differ, they all go through the same developmental stages and have the same basic needs. No matter what childrearing strategy the parents follow, they must meet these needs.

The parental role sounds so simple—to meet the needs of children so they can grow. In what ways does a child need to grow? What must parents do to satisfy all of the child's needs?

The parental role sounds simple: to be sensitive to and meet the needs of children so that they can grow (Swafford and Jolley 2012). Within all children are the seeds of growth, that is, a natural inclination to develop to maturity. Parents do not have to teach children to grow physically, for example. The tendency to grow is so strong that only by extreme physical deprivation can parents prevent physical development, and even then some development takes place. The parental task is to discover the needs of the child and to fulfill those needs (Clark-Jones 2013).

Sometimes children's needs are not met because parents either cannot or will not fulfill them. For example, children do not receive proper food and rest; they are not loved or socialized; and they are deprived intellectually and spiritually. When this happens, children become physically, emotionally, socially, intellectually, or morally limited (Clark-Jones 2013). Optimum growth and development take place when needs are fulfilled.

In other circumstances, children are born with special needs or are injured or have an illness resulting in special needs. Most parents do not expect to have a child with special needs, and yet about one-fifth of U.S. families face the daily challenges of raising children with disabilities. Some estimates are that 14% to 18% of the nation's children (10.2 million children) age 18 and younger have a chronic physical, developmental, behavioral, or emotional condition and have a need for health and related services that is greater than that typically required by children (A. F. Lee 2013; Newacheck et al. 2000; UPI 2008). Mothers of children with special health needs typically provide extensive amounts of in-home care for their children and experience curtailed and suspended employment histories (Leiter et al. 2004). Some 24% of families have had a parent quit or reduce work to care for a child with special needs (UPI 2008). This pattern of employment, which affects family wages and job security, is particularly problematic given the added financial demands of raising a child with special needs. When a child has a disability, parents may be faced with caring for that child for the rest of his or her life. This caregiving is usually much more expensive, longer, and over many life-course transitions compared to the relatively shortened period of caregiving for an older parent or ailing spouse.

Stress and Children

Two of the most pressing challenges for modern parents are to help their children learn how to deal effectively with stress and to create an environment for their children that minimizes stress. Unfortunately, many children today experience a great deal of stress in their lives. Stress-related conditions such as headaches, ulcers, upset stomachs, and anxiety have increased significantly in children in recent years (Dutro and Selland 2012).

Much of the stress children experience is influenced by stress in their parents' lives, which may be a result of factors such as time pressures, loneliness, insecurity, divorce, strains of being a single parent, marital conflict, or financial problems (Ravitch 2010). Many children find the complexities of adjusting to a blended family (stepparent and stepsiblings) while also maintaining a relationship with a noncustodial parent to be taxing (Knox and Schacht 2016). Other children are lonely because their parents are too busy with work and other demands to spend as much time with the children as they need (and want).

The hectic, fast-paced lifestyles that characterize our modern society are a source of stress for children. The emphasis on accomplishing goals quickly and at younger ages means many children are pressured to achieve academic, social, and athletic goals and to make decisions with regard to certain areas such as careers and sexual relationships before they are developmentally ready. Children are pushed to look, dress, and act—at least superficially—like adults. This stressful environmental pattern is referred to as the *hurried child syndrome* (Elkind 2001).

Parents can unwittingly place enormous pressure on their children by expecting them to act and look older than they are—to be "superkids" who can read by age 3, make all A's, star in athletics, take music or dance or karate, be a scout, and on and on. It is easy for these children to be overwhelmed and to feel discouraged. Their lives are so structured, scheduled, and rushed that they have little or no time for play or fun. They have little opportunity to experience childhood (Dutro and Selland 2012; Elkind 2001).

The competition to get good grades and to perform well on standardized tests is a source of chronic anxiety for many children. Standardized testing is inappropriate and unfair for some children, such as those who are disadvantaged or disabled. Also, the emphasis on standardized test scores can limit the range of educational experiences children receive; they may not be taught to think creatively or critically because these traits are typically not tested. Consequently, their enthusiasm for learning may be diminished (Ravitch 2010).

There are specific actions that parents can take to create an environment for a child that minimizes stress and to help children learn how to deal with the stress that cannot be avoided. The following are some helpful steps for parents to consider:

- Place priority on developing a strong, stable, and healthy family environment.
- Spend regular, relaxed time with the child.
- Create a relationship with the child (early in life) that makes the child feel comfortable talking to the parent about concerns, worries, or fears. Be a good listener. Do not judge or criticize.
- Help the child learn positive, healthy coping skills. Model effective coping skills for the child.
- Give the child opportunity for unorganized, free play times.

- Avoid overloading the child with extracurricular activities.
- Avoid excessive and developmentally inappropriate expectations of the child.
- Take leadership in fostering a partnership among other families, schools, and communities to create an educational system that is more relevant, more family and community centered, and less stressful.

Fostering Cognitive and Intellectual Growth

The capacity for intellectual growth is inborn. Children are born naturally curious: they want to learn about everything. The parental role is to encourage cognitive growth and to satisfy intellectual needs by providing sensory stimulation and a variety of learning experiences. Parents facilitate intellectual growth by providing opportunities for observation, experimentation, reading, conversation, and contact with others and with the natural world. A stimulating environment encourages a child's curiosity, and his or her cognitive development will proceed rapidly. But

Serendipity

Serendipity is a fun word that means finding good things that were not sought. Much of the good that comes when parents and children spend time together is serendipitous. It springs naturally from the moment—unplanned and unscheduled.

It was early spring at the beach and unseasonably bitter cold. We decided to bundle up and take one short walk before going home early. We drove a few miles to a section of Gulf Islands National Seashore, pulled into an empty parking lot, and were immediately greeted by a flock of seagulls. As we got out, we tossed some snack leftovers to them. In a flash, we were in a cloud of seagulls. Caught up in the fun of it, we fed the gulls a box of saltines, a

loaf of bread, and a box of Moonpie cakes from our picnic supplies. They'd hover just above our heads to catch the goodies we tossed—or take pieces of bread from your hand. I've never seen gulls so close; their wings brushed our hair.

When I was growing up, there was a mimosa tree in our yard. It was large and umbrella-like with fragrant pink flowers in the summer. We—Mom, Sis, and I—would spread a blanket under the tree, stretch out and watch the hummingbirds come for the nectar in its blossoms. You had to lie very still, and of course, you couldn't talk or the hummers wouldn't come.

if a child's surroundings are sterile, unchanging, and uninteresting or if his or her human contacts and experiences are limited, growth will stop or slow down because of intellectual deprivation.

The word **cognition** (derived from the Latin *cognoscere*, "to know") refers to the process of becoming acquainted with the world and objects in it, including ourselves. We do this by taking in information through the senses of vision, touch, taste, hearing, and smell; processing this information; and acting on it. This process goes on constantly, so children are developing cognitively all the time.

Parental Contributions

Parents can assist their children's cognitive development in several ways. One way is by providing secure human relationships from which exploration can take place. Children who feel secure and safe will explore (and learn) more readily (Clark-Jones 2013; Swafford and Jolley 2012). Older children who experience fear and anxiety as a result of family or school violence—bullying, for example—often have academic difficulties. A child who is concerned with staying out of harm's way is not able to learn to spell or do multiplication tables (Fullchange and Furlong 2016).

Starting with a base of security, parents can further enhance their child's development by providing intellectual stimulation. This means talking and singing to babies; playing music; offering objects that vary in shape, texture, size, and color; and offering playthings to look at, hold, squeeze, mouth, smell, hear, and examine. It means providing toddlers playthings they can climb onto, crawl under, push, pull, and ride. Music, books to read, and conversations are important to preschool-age children, too, as are sand and water play. Simple excursions to the grocery store, zoo, or park expand the child's world.

When children enter school, parents can foster learning by taking an active interest in what goes on at school. Make a quiet place with tools (paper, pencils, etc.) for homework. Continue to read to and with children. Find opportunities to learn outside of school and for fun: learn about seashells on a trip to the beach, for example, or visit historical sites as you travel.

Compared with children who receive stimulation, children who are environmentally deprived do much more poorly on IQ tests because of cognitive delays. Specifically, intervention by the age of 18 months is recommended for infants who are markedly environmentally deprived (Berk 2013).

Language Development and Cultivation

In the beginning, babies produce coos (vowel sounds) and babbles (da-da-da or ba-ba-ba, for example) and a variety of vocal explorations such as squeals and gurgles. Between 8 and 12 months, babies show they understand words and respond to them. For example, a baby may open her mouth when her mom asks, "Want a cracker?" And babies of this age use gestures (wave bye-bye) and simple sign language. A child's first words are uttered at about 12 months; by 18 months, spoken vocabulary is about 50 words and grows rapidly to about 200 words by the second birthday.

Parents do much to facilitate language development. They coo and babble back to their infants; they sing. Parents talk—a lot—to their children: They label ("That's a banana"); they ask questions; they read books. The timing and amount and the warmth of the vocalization of parents all are related to their children's vocalization. For example, moms who smiled and touched their infants (8 months old) immediately after the babies cooed and babbled had babies who made more complex, speechlike sounds (M. H. Goldstein, King, and West 2003). Furthermore, communication skills (such as not interrupting and using a pleasant voice tone) that parents teach their children have a definite effect on the children's peer acceptance. In other words, there is a positive relationship between children's popularity in their peer group and their communication skills.

Educational Goals

Parents will help determine their children's educational goals and whether they attain them. Parents transmit their educational values to their children in a variety of ways. Parents who are well educated serve as examples of what they hope their children will achieve. Those who take an interest in their children's schooling are teaching them that education is important and that they are expected to do well (Weale 2014).

Meeting Emotional Needs

Another part of the parental task is to fulfill emotional needs so that children become emotionally secure and stable people. If children's needs for love, affection, security, understanding, and approval are met, they are likely to develop positive feelings. But if their emotional needs are unmet, children may become fearful, hostile, insecure, anxious, and rejecting.

Children's basic emotional needs are for security, trust, love, affection, and self-esteem. The psychoanalyst Erik Erikson (1959) concluded that developing trust is the basic **psychosocial task** during the first year of life. When infants receive prompt, consistent, loving care, they develop trust and security and a basic optimism. When care is inconsistent, lacking, or brusque, they become insecure and mistrustful. Overall, infant affect (positive emotion) is positively correlated with the quality of the home environment in which they are brought up (Berk 2013; Kail and Cavanaugh 2016).

During the first year of life, parents can best meet these emotional needs by fostering their children's feelings of dependency, helping them feel totally secure. This is accomplished in several ways. The home environment is important. If it is reasonably relaxed, free of tension and uncertainty; if it is a pleasant, happy place, children develop a feeling of well-being merely by living there.

The emotional tone and stability that parents convey also is important. For example, research indicates that parental depression is associated with depression and anxiety in children (L. T. Ross and Wynne 2010). Also, a parental history of a suicide attempt is associated with a significantly increased risk of suicide attempts by their offspring (Brent et al. 2015). Warm, loving, pleasant parents who are themselves calm and relaxed convey these feelings to their children. Being able to depend on parents for need fulfillment, whether it be for food when hungry or for comfort when upset, also develops infants' sense of security and trust. Physical contact and closeness are important. Young children feel secure when held close to a parent's warm body or when they feel the comfort of loving arms. Above all, children must feel they are wanted and accepted, that their parents truly like and approve of them. These feelings, when transmitted to children, build their own sense of self-esteem. Several studies have found that children who are exposed to high levels of negative parental emotions are less well accepted by their peers, whereas high levels of positive parental emotions are associated with greater peer acceptance (Bergin and Bergin 2012).

Parents meet important emotional and social needs of children by establishing a pattern of positive, healthy communication with the child from an early age. Open, positive communication in parent–child relationships is related to positive psychosocial development, academic achievement, and higher self-esteem. Nonexistent or low levels of communication are directly linked to behavioral issues and depression among adolescents. In contrast, adolescents who have positive perceptions of open communication with their parents are more likely to express healthy psychological and social adjustments (Xia, Li, and Stanton 2011).

Parental support in the form of praise, affection, and encouragement is extremely important in developing self-esteem. In contrast, parental criticism, shaming, and belittling are associated with low self-esteem and high levels of depression, substance abuse, and various forms of emotional disturbance (Kreisman and Straus 2010; Stinnett and Stinnett 2010).

Emotional Attachments

Research has shown that children begin to make emotional attachments early in their development. Although many babies are able to distinguish their mother from other people by 1 month of age, they begin to develop emotional attachments to people in general before they become attached to one person. Specific attachments, including attachment to the mother, begin at about 7 months. Securely attached infants have been found to have mothers who respond quickly to their indications of need.

Attachment is measured by the intensity of the child's distress when the object of attachment, usually the mother, leaves him or her alone or with a stranger. Securely attached children are less upset by the mother's disappearance and more easily soothed. The child whose attachment is less secure will be more upset by the mother's departure and, if soothed, will be more likely to become upset and possibly angry when the mother returns. Soothing takes longer, and the child, wary that the mother may leave again, may need visual or physical contact to remain calm.

cognition Literally, the act of knowing; the act of becoming acquainted with the world and the objects, people, and conditions in it.

psychosocial task The skills, knowledge, functions, and attitudes individuals must acquire at different periods in their lives.

The quality of children's attachment to their parents has been studied extensively. For example, children's early positive attachments lead to more frequent, sociable, and positive interactions with parents and peers in later life (Bergin and Bergin 2012; Berk 2013; Fish 2004). Attachment style is also thought to influence how a person relates to a romantic partner as well as to his/her parenting style (Swafford and Jolley 2012). Conversely, children with insecure attachments are more likely to cling to their parents, interact negatively with them and with their peers, and show signs of anxiety around their parents. Children form secure attachments to their parents through positive, reciprocal interactions over time. When attachments with parents are severed by separation, children feel threatened, which can be detrimental to their self-esteem and interpersonal relations such as romantic relationships as adults (Swafford and Jolley 2012; R. A. Thompson 2006).

Insecurity and anxiety about attachment are related to parenting behaviors (great inconsistency and unpredictability or cold, indifferent parenting, rejection, or neglect) and/or psychotraumatic events. Sometimes the parenting is supportive and loving but the child still develops attachment anxiety and insecurity because of psychotraumatic events experienced in childhood (the death of a loved one or the chronic, major depression of a parent, for example), which generate fears of and preoccupation with being abandoned. Clinical evidence indicates that severe attachment anxiety or insecurity is frequently associated with the diagnosis of borderline personality disorder (Neborsky and Bundy 2013). Because many children grow into adults who struggle with this disorder, it is important for all parents to have an awareness of it.

Borderline personality disorder (BPD) is one of 10 personality disorders listed in DSM–IV–TR. Several studies indicate that 18 million Americans exhibit primary symptoms of BPD and other studies suggest this is an underestimation. It is one of the most common of all personality disorders (Gunderson 2009; Cloud 2009). The nine symptoms (five must be present for diagnosis) of BPD are as follows:

- Frantic efforts to avoid real or imagined abandonment.

- Unstable and intense interpersonal relationships.

- Lack of clear sense of identity.

- Impulsiveness in potentially self-damaging behaviors, such as substance abuse, sex, shoplifting, reckless driving, binge eating.

- Recurrent suicidal threats or gestures or self-mutilating behaviors (cutting or burning, for example).

- Severe mood shifts and extreme reactivity to situational stresses.

- Chronic feelings of emptiness.

- Frequent and inappropriate displays of anger.

- Transient, stress-related feelings of unreality or paranoia.

A lack of a sense of core identity is central to borderline personality syndrome. Persons struggling with BPD have difficulty regulating their feelings, which can generate a variety of impulsive, self-destructive behaviors, including drug and alcohol abuse, eating disorders, gambling addiction, sexual promiscuity, self-mutilation, and unpredictable outbursts of rage at loved ones, particularly parents, friends, and romantic partners. Because persons with BPD have attachment issues, they have difficulty judging an appropriate emotional distance from significant others; they fear abandonment, but are uncomfortable with intimacy; they swing back and forth between clinging desperately to someone and pushing that person away. The relationship can be described as, "I hate you! Don't leave me!" (Kreisman and Straus 2010).

The family background of individuals with BPD is frequently characterized by depression, emotional disturbance, and alcoholism or drug addiction. They often have experienced childhood emotional deprivation, abuse, and parents who were rejecting, indifferent, or absent (Kreisman and Straus 2010).

A common therapy approach for BPD provides a balance of acceptance of the person with the development and implementation of strategies for positive change. This therapy approach includes formal skills training in four modules:

- Learning to regulate emotions;

- Developing distress tolerance;

- Becoming aware and mindful of one's own feelings and the "triggers" for self-destructive behavior; and

- Developing interpersonal skills and effectiveness (Jacobson and Mufson 2012).

This particular psychosocial intervention is also effective for the treatment of the self-destructive behavior of mutilating, burning, or cutting one's own body, which research indicates that 13%–23% of high school students experience (Jacobson and Mufson 2012).

The clinical evidence and this commonly used, effective psychosocial therapy intervention for BPD have important implications for parenting. Parents can do much to promote the psychological and emotional health of their children by doing the following:

- Creating a stable, strong family life;
- Providing acceptance, warmth, and love for the child;
- Meeting the child's need for trust, security, and protection;
- Helping the child learn to regulate emotions;
- Developing distress tolerance and problem-solving abilities in children; and
- Helping the child to develop effective, productive coping strategies and stress management skills.

Autonomy

Children start demonstrating their need for autonomy at about 18 months, and that need is foremost for the next 2 years. **Autonomy** is the assertion of independence and self-will (Erikson 1959). "No!" and "Me do it!" are familiar sounds during this period.

If children are to function as individuals, they must learn to do things for themselves: to walk, to feed, and to dress themselves, for example. However, because toddlers are not as capable as they would like to be, frustration and anger are frequent, and temper outbursts increase. Anger outbursts peak during the second year and decline thereafter (Kail and Cavanaugh 2016). Physical factors can influence anger responses—for example, being too tired or hungry and illness, even slight colds or constipation.

The parent's role is to encourage independence in things such as eating, playing with toys, and dressing and to guide their child through substitution, distraction, and tactful control, trying to avoid direct confrontation as much as possible. For example, toddlers can be allowed to make simple choices: milk or juice for snack? Puzzle or book for quiet time? Teddy bear or train pajamas?

Children's performance at school is enhanced if their parents often read to them and provide other early literacy experiences.

If the home environment is relaxed and free of tension and anxiety and if the home is a pleasant, happy place, children develop a feeling of well-being.

Connectedness

Children also have an ongoing need to feel connected to others—their family, friends, their school, and the community. Having a sense of connectedness or

autonomy The assertion of independence and self-will.

belonging is an important component in self-esteem (along with innate worth and feelings of competence). Parents foster positive self-esteem when they nurture connections for their children.

One way that parents can develop a sense of belonging is through the formation of a family identity. "We're the _____ family. This is our history. This is what we believe in. This is what we love to do together. These are our dreams." Family stories (usually with photos)—often told by grandparents—are family history. Family reunions or vacations with aunts and uncles and cousins build connections within the family.

Parents who encourage children to participate in extracurricular activities (band, softball team, scouts, etc.) help them with connections to peers and other adults. When children are part of a team or group of friends, they have opportunities to practice social skills (manners, for example), communication, and problem solving.

Identity

During the teenage years, children face the psychosocial task of developing a sense of identity (Erikson 1959). In some ways, this seems akin to the striving for independence of the toddler years. Adolescents are making lifestyle decisions (career, marriage, etc.) and moving toward adulthood. Naturally, some conflict with parents usually happens as teens "try on" various

---

AT ISSUE TODAY

Family Happiness and Material Wealth

For most of us, happiness is a fundamental goal in life. Although most people believe that material comforts should be grasped whenever they can be and that these will improve the quality of life, wealthy children report being less happy than children of lower socioeconomic status (Csikszentmihalyi 1999; Csikszentmihalyi and Schneider 2000).

Why might this be the case? Csikszentmihalyi (1999) suggests three reasons that material rewards do not necessarily ensure happiness. First, people's expectations are continually increasing. Studies on happiness confirm that goals keep getting pushed upward as soon as a new level is reached. Thus, people are never satisfied for long with their achievements. Second, people are constantly comparing what they have with what wealthier people around them have. Those individuals with decent incomes can feel poor relative to those who have more, which can lead to unhappiness. Third, despite an almost universal obsession with wealth, nobody has ever claimed that material rewards alone are sufficient to make us happy. If people devote most of their time to making money, they often neglect other aspects of their lives that might ultimately be more important for happiness, such as family life and friends. Eventually, they might even develop a dependence on material rewards and lose the ability to derive happiness from other sources (Benedikt 1999).

An alternative to the materialist approach to happiness is a psychological approach in which happiness is a mental state that a person can control. The key to achieving happiness is finding meaning in everyday experiences, and one does not need material wealth to accomplish this (Csikszentmihalyi 1999). In fact, studies have shown that in comparison to less wealthy adolescents, affluent teenagers have more difficulty finding meaning in activities and tend to exhibit more boredom and less involvement, enthusiasm, and excitement.

The family environment, especially the prevailing attitudes or emotional tone of parent–child interactions, has long been recognized as an important factor in family happiness. Home environment is related to a variety of developmental variables, including independence, self-esteem, moral development, anxiety, conduct problems, and school adaptation and achievement. When families place meaning on activities derived from active physical, mental, or emotional involvement, as opposed to material wealth, children's chances for a happy family life improve.

lifestyles (purple hair, body piercings, language, etc.). Adolescents, even as they push away from parents toward independence, continue to need the secure base of parents and family (Kail and Cavanaugh 2016). The challenge for parents is to allow teens to make more and more decisions as they are ready.

Child Care

Many parents in the United States need assistance in caring for their children—usually while they work; many also worry about the effects of such care on children. About 3.5 million children (under age 14) are in formal child care (such as a child-care center or a licensed home/family day care); uncounted millions are cared for by relatives, babysitters, or in unlicensed home/family day cares.

Several factors influence the type of child care parents choose, including number and age of children, availability of relatives or other child care, cost and ability to pay, and parents' goals and child-care preferences. Infants and preschool-age children are often cared for by relatives or in home/family day care. According to the U.S. Bureau of the Census (2012), grandparents take care of 21% of preschoolers and 13.5% of grade-school–age children. Grandparents and other relatives provide convenient, loving, and relatively inexpensive care. (Nana may even be free and fold laundry to boot!) Because home/family day care is typically less expensive than center-based care

and has more flexible hours, it is often chosen by parents with more than one child and/or those needing early-morning, late-evening, or overnight hours (because of shift work, for example). Parents who value their child's knowing the caregiver or having a more homelike environment also often choose home/family day care.

Professional child care becomes more common the older the child, the fewer the relatives available locally, the higher the family income, and the higher the mother's educational level. Parents who value developmental characteristics more often choose day-care centers. Type of child-care arrangements also varies by ethnicity, with Hispanic families using the least amount of formal child care (see Figure 13.1).

Since 1991, the National Institute of Child Health and Human Development has conducted a longitudinal study of child care in the United States. Evaluations of quality of care are based on characteristics such as child–adult ratio, physical environment (clean, bright, comfortable), caregiver characteristics (such as specialized training or education), and caregiver behavior (sensitivity to children, positive talk). Unfortunately, much care—especially for young children—is of low or mediocre quality.

Quality of child care is important because the relationship between child-care quality and children's social and cognitive development is well established. Children who experience high-quality care score higher on a variety of child development measures (such as cognitive and social development, language,

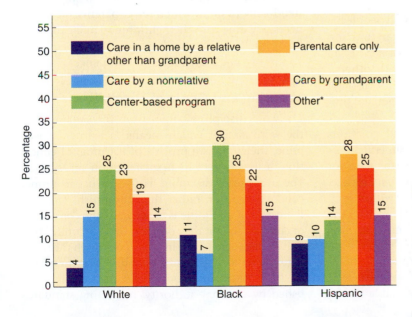

FIGURE 13.1 Type of Child-Care Arrangements for Children under Age 4 by Ethnicity

Note: Federal Interagency Forum on Child and Family Statistics. American children: Key national indicators of well-being 2014. Table FAM 3.A. http://www.childstats.gov.

Includes children in kindergarten or self-care or with no regular arrangement.

cooperation) than children who experience low-quality care. *Quantity* of child care is also important in the effect it has on children. Children who spend more than 30 hours a week in child care experienced less-sensitive interactions with their mothers, showed more behavior problems, and had higher rates of illness (Ramey 2005; Vandell 2004).

Social Competence, Socialization, and Discipline

Children also have social needs and must develop social competence. They are naturally gregarious, want to be with others, generally like other people, and ordinarily try to please them and be accepted by them. However, these natural tendencies are unsophisticated. Children want to make friends but do not know how to relate; they want others to like them but do not know how to please. Their need, therefore, is for socialization—to build on their normal desire to belong and to relate by learning group mores, customs, manners, and habits so that they can fit into the group. The parents' task is to provide their children with opportunities for socialization so that they can become part of society. Furthermore, certain parental practices, such as a high degree of parental affection and authoritative childrearing, may stimulate a child's positive orientation toward others and influence the child's acceptance by a peer group.

Socialization is the process by which people are taught the ways of society so that they can function appropriately. One dictionary defines *socialize* as "to make fit for life in companionship with others." Children are taught social roles and norms through contact with already-socialized individuals, initially the family.

Social roles are culturally defined positions such as mother, father, grandparent, supervisor, or student. **Social norms** are expectations for behavior as one performs his or her role. Norms vary by age, gender, and social class, and they differ within societies and change over time. For example, in the United States during the 1950s, norms informed the mother that she must see that the children were clean, appropriately dressed, and on time for school. She was expected to see that the house was tidy and that meals were served at reasonable times.

However, today, the mother may be expected to share in the financial support of her family and to be a partner in the management of the home.

Among the many tasks that parents undertake, the socialization of children is one of the most important. Through the socialization process, attitudes and behaviors necessary for effective functioning in society are transmitted. If parents are absent from the home a great deal, other adults may exert more socializing influence on small children than do the parents. As the children grow older, the peer group may begin to exert more influence in developing values. Bronfenbrenner (1975) suggested that in many urban and suburban homes, where the parents of school-age children are not often home and the children themselves are with their peers most of the time, peers have the greatest influence on values. Ordinarily, it is adults who are able to teach values such as cooperation, unselfishness, consideration for others, and responsibility. Peer values for boys often emphasize aggressive, antisocial behavior. In an interview, Bronfenbrenner commented,

> If parents begin to drop out as parents even before the child enters school, you begin to get children who become behavior problems because they haven't been "socialized." . . . They haven't learned responsibility, consideration for others. You learn that from adults. There's no way that you can learn it from kids of your own age. (49)

Bronfenbrenner was pointing to an important trend—the trend in which fewer parents spend the necessary time with their children to make their influence felt. When this happens, other people or groups become more important influences.

Meaning and Goals of Discipline

The word **discipline** comes from the same root as the word *disciple*, which means "a learner." Discipline, therefore, is a process of learning, of education, a means by which socialization takes place. The purpose of discipline is to instruct in proper conduct or action rather than to punish. The ultimate goal of discipline is to sensitize the conscience of children so that they develop the self-control that will enable them to live in accordance with the rules, regulations, and standards established by the group.

In the beginning, control over the child is established by external authority, by setting standards and rules of behavior. But children gradually are encouraged to adopt these principles for themselves, not because they have to but because they want to. When this happens, these internalized truths become their own standard of conduct.

At very young ages, discipline may be accomplished through wise management: providing interesting toys and activities; equipping sections of the residence, such as a playroom or play yard; and child-proofing the house by placing dangerous objects out of reach. Young children may be disciplined through distraction and offering substitute activities. For example, give your toddler his or her own toy cell phone or set of keys (to leave yours alone). Suggest to a child who is throwing wooden blocks, "Bean bags are for throwing." Sometimes the wisest discipline is through environmental manipulation: removing the child from the situation or the situation from the child (put up Aunt Jane's crystal candy dish, for example). Parents can discuss issues with older children and arrive at joint decisions, whereas instruction to preschoolers necessarily involves more imperatives. Even then, explanations and reasons can be helpful, depending on the child's level of understanding. A combination of reasoning and mild punishment is often most effective. For example, "Biting hurts! No biting. Come sit here (in time out) for a few minutes."

Principles of Discipline

If discipline is to accomplish the goal of development of inner controls, a number of principles should be followed. These may be summarized as follows:

- **Children respond more readily to parents within the context of a loving, trusting relationship of mutual esteem.** Children who receive nurturance and emotional support from parents show lower levels of aggression than do those who do not receive this support; consequently, the most effective discipline balances control with warmth and judicious demands with responsiveness (Baumrind 1996).

- **Discipline is more effective when it is consistent rather than erratic and when behavioral expectations are clearly specified.** Discipline that is harsh or inconsistent is not likely to be effective. Tell children what you want them to do (not what you do not want); for example, "Use a quiet voice inside" (not "Stop yelling!").

- **Learning is enhanced if responses involve positive reinforcement.** A smile and "Good job" when the trash is taken out helps to make it happen again.

- **Discipline is more effective when it is applied as soon after the offense as possible.** Young children, especially, have trouble connecting the two events if too much time lapses.

- **Severe punishment, especially if it is cruel and abusive, is counterproductive.** It merely serves to stimulate resentment, rejection, and similar harsh, cruel behavior on the part of children.

- **Discipline becomes less effective if it is too strict or too often applied.** A parent who continually criticizes a child no matter what the child does is teaching the child that it is impossible to please the parent.

- **Discipline must be developmentally appropriate, depending on the child's age and level of understanding.** All children need external controls in the beginning, since they are not yet mature enough to exert control over their own behavior. Appropriate methods of discipline will vary according to the child's age and level of understanding. However, extremes of either permissiveness or authoritarianism are counterproductive.

- **The internalization of appropriate social and moral norms is the result of successful socialization.** It is a major means by which social order and control are maintained in a society because it involves the individual's voluntary compliance. Effective socialization motivates the child to behave in accordance with society's values and norms by making these values an important part of the child's self-concept.

socialization The process by which people learn the ways of a given society so that they can function within it.

social roles Culturally defined social positions such as mother, grandparent, supervisor, or student.

social norms Expectations for behavior as one performs social roles.

discipline A means by which socialization takes place; the process of instruction in proper conduct or action.

- **Methods of discipline to be avoided are those that threaten the child's security or development of self-esteem.** Some examples are threatening to give children away if they are not good or to call a police officer to put them in jail. Similarly, threatening to withdraw love if children are not good is a harmful means of disciplining, but it is one that some middle-class parents employ in subtle ways to control their children's behavior. It may work to temporarily control behavior, but it is devastating to the child's sense of security if regularly employed.

- **In general, authoritative methods of discipline, those that give children choices, are more effective than more authoritarian methods.** Mothers and fathers who use authoritative methods of discipline stimulate prosocial behavior on the part of their children (Benchaya et al. 2011; Choe, Olson, and Sameroff 2013). Research has repeatedly found a positive relationship between authoritative parenting and secure attachment (e.g., Karavasilis, Doyle, and Markiewicz 2003; Neal and Frick-Horbury 2001). Higher levels of authoritative parenting also have been found to be associated with more healthy, loving children across all income levels (Horning and Rouse 2002); lower levels of drug use among adolescents (Adamczyk-Robinette, Fletcher, and Wright 2002; Benchaya et al. 2011); better family functioning as measured by family adaptability and cohesion (Mupinga, Garrison, and Pierce 2002); fewer child behavior problems (Querido, Warner, and Eyberg 2002); higher self-esteem (Carlson, Uppal, and Prosser 2000); and better academic adjustment (Hickman, Bartholomae, and McKenry 2000).

The Stress of Discipline

One of the difficult issues with which parents must cope is discipline. Parents often think of discipline as a way to control the behavior of their children. This perception causes much stress for both parents and children for two reasons. First, it is difficult for anyone to control the behavior of another over a prolonged period of time. Ask any parent who has tried to make a child eat his peas or stay out of the candy dish. And it becomes increasingly difficult as the child becomes older (and gets a driver license!). Second, attempts to control the behavior of another often create conflict and set up a perpetual power struggle.

Parents can avoid some of this stress and these power struggles with their children using the coping strategy of *reevaluating their goals*. Is the goal of discipline to control a specific behavior of the child at the present moment? To pick up toys? Or feed the cat? Or is the goal to help the child learn to control his or her own behavior—not only in the present, but also in the future—and without parental nagging? To develop the habit of putting away toys, books, tools when done—even if no one says so? Or to remember to feed the kitty because she gets hungry?

Discipline may best be defined in terms of parental behaviors that assist children to do the following:

1. Control their own behavior and develop self-direction;

2. Accept responsibility for the consequences of their own behavior; and

3. Become sensitive to and respect the needs and feelings of others.

This approach to discipline is holistic, places the emphasis on assisting the child to develop self-discipline, and avoids setting up the parent for ongoing power struggles with the child. This model of discipline can best be considered guidance rather than simply punishing undesirable behavior or rewarding the good (Stinnett and Stinnett 2010).

Discipline Styles

How to discipline children is a challenge: every child is different, every situation is different, and to know the right course of action in so many different circumstances is impossible. Parents often are not consistent in their styles of discipline and have different styles for different children. Most children know when they are disciplined differently from their siblings and are quick to point out "unfair" treatment. Many different parenting styles have been discussed in the literature, but four classic styles sum up much of the discipline experience. Baumrind (1967, 1991) identified styles according to support and control and has written extensively about parents who are authoritative, authoritarian, permissive (indulgent), or neglectful. In fact, parents can be some combination of these or be so inconsistent that they change styles depending on the circumstance. Authoritative parenting has consistently been reported to be the best discipline strategy. Authoritative (or democratic) parenting has been described as being warm, supportive, nurturing, and accepting (Swafford and Jolley 2012). Authoritative parents have clear rules and boundaries, but they are willing to discuss them with their children. Children know parents care and know what is expected of them. In general, children who have authoritative parents tend to score higher on various dimensions of social competence (self-reliant, achievement oriented, energetic, friendly, able to cope, for example) and life satisfaction (Benchaya et al. 2011; Choe, Olson, and Sameroff 2013; Suldo and Huebner 2004; Yamagata 2013) than children whose parents are authoritarian or permissive.

Authoritarian parents have definite rules and expectations and enforce them. They expect unquestioning obedience from children. Children reared in this style of parenting tend to show problems in a variety of areas (lower self-esteem, moodiness, unhappiness, vulnerability to stress, less academic achievement) (Rudy and Grusec 2006).

Permissive (indulgent) parents tend to be warm and supportive with their children. However, they rarely force children to follow rules or meet parental expectations. These children are apt to be impulsive, rebellious, and domineering ("spoiled brats").

Neglectful or indifferent parents typically ignore children's needs; they are not warm or supportive. They do not have or enforce expectations or rules. As a result, children tend to feel unloved and lonely—abandoned. This parenting style is the

Discipline is most effective in the context of a loving, trusting relationship. Time-outs and discussions about appropriate behavior are constructive discipline methods to use with young children.

most damaging to children's development because it lacks parental support.

Parental support has been defined as the nurturing behavior of parents toward their children, which includes affection, acceptance, warmth, encouragement and praise. Research has consistently shown that parental support reduces the risk of antisocial behavior in children and may help insulate adolescents from peer pressure to use drugs (Dorius et al. 2004).

Corporal Punishment

Corporal punishment—the use of reasonable (or not excessive) physical force by a parent or legal

---

corporal punishment Physical or bodily punishment with the intention of inflicting pain but not injury for the purpose of correction or control.

guardian, with the intention of causing pain but not injury for the purpose of correction or control—is legal in nearly every state (Kidjacked 2013). In a study of 20,000 parents of kindergarten-age children, 89% of African American, 80% of Hispanic, 79% of white, and 73% of Asian American parents reported spanking their children (Gershoff 2010). Parents who use corporal punishment tend to do so frequently. In fact, 7.5% of the mothers of children ages 3 to 5 interviewed for the National Longitudinal Study of Youth hit their child *during the interview.*

Just over half of parents continue corporal punishment into their children's adolescence; in one study, parents had hit their teenagers an average of eight times during the previous 12 months (Straus and Donnelly 1993). A majority of Americans seem to feel that a spanking is sometimes necessary.

However, studies have shown that, compared with those who are spanked, children who are not spanked tend to do better in school, behave better, grow up to have better marriages, earn more money as adults, and basically live better lives (Straus

---

A QUESTION OF POLICY

Family-Friendly Policies

Most public policies directed at families are generally designed to strengthen perceived at-risk families (P. Cowan and Cowan 2003). Dual-earner families (which make up the majority of U.S. families today) with young children are not considered at risk, but they are under substantial stress because of role overload and interrole conflict. Policy could be enacted to address some of the tensions experienced by millions of American families with young children. P. Cowan and Cowan (2003) argue that contemporary couples in two-parent lower- to middle-income families deserve the attention of policy-makers as well.

As discussed in Chapter 8, the United States does have a family leave policy that allows up to 12 weeks of unpaid leave after the birth or adoption of a child. However, many families cannot afford to take 12 weeks of unpaid leave, and many employers discourage taking that much time off although it is federally authorized. Compared to other countries such as Sweden and Norway, which provide 2 years of paid maternity leave to mothers, the U.S. government is not prepared to provide extensive paid leave with a guaranteed return to a job, in part because of the great expense of such a policy.

Aside from allowing maternity and paternity leave, workplaces could become more family-friendly through such benefits as flextime and on-site child care. Finding affordable

high-quality child care is an important issue for many dual-earner families. However, on-site child care could add a significant expense to business owners, and many businesses are reluctant to cater to the needs of families if doing so infringes on profit margins. Unless mandated through law, most businesses would not freely adopt family-friendly policies.

Questions to Consider

How are existing laws or policies harmful to families with young children? How can policies help reduce tension in families with young children? For example, should longer maternity leaves be granted, or should policy (e.g., tax incentives) encourage employers to establish flexible hours and on-site child care?

What would be the effects of encouraging (enabling) one parent to stay home?

How can a competitive, capitalist society help support families in nurturing, caring for, and attending to their children? What responsibilities do companies or communities have with regard to families' well-being?

What are specific practices that would make workplaces more family friendly? Communities?

How might family-friendly practices in the workplace be beneficial to businesses? To the community?

2001). After reviewing 50 years of research on spanking, Straus concluded that it is not the most effective method of discipline and that it has harmful side effects that may take years to manifest. After her similar review, Gershoff (2010) reached similar conclusions.

More attention must be paid to the possible harmful effects of corporal punishment. Corporal punishment of children is associated with aggression toward other children and a less-well-developed conscience. A number of studies also have found a link between corporal punishment and physical abuse by parents. It is not uncommon for physical abuse to occur at the end of a continuum that begins with verbal threats, escalates to corporal punishment, and gets out of hand; thus, corporal punishment increases the risk of physical abuse (Straus and Yodanis 1996).

Social learning theories suggest that children learn to use and value violence by observing and modeling the behavior of their parents, especially when the violence is in the form of corporal punishment of children. Since corporal punishment is a socially approved behavior, parents' use of corporal punishment to correct and teach contains hidden messages. Two of the hidden lessons are (1) that violence can and should be used to secure positive ends and (2) that the moral rightness of violence is permissible when other things do not work. Corporal punishment teaches children that, when someone misbehaves and will not listen to reason, it is appropriate to use violence. Lessons learned in childhood may persist in adulthood and affect marital relations. It is almost inevitable that, sooner or later, a spouse will "misbehave" and "not listen to reason," as the partner sees it. Persons who as adolescents were hit for misbehavior are more likely as adults to hit a spouse who goes against their wishes (Straus and Yodanis 1996).

Parenting is probably the hardest job a person ever takes on and usually a job he or she never regrets. It is important to create a home where family members support and relate to one another. That will require fine-tuning parenting practices, discipline, and meeting children's needs. Although all children are different, they all go through the same developmental states and have the same basic growth needs. No matter what childrearing strategy parents follow, satisfying children's needs is the essence of parenting. Growth takes place when needs are fulfilled; development is delayed when children are deprived.

Summary

1. Childrearing philosophies change from one generation to the next, so parents must sort out conflicting advice. Men and women often differ on basic philosophies of childrearing.

2. Parents and children often disagree in their perceptions of each other's behavior.

3. Cultural differences play an important role in parents' priorities.

4. Life circumstances affect parent–child relationships, particularly the amount of stress people experience. Maternal age at first birth affects the degree of supportive maternal behavior.

5. Children are different, so no one method of discipline can be considered best for all children.

6. The parental role is to meet the physical, emotional, social, intellectual, and moral needs of children. Optimal growth and development take place when needs are fulfilled.

7. Most parents do not expect to have a child with special needs, and yet millions of families face the daily challenges of raising children with disabilities. Some estimates are that as many as 14% to 18% of the nation's children younger than age 18 have a chronic physical, developmental, behavioral, or emotional condition and need health and/or related services beyond those typically required by children.

8. Modern parents are challenged to help their children deal with the considerable stress that they face. Some children experience stress from the spillover of parental stress or the strain of adjusting to life in a blended family or missing a noncustodial parent. Others are stressed by hectic schedules and unrealistic

pressures to do everything at an extraordinary level—to be "superkids." Parents can take some practical steps to help their children deal with stress.

9. *Cognition* means knowing and understanding. Parents can assist in cognitive development by providing secure human relationships from which exploration can take place and by offering a stimulating and intellectually rich environment. Environmental deprivation retards cognitive development. Language development is enhanced by talking and reading to children. Parents also serve to define children's educational aspirations and attainment.

10. An infant's emotional needs include trust, love, affection, security, and self-esteem. Children's self-esteem develops in relation to the home environment; the emotional tone between parents and child; and the willingness of parents to fulfill emotional needs, to offer physical contact and closeness, and to help children feel wanted, accepted, and connected.

11. Autonomy is a fundamental emotional need for children. Striving for autonomy begins at 18 months and continues for the next 2 years.

12. During the teen years, children develop an identity and grow in independence. They continue to need the secure base of family.

13. The type of child care parents choose is related to cost, availability of other adults, parental goals, quality of caregiving, and the range of child-care alternatives available.

14. Socialization is the process by which people are taught the ways of a given society or social group; it conveys the norms, roles, and values necessary for living within the society. Parents enhance children's socialization by maintaining close, affectionate relationships with them and by providing appropriate role models.

15. The purpose of discipline is to teach. It is a means by which socialization takes place. The goal is to sensitize children's consciences so that they internalize truths and standards.

16. How to discipline children is a challenge for most parents. Every child is different, every situation is different, and to know the right course of action in so many different circumstances is stressful. Parents are often not consistent in their styles of discipline and have different styles for different children.

Key Terms

autonomy

cognition

corporal punishment

discipline

intergenerational stake

psychosocial task

socialization

social norms

social roles

Questions for Thought

1. All parents do some things well and also make some mistakes. What are some practices that your parents used in rearing you that you want to use with your children? What are some that you want to avoid?

2. What are the pros and cons of the disciplinary techniques of time-out, spanking, and natural consequences?

3. What are the added challenges or demands on parents of children with special needs?

4. What are some of the things that happen in school or from the media that decrease self-esteem in children? How can parents offset negative out-of-family influences?

5. Uri Bronfenbrenner suggested that when parents are absent, others—other adults, peers—will become important socializing influences. With regard to the socialization of children, what part does the media (movies, television, video games, etc.) play?

6. What are some strategies for parents—both mothers and fathers—to manage their many responsibilities?

7. What are some things parents can do to promote their children's emotional and intellectual development?

For Further Reading

Bigner, J. (2005). *Parent–child relations: An introduction to parenting.* Upper Saddle River, NJ: Pearson Education. Presents a comprehensive review of parent–child relations and parenting.

Borkowski, J. G., Ramey, S. L., and Bristol-Power, M. (2002). *Parenting and the child's world: Influences on academic, intellectual, and social-emotional development.* Mahwah, NJ: Erlbaum. Describes when, where, and how parenting matters and the major antecedents and moderators of effective parenting.

Crittenden, A. (2001). *The price of motherhood: Why the most important job in the world is still the least valued.* New York: Metropolitan Books. Reviews current social scientific literature on motherhood.

Heymann, J. (2005). *Forgotten families: Ending the growing crisis confronting children and working parents in the global economy.* New York: Oxford University Press. Discusses the relationship between parents' working conditions and children's overall health and well-being.

Rubin, K., and Chung, O. (2005). *Parenting beliefs, behaviors, and parent–child relations: A cross-cultural perspective.* New York: Psychology Press. Reveals a cultural perspective on parenting, parent–child relations, and families.

Check the Child Discipline Directory at WebMD for articles dealing with a variety of topics about discipline: setting limits for school-age children and teens, types of discipline, gentle discipline tips, and how to recognize danger signs that your child needs professional help. http://www.webmd .com/parenting/children-discipline-directory.

Learn more about children with special needs at http://www.childrenwithspecialneeds.com. This site includes links to sites devoted to many specific special needs—children who are hearing or vision impaired, children with ADHD, children with Down syndrome, or children with autism, for example. It also has a link to job opportunities and to a site (Something Sew Special) offering clothing/accessories items for children with special needs.

The site of the National Center for Children in Poverty, http://www.nccp.org, has much information about the effects of poverty on the lives of children, demographic information by state, a library of publications, and a list of their projects to help children in poverty. Find the "Basic Needs Budget Calculator" under the "Data Tools" tab to calculate how much a family requires to meet basic needs in your part of the United States.

Parents and Extended Family Relationships

CHAPTER OUTLINE

Learning Objectives

Parent–Adult Child Relationships

- When Parents Disapprove of Choice of Partner
- Children's Identification with Parents
- Interdependence between Generations

CULTURAL PERSPECTIVE: *Emerging Adulthood*

- Parent–Adult Child Relationships and Psychological Functioning
- Elder Care

PERSONAL PERSPECTIVE: *Mother–Daughter Relationships*

In-Laws

- Successful In-Law Relationships
- The Roots of Conflict

FAMILY STRENGTHS PERSPECTIVE: *Family Reunion*

Living with Parents or In-Laws

- Effects of Co-residence

COPING FEATURE: *Reframing*

- Sources of Stress

Grandparents

AT ISSUE TODAY: *Fictive Kinship*

- What Grandparents Can Do for Grandchildren

- Grandparents Who Parent Their Grandchildren
- Adolescents, Young Adults, and Grandparents
- What Grandchildren Can Do for Grandparents

Adult Sibling Relationships

A QUESTION OF POLICY: *Grandparents' Rights*

Summary

Key Terms

Questions for Thought

For Further Reading

LEARNING OBJECTIVES

AFTER READING THE CHAPTER, YOU SHOULD BE ABLE TO DO THE FOLLOWING:

- Explain how family-of-origin experiences continue to exert an influence after marriage.

- Discuss the causes of and alternatives to parental disapproval of partner choice.

- Identify some of the effects of positive and negative identification with parents and the way these affect a person in adulthood.

- Describe the realities of care provided by families to their elderly family members.

- Discuss important considerations relating to intergenerational bonds.

- Discuss important issues in relation to conflicts between parents and adult children.

- Summarize some of the basic information about relationships with in-laws, including the relationship of in-law adjustment to marital happiness and the causes of and alternatives to in-law conflict.

- Identify considerations in living with extended families during middle age.

- Discuss relationships with grandparents: how grandparents are different today than in former generations, what grandparents can do for grandchildren, how adolescents and young adults relate with grandparents, what grandchildren can do for grandparents, and how grandparents parent their grandchildren.

In her book *Families*, Jane Howard wrote,

> Call it a clan, call it a network, call it a tribe, call it a family. Whatever you call it, whoever you are, you need one. You need one because you are human. You didn't come from nowhere. Before you, around you, and presumably after you, too, there are others. Some of these others . . . must matter a lot to you and, if you are very lucky, to one another. Their welfare must be nearly as important to you as your own. . . .
>
> For most of human history, looking for a tribe was the least of anyone's worries. Our tribes and clans were right in plain sight, like our kneecaps. We were born into tribes, or married into them, or they enslaved us, and that was that. Our tribe kept the howling wolves at bay, and shielded us from savage aliens. It made our decisions for us. It named us, bred us, fed us, taught us how to earn a living, found us our mates, and willed us its property. It told us who we were, what we stood for, and what we might hope to become. After we died, it honored our memory. . . .
>
> A couple such anachronistic tribes of this sort still survive today, but most such august and enveloping clans have long since evolved into families. (277–278)

The couple relationship in marriage does not exist in isolation. Not only do the spouses continue to maintain relationships with their own parents, but also each has acquired a whole new set of in-laws. How the spouses relate to their own parents and to their parents-in-law has important influences on their marriage and their children.

In this chapter, we are concerned with these extended family relationships and their effect on the couple. We also are concerned with some special situations: problems created by parental disapproval of choice of partner, positive and negative parental identification, interdependence between generations, mother–daughter relationships, and conflict between parents and adult children.

Special attention is given to in-law and grandparent relationships. What kinds of in-laws and grandparents do people like? What are important roots of conflict? What are some special considerations when couples live with in-laws or grandparents? What are some positive aspects of such relationships? What can grandparents do for grandchildren and vice versa? In answering all these questions, this chapter emphasizes working out harmonious relationships among generations.

Parent–Adult Child Relationships

Parent–child relationships are considered among the most important relationships individuals will ever have (A. Shapiro 2004). The relationship a person experienced with his or her parents while growing up continues to exert a profound influence on that person as an adult. If the relationship with the parents has been satisfying, pleasant emotional reactions and memories are carried into adulthood. However, dysfunctional relationships involving frustration, deprivation, fear, or hurt produce unpleasant emotional experiences and memories that evoke stress. In some cases, time moderates the distress; in others, parent–child misunderstandings influence family relationships across the life span (Kail and Cavanaugh 2016).

When Parents Disapprove of Choice of Partner

Parent–young adult child relationships become particularly important in the spouse selection process. Parental influence may begin when an adolescent first starts dating because parents are appropriately interested in their child's choice of friends and dating partners. The key to maintaining a harmonious relationship and to continuing dialogue lies in how they express that concern. If the parents object to the choice, the couple are sometimes pushed into each other's arms for comfort and solace. This "Romeo and Juliet" effect may result in a hasty, poor partner choice that would not have been made if the relationship had been allowed to evolve or dissolve naturally.

Parental objections are usually based on one or more of the following reasons:

- **The parents do not like the person their son or daughter has chosen:** "He's rude." "She's crude." "He's not a very nice person." "She's too domineering." These objections are based on dislike of the person's personality.

- **The parents feel the other person has a problem:** "He drinks too much." "She's too emotional." "He can't hold a steady job." "She can't get along with anybody."

- **The other person is different from the parent's family:** "Her family are rather common people." "He's not educated." "She's not of our faith." "Why couldn't he have picked some nice Italian (or Irish, Jewish, African American, or Latino) girl?"

- **There is a significant age difference:** "She's too young." "He's too old for her."

- **The person has been married before:** "This is his third time around." "She has three children by a previous marriage. Why does he want to get stuck with her?"

- **They are in too much of a hurry:** "They've only known each other for 3 months." "We don't even know him (her)."

Some families would object no matter whom their son or daughter selected. Such families may be possessive of their offspring and unwilling to let them leave home or grow up. Or they want to keep their children home to help the family.

Parental disapproval may be expressed in a number of ways. Parents who object before marriage may not back off after the wedding, so they continue to object and criticize, exerting an adverse influence. Parents may come between the partners by taking sides in disputes. For the children's part, choosing a spouse in opposition to parental acceptance may be indicative of problems in the parent–young adult relationship, which may find disruptive expression in the marriage. Furthermore, the selection of a partner to whom parents object can be motivated by rebellion against parental values, a motivation that impairs judgment in choosing a partner.

Of course, young adults can try to get their parents to like their partner. If objections are based on

The relationship a child experiences with his or her parents while growing up continues to exert a profound influence on that person as an adult.

lack of knowledge, given time and opportunity to get acquainted, some parents end up approving. But parents are not always wrong. If there are serious differences, this may be a warning signal to go slowly, to take more time and not rush into marriage. Premarital counseling also may help the couple clarify issues.

Children's Identification with Parents

As we have seen, in healthy families, children form close emotional attachments to parents. In the process, gender-role socialization takes place. That is, girls learn what it means to be a wife and mother, and boys learn what it means to be a husband and father. Each child also forms expectations of what traits and behaviors to expect from the opposite sex based on the role models they have observed. This identification, particularly with parents, influences marital expectations and behavior. However, identification may be positive or negative.

Positive identification is the attachment of the child to images of desired loving behavior. In this situation, the young adult child seeks to duplicate family-of-origin relationships in his or her own marriage. Such situations become troublesome when the spouse is not like the beloved parent—for example, when a woman cannot be like her spouse's mother or a man like his spouse's father. As one man said, "I'm not like your father, so don't expect me to be." The man who expects his partner to play the same role in their marriage that his mother did in hers is suggesting, "I can only love you if you're like my mother." People may develop unrealistic expectations from the example set by their own parents.

Negative identification is an avoidance of undesired behaviors. In situations of negative identification, differences rather than similarities underlie spouse selection and facilitate marital harmony. For example, a man reared by a demanding mother might always be wary lest a female dominate him. A woman may avoid men who drink because, as a child, she was frightened when her father came home drunk. She may find her partner's restraint particularly appealing. In marriage, two personalities interact. How they deal with the partner's conscious and unconscious needs will partly determine the success of the marriage.

Interdependence between Generations

For many years, the myth prevailed that elderly people were alienated from their families (especially their adult children), that families did not care for their elderly relatives, and that children had abandoned their elderly parents to institutions for care. Families as primary social units were believed to be dying out or at least were irresponsible toward elderly members. The belief was substantiated by the decrease in family size and the geographical mobility of families (understood as widening the generation gap), the development of an advanced society that supported nonworking members, and the proliferation of nursing homes to care for chronically ill and frail elderly persons.

We now know that the myth is indeed just that. Although independence and autonomy remain a cultural ideal, families are typified by interdependence. Interdependence refers to cooperation between persons and groups; each person gives to and receives from others in the group. Families tend to maintain varying degrees of interdependence throughout the life course. The flow of resources typically is from the older generations to the younger ones, even when elderly members are receiving some form of assistance. Families were and still are a major source of help to older people (Lei et al. 2012). Families often go to great lengths to care for their elderly members and do not enter into decisions to institutionalize them lightly. They also maintain strong bonds with older members and visit the older relatives who are institutionalized and mentally or physically disabled. Nevertheless, the myth was laid to rest only after several decades of research on the part of gerontologists.

Bengtson (2001) sees an increasing importance placed on multigenerational bonds and the diversity of intergenerational family styles; he proposes that "relations across more than two generations are becoming increasingly important to individuals and families in American society; that they are increasingly diverse in structure and functions; and that in the early 21st century, these multi-generational bonds will not only enhance but in some cases replace nuclear family functions, which have been so much the focus of sociologists during the 20th century" (2). Silverstein and Bengtson (1997) identified five types of intergenerational relationships, with most being strong, positive, and mutually supportive. They found that 25% of family generational relationships were tight-knit or emotionally and psychically close and supportive; 25% were sociable, with high levels of affinity; 16% were obligatory, with low levels of attachment and mutual exchange of help, but with potential for future support; 16% were intimate but distant, with promise of possible future support; and only 17% were detached with low levels of connectedness.

Research has shown that some late-life events are associated with increased intergenerational involvement. For example, adult children are more likely to co-reside with their mothers if their mothers are widowed. Moreover, widowhood increases intergenerational contact because mothers and adult children share their grief and offer mutual support (Ha and Ingersoll-Dayton 2008).

Two demographic changes have impacted the roles of older parents and their adult children. First, with the aging of the population, the size of current and future generations of older persons will challenge public and private organizations' ability to provide formal support to older adults. Second, high divorce rates and low fertility rates will make fewer children available for older adults to rely on to provide informal support (A. Shapiro 2004; Wijkmans and Van Bavel 2013).

Despite social changes such as geographic mobility, divorce, and women's participation in the labor force, adult children, especially daughters, remain the most reliable source of instrumental social support for their parents. There are two major reasons for support: (1) the ties of affection and (2) the sense of responsibility. Strong affectional ties are powerful motivating factors in providing support. Daughters are more likely to be directly motivated to act by feelings of emotional intimacy. Sons are more inclined to help parents out of a sense of obligation regardless of the quality of their relationship.

When men and women have jobs outside the home, their ability to provide help to parents is reduced, and employed women and employed men give equal amounts of help to parents and parents-in-law. However, women and men typically differ in their employment characteristics because there are more unemployed or partially employed women than men and thus they differ in the amount of help they give to parents (Sarkisian and Gerstel 2004).

Dependence between generations is not limited to what the middle-age generation does for the older generation, however. It includes the contributions that the older generations make to younger family members as well. These contributions are sizeable and take the form of shared meals; loans for household appliances and furnishings; transfers of deeds and titles; and bargain-rate sales of homes, businesses, and vehicles. Some elders cosign loans for their children and grandchildren or save money for the grandchildren's tuition. Others provide child care or other services that allow the parents to work or do other things. Gifts also are common. Overall, more resources flow down the generations than flow up.

The social support patterns between middle-age parents and their adult children differ according to marital status. Parents in first marriages are more likely overall than parents in other marital situations to report giving support. Middle-income widows also are inclined to help their children financially through gifts, loans, and asset transfers. Giving social support to children, whether reciprocated or not, is associated with better psychological well-being than is only receiving social support from children. Parents benefit psychologically by being able to give support as well as receive it (Igarashi et al. 2013).

Interestingly, research shows that older parents and their adult children may have different ideas about their relationship. One study compared the perceptions of intergenerational solidarity among 2,590 adult-child/older-parent dyads from the National Survey of Families and Households (A. Shapiro 2004). The findings indicated that there was a high degree of disagreement between how adult children and their parents viewed their relationship. Parents were more likely to report greater relationship quality, whereas children reported greater contact and exchanges of assistance. Adult children were likely to over-report both the amount of contact and the exchanges of assistance they had with their parents. In general, parents tended to have a more positive outlook on their relations with their adult children than did their children. Parent–child agreement was most likely achieved when parents and children were of the same sex and when the parent was female (A. Shapiro 2004).

Investigations of the sources of tension between aging mothers and adult daughters have revealed some interesting findings (Bernstein 2012). One source of tension in the mother–daughter

positive identification The attachment of a child to positive images of desired loving behavior.
negative identification The avoidance of undesired behaviors.

Emerging Adulthood

The definition of when a person actually becomes an adult varies from culture to culture. In the United States, for example, there is now a term called "emerging adulthood," which is a time when young people are no longer children or adolescents, but they have not fully taken on the responsibilities of adulthood (Arnett 2000, 2003). This period is typically seen as between ages 18 and 25. In essence, people have postponed the full responsibilities of adulthood. A good example of this in the United States is a typical 21-year-old college student who is living independently but is still financially dependent on his or her parents. Although typical college-age students do not consider themselves adolescent, neither do they consider themselves fully adult. Research in this area shows that people's perceptions of when they actually become an adult are when they begin accepting responsibility for themselves, become capable of making independent decisions, and become financially independent (Arnett 2003). It is interesting to note that the traditional markers of adulthood, such as marriage and parenthood, are not seen as criteria for adulthood. Instead, a more individualistic criteria of self-sufficiency is seen as the marker of adulthood (L. J. Nelson, Badger, and Wu 2004). This is in contrast to many traditional, non-Western countries that still see marriage as the onset of adulthood.

The traditional Chinese culture is a good example of a culture with a much earlier age of adulthood. Many Chinese children grow up with the idea that they will help take care of their parents when they get older and believe that the wishes of the family are more important than their own desires. This idea is so strong that many children forgo their own dreams and aspirations to fulfill their family obligations. One study investigated the emergence of adulthood in the Chinese culture by interviewing students from a Chinese university (L. J. Nelson, Badger, and Wu 2004). Findings showed that most Chinese students (59%) felt they were adults. Similar studies using students from the United States show much lower percentages (e.g., 27% [Arnett 1998]; 36% [Arnett 2003]; and 24% [L. J. Nelson 2003]). The criteria cited most often by Chinese students as markers for adulthood were accepting responsibility for the consequences of your actions, learning always to have good control of your emotions, becoming financially independent from your parents, becoming less self-oriented and developing greater concern for others, and becoming capable of supporting your parents financially. These items signify the importance of putting the needs and interests of the family and community above one's own needs and demonstrate the influence of culture in determining the status of adulthood. In sum, Chinese young people are experiencing the years between 18 and 25 differently because of their unique cultural beliefs and values. They are influenced by a collectivist culture and place more emphasis on the needs of family and society, whereas young people in the United States are influenced by an individualistic culture and place more emphasis on the self. Indeed, culture influences the beliefs and behaviors of emerging adulthood (L. J. Nelson, Badger, and Wu 2004).

relationship is conflicting ideas of inclusion and exclusion. Most mothers and daughters consider the other person important in their life, yet mothers seem to feel closer to their daughters emotionally than daughters feel to their mothers. Mothers are more likely to name their daughter as their preferred confidante or the person with whom they most enjoy spending time. Another area of conflict is that mothers continue to offer advice and sometimes criticism about their daughters' lives, housekeeping, lipstick color, etc. Daughters are very influenced by the comments from their mothers; the daughters may feel disrespected or guilty (Bernstein 2012; Fingerman, Hay, and Birditt, 2004).

Parent–Adult Child Relationships and Psychological Functioning

Adult children's lives can affect their parents' well-being. Parents continue to worry about their children no matter how old the children are. When the children have marital problems, financial difficulties, health problems, vocational difficulties, or other problems, their parents are bound to be affected. For example, the participants (middle-age or older parents) of several studies whose adult children had problems indicated poorer psychological well-being and more family relationship strain (Cichy et al. 2013; Fingerman et al. 2012).

Parents remain heavily invested in their children throughout the course of their lives. All parents hope that their children will become successful, functioning adults. If the children do not do so, parents become concerned and upset. Children who have not successfully negotiated leaving their parents' home and who have not become independent serve as a reminder that parents have not achieved their task of socialization (Birditt et al. 2009; Fingerman and Pitzer 2007). Generally, parents whose adult children have mental, physical, or stress-related problems experience greater depression than parents of children who do not have these problems (Birditt et al. 2009; Willson et al. 2006).

The relationships between adult children and their parents have psychological consequences for the younger generation, too. Sons whose relationships with their parents are positive have lower levels of psychological distress than do sons whose relationships are negative. It is important to note that positive relationships with mothers and with fathers are significant predictors of adult sons' psychological distress. The more positive the relationships with their mothers or fathers, the lower the level of distress (Barnett, Marshall, and Pleck 1992; Birditt et al. 2009).

Similarly for daughters, having a positive relationship with a parent is associated with a high sense of well-being and low levels of distress. Distress is often conditioned by family-role patterns. For example, having a poor relationship with one's mother is associated with psychological distress, particularly among daughters who are single or childless (Bernstein 2012; Birditt et al. 2009). Thus, the quality of the relationships between adult children and their parents is associated with the psychological functioning of both

generations. This idea is consistent with a family life course perspective that has a central proposition that people in intimate relationships share developmental trajectories that are interlocking and that influence each other (Cichy et al. 2013; Fingerman et al. 2012).

Elder Care

As people live longer and a greater percentage of the population is considered elderly, families are now providing more care to their older members, who may need considerable help. According to the U.S. Bureau of the Census (2016), by 2030, the older population is expected to grow to over 20% of the U.S. population. This translates to about 71.5 million (compared to 41.4 million now) persons age 65 and older. Although the majority of older adults are self-sufficient and capable of caring for themselves, the older they get the more likely they will be to need some sort of long-term care.

The majority of older people with disabilities live in the community and receive assistance from spouses, adult children, and other family members. Caregiving for an aging parent or spouse presents many tough challenges. As discussed in Chapter 7, each situation is unique and families have different options for care based on different resources. For some, nursing homes may be the best option, whereas for others assisted living, elder day care, or

As people are living longer and as a greater percentage of the population is considered elderly, families are now providing more care to their older members.

informal family care may be most appropriate. A senior's medical history, financial resources, personality, relationships with potential caregivers, proximity to services, and other factors all determine the best approach to take.

We focus here on elder care that is provided by families because millions of Americans provide unpaid assistance each year to elderly family members. This typically involves a middle-age (half are over 50 years old) female caregiver who is either the daughter or the daughter-in-law of the elderly person. Because these caregivers often are also helping their children as well as their parents, they have been termed the "sandwich generation."

Caregiving exacts a heavy toll physically; many caregivers are still employed; about 30% care for more than one person. The emotional toll is heavy, too, as the elder experiences physical and or cognitive declines (Administration on Aging 2015).

To help families who are caring for elderly members, the National Family Caregiver Support Program, an amendment to the Older Americans Act, was established in 2000. Funds have been allocated to states to work in partnership with area agencies on aging and local service providers to put into place multifaceted systems of support for family caregivers. A specific component of these systems is respite care, which could include, for example, a care provider coming into the home to give the family caregiver time off to relax or take care of other responsibilities. It also could include temporary placement of the elderly person in a nursing home or assisted-living facility to help relieve the family caregiver (Administration on Aging 2015). Other programs and services provided under the Older Americans Act include congregate meals, home-delivered meals, nutrition education, transportation, and home repair, to name only a few. These programs and services help preserve the independence of many older adults who are at risk for institutionalization and allow them to stay in the community, while providing needed relief for families.

Caring for elderly family members, as well as respect for elderly persons and willingness to access services, varies from culture to culture. In a study

---

PERSONAL PERSPECTIVE

Mother–Daughter Relationships

Beth is the mother of a 5-year-old daughter and vows to have a different mother–daughter relationship than the one she had with her own mother. She and her mother live close to each other and see each other often, but there has always been and continues to be conflict in their relationship.

I can't imagine life without my mom, and I consider us very close, but she is the one person who can still manage to drive me crazy in 2 seconds. I am a grown woman, but when I am with my mom I go back to feeling like a child. I feel like she criticized me the whole time I was growing up, and that I never did anything right. I still feel criticized by her, or that I don't measure up when she comments on my hair, what I wear, or how I interact with my daughter. Of course, she doesn't see it like that. She thinks I am too sensitive, and maybe I am, *but I have a lifetime of feeling inferior and it just doesn't go away when you grow up. I try never to criticize my daughter, and I tell her all the time how much I love her just the way she is. I know my mom thinks I am coddling her, and maybe I am, but I can't bear to have a similar relationship with my daughter as I do with my mom. I have been to years of therapy to help figure out how I feel toward my mom. She had a very hard marriage and went on to be a single mother while I was growing up, and that couldn't have been easy. I think she took a lot of her unhappiness out on me, and now I need to forgive her for that. The hard part is that she doesn't see any of that, and so how can I hope for an apology if she feels she doesn't have anything to be sorry for. She feels she did the best job she could. And I guess that's what I am trying to do too.*

examining Asian American caregivers, H. Li (2004) found that more than half of the caregivers he sampled reported personal or cultural barriers to utilizing services. The barriers they identified most often were that they felt too proud to accept services and they did not want outsiders coming in. In another study comparing white female caregivers with Latina caregivers, the researchers found that when dealing with a family member with dementia, Latinas delayed institutionalizing significantly longer than their white counterparts. Latinas who were less acculturated were significantly more likely to identify positive aspects of caregiving than more acculturated Latinas. The researcher concluded that Latino cultural values and the more positive views of the caregiving role are important factors that may significantly influence a family's decision to institutionalize loved ones (Mausbach et al. 2004).

Significant cultural differences also have been found in examining caregiver and care recipient characteristics, types of assistance provided, and workplace support among black, Hispanic, Asian, and white employed family caregivers. One study showed that although minority caregivers were more economically disadvantaged than their white counterparts, they also provided the highest level of care. In addition, the same study showed that employed white female caregivers reported higher levels of role strain than did black and Hispanic caregivers (Fredriksen-Goldsen and Farwell 2004).

Typically, the caregiver's perceived burden and level of depression increase as a patient's functional status declines (Grunfeld et al. 2004), and many women become more depressed as their caregiving role increases. However, there are benefits to caregiving, and adult children often experience more rewards than do the spouses of the elderly person being cared for (Raschick and Ingersoll-Dayton 2004). The challenges typically associated with elder care can provide possibilities for caregiver growth, a chance to discover and create meaning in life, and a means to teach future generations the importance of looking after the older generation.

The way in which we age and who cares for us are both affected by a variety of factors such as gender, socioeconomic status, ethnicity, health, and social networks (Karasik 2005). It can be a difficult process for some, and yet many people welcome the opportunity to live to old age or to have their parents live to old age, even with the inevitable declines in health. No one can know what the future will bring, but understanding both the positive and the negative outcomes can help us to prepare for our own aging as well as the aging of our family members.

In-Laws

In-law disagreements are most common in the early years of marriage. Some young couples are able to work out their relationships with in-laws, including the spouse's parents, siblings, and other relatives, so that good accommodations are reached. Others settle into a permanent state of friction with their in-laws. This friction may not break up the marriage, but it can cause unhappiness.

Successful In-Law Relationships

In a longitudinal study of the influence of in-laws on marital success among couples who were married on average for 20 years, researchers found that in-laws are influential in the overall success of the marriage. Indeed, even after an average of 20 years of marriage, unhappiness and conflict with in-laws led to decreased perceptions of marital success. The influence of in-laws thus continues far beyond the early years of marriage, and perhaps vulnerability to the opinions and behaviors of those who are close to us never ends (Bryant, Conger, and Meehan 2001).

Lauer and Lauer (2011) surveyed people married slightly more than 11 years on average to ask how their in-law relationships had affected their marriages and which in-law relationship had been most significant, in either a positive or a negative way. All of their subjects reported that in-law relationships had been significant in some way in their lives. The mother-in-law was most often named (by 47%) as the most significant in-law relationship, with about half citing the relationship as positive and half as negative. Father-in-law was second (19%), followed by brother- or sister-in-law (18%) and both mother- and father-in-law (13%).

One of the most comprehensive studies on in-laws was reported in the book *In-Laws: Pro and Con* by Duvall (1954). Her classic study is an old one, but it is still a rich source of relevant information and shows that in-law problems are not a new phenomenon. Her findings form the basis for the discussion that follows.

Duvall's research indicated that the major complaints parents-in-law made about their daughters-in-law and sons-in-law were that they were: (a) indifferent, (b) distant, (c) thoughtless and inconsiderate, and (d) too busy to be interested in parents or parents-in-law. In contrast, the most frequent complaints by sons- and daughters-in-law were that their parents-in-law were: (a) meddlesome, (b) naggers, (c) critical, (d) possessive, (e) aloof, and (f) thoughtless. M. J. Turner, Young, and Black (2006) interviewed wives about their relationship with their mothers-in-law and found a major challenge for the younger women was to feel "a part of the family" of the in-laws. Only a few felt fully accepted, the majority were ambivalent or uncertain about their belonging and a few felt disillusioned by their difficulty in being an integral part of their in-laws' family.

About one-fourth of all couples in Duvall's study had a fine relationship with their in-laws. Couples give the following reasons for liking their in-laws:

- "They are the kind of people we admire: sincere, interesting, young in spirit, good-natured, pleasant and fun, generous, tolerant, and understanding."
- "They do many things to help us." "They take care of the baby." "They help us when we're sick or when my husband is away." "They give us so many things, like furniture, clothes, and money."

Many couples have a fine relationship with each partner's family. How important are in-laws to marital success?

- "They are more like parents to me than my own parents." Orphans and people who are estranged from their own parents may be especially close to their in-laws.
- "They are the parents of my spouse, who is a fine person."
- "We're in-laws ourselves so we can appreciate what it means." Such couples objected to stereotyped prejudices against in-laws, which they felt were unfair.

The Roots of Conflict

Timmer and Veroff (2000) report that low levels of conflict with in-laws among newlyweds predict marital happiness for both husbands and wives. Yet, the literature on family and couple therapy often cites in-laws as a significant source of stress in couples' relationships (Bryant, Conger, and Meehan 2001). There are many reasons for in-law conflicts. Although spouses are more or less obligated to form family relationships with in-laws, often this obligatory relationship is not a good match of compatible personalities. Sometimes the problem is with the parents-in-law, but more frequently it is with the partners themselves, who in many cases are more critical of their in-laws than the in-laws are of them (D. Olson, DeFrain, and Skogrand 2014; Stinnett ad Stinnett 2010).

According to family developmental theory, at the time of marriage, the new husband and wife face a series of difficult tasks. Each must redefine the relationship with his or her own parents; the child role of earlier times must be left behind. Loyalties and priorities must be shifted, too, from parents and siblings to spouse. Each also faces the task of building a relationship with his or her new in-laws and learning to respect their values, rituals, and traditions.

Achieving independence causes trouble for both the new couple and their parents. The newlyweds have difficulty because true independence takes years of maturing. First attempts at independence may be severe to the point of rebellion. Young adults' reactions to real or presumed threats to their autonomy may be inappropriate or alienating. It is not easy to balance loyalty to a spouse and loyalty to one's parents. The complaints (as noted by Duvall) against children-in-law that they were indifferent, distant, thoughtless, inconsiderate, and too busy to be interested in the parents' lives may

Family Reunion

Many persons enjoy an opportunity to get together with the "whole" family—aunts, uncles, cousins, and so on. It provides a time to renew relationships, to see the new babies born into the larger family, and to mourn the passing of family members who have died. People who have had family reunions offer some practical suggestions for planning one.

1. Select a location as convenient to as many family members as possible. Using the same location year after year has some advantages: continuity and fewer decisions to make. On the other hand, if families are scattered, it may help some to attend if the location is closer part of the time. And one family (or group of families) does not always have host duty. Consider a community center or church fellowship hall to relieve the pressure of finding someone's home that is large enough.

2. Pick easy activities: a band for listening and dancing or badminton, croquet, horseshoes for the yard; chairs for sitting and talking; cards, dominoes, checkers.

3. Keep the decorations simple. Use homemade tablecloths and disposable tableware. Flowers from the garden or roadside make casual bouquets. Plain white candles and greenery are nice, too. Decorate the walls with pictures of past reunions and/or big events in the family.

4. Make the meals potluck. Have everyone bring a favorite dish or two (and the recipe) and a cooler of drinks.

5. Hire local teenagers to help with setting up tables and chairs, cleaning up, and entertaining younger children.

6. Appoint some family members to take photographs or videos. (Every family has a couple of shutterbugs.) Record oral history from older family members. Update address books and phone numbers.

---

be reflections of unskilled or extreme attempts to assert their independence.

At the time of a marriage, the parents of the new couple face a series of challenging tasks as well. They, too, must build new relationships—with their own child and with a new son- or daughter-in-law. Relinquishing the parental role may be hard; it is a role most have played for more than 20 years, and habits are hard to change. To parents, children do not cease to be children just because they marry. And opening themselves to strangers who have become official family members through a marriage ceremony is stressful to many. It is not surprising that married couples consistently report that their mothers- and fathers-in-law are meddlesome, nagging, criticizing, possessive, aloof, and thoughtless. Many of these may be the result of an inability to drop the parental role (meddling, nagging) or the result of an extreme attempt to give the new couple autonomy (being aloof).

Some parents create problems because they resent the person their son or daughter married. They may find it hard to accept a son- or daughter-in-law who comes from a different national, religious, economic, or social background. Others resent anyone a son or daughter married because the person "is not the right one" or "is not good enough." In these cases, the parents' intolerance is the primary problem.

Living with Parents or In-Laws

Co-residence by parents and adult children is not uncommon. Some 21.6 million adults ages 18 to 31 live with their parents, up from about 12.5 million in 1970. This is 56% of all adults ages 18 to 24 and 16% of the adults ages 25 to 31 (Fry 2013). Research has indicated that co-residence typically reflects the needs of adult children rather than the caregiving needs of parents and that it does not generally have negative effects on parent–adult child relationships (Warbelow and Bass 2012).

Adult children usually live with their parents because of financial or housing needs or other circumstances (Warbelow and Bass 2012). One-third to half of the young adults still living with parents are college students; others are at home because of unemployment (Fry 2013). Most young couples do not want to live with either partner's parents after marriage, but the younger they are when they get married, the greater the likelihood that they will do so for a while, since they cannot afford living quarters of their own. This "doubling" sometimes adds to the stress of family relationships.

Effects of Co-residence

Whether adult children and parents living together is seriously stressful depends on the circumstances. For example, if co-residence implies failure to attain adult status or crisis, such as unemployment, it may create significant parental stress (Cichy et al. 2013; R. A. Ward and Spitze 2004).

According to the National Survey of Families and Households, parental satisfaction with the presence of adult children (ages 19 to 34) in the home was highly related to parent–adult child conflict and to the level of positive social interaction between parent and child. The negative consequences of dependency also are influenced by the children's marital and parental status. Parents whose adult children move back home after marital breakups report more negative effects of co-residence than do parents of never-married children. Also, supporting adult children who are unemployed and continually financially dependent becomes more burdensome as the share of adult children's basic needs paid for by parents increases. Supporting grandchildren as well as adult children exerts additional negative influence (Aquilino 2005). However, many parents are highly satisfied with the co-resident living arrangement and describe mostly positive relationships with their adult children (Warbelow and Bass 2012).

One research study focused on the implications of adult–child co-residence for parents' marital relations in midlife. Longitudinal data assessed change in parents' time together and marital quality in

---

COPING FEATURE

Reframing

Reframing is a coping strategy that can be important in minimizing dissatisfaction with in-law relationships. Reframing is redefining or reappraising a situation in a more positive way.

For example, Liz, a young wife and mother, is frustrated with her mother-in-law's interfering and meddling with suggestions for decorating the house, recipes for nutritious meals, advice on disciplining the children, and tips for balancing the household budget. Since she cannot control or change her mother-in-law's behavior, Liz is left with two options: (1) continue to feel frustrated by the interaction and be quiet about it (and seethe inside at every comment that is made) or be snappish and irritable; or (2) reframe her appraisal of her mother-in-law's behavior.

Liz can reframe by considering her mother-in-law's meddlesome behavior and asking herself, "What *good intentions* could possibly be at the root of her interfering?" Possible answers to this question are, "She wants to be helpful (she does have lots of recipes to share)." "She is interested in Liz and her family (she wants to get to know them and spend time with them)." "She wants to help Liz avoid mistakes (ones that she made in budgeting or decorating)." Or "She wants the best for her son and his family (a nice home and meals and financial security)."

Liz may then be able to reason, "I still don't like so many suggestions, but at the heart of her meddlesomeness are good qualities. She is interested in us and wants to be helpful." This reframing will help Liz feel less defensive and to respond more positively to her mother-in-law.

response to adult children's moves into and out of the nest. When adult children move out, parents increase their time together as a couple, and, if a child moves back in, parents reduce their time together as a couple. However, an examination of marital happiness and disagreements found no effects of co-residence. Thus, co-residence with adult children does not appear to be an experience that disrupts the quality of marital relations. It may be that the quality of the relationship between the parents and adult child matters much more to the overall quality of family life than the fact of co-residence (R. A. Ward and Spitze 2004).

Sources of Stress

The type of living arrangement affects the amount of stress. If doubling up takes place under one roof but in two separate apartments or living quarters, the situation is not any more stressful than if the two families lived next door to each other. But when families share living space, the likelihood of conflict is greater. Some families even end up sharing the same sleeping quarters. If at all possible, it is helpful if each couple/adult has at least one room they can call their own and to which they can retreat for privacy.

When it is not possible to be completely separate, conflict is less likely if families develop a clear understanding of financial and household obligations ahead of time. Who pays for what and how much? What household and yard work is each person expected to do? The division of household labor and responsibilities is particularly challenging. In the National Survey of Families and Households, adult children reported doing substantial amounts of weekly housework; parents reported doing lower amounts. Adult children did more housework in one-parent households than in two-parent households and did increasing amounts with age. Daughters spent somewhat more time on household work than did sons. Also, when a parent was in poor health, the adult children did more housework. Some adult children might have been doing extra housework that they themselves generated, so they were probably not relieving their parents of any substantial amount of housework in exchange for living in the house.

Another potentially stressful situation is created when parents and adult children share responsibilities for a family business. The overlapping of work and family roles creates a special dilemma for family

members who not only live together or close by but also work together. Some of the difficulties can be lessened when clear boundaries are established between work and family, for example, treating each other as colleagues at work and discussing work issues during business hours—not around the dinner table. Family time must be separate. It also helps to have a business plan that specifies procedures for hiring, firing, and airing grievances (Family Business Institute 2013).

Grandparents

Recent demographic trends have contributed to a rise in the number of grandparents and to fewer grandchildren per grandparent. For most, grandparenthood begins in middle age and spans several

Many elderly people will give up their independence and share a residence with an adult child. One advantage, confirmed by research, is the unique emotional attachments between grandparents and grandchildren.

decades, lasting well into the grandchild's adult-hood. More people living longer means that adults today can expect to share their role as grandparent with other grandparents and that some can expect to be great-grandparents.

Today's grandparents usually do not fit the stereotypic image. For example, the modern grand-mother is far less likely to be wrapped in her shawl, rocking and doing needlework before the fireplace. She is apt to be youthful (average age is 48), vigorous, and energetic, with plenty of ideas and enthusiasm. She is also likely to be employed.

Today's grandparents are different from previous cohorts in a number of ways. Increasingly, each generation of grandmothers and grandfathers will span a greater range of ages because of teen births and delayed parenthood. Improved nutrition and medical care have made it possible for people to stay healthier longer.

Modern grandparents have a chance to be vigorous in mind and spirit as well. Many middle-income grandparents keep up in appearance, taste, vitality, and knowledge with their juniors; most are online, many use social media and play video games; nearly half volunteer. They continue to think creatively and take courses related to their work or their interests (or they teach the courses). They travel.

Finally, modern grandparents differ from the grandparents who preceded them because they are more likely to have intergenerational lineages.

Fictive Kinship

Fictive kinship is described as a relationship with someone who is not related through blood, marriage, or adoption but who takes on the role a family member typically plays in society. That is, fictive kin are family-type relationships based on community or friendship ties. They are fictive in the sense that the ties that bind individuals together are not the same ties that bind relatives, but not in the sense that these relationships are any less important. In many societies, fictive kinship ties are as important as or more important than family ties created by blood, marriage, or adoption. Unlike family bonds, fictive kin ties are usually voluntary and require the consent of both individuals in establishing the relationship because one can pick who they would like to be fictive kin (E. K. Shaw 2008; Rank 2015).

Fictive kin relationships are not new and numerous accounts of such relationships exist throughout history. For example, godparents, religious movements creating brotherhoods and sisterhoods, crime networks and gangs referring to each other as part of a blood brotherhood, and those who take on the title of aunt or uncle to their friends' children are all considered fictive kin. In addition, African American and Native American communities have a long history of establishing fictive kin relationships to help raise children and support families.

What is new is the increased importance placed on fictive kin for many families because of geographic and social mobility, divorce, single parenthood, gay and lesbian relationships, smaller family size, and increased life expectancy. Many individuals today find themselves living in communities with no relatives to help them raise their children, care for them when they are sick, or depend on in times of need. Fictive kin relationships create a vital sense of family for these people. As individuals continue to move away from nuclear and extended family members, they will continue to foster deeper connections with friends and create surrogate family members.

Raising children, growing old, forming partnerships, moving to a new place, and just surviving on one's own can be overwhelming at times, regardless of the situation, and everyone needs help, support, and a sense of community to deal with life's inevitable challenges. Most people need to feel they belong to a family and have someone to turn to in times of need. When family members are not there or are unable to provide help and support, fictive kin can fulfill those roles.

Today, grandparents may have living parents and even grandparents. When the age at first birth is during early adolescence for a number of generations in a row, intergenerational lineages are more likely. Although not numerous, grandmothers can be in their thirties and have living mothers and grandmothers. Conversely, when young adults delay the age of first birth, the time between generations increases, and intergenerational lineages are less likely.

What Grandparents Can Do for Grandchildren

Social scientists have come to recognize and appreciate what children have known for years: grandparents have a role that is central to family dynamics and they are a valuable resource to the family. Brhel (2013) describes grandparents as being the "secondary attachment" figures for children. The emotional attachments between grandparents and grandchildren have been described as unique because the relationship is exempt from the psycho-emotional intensity and responsibility that exist in the parent–child relationship.

However, the relationship between grandchildren and grandparents is mediated by the parents. Usually, the connections with the maternal grandparents are stronger than those with the paternal grandparents. However, if the parents align more closely with the paternal grandparents, the grandchildren are likely to do so as well (Chan and Elder 2000). The relationship between grandparents and grandchildren also is influenced by changes in family life, such as a move or a divorce. Following a parental divorce or separation, contact between grandchildren and maternal grandparents often increases or at least is maintained, whereas contact with paternal grandparents often declines.

Grandparents can have a major positive influence on grandchildren. For example, they can help children feel secure and loved. Children can never have too much of the right kind of love—love that helps them grow and develop and that alleviates anxiety, tension, and emotional pain. Love that adds security and trust, that accepts and understands, is always needed (Brhel 2013). That love is just as important, if not more important, during difficult times in the family.

Grandparents can play a crucial role during family transitions, such as illness, birth of a child, or divorce. They are a source of family continuity and stability. Because of their function in maintaining the family system, grandparents may be seen as "family watchdogs." Although they usually play a relatively passive role in the family, during crisis grandparents often become actively involved in the family. A large percentage of divorced adult children, for example, are dependent on their parents for help. Contact between grandchildren and grandmothers usually increases after the separation or divorce of an adult child. In addition, grandmothers report that they provide more support (babysitting, teaching family history and tradition, giving advice) after the separation or divorce. They play an even more important role in families in which there are unwed teenage mothers. For example, grandmothers may take over responsibility for the care of babies and assist by giving directions to the teenage mother (Brhel 2013; Dunifon and Bajracharya 2012).

Grandparents can help children learn to know, trust, and understand other people. Children can find that grandmother's arms are comforting. They can discover that grandfather's house is a safe and happy home away from home. They learn how to be flexible and to adjust to the ways their grandparents think, feel, and behave, which are different from the ways their parents do.

Grandparents bridge the gap between the past and the present and give children a sense of history and their ethnic/cultural heritage. Most children enjoy hearing grandparents talk about what life was like when they were growing up. Grandparents can thus provide a foundation for children to depend on as they grow and develop. Stories about their family give them a broader and deeper sense of what life can bring and how people cope, survive, and flourish. This knowledge about their cultural and family heritage helps adolescents' identities develop (Brhel 2013; Dunifon and Bajracharya 2012).

Grandparents can provide children with experiences and supervision that their parents do not have time or money to provide. For example, they may provide day care while parents work or outings to the zoo or music lessons. One grandfather shared,

> I've done swimming lessons with our grandsons for the last three summers (I have signed them up and paid the fees and attended the lessons). One of the four parents

always comes—sometimes more as their work permits. We usually stay after the lesson and swim some more—and often have lunch from the snack bar or a picnic. All four boys love the water and are good swimmers. I've loved doing it—and have lost about 30 pounds—a nice bonus!

This is especially important given the increase in one-parent families and the increase in time spent at work.

Grandparents can give children a sense of values and a philosophy of life that is the result of years of living. Valuable life experiences and lessons must be shared; in this regard, grandparents play the traditional role of valued elder (Brhel 2013).

Grandparents may play the role of arbitrator between their adult children and grandchildren. Grandparents may be the negotiators between the young and the middle aged regarding behaviors and values. They may serve as interpreters in helping each generation understand the other's perspective, and they may provide a refuge for both adult children and grandchildren (Brhel 2013).

Finally, grandparents can give children a wholesome attitude toward old age. In Western culture especially, in which youthfulness is almost worshipped, children must know and learn to respect their elders. Older people who are living rich, fruitful, meaningful lives are a good example for children. They are role models for the future role of grandparent, for aging, and for family relationships.

Grandparents Who Parent Their Grandchildren

As discussed in Chapter 1, there has been a dramatic increase in the number of grandparents who are raising their grandchildren. According to the U.S. Census Bureau, more than 6 million grandchildren live with their grandparents and, of these, 23% were living with grandparents with no parents present (Ellis and Simmons 2014; Kreider and Fields 2005; U.S. Bureau of the Census 2013). This equates to approximately 1.5 million children being raised solely by grandparents. Most of these caretakers are grandmothers, rather than grandfathers. Often the grandparent is raising grandchildren because of a child's death, teenage pregnancy, divorce, drug and alcohol abuse, physical and mental illness, or incarceration. In some cases, the parents have lost custody of their children because of abuse or neglect (Dolbin-MacNab 2006; Ellis and Simmons 2014).

The arrangement of grandparent as caregiver has benefits for both grandparents and children. Grandparents may experience a greater sense of purpose for living, a renewed vitality, and a feeling of rejuvenation. They may relish the opportunity to raise a child differently or to nurture family relationships, and they may be rewarded with love and companionship they did not have previously with the grandchild. Children also may benefit from living in grandparent-maintained households. Compared with children in foster care, those in grandparent-maintained households may be less traumatized, enjoy the continuation of family identity and culture, and maintain a connection to their extended family.

Much of the research, however, puts more emphasis on the negative effects of grandparents rearing grandchildren (Bachman and Chase-Lansdale 2005; C. C. Goodman and Silverstein 2006; M. E. Ross and Aday 2006). The media have referred to these grandparents as the "silent saviors," "the second line of defense," and "the safety net" because they are grandparents who thought their childrearing days were over but now take on the responsibility of raising their children's children. This responsibility comes with many adjustments and challenges; common complaints from grandparents are fatigue, guilt, lack of emotional support, and financial constraints.

Grandparents can be important in the lives of adolescents and young adults. Research shows that grandparents share family history and help the young understand their parents.

Grandparents must be healthy and energetic enough to deal with the physical demands of child-rearing, and they must be able to support a child both emotionally and financially. Some grandparents experience increased health problems and loss of stamina. Many report feeling emotionally and physically drained from having to care for their grandchildren. Other drawbacks include loss of time for themselves that they had rediscovered after their own children left home, isolation from their social networks, and resentment based on jealousy and role confusion on the part of other grandchildren and family members. In addition, grandparents struggle with school enrollment, medical coverage, and help with child care (Zimmerman 2005).

As stated before, economic difficulties are prevalent in grandparent-maintained households. When a grandparent is raising the children alone, without the presence of a parent, 35% of the children are living in poverty. This figure is considerably higher than the 17% of children who live in poverty with two parents. Yet it is slightly lower than the 39% of children living in poverty in mother-only households without the presence of a grandparent (Ellis and Simmons 2014; Kreider and Fields 2005). Most older adults are on limited incomes and, as discussed in Chapter 8, the financial responsibility for raising a child can be great.

In three-generational households where the parent is still present but the grandparent is raising the child, grandparents report that they walk a thin line in trying to provide a stable environment for their grandchildren without overstepping parental boundaries. The parent retains decision-making responsibilities, but the grandparent is left with the physical care of the grandchild. Such a relationship gives the grandparent great responsibility without any authority. In situations where the parent is not living in the house but the grandparent does not have legal custody of the child, the grandparents never know when the grandchild's parent might take the grandchild back. They have no legal way of protecting the child from an unsuitable or even dangerous parent. These grandparents also experience considerable strain between their beliefs about what grandparenting would be like and how it actually is.

For many grandparents, the responsibility of raising grandchildren is too difficult without some type of legal authority to make decisions for the child's upbringing. For example, without legal guardianship, grandparents cannot give a doctor permission to treat their grandchild, cannot enroll a grandchild in school, and may be denied financial help in raising the child. Obtaining legal custody of a child can be difficult, particularly if the parent is unwilling to give up parental rights. This can tear a family apart. Typically, one must prove that a legal relationship between grandparent and grandchild is in the best interest of the child (for example, the parent is unfit) before legal custody is granted.

The legal options available to the grandparents differ from state to state. In some states, grandparents may be able to become foster parents to their grandchildren and receive state aid to help raise them. In others, however, grandparents may be denied foster-parent financial benefits because of their blood relation to the children. Some states allow grandparents to fill out a form that lets them get services such as medical care or school enrollment for their grandchildren, whereas other states have a legal guardian program that provides some subsidies for raising grandchildren.

Because of the wide variation from state to state, it is important for individuals to check with their local Area Agency on Aging for current state policies. The federal government does offer benefits and programs that some grandparents may qualify for, as well as a wide variety of information to help grandparents raise their grandchildren. The link to resources sponsored by the U.S. Administration on Aging can be found on its website at www.aoa.gov.

Adolescents, Young Adults, and Grandparents

Grandparents can be especially influential in the lives of adolescents and young adults. They can tell adolescents and young adults about the family history and help them understand their parents. This in turn can help adolescents form their identity—this is who I am, this is what my history is. Grandparents also function as confidants and provide outlets when parent–teen relations become tense (Brhel 2013; Dunifon and Bajracharya 2012).

Research on the relationship between college-age men and women and their grandparents revealed that when there is high contact between generations, the maternal grandmother–granddaughter bond is the strongest. In addition, grandmothers describe a closer relationship with grandchildren than do grandfathers (Brhel 2013). Research shows that rural youth enjoy more frequent contact with paternal grandparents and receive more help from all grandparents than do urban youth. Adolescents who grow up on a farm have the most contact and receive more help from paternal grandparents than rural children who do not grow up on a farm (V. King et al. 2003). Proximity significantly affects the frequency of contact between grandchildren and grandparents.

What Grandchildren Can Do for Grandparents

The grandparent–grandchild relationship is not a one-way street, with benefits flowing only from grandparent to grandchild. Grandchildren can enhance the lives of their grandparents in several ways. First, grandchildren are a source of biologic continuity and living evidence that the family will endure. All individuals wish a part of themselves to survive after death, and grandchildren allow a grandparent to glimpse his or her own immortality. Second, grandparents' self-concept is enhanced by playing the role of mentor, historian, and resource person. Third, grandchildren can help keep grandparents up to date by introducing them to the new ideas, customs, and traditions of the younger generation. Finally, grandchildren who have grown past early childhood can provide a variety of types of assistance to help grandparents maintain an independent lifestyle. Adolescents can help with lawn care, household chores, and other tasks related to maintaining a home. Such help plays a crucial role in enabling older adults to stay in their homes as long as possible.

Adult Sibling Relationships

Sibling relationships create significant bonds for many adults. In contrast to typical relationships with parents and children, sibling relationships have the potential to last a lifetime. Siblings have the potential to know us for a longer period of time than any other human beings. Whereas our parents may know us for 50 years and our children may know us from adulthood on, siblings could know us for more than 80 years. They are the most enduring and permanent relationships for most family members. For many, the rivalry experienced between siblings throughout childhood and adolescence fades in adulthood and gives way to more emotionally mature relationships with greater degrees of closeness and warmth (Scharf, Shulman, and Avigad-Spitz 2005).

However, although rivalry tends to decrease after adolescence when siblings leave home to establish their own lives, it is not unusual for their relationship to lapse during the early and middle years of adulthood, particularly if they do not live in close proximity to one another. Yet in times of illness or crisis, siblings provide emotional and psychological support to one another regardless of whether they live close or far away. During late middle age, siblings often establish close ties again (Price 2001).

What tends to bring many adult siblings back together is the need to care for their aging parents (Brintnall-Peterson 2004) as well as their own mortality and need for care as they age. After age 70, exchanges of giving and receiving help between siblings appear to rise (J. White 2001). Possibly because of

Most older adults have at least one living sibling, often whom they consider one of their closest friends. This is not surprising given siblings share biological and cultural heritage, as well as a lifetime of family memories.

Grandparents' Rights

Families break up for many reasons—death of a parent, divorce, drug and alcohol addiction, or incarceration. Although grandparents have custody rights of the grandchildren or court-mandated visitation in these cases, these rights are not constitutional in nature nor do they exist in common law. Federal legislation does require each state to recognize and enforce the custody and visitation decrees or orders of other states. However, each state determines the conditions under which custody to or visitation by grandparents can take place, and these vary considerably from state to state.

All states require grandparents to prove that custody or visitation is in the best interests of the child. Courts first consider the relationship of the parents with the child before considering whether granting custody to grandparents is appropriate. Several states include consideration of grandparents as custodians when both parents are deceased. If a parent is alive, courts typically presume that the parent should retain custody unless the grandparents can prove the parent(s) unfit (unable to provide or care for the child because of substance addiction or incarceration, for example). Even if the relationship between grandparents and grandchildren is close and strong (even if grandparents have had responsibility for the daily care of the child), it is difficult for grandparents to get custody against the wishes of the parent.

State statutes also provide visitation to grandparents (against parental objections) when certain conditions occur. Some states are more permissive: in Connecticut, Hawaii, Idaho, Kentucky, Maryland, and New York, for example, grandparents can file for visitation based only on the premise that visits are in the best interests of the child. In other states (Alabama, Iowa, Mississippi, Oregon, Rhode Island, and Utah), grandparents can file a suit for visitation only when they have been denied visits altogether. If they see grandchildren—even infrequently—they do not have a case. In some states, when one parent is deceased, grandparents can petition for regular visitation.

In the most restrictive states (Florida, Minnesota, and Pennsylvania), grandparents cannot make a legal case unless they can demonstrate that they have or had a surrogate-parent type relationship with the child. For example, they may have to show that they cared for the child full-time while parents were gone for extended periods of time. Grandchildren may have had a warm, loving relationship with Grandma—including Sunday dinner at her home each week—and still be denied visits with her if parents decide against it. And in some states, adoption of the child by anyone (including a stepparent) terminates the visitation rights of a grandparent. (From "Third-party visitation." *Family Law Quarterly, 46*(4), 537–541. American Bar Association, 2013.)

Questions to Consider

What rights should grandparents have with regard to consideration for custody and visitation?

Under what conditions should a parent or parents be able to deny visitation to grandparents?

What factors should be considered in deciding "the child's best interests"?

Should relatives other than grandparents—aunts and uncles, for example—have rights with regard to custody or visitation? When?

How much and when should the child's wishes be a factor in custody and visitation decisions?

---

these exchanges, people with siblings report higher levels of life satisfaction and lower rates of depression in later life.

Most older adults have at least one living sibling, often whom they consider one of their closest friends. This is not surprising given siblings share biological and cultural heritage, as well as a lifetime of family memories (Brintnall-Peterson 2004). For example, your sisters and brothers may be the only people alive who remember the family vacation to the beach when the dog got lost or the family secrets that have never been fully exposed. This shared history appears to become more important and valuable as we age (Price 2001), although shared histories can cause mixed sentiments because of past tensions, irritations, and jealousies (Fingerman, Hay, and Birditt 2004).

Summary

1. The relationship a child experiences with his or her parents while growing up continues to exert a profound influence on that person as an adult. Both satisfying and disruptive memories and emotions may be carried into marriage.

2. Parent–child relationships become particularly important in the mate selection process. Parents may try to influence a child's choice of spouse. Parental objections to a child's choice of spouse may drive the couple into each other's arms. Rebellion against parents also impairs children's judgment in choosing a spouse.

3. People can do several things when parents disapprove of their spouse choice. They can try to get their parents to like their spouse and can give their parents time and opportunity to get acquainted. They can discuss the situation with their parents, and they can get premarital counseling.

4. In healthy families, children identify with the roles of their parents and learn what mother, father, and spouse are like from their parents. Identification may be positive or negative.

5. People may develop unrealistic or unhealthy expectations about marriage from the example set by their own parents.

6. Despite myths to the contrary, families are a major source of help to elderly persons.

7. Conflicting ideas of inclusion and exclusion are a source of tension in mother–daughter relationships. Daughters may feel mothers are intrusive; mothers may feel excluded.

8. Conflicted relationships between adult children and parents can be a source of stress for all generations.

9. Because people are living longer and because a greater percentage of the population is considered elderly, families are now providing more care to their older members who may need considerable help.

10. The roots of in-law conflict may include the following: partners' negative conditioning to expect trouble, their immaturity, the parents' resentment of the spouse selected, and parents who cannot let their child go and who are overprotective and meddling.

11. Most young couples do not want to live with their parents after marriage, and parents do not want to live with them. When doubling up is necessary, harmony is more likely when each couple has their own space and when obligations and responsibilities have been discussed ahead of time.

12. There has been an increase in the number and percentage of young people who accept the idea of sharing a home with an elderly relative, but older people give up their independence and share residence with an adult child typically when forced to by circumstances such as economic difficulties or divorce.

13. Demographic trends have resulted in more living grandparents and fewer grandchildren per grandparent.

14. Today's grandparents are healthier and live longer than their predecessors and are typically open to continued growth, experiences, and development well into late life.

15. Many couples appreciate grandparents for all they do for them and their children.

16. Grandparents can help grandchildren feel secure and loved; play a crucial role during family transitions such as divorce; help grandchildren learn to know, trust, and understand other people; give grandchildren a sense of

history; provide grandchildren with supervision and experiences that parents do not have the time or money to do; give grandchildren a sense of values and a philosophy of life based on their years of living; play the role of arbitrator between adult children and grandchildren; and give grandchildren a wholesome attitude toward old age.

17. There has been a dramatic increase in the number of grandparents who are raising their grandchildren.

18. Grandparents also can be important in the lives of adolescents and young adults. The maternal grandmother–granddaughter bond is the strongest of the grandparent–grandchild bonds, but paternal grandfathers and grandsons have a more intense bond than do maternal grandfathers and grandsons. Parents heavily influence the grandparent–grandchild relationship.

19. Grandchildren also can do many things for grandparents: provide a source of biologic continuity and a sense that the family will endure, enhance grandparents' self-concept, help grandparents overcome social isolation, and provide physical assistance.

20. For many, the rivalry experienced between siblings throughout childhood and adolescence begins to diminish in adulthood and gives way to more emotionally mature relationships with greater degrees of closeness.

Key Terms

negative identification

positive identification

Questions for Thought

1. What are some important family-of-origin experiences you have had, and how have they influenced you or how may they influence you after marriage: for example, roles of men and women (who cooks? mows?), power and decision making, and life goals?

2. To what extent and in what ways have your parents influenced your spouse selection (either present or future)? What characteristics would your parents like to see in your ideal mate? How does your parents' ideal view compare with your own view?

3. Most of the conflict in in-law relationships is between mother-in-law and daughter-in-law. Why do you think this is so?

4. What are some approaches a couple can take to build a healthy relationship with parents-in-law? Parents with children-in-law?

5. Under what circumstances is it acceptable for young adults to live with their parents? Parents with their grown children?

6. What have been the major characteristics of your relationships with your grandparents? What benefits have they provided to you? How have you assisted them?

For Further Reading

The website of the American Association of Retired Persons has a wealth of information on grandparenting (do's and don'ts for grandparents, activities to do with grandchildren, etc.), getting along with your aging parents, being a caregiver to an elderly family member, and grandparents who are rearing their grandchildren. http://www.aarp.org.

Bornstein, M. (2003). *Well-being: Positive development across the life cycle.* Mahwah, NJ: Erlbaum. Discusses positive development in relationships between family members across the life course.

Caputo, R. (2005). *Challenges of aging on U.S. families: Policy and practice implications.* New York: Haworth Press. Presents a comprehensive overview of challenges facing the country as well as families with regard to an aging population.

"Listen sister: 7 steps to healing adult sibling rivalry" by Deborah Dunham has practical suggestions and a link to a book by sisters Cathy Jo Cress and Kali Cress Peterson, *Mom loves you best: Forgiving and forging sibling relationships*, for those who want to read more. http://www.mydaily.com/2011/02/23.

CHAPTER

15

Conflict, Family Crises, and Crisis Management

Learning Objectives

Conflict and Children

- The Family Environment
- Interparent Conflict

CULTURAL PERSPECTIVE: *The Plight of Immigrant Families*

Sources of Conflict

- Personal Sources
- Physical Sources
- Interpersonal Sources
- Situational or Environmental Sources

PERSONAL PERSPECTIVE: *What Would You Like to Change about the Way You Deal with Conflict?*

Methods of Dealing with Conflict

- Avoidance
- Ventilation and Catharsis
- Constructive and Destructive Conflicts
- Levels of Marital Conflict Model

Family Crises

- Stage 1: Onset

- Stage 2: Disorganization
- Stage 3: Reorganization

COPING FEATURE: *Search for Meaning in Tough Times*

The Crisis of Infidelity

- Reasons for Infidelity

FAMILY STRENGTHS PERSPECTIVE: *Affair-Proofing Your Marriage*

AT ISSUE TODAY: *Cheating in Cyberspace*

- Affairs as Crises for Married People

The Crisis of Economic Distress

- Types of Economic Distress
- Effects on Individuals and on Family Relationships
- Coping with Economic Distress

The Crisis of Addictions

- Characteristics of Addiction
- Reasons for Addiction
- Effects on the Family

- Overcoming Addiction: The Addicted Person
- Overcoming Addiction: The Family and the Addicted Person Working Together

The Crisis of Violence and Abuse

- Factors Related to Violence
- Child Maltreatment
- Treatment for Spouse and Child Abuse
- Detecting Child Maltreatment
- Elder Abuse

The Crisis of Death and Grief

A QUESTION OF POLICY: *Abused and Neglected Children*

Summary

Key Terms

Questions for Thought

For Further Reading

LEARNING OBJECTIVES

AFTER READING THE CHAPTER, YOU SHOULD BE ABLE TO DO THE FOLLOWING:

- Explain why conflict is inevitable in family relationships.

- Identify the sources of conflict in the family: personal, physical, interpersonal, and situational or environmental.

- Discuss the effects of conflict on children.

- Discuss methods of dealing with conflict.

- Describe the meaning of family crises and the definable stages of coping with one.

- Explain the reasons for infidelity and the crisis it creates.

- Discuss the crisis of economic distress, the effects on individuals and family relationships, and means of coping with it.

- Identify the characteristics of addiction; describe the effects on the family and how the family can help the addicted person overcome addiction.

- Describe the crisis of violence and abuse in the family; the factors related to violence; the facts about spouse abuse and child abuse, including sexual abuse; and the treatment for spouse and child abuse.

- Describe the stages of grief and people's reactions during each stage.

Over the 10-year marriage, she had endured repeated abusive episodes that had gotten worse. The occasional slap or shove had given way to punches and kicks, bruises, and black eyes. She called her mom after one beating, ready to leave (again). He confronted Mom on the porch, yelling and pushing her down.

He was kept away for a few weeks by a restraining order. Then he began calling. Would she drive him to a nearby city for counseling? She decided against it. He wanted to come to the house to talk about the kids. She refused. He followed her around town, showing up at her work.

On Mother's Day he showed up unexpectedly and burst into the house. He raged from one room to another, breaking windows, pushing over furniture, throwing toys and other things. He broke off a chair leg and began beating her. A friend who was visiting tried to stop him, but could not. The friend escaped out the back door (with her cell phone); the children scattered to their rooms or the front yard.

Convinced she was unconscious, he piled dish towels on the stove and lighted them. He told the oldest child (in the front yard) that he was going to burn down the house with her and the younger children inside. The child ran back inside and was pulling off burning towels when the sheriff arrived.

Although most couples do not experience anything like this, some conflict and discord is a normal part of every relationship. Two people will never agree on everything. Tensions build up and misunderstandings occur in the process of living. The numerous decisions that couples must make and the disappointments, frustrations, and adjustments they must face will result, at some time, in a hurt look, an angry word, or a quarrel. Some couples have less conflict than others, and some are able to deal with it more constructively than others, but conflict is present in every human relationship.

How conflict is managed, rather than how much conflict there is, distinguishes satisfied from dissatisfied couples. Although some conflict is inevitable, that does not mean it is always desirable or helpful. Conflict can destroy love and even an otherwise good marriage. But it also can relieve tensions, clear the air, and bring two people closer together than ever before (Harrar and DeMaria 2007). It depends on the total circumstances, the focus of the conflict, the way it is handled, and the ultimate outcome.

In this chapter, we look closely at conflict—its causes, its functions in marriage, some ways couples deal with it, and its effects on children. Then, we discuss typical patterns of family adjustment to crises and describe the processes of adjustment. In addition, we discuss five major crises families may face: infidelity, economic distress, addiction, violence and abuse, and death.

Conflict and Children

When children are involved, conflict necessitates additional considerations. How are children affected by conflict? Are older children and adolescents affected to the same extent as younger children? Should parents quarrel in front of the children? Is it best to try to hide marital problems from them? These are questions of significance for families' and children's well-being.

The Family Environment

When the family environment is characterized by positive affect—love, warmth, faith, trust, consideration, and empathy—children thrive. Such an environment helps them feel good about themselves and know that they are loved and wanted. Conversely, researchers have found that childrearing environments in which interpersonal relations are characterized by anger and conflict place children at risk for lack of appropriate affection (Fauchier and Margolin 2004) and the development of emotional and behavioral problems such as engaging more often in high-risk behaviors (Lam, Solmeyer, and McHale 2012).

A general family atmosphere of anger and discord has a greater impact on children than marital discord. Some parents who have discordant marriages may maintain the image of a harmonious relationship and keep their disputes hidden from their children. However, children are observant, and it is impossible for them to escape a general climate of anger and conflict in the home. The effects of conflict on children are less if they can withdraw when their parents are fighting, even if they cannot withdraw completely from a negative home environment.

Interparent Conflict

Exposure to interparent conflict is a source of stress for children and is predictive of problems in child adjustment (El-Sheikh and Elmore-Staton 2004; L. M. Papp, Cummings, and Schermerhorn 2004). The more disruptive of family functioning parental conflicts are, the more likely they are to be perceived by children as stressful and to reduce children's reliance on the family as a safe emotional environment. Consistent with this, empirical evidence has confirmed that children who perceive their parents' fights as frequent and intense also have a higher incidence of maladjustment and behavior problems. For example, when children repeatedly witness their parents fighting and expressing negative emotions, they are more likely to exhibit aggressive behavior, whereas when parents use constructive conflict tactics and express positive emotions, the probability of children exhibiting aggression decreases (Cummings, Goeke-Morey, and Papp 2004; Y. Li, Putallaz, and Su 2011; Underwood et al. 2008).

Quarrels between parents that are directly related to their children, such as disagreements about childrearing practices, have a more negative impact than quarrels that are not related to the children. Children begin to see themselves as a source of conflict and to blame themselves for their parents' difficulties. As a result, they are more disturbed than if the conflict does not involve them. Furthermore, parents who quarrel with each other may take out their anger on their children. Sometimes older

Some conflict and discord may be a normal part of every relationship. Research suggests that couples who are closer and have the greatest potential for satisfaction in their relationship also have the greatest potential for conflict.

The Plight of Immigrant Families

Many immigrant families experience crises as a result of existing immigration policy or lack thereof. Immigration policy impacts marital, parent–child, and extended family relationships of many families from different cultures. Immigration reform is a major social issue directly affecting thousands of families. The issue is increasingly the subject of policy debate. Unfortunately, it has been politicized and used as a way to try to influence elections. Politicizing the issue, mega-marches, networking with labor unions, and lobbying have resulted in some gains. For example, the Deferred Action for Childhood Arrivals was an important development at the federal level; it stops deportation of qualified but undocumented youth.

However, politicizing the immigration issue has also been counterproductive. It has often been driven and controlled by political gamesmanship and a quest for electoral power rather than by a genuine desire to help families. This has resulted in a milestone of some 2 million deportations during the Obama administration, the criminalization of immigrant workers, and many immigrant families hurt by separation.

At the heart of immigration reform—beyond the politicizing and gamesmanship—are hurting families stressed by uncertainty and separation. There are 11 million undocumented workers in the United States and 13 million legal, permanent immigrant residents, of which 8 million are currently eligible for citizenship. It is estimated that each day an additional 1,100 families are separated because of deportations. This results in great emotional, relationship, and financial stress among these families (Azemun and Benito 2014).

What criteria should be considered in developing immigration reform with regard to deportation of illegal immigrants whose families are legal immigrants?

What are some of the major difficulties or stresses that immigrant families face on an everyday basis? What kinds of programs would help these families?

---

children are drawn into the argument and pressed to take sides; they may try to keep their parents from fighting. Failure to achieve peace is disturbing to them, and children blame themselves for not being able to do anything about their family's difficulties.

Moreover, the effects of family conflict are heightened by direct exposure to conflict and aggression. Repeated conflict in the family sensitizes children to interparent aggression and causes them to be more affected by subsequent conflict than they would have been otherwise. Consistent with a sensitization hypothesis, interparent physical aggression during the previous year is related to child withdrawal and anxiety. Children who are exposed to interparent aggression tend to have a higher incidence of emotional and behavioral problems (Li, Putallaz, and Su 2011) and are at greater risk for lack of parental support and affection (Margolin, Gordis, and Oliver 2004). Research also indicates that adolescents exposed to marital violence during childhood are more likely to justify the use of violence in dating relationships and to possess more traditional attitudes of male–female relationships (E. L. Lichter and McCloskey 2004).

Marital conflicts that include physical aggression seem to be especially distressing to children and to have a lasting effect on how they react to subsequent interadult conflicts. Tensions between spouses may become intertwined with tensions among other family members, especially the children. Dysfunctional families are characterized by the spread of tensions from one subsystem to another, particularly from the parents to the children (Kanel 2007).

Sources of Conflict

Conflict may have its origin in (1) personal sources, (2) physical sources, (3) interpersonal sources, or (4) situational or environmental sources.

Personal Sources

Personal sources of conflict are those that originate within the individual when inner drives, instincts, and values pull against each other. The conflict is not with one's partner but with oneself, and tensions arise from the internal battle. As a result of these inner tensions, the individual has disagreements or gets into quarrels in situations that heighten the tension. Consider this case:

> Mr. M. was brought up by parents who rejected him and made him feel unwanted and unloved as a child. As a result, he became the kind of man who was afraid to show love for his wife or to let her get close to him. He needed her and wanted her attention and companionship; but whenever she tried to develop a close, loving, intimate relationship, he became anxious and fearful and would end up rejecting her or pushing her away. She was very hurt and became frustrated and angry, which, in turn, made him mad. They always ended up in a fight when they started getting close to each other. (Counseling notes)

In this example, the man had deep-seated fears of being lonely, but also anxiety about being vulnerable.

Irrational fears and anxieties and neurotic needs can be the basic sources of spousal friction. For example, a spouse who has a deep-seated fear of losing his or her partner becomes extremely jealous, even with regard to superficial contacts. Emotional illness is another source of friction and arguments. For example, when a spouse is depressed, the couple may experience disruptive and hostile behavior when the partners interact with each other (Rapini 2012). Even emotionally healthy people have mood swings that influence their behavior.

The basic cause of personal conflicts lies deep within the psyche of the individuals involved. Usually, the anxieties have their origins in childhood experiences and early family relationships. For this reason, troubles that arise in marriage because of these previous experiences are difficult to deal with. Permanent solutions can be found when the internal tensions within the individual are relieved.

Physical Sources

Physical sources of conflict are inner tensions having a physical origin. Physical fatigue is one such source. Fatigue causes irritability, emotional upset, impatience, distorted reasoning, and a low tolerance for frustration. It causes people to say and do things that they would not say or do ordinarily. Hunger, overwork, and pain are also potential sources of tension. A pounding headache may be just as much a source of conflict as a serious disagreement.

Interpersonal Sources

Interpersonal sources of conflict are those that occur in relationships between people. All couples have marital problems, but unhappily married people are more likely to complain of neglect and lack of love, affection, sexual satisfaction, understanding, appreciation, and companionship than are happily married couples. Furthermore, their self-image suffers; their spouse may magnify their faults, belittle their efforts, and make false accusations. They feel worthless, and the complaints become the focus of the conflict that ensues. Difficulty resolving differences, lack of communication, or emotional withdrawal by a partner could also contribute to an unhappy marriage.

Although it seems contradictory, one of the reasons for conflict is the intimate nature of the marriage relationship. Any close relationship will involve conflict; people who spend much time together and who share many aspects of their lives encounter numerous opportunities for disagreement (Stinnett and Stinnett 2010).

Another obvious reason for conflict between two persons is that they have basic differences. Even people who share similar backgrounds usually have some differing experiences, family traditions, attitudes, habits, goals, religious beliefs, or values.

Conflict may also arise when each partner has strong power needs, and interaction becomes a contest to determine who exercises the most power. Conflict may even be regarded as necessary to resolve the power struggle—to see who "wins." One person may enhance feelings of self-worth

personal sources of conflict Those that originate within the individual when inner drives, instincts, and values pull against one another.

physical sources of conflict Inner tensions having a physical origin, such as fatigue, hunger, or a headache.

interpersonal sources of conflict Tensions that occur in the relationships between people.

by dominating the other (Anderson, John, and Keltner 2012; Hartwell-Walker 2015).

In American society, competition is emphasized in work, school, and sports. Not surprisingly, the spirit of competition sometimes carries over into marital relationships; spouses may compete in terms of salaries, status, or just everyday decisions. A competitive style of dealing with conflict is where the partners are both assertive and uncooperative. There is an attempt by each partner to force his or her will on the other so that there is a loser and a winner (Knox and Schacht 2016). Therapists report that problems involving power struggles are difficult to treat (R. B. Miller et al. 2003).

There is an adage, "It's not the great storms that destroy the oak tree; it's the little bugs." The little bugs might be compared to the tremendous trifles that can add up and damage a relationship if they are not dealt with effectively. Slurping coffee, leaving the cap off the toothpaste tube, throwing dirty clothes in the corner, muttering, jingling coins or keys in a pocket, and irritating verbal expressions—these are examples of tremendous trifles.

Unfortunately, many things that truly irritate us seem so petty that we are reluctant to discuss them. Petty irritants are most damaging to a relationship when they are kept inside and resentment is allowed to build, eventually becoming a source of conflict. And, unfortunately, we sometimes disregard a partner's irritation over a matter as being too trivial to honor.

The patterns and relationships of intimate interaction between partners far outweigh other ("outside") sources of conflict. People feel hurt, resentful, and frustrated when their partners do not meet their sociopsychological needs. Relationships with kin, the community, or others outside the family do not affect the partners as much as their relationship with each other does. They expect that their needs for understanding, communication, love, affection, and companionship will be met. If those needs are not met, the couple may become dissatisfied and discontented.

It can be difficult to sort out all the causes of conflict because there are often multiple interrelated problems. Marriage counselors know that the problems couples complain about in the beginning of counseling may be only symptoms of the focal point of conflict. The real causes of difficulties often run much deeper. For example, a spouse's lack of sexual interest may be correlated with quarreling, lack of communication, dislike of the partner, mental health problems, infidelity, or general alienation. Sometimes, the couple may not realize the basic reasons for the difficulties. These causes often are found in the psyche of one of the individuals or in the pattern of the couple's interpersonal relationship.

Situational or Environmental Sources

Situational or environmental sources of conflict include things such as living conditions, societal pressures on family members, cultural strains among minority group families (such as discrimination and assimilation), and unexpected events that disturb family functioning. A major source of stress for families can be caring for someone with a chronic illness. Typically, the caregiver is a female who has other family and work responsibilities in addition to caring for a sick family member. Such caregivers are under extended, chronic stress because of the demands placed on them, which in turn can compromise their own health and well-being (Mayo Clinic Staff 2015; Vitaliano, Young, and Zhang 2004). This is a good example of how one family crisis can create another (i.e., the situational crisis of caregiving can lead to a physical crisis of poor well-being of the caregiver).

Sometimes a marital relationship remains in a state of relative equilibrium until some traumatic event occurs to disrupt the relationship. Sometimes a long-standing marriage suddenly becomes conflictual. For example, one man could not work through his feelings of isolation and deprivation following the death of his father; he felt he had been an undutiful son and withdrew from his spouse and family while he struggled with his guilt and grief. In this instance, a specific event triggered the conflict. Unexpected events such as unemployment, change of jobs, disaster, illness, pregnancy, death, or a forced separation or move may be enough to trigger a crisis. Couples who are emotionally insecure or unstable usually have far more difficulty coping than do other couples. Couples characterized by high levels of tension may even have conflict when their time together increases because of vacations, retirement, illness, or reduced hours of employment.

Another example of the situational source of conflict can be seen among divorced families with children. Cashmore and Parkinson (2011) conducted a research study to identify reasons for disputes in high-conflict, divorced families. Two major reasons were identified. One reason involved breaches of

What Would You Like to Change about the Way You Deal with Conflict?

Following is a sample of answers given to this question by college students:

"I would like to stop getting so mad. I get extremely angry at my boyfriend, start yelling and throwing things. I get out of control. My dad had a hot temper—guess I got it from him."

"I want to be more open-minded and less judgmental."

"I get so defensive—sometimes see criticism where there isn't any intended. My feelings get hurt or I get mad."

"I say really harsh things—things that I don't truly mean. But I feel like I have to keep people from walking all over me."

"I hold a lot of things inside—fret and fume—until one day I overreact to some small thing."

"A lot of times I am too 'nice' and polite about things. I may not like something that is said or done, but won't speak up about it. I need to be more assertive—not hostile or mean, of course—in communicating my feelings."

court orders: about two-thirds of the parents reported they were denied visitation or contact with their children by their former spouse. The second reason for conflict involved parenting arrangements as well as the frequency, type, and flexibility of the contact arrangements. Parents with primary custody indicated that their resistance to additional contact (by the noncustodial parent) was because of concerns about the other parent's parenting style and its negative effect on the children, as well as because of the introduction of a new partner.

Methods of Dealing with Conflict

It is not the existence of conflict per se that is problematic for the family, but the methods of managing and resolving the conflict. The methods discussed in this section include avoidance, ventilation and catharsis, and constructive and destructive arguments. Some couples have substantial conflict but resolve their tensions and problems. Other couples are unable to minimize tension or solve anything, so small problems grow into big ones.

Avoidance

Some couples try to deal with conflict through **avoidance**, that is, they try to prevent conflict by avoiding the people, situations, and issues that stimulate it. Or they refuse to acknowledge it or be involved with it. Although disagreement, anger, and frustration are felt, they are not expressed. The motivations for avoiding conflict vary: conflict may be regarded as cruel, vulgar, or indicative of a lack of love. Engaging in conflict may represent failure of the relationship; alienating others or being hurt may be regarded as unacceptable consequences.

A person or couple may consistently avoid conflict by being unresponsive; they are silent, withdrawn, or refuse to talk about the issue. Another strategy is to change the subject every time the conflict issue comes up. Humor also may be used to avoid dealing with the issue. A person may make jokes or funny remarks one after another, thus refusing to treat the issue seriously. This can be frustrating to a partner. Always being too busy to discuss a problem is another example of avoidance.

Avoiding conflict when people are hungry or tired may provide temporary calm, but when problems are not resolved it can lead to long-term

situational or environmental sources of conflict These include living conditions, societal pressures, cultural strains, and unexpected events.

avoidance Method of dealing with conflict by avoiding the people, situations, and issues that stimulate it.

eroding of the relationship. Partners who never address important issues gradually withdraw from each other. Disengagement and alienation occur when partners stop communicating with each other. As a result, there is increased loneliness, less reciprocity in attempting to settle issues, a loss of intimacy, and a decline in other forms of interaction, such as sexual intercourse.

The avoidance pattern of dealing with conflict is described as antisocial and is unhealthy for individuals and relationships if used routinely. As mentioned earlier, unexpressed conflict leads to high levels of frustration and resentment. Nondistressed couples differ from distressed couples in that they more often discuss conflict situations (D. Oson, DeFrain, and Skogrand 2014; Stinnett, Hilliard, and Stinnett 2000).

Sometimes, however, temporarily avoiding (as in postponing) conflict is the wisest choice. Positive solutions can be found only after intense negative feelings have subsided and people can think straight. Thus, upset individuals might want to engage in physical activity, go to a movie, visit a neighbor, or discuss things with a counselor before confronting the problem.

Stressful living conditions or unexpected events that disturb family functioning affect every member of the family, not just the adults. The more children in a family, the more strain, stress, and conflict are naturally introduced.

Ventilation and Catharsis

The opposite of avoiding conflict is ventilating it. **Ventilation** means expressing negative emotions and feelings. This concept has been used in psychotherapy for years. It involves encouraging people who are upset to talk out or act out their feelings to get them in the open; only then can the individuals scrutinize their feelings, understand them, and channel them in less destructive directions. This therapeutic approach, which emphasizes the importance of "letting it out," is based on the idea of **catharsis**, or draining off negative emotions and feelings so that they can be replaced by more positive ones. This assumes that people have a tendency toward aggression that cannot be bottled up. If they attempt to repress this tendency, it will only result in a more destructive expression at some later time. Therefore, it is better to let out the aggression through a series of minor confrontations than to let negative feelings accumulate until they become a potential relationship bomb.

This approach to dealing with conflict can be helpful psychotherapy for people with feelings of hostility and emotional problems. But venting one's hostilities on the psychiatrist's couch or in the counseling center and in the presence of a trained therapist is far different from doing the same in one's own home, where the hostilities are directed toward one's spouse or children. In therapy, an adult may express hostilities toward a family member verbally or a child may express them physically, in the presence of the therapist, but not actually in the physical presence of the person. Telling a therapist "I hate my spouse" is far different from actually telling a spouse "I hate you." In the first instance, the hostilities may be drained off harmlessly, such that when the individual gets back home he or she feels less hateful; but in the second instance, although the individual feels better, the spouse feels worse and will usually retaliate in some fashion. This may result in an increase of hostile feelings between the two people.

The reason is that the family is an intimate, closely confined group, with members intensely involved with one another. If excessive hostility is directed at other family members, they typically feel angry, hurt, or misunderstood. When their reactive emotions are not dealt with, additional disagreements arise and tension mounts, sometimes to intolerable levels. Furthermore, family members cannot get away from the source of friction without splitting up the family, even if only temporarily. Of critical importance here, too, is the possibility that when verbal aggression becomes excessive, it can lead to physical aggression (Halpern-Meekin 2013).

What about more intellectual, rational approaches to problem solving? Evidence suggests that families that take the calm, rational, intellectual, emotion-suppressing approach have much lower levels of physical violence. Intellectual approaches that observe "civility" and "etiquette" in interpersonal relationships are more helpful in the long run in promoting marital harmony and stability and in resolving conflicts (Gottman Institute 2015). Some families actively teach their children about communication and how to deal with their emotions appropriately, whereas other parents discourage or even punish children for expressing their emotions (Fitness and Duffield 2004).

Constructive and Destructive Conflicts

Every family has conflicts, and how a person manages conflict affects his or her personal development (Sillars, Canary, and Tafoya 2004). A distinction must be made between conflicts that are constructive and those that are destructive. **Constructive arguments** are those that attack the problems, stick to the issues, and lead to a more complete understanding and to consensus, compromise, or other acceptable solutions to the problem. Confrontations are a cooperative effort to handle a difficulty—not a competitive struggle to hurt each other. People (spouses or parents and children, etc.) are respectful of each other and keep their focus on solving the problem (instead of attacking each other). They are adaptable and willing to modify their behavior. This pattern of behavior is described as *issue centered* and prosocial in nature. It includes several key elements, including the following:

- Acceptance that we are different;
- Respect for the rights of people to disagree;
- A clear, specific identification of the problem;
- Expression of each person's feelings about the problem;
- Identification of alternative solutions to the problem;
- Evaluation of alternatives; and
- Choice of alternative that is best for everyone.

Constructive conflicts minimize negative emotions, foster respect and confidence, and bring a

couple closer together. They take place in a nonhostile, trusting atmosphere in which honest disagreements may be discussed and understood and in which the argument progresses according to fair rules. They involve a low level of negative verbal responses. Forgiveness is a part of constructive arguments that generates intimacy (Fincham, Beach, and Davila 2007; Siassi 2015).

Cooperative behaviors are positively related to marital satisfaction and successful conflict resolution, whereas conflict-oriented behaviors (such as frequent disagreements and serious quarrels) are negatively related to marital satisfaction and conflict resolution (Leggett et al. 2012). Also, commitment to the marriage serves as a buffer or protection from high, destructive conflict (and is positively associated with marriage happiness) (Dush and Taylor 2012; Lauer and Lauer 2011).

Destructive arguments are those that attack the other person rather than the problem. The aim is to shame, belittle, or punish the other person through name calling or by attacking sensitive issues in a spirit of ill will, hatred, revenge, or contempt. Criticism and negative personal comments are used to bully the other person. The frequent use of hostile and volatile conflict styles is significantly related to higher levels of disengaged, distant relationships and lower levels of family satisfaction (Baptist et al. 2012; Leggett et el. 2012; Stinnett and Stinnett 2010).

Destructive arguments are characterized by a lack of genuine communication and by suspicion, and they often involve interpersonal strategies of threat or coercion. The attacker may bring up side issues as he or she relieves personal tensions at the expense of the other person.

---

ventilation The process of airing, or expressing, negative emotions and feelings.

catharsis Venting negative emotions to rid oneself of them so that they can be replaced by more positive ones.

constructive arguments Arguments that stick with the issues; that attack the problem and not the other person; that employ rational methods; and that result in greater understanding, consensus, compromise, and closeness between two people.

destructive arguments Arguments that attack the other person rather than the problem; that increase resentment and hostility and undermine trust, friendship, and affectionate feelings; that result in greater alienation; and that do not solve the problem.

Some couples become locked in a competitive style of conflict where the focus is on *winning* a conflict at the expense of the other partner's goals and desires. They may enjoy the excitement of engaging in verbal fights and perceiving themselves as the "winner." They find it difficult to stop a heated argument. The competitive style is destructive and usually not conducive to intimacy because it is based on there being a winner and also a loser (D. Olson, DeFrain, and Skogrand 2014; Wilmot and Hocker 2007).

When this competitive, antisocial pattern is utilized, conflict becomes a game of wits where victory means the enhancing of one person's ego by belittling another's. The objective is not solving the problem or gaining insight about the issue; rather, it is attacking the person who takes a different viewpoint. Attacks lead to counterattacks as each mate becomes hypnotized by his or her virtues and by a mate's faults. Real issues get lost in the fray, and any true conflict resolution is prevented.

Destructive arguments elevate tension levels; increase resentment and hostility toward the other person; undermine confidence, trust, friendship, and affectionate feelings; result in loss of companionship; and engender greater alienation. One of the characteristics of destructive arguments is that the conflict or disagreement gets worse—not resolved.

Levels of Marital Conflict Model

The Levels of Marital Conflict Model (LMCM) was originated by a conflict management specialist and was adapted for use in marital therapy. It is one of the clearest and most helpful models for understanding marital conflict. The LMCM identifies five levels of interpersonal conflict. Each level, with associated objectives, assumptions, emotional climate, and negotiation style, is shown in Table 15.1.

The LMCM is used as a tool in marital therapy because it enables the therapist to focus on the dimensions of conflict interaction and to organize a confusing array of information in a manageable manner. The therapist's approach will be different for a couple in Level II than for a couple in Level V. One aim of the therapist is to deescalate the conflict level to a level where resolutions are easier to achieve and more likely.

LEVEL I: PROBLEMS TO SOLVE Discord at this level is not over issues that threaten the relationship. Real issues do exist, and tensions arise from awareness by the partners that their goals, needs, or values are in conflict. Issues may be serious (whether to have children, for example) or not so serious (where to vacation, for example). Partners at this stage perceive they have a problem but believe it can be solved.

TABLE 15.1 Level of Marital Conflict Model

LEVEL	MAJOR OBJECTIVE	KEY ASSUMPTION	EMOTIONAL CLIMATE	NEGOTIATION STYLE
I. Problems to solve	Solve the problem	We can work it out	Hope	Open; direct; clear and nondistorted; common interests recognized
II. Disagreements	Protect oneself	Compromise is necessary	Uncertainty	Cautious sharing; vague and general language; calculation beginning
III. Contest	Win	Not enough resources to go around	Frustration and resentment	Strategic manipulation; distorted communication; personal attacks begin; no one wants to be first to change
IV. Fight/flight	Hurt the other	Partner cannot or will not change; no change necessary in self	Antagonism and alienation	Verbal/nonverbal incongruity; blame; perceptual distortions; refusal to take responsibility
V. War	Eliminate the other	Cost of withdrawal greater than cost of staying	Hopelessness and revenge	Emotional volatility; no clear understanding of issues; self-righteous; compulsive; inability to disengage

Note: Weingarten, H., and Leas, S. (1987). Levels of marital conflict model: A guide to assessment and intervention in troubled marriages. American Journal of Orthopsychiatry, 57, 407–417. Reprinted with permission from The American Journal of Orthopsychiatry. *Copyright (1987) by the American Orthopsychiatric Association, Inc.*

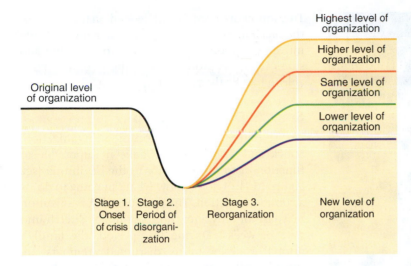

Highest level of
organization

Higher level of
organization

Same level of
organization

Original level
of organization

Lower level of
organization

Stage 1. | Stage 2. | Stage 3. | New level of
Onset | Period of | Reorganization | organization
of crisis | disorgani-
| zation

FIGURE 15.1 Family Adjustment to a Crisis

LEVEL II: DISAGREEMENTS At this level, partners perceive disagreement as arising from the relationship rather than from a problem. Clashes are motivated more by the need for self-protection than by the need to solve a problem. Because trust is lowered and partners feel uncertain about each other, they may avoid confrontation and may become defensive in communication. Third-party support from friends and family is often sought.

LEVEL III: CONTEST Conflict issues have accumulated at this level and are hard to disentangle. Hope has diminished; frustration has grown. Because they perceive resources as limited, power struggles and competition are easily triggered. Marital partners have lost sight of their common interests and goals; they seek to end disputes by changing each other.

LEVEL IV: FIGHT/FLIGHT Alienation and antagonism are characteristics of this level. The partners believe that neither can nor will change; the relationship satisfies few of their needs. The aim of interaction is to hurt each other; outsiders may be enlisted in the struggle, not in support of the marriage (as in Level II), but as alternative sources of gratification. Couples who end their relationship at this level are often willing parties to hostile divorce proceedings. Couples who stay together may exclude each other more and more—stop eating together, forget anniversaries, and so on.

LEVEL V: WAR The discord at this level includes not only issues but also personalities. Partners believe they cannot resolve differences and cannot escape the relationship except by destroying each other.

Perception is distorted; irrationality is high. Violence is common because partners use compulsion and force to accomplish their aims.

Family Crises

A **crisis** may be defined as a drastic change in the course of events; it is a turning point that affects the trend of future events. It is a time of instability, necessitating decisions and adjustments. Sometimes the crisis develops because of events outside the family: a hurricane, earthquake, flood, war, economic depression, or plant closure. Other times, the crisis happens within the family: death, divorce, violent conflicts, sudden and/or prolonged illness or incapacity, or substance abuse. Internal crises tend to demoralize a family, increasing resentment, alienation, and conflict. Sometimes a crisis develops out of a series of smaller external and internal events that build up to the point at which family members cannot cope. Broderick (1984) explained:

> Even small events, not enough by themselves to cause any real stress, can take a toll when they come one after another. First an unplanned pregnancy, then a move, then a financial problem that results in having to

crisis A drastic change in the course of events; a turning point that affects future events.

Families who experience crises, such as the loss of their home because of a natural disaster, like this family who survived Hurricane Katrina, will pass through the predictable stages of disbelief, disorganization, and reorganization before they begin rebuilding their lives.

borrow several thousand dollars, then the big row with the new neighbors over keeping the dog tied up, and finally little Jimmy breaking his arm in a bicycle accident, all in three months, finally becomes too much. (310)

Broderick calls this situation **crisis overload**.

During a family crisis, families go through three stages—onset, disorganization, and reorganization—before reaching a new level of organization (Chatham 2012; Lavee, McCubbin, and Patterson 1985). The new level may be higher or lower than the level before the crisis.

Stage 1: Onset

The first stage is the onset of the crisis and the increasing realization that a crisis has occurred (see Figure 15.1). An initial reaction may include disbelief. Family members may define a situation differently; what is a major crisis to one person may not be to another. One spouse, for example, may be on the verge of asking for a divorce; the other may refuse to accept the fact that there is a problem, believing that the spouse is "making too big a deal out of it." The first step, therefore, is to define the problem and gradually accept that a crisis exists—for example, recognizing and accepting a child's disability.

The impact of the crisis will depend on the nature of the precipitating event, the interpretation and cognitive perception of it, the degree of hardship and stress the crisis produces, and the resources available to handle the problem.

Stage 2: Disorganization

The second stage is a period of disorganization. Shock and disbelief may make it impossible to function or to think clearly in the beginning (see Figure 15.1). "I don't know what I'm going to do" is a common reaction. The period of disorganization may last for only a few hours or it may stretch into days or weeks. During this period, the family's normal functioning is disrupted. Tempers are short, loyalties are strained, tension fills the air, friction increases, and family morale declines. Child or spouse abuse is more likely to develop during the time of maximum disorganization than at any other time.

When the volcano Mount Saint Helens erupted on May 18, 1980, thousands of people felt the stress. Associated Press reports from Washington after the eruption indicated that, locally, criminal assaults rose 25%, suicide threats and attempts doubled, and the number of cases of battered women increased 45%. The situation was particularly stressful because of the violence of the explosion (500 times the force of the atom bomb dropped on Hiroshima) and the uncertainty of subsequent explosions. People did not know what would happen next or how long the catastrophe would last. The effects of stress were delayed, however. The greatest increase in spouse abuse cases did not occur until about 30 days after the major eruption.

Other studies concur. The use of alcohol and other drugs sharply increases during times of stress and may lead to a deeper level of disorganization or serve to handicap the individual's and family's capacity to bounce back from the crisis (Kanel 2007; D. Olson, DeFrain, and Skogrand 2014).

Stage 3: Reorganization

The third stage is one of gradual reorganization, during which family members take remedial action (see Figure 15.1). If the crisis is financial, family members may borrow money, sell the family car, or cash in some savings. Other family members may get temporary employment to help out, or a former

Search for Meaning in Tough Times

In times of major crisis or loss, such as when a loved one dies or a tornado destroys entire neighborhoods, people search for a meaning to the event. Why did it happen? Is there any good that can come out of it? How do I deal with this loss? What remains?

Meaning-making coping describes using values, goals, and beliefs to define the meaning of a stressful event or situation. This coping strategy is typically used in the context of one's spiritual faith and can be effective—especially in high-stress circumstances. Spiritual faith and religious practices can serve as a system of finding meaning that helps one reframe a catastrophe, maintain hope, and move toward recovery. For example, research indicates that those who are religious (and use meaning-making coping) have a better long-term adjustment and less depression following the death of a loved one (C. L. Park 2005; Santrock 2015).

Meaning-making coping is effective in high-stress situations because of our desire for a life of consequence—a life that "counts for something." The following needs influence how we try to make sense of our lives: (a) the need for purpose; (b) the need for values that provide a positive characterization or a sense of "goodness" to life (for example, "Every cloud has a silver lining"); (c) the need for a sense of efficacy—the belief that "I can make a difference;" and (d) the need for self-worth (Baumeister and Vohs 2002).

Parents who have lost a child to a disease use meaning-making coping strategies when they establish a website to raise awareness of the disease or to support other families in a similar situation. A survivor of Hurricane Katrina remarked, "We are all OK. We lost our house with lots of antiques from my mother and his mother. But we have insurance and, frankly, I didn't really like most of the old furniture. Now no one's feelings will be hurt when I get some that I do like!"

Viktor Frankl, a psychiatrist and the author of *Man's search for meaning* (2006), was a survivor of a Nazi concentration camp. His wife, parents, brother, and sister died in the concentration camps. Frankel concluded that those most likely to survive the camps were those who had developed a positive meaning for their experience by deciding they could make a difference in the quality of life for other prisoners. They made it their purpose and daily mission to minister to those who were physically ill and to encourage and counsel those who were losing hope.

wage earner may start drawing unemployment. If the financial crisis persists, the stock of resources begins to run out. The family must think about taking out a second mortgage, selling the house, or moving to another neighborhood.

Often, once the family hits bottom, things begin to improve. The unemployed wage earner gets a new job, and bills are gradually paid off; the family begins to recoup its emotional and physical resources. Eventually, after a period that may range from days to months to years, the family is reorganized at a new level. Sometimes the new level is not as satisfactory as the old; at other times, the level of organization is superior to the old. For example, in the case of a financial crisis, family money management may improve, total income may be higher, or both. At any rate, the level is high enough and stable enough to mark the end of the period of crisis.

It is helpful to understand what happens when families have various kinds of crises. Although a wide variety of crises exist, we have selected five types for detailed discussion here: (1) infidelity, (2) economic distress, (3) addictions, (4) violence and abuse, and (5) death and grief.

crisis overload A series of crises occurring one after another until they become more than a person can handle.

The Crisis of Infidelity

The majority of Americans still enter marriage expecting and committed to sexual fidelity; most strongly disapprove of a married person having a sexual relationship with someone other than a spouse (Willetts, Sprecher, and Beck 2004). Because sexual fidelity is expected and is a key norm regulating the institution of marriage, infidelity could cause a relationship to dissolve (Previti and Amato 2004). The National Health and Social Life Survey found that 80% of married women and 65% to 85% of married men of every age reported that they had no partners other than their spouse while married (Michael et al. 1994). Ninety percent of married adults had only one sex partner in the previous 12 months. Recent research reveals similar findings: slightly more than 80% of women and 66% to 77% of men are faithful to their partners (Mark, Janssen, and Milhausen 2011; Tafoya and Spitzberg 2007).

These figures reflect the fact that a large majority of married Americans are faithful; here we will discuss those who are not.

Reasons for Infidelity

Why do people become involved in extramarital affairs although they say they do not believe in them? There are a variety of reasons.

EMOTIONAL NEED For some people, extramarital affairs represent an effort to fulfill emotional needs. Affairs are often an expression of personality problems. A woman may unconsciously seek an older father figure (who is already married) to comfort her and love her and to replace the father she lost in childhood or who rejected her as a child.

Extramarital affairs can be an important validation of attractiveness and self-esteem. Affairs may result from insecurities about one's self-worth or sexual attractiveness or sexual performance (Mark, Janssen, and Milhausen 2011). The affairs become

---

FAMILY STRENGTHS PERSPECTIVE

Affair-Proofing Your Marriage

Commitment in marriage and sexual fidelity are so closely linked in the minds of most people that an extramarital sexual affair is regarded as the ultimate threat to a marriage. Affairs have negative consequences to the marriage relationship and often contribute to divorce. Affairs are a significant threat because of the great sense of betrayal that is felt, the loss of trust, the emotional hurt, and the damage to self-esteem. It is possible to take some precautions to reduce the chances that an affair will happen. Taking the following steps demonstrates a commitment to remain faithful:

- *Consider the consequences.* Even if an affair did not mean a divorce, how would the marriage change? What is the *least* harm that could happen? (Extreme hurt to a spouse? Loss of trust?) What is the *worst*?

- *Be wary of rationalization.* Many affairs begin with, "She needs my help. She's new at this job." Or "His wife doesn't understand him. He's so lonely. We're just talking."

- *Avoid "dangerous" situations.* These are times when opportunity is present and temptation is high, such as an out-of-town convention or long hours working alone with someone.

- *Build a spouse's self-esteem.* Do things to make a spouse feel attractive and interesting. Be attentive and do not take each other for granted.

- *Keep romance alive.* Marriages need a sense of adventure and spontaneity. Court each other; go out on dates; take your spouse to the conventions (and enjoy sightseeing and romantic times without the kids); send flowers; have fun together.

- *Deepen intimacy.* True intimacy means sharing many aspects of life. It is being partners, best friends, companions, and lovers. Intimacy requires much quality time together (Stinnett and Stinnett 2005).

an attempt to feel better about oneself. For example, a new sex partner does not know about one's performance in the past, thus easing insecurities about it. More generally, infidelity may be a symptom of emotional difficulties in the individual and an attempt to resolve these difficulties.

UNRESOLVED MARITAL PROBLEMS Infidelity also can be a symptom of unresolved problems in the marriage itself (Maisel et al. 2008; Mark, Janssen, and Milhausen 2011). Problems build up year after year if they are not successfully addressed. Both men and women are more likely to pursue sex outside of marriage when the marital sexual relationship is not satisfactory—monotonous or too infrequent (Krishnamurti and Loewenstein 2008; Mark, Janssen, and Milhausen 2011).

Unresolved issues can include a lack of communication, the efforts of one person to dominate the other, a failure to show affection, and a lack of social life and companionship. People repress their feelings because they do not like to be upset and frustrated all the time. Eventually, they shut off their positive feelings of warmth and affection as well. The marital partners may be at a stalemate, unable either to revive the marriage or to end it. However, they are still vulnerable and will respond to people who fulfill the needs not being met in their marriage.

If hostility builds up between marital partners, an extramarital affair becomes a way of balancing the animosity felt toward a spouse or a way of getting even for hurts suffered in the marriage. Most people are not interested in extramarital relationships when everything is going smoothly in their marriage. For this reason, an affair can be a symptom of problems rather than the problem itself.

AMBIVALENCE ABOUT MARRIAGE Single people who are ambivalent about getting married may seek sexual partners who are already married because they feel "safer" knowing they will not have to make a permanent commitment. They escape the responsibilities of being a spouse but gain the benefits of having a lover.

PLEASURE AND EXCITEMENT Some people have affairs simply because they want the excitement of sexual variety. Other people enjoy the sense of competition, and the married person's unavailability

---

AT ISSUE TODAY

Cheating in Cyberspace

With the widespread availability of the Internet have come opportunities for sexual encounters not imagined in earlier times. The Web offers accessibility to large numbers of potential partners plus anonymity that reduces inhibitions and certain risks.

Cybersex takes several forms. One of these is the consumption of online pornography. Only about 11% of people regard this as being "unfaithful." Even so, pornography portrays women in a demeaning manner—as sex objects—to be used for men's pleasure. Such attitudes may seriously interfere with developing a caring, committed relationship with a spouse.

Much use of pornography is solitary; however, another form of online sex involves interaction with someone else. This may be just flirting and suggestive talk or may escalate to sexual chat for the purpose of sexual gratification—for example, sharing explicit sexual descriptions while masturbating (Daneback, Cooper, and Mansson 2005). About 45% of people regard this as infidelity although cybersex of this sort is typically anonymous, with strangers who never meet.

The final form of online sex involves two people who form an emotional relationship. These are usually personal, intimate connections—regarded as infidelity by about 39% of people. However, individuals who become emotionally involved with each other online are much more likely to want to meet face-to-face and real sex may follow (Henline, Lamke, and Howard 2007). Some estimate that as many as half of all emotional affairs (counting both in-person and online affairs) become sexual (Harrar and DeMaria 2007).

only serves to increase the challenge. They like the thrill of illicit sex. And for some, high-risk situations help to overcome arousal problems (Mark, Janssen, and Milhausen 2011).

There is risk, of course. One is the possibility that they will become emotionally involved, whether they intended to or not. To other people, a one-night stand provides excitement and freedom from the responsibilities of an emotional commitment. The risks include the possibility of STD (or a pregnancy) and the negative effects on the marriage because marital vows have been violated.

PERMISSIVE VALUES Some individuals do not really see anything wrong with extramarital sex—as long as their spouses do not find out or it does not hurt anyone. Some people have numerous partners before marriage and continue to do so afterward because permissiveness is part of their value system. They may have attitudes that sex has little to do with love or commitment; they often are sociable, dynamic, flirty, and open to the possibility of another sex partner (A. P. Clark 2004; Ostovich and Sabini 2004; Simeon and Miller 2005).

Affairs as Crises for Married People

Extramarital affairs have varying effects on married people and their marriages. Both men and women have affairs, and some marriages are never the same afterward. A sense of betrayal and the ensuing distrust are common. One woman remarked, "I don't know if I can ever trust him again. Every time he's out of town I wonder what he is doing and who he's with." Another woman commented, "All I can think of is that he was doing this with that other woman. I can't give myself to him." In such cases, extramarital affairs may be a major factor in precipitating divorce.

Do existing problems in a marriage lead to infidelity or does infidelity lead to problems in a marriage? In a 17-year longitudinal study of 1,475 individuals, researchers assessed whether extramarital sex preceded or followed deteriorations in marital quality. The results were mixed. Couples with marital problems and who appeared prone to divorce had a higher occurrence of extramarital sex. However, extramarital sex lowered subsequent marital happiness and quality, increased subsequent divorce proneness, and increased the odds of divorce. Thus, the study concluded that infidelity is both a cause and a consequence of relationship deterioration (Previti and Amato 2004). Sometimes, however, the crisis of

an affair stimulates the couple to finally accept the fact that their marriage is in deep trouble and that they need help. One woman explained:

> I've been trying to tell my husband for years that I was unhappy in our marriage, but he didn't listen. Now, I've met someone else, and for the first time my husband is listening and is willing to go to a marriage counselor. (Counseling notes)

In this case, the affair had a positive value.

A few marriages are not affected much by an affair. One of the spouses is having an affair, but the other does not care. These are often marriages in which the emotional bonds between the spouses are already broken, so the extramarital relationship is simply evidence of the fractured marriage. In still other marriages, the spouses may agree that they have the freedom to have affairs. And in some situations, one spouse discovers that the other has been unfaithful but chooses not to confront the situation because he or she does not want to divorce—perhaps because of the children.

Affairs that are most threatening to the marriage are ongoing ones that include emotional involvement, as well as sexual relations (M. C. Green and Sabini 2006). Women are more likely than men to be emotionally invested in an affair and to be more distressed by emotional infidelity (Penn, Hernandez, and Bermudez 1997; Schutzwohl 2006, 2008). People who believe that they have fallen deeply in love do not want to give up the affair, which seems both meaningful and exciting. One person involved in an affair remarked, "I haven't felt like this for years. I can't give up something that makes me feel alive again." Of course, what people do not realize in the beginning is that the intense emotional excitement will pass. One man related, "When my first wife and I met, we could hardly wait to get married; the sexual attraction was so intense! After a few years and a baby, things cooled off considerably. About then a new neighbor moved in; she was friendly; soon we were very attracted to each other. A divorce happened and we married. That was three years ago. She ran out on me about four months ago." If the relationship is to endure, the couple must have many other things going on in the relationship.

From many points of view, extramarital relationships typically are a crisis in the marriage that requires considerable effort to resolve.

The Crisis of Economic Distress

Many families must face the crisis of economic distress because of employment instability or uncertainty; underemployment; reduced income caused by demotion, cutbacks, or retirement, or poor income potential resulting from unmarketable skills, disability and health problems, or inadequate education. Economic distress has profound effects on individual and family functioning. In this section we examine some of these effects.

Types of Economic Distress

The effects of an economic crisis depend on the type of crisis and its duration. For example, a permanent closure of one's office or plant is more stressful than a temporary cut in hours.

EMPLOYMENT INSTABILITY Even during prosperous times, the unemployment rate in the United States hovers at around 5% of the labor force. During periods of recession, the percentage increases considerably. In 2005, the overall unemployment rate was about 5%; in early November 2009, it reached 10.2% during an economic recession and dropped gradually to just under 5% in April 2016. The rates are always highest among minority groups and among individuals younger than 20 years of age. During recessions, unemployment rates are usually higher in the construction and agricultural industries. People with the least education and seniority have the highest rates of attrition (Bureau of Labor Statistics, 2016).

The effect of unemployment on individuals and families depends partly on how long it lasts, whether it involves permanent job displacement or a temporary layoff, whether other comparable or replacement jobs are readily available, and whether there is more than one wage earner in the family. Young couples and single mothers with a number of children, especially young children (requiring child care), are most affected by unemployment. Many have minimal skills and experience or resources, so they must turn to others for help.

EMPLOYMENT UNCERTAINTY Families may suffer the stress of unemployment before, during, and after an actual layoff. For example, when a large national corporation announces that it is closing an assembly plant, families may wait for months to learn whether the plant to be closed is in Michigan or Texas. Individuals and families wait while the armed services decide which base to close. Workers in a particular plant are told to expect layoffs but do not know which workers will be let go. Once the job has ended, families must live with the anxiety produced by not knowing where or when they will find employment and what other sacrifices a new job will require of the family.

UNDEREMPLOYMENT Underemployment is also a source of economic distress. It may involve working at a job below one's skills or working fewer hours or at lower pay than one would like. For example, to avoid laying off employees, some companies will reduce hourly employee hours from 40 to 30 hours per week. During recessions, many white-collar workers—even those at middle-management levels—and highly skilled blue-collar workers are laid off and forced to accept whatever type of employment they can find.

Economic distress also can be caused by declining income. Some causes of income reduction are a cut in hours or rate of pay, a demotion, reduced or restructured commission, forced early retirement, or voluntary pay cuts because of a reduction in company profits. Typically, when companies' profits are reduced, they seek concessions in labor agreements that may result in reduced income or benefits for workers. Employees could find themselves faced with the choice of reduced wages or no job at all. Adverse economic changes require families to adjust to a lower income by changing their lifestyle, reducing their consumption, or increasing their income by changing jobs or by having another family member go to work. In addition, divorce often brings economic decline for the custodial parent. This also can occur when a spouse dies and the widow or widower must survive on less income.

Effects on Individuals and on Family Relationships

Economic distress has a significant impact on the individuals and families involved. Unemployment and employment uncertainty are associated with unemployed individuals having lower psychological and physical well-being (McKee-Ryan et al. 2005). The level of economic status affects mortality; the advent of poverty, for example, increases the hazard of dying for both men and women. Men's unemployment also is associated with increased psychological distress for their spouses (Howe, Levy, and Caplan 2004).

The effect of economic distress on families is extensive and wide ranging. For one thing, families need a minimum level of income and employment stability to function. One study of European American and Mexican American families found that economic pressure was linked to depressive symptoms for mothers and fathers of both ethnicities. In turn, depressive symptoms were related to marital problems and hostile parenting (R. D. Parke et al. 2004). Other studies have shown that income loss and economic strain are negatively associated with marital quality and family satisfaction because of financial conflicts, the man's psychological instability, marital tensions and hostility, and lack of warmth and support (James and Gilliland 2013). Mounting economic pressure makes men irritable and short-tempered, increasing their hostility in the marital relationship and causing them to behave more punitively in their parent role.

Economic pressure and distress impacts the emotional status and parenting behavior of parents which in turn affects the children. Family hardship and strong economic pressure diminishes the sense of parental competency: Parents become depressed and demoralized under economic pressure and lose confidence in their parenting ability. Families with fewer economic resources to begin with are likely to experience greater emotional distress, so any economic distress may more seriously diminish their confidence in their ability to effectively meet their children's needs (Zilanawala and Pilkauskas 2010).

Economic hardship appears to have a spillover effect in families—affecting not only people and their children, but also the next generations (Conger et al. 2012). When people (termed "generation 1 or G1" in this study) experienced economic hardship, their children ("G2") had diminished contact with conventional peers, reduced participation in extracurricular activities, and lesser later educational attainment and assistance with college. Also, G2 had higher levels of negative emotionality and lower conscientiousness. As a result, G2's personal and social resources (friends, higher education, skills, etc.) are diminished. This, of course, affects their ability to be parents to G3 (Conger et al. 2012).

Problems within marriage also can spill over to work, resulting in loss of income. Marital distress is often associated with work loss. Work loss associated with marital problems translates into a loss of several billion dollars per year. Preventing marital problems may thus result in important economic benefits for society.

Coping with Economic Distress

Individuals and families use various strategies in coping with economic distress. Avoidance coping involves keeping one's feelings to oneself; refusing to believe the economic crisis is real; and eating, using alcohol or drugs, and smoking to relieve tensions. Avoiding the problem may allow more positive interaction with one's spouse and fewer arguments about finances and partially lessen the impact of financial distress; however, it does not solve the problem. Instead, families are better served by developing skills in conflict management and problem solving.

A more positive approach is to cut back on expenditures wherever possible and postpone major purchases, such as a new car or furniture. Selling property or possessions is sometimes necessary. Some families take in boarders or supply child care for others. Many families borrow from savings or life insurance policies. Finding part-time or temporary employment may be possible. Teenagers or other family members may have to go to work. Other families start small businesses at home. Skills such as sewing or carpentry can be tapped to earn additional income. Generally, married men spend significantly less time unemployed than do single men, probably because of the greater pressure to support their families.

Before their resources are exhausted, families may turn to relatives, friends, coworkers, neighbors, their faith community, self-help groups, human service professionals, or helping agencies. Major types of support may include money, goods, services, emotional support, babysitting, transportation, job-hunting aid, and advice and feedback. There are also many types of social and government programs designed to help people who are in financial distress. However, many families find these sources of help frustrating and humiliating to access and use, so they avoid them as much as possible.

Instead, family members frequently seek the social support of relatives and friends as they try to cope with economic distress. External support can reduce the stress of individuals, but it also may generate costs for the persons involved. In theory, for example, the woman's support from external sources reduces her stress, but it also can reinforce the man's sense of failure as a breadwinner and evoke more negativity on his part in family relationships. In general, research shows that families who are resilient in the face of declining income and poverty have adequate support systems, possess an inner locus of control, and believe in a higher power (C. Juby and Rycraft 2004).

The Crisis of Addictions

Addictions have a severe, negative impact on families. America has experienced a dramatic increase in drug addiction in the past 50 years. More than 23 million people in America abuse alcohol and drugs enough to need treatment critically (NCADD 2016). About 50% of all highway accidents are alcohol related and it is estimated that 25%–40% of hospitalizations in the United States are directly or indirectly related to alcohol. Alcohol and drug abuse contribute to much of family violence (James and Gilliland 2013). There are numerous other types of addiction including drugs and alcohol, gambling, pornography, work, shopping, computer/Internet, and television.

Characteristics of Addiction

Regardless of the type of addiction, certain characteristics are the same:

- Loss of control;
- Compulsive behavior;
- Persistent behavior (drinking, gambling, etc.) despite severe consequences;
- An inordinate amount of time and money spent pursuing the addiction;
- Work and family commitments sacrificed to pursue the addiction;
- Lying and dishonesty used to conceal addictive behavior;
- Addictive behavior takes priority over everything else; and
- An increased amount of substance or experience required to achieve the desired effect (Bradford Health Services 2016; Insel and Roth 2013).

Reasons for Addiction

Why do people engage in addictive behaviors? Some initially use drugs, for example, because it is exciting—illegal and rebellious. Adolescents may be influenced by peer pressure to be part of the group, to fit in. Imitation or modeling of behavior of celebrities or significant others in their lives is another possible reason. Many engage in addictive behaviors because they wish to alter their mood or escape depression or low self-esteem (Insel and Roth 2013). They engage in the addiction, regardless of the type, as a way to cope. Unfortunately, the addictive behavior only makes it more difficult to cope successfully. Instead, the addiction creates problems.

Effects on the Family

Whether it is a spouse, child, or parent who is an addict, addiction is a family crisis because the stress it creates is so great and so chronic that family members feel unable to deal with it. The family feels overwhelmed because the nature of addiction is complicated. The addict often has unresolved emotional issues: many have experienced the trauma of having been abused, raped, or bullied; having seen their parents divorce; or losing loved ones to death. Others have a genetic vulnerability to an addiction such as alcohol. The addict's emotional distress often includes guilt over things he or she has done that have hurt others.

Another reason addiction is overwhelming is because of the many negative emotions that are produced. Fear is one of these; family members do have legitimate cause to be concerned for the safety and well-being of the addict. With drug addiction, family members are concerned about drug overdose, violence, and legal problems. For example, there are more arrests for drug abuse and alcohol violations (more than 3 million a year) than any other specific offense (Federal Bureau of Investigation 2015). There are approximately 2.5 million drug abuse– and alcohol abuse–related visits to hospital emergency rooms per year. About 51% of those visits involve illicit drugs and 25% involve alcohol (Substance Abuse and Mental Health Services Administration 2014).

Family members also feel anger and resentment toward the addict for continuing behavior that causes so many problems for himself or herself and the family. Characteristically, much money is spent (wasted) on the addiction—sometimes huge amounts. The addict may steal money, checkbooks, or credit cards as well as property. Addicts typically have trouble getting and keeping jobs. If the addict has been a major breadwinner, the family may lose a home or car. Anger, anxiety, and mistrust are aroused because of the financial strain and uncertainty.

Because the person in addiction typically spends an inordinate amount of time pursuing the addiction, time with family is sacrificed. Children may feel abandoned, ignored, or unloved; family members may feel angry, lonely, and "second-best" to the addiction.

The addict frequently lies and engages in other dishonest behavior to conceal the addiction. He or she may become increasingly manipulative of others. Naturally, deceit and manipulation make others feel distrustful, confused, and hurt. One mother remarked, "She [her daughter] lies all the time—even about stupid things. I want to believe her, but just as soon as I do, I discover it was foolish on my part."

Those in addiction frequently do not keep their commitments to other family members because the addiction takes priority over everything else. They do not show up for family get-togethers; they miss children's ballgames and recitals, for example. This leaves family members disappointed because the addict cannot be depended on—and angry or hurt when plans are spoiled repeatedly.

Family members also experience frustration and feelings of futility because their attempts to control the behaviors of the addict (pouring out "stashes" of alcohol, flushing drugs, nagging about sobriety, for example) inevitably fail. These attempts to control are termed *codependency*, which means that, in reality, the addict is the one in control. For example, to "help" the addict not lose a job, a spouse calls the boss and lies: "She can't come in today. She's just so sick." Parents provide a place to live, a car, and cash to an adult child to help him or her stay off the street. The addicted person may skillfully manipulate others into such behaviors by making them feel that this demonstrates their love and regard. However, most codependent behaviors only enable the addict to continue in the addiction. Other codependent actions such as staying up all night worrying whether the addict is OK and neglecting one's own health while "taking care" of everyone else are not effective in changing the addict's behavior either.

Addiction results in enormous amounts of stress in a family because it creates a situation filled with dishonesty, dysfunctional communication, conflict, anxiety, distrust, anger, fear, guilt, alienation, and financial distress. Furthermore, these experiences are chronic—they are not over in a month or a year.

Overcoming Addiction: The Addicted Person

Many individuals and their families have and do successfully overcome the pain and frustration of addiction. First, the addict must come to want to change. This desire to change usually is the result of a crisis—a low point ("hitting bottom")—that may be a serious automobile accident, illness, legal troubles, or great financial loss. Then the addicted person gets needed help through professional assistance, a rehabilitation program, support groups, and the positive influence of good friends and family. The 12-step program has been the most effective and prevalent treatment/support program for addictions. Programs are available for both the addicted person (Alcoholics Anonymous, Narcotics Anonymous, Gamblers Anonymous, for example) and family members (Alanon, Narconon, Adult Children of Alcoholics, for example). The 12 steps are summarized and paraphrased as follows:

STEP 1—Admit there is a problem and that it is unmanageable; realize one's powerlessness.

STEPS 2 AND 3—Turn to a power greater than oneself for help. Talk to professionals; turn to a Higher Power for guidance. Realize one cannot fix it alone.

STEPS 4 AND 5—Realize that past behavior has led to present problems; continuing those same behaviors will affect present life negatively.

STEPS 6–9—Become willing to change; ask for forgiveness and be willing to make amends for wrong done to others, if possible.

STEPS 10–12—Commit to a new way of living, characterized by peace and serenity; seek spiritual guidance. Realize life is a spiritual journey—a process rather than a destination. Correct wrongs on a daily basis. (Bradford Health Centers 2016)

Overcoming Addiction: The Family and the Addicted Person Working Together

The nonaddicted family members play an important role in the recovery process. Couples and families who have overcome the problem of addiction report several principles that are most important.

LEARN ABOUT THE NATURE OF ADDICTION AND GET SUPPORT Get involved in a support group for families, such as Alanon or Narconon. This action by the family communicates a message of support and commitment to the addicted person.

ACT WITH MATURITY It is beneficial for family members to possess a high degree of emotional maturity, patience, kindness, and rationality. This is critical because an addiction tends to magnify immature and self-centered behaviors in the addicted individual. If other family members are also behaving immaturely, communication is shut down and conflict escalates; feelings are hurt and stress builds (Stinnett, Hilliard, and Stinnett 2000).

SET BOUNDARIES Boundaries communicate what is not acceptable and will not be tolerated to the addicted person. This is not to suggest that family members become tyrants or extremely rigid, but simply that clear limits must be established. Examples of boundaries are as follows:

1. I will not allow you to physically or verbally abuse me.
2. I will not allow chemical abuse in my house.
3. I will not finance your addiction.
4. I will not lie to protect you from your addiction.
5. I will not rescue you from the consequences of your addiction (pay bail, legal fees, fines; pay bill collectors; etc.).

The setting of boundaries provides a healthy balance to the support, patience, and kindness being shown to the addicted person.

BE GOOD PROBLEM SOLVERS A common theme among families who have successfully overcome addiction is that they are (or have become) good problem solvers. Rather than blaming one another or becoming hypnotized by the pain they are experiencing, they keep their focus on dealing with addiction as a problem to be solved. A critical part of problem solving is doing the homework to determine what options are available. A persistent search for the best treatment and course of action (residential, outpatient, counseling, parenting class, vocational retraining, etc.) and an ongoing effort to reduce stress (good nutrition, effective communication, recreation, meditation, exercise, etc.) are aspects of effective problem solving (Stinnett, Hilliard, and Stinnett 2000).

USE POSITIVE COPING STRATEGIES Staying positive is extremely important because of the chronic and often high levels of frustration and stress associated with addiction and also because the coping strategies typically used by addicts are negative and counterproductive. Following are some examples of positive coping strategies:

1. Set realistic goals that can be achieved.
2. Focus on what can be controlled or improved (one's own exercise and nutrition) rather than what cannot be controlled (e.g., someone else's behavior or attitude).
3. Maintain a balanced perspective instead of being overwhelmed with the negative. For example, attending meetings, making new friends (nonaddicted), or spending less time on the Internet or the addicted person securing a part-time job are positives.
4. Be proactive in terms of taking positive actions rather than being reactive to the dysfunctional, irrational, blaming behaviors often expressed by the addicted person. For example, securing checkbooks, credit cards, and car keys rather than being outraged by those things being stolen (Bradford Health Services 2016; Stinnett, Hilliard, and Stinnett 2000).
5. Forgive. People in families affected by addiction experience hurts, manipulation, and deceit. As a result, they consistently have significant amounts of anger. It is appropriate to consider forgiveness as an antidote to anger. Forgiveness does not mean you approve or necessarily "forget" what someone else has done. When you forgive, you make the decision not to dwell on the negative feelings associated with the mistreatment. You also make the decision to accept that the other person is not perfect. Your act of forgiving is liberating—releasing you from carrying a burden of resentment and anger. Instead of being caught up in destructive emotions, you can move forward with life in positive, productive ways (Lawford 2014; Siassi 2015). Forgiveness helps you avoid being controlled by the hurtful actions of others.

ENCOURAGE THE CULTIVATION OF NATURAL, HEALTHY JOY EXPERIENCES Addicts are driven by a desire to experience a "high," a feeling of excitement. Unfortunately, the drug abuse, gambling, and other addictive behaviors are destructive and have severe consequences (T. Rosen 2014). Family members can help their loved one in recovery by encouraging them to search for natural, healthy joy experiences to replace destructive, addictive substances and behaviors (Lawford 2014).

Research has shown that exercise such as working out in the gym, running, swimming, yoga, tennis, or golf stimulates oxygen flow and boosts serotonin levels in the brain, triggering the release of endorphins, which promote feelings of well-being and positive mood. Many people in recovery feel that exercise reduces stress, enhances their mood, and helps to prevent relapse (Lawford 2014; T. Rosen 2014).

As Brenda Schell, program director at the Missouri Recovery Network, observes, anything natural that promotes the release of brain endorphins is a natural "high." These may include watching a sunset, photography, music, genuine humor and laughter, or gardening. Helping other people or becoming involved in community service can also elevate a person's mood.

Family members can play an important role in helping the recovering loved one find his or her specific natural joy experiences. The family can be a positive influence on the member in recovery, as well as on the broader society, in learning how to experience healthy joy experiences without drugs, alcohol, or other addictive behaviors.

MAINTAIN A SPIRITUAL PRACTICE For most people, the path to sobriety and recovery from addiction becomes a spiritual journey (Lawford 2014). Addictions often develop, in part, as an unproductive attempt to fill a spiritual void. This was observed many years ago by one of the world's greatest pioneers in psychotherapy, Dr. Carl Jung. Dr. Jung stated, "Alcohol dependence is the equivalent, on a low level, of the spiritual thirst of our being for wholeness."

Many in the recovery community indicate that those in addiction unsuccessfully attempt to satisfy this "spiritual thirst" by "the quick-fix" short cut of pills, alcohol, marijuana, of other substances and addictive behaviors. They come to discover that true and lasting recovery is experienced by beginning and maintaining a personal, spiritual practice (Lawford 2014).

Our spiritual dimension is multifaceted. Those in recovery have discovered that believing in a power greater than themselves brings hope and is an important step in recovering successfully from addiction (Lawford 2014). Other spiritual principles that are important aids to recovery include helping others, community service, engagement with a faith community, prayer and meditation, compassion, grace, forgiveness, doing a moral inventory of oneself, thankfulness, integrity, and commitment.

Family members can provide major support by practicing these spiritual principles themselves. The family may help connect the loved one in recovery to a church or synagogue, for example. They may encourage their loved one to participate in a 12-step program. Introducing the person in recovery to an opportunity to help others on an individual basis or through a community service or faith-based program can be a helpful contribution by the family.

The Crisis of Violence and Abuse

Violence in the family crosses color, class, and ethnic lines; occurs across all age groups; and affects people in heterosexual and homosexual relationships. It is estimated that about 4.8 million women and more than 800,000 men are victims of partner violence and one in three murders are partner murders (Centers for Disease Control and Prevention 2015; James and Gilliland 2013). The great majority of partner violence is male to female. Fortunately, research indicates a decline in husband-to-wife violence. However, other recent research reports an increase in wife-to-husband violence, an increase in female-to-male violence among the dating/nonmarried population, and even comparable levels of female- versus male-initiated violence (Bowen 2009; D. A. Hines and Douglas 2011; Randle and Graham 2011).

Family violence generally refers to any rough or extended use of physical force or aggression or of verbal abuse by one family member toward another. Violence may or may not result in the physical injury of another person. Thus, a man who throws and breaks dishes, destroys furniture, or punches out walls when he is angry may not injure his spouse or children, but he is certainly being violent. Family violence is not easily defined, however, because there are disagreements surrounding what use of force, if any, is appropriate, and because there is often a discrepancy between spouses' perceptions of family violence.

Spouse abuse and *child abuse* are more limited and specific terms than *family violence*; they refer to acts of violence that have a high probability of injuring the victim. An operational definition of **child abuse**, however, includes not only physical assault that results in injury but also malnourishment, abandonment, neglect (defined as the failure to provide adequate physical and emotional care), emotional abuse, and sexual abuse. Sexual abuse by a relative is incest. **Spouse abuse** may include not only battering, but also sexual abuse and marital rape.

Attitudes toward violence have a significant effect on whether people act violently toward a spouse or children. To understand domestic violence, one must examine issues of power and control in a relationship (Harway 2003). Harway explains feminist perspectives about domestic violence by describing battering as an act of control by one intimate partner over another. It may involve physical violence, that is, using one's physical strength or presence to control another, or it may involve verbal and emotional abuse, that is, using one's words or voice to control another. Battering includes a variety of behaviors ranging from the moderate to the extreme. "To recognize that batterers use a spectrum of violent behaviors is to recognize battering not as a response to anger but as a strategy to maintain power in the relationship" (Harway 2003, 320).

Another example of the influence of attitudes toward violence is seen in that in Sweden, a parent can be imprisoned for a month for striking a child. In contrast, many Americans believe that spanking children is normal and necessary and sometimes even good. In fact, a high percentage of families use corporal punishment to discipline their children. And although most parents define "spanking" as a swat or two on the bottom with an open hand, others have a definition closer to beating.

Some men and women believe that it is acceptable for spouses to hit each other under certain circumstances. Many abusers deny they are "real" abusers because "I just pushed her around a little" or "Yes, I hit him, but he's a big man, and I didn't hurt him all that much," although many have, in fact, badly injured the other person (D. A. Hines and Douglas 2010a, b; Wood 2004). Even civil authorities hesitate to interfere in family quarrels because of the different beliefs about legitimate force and illegitimate violence in the family.

Some writers argue that there are three distinct forms of couple violence taking place within families. Some families suffer from occasional outbursts of violence from either or both spouses, typically as part of an argument that has escalated to the point that spouses are angry and out of control (for example, at Level IV of the LMCM). This *situational couple violence* (*SCV*) is usually mild to moderate, happens a few times a year, and rarely leads to life-threatening actions.

In another form of relationship violence, one partner controls and oppresses the other through violence, threats, isolation, and economic subordination. This *intimate terrorism* (*IT*) is typically one sided, gets worse over time, and is apt to involve serious injuries (D. A. Hines and Douglas 2010a, b; M. P. Johnson and Leone 2005).

The third type of couple violence, *violent resistance*, occurs when a partner fights back against IT. This is the least frequent type of intimate violence and usually involves only self-protection, not an attempt to control the spouse.

It must not be assumed that SCV is unimportant or that psychological abuse is not hurtful. Suggesting that only physical IT counts as a problem comes disturbingly close to minimizing both situational intimate partner violence and verbal and psychological abuse. Even occasional and moderate violence is associated with a host of negative consequences, such as health conditions (asthma, gastrointestinal disorders, and migraines, for example), psychological difficulties (anxiety, depression, and post–traumatic stress disorder, for example), and poor family functioning (emotional detachment or inability to trust,

family violence Any rough or extended use of physical force or aggression or verbal abuse by one family member toward another.

child abuse May include not only physical assaults on a child but also malnourishment, abandonment, neglect, emotional abuse, and sexual abuse.

spouse abuse Physical or emotional mistreatment of one's spouse.

Violence may or may not result in physical injury of another person. Family violence refers to any rough or extended use of physical force or aggression or of verbal abuse by one family member toward another.

for example) (Black 2011; Black et al. 2011; Crofford 2007; Leserman and Drossman 2007).

Intimate partner violence is not uncommon and is costly in the United States. About one-third of women and 25% of men in the United States have experienced rape, physical violence, and/or stalking by an intimate partner—with 15% of women and 4% of men having been injured as a result (Black et al. 2011; Centers for Disease Control and Prevention 2016). Estimates of the economic cost of intimate partner violence perpetrated against women in the United States, including expenditures for medical care, mental health services, and lost productivity from injury and premature death, total more than $8.3 billion (Centers for Disease Control and Prevention 2012b).

Factors Related to Violence

Family violence is a multifaceted phenomenon that can best be understood from a multidisciplinary perspective. Indeed, no single theory or discipline has adequately explained it. The factors related to SCV may differ from those related to IT.

Eli Finkel (2008) has proposed a model of the influences on SCV—categorizing them as *instigating triggers*, *impelling influences*, and *inhibiting influences*. Instigating triggers are conditions that cause the partners to be stressed or frustrated in general (a disagreement, hunger, stress from work, etc.). Impelling

influences make it more likely that couples will move toward SCV; inhibiting influences encourage couples to restrain themselves. Impelling and inhibiting influences can be subdivided into *distal*, *dispositional*, *relational*, and *situational* factors.

Distal factors come from a person's background, such as family experiences and cultural beliefs. Dispositional influences refer to the person's personality, temperament, or personal belief system. Relational influences arise from the condition of the couple's relationship and situational influences come from the immediate situation (Table 15.2 gives examples). For example, he and she come in from work, hungry and tired, look at the mail, and discover that they have just bounced *more* checks. These are strong instigating triggers toward SCV. The risk of SCV may be high or low depending on impelling or inhibiting influences. If either has grown up in a violent family or neighborhood (Hughes et al. 2007) and/or is impulsive; if they have faulty communication or conflict-resolution skills (Simpson et al. 2007) and either is prone to push, hit (Holt 2006), or verbally provoke a partner, they are impelled toward a violent episode. In contrast, if they have cultural values of gender equality (Archer 2006) and personal values of restraint and respect coupled with good problem-solving skills; a committed, basically happy marriage (Hellmuth and McNulty 2008); and sobriety (M. P. Johnson 2006), they are inhibited from SCV. The factors related to SCV are both somewhat stable (low self-esteem, moodiness, family and cultural background and beliefs, and neuroticism, for example) and more temporary. Temporary or situational factors include employment or financial troubles, unplanned pregnancy, and alcohol or drug abuse (A. L. Coker et al. 2000; Jasinski 2004), as well as relational difficulties (jealousy, for example).

IT seems to have a different set of influencing factors and a different motivation than SCV. At the heart of IT is a need to exercise power and control—a way to get what one wants (M. Smith and Segal 2012). Background and cultural factors such as having had a violent family of origin, holding traditional gender role ideas, and being antisocial incline men (more intimate terrorists are male) to view women as people who should be dominated and controlled by force, for example (Porcerelli, Cogan, and Hibbard 2004; K. Robertson and Murachver 2007).

Furthermore, lower-income individuals who are more dependent economically on their spouses may

TABLE 15.2   The Model of Situational Couple Violence Influences on Perpetration

INSTIGATING TRIGGERS	IMPELLING INFLUENCES	INHIBITING INFLUENCES	
Conflict	DL: violent family of origin	DL: gender equality	
Hunger		DP: easy going	
Too hot/too cold	DP: impulsive	RL: commitment; generally happy	
Stress at work	RL: poor communication		
	ST: pushing, yelling by partner	ST: sobriety	
Are these strong?	Are these strong?	Are these weak?	
Yes	Yes	Yes	High risk of SCV
→	→	→	
No	No	No	Low risk of SCV
→	→	→	

DL = Distal; DP = Dispositional; RL = Relational; ST = Situational

Note: From "Intimate partner violence perpetration: Insights from the science of self-regulation," by E. J. Finkel, 2008, in Social Relationships: Cognitive, Affective, and Motivational Processes (pp. 271–288), by J. P. Forgas and J. Fitness (Eds.), New York: Psychology Press.

feel locked into an abusive relationship. Middle- and upper-class families have many more resources to mediate stress, such as greater financial resources; better access to contraception and medical and psychological personnel; and more opportunities to utilize babysitters, nursery schools, and camps to provide relief from family responsibilities.

Intimate terrorists may seem to be ordinary citizens in other aspects of their lives, but a positive social facade frequently conceals disturbing personality characteristics. Spouse abusers have been described as having Jekyll-and-Hyde personalities. They typically have poor self-images. Excessive jealousy and alcohol or drug abuse are also common among abusers. Because they are insecure individuals who do not feel powerful, abusers typically seek a partner who is passive and compliant, whom they can bully, and whom they can blame for all of their problems.

Intimate terrorists are controlling. They want to know everything a spouse does, so they engage in surveillance or constant phone (text) contact (M. Smith and Segal 2012; S. L. Williams and Frieze 2005). Control also includes isolating the victim from family, friends, and outside activities such as school or work. Economic abuse involves restricting the victim's access to money, stealing her/his money, and interfering with the victim's work. Emotional abuse adds in humiliation such as name-calling, insults, and public put-downs or crazy-making mind games.

Negative attitudes about women held by men who feel inadequate, inferior, or threatened (by a wife's intellect or earning, for example) (Kaukinen 2004) seem to move them toward using violence (intimidation and threats) to gain power—perhaps because they have few other sources of power. This is also supported by the association between poverty and violence (Cunradi, Caetano, and Schafer 2002; Leone et al. 2004). It may also be that violence is underreported in more affluent families.

Controlled studies indicate that men who physically abuse their spouses are characterized by generalized aggressive tendencies, impulsive and defiant personality styles, an external locus of control, type A behavior, rigid authoritarian attitudes, a traditional role identity, and low self-esteem and self-concept (G. Cowan and Mills 2004; T. M. Moore et al. 2008). They perceive their spouse as less physically attractive than do men in distressed but non-abusive marriages. Abusers report lower levels of marital satisfaction and significant problems in communication. Anger, verbal attacks, and withdrawal appear to dominate the problem-solving interactions in abusive marriages. Abusive relationships also have been found to be associated with sexual dysfunction. Abusive men evidence significantly lower relationship closeness and less sexual assertiveness and sexual satisfaction in their marriages than do nonabusive men. They demonstrate more negative attitudes toward sex and greater sexual occupation; victims may be forced into degrading or undesired sexual behaviors (M. Smith and Segal 2012).

Abusers are not only males. A number of studies indicate that women are also capable of emotional, verbal, and physical aggression (D. A. Hines and Douglas 2010a, b; Swinford et al. 2000). However, to get a more complete picture of the complex nature of intimate partner violence, it is necessary to distinguish between the kind and frequency of aggressive acts and the severity. For example, women are more likely to engage in indirect aggression such as gossip or rumors to hurt someone (N. H. Hess and Hagin 2006). In addition, women tend to throw things, slap, kick, or punch, whereas men are more apt to choke, strangle, rape, and murder (Archer 2002). The greater average strength and size of men enable them to do more injury.

Figure 15.2 shows the primary tactics and behaviors abusers manifest to get and maintain control in relationships. Battering is an intentional act used to gain power and control over another person. Physical abuse is only one part of a whole system of abusive behavior that an abuser uses against his/her partner. Violence includes not only the acts of physical aggression but also patterns of oppression occurring over time, including events leading up to and following the use of force itself.

In trying to understand domestic violence—especially IT—people often wonder, What about those who are abused? What are they like? Why do they allow themselves to be mistreated? These questions denigrate the victim and many are based on inaccurate assumptions. People from any background can find themselves in abusive relationships. The abuse can be insidious (emotional, indirect) and intermittent, leaving the victim with mixed messages and an unclear picture of the situation. Some abused women have experienced childhood abuse, which has been shown to elevate the probability that they will become the victims of domestic assault. Women subjected to abusive parenting tend to develop hostile, rebellious orientations and are likely to affiliate with and marry men with similar characteristics who engage in a variety of deviant behaviors, including violence toward a spouse (Zayas and Shoda 2007).

Sometimes, too, her partner is nice and says he loves her and needs her. Or the IT may try to make the victim feel that she/he has done something wrong. The victim can be convinced of the need to become a better person or to search for a correct way to behave. The victim acts compliant and gives up her/his freedom if asked (demanded)—including job, activities, interests, and friends. Every part of the victim's life is controlled. The most widely held theory of the pattern or cycle of violence outlines at least three phases—the tension-building phase, the acute battering phase, and the loving contrition phase—that ensnare victims in a web of punishment and deceit (Wolf-Smith and LaRossa 1992).

Many victims do not leave because they hope things will change or they are committed to the marriage; they may lack the financial resources to leave. Others are fearful of what their intimate terrorist might do (kill them or commit suicide, for example) if they try to leave (McHugh, Livingston, and Frieze 2008). A man who is abused may fear that he will lose custody of his children or that a spouse will mistreat/kill them in his absence (D. A. Hines and Douglas 2010a, b).

Women who remain in abusive relationships report that there is little or no change in the frequency or severity of abuse or the amount of love and affection expressed, and they often report that their relationship is not as bad as it could be (P. J. Marshall, Weston, and Honeycutt 2000).

For example, many women underestimate the severity of the violent situation in their home. A national study showed that only one-half of women who were killed or almost killed by a husband, boyfriend, ex-husband, or ex-boyfriend accurately perceived their risk of being killed by their abusive partner (J. C. Campbell 2004). Men who are victims face the challenges of being believed by professionals in counseling and in law enforcement; a man who calls the police may find himself under arrest—because of the assumption that she cannot be an abuser. Even among professionals, many believe that IT by women is humorous or annoying, not truly serious or damaging to a spouse (D. A. Hines and Douglas 2010a, b).

Child Maltreatment

Public concern about child maltreatment has increased in part because it is particularly common in large, industrialized nations. Approximately 2.2 million children in the United States are victimized every year. The actual numbers are likely higher because

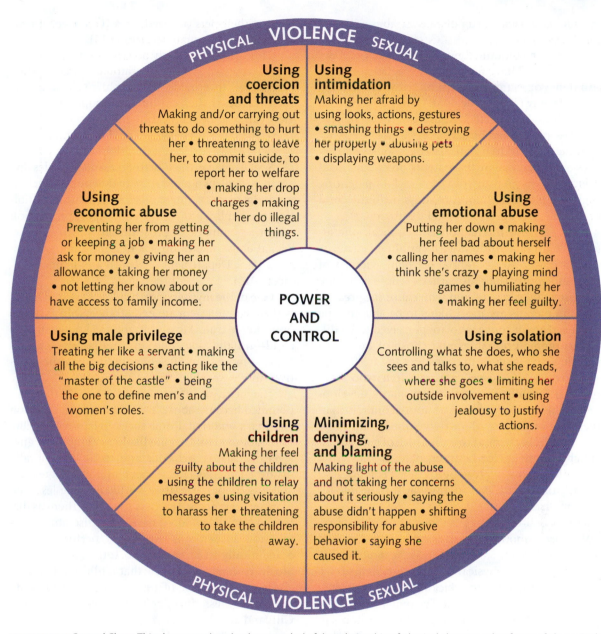

FIGURE 15.2 Control Chart. This chart uses the wheel as a symbol of the relationship of physical abuse to other forms of abuse. Each spoke represents a tactic used to control or gain power, which is the hub of the wheel. The rim that surrounds and supports the spokes is physical abuse. It holds the system together and gives it strength.

Note: From Domestic Abuse Intervention Project (202 E. Superior Street, Duluth, Minnesota 55802. 218-722-2781.) All rights reserved.

most cases are unreported (Berk 2013; U.S. Department of Health and Human Services 2016).

Early studies attempted to show that abusive parents suffered from mental or emotional illness, that the reason people abused their children was that they suffered from psychoses, neuroses, or psychopathic problems of one kind or another. More

recent research has shown that child abusers are not necessarily emotionally ill. However, they usually exhibit more psychological problems than other parents do, such as having negative concepts of self, which they project onto the child. A number of abusers were themselves abused as children (Cicchetti and Toth 2006). Other personal liabilities include depression, drug or alcohol abuse, illness, and social isolation.

Many are ignorant about the basics of child development and have unrealistic expectations about children. For example, a typical 2-year-old striving for autonomy ("No!" "Me do it!") may be viewed as defiant and disrespectful. Abusers may also believe that discipline must be severe to be effective. Maltreatment of children may also be a spillover from stress and conflict in the parents' lives. Financial difficulties, marital discord, or a lack of parenting skills result in a high level of stress, with the child becoming the target of parental frustration.

Parent–child interaction is reciprocal; one affects the other. Children with certain characteristics have a greater potential for being victims of parental abuse than do others. Those who are hardest to take care of and who cause the greatest stress in parents are most likely to be abused. The same is true for those who are perceived to be different: premature babies and those of low birth weight, who are likely to be restless and fretful and who require intensive care; children who have physical disabilities; or children whose development is delayed. Parents with more children than their resources can adequately support are more likely to abuse them. If there is a lack of emotional-attachment behavior between parents and child, the child is more likely to be abused. (This does *not* mean children are ever in any way responsible for their maltreatment.)

Child maltreatment takes four main types: physical abuse, emotional abuse, neglect, and sexual abuse (Berk 2013; Santrock 2015). *Physical abuse* is the infliction of physical pain and/or injury as a result of hitting, beating, kicking, biting, burning, or using a weapon on a child. The injury may not be intentional, but rather punishment gone too far. Physical abuse is easiest to detect because it leaves bruises and broken bones. Physical abuse represents 17% of reported cases of child maltreatment (U.S. Department of Health and Human Services 2016).

Emotional abuse (psychological/verbal) includes those acts that damage a child's emotional development or well-being (Santrock 2015). It constitutes 9% of reported cases of child maltreatment and consists of belittling, humiliating, threatening, isolating, or corrupting (involving in illegal activities) a child. Emotional abuse also involves repeated unreasonable demands, terrorizing a child, withdrawal of love and destroying a child's possessions, or

hurting their pets or loved ones (U.S. Department of Health and Human Services 2016).

Child neglect, which accounts for 75% of reported cases of child maltreatment, occurs when parents fail to provide for the child's basic needs, such as food, shelter, clothing, and supervision. Neglect can also be medical or educational in nature (Berk 2013; U.S. Department of Health and Human Services 2016).

Sexual abuse is the fourth type and includes any act that involves a child in sexual activity—such as fondling, oral sex, intercourse, sodomy, and exhibitionism. Exploitation of the child in the production of pornography or in prostitution is also abusive. Sexual abuse makes up 9% of child maltreatment cases (U.S. Department of Health and Human Services 2016).

One of the myths concerning child sexual abuse is that the molesters are evil strangers. In fact, the opposite is true. Most abusers are known to the child—usually someone in the family. Parents commit more than 80% of abuse while other relatives are responsible for 5% (Berk 2013).

The negative effects of child abuse are compounded because abuse has a detrimental effect on children's emotional and social relationships. Because abused children are likely to exhibit a higher level of negative behavior and to be behaviorally disturbed, less socially competent, more aggressive, and less cooperative, they are likely to be less well liked by their peers. Teachers may view them as disturbed. Abused children have more discipline referrals and suspensions and often perform poorly academically (Cicchetti and Toth 2005, 2006). Much research indicates that childhood sexual abuse is a predictor of the development of post–traumatic stress disorder in later life (James and Gilliland 2013).

Adults who were abused as children may show increased use of alcohol and drugs, anxiety, and depression (Sachs-Ericsson et al. 2005; Shea et al. 2005). They also often have problems with establishing and maintaining healthy intimate relationships (Colman and Widom 2004).

One study examined whether abusive experiences in childhood would influence coping strategies used by undergraduate women to deal with new stressful events in young adulthood. The results showed an increased reliance on disengagement methods of coping (wishful thinking, problem avoidance, social withdrawal, and self-criticism) in women with more extensive child abuse histories. This study concluded that undergraduate women with abusive childhood histories are particularly at risk for relying on maladaptive disengagement coping strategies to deal with various new stressors later in life (Leitenberg, Gibson, and Novy 2004).

Other research indicates that it is not only the child who is abused who is affected, but also his or her siblings. Moreover, abused children who have adjustment problems in adolescence are more likely to perpetuate violence in their adult intimate relationships (Sachs-Ericcson et al. 2005; Santrock 2015; Shea et al. 2005).

Treatment for Spouse and Child Abuse

Those who have been abused may exhibit psychological symptoms such as **post–traumatic stress disorder** (severe stress reactions that occur after a person has suffered a trauma) and high levels of depression, avoidance, and anxiety, and they may show borderline psychotic and passive-aggressive behavior patterns. Many of the aftereffects of trauma hamper an individual's ability to function in relationships. Common problems include an inability to trust, difficulty in sharing emotions, sexual dysfunction, and poor parenting skills.

Crisis shelters, transition houses, hotline services, police intervention teams, the legal system, trained social service workers, family therapy services, and other organizations are involved in dealing with abuse. Considerable progress has been made in treating both the abused and the abusive, and every effort should be made to get professional help for them. Research shows that victims of abuse who receive intervention services quickly are at lower risk for later psychosocial difficulties such as post–traumatic stress disorder and major depression (Ruggiero et al. 2004).

Because of the value of early intervention, professionals who work with children (teachers, nurses, doctors, day-care workers, coaches, etc.) are required by mandatory reporting laws in all 50 states to report known or suspected abuse. Child protective services or the police then investigate the situation and intervene if necessary. In addition, persons in the general public can (and should) report known or suspected abuse. Some people are reluctant to report their suspicions because they might be wrong or they are not absolutely sure; however, reporters do not have to prove the abuse. And reports made in good faith are not subject to legal action even if a mistake is made.

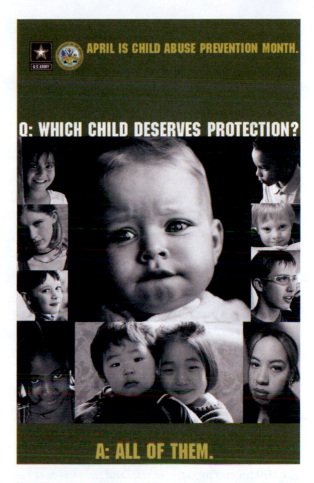

Whether verbal or physical, child abuse is usually a result of the parents' inability to cope with the frustrations of their lives and their lack of knowledge about children and parenting. For their own sake and for the sake of their children, abusive parents must be encouraged to seek out the many kinds of help available to them.

Detecting Child Maltreatment

A number of clues point to the possibility of child abuse or neglect. One sign alone may not mean abuse; however, the possibility of abuse should be considered when several signs are present. These signs include when the child:

- Has unexplained injuries, burns, bruises, or a limp;
- Has injuries, bruises, etc., for which the explanation does not really "fit";

post–traumatic stress disorder Severe stress reactions that occur after a person has suffered a trauma.

- Does not want to go home; seems fearful of parents (others at home);
- Is overly compliant and passive;
- Is nervous, disruptive, or destructive;
- Has genital bruises or injuries or discharge;
- Has an STD or is pregnant;
- Is too thin, always hungry, or steals food; is constantly tired;
- Is dirty; has bad teeth; or
- Has no coat, etc., for cold weather; wears long sleeves in hot weather to conceal bruises.

Child sexual abuse may be a causative factor in many severe disorders, including dissociative, anxiety, eating, and affective disorders and sexual and substance abuse problems. It also may be a contributing factor in many other conditions, such as paranoid, obsessive-compulsive, and passive-aggressive disorders. Many studies have found sexual abuse victims to have high levels of anxiety and depression, suicidal tendencies, and difficulty with intimate relationships (Kanel 2007). Mood disturbances (depression, guilt, and low self-esteem) are frequent. Depression is the most common consequence, and victims tend to be more self-destructive and suicidal than are nonabused depressed individuals. They can suffer from anxiety attacks and phobias and experience sleep and appetite disturbances. They may suffer from all kinds of somatic disorders, especially gastrointestinal problems, chronic pelvic pain, headaches, backaches, skin disorders, and genitourinary problems (SECASA 2015).

Incest is sexual activity between people who are closely related. The relationships that are forbidden by law vary from state to state. Most social scientists consider all forms of sexual contact, sexual exploitation, and sexual overtures initiated by any adult who is related by blood or surrogate family to the child as incest. In other words, the abuse is considered incestuous if the adult shares a primary relationship with the child, whether they are related by blood (father, for example) or not (stepfather, for example).

Much of the research has focused on father–daughter relationships. Such incest usually takes place in unhappy and disorganized family contexts. In most cases, the spouses' sexual relationship is unsatisfactory, so the man turns to his daughter for affection and sex. However, in these cases, the sexual abuse of his daughter is not basically a sexual problem; rather, it represents the sexual expression of nonsexual problems, such as depression, low self-esteem, and feelings of inadequacy.

The incestuous contact is usually premeditated and initiated by the father and passively tolerated by the daughter. The father begins by cuddling, hugging, and kissing his daughter, which both may enjoy. The contact expands to include touching (such as feeling the daughter's buttocks or breasts), playful wrestling, prolonged kissing, or genital caressing. It usually takes place without any force being used and may develop into full intercourse. Father–daughter incest may continue over many years, until the daughter is old enough to understand, resist, or leave home. She rarely goes to the police but may tell a friend, family member, or her mother. Maternal supportiveness is a crucial component of helping children cope effectively (Corcoran 2004).

Mother–child incest is also a problem but is rarely discussed. The National Center on Child Abuse and Neglect estimates that the sexual abuse of children by women, primarily mothers, constitutes approximately 25% of such abuse, but that this is probably an underestimate because of the tendency for victims not to disclose the abuse (Boroughs 2004).

Elder Abuse

Elder abuse is a significant problem in the United States, affecting possibly thousands of older Americans every day (Anetzberger 2005). It is difficult to estimate the number of elders abused because so many cases go unreported. The National Center on Elder Abuse (2015) reported that only 1 in 14 of abusive situations are referred for help and that conservative estimates put the number of elders who have been mistreated at about 1 in 10. As America's population ages, the incidence and risk of elder abuse likely will increase.

The major types of **elder abuse** involve physical abuse, sexual abuse, emotional and psychological abuse, neglect, abandonment, and financial or material exploitation. One study of 95 abused women age 60 or older found that the most common types of mistreatment reported were neglect, exploitation, and physical abuse. The women typically had several functional limitations and were dependent on their family members for care (Roberto, Teaster, and Duke 2004). Social isolation and mental disability are two factors that make an older person vulnerable to abuse.

A common assumption is that most elder abuse occurs in institutional settings such as nursing homes.

Although there are cases of abuse in institutions, most abuse occurs in domestic settings by family members—most often an adult child or a spouse.

If abuse is reported, Adult Protective Services investigates the allegations. If abuse is confirmed, they provide assistance to the victim and help ensure his or her health and safety. Law enforcement may be involved if there is a possibility of criminal prosecution. If an older adult is not mentally capable of managing his or her affairs or personal care and a suitable family member is not available or willing, a court may appoint a guardian to make decisions for the older adult.

The Crisis of Death and Grief

Another crisis that affects all families is death. Loss and grief are part of the human experience and everyone is affected by the experience of the death of a loved one at some point in their life. Death, especially of a spouse, child, or other close relative, is among life's most stressful events. It creates considerable physical, mental, and emotional stress and tension, which may take a long time to subside.

People react to grief emotionally, behaviorally, cognitively, and physically: studies show that bereavement is associated with increased incidence of physical illness, morbidity, and psychological disorders (James and Gilliland 2013; Worden 2002). In the case of a partner's death, the severity of the sense of loss and grief can be related to the length of the relationship, age of the partner and of their children, existence of a support network, quality of the relationship, and whether the partner's death was sudden or followed a long illness (Kaslow and Kaslow 2004).

However, no matter what circumstances surround a person's death, it still may come as a shock. In fact, people who have watched loved ones suffer through chronic illness before dying are sometimes affected as much as or more than those whose loved ones died after a short illness.

Many people grieve in a similar way, and understanding the way grief typically works can help people through this difficult process. Most people experience a feeling of shock or numbness after first learning of a death. They may appear unemotional as they carry out funeral plans and make other necessary arrangements. As reality sinks in and the

business of the funeral is over, many people break down and begin a process of grieving. Grief can be expressed emotionally, physically, and psychologically. Crying may be a physical expression of sorrow, whereas depression may be a psychological expression. Numbness, disbelief, denial, anger, confusion, shock, sadness, yearning, humiliation, despair, and guilt are all part of the process. Grieving is personal and may last months or years, but it is important for the bereaved person to allow himself or herself to mourn (Coleman and Ganong 2002; Kail and Cavanaugh 2016). Many people experience loneliness and despair while grieving, but the weeks and months following the death of a loved one can also be a time of personal growth (Neimeyer, Prigerson, and Davis 2002).

Hiltz (1978) described three stages of grief. The first is a short period of shock, during which the surviving family members are stunned and immobilized with grief and disbelief. The second is a period of intense heartache, during which individuals experience intense physical and emotional symptoms. Physical reactions may include disturbed sleep, stomach upset and loss of appetite, weight loss, loss of energy and muscular strength, and shortness of breath or tightness in the chest. Emotional reactions may include anger, guilt, depression, anxiety, and preoccupation with thoughts of the deceased. During this stage of intense grief, people must talk with friends or family about their loss. But since grief and death are uncomfortable subjects, this opportunity is often denied, and recovery from the loss is more difficult and prolonged. Finally, in the third stage, there is a gradual reawakening of interest in life.

For anyone who has lost a loved one, it is important to work through one's grief. Worden (2002) described the tasks of mourning as accepting the reality of the death of a loved one, working through the pain of loss, adjusting to the new environment without the loved one, and moving on with life in a healthy way. Although not defined as stages, these are seen as important tasks one must successfully accomplish to recover from the loss of a loved one.

incest Sexual activity between two people who are closely related.

elder abuse May include physical abuse, sexual abuse, emotional and psychological abuse, neglect, abandonment, and financial or material exploitation of an elderly person.

Men and women may respond differently to bereavement. Men generally find it more difficult to express sorrow; however, they usually have more money than widows do and they are more likely to remarry. Widows are better able to continue working during bereavement than are men and they have better networks of friends and closer relationships with family. Nonetheless, loneliness is still a problem, as are finances (Antonucci et al. 2001). After the death of a spouse, men are more apt to describe their loss as the loss of part of themselves; women may frame their loss in terms of being deserted and left to fend for themselves.

The negative impact of the loss of a loved one cannot be overstated. The degree and duration of this damage depend on a number of factors, including the relationship to the deceased (loss of a child vs. a spouse vs. a cousin, for example); the nature of the death (natural death is easier to accept than accident, murder, or suicide); the age of the deceased (loss of a 95-year-old grandmother is easier than that of a 9-year-old child); general mental health; age of the bereaved (older people usually cope better); and one's religious/spiritual beliefs (Kail and Cavanaugh 2016). Spiritual faith and/or religion is a major help and way of coping with bereavement for many. Spiritual resources and religion provide meaning, comfort, hope, support, and connection for those mourning the loss of a loved one (Walsh 2009).

The death of a family member often affects the health and well-being of other family members. It also affects the structure and dynamics of the family, including the relationships between survivors, possibly leading to increased closeness or strain in these relationships.

One of the most common deaths faced by adults is the death of a parent. Demographers report that the death of a parent is most likely to occur when adult children are ages 35 to 64. The death of a parent is also a significant predictor of change in marital quality. The decline in marital quality may occur because a partner fails to provide emotional support, cannot comprehend the significance and meaning of the loss, or is disappointed by the bereaved individual's slow recovery. Some partners feel imposed on by the continuing depression of the bereaved person.

Although not common, the death of a child is possibly the most devastating of losses. The death of an elderly parent or spouse is an expected life transition; the loss of a child is always untimely (parents

The emotional impact of an unexpected death, such as that of a young mother, is gauged by how alive and engaged the person was at the time of death. Responsibilities often shift suddenly and heavily onto surviving family members.

are not "supposed" to outlive their children). The relationship between surviving marital partners is usually at risk, especially if their child's death was unexpected (as an accident or suicide). Grieving parents report feeling as if all of life has changed—that nothing will ever be the same again, that they cannot get along with others and cannot concentrate. Their partner's failure to provide support or any strains that are initiated by their partner may lead to a decline in marital quality for recently bereaved individuals.

Conflicts, family crises, and how the crises are managed affect all members of the family. Children are deeply affected by family conflict and crisis not only at the time of the occurrence, but possibly throughout the rest of their lives. It is helpful to recognize that there are positive approaches for dealing with conflict and that crises go through a cycle that will end.

Abused and Neglected Children

Since the late nineteenth century, most states have enacted child abuse and neglect laws to protect children. The Child Welfare Service is a branch of the U.S. Department of Health and Human Services intended to protect the welfare of children by intervening in cases of neglect and abuse. However, many children do not get the help they need because there is often not enough staff or money to provide in-home services to successfully monitor at-risk family situations.

Children are sometimes removed from the home and placed in foster care; however, appropriate foster care is not only expensive but also often difficult to find. Many social workers are concerned about maintaining cultural and racial continuity and are reluctant to place a child in a foster home with a different cultural identity. Also, foster care is not a panacea for all neglected children. Being transferred between many different homes causes a lack of stability in their daily lives.

Many agencies are pushing for swifter termination of parental rights in abuse cases and, subsequently, faster legal adoptions for abused and neglected children. These ideas are reflected in the change of the Adoption Assistance and Child Welfare Act of 1980 to the Adoption and Safe Family Act of 1997. The emphasis of the policy shifted to protecting children, even if that means a child will not live with his or her natural parents. With the new policy in place, agencies can simultaneously plan for reunification with natural parents and adoption planning for children who are unlikely to go home. The new policy calls for shorter time limits for children in foster care so that termination of parental rights and placement in an adoptive home can be pursued after 12 months. "The balance of the law has clearly moved against the presumption that every child must be reunified no matter how treacherous the child's home environment and no matter how long it takes to complete the job. The emphasis is on more quickly freeing children, who are not safe to go home, for adoption" (R. Barth 2003, 273).

Not everyone is in favor of this policy change. Roberts (2002) suggests that black children are too quickly removed from their homes and dumped into the foster care system, and it is troubling that now policy makers want to speed up the process to adoption. Roberts indicates that African American children make up almost half of the foster care population, are moved more often and remain for longer periods in foster care, and are less likely to be returned to their mother or adopted than children of other races.

Questions to Consider

What objections might there be to endorsing the adoption of foster children?

To what extent should race and ethnicity matter in the placement of children in foster care?

Is it preferable to place abused and neglected children in foster care or should they be united with their parents as soon as possible? Defend your answer.

Should foster parents have parental rights after a certain period of time? Why or why not? How long should a child in foster care have to wait before being eligible for adoption?

Who is an unfit parent? If someone is deemed to be an unfit parent, how long can he or she retain parental rights? Under what circumstances should a parent be able to redeem parental rights?

Summary

1. Conflict is part of every relationship. It arises from various sources: personal, physical, interpersonal, and situational or environmental.

2. Conflict and a negative family environment have a negative effect on children and may place them at increased risk for behavioral and emotional problems.

3. Avoidance is a method of dealing with conflict. The opposite of avoidance is ventilation and catharsis: letting out all feelings in an unrestrained manner. Rational, tactful, thoughtful, and considerate approaches to solving conflict work better.

4. Conflict is constructive if it sticks to issues, generates solutions, and builds better feelings between people. Conflict is destructive if it attacks the ego rather than the problem or if the discussion gets off track, increases tension and alienation, and leaves the initial issue unresolved or unaddressed.

5. A crisis may be defined as a drastic change in the course of events; it is a turning point during which the trend of future events is affected.

6. Researchers identify three stages in family adjustment to crises: (1) the onset of the crisis, (2) a period of disorganization, and (3) reorganization. After reorganization, the new level of family organization may be lower, at the same level, or higher than it was before the crisis.

7. Infidelity is a crisis in many marriages because Americans enter marriage expecting and committed to sexual fidelity. People get involved in extramarital affairs for a variety of reasons.

8. Extramarital affairs have varying effects on married people: some marriages are never the same afterward; some end in divorce; some spouses are motivated to solve the problems of their marriage; and some marriages in which the emotional bonds are already broken are not affected much by the affair.

9. In some situations, a partner discovers that his or her spouse is unfaithful and chooses not to confront the other person regarding the infidelity. The affairs that are most threatening to marriage are ongoing affairs that include emotional involvement as well as sexual relations.

10. Many families have to face the crisis of economic distress because of employment instability or uncertainty, underemployment, or declining income.

11. Economic distress is associated with both physiological distress and psychological distress, and it has far-reaching effects on families. It increases the possibility of divorce because of lower levels of consensus, poorer communication, disharmony, and stress in the relations between spouses and between parents and children.

12. Individuals and families use various methods for coping with economic distress: avoiding the issue, cutting back on expenditures, selling property, renting rooms, borrowing money, finding part-time or temporary employment, starting home businesses, or turning to various social supports.

13. Addiction is an overwhelming family crisis. Family members experience anger, fear, and frustration. Persons with addiction often are dishonest and withdraw from their families. Addicted persons and their families can get help through professional assistance, rehabilitation programs, support groups, and good friends and family.

14. Family violence is any rough and extended use of physical force or aggression or of verbal abuse by one family member toward another.

15. Couple violence can take the form of situational couple violence, intimate terrorism, or violent resistance.

16. Child abuse may include not only physical assault but also neglect, emotional abuse, and sexual abuse.

17. Abusers are likely to have a poor self-image, rank higher in general aggression, be jealous, abuse alcohol and drugs, and be insecure individuals who need a scapegoat for their problems.

18. Although both women and men use verbal and physical aggression against their spouse, men are more likely to inflict injury because of their size and strength.

19. Child abusers exhibit more psychological problems than nonabusers, have a negative self-concept, lack knowledge of parenting, overreact to stress in their life, and—because of immaturity and inexperience—are unable to cope.

20. Children who are born prematurely or are fretful, disabled, or otherwise difficult to care for are more likely to be abused.

21. The great majority of those who sexually abuse children are people in the child's immediate family whom the child loves and trusts.

22. Incest is sexual activity between people who are closely related or are surrogate family members. Father–daughter incestuous relationships usually take place in unhappy and disorganized

family situations in which a maladjusted father turns to his daughter as a sexual expression of nonsexual problems such as depression, low self-esteem, and feelings of inadequacy.

23. Elder abuse is a growing problem in the United States. The major types of abuse include physical abuse, sexual abuse, emotional and psychological abuse, neglect, abandonment, and financial or material exploitation.

24. The three stages of grief include a first period of shock, a second stage of intense suffering, and finally a third stage of gradual reawakening of interest in life.

Key Terms

avoidance

catharsis

child abuse

constructive arguments

crisis

crisis overload

destructive arguments

elder abuse

family violence

incest

interpersonal sources of conflict

personal sources of conflict

physical sources of conflict

post–traumatic stress disorder

situational or environmental sources of conflict

spouse abuse

ventilation

Questions for Thought

1. What were the major sources of conflict in your family of origin? What were the effects on you? On other family members?

2. In one of your intimate relationships (spouse, close friend, sibling), what are the major sources of conflict? What can be done to minimize this conflict?

3. Should the consumption of pornography be considered infidelity? Anonymous cybersex?

4. Recollect times when meaning-making coping strategies have been used by someone you know.

5. Knowing what you do about the stages of grief and people's reactions during different stages, what would be some positive steps that a grief-stricken person could take to overcome grief? What would be some positive steps that other family members could take to help a grief-stricken person overcome his or her grief?

For Further Reading

Barnett, O., Miller-Perrin, C., and Perrin, R. (2005). *Family violence across the lifespan: An introduction.* Thousand Oaks, CA: Sage. Presents a broad overview of family violence and how it changes across the life course.

The Bradford Health Services website has information about the nature of alcohol and drug addiction, treatment, and after treatment. http://bradfordhealth.com.

Carp, F. M. (2000). *Elder abuse in the family: An interdisciplinary model for research.* New York: Springer. Reviews research on elder abuse, introducing a broad theoretical model.

Frieze, I. (2005). *Hurting the one you love: Violence in relationships.* Belmont, CA: Thomson Wadsworth. Examines violence in intimate relationships and reasons why people abuse.

Loseke, D., Gelles, R., and Cavanaugh, M. (2005). *Current controversies on family violence.* Thousand Oaks, CA: Sage. Presents various sides of controversial issues in family abuse.

McKenry, P., and Price, S. (2005). *Families and change: Coping with stressful events and transitions.* Thousand Oaks, CA: Sage. Discusses various aspects and theories of family stress.

The Safe Horizon website provides information about domestic violence, child abuse and incest, stalking, rape, and family justice centers. They also provide a hotline for victims. http://www.safehorizon.com.

Schewe, P. A. (2002). *Preventing violence in relationships: Interventions across the life span.* Washington, DC: American Psychological Association. Examines violence prevention in intimate relationships and families.

CHAPTER 16

The Family and Divorce

CHAPTER OUTLINE

Learning Objectives

Probability of Divorce: Social and Demographic Factors

- Marital Age
- Religion
- Socioeconomic Status
- Geographic Area
- Parental Divorce
- The Presence of Children
- Quality of Marriage and Parent–Child Relationships

Causes of Marital Breakup

- Spouses' Perceptions
- The Marital Disaffection Process

The Divorce Decision

Alternatives to Divorce

- Marriage Counseling

PERSONAL PERSPECTIVE: *Getting Divorced*

- Marriage Enrichment
- Separation

AT ISSUE TODAY: *Why Marriage Counseling Sometimes Does Not Succeed*

No-Fault Divorce and Mediation

CULTURAL PERSPECTIVE: *Adjustment to Divorce*

Adult Adjustments after Divorce

- Emotional Trauma
- Societal Attitudes toward Divorce
- Loneliness and Social Readjustment
- Adjustments to Custody Arrangements
- Finances
- Realignment of Responsibilities and Work Roles

- Contacts with the Ex-Spouse
- Kinship Interaction

COPING FEATURE: *Anger*

Children and Divorce

- Child Custody

FAMILY STRENGTHS PERSPECTIVE: *Forgiveness and Conflict-Resolution Skills*

- Child Support
- Visitation Rights
- Reactions of Children
- Adjustments of Children

A QUESTION OF POLICY: *Divorce and the Single-Mother Family*

Summary

Key Terms

Questions for Thought

For Further Reading

LEARNING OBJECTIVES

AFTER READING THE CHAPTER, YOU SHOULD BE ABLE TO DO THE FOLLOWING:

- Identify social and demographic factors that increase individual probability of divorce.

- Summarize the causes of divorce as identified by divorced men and women.

- Describe the process of disaffection.

- Describe the important factors to consider in making a decision about whether to get divorced.

- Discuss marriage counseling, marriage enrichment, and structured separation as alternatives to divorce.

- Compare ways to get divorced—no-fault divorce and mediation—in terms of property and finances, child support, legal fees, and children.

- Describe the major adjustments that adults make after divorce.

- Discuss the following in relation to children and divorce: child custody, child support, visitation rights, and the reactions of children.

"When the divorce happened, I felt like I was in another world and another life—literally. My wife got custody of the children and she makes it difficult for me to see them. It's always hard to get in touch with her to make visiting arrangements or she has some special plans or something. My finances have been pretty much devastated; child support takes a big chunk of my salary. I usually don't have money for the 'extras' like karate lessons or camp—and I hate that my kids miss out and, of course, it is always my fault. I also resent that their new stepdad sees them every day. It's good that he helps with homework and rides bikes with them, but I'm jealous. I feel replaced. I had to move to a small apartment—lost my home; I lost some friends and neighbors; I feel like I'm losing my kids, too."

The United States has one of the highest divorce rates in the world. The divorce rate surged during the 1960s and 1970s and reached an all-time high in 1981 at 5.3 (rate per 1,000 population). Since 1981, the divorce rate has declined steadily, reaching 3.4 in 2012, the lowest in the past nearly 40 years (National Center for Health Statistics 2016). The declining divorce rate since 1981 is probably a result of a combination of factors: the HIV/AIDS epidemic; a trend toward greater sexual fidelity and monogamy; a growing awareness of the importance of marriage and family stability to the prevention of many of the social problems in our nation; and an increase in marriage and family education and enrichment programs.

Although the divorce rate has stabilized and declined slightly, it remains high. Demographers estimate that about 40% of first marriages will end in divorce. Based on surveys of individuals 18 or older and conducted by the U.S. Bureau of the Census (2016), the percentage of individuals who were divorced increased from 1.9% in 1950 to 10.1% in 2015. The highest percentages of divorced adults are in the 45 to 54 age range (29% for men and 29% for women), followed closely by the 55 to 64 age range (16% for men and 19% for women). The average age of first divorce is 32 for men and 30 for women; first marriages that end in divorce last a median of eight years (Lewis and Kreider 2015; Spangler and Payne 2014).

The high divorce rate does not mean that marriage is in a state of breakdown. Many marriages last a lifetime and marriage is highly valued by most people. Also, remarriage rates remain high,

indicating that people are not disillusioned with the institution of marriage (Lewis and Kreider 2015). The high divorce rate does suggest that our society has become more accepting of divorce; when couples become disenchanted or unhappy, they are more likely to end the marriage than was true in the past.

The increasing numbers of divorcing people have resulted in numerous books on the subject—everything from do-it-yourself divorce to divorce as a creative experience. There has also been an examination of divorce laws, which in their old forms created suffering for millions of couples and their children. Most state legislatures have now changed their laws and encourage reconciliation counseling, divorce mediation, and no-fault divorce.

All of the statistics, laws, and court cases, however, involve human beings: parents and children who are trying to make the best of difficult situations. Therefore, we must take a careful look at the facts and causes of divorce, at our divorce laws, and at children's reaction to divorce and its effects on them. We must also understand what couples go through and how they struggle to adjust following a divorce.

Probability of Divorce: Social and Demographic Factors

In looking at divorce rates, let us examine first those social and demographic factors that increase or decrease the probability of divorce. As stated in Chapter 1, divorce rates vary from group to group and relate to factors such as age at marriage, religion, occupation, income, education, ethnicity, geographic area, and parental divorce. However, although it is true that many marriages end in divorce, the divorce rate must be viewed with caution. For many people, the actual chance of divorce is far below 40%. For example, if a person is reasonably well educated with a decent income, comes from an intact family, is religious, and marries after age 25 without having a baby first, the chances of divorce are considerably lower than the national average (U.S. Bureau of the Census 2016; Whitehead and Popenoe 2005).

No one factor or set of factors will pinpoint which individuals will get divorced, but they do

Divorce is a stressful and troubling experience for everyone involved.

indicate statistical probabilities for different groups. The causes of divorce indicated in the research include women's independence; early marriage; economic factors; poor intellectual, educational, and social skills; liberal divorce laws; sexual factors leading to incompatibility; role conflicts; alcoholism and substance abuse; risk-taking behavior; differences between partners leading to acrimony; religious factors; attitudes about divorce; and various other reasons (Ambert 2009; Lowenstein 2005). We focus here on some of the more reliable social and demographic correlates of divorce and separation in the United States.

Marital Age

Age at first marriage is one of the most important predictors of marital success: people who marry young are more likely to divorce than are those who wait until they are older (Amato 2010; Kaperberg 2014). In fact, some research suggests that age at marriage is the strongest predictor of divorce in the first 5 years of marriage and that the negative effects of early marriage last far into marriage. References to growing apart, as well as problems with alcohol

and drug use, are more commonly cited as reasons for divorce in people who married relatively early (Amato 2010; Amato and Previti 2003).

Data from the National Survey of Families and Households show that after 10 years of marriage, 48% of first marriages of brides under age 18 have ended in divorce or legal separation, compared with only 24% of first marriages of brides who are age 25 or older at marriage (Bramlett and Mosher 2002). Note, however, that this difference is not seen among Hispanic women (see Figure 16.1).

As discussed in Chapter 1, the age at first marriage has been increasing since the mid-1950s. This relative delay in marrying is a result of people staying in school longer, women entering the work force in greater numbers, and rates of cohabitation increasing dramatically. Because more people are older today when they experience their first marriage, we may continue to see a slight decline in the divorce rate.

Religion

Frequency of attendance at religious services is correlated strongly and negatively with divorce or separation. That is, those who attend church/synagogue/mosque regularly are less likely to divorce or separate. In addition, those who are religious have a greater likelihood of marital happiness (Ambert 2009; Clements, Stanley, and Markman 2004; Harrar and DeMaria 2007). Religious teachings and values can be powerful factors in motivating couples to try to make their marriage succeed (Stinnett and Stinnett 2010). The National Survey of Families and Households indicated that the higher the importance attached to religion, the lower the likelihood of marital breakup (Bramlett and Mosher 2002). Those who have strong religious beliefs may be more likely to reconcile when difficulties arise; and most religions teach about forgiving which likely increases the success of their reconciliation.

Socioeconomic Status

Socioeconomic status includes education, income, and occupation. Figure 16.2 shows the relationships among several economic measures (median family income, male unemployment rate, and receipt of public assistance, for example) and the probability that the first marriage will end within 10 years. Studies show that rates of divorce or separation are higher at lower socioeconomic levels. In general,

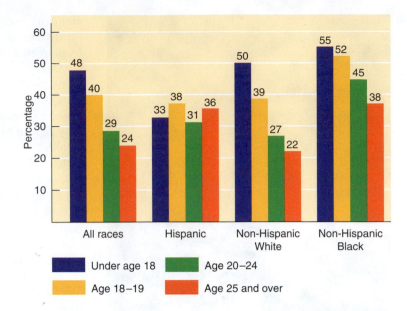

FIGURE 16.1 Probability That the First Marriage Breaks Up within 10 Years by Race/Ethnicity and Age at the Beginning of the Marriage: United States

Note: From the National Center for Health Statistics, *2002 (Figure 19).*

couples facing more financial problems and those spending less time together have a higher divorce rate (Ambert 2009; Poortman 2005).

Individuals of low socioeconomic status also tend to divorce for different reasons. As education and income level increase, reasons cited for divorcing are more likely to include relationship-centered causes, such as incompatibility and personality problems, and less likely to include reasons such as problematic behavior or abuse (Amato and Previti 2003).

Risk of divorce increases when wives contribute between 40% and 60% of the total family resources, particularly when marital happiness is moderate to low, as opposed to high (S. J. Rogers 2004). It may be that when spouses' resources are similar, it lowers her dependence on him; she has greater resources to leave. Then, too, her equal contribution to family income likely means she is working full-time—perhaps because he is unemployed or underemployed (with the increased stress, fatigue, etc.), one of the characteristics of women associated with a greater probability of marital dissolution (Sayer et al. 2011).

Geographic Area

Divorce rates tend to be higher in large cities and lower in small cities or rural areas, even when adjusted for other variables such as ethnic, religious, and socioeconomic differences. This is explained partly by the higher levels of residential mobility among people in large cities and urban areas compared to that among people in small cities and rural areas. Rapid economic growth, demographic changes (birthrates, death rates, proportion of elderly people), and employment rates are all correlated with divorce rates. Overall, first marriages are more likely to be disrupted in communities with higher unemployment, lower median family income, and a higher percentage of families living below poverty level or receiving public assistance (see Figure 16.2) (Lewis and Kreider 2015). First marriages also are more likely to be disrupted in central cities and in communities with a lower percentage of college-educated members and a higher crime rate.

Parental Divorce

Research studies have consistently found that people whose parents have divorced are statistically more likely to divorce themselves (Cui, Fincham, and Durtschi 2011; Ming, Fincham, and Durtschi 2011; Stinnett and Stinnett 2010). However, it is important to recognize that many children of divorce have successful marriages and do not divorce. Perhaps they learn from their parents' mistakes, develop better relationship skills, and/or have a greater level of commitment than did their parents. Dr. Carlfred Broderick (1996), a psychologist and former president of the National Council on Family Relations, described a process whereby some individuals make a decision to "filter" family dysfunction from their family line.

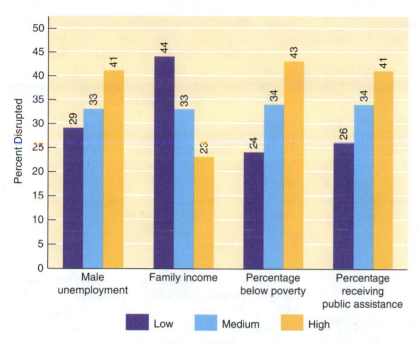

FIGURE 16.2 Probability That the First Marriage Breaks Up within 10 Years by Community Male Unemployment Rates, Median Family Income, Percentage below Poverty, and Percentage Receiving Public Assistance

Note: From the National Center for Health Statistics, *2002 (Figure 26).*

Why are children whose parents have divorced more vulnerable to also become divorced? One possibility is that they have modeled dysfunctional communication and relationship patterns. Another reason is that because their parents are divorced, the children may be more likely to consider divorce (when marital dissatisfaction occurs) themselves.

Research by Cui, Fincham, and Durtschi (2011) provides an insight into why parental divorce is a predictor of divorce among their children. Their research found that young adults from divorced families expressed a more favorable attitude toward divorce than did those from intact families. Interestingly, their more favorable attitude toward divorce was significantly related to a lower level of commitment in their own romantic relationships, which, in turn, was associated with dissolution of their relationships.

If both spouses experienced parental divorce, their risk of divorce is increased. The risk of divorce is particularly high if parental divorce occurred when the spouses were 12 years of age or younger. People whose parents divorced are more likely to have problems with anger, jealousy, hurt feelings, communication, infidelity, and so on. As children, they may have been exposed to poor models of behavior and may not have learned the skills and attitudes that facilitate successful functioning within their married role. Therefore, they may be more likely to become divorced themselves (Lauer and

Lauer 2011) or to have more negative intimate relationships (van-Schaick and Stolberg 2001). After examining national longitudinal data that spanned almost 20 years, Amato and DeBoer (2001) concluded that parental divorce approximately doubled the odds that offspring would see their own marriages end in divorce. This may be because they hold a comparatively weak commitment to the idea of an enduring marriage. Amato and Booth (2001) reported that parental behaviors most likely to predict problematic marriages for offspring include jealousy, being domineering, getting angry easily, being critical, being moody, and not talking to the spouse.

Interestingly, research has even suggested that divorce has consequences for subsequent generations, including individuals who were not yet born at the time of the original divorce. Using data from a 20-year longitudinal study to determine whether divorce in the grandparent generation had implications for well-being in the grandchild generation, Amato and Cheadle (2005) found that divorce between grandparents was associated with a variety of problematic outcomes for grandchildren, including lower educational attainment, greater marital discord, and poorer quality relationships with mothers and fathers.

However, although research shows that parental divorce increases the likelihood of offspring divorce, Teachman (2002) found that living apart from both parents, irrespective of the reason, is associated with an increased risk of divorce. In particular, he found that children who were born to a mother who was not married and who did not experience parental divorce or death experienced a very high rate of divorce. He found that neither the number of transitions in childhood living arrangements nor parental remarriage affected the risk of an offspring's marriage ending in divorce, and he suggested that "there is strong evidence that children who were born out of wedlock (and who did not experience parental divorce or death) are as likely, if not more likely than children of divorce to see their own marriages dissolve" (Teachman 2002, 728).

The Presence of Children

The risk of marital dissolution is highest among childless couples, possibly because they are not constrained to stay together by the presence of children (Heaton 2002). There are differences in the risk of marital dissolution depending on the ages and number of children. The likelihood of marital dissolution decreases as the number of children rises, to a maximum of four. Once couples have five or more children, the likelihood of marital dissolution increases. The rates of divorce are relatively low when the youngest child is under age 3, but rise sharply when that child reaches early adolescence and decline substantially after he or she reaches age 17. Thus, children's stabilizing effect on marriage is strongest when they are very young or when they have reached adulthood.

Other research has found that, if the family includes at least one son, fathers spend increased time with their children. If there is more paternal involvement in family life, through either the father's investing more time with the children or his doing household chores, his wife has a greater perception of fairness in the relationship and is more satisfied with the marriage (Schlindler and Coley 2012).

Quality of Marriage and Parent–Child Relationships

Couples who have lower-quality marriage relationships and who experience less marital happiness and satisfaction are significantly more likely to divorce. Much research has found that marriage conflict, low positive affect, and low commitment to marriage are strong predictors of divorce. These factors are also strongly predictive of less effective and

less involved parenting, resulting in more stressful parent–child relationships, which, in turn, may contribute to more strain in the marriage relationship (Amato 2010; Schindler and Coley 2012).

Less warm and more confrontational behaviors by both mothers and fathers toward each other predict a higher probability of divorce. However, such negative marital behaviors by the mother toward the father are more predictive of divorce (Cherlin 2009; Shindler and Coley 2012). These research findings are consistent with other research indicating that men's feelings of affirmation and affection from their partners are more predictive of marriage stability than are women's feelings of affirmation from their partners (Cherlin 2009; Shindler and Coley 2012).

Consistent with family systems theory, the quality of the parent–child relationship influences and is influenced by the quality of the marriage relationship and, as a result, may be an important predictor of divorce. Keep in mind, of course, that marital dissolutions are related to complex family relationships. Even so, some research indicates that parents who divorce are more likely to experience negative parent–child relationships. In a large, national study of couples with young adolescents, Schindler and Coley (2012) found that marital separation was predicted by lower father–child relationship closeness, but by higher mother–child relationship closeness.

Perhaps, as role identity theory suggests, fathers who experience a close parent–child relationship develop a strong connection to their fatherhood role and are more committed to maintaining a successful, stable relationship with their spouses. Another possible explanation is that fathers who are highly dissatisfied with the marriage relationship and are considering divorce will begin to remove themselves from active parenting as part of the process of distancing themselves from the family. This parenting withdrawal may also be influenced by a father's anticipation that the mother will be given custody.

It is interesting that fathers' negative and harsh parenting did not predict marital separation. Instead, it was the presence of positive and connected father–child relationships that was significantly related to a lower probability of marital separation (Schindler and Coley 2012).

The findings that greater mother–child closeness predicted a higher likelihood of marital separation may be a result of mothers' transferring their emotional energies from unhappy marriage relationships to their children. This positive relationship between mother–child closeness and a higher probability of marital separation may be because a close mother–child relationship, in combination with a low level of marital satisfaction, pushes the father from the family system and, therefore, decreases his parental involvement. This is consistent with family systems theory (Schindler and Coley 2012).

Causes of Marital Breakup

Social and demographic factors indicate the probability of divorce, but they do not reveal the actual causes of marital breakup. Causes may be determined by studying people who are divorcing to find out their perceptions of the reasons that their marriages have failed.

Spouses' Perceptions

The research on divorce and marital satisfaction indicates two critical times in a marriage when divorce is most likely: (1) the first 8 years of marriage, during which half of all divorces occur, and (2) at midlife, when people often have young teenage children. The latter period has been described by some researchers as possibly the lowest point in marital satisfaction during the life course.

Gottman and Levenson (2000) studied the predictors of divorce in these two critical periods of a marriage. They found that different sets of variables predicted early divorce and later divorce. Negative affect during conflict (for example, criticism, contempt, or defensiveness) predicted early divorcing, but it did not predict later divorcing.

By contrast, the lack of positive affect in discussing the events of the day (for example, being excited or showing interest in what a spouse had to say) predicted later divorcing, but it did not predict early divorcing. Thus, it could be that marriages characterized by criticism, contempt, and intense fighting dissolve sooner than do those without positive affect. In marriages without positive affect, people may stay together but become emotionally detached and postpone divorce until their loneliness becomes unbearable and they no longer feel the need to remain married for the sake of the children (Gottman Institute 2015; Gottman and Silver 2015). This is consistent with other research indicating that couples and families who establish a daily pattern of taking time to communicate interest in and concern for each other as they discuss events of the day report the highest levels of family satisfaction (Burns and Pearson, 2011).

Indeed, showing positive affect may be one of the most important aspects of a successful marriage (Gottman and Silver 2015; Harrar and DeMaria 2007). Among the most common reasons for divorcing, cited by both men and women are a gradual growing apart, a loss of a sense of closeness, and a lack of feelings of being loved and appreciated. Severe and intense fighting is cited much less frequently. Gottman and Levenson (2000) suggest, "Perhaps changing the affective nature of the way couples discuss such mundane topics as the events of their day, in which they either make an emotional connection upon reunion or fail to do so, could affect the way they resolve conflict, and possibly the future course of the marriage" (743).

The relationship before marriage, particularly how the couple communicates and handles conflicts, may be the best indicator of marital stability and happiness. Clements, Stanley, and Markman (2004) followed 100 couples for 13 years from the premarital period through the primary risk period for divorce. They found that couples who would remain satisfied, become distressed, or divorce could be reliably predicted based on premarital data. Not surprisingly, couples who reported having lower premarital happiness were the same couples who became distressed in marriage. Another longitudinal study of newlyweds yielded similar findings (Carrere et al. 2000).

In yet another study of newlywed couples, Huston and colleagues (2001) found that disillusionment—such as an abatement of love, a decline in overt affection, a lessening of the conviction that one's spouse is responsive, and an increase in ambivalence—determines which couples will divorce and which will have a stable marriage. It is not surprising that spouses who are zestful and take a positive attitude toward life are more likely to maintain a happy marriage, whereas those who are moody, emotionally unstable, and have high levels of negativity have lower levels of marital happiness (Gottman 2012).

In a longitudinal study of 208 people, Amato and Previti (2003) found that infidelity was the most commonly reported cause of divorce. However, they note that it is difficult to determine whether infidelity is a cause or a consequence of problems in a marriage. Other reasons cited for divorce included incompatibility, growing apart, personality clashes, and lack of communication. Women were more likely to report problematic behavior on the part of a husband, and men were more likely to report that they did not know what caused the divorce.

Much research indicates that individuals tend to attribute the cause of the divorce more often to their former spouses than to themselves; they also tend to feel they had been wronged (Rye and Moore 2015). Both men and women agree that women more often initiated the divorce.

Why do couples with a high level of marital happiness in the early years of their marriage eventually divorce later? In two different longitudinal studies among low-distress couples with high levels of marital happiness during the early years of marriage and with a low projected likelihood of divorce, it was found that those couples who eventually divorced a few years later tended to be younger at marriage, were more likely to have divorced parents, and held more liberal and positive views of divorce (Amato and Hohmann-Marriott 2007; Lavner and Bradbury 2012).

Both studies found that those couples who eventually divorced displayed (during early marriage) more negative affect, contempt, and blame while expressing lower levels of support. In addition, Lavner and Bradbury (2012) reported that those couples with a high degree of happiness in their early years of marriage who eventually divorced were characterized by husbands who were verbally aggressive and by wives with more negative personalities and higher average acute stress compared with individuals in couples who did not divorce.

Perhaps these negative characteristics were minimized, rationalized, or offset by strengths and assets of the couple early in the relationship. In time, however, the couples' ability to cope may have been challenged or overwhelmed by the presence of these negative characteristics—especially in combination with the cumulative stress of more severe relationship issues, plus daily hassles and the outside strains of job and life changes (Lavner and Bradbury 2012).

The Marital Disaffection Process

When couples cease to love each other and to create intimacy between them, they set up conditions for the marriage to end. Many scholars agree that one of the reasons for divorce is the unrealistic expectation placed on marriage as an avenue to personal fulfillment—an expectation it cannot possibly fulfill (Gillis 2004; Knox and Schacht 2016), regardless of how good a marriage may be.

Marital disaffection involves the gradual loss of emotional attachment, a decline in caring, emotional estrangement, and an increasing sense of apathy and indifference. Positive feelings are replaced over time by neutral or even negative feelings. However, it is important to emphasize that mutual disaffection is the result of other problems in the relationship, rather than the initial cause. Spouses report they want a divorce because they do not love each other, but falling out of love is usually a consequence of years of unresolved tensions in the relationship.

The development of marital disaffection is divided into three phases. The first phase is characterized by increased disappointment, disillusionment, and feelings of hurt and anger. One partner's (or both partners') thoughts begin to center on the other partner's negative traits because that partner's behavior is not what was expected. The partners are still optimistic about the future of their marriage and attempt to solve the problems by asserting their feelings or by attempting to please a spouse.

During the middle phase, anger and hurt increase in frequency and intensity. Spouses begin to expect their partner to behave in negative ways, and apathy increases. Some partners begin to weigh whether to leave the marriage as they sort out factors relating to the children, finances, or religion. Attempts to please the partner decrease.

During the end phase, anger again is the most frequent feeling. Feelings of trust decline, and apathy and a sense of helplessness increase: "I've just put up with the same behavior so long now—I just want out because I don't see him ever changing. . . . It's too late to rekindle the feelings. . . . I don't want to try." The most frequent thoughts during this stage concern wanting to end the marriage and determining how it can be done. However, there may still be some ambivalence. Before this stage, counseling is infrequently pursued, but now many couples seek marital therapy in a last attempt to save the marriage or to get assistance in leaving it (Kayser and Rao 2006).

Basic to the dissolution of the relationship is the perception that the costs of staying together outweigh the rewards. Partners focus on the negative traits of their spouse (and not their own negative traits), so it is difficult to change their feelings. Sometimes changes are made (by one or both) and feelings do become positive again, but it takes a lot of hard work. If the marriage is dissolved, the disaffected spouse continues to focus on the negative traits of the ex-spouse, convincing himself or herself that dissolution was justified (Rye and Moore 2015).

The Divorce Decision

The decision to divorce is a difficult one that few couples are able to make easily and quickly; rather, they usually agonize for months or years before finally deciding. Even then, the partners may change their minds a number of times, repeatedly separating and then moving back together. Many couples file a petition for divorce only to withdraw it. Others even go to court and then change their minds at the last minute.

From a counselor's point of view, it is hard to predict who will or will not get divorced. Some couples have relatively minor problems but give up easily. Other couples seem to be likely candidates for divorce, but through intense effort and motivation overcome all obstacles and end up with a good marriage. The outcome depends partially on the motivation and commitment of the partners.

There are, of course, some couples who never divorce, but not necessarily because the two people love each other or are compatible. Consider this case:

> Mr. and Mrs. P. have been married 43 years. He's 79 and she's 76. They absolutely hate each other. They say and do horrible things to each other. They constantly criticize each other and are in chronic conflict. They have no companionship, never share any social activities together. He's gay, has male lovers on the side, and never has intercourse with her. He's intellectual, verbal, and artistic. She's none of these things. He's a dreamer, she's practical. The only reason they give for living together is to have two Social Security checks instead of one. (Counseling notes)

According to exchange theory, reconciliation is more likely when the costs of divorce are high, the barriers to getting out of the marriage are great, and the alternatives are few. Levinger (1979) proposed a three-factor theory of marital cohesion, identifying three basic considerations in deciding whether to remain married:

1. **Satisfaction with or attractions of the marriage.** These are the forces that strengthen the marriage bond. They include sexual fulfillment, emotional bonding, care, concern, and need (even neurotic need) for each other. Attractions also include socioeconomic rewards: a better income, an improved standard of living, superior social status, a nice house, more economic security, or the need for the physical services that a spouse can provide.

2. **Barriers to getting out of the marriage.** These are the forces that prevent marriage breakdown. In one study, three perceived barriers were cited most often by participants as being very important: (1) the possibility of children suffering (50%), (2) the threat of losing a child (46%), and (3) religious beliefs (41%). About 33% of married individuals felt that their dependence on their spouse was very important in keeping their marriage intact, whereas 31% cited their spouse's dependence on them as very important. Although married couples perceived financial security to be important, it was not important enough to keep them from divorcing (Knoester and Booth 2000).

   When the perceived barriers were analyzed as to how well they actually deter divorce, only two decreased the odds of divorce: (1) the importance of religious beliefs and (2) dependence on one's spouse. When responses were separated by gender, it became evident that women rank perceived dependence on their spouse and religious beliefs as more essential barriers to divorce and that men rank more highly the threat of losing a child and the influence of family and friends. Responses to other barriers did not differ significantly between women and men. Neither of the perceived barriers that involve children were found to be deterrents to divorce. Overall, although many people perceive certain barriers to divorce and value them as important, these barriers apparently do not keep couples together (Knoester and Booth 2000). Couples who mention only barriers (and not rewards to staying) as reasons for not divorcing are the most unhappy and are most likely to divorce eventually (Previti and Amato 2003).

3. **The attractiveness of alternatives to the marriage.** These include an evaluation of personal assets: sexual attractiveness, appearance, age, and other factors that influence the possibilities of remarrying, if desired. People with high self-esteem and a sense of personal competence are more likely to feel that they can get along on their own. People with good education, high income, and intelligence realize that even if they are cut off from their spouse's earning power, they still are capable of living a good life.

A powerful motivating force in divorce is the desire to marry another person. A person who is involved in an ongoing emotional and sexual relationship outside of marriage may not be as hesitant about getting a divorce as a person who has no one else on the side. Although an extramarital affair is often a result of an unhappy marriage, it also may be the added incentive to terminate the marriage.

A fourth factor affects the decision to stay married or get divorced. This factor was not discussed by Levinger, but it is important: the intensity of the emotional pain generated by an unhappy marriage. One man explained:

> I've remained in the marriage for 28 years because I didn't believe in divorce and because I didn't want to desert my children. But I can't take it any longer. My wife hates me and takes every occasion to let me know. She tells me she hopes I'll die so she can collect my life insurance. There is no love, companionship, or anything positive left in our relationship. (Counseling notes)

A woman commented,

> You can't imagine what it was like being married to my alcoholic husband. He was completely irresponsible. I did literally everything around the house, yard, and in raising our five children. Yet, he wouldn't admit that he had an alcohol problem. (Counseling notes)

In these situations, there was no question in the minds of the individuals that divorce was the only acceptable course.

One very debated question is whether couples should stay together for the sake of the children. Some social scientists believe the answer is yes, unless abuse is occurring in the relationship, because many marriages that end in divorce could be salvaged. Booth and Amato (2001) studied national longitudinal data from parents and their adult children to examine the way in which the amount of marital conflict influences the impact of divorce on children. They found that many marriages that end in divorce are low conflict. Divorces in these low-conflict marriages can be damaging to children because children can be unaware of the unhappiness and may be shocked when their parents divorce.

Booth and Amato (2001) also found that high-conflict marriages that end in divorce appear to have a neutral or even beneficial effect on children: "Presumably, escape from a high-conflict marriage benefits children because it removes them from an aversive, stressful home environment. In contrast, a divorce that is not preceded by a prolonged period of overt discord may represent an unexpected, unwelcome, and uncontrollable event, an event that children are likely to experience as stressful" (210). Booth and Amato noted that two categories of children are most at risk for psychological problems: those who grow up with parents who stay married but remain conflicted and hostile and those whose parents are in low-conflict marriages but divorce anyway.

However, not everyone agrees that couples should stay together when they are in low-conflict marriages. Some studies show that 5- and 6-year-olds perceive their parents' low-conflict marriages to be high in conflict. Other research shows that boys raised in two-parent families where the parents were cold to each other have a harder time showing intimacy than those raised in divorced families (Coontz 2001).

In reality, however, few marriages are happy or unhappy all the time. Waite and Gallagher (2000) found that couples who rank in the lowest percentile on marital satisfaction but who do not divorce often say they are very happy 5 years later. Using the National Survey of Families and Households data, they found that 64% of those who said they were unhappy but stayed together reported they were happy 5 years later and another 25% reported improvement in their marriage. Interestingly, almost 75% of the spouses of those who reported to be unhappily married reported for themselves that they were happy in their marriages. Thus, perception varies within a marriage as to whether it is a happy one (Waite and Gallagher 2000).

Alternatives to Divorce

When spouses are dissatisfied with their marriage, they might consider marriage counseling, marriage enrichment programs, or separation as alternatives to divorce.

Marriage Counseling

Although couples cannot be expected to live together unhappily, breaking up the marriage may not always be the best option. Divorce often substitutes one set of problems for another. Another option is to see whether, with professional help, the unhappy marriage can become a satisfying one. Couples are often skeptical about the outcome of counseling, especially if they have never been to a counselor before or if they have had unhappy experiences with therapists. Of course, therapists vary in their philosophy, style, and degree of competence.

In a survey by the American Association of Marriage and Family Counselors, 93% of persons who had received marital counseling said they had more effective tools for dealing with their problems (Tasker 2015). Other research has indicated that marital therapy is effective, at least in the short term, in reducing marital conflicts. In addition, research has shown marital therapy to be effective over the long term in promoting marital stability, reducing marital conflicts, and preventing divorce (D. Olson, DeFrain, and Skogrand 2014). There is a greater chance of a positive outcome when spouses are treated together rather than individually, and that positive results typically occur in treatments of short duration—from 1 to 20 sessions.

Marriage therapy or counseling has become a growing business as more people have come to feel comfortable asking for help with their relationships. Therapists have benefited from decades of research documenting the underlying variables in a strong

---

PERSONAL PERSPECTIVE

Getting Divorced

Anthony was in his early twenties when he married his high school sweetheart. He remembers that they dated throughout high school and were excited to be getting married. After 15 years of marriage and shortly after the birth of their third child, Anthony asked for a divorce.

I was so miserably unhappy I couldn't stand it. I didn't want another child, but I think my wife thought it would help our marriage or maybe make me stay. It only proved to make matters worse. We stopped sharing a bedroom, and then stopped talking altogether. I began working long hours to stay away from home and started to have meaningless affairs because I was lonely. I had to leave. Nobody understood why because from the outside it looked like the perfect family. I know I looked like a jerk, particularly since my wife had just had a baby. People don't always understand other people's unhappiness. I had changed so much since high school and my wife and I were no longer the same people we once were. We no longer were good for each other, and I don't even know if we liked each other anymore. The thought of a lifetime of living together was too much for me, and I felt too young to spend the rest of my life in a miserable marriage. I may have been a bad husband, but I don't think I have been a bad father. I insisted on joint legal and physical custody: my children spend half of the week at my house and half of the week at their mother's house, and all decisions concerning the children are made jointly. It is important for me to be responsible and available to my children, and I am committed to being a big part of their lives. It isn't always easy, as it has been very stressful coparenting with my ex-wife, but it is worth it.

and happy marriage versus an unhappy one. In addition, some states require **conciliation counseling** before a divorce may be granted. Florida has implemented a 3-day waiting period for marriage licenses if couples do not seek premarital education. Some states are trying to create a 60-day waiting period for a marriage license unless the couple has received 4 hours of premarriage education or counseling. In addition, some states provide incentives and subsidies for premarital education and require marriage education in high school (Hawkins et al. 2002).

Marriage Enrichment

The basic idea behind marriage enrichment is that a married couple can be active in the growth of their marriage relationship. Marriage enrichment programs combine education with group discussion to assist couples in improving marital communication, relationships, and problem solving. Programs are conducted in groups of couples—often over a weekend. Many also offer videos and online resources. The central purpose of such programs is preventive: to address issues before they become unmanageable conflicts.

One such program, the Prevention and Relationship Enhancement Program (PREP), was designed to teach partners skills for handling conflict, promoting intimacy, and dealing with differences and negative affects, such as anger and frustration. PREP is educational; it is not presented as therapy or

counseling. Leaders outline the course themes in brief lectures. PREP couples practice key techniques in sessions with trained consultants and in homework. Specific readings are also assigned. Numerous studies of the efficacy of PREP show improved communication, commitment, and intimacy after participation in the program (NREPP 2015). In one specific instance, military couples experiencing infidelity were assigned to either a PREP group or a control group; those in the PREP group had a divorce rate one-third (2.0%) that of the control group (6.2%) (Allen et al. 2012).

Separation

A trial separation is another alternative before divorce. Couples ask, "Do you think if we separated for a while it would help us to decide what we should do?" Separation can be effective in some instances, especially if the separation is carefully structured and if marital therapy continues during the separation. Separation is not to be taken lightly. It is a time of emotional upheaval and extreme stress—for spouses and for children—and it has both potential benefits and potential risks (Gold 2009).

Structured separation may be defined as a time-limited approach in which the couple terminates cohabitation, commits to regularly scheduled therapy, and agrees to regular interpersonal contact, with a moratorium on a final decision to either reunite or divorce. The objective of the separation is change; it is designed to interrupt old interactional patterns through the creation of an environment conducive to change. It is characterized by ambivalent feelings between the spouses and toward the marriage. The anticipated result is that spouses will move either closer together or farther apart (Gold 2009).

A number of different situations may support the decision to consider structured marital separation as a treatment method:

- **Extreme conflict.** The frequency, intensity, and duration of conflict are so overwhelming that the couple cannot tolerate it. Physical or emotional abuse and verbal aggressiveness may be so debilitating that no positive change can take place in the relationship.

- **Absence of spousal reinforcement.** There is little or no reward, pleasure, or satisfaction from the marital relationship, and separation may help raise the level of mutual positive exchange.

Some states require conciliation counseling before a divorce may be granted. Can voluntary counseling be more effective?

Why Marriage Counseling Sometimes Does Not Succeed

Marriage counseling may fail to preserve the marriage for any combination of the following reasons:

- **One of the spouses does not want the counseling to succeed.** He is so tired of the marriage that he absolutely does not want it to continue. Or she does not believe that counseling works, so she sabotages it (misses appointments, for example). Or one of them has someone else he or she wants to marry.

- **The spouses lack commitment to the counseling process.** They do not really try. There is no motivation to try to do their very best.

- **Each spouse blames the other and refuses to take personal responsibility.** Each spouse believes that the entire problem lies with the other person. Or they refuse to admit there is a problem. They are not both willing to take responsibility for part of the problem and for making the solution.

- **One of the spouses is rigid and inflexible.** Sometimes counseling can go on for years, but one of the spouses is not willing to make the changes necessary for the relationship to work.

- **The spouses are incompatible.** They may be decent people, but they have different philosophies, values, habits, and ways of doing things. It is not that they do not want to live together, but they find that they simply cannot.

- **One of the spouses is too immature.** A spouse may be so insecure, unstable, irresponsible, or angry that he or she causes a great disruption in the relationship and destroys anything valuable in it. Personality problems prevent the person from working out relationship problems.

- **One of the spouses is mentally ill.** A person who is very depressed, paranoid, or manic is not capable of living together in a positive way with another person.

- **The couple does not come to counseling long enough to achieve success.** They may expect instant results and quit coming before the counseling can be of permanent help.

- **The spouses possess poor communication skills.** One person will not talk; the other monopolizes the conversation; they get in highly destructive arguments; they will not stick to the subject; or they are not able to discuss issues in a positive way, so they never resolve any problems.

- **The spouses' pasts constantly intrude on the present.** Dysfunctional family backgrounds are carried over into the present relationship. Without resolving issues in their respective parent–child relationships, they are unable to work out their present relationship.

- **Spouses listen to wrong advice from family or friends.** Instead of making their own decisions, they try to follow what other people tell them to do. Many times, the advice is exactly the wrong way for them to behave.

- **The couple selected the wrong counselor.** Each counselor has particular skills, qualifications, education, and specialties. The couple must select a person with the appropriate education, background, and interests to deal with their particular problems.

- **Feeling constricted or smothered.** One or both partners need more personal and emotional space, relief from spousal control and jealousy, and an opportunity for personal growth and individual freedom while they restructure their relationship.

- **A situational or midlife transition.** Situational transitions may include loss of a loved one, a job change, a move to a new community, or

conciliation counseling Marriage counseling ordered by the court in which spouses try to decide whether they want to dissolve their marriage or agree to try to solve their problems.

structured separation A time-limited approach in which partners terminate cohabitation, commit themselves to regularly scheduled therapy with a therapist, and agree to regular interpersonal contact, with a moratorium on a final decision either to reunite or to divorce.

children leaving home. A midlife transition is characterized by evaluation of one's achievements relative to one's goals. It may result in increased satisfaction with the status quo, recalibration of one's current direction, or the identification of entirely new goals. In extreme cases, it can include disillusionment, depression, directionlessness, and emotional upheaval. For these individuals, respite from the marital relationship may allow them to deal with the crisis before they are confronted with an intense effort to change the marriage.

- **Indecision regarding divorce.** If couples cannot decide, a structured marital separation may effect a break in the decision-making dilemma.

Some people want a separation to pursue other sexual relationships. One man explained, "I have to be free to find out if my love for Sarah [the other woman] is genuine and will last." In this situation, his spouse was understandably upset: "You want to see if it's going to work out, then if it doesn't, you're coming home to me. I'm not going to be anybody's second choice" (Counseling notes).

Few spouses will agree to a separation to free the other to pursue extramarital affairs. If the couple is really serious about straightening out the marriage, it is most helpful to first give up the affair and work on the marriage. If the spouse pursues the affair, there usually is not any marriage left to come back to.

No-Fault Divorce and Mediation

Divorce is the legal method of ending a marriage. Legally, following the divorce, (1) the parties can marry someone else; (2) their property is divided, as are their debts; and (3) if children are involved, their care and custody are decided. In some circumstances, spousal support on a permanent or rehabilitative basis is awarded. These issues can be difficult to negotiate even if both parties want the divorce.

Traditionally, divorce was granted only if one party could be found guilty of some type of marital misconduct, such as adultery or physical abuse. The party accused of being guilty was punished by getting a smaller share of the couple's property or being denied custody of their children, whereas the other spouse was rewarded for being faithful to the vows of marriage. In 1970, California passed the first **no-fault divorce** legislation, and currently all 50 states have a no-fault divorce law or provision.

The essence of no-fault divorce laws is that they do not attribute fault and thus do not require one of the spouses to be considered innocent and the other guilty. No-fault divorce laws recognize the breakdown of the marriage and the inability of the spouses to function as a married couple. The no-fault law removes any question of who is "to blame" (legally) and reduces the grounds (reason for divorcing) to irreconcilable differences or an irremediable breakdown of the marriage. Consent of both spouses is not required; rather, one spouse can decide unilaterally to divorce. No-fault divorce laws are gender neutral in that both spouses are responsible for spousal and child support and both spouses are eligible for child custody. Financial rewards in terms of spousal support, child support, and property distribution are linked not to issues of fault or blame, but to the spouses' current financial needs and resources. Probably the most important feature of no-fault divorce laws is that they improve the sociopsychological and communication climate of divorce by abolishing the concept of fault and tempering the adversarial process surrounding divorce proceedings.

There are those who feel that this approach makes divorce too easy. Divorce may be extremely easy if it is not contested (and there are no children), requiring only a perfunctory hearing in court. But the process of trying to work out the settlement is often challenging. Couples may still fight bitterly, and the adversarial nature of divorce is hardly eliminated.

It is debatable whether no-fault divorce has led to an increase in divorce rates. Some researchers believe it has, particularly among couples of median family income. Others believe that no-fault divorce was a response to the already-occurring loosening of divorce restrictions and has not caused a significant increase in the divorce rate. Almost everyone who wanted to divorce and who was willing to pay the costs was probably able to divorce even before the implementation of no-fault provisions. But the removal of high attorney fees from the adversarial process of divorce may have made divorce more financially attainable for many unhappy couples and eliminated a great deal of human suffering.

Mediation and other forms of dispute resolution have grown rapidly in the past few decades. This is a

Adjustment to Divorce

Studies conducted among culturally diverse populations indicate that divorce, like other family patterns, is a cultural phenomenon and that both the problems that individuals experience and how they deal with those problems are affected by their culture and society. Some cultures stigmatize divorce more than other cultures, which causes more stress on the divorcing family. One example is found in the ultra-Orthodox community in Israel. According to the Jewish religion, divorce is legally legitimate; however, especially in the Orthodox subculture, divorce is highly unwanted and a forbidden religious act (A. Barth and Ben-Ari 2014).

The ultra-Orthodox community is collective (within the larger individualistic culture) and patriarchal; family is a foundation of society; men are religious scholars, with the family supported by the women. Divorce is regarded as both a personal failure and a social disappointment. Because of the strong social stigma, divorced women may be forced to leave the apartment building where they live and may lose their jobs (no longer being "acceptable" models as teachers, for example). Remarriage is out of the question; marriages are arranged and a divorced woman is downgraded (Barth and Ben-Ari 2014).

Another case in point is Middle Eastern Muslim women. In many Arab Muslim societies, divorce is not readily accepted and divorced individuals, particularly women, are regarded as socially deviant (Asante, Osafo, and Nyamekye 2014; Cohen and Savaya 2003a; Esmaeili et al. 2015).

One study reported that divorced Arab women in Israel suffer from psychosocial problems because of social censure, restricted liberty, and reduction in social status (Al Krenawi and Graham 1998). Another study found that divorced Muslim women in Israel struggle against their society's perception of them as "licentious temptresses who are fair game for sexual advances, and that they attempt to adjust by proving to their doubting neighbors and relatives that they can preserve their chastity, keep a clean house, and take good care of their children" (Cohen and Savaya 1997 in Cohen and Savaya 2003a, 272).

Cohen and Savaya (2003b) examined factors associated with adjustment among divorced Muslim Arab men and women living in Israel. They found that participants perceived their society as stigmatizing divorced women more than divorced men and that they saw women as bad parents and spouses. These negative perceptions affected their adjustment to divorce. Adjustment to divorce was directly related to the individual's perceptions of the societal image of the divorced person on his or her own sex. Divorced Muslim women living in Israel scored lower than their male counterparts on mental health, showing they suffered more psychological difficulties than did divorced men. These findings are in contrast to research that shows that, in Western divorced couples, women score better on adjustment and tend to be happier than divorced men (Cohen and Savaya 2003b).

---

result of high divorce rates, frequent conflicts between parents, the resulting administrative burden on courts, and concerns about the damaging effects on children and postdivorce family relationships (Emery, Sbarra, and Grover 2005). Both private mediators and public or court-appointed mediators provide services throughout the United States. One advantage of using mediators is that they can objectively represent the interests of both parents and of the children. Successful mediation requires parental cooperation, the opportunity to address

underlying emotional issues, establishment of a businesslike relationship between parents, and the avoidance of divisive negotiations (Emery, Sbarra, and Grover 2005).

no-fault divorce A legal approach that eliminates fault as a precondition for access to courts and recognizes the right of individuals to petition for divorce on the grounds of irretrievable breakdown of the marriage or irreconcilable differences.

Mediators of property and money settlements can ask for complete financial disclosure, get a property appraisal if needed, and hire an accountant if many assets are involved. Settlements that are agreed on do not become binding until they are approved by the court. One advantage of a mediated settlement is that the partners are more likely to comply with decisions they make jointly than with financial judgments that are ordered by the court against the will of the couple. Disputes regarding child custody and visitation rights and responsibilities ideally are settled on the basis of the best interests of the children. Research has shown that people who use divorce mediation have better relationships with their ex-spouses, are generally more satisfied with the outcomes of divorce, have less need for relitigation, and feel more satisfied with the process and the results. Mediation is a beneficial alternative to litigation (Palihapitiya and Eisenkraft 2014; Shaw 2010).

In summary, the process of no-fault divorce requires less extensive litigation (many couples file without benefit of attorneys), reduces legal expenses, and makes a "friendly" divorce easier than under the old adversarial system. It has partially removed the punitive element of moral condemnation that pervaded divorce for centuries from the legal process.

However, some other changes bring up important questions. Because one spouse is no longer considered "guilty" or "at fault" (and hence, the bad guy), spousal support has been awarded less frequently, for shorter periods of time, and in smaller amounts. In addition, household property and furniture are less likely to be awarded exclusively to the woman, and attorney's fees are more likely to be paid by both spouses. Fewer women are awarded full custody, and joint custody arrangements have increased. The effect on child support payments to the custodial parent has been variable. Overall, the loss of bargaining power by women has resulted in a less favorable financial settlement to many women, particularly older homemakers. Those who do not have substantial earning power of their own are affected greatly, with many having to reduce their standard of living significantly because of inadequate support from their ex-spouse. So, although no-fault divorce has many advantages, it also has created some inequities and contributed to economic hardship for many custodial parents (usually moms) and their children.

Adult Adjustments after Divorce

Adjustment after divorce may be grouped into a number of categories: (1) the emotional trauma of divorce, (2) the attitudes of society, (3) loneliness and social readjustment, (4) adjustments of the noncustodial parent, (5) finances, (6) realignment of responsibilities and work roles, (7) contacts with the ex-spouse, and (8) kinship interaction.

Emotional Trauma

In the best circumstances, divorce is emotionally disturbing. Under the worst conditions, it may result in a high degree of shock and disorientation. For many people a divorce (or breakup of a relationship) creates a lingering grief and feelings of abandonment, which cause problems in future relationships and remarriage (S. Anderson 2014). Divorce is often an emotional crisis involving emotional turmoil before and during the divorce, the shock and crisis of separation, mourning as the relationship is laid to rest, and disruption as one attempts to regain balance and reorganize (Rye and Moore 2015). A drawn-out and bitter legal battle tends to heighten the emotional trauma of divorce. In these cases, the actual divorce decree comes as a welcome relief from a long period of pain.

The trauma is greater when one spouse wants the divorce and the other does not, when the idea comes unexpectedly, when one spouse continues to be emotionally attached to the other after the divorce, or when friends and family disapprove.

For most couples, the decision to divorce is viewed as an end-of-the-rope decision that is reached, on average, over a period of about 2 years. One spouse usually wants a divorce more than the other, and spouses who want the marriage to end are likely to view divorce differently than those who would like the marriage to continue. H. Wang and Amato (2000) found that spouses who wanted and initiated the divorce exhibited less attachment to their ex-spouse and better overall divorce adjustment. Thus, the partner who leaves often experiences less postdivorce distress than the partner who is left.

Most studies reveal that during the pre- and postseparation periods both men and women report a decline in psychological adjustment. The early postseparation period is the hardest time for some, as they struggle to come to grips with the loss of a spouse and with the personal cost that loss entails. The time of greatest trauma for others is at the time of final separation. After that comes a long period of realization that the relationship is over, emotionally as well as legally. Research examining the relationship between divorce and psychological stress shows that stress and depression increase significantly soon after the divorce and then diminish over the next 3 years (Amato 2010; Gottman and Silver 2015). Interviews with women who divorced after a long-term marriage indicated that midlife divorce is a complicated process consisting of multiple endings and new beginnings that take place over an extended period of time (McDaniel and Coleman 2003). That physical health is poorer, alcohol consumption is higher and the suicide rate is much greater for divorced men and women than for married people indicates that getting divorced can be traumatic (Kposowa 2003).

Societal Attitudes toward Divorce

Part of the trauma of divorce stems from the attitudes of society toward divorce and divorced persons. In the eyes of some, divorce reflects moral failing or personal inadequacy. "Friends," one woman remarked bitterly, "they drop you like a hot potato." However, negative attitudes have lessened as divorce has become more common. One reason is that people today who recall their parents' marriage as being unhappy or who experienced parental divorce have more accepting attitudes toward the possibility of their own and other people's divorces (Amato 2010).

In general, people who hold negative attitudes toward divorce are likely to view their own divorce as a moral failure. People who hold positive, accepting attitudes toward divorce when they are married report less attachment to the ex-spouse following divorce and better postdivorce adjustment than do people who hold negative, rejecting attitudes (H. Wang and Amato 2000).

Loneliness and Social Readjustment

Even if two married people did not get along, at least they knew that someone else was in the house. After divorce, they begin to realize what it is like to live alone. This adjustment is especially hard on those without children or those whose children are

Disputes over custody may need to be solved by employing a mediator. Child custody and visitation rights issues resolved in mediation seem to have more positive outcomes than court-imposed determinations.

living with the other parent. Holidays can be particularly difficult.

Numerous authorities suggest that the friendship and companionship of other people are among the most essential ingredients for a successful readjustment after divorce; finding new relationships that are positive and supportive helps heal the psychological injury caused by the divorce. Several studies have shown that social network size is a significant predictor of postdivorce adjustment: the more friends one has, the better one adjusts (Amato 2010).

The strongest predictor of divorce adjustment seems to be involvement in an intimate relationship. People with a new dating (or cohabiting) partner report better overall adjustment, less attachment to their ex-spouse, and a more positive outlook on life (H. Wang and Amato 2000). Remarriage also leads to better overall adjustment and a more positive appraisal of life possibly by providing a confidant and a regular sexual partner as well as by increasing economic security.

There seems to be some difference in the social readjustment of divorced people according to their age at the time of divorce, with older individuals having a more difficult time adjusting than do younger individuals (H. Wang and Amato 2000). Older women in particular have a hard time; fewer women than men older than age 40 at the time of divorce remarry. Many of these women have inadequate income to support themselves and their children and miss the economic benefit of marriage.

Additionally, among people who do not remarry, loneliness represents one of the grave consequences of divorce (Gold 2009).

Adjustments to Custody Arrangements

Adjustments to custody arrangements vary. Caring parents miss their children and seek every opportunity to be with them. They often suffer from anxiety and guilt that they cannot be with their children more. Other parents virtually abandon their children, never seeing, calling, or writing them or remembering holidays and birthdays. A third category of parents would like to see their children more often but are prevented from doing so by geographic distance or other circumstances. Overall, research shows that divorce reduces the closeness between noncustodial parents and their children and that there are fewer contacts between older divorced parents and their adult offspring later in life (J. B. Kelly 2007; Santrock 2015).

V. King and Heard (1999) and V. King and Sobolewski (2006) studied family interactions following divorce. They considered father visitation, mother satisfaction with the visitation, and the parental conflict that surrounds the visitation. Overall, they found that mothers prefer involved fathers even if some conflict occurs as a result. Only a small number of mothers were content to have the fathers relatively absent from involvement with them and the children. Interestingly, the quality of the father–child relationship seemed to have a small or modest effect on child well-being. Instead, mother satisfaction appeared to play an influential role in child outcomes: Child well-being suffered when mothers were dissatisfied, whatever the arrangements.

Research examining the effects of divorce on the quality of the father–child relationship and on father well-being has found that divorced fathers with custody perceive poorer relationship quality with their children than do continuously married fathers. Fathers with joint physical custody (co-resident) continue daily involvement with their children but usually have to fight to get it. They feel more in control, and the role of father is likely to be highly salient to them. Nonresident fathers perceive the poorest relationships, have the least contact with their children, and probably feel a loss of control. However, both co-resident and nonresident fathers experience higher levels of depression and unhappiness than continuously married fathers (J. B. Kelly 2007; Shapiro and Lambert 1999).

Noncustodial parents must be concerned about spending enough time with their children.

Stone (2002) explored the role that varying types of social support have on the psychological well-being of nonresidential fathers following divorce. He found that the psychological well-being of nonresidential fathers was associated with a combination of support from the father's workplace, from the father's new intimate partner, from the father's former spouse, and from the father's former in-laws.

Interestingly, the most important variable for fathers was the level of support they reported from their workplace. This suggests that the workplace is an important place for receiving support and encouragement to enhance psychological well-being after a divorce.

Unfortunately, workplaces are typically more mother friendly than father friendly. Numerous changes in the workplace environment could help: valuing fatherhood and the importance of fathers in children's lives; offering father education and training programs; encouraging fathers' participation in their children's schools; supporting fathers who must stay home when a child is ill; and allowing flextime and flexible work hours to help meet the demands of parenthood.

Finances

Speaking about her financial change after a divorce, Amber Rodgers shared, "When you go from a dual income into a single income, it's traumatizing. I literally had my electricity turned off because I just couldn't pay my bills. I had to borrow money from friends" (Malcolm 2012). Going through a divorce and shifting from a dual income to a single income can be stressful and difficult for both men and women, but particularly so for women.

As discussed in Chapter 8, despite some advances, women still generally earn less than males. Furthermore, the mother still ends up with primary custody of the children in a bit more than 80% of cases, although many receive only a little or irregular support from their ex-spouse. Consequently, although most divorced mothers work, mothers with custody of their children often experience serious economic hardship. The custodial parent typically suffers about a 50% decrease in income (Fagan, Kidd, and Potrykus 2011; Kreider 2005).

As will be discussed later, although the court may mandate a parent to pay child support, many custodial parents do not actually receive the full amount awarded to them and some receive no financial support from their ex-spouse to help with the cost of raising their children. The rate of custodial parents and their children living below the poverty level is about three times higher than the rate for married-couple families with children. The poverty rate for custodial mothers compared to custodial fathers is 31% versus 16%, respectively (U.S. Bureau of the Census 2015).

Many divorced female retirees also find themselves struggling financially. More divorced female retirees live in poverty than do widows. Part of this problem stems from divorce settlements that do not take into account retirement and pension benefits for women. Also, many women negotiate to keep the house and primary custody of the children in the divorce settlement, but the house becomes too costly to maintain on their own income and thus becomes a financial drain, preventing them from saving for retirement. Many women do not get a share of their ex-spouse's pension benefits or retirement plans, and women who have stayed at home to raise a family typically have no pension plan of their own. Imagine a scenario in which a couple decides that the woman will stay home to raise the children while the man will work outside the home. After 20 years of this arrangement, they decide to divorce. She is forced to go to work outside of the home at age 45, whereas he maintains his job status and has a 20-year jump on his retirement savings. Given their uneven work history and lower salaries than men, older women are particularly vulnerable to poverty.

Because divorce usually means a dramatic change in finances for both men and women, there are financial strategies that can be beneficial:

- Seek financial help. Meet with a financial advisor before the divorce is finalized.
- Review your bank accounts and any other jointly held assets with your spouse. Know your financial assets.
- Review your financial liabilities. Know the bills for which you will be responsible.
- Cancel anything in the spouse's name that is a credit card.
- Review beneficiary designations on bank accounts, life insurance, and retirement funds. People typically name a spouse on these. If the designation is not changed, an ex-spouse will receive the benefits rather than one's children.
- Reevaluate lifestyle choices such as how much can be spent on cell phones, cable television, entertainment, clothing, or travel.
- Know how you will support yourself on a single income. This is especially crucial to those reentering the workforce.
- Establish an emergency financial fund and, as soon as possible, a longer-term financial investment fund (Malcolm 2012).

Realignment of Responsibilities and Work Roles

A divorced parent with custody of the children is faced with the prospect of an overload of work. Now one parent must perform all the family functions that were formerly shared by two people. She or he also must readjust the parenthood role to include taking over functions formerly fulfilled by the noncustodial parent. As a consequence, the custodial parent devotes less time to the children, listens less, and often has more problems controlling and guiding the children. So, whether male or female, the solo parent must fulfill all family functions and may have little relief from that responsibility.

Contacts with the Ex-Spouse

Understandably, many people are so angry at their spouse when they divorce that they carry these feelings through the divorce process and sometimes for many years after. It is important for the marital partners to work through their anger so as not to taint the relationship with their children and not to place the children in the middle of their disagreements (Gold 2009). Forgiveness is a key step in working through the negative emotions of divorce. Research indicates that forgiveness of a former spouse is associated with a more positive mood and less depression (C. McCabe 2013; Rye and Moore 2015).

The more upsetting the divorce has been and the more difficult the ex-spouse, the less the other person wants to have any postdivorce contact. This is particularly true in cases of remarriage. Most second wives or husbands object to contacts with former spouses, because this usually leads to resentment and conflicts, especially if a bitter ex-spouse tries to cause trouble for the new couple.

When contacts are maintained, it is usually in relation to the children or support money or both. When the children have problems, both parents must be involved and correspond or talk to each other about the problems. In this case, an amicable relationship helps them work things out and makes

things easier on the children (Gold 2009). Sometimes, however, couples must turn to the courts to settle disputes after the divorce.

Most postdivorce disputes are related to visitation rights and child support. Some communities have "father's day" in court, when fathers are taken to task for not making support payments on time. Other disputes may involve spousal support payments.

Some spouses have difficulty breaking emotional attachments following divorce. This increases the subjective stress experienced. The greater the attachment, the more difficulty spouses have adjusting to divorce.

In contrast to these situations, some couples remain friends. One woman commented,

My former husband and I get along better now than when we were married. He came over for dinner the other night; I cooked, and we had a pleasant evening. It's strange, but when we were married, we fought all the time. Now we are really good friends. (Counseling notes)

Kinship Interaction

Both divorced men and women rely on kin in times of divorce, especially for practical support but also for social-emotional support. Most parents are active in easing the strains in the lives of their divorcing adult children and their grandchildren (Gurmen 2015). Men are more likely to rely on kin in the early stages of divorce and women over longer periods of time.

COPING FEATURE

Anger

Anger is a common emotion that can take many forms, such as rage, hostility, irritability, jealousy, resentment, and bitterness. Anger is one of the first emotions displayed by infants (Berk 2013; R. D. Parke and Gauvain 2009) and is typically expressed in response to restraint, discomfort, or hunger. Anger is experienced in a similar pattern among adults. For example, many adults become most irritable when they are hungry, tired, or just do not feel well. The two major reasons for anger are (1) that our pursuit of a desired goal has been frustrated or interrupted by something, and (2) we perceive someone has mistreated us or abandoned us (S. Anderson 2014).

Anger can cause major interpersonal problems and is counterproductive to successful conflict resolution. When we become angry, our brain functioning changes in such a way that we are less capable of effective problem solving. Anger can also contribute to high blood pressure and other physical problems. It is in our best interest to learn to cope effectively with anger. The following are helpful coping strategies:

- **Calm down, relax, and coach yourself through the anger situation.** Deliberately calming down and relaxing can help you think more clearly and maintain self-control. Coach yourself by making statements to yourself such as, "Stay calm and relaxed," "I do not have to allow the other person's behavior to make me angry," or "Take a deep breath; I can be more effective if I don't blow up."

- **Analyze your appraisal of the anger-provoking situation.** Is this really worth getting angry about? Am I angry because of what the other person did or am I really angry because I just do not feel well? Sometimes our anger is irrational because we are making unreasonable demands based on irrational beliefs such as the following:

  1. Everyone should agree with me and, if they do not, they are stupid, morally corrupt, or misinformed.

  2. I am a nice person and everyone should treat me nicely at all times and, if they do not, they are no good.

  3. I should never experience frustration.

  If we have these unrealistic beliefs and make corresponding irrational demands, we are certain to become angry. An effective coping strategy is to become aware of such irrational beliefs and replace them with more rational statements such as, "I do not like to be frustrated and I prefer that people treat me well, but not everyone will treat me nicely. Other people have bad days, too. Actually, most people are nice."

- **Understand how others react to anger.** An effective interpersonal skill is to be aware of how our anger will impact the other person. Not surprisingly, research indicates largely negative reactions to anger. Among the most common reactions are hostility, hurt feelings, rejection, defiance, indifference, or lack of concern. Clearly these are not in the angry person's best interests.

- **Be assertive, not aggressive.** Being assertive is an effective way to cope with anger because it prevents anger from building up and it prevents misunderstandings. Assertiveness means communicating your feelings, wishes, and thoughts directly and honestly. It means standing up for your rights. Assertiveness means you do not allow others to take advantage of you or push you into doing something you do not wish to do. Being assertive increases feelings of self-efficacy (feeling that you can cope successfully with difficult circumstances). Assertiveness does not mean being pushy or aggressive. Aggression, on the other hand, involves hostility, is often aimed at taking advantage of others, typically increases anger, and tends to have a destructive effect on relationships.

- **Forgive.** Since a great deal of anger is experienced because we perceive someone has mistreated us in some way, it is appropriate that we consider forgiveness as an effective way to cope with anger. Forgiveness does not mean you approve of or necessarily forget what the other person has done. When you forgive, you make the decision not to dwell on the negative feelings associated with the mistreatment. You also make the decision to accept that the other person is not perfect. Your act of forgiveness is liberating and releases you from the burden of carrying resentment and anger. Instead of being caught up in bitterness and revenge, you can move forward with your life in a positive way. Forgiveness helps you avoid being controlled by the hurtful actions of another (Kleinke 2002; C. McCabe 2013; Rye and Moore 2015).

Divorce is a multigenerational process that affects parents and other kin, as well as the divorcing couple and their children. Positive support from parents can have an important effect on the divorcing person's adjustment. Helpful behavior includes the following:

- **Emotional support.** This involves listening, showing empathy, and affirming love and affection.

- **Child care.** This might mean occasional babysitting or taking the grandchildren for weekends.

- **Good, rational advice.** Examples include helping think through decisions and solving problems.

- **Respect for autonomy and regression.** Divorcing people have contrasting needs. Some want autonomy in decision making; others want to regress to dependency for a while.

Overall, continued contact with former in-laws after divorce is not as frequent as with one's own family. Most of the positive relationships with ex-kin involve grandchildren, with custodial parents maintaining more contact than noncustodial parents (Gurmen 2015).

Children and Divorce

There has been considerable concern over the number of children exposed to parental divorce and how both the short-term and the long-term aspects of divorce affect a child. There is no set answer to how divorce affects children because children are as varied as their parents' marriages. However, there is a need to discuss the whole subject of children and divorce in more detail and to examine the many facets of the sometimes conflicting and controversial research on the topic.

Child Custody

The term **custody** refers to both legal custody (who holds decision-making rights) and physical custody

---

Forgiveness and Conflict-Resolution Skills

Although it might seem contradictory at first glance, knowledge of the characteristics of strong families can be useful in divorce. These traits help minimize the stress and hurt of the divorce process and promote the positive adjustment and recovery of everyone concerned.

Many of the subtraits in spiritual well-being are helpful—honesty, faith, hope, compassion, and dependability, for example. One that is especially helpful is the practice of forgiveness. Dwelling on hurts and grievances builds resentment and bitterness; the ability to forgive is a quality of couples who enjoy a high degree of marital success. It is also a quality of "successful" divorces. Forgiving helps ex-spouses move forward in their lives in positive ways (Rye and Moore 2015). The absence of antagonism and resentment helps children maintain positive relationships with both parents, thus helping them through a difficult transition.

A second quality of strong families that is certainly relevant to minimizing the devastation of divorce is constructive conflict resolution. Avoiding the escalation of conflict is critical to keeping civil interactions among all the individuals involved. When conflict builds in intensity, they magnify one another's negative traits and behaviors, become convinced that the others will not change (and that they do not need to), and can come to an emotional climate of wanting to destroy one another. It is, of course, essential to retreat from such a destructive level of conflict to come to a problem-solving level, where the focus is on solving the problem (for example, custody arrangements and child support) rather than on revenge. Key elements to problem solving are respecting disagreement; identifying the specific problem that must be solved; identifying and evaluating different options for solving the problem; and choosing the option that is best for everyone.

(where the children will live). In **sole legal custody**, the noncustodial parent forfeits the right to make decisions about the children's health, education, or religious training; in effect, the custodial parent is given control over childrearing. In **joint legal custody**, custody is shared between the two parents, with parental rights and obligations left as they were during the marriage. There are advantages and disadvantages to both arrangements.

Traditionally, sole custody of the children has been granted to the mother unless it can be established that she is unfit. It is not surprising that mothers tend to be more satisfied than fathers with custody arrangements. When mothers have physical custody and thus primary control of their children, fathers' access to their children can be significantly reduced, leading fathers to feel distant from their parental roles (Cherlin 2009; Schindler and Coley 2012). However, more men are becoming custodial parents because courts are taking into consideration the best interests of the child and awarding joint custody—in which both parents are responsible—more often. The growing popularity of shared custody is largely a response to the changing gender roles in society, such as the gradual move toward a more equal sharing of family responsibilities between mothers and fathers (H. Juby, Le Bourdais, and Marcil-Gratton 2005). Studies show that joint custody has advantages for some children by maintaining an ongoing involvement with both parents and that children in joint physical or legal custody are better adjusted than children in sole-custody settings (Bauserman 2002; Berk 2013). However, not everyone agrees that it is the best for children, particularly when parents cannot reach the necessary level of cooperation to make it work (H. Juby, Le Bourdais, and Marcil-Gratton 2005).

In cases of custody dispute, a mediator may be employed or a child development expert appointed to investigate the family situation and to recommend custody arrangements to the court. The wishes of older children are usually taken into consideration in deciding with whom they will reside.

Child Support

Providing for continued support of children is one of the obligations of parenthood. Under law, this is an obligation of both the mother and the father, whether the parents are married or not. In situations where one parent has physical custody, child

After the first year or so following separation, problems of communicating, showing affection, and spending time together tend to diminish for the noncustodial parent and the children.

support awards are the most common mechanism by which noncustodial parents are required to transfer economic resources to their children. These transfers are often critical to the well-being of the children.

According to the U.S. Census Bureau data, an estimated 13.7 million parents had custody of 22 million children under age 21 whose other parent lived somewhere else. Overall, about one-quarter (26%) of all children under 21 living in families had a

custody A term that refers to both legal custody (the parent's right to make decisions regarding the welfare of the child) and physical custody (the parent's right to have the child living with him or her).

sole legal custody Situation in which the noncustodial parent forfeits the right to make decisions about the children's health, education, or religious training.

joint legal custody Custody shared by both parents, both of whom are responsible for childrearing and for making decisions regarding the child.

parent not living in the home. The percentage of black children in families who lived with their custodial parent while their other parent lived elsewhere (49%) was more than twice as large as the percentage for white (22.4%) or Hispanic (23.4%) children. Among children of other races, including Native American and Asian, about 13% lived in custodial-parent families. The large majority (82%) of the custodial parents were mothers, whereas 18% were fathers (Grall 2011).

About half (51%) of custodial parents have either legal (91%) or informal (9%) agreements regarding child support they are to receive. No legal agreement may be made (or the parties may use an informal arrangement) for several reasons: the custodial parent does not feel a need for an agreement; the other parent provides what he/she can; the other parent cannot afford to pay; the child stays with the other parent part of the time; or the custodial parent does not want the other parent to pay or/and does not want contact with the other parent (Grall 2011). Custodial parents who were due child support payments under the terms of legal awards or informal agreements were due an average of $5,500 per year, or slightly less than $500 per month (Grall 2011; U.S. Bureau of the Census 2012).

Of those custodial parents who were awarded child support, some 71% received at least a portion of the money. Forty-two percent of mothers and 34% of fathers received the full amount. Some 29% received no payments. The average amount of child support received by custodial parents was about $3,630 a year, or about $300 per month. About 60% of custodial parents also received noncash support on behalf of their children, such as gifts for birthdays or holidays, clothes, groceries/food, medical expenses, and payments for child care or summer camps (Grall 2011).

There are essentially three systems for determining the amount of child support awards: (1) specifying a straight percentage of the noncustodial parent's income based on the number of dependent children; (2) calculating support according to the combined income of both parents, with each paying the percentage that is his or her share; and (3) taking both parents' incomes into consideration but allowing for exemptions such as providing health insurance or child care, work-related expenses, or new dependents of a noncustodial parent.

In an attempt to establish fairer standards for child support obligations, federal legislation requires each state to establish standards for determining child support, and judges who deviate from this standard must provide grounds, in writing, for doing so. This legislation gave the courts less discretion than they previously had held, but standards still vary widely from state to state. There is considerable disagreement about how much money parents should pay for child support, with a large discrepancy between what states recommend and what parents think is fair. Many parents feel that there should be a reduction in the father's obligation if the mother remarries but not if only the father remarries. Thus, a reduction of financial support appears to relate mostly to the mother's perceived increased income and not to additional financial responsibilities assumed by the father.

The legal system has three approaches to promote compliance with support orders. The deterrence-based approach uses legal punishment to ensure payment of support. It can be either specific, which involves punishing an individual who is delinquent in payment to prevent future delinquency, or general, which involves punishing offenders to discourage others from becoming delinquent. These punishments include interception of tax refunds, liens on property, suspension of driver's license, garnishment of wages, or imprisonment. There is some statistical evidence that the deterrence-based approach does increase child support payments.

Another approach is based on compliance. Rather than relying on punishment after the fact, this approach intervenes before the law is broken. The compliance approach uses random checking, or checking of potential offenders, resulting in funds being withheld from earnings before a child support payment is missed. This approach also has been shown to have a positive effect on payments.

Finally, the consensus-based approach relies not on fear of punishment or on payment regulation, but on societal acceptance and concurring norms. There are two strategies for establishing the proper norm: (1) enforcing the law consistently until behavior changes and (2) using the media to convince the public that the norm has merit. Establishing standards for determining child support and encouraging judges to use consistent criteria when awarding child support are two examples of the consensus-based approach.

Studies have shown that compliance with support orders is positively affected by both income withholding and the father's perception of fairness.

They also have revealed that, once a parent feels that the order is fair, withholding no longer has an impact on compliance and withholding does not reduce compliance among those who perceive the order to be fair. These results suggest that policy makers should focus on improving perceptions of fairness while continuing to promote income withholding in efforts to improve compliance (I. Lin 2000).

Making regular child support payments is important to children's welfare. It lets children know that they are cared for by both parents. It better enables the children to have the necessities of life; to live in better neighborhoods and housing; and to have adequate food, clothing, and education. For custodial parents who receive the full amount of child support payments due, child support makes up 21% of annual income. For custodial parents below the poverty level who receive full payments, child support makes up 61% of annual income (Grall 2011). Conscientious payment of child support helps prevent children from being penalized because of the actions of parents. Children must be loved and nurtured by both parents, regardless of their parents' marital status.

Visitation Rights

Ordinarily, visitation rights are granted to the noncustodial parent. These rights may be unlimited—allowing visitation at any time—or they may be restrictive—limiting visitation only to specific times. The majority of parents not living with their children had joint custody or visitation privileges. If the parents had an agreement for child support, 83% had visitation or joint custody. If there was no agreement or no child support was awarded, 68% had visitation or shared custody (Grall 2011). A vindictive ex-spouse can make life miserable by managing to be away with the children when it is time for the other parent to visit, poisoning the children's minds against the other parent, refusing to allow the children to phone or write, or using visitation rights as a weapon—for example, denying visitation if child support is late (even for a legitimate reason).

Of course, noncustodial parents can be difficult, too. They may pick up or return children early (or late); they, too, may be critical of the other parent or "pick" the children for information. In a pattern that is emotionally devastating to children, some noncustodial parents repeatedly build up a child's hopes ("We'll go to the zoo this weekend") but then fail to follow through or often cancel visits without a reason (or just do not show up).

Reactions of Children

A significant number of clinicians emphasize that children perceive divorce as a major negative event that stimulates painful emotions, confusion, and uncertainty (Amato 2005; D'Onofrio et al. 2006; Lansford et al. 2006; Uphold-Carrier and Utz 2012). As discussed earlier, children of divorce are often cited as having poorer relationships with family members and more social and emotional problems than children of intact families (Santrock 2015). For example, adolescents of divorced parents report higher levels of aggression than do adolescents of intact marriages (Hamama and Ronen-Shenhav 2012). A large national study of more than 2,000 adults, ranging in age from 25 to 86 years old, indicated long-lasting effects of divorce, regardless of the age at which the child experienced the divorce of parents. The results suggested that experiencing parental divorce appears to have long-term impact on the child's mental health and on family solidarity (the levels of family support and family strain). Specifically, those children who experienced the divorce of their parents showed a significantly higher risk for depression and for lower levels of family solidarity during midlife and older ages than children of intact marriages. The higher risk for depression and for lower levels of family solidarity was a consistent pattern regardless of whether the parental divorce was experienced during childhood or adulthood (Uphold-Carrier and Utz 2012).

This research suggests that parental divorce may set a chain of negative consequences in motion. Conflict between the parents during and after their divorce can generate emotions such as anger, hurt, anxiety, and depression in the parents—which often leads to a decrease in the quality of parenting and/or disrupted parent–child relationships. Contacts the child has with other family members such as grandparents may also be reduced. For many children (of divorce), the long-term detriments in both the quality and the quantity of contact between family members can lead to less social support and feelings of connectedness, lowered sense of control, less stability and sense of life predictability, less trust, and unhappy marriages or failed romantic relationships—which are associated with higher risks for later-life depression and lower levels of emotional well-being. These long-term effects are experienced by many children of divorce, regardless of whether the parental divorce was experienced by a young child or by an adult child (Bulloch et al. 2009; Riggio and Valenzuela 2011; Uphold-Carrier and Utz 2012).

Even so, many clinicians feel that the majority of children regain psychological equilibrium within a few years and resume a normal curve of development. In fact, some children of divorce believe, as adults, that their parents' decision to divorce was the right one and do not wish their parents had remained married (Ahrons 2004).

One of the debates in the divorce literature is the "good enough marriage" versus the "good enough divorce" argument (H. Harvey and Fine 2004). Research consistently finds that children whose parents are separated or divorced are more likely to have behavioral problems (for a review of this literature see Amato 2001; Reifman et al. 2001; or Wallerstein and Lewis 2004). However, children in intact families with high levels of parental conflict also have high levels of problem behaviors. Thus, although divorce is disruptive to children, living with two quarreling parents is also problematic. Some researchers conclude that parent conflict poses a greater threat to children's well-being than does family structure per se (Amato 2005), although other researchers strongly disagree (see Wallerstein and Lewis 2004).

Some researchers feel that, for a substantial portion of children, the upheaval in their lives interferes with normal social-emotional growth. This view is substantiated by Judith Wallerstein in a 25-year study of 60 divorced families, involving 130 children, living in Marin County, California (Wallerstein and Lewis 1998). Wallerstein found that 10 years after divorce, half the women and one-third of the men were still so angry at their former spouse that this anger colored their relationship with their children.

The children in her study had memories of abandonment, terror, and loneliness. They felt that they had been denied the basic security with which to grow and that they had lost their childhood by feeling compelled to assume responsibility for their parents' well-being.

The effects of divorce did not disappear over time. High levels of alcohol abuse, promiscuity, and delinquency showed up 10 to 15 years after the parents' divorce. Half the children entered adulthood as underachieving, self-deprecating young men and women. Financial support for college was often missing because few fathers offered consistent financial support throughout childhood and toward higher education. Overall, Wallerstein concluded from decades of research that divorce causes serious harm to children who experience it.

Wallerstein and Lewis (2004) conducted a follow-up study of the original group of children after 25 years and added a comparison group of peers from the same community. The conclusions were similar: there was a wide gulf between growing up in intact versus divorced families, and children of divorce experienced difficulties achieving love, sexual intimacy, and commitment to marriage and parenthood. They attribute the problems in the children of divorced parents to the divorce itself,

Children often perceive divorce as a major negative event that stimulates painful emotions, confusion, and uncertainty.

rather than to the conflicted marriage or the emotional health of their parents.

However, it is important to note that Wallerstein's original sample (Wallerstein and Lewis 1998) came from an affluent area during years of rapid social change in the United States. There was no control group with which to compare findings. No study was done of how tension prior to divorce affected children. So how widely these findings can be applied to other children from divorced families is not certain.

We do know that the effects of divorce on children depend on many variables. One important variable is age of the child at the time of the divorce. Younger children (under 5) often experience guilt and blame themselves for their parents' divorce. They may also have nightmares and anxiety; they may regress to younger-age behaviors such as having toileting "accidents" long after they have been "potty-trained."

Children between the ages of 5 and 8 at the time of the divorce tend to react with great sadness and are fearful and insecure; they frequently feel they have been abandoned. Children 9 to 12 years of age at the time of the divorce are distinguished from children of younger ages by their frequent feelings of confusion, intense anger, and often the rejection of one parent. A significant number of school-age children show a decline in math and reading scores (Amato and Anthony 2014).

Adolescents, in addition to experiencing the emotions of loss, sadness, and anger, also often engage in "acting-out" behaviors such as sexual promiscuity, drug and alcohol abuse, and aggressive behavior. Adolescents tend to have the most difficult time dealing with parental divorce (Weston 2009).

Other factors that influence the effects of divorce on children include whether divorce improves or reduces the quality of parenting, whether divorce improves or worsens the emotional atmosphere of the home, whether the divorce is amicable or bitter, what the effect of divorce is on the parents, and what custody and living arrangements are worked out. Regardless of the variables at play, divorce is a challenging adjustment for children.

In the time immediately surrounding the divorce, children may go through a period of mourning and grief, and the mood or feeling may be one of sadness and dejection. Another common reaction of children is to blame themselves. If the children are a major source of stress or conflict for the couple, the children may feel they are responsible. Some children think that the departing parent is abandoning them because they have not been "good boys or girls." Yet another common reaction is for children to try to bring their parents together. They wish that everyone could live together and be happy (a reconciliation fantasy). The longing for a reunited family may go on for a long time, until children are able to understand the realities of the situation.

Adjustments of Children

Children must make numerous adjustments when their parents divorce. One ongoing adjustment may be to being caught "in the middle" of parental conflict and misery. The following are five common ways in which divorced parents put children in this unhappy situation:

- Demeaning each other in front of the children.
- Asking children to deliver hostile messages to each other.
- Encouraging children to keep secrets from the other parent.
- Asking children to reveal intrusive personal information about the other parent ("pumping them").
- Undermining each other's parenting authority (J. B. Kelly 2010; Rye and Moore 2015).

Children have other adjustments to make. They must adjust to the absence of one parent, often one on whom they depended deeply for affection and help. One teenage girl remarked, "The hardest thing for me was to get used to living without my father. I never really realized how much I needed him until he left" (Counseling notes).

Older children also may be required to assume more responsibility for family functioning: cooking, housekeeping, even earning money to help support the family. This is usually a maturing experience for them, but it is also a difficult adjustment. Some children, used to having everything, have a difficult time realizing that money is short and that they cannot buy the clothes and other things they used to buy.

Parental divorce when children are preteens to teens may interfere with sibling relationships. In a study of sibling relationship quality among young adults who had experienced childhood parental divorce, Riggio (2001) found that individuals who experienced parental divorce between ages 8 and 19 experienced significantly fewer positive feelings toward siblings in adulthood. They also recalled fewer positive feelings, beliefs, and behaviors toward siblings in childhood compared to individuals who experienced parental divorce before age 8 and compared to individuals from intact families.

Of course, special adjustments are necessary for children of divorced parents. For example, when a parent begins to date again and to become emotionally involved with another person, the children must share their parent with another adult. If the parent remarries, as the majority do, the children are confronted with adjustment to a stepparent and perhaps stepsiblings. (This will be discussed in more detail in Chapter 17.) Parents, as well as grandparents, will be required to work on new roles in their children's lives as children pass through various developmental stages (Wallerstein and Blakeslee 2003).

Research by Storksen et al. (2006) of more than 9,000 adolescents and their parents suggests that children may hide problems stemming from parental divorce during childhood that may later manifest in adolescence. The adolescents experienced a "double exposure" effect of being exposed to the divorce and to parental depression and anxiety. The adolescents in this study who were from divorced families reported more symptoms of anxiety and depression, lower feelings of well-being, and more school-related problems than did adolescents from nondivorced families. Depression and anxiety increased with age and were higher among girls.

The availability of social support is an important resource that can serve as a protection or buffer from the effects of the depression, anxiety, and anger that many children of divorce experience. For example, research evidence indicates that adolescents with greater social support express less hostility and aggression (Hamama and Ronen-Shenhav 2012). Social support may be provided by grandparents, siblings, other relatives, teachers, friends, social service agencies, and—hopefully—one or both parents. The most important message the child needs to hear, regardless of the source of the support, is, "You are important to me! I care about you."

Some parents and children attend programs designed to help the children cope with divorce. Other parents attend skill-building intervention sessions that have been shown to improve children's postdivorce adjustment (Wolchik et al. 2005). One study conducted focus groups for children to talk about their problems and feelings about being caught in the middle of their parents' disputes, parents not keeping them informed, and complications arising when a parent's new partner enters the family. Children expressed that the best way a friend could help them cope with divorce was by discussing it, provided the friend had also been through a divorce (Hans and Fine 2001).

Other research has found that short coping programs can help ease the pain in children's lives caused from divorce (Gilman, Schneider, and Shulak 2005). For example, a program designed to strengthen a mother's parenting skills and her child's ability to cope after a divorce made a significant difference in the overall well-being of the child. Adolescents who had participated in the program compared to those who did not showed fewer mental health problems, had less alcohol and drug use, had fewer sexual partners, and showed fewer externalizing problems such as acting out. Another study examined an intervention program designed to assist the parents of children age 6 or younger as they began the separation/divorce process. They found that the program benefited the participating families by resulting in lower conflict, greater father involvement, and better outcomes for children compared to a control group that did not participate in an intervention program. Parents also were more cooperative and less likely to need custody evaluations and other costly services (Pruett, Insabella, and Gustafson 2005). Thus, it appears that programs designed to help families cope with the changes and challenges that are inevitable with a divorce can be helpful.

Difficulties may persist in parent–child relationships as children from divorced families grow into adulthood (Lewis, Johnson-Reitz, and Wallerstein 2004). Yet, it is important to note that divorced and blended families have some of the same forms of resiliency as intact families (Rodgers and Rose 2002). Although children of divorce may have a difficult time in the beginning, most learn to adjust and do well. Divorce reorganizes a family, but it does not destroy it (Berk 2013).

Divorce and the Single-Mother Family

There are many different types of single-parent families, from wealthy older widowers to poor, young teenage mothers. There are also many different types of concerns, from children growing up in poverty to the belief that single-parent families deprive children of a vital need to be raised by both a mother and a father. Our focus here is on single-mother families created through divorce.

One public policy that has been put into place to address the economic difficulties of many single-mother families is the collection of child support from what are typically described as "deadbeat dads." As discussed in the text, federal law mandates that noncustodial fathers pay child support, and one means of collecting this support is to garnish wages. However, because fathers typically remarry and form new families, some argue that this policy merely takes money from one child to feed another. Sugarman (2003) reports that for policy to really address the economic disparity of single-mother families, it must focus on the feminization of poverty, wage disparity, and a living wage.

Even if single-mother families were economically on par with other families, there are still the concerns that single-parent families are inferior to two-parent families and that single motherhood undermines the importance of fathers in families. Some people believe that policy should be directed at encouraging marriage and making divorce more difficult to obtain. Sugarman (2003) points out that many conservatives construe several current policies as actually encouraging single

parenting (e.g., easy access to divorce and welfare, coddling of pregnant schoolgirls, and poor two-parent families generally not qualifying for welfare in contrast to single-parent families). Indeed, public policy could eliminate no-fault divorce and make divorce more difficult to obtain. However, this would probably make divorce more expensive and acrimonious, and people would have to grapple with the question of what circumstances constitute grounds for a divorce.

Questions to Consider

Should noncustodial fathers be forced to pay child support? Why or why not?

Should a father's child support amount be reduced when he remarries? When he has another child?

Should a custodial mother receive less child support when she remarries?

Why do you think many single mothers cannot earn enough money to support their children? What policies might help?

Should men who impregnate women, and who have no intention of claiming responsibility for the child, somehow be made accountable for child support? Why or why not?

Should policy discourage people from forming single-parent families? For example, should there be incentives for pregnant women to marry? Should divorce be more difficult to obtain when children are involved? Discuss.

Summary

1. A number of factors affect the probability of divorce: age at first marriage, early childbearing, frequency of attendance at religious services, socioeconomic status, ethnic background, geographic area, parental divorce, and the number of children in the family.

2. Disaffection, or the loss of intimacy and love, is a major component of marital dissolution. It develops in three phases, during which feelings of anger, disappointment, apathy, and hopelessness grow until the costs of staying together are perceived as outweighing the rewards.

3. The decision to divorce is difficult. There are four basic considerations in deciding whether to remain married: satisfaction with or attractions of the marriage, barriers to getting out of the marriage, the attractiveness of alternatives to the marriage, and the intensity of the emotional pain generated by the unhappy marriage.

4. There are three major alternatives to divorce: marriage counseling, marriage enrichment programs, and structured separation, during which couples try to resolve their problems.

5. Five types of situations may support a couple's decision to consider structured marital separation: extreme conflict, absence of spousal reinforcement, feelings of being constricted or smothered, a situational or midlife transition, and indecision regarding divorce.

6. In no-fault divorce, the spouses petition for divorce on the basis of irremediable breakdown of the marriage or irreconcilable differences.

7. Sometimes spouses fight over property and finances, spousal support, child support, and child custody, using the children as pawns to win concessions. Such actions are particularly hurtful to the children.

8. One of the most helpful solutions to property, custody, child support, and other issues is to use a mediator to help resolve differences.

9. Many of the effects of no-fault divorce have been helpful: less extensive and less expensive litigation, the greater possibility of friendly divorce, and partial elimination of the punitive element of moral condemnation that pervaded divorce for centuries.

10. Some effects of no-fault divorce are not always helpful. More men are filing because the threat of recrimination has been removed. Although this may be of some advantage to them, their spouses have been placed at a disadvantage in trying to attain fair financial and property settlements. Overall, men may be better off financially after the divorce; many women and their children are forced to live in poverty.

11. The major adjustment problems of adults after divorce involve emotional trauma, the negative attitudes of society, loneliness and social readjustment, adjustments of the noncustodial spouse, finances, realignment of responsibilities and work roles, contacts with the ex-spouse, and kinship interaction.

12. The mother's satisfaction with the father's involvement following divorce is an important predictor of children's well-being.

13. Custodial fathers report better relationship quality with their children than do noncustodial fathers. However, continuously married fathers report the highest level of relationship quality with their children.

14. The term *custody* refers to both legal and physical custody. In the past, the mother typically got sole custody of the children. Today, the courts strive to consider the best interests of the children.

15. In joint legal custody, the responsibility for parenting is given to both parents. They both have parental rights and responsibilities for childrearing, as they did during the marriage. Joint custody requires the active cooperation and responsibility of both parents, as well as the ability to get along with each other.

16. Providing for continued support of the children is the responsibility of both the mother and the father, even if they are not married. Although many custodial parents get child support awards, a large number of parents do not actually receive even a portion of the award. There are different systems for calculating the amount of child support payments. Laws have been enacted to force delinquent parents to pay. Making regular child support payments is important to children's welfare.

17. Ordinarily, the parent not given custody has visitation rights. Although frequent visitation is associated with good noncustodial parent–child relationships and benefits the child, the association is mediated by the quality of the postdivorce parental relationship.

18. Many parents have problems in their marriage that begin years before a divorce. This marital discord affects children negatively because parents are unable to meet their children's needs.

19. Children perceive divorce as a major negative event that stimulates painful emotions, confusion, and uncertainty. The effects of divorce on children depend on many variables.

20. Wallerstein found long-term negative effects of divorce on children that continued to show up in adulthood.

Key Terms

conciliation counseling

custody

joint legal custody

no-fault divorce

sole legal custody

structured separation

Questions for Thought

1. What behaviors or problems are most damaging to a marital relationship? Explain the reasons for your selection.

2. What do you think are some of the common emotional and physical effects of divorce?

3. What can a couple do to minimize negative feelings and destructive behavior in a divorce?

4. In your opinion, why does marriage counseling at times *not* succeed? Contrast your views with what is presented in the "At Issue Today" box.

5. Neither an unhappy home nor a divorce is easy for children. With this in mind, what recommendations would you make for a husband and wife with children involved in a very unhappy marriage? What might these parents do to help their children if they divorce? If they do not?

For Further Reading

Ahrons, C. (2005). *The good divorce: Keeping your family together when your marriage comes apart.* New York: Perennial Currents. Shows couples how they can move beyond the early stages of breakup and learn to deal with the transition from a nuclear to a "binuclear" family.

http://www.DadsDivorce.com has resources for fathers and men going through divorce, including information about custody and child support. Check out child support for your state on the child support calculator.

Gold, L. (2009). *The healthy divorce.* Naperville, IL: Sphinx. Provides divorcing parents with the tools to negotiate the ending of a marriage without harming their children.

McWhorter Sember, S. (2005). *No-fight divorce: Using mediation to end your marriage with less conflict, time, and money.* New York: McGraw–Hill. Presents options for a more amicable divorce.

Oliver, K. Kim Oliver explores "Divorce causes: 5 Marriage mistakes that lead to divorce." http://www.huffingtonpost.com/2013/03/06.

Teyber, E. (2001). *Helping children cope with divorce.* New York: Lexington Books. Teaches divorcing parents what they can do to help their children successfully adjust to divorce.

Wolfinger, N. (2005). *Understanding the divorce cycle: The children of divorce in their own marriages.* Cambridge, UK: Cambridge University Press. Discusses how parental divorce affects offspring marital behavior.

CHAPTER **17**

Coming Together
Remarriage and Stepparenting

CHAPTER OUTLINE

Learning Objectives

Remarriage
- Divorce or Success in Remarriage?

FAMILY STRENGTHS PERSPECTIVE: *Happy versus Unhappy Stepcouples*
- Courtship and Mate Selection in Remarriage
- Preparing for Remarriage
- Facets of Remarriage

Challenges of Remarriage
- Complex Relationships
- Ambiguous Family Boundaries
- Ambiguous Cultural Norms
- Carrying Expectations from One Marriage to Another

AT ISSUE TODAY: *Merging Families and Finances*
- Finances
- Relationships with the Ex-Spouse
- Family Relationships from a Previous Marriage

COPING FEATURE: *Humor*

Stepfamilies
- Stepfathers
- Stepfamily Turning Points

Stepparent–Stepchild Relationships

CULTURAL PERSPECTIVE: *Stepfamilies in Cultural Context*
- Child Well-Being in Stepfamilies

- Facilitating Bonds between Stepparents and Stepchildren
- Coparents and Parenting Coalitions

Stepsibling Relationships

PERSONAL PERSPECTIVE: *Being a Stepmom*

A QUESTION OF POLICY: *Stepfamily Rights*

Summary

Key Terms

Questions for Thought

For Further Reading

LEARNING OBJECTIVES

AFTER READING THE CHAPTER, YOU SHOULD BE ABLE TO DO THE FOLLOWING:

- Identify trends relating to remarriage and stepfamilies.
- Discuss various factors in relation to remarriage: types of remarried families, divorce and success in remarriage, courtship and mate selection in remarriage, finances, and marital satisfaction.
- Describe six facets of remarriage.
- Compare family relationships in primary families and stepfamilies, giving both similarities and differences.
- Discuss the major challenges in stepparent–stepchild relationships.
- Explain the implications of ambiguous family boundaries and cultural norms for blended families.
- Describe coparenting and parenting coalitions.
- Discuss basic information about stepsibling relationships.

"My mother remarried when I was 23. I am 25 now and I am not really comfortable with the new family situation. My stepfather has two sons and one daughter who are all a good bit younger than me. They're nice enough, but I have little in common with them—after all, I've moved out on my own and am engaged to be married. My mother is happy in her new marriage and I am glad for her; however, it just seems strange for me. We rarely talk anymore and we used to tell each other everything. She spends all her time with her new husband and *his* family. And there is an inheritance issue. My mother owns a successful business that she started about 20 years ago. Now she says that inheritance will be shared with my new stepsiblings. It isn't fair to me and I don't feel right about it. I just don't feel a part of this family."

According to the cultural ideal, marriage lasts until "death do us part." Historically, this marital commitment was largely borne out, and most marriages ended with the death of a spouse, often when dependent children were still present. As life expectancy has increased and as cultural norms for divorce have changed, more marriages are ended by divorce than by death. Whether the marriage ends by divorce or death, remarriage and the formation of stepfamilies have become common.

Remarriage

Today, close to one-fourth of married couples have been married before (Livingston 2014; Siordia 2014). More than 2 million people in America divorce each year; the majority (57%) eventually remarry and do so rather quickly. The median time for remarrying after a divorce is about 3.5 years for both women and men. The median age for second marriages is 35 for men and 33 for women. The median duration for second marriages is 8.6 years for men and 7.2 years for women—similar to the duration of first marriages (U.S. Bureau of the Census 2015).

Many widowed persons also remarry, although they are less likely than divorced individuals to consider remarriage and take longer to become interested in dating. A certain amount of time is needed before remarriage in either situation. Divorced people who remarry too quickly may not have worked through the pain and troubling issues of the previous marriage. Widows and widowers who remarry too soon may not have dealt with grief and loss sufficiently to

be emotionally prepared to enter a new intimate relationship. Although there is no specific time that is right for every person who remarries, a period of 3 to 5 years before remarriage is considered desirable (Lauer and Lauer 2011).

A good number of people remarry quickly; this is likely a factor contributing to greater instability in remarriages; about 39% of divorced women remarry within 3 years of the divorce. Research indicates that 50% of divorcing custodial parents were already dating *before* officially filing for divorce (E. Anderson et al. 2004).

Spouses who initiate a divorce tend to remarry more quickly than those who did not initiate the divorce, but this differential diminishes after about 3 years of being separated. The initiator status is a stronger predictor of remarriage among relatively older women than among younger women, which suggests that older women may be more willing to stay in an unhappy marriage until the likelihood of finding a better relationship is good (Sweeney 2002).

Remarriage rates vary by ethnic background. Whites are most likely to remarry; 60% of those who were previously married will remarry. This compares to 51% of Hispanics, 48% of blacks, and 46% of Asians (Livingston 2014).

Divorce or Success in Remarriage?

The majority of survey studies have revealed that the probability of divorce is greater in remarriages than in first marriages (Karney 2015; Whitton et al. 2013). It has been estimated that some 67% of second marriages and 73% of third marriages will end in divorce; this compares to 40% to 50% of first marriages (Banschik 2012).

Major reasons for why remarriages have a higher rate of divorce than do first-time marriages include the high degree of complexity in remarried relationships, the challenges of stepfamily integration and dealing with a series of complex changes. These challenges range from predivorce tensions to separation and reorganization of households, and reorganization of parent–child relations/establishment of stepparent–stepchild relationships (Brown and Robinson 2012; Karney 2015).

Although these stressors and challenges of remarried families are well documented by research, it is important to understand the strengths that help many remarried families to adapt successfully. Family resilience is one such strength; this is the ability of a

FAMILY STRENGTHS PERSPECTIVE

Happy versus Unhappy Stepcouples

David Olson (2009) conducted a large research study in which 19,198 happy, satisfied stepfamily couples were compared with 15,433 unhappy, unsatisfied stepfamily couples with regard to specific aspects of their relationships. Following are the percentages of couples who agreed in each area and who viewed it as a strength:

Issue/Area/Statement	% Happy Couples	% Unhappy Couples
We have good conflict resolution.	91	16
We understand each other's feelings.	93	21
A partner's moodiness is not a problem.	79	12
We agree on how to spend money.	80	26
We enjoy many of the same leisure activities.	85	32
Jealousy is not an issue.	89	44
We are satisfied with how our spiritual natures and beliefs are expressed.	88	47
We have resolved issues and hurts from past relationships.	61	21

family to emerge stronger over time after encountering challenging and difficult circumstances—rather than being defeated or destroyed by them.

Research, using both quantitative and qualitative measures, identified the following factors as important in enabling remarried families to adapt successfully—to be resilient—when faced with the challenges of remarriage and stepfamily living (Brown and Robinson 2012; Orbuch 2012; Shafer, Jensen, and Larsen 2014; Whitton et al. 2013):

- Family hardiness: a high degree of commitment and persistence in meeting challenges;

- Good problem-solving skills;

- A high degree of time together and engagement in family routines;

- Spirituality: receiving strength through prayer; feeling a spiritual closeness with God; and relying on God for help with coping;

People who remarry typically are older, more emotionally mature, and more experienced than when they married for the first time.

- Respecting boundaries: maintaining clarity about roles and rules; accepting and including each person as a valued member of the remarried family; avoiding exclusive/closed systems such as a close relationship between biological parent and child that does not include the stepparent or stepchildren;
- Love and compassion;
- Good communication; and
- Flexibility.

These eight qualities are important not only in promoting resilience among remarried families, but also in generating positive interactions within them (not only do the families survive, but also they are pleasant, happy places to live). Many of these qualities have been identified by research as major characteristics of strong families, including both intact, never-divorced families and remarried families (DeFrain and Asay 2007; D. Olson, DeFrain, and Skogrand 2014; Stinnett and Stinnett 2010).

From one point of view, remarriage should be more successful than first marriage. After all, remarried people are older, more mature and experienced, and often highly motivated to make their marriage work. Indeed, some research has shown that remarriages are similar in happiness to first marriages, with little difference in partners' well-being (Pasley and Moorefield 2004). Whereas spouses in long-established stepfamilies view their marital relationship as just as happy as their first marriage, they also view their second marriage as more egalitarian in terms of housework and child care (Hetherington 1999; Hetherington and Kelly 2002), more open and pragmatic, and less romantic; and they are more willing to confront conflict. Although the risk of divorce is higher for remarried couples, many eventually establish strong, positive marital relationships and an adaptive, well-functioning parenting environment (Knox and Schacht 2016).

Remarried couples with children from prior marriages are more likely to divorce than are remarried couples without stepchildren (Karney 2015). Research shows that the extent to which children are a source of marital arguments increased more in stepfamilies than in biological families (Jenkins et al. 2005; Whitton, Nicholson, and Markman 2008; Whitton et al. 2013). Since mothers still most often get custody, their children likely are living with her and her new spouse, who becomes a stepfather. A biological parent and the children may be a "closed system" of social interaction, which is difficult for a new stepparent to enter. Lofas (2013) likens this to what happens in organ transplants when the body produces an immunological rejection of foreign tissue, thus causing the transplant to fail.

Courtship and Mate Selection in Remarriage

Courtship and mate selection in remarriage differ from those in first marriage in a number of ways. One difference is that the two people typically are older and in a different life-cycle stage. Overall, people who remarry are likely to be more emotionally mature and more experienced than when they married the first time around.

Another difference is that the majority have children (with a mean age of 6 to 8 years), meaning that the couple do not ever have a time of being a twosome. Children may not immediately accept the new stepparent; rapport, love, and trust take time to develop.

Remarriages in which one or both partners have been divorced receive less enthusiastic support and celebration from family and friends than do first marriages. They are less likely to involve presents and bridal showers, for example. There is less optimism among family and friends—regardless of how accepting family and friends are of divorce; some family members may even oppose the remarriage. New partners enter a family system that has an established history, and there are no guidelines for how they should fit in. Sometimes, too, ex-spouses become involved; they may try to break up the relationship or turn children against the new stepparent.

Preparing for Remarriage

As previously mentioned, divorced persons need time to work through the pain and difficult issues of the previous marriage. A widow or widower needs time enough to grieve. Professional counseling—including grief counseling for widowed individuals—may be helpful. Unfortunately, most people do not seek counseling before remarriage.

Another way to prepare for remarriage is to spend time developing relationships with the potential partner's family of origin before a remarriage actually takes place. This step of preparation increases the probability of developing positive in-law relationships; it may help avoid stressful, unsupportive experiences with the potential in-laws.

Taking this step increases the chances that the families of the couple will be a positive resource rather than a major stress for the remarriage. Sadly, a sizeable number do not even meet their potential in-laws until the time of the wedding or after.

Among couples where one or both have children from a previous marriage, a critical step in preparing for remarriage is to develop a relationship with each other's children. Including the children in many of the couple's social, recreational, and entertainment activities helps children feel more secure and optimistic about entering a new, blended family.

Another important preparation for remarriage is for the couple to discuss significant issues and potential problems (Lauer and Lauer 2011; Lofas 2013). How finances will be managed, how children will be disciplined, and whether there will be more children are examples of a few important issues. For many persons, the problems that contributed to the termination of a previous marriage will be carried over into the next unless changes in interacting and responding are made.

Participating in stepfamily education that includes children is beneficial to both children and parents. Children who participate in a research-based stepfamily education program learn to better express their feelings and develop relationship skills. They experience social support from participating in the program and also report feeling more "normal" when they realize that other children in stepfamilies have similar experiences. Parents who participate in these types of programs benefit in the following ways: (1) they develop greater awareness and empathy about the issues their children are facing; (2) they become more involved in family activities; and (3) they improve their parenting skills (Higginbotham, Skogrand, and Torres 2010).

Pre-remarriage counseling can be helpful preparation to a couple by addressing remarriage or blended family concerns and preparing for the unique challenges of blended families (Gonzales 2009). The services of a marriage and family counselor can be effective in helping a couple to examine their relationship and to identify strengths as well as potential problems.

Facets of Remarriage

A number of issues and tasks must be dealt with by those who marry. It has been suggested that persons who remarry must undo some of the adaptations they have made to divorce. Six of the "facets" of remarriage closely parallel the adaptations of divorce; there is also the challenge of maintaining boundaries.

EMOTIONAL REMARRIAGE Emotional remarriage is the slow, sometimes painful process by which the divorced person reestablishes a bond of attraction, commitment, and trust with someone. Divorced persons may find the establishment of a new marital-type relationship difficult because they have been hurt and disappointed.

PSYCHIC REMARRIAGE Psychic remarriage involves relinquishing the autonomy and personal freedom of being a single person. The remarried person once again is one component of a partnership.

COMMUNITY REMARRIAGE Reentrance into the "couples" world takes place in community remarriage. Unmarried friends typically are lost because of a lack of common interests; new friendships among other couples are formed.

PARENTAL REMARRIAGE For couples with children, the parental remarriage may be the most difficult part of remarriage. Children are a tie to the previous marriage and, as such, are a potential source of marital disruption if they make a new spouse feel like an outsider. Also, because a new marital relationship and new parental relationships must be assumed simultaneously, the remarried couple may feel cheated of the opportunity to establish a primary couple bond without the intrusion of children. Marital and parental problems compound each other. Finally, stepparents are often confused about the exact nature of their role. They frequently share parenting roles with natural parents without the benefit of any social guidelines for this joint parenting. Confusion, resentment, and frustration are common (Lofas 2013).

ECONOMIC REMARRIAGE Economic remarriage entails the establishment of a household. Typically, the economic situation of remarried couples improves because of pooled resources. Many blended families, however, are unsure about how much money they will have each month. Child support payments may not arrive regularly. Equitable division of resources is also a difficult area. If his son is given music lessons, is her son entitled to join Scouts?

LEGAL REMARRIAGE Remarriage has special legal considerations because of relationships from the earlier marriage—his or her former spouse; his, her, and/or their children. Questions arise, such as whether his life insurance and retirement benefits should go to his ex-wife, who is the custodial mother of his young children, or to his current wife. Inheritance laws typically favor the current spouse and natural children. Consequently, anyone wishing to provide benefits to stepchildren or a former spouse needs a clearly defined will.

MAINTAINING BOUNDARIES One aspect of boundary maintenance involves "ghosts" of the first marriage with respect to the former spouse. For example, it is easy to respond to memories of dysfunctional behavior of an ex-spouse within the new marriage as if the new spouse is behaving the same way. Her ex-husband was in an extramarital affair that ended the marriage; now she is suspicious when her new husband is late getting home from work (although he is not having an affair).

Parents must decide how to relate to a former spouse to ensure that their children maintain a good relationship with both biological parents, while maintaining an emotional distance from the former spouse (to avoid causing problems with the new spouse). Problems can develop if a person continues to be emotionally attached to the ex-spouse (even negatively) and cannot detach and move forward.

Challenges of Remarriage

Complex Relationships

Remarried families (sometimes called blended or binuclear families) may be grouped into categories according to family configuration. Blended families include couples with (1) no children, (2) children-in-common only, (3) her children (stepfather families), (4) his children (stepmother families), (5) children-in-common plus her children (natural parent plus stepfather), (6) children-in-common plus his children (natural parent plus stepmother), (7) children of both spouses (two stepparents), (8) children-in-common plus their children (natural parents plus two stepparents), (9) custodial children of the mother plus relationships with the father's children on a noncustodial basis, and (10) custodial children of the father plus relationships with the mother's children on a noncustodial basis.

When one or both spouses bring children from a previous marriage, stepsibling relationships can pose challenges of competition and jealousy among the children. Add to that the children born to the new husband and wife and the relationships are numerous and complicated.

Being a stepparent can be a more trying task than being a biological parent because children often have difficulty accepting a substitute parental figure. The spouse of a noncustodial parent must try to develop a friendly relationship with stepchildren during visits. All the adults are coparenting; the children are growing up in two households with three or four parent figures and role models.

Children may have natural parents plus stepparents; siblings, stepsiblings, and half-siblings; both grandparents and stepgrandparents; and aunts and uncles plus stepaunts and stepuncles, not to mention cousins and other relatives. Adult spouses relate to each other, to their own parents and grandparents, and to new in-laws. They also may continue to relate to their former in-laws. It is no wonder that family integration is challenging. The website for the Stepfamily Foundation (www.stepfamilies.org) (2016) puts it another way, "Often stepfamilies don't blend, they collide!"

Ambiguous Family Boundaries

A concept from family systems theory that is helpful in understanding remarried families is that of family boundaries. *A family boundary* is defined as the set of rules and parameters concerning who is included in the family (and who is not), as well as how much each member participates in the family. Family boundary ambiguity is much more common in remarried families; such vagueness increases stress and confusion and hampers family functioning (Doodson and Morley 2006; Lauer and Lauer 2011). Is it acceptable, for example, for the ex-spouse to show up unannounced to see the children? Some grandparents have difficulty seeing or communicating with grandchildren because the remarried parent (who has custody) and stepparent do not consider those grandparents (the parents of the noncustodial ex-spouse) part of the family. Yet the grandparents and grandchildren continue to love one another and want to be together.

Sometimes the children in the family and the adults differ concerning who is family and who is not. For example, a parent may view a nonresidential biological child as a member of the blended family who can come into the house at any time. The residential children in the family may consider the nonresidential child as more of a guest or visitor who should not just come barging in. Also, some children (as many as one-third in some research) view both of their biological parents as family but do not consider the stepparents part of the family. Other children count both biological parents and stepparents as family (Lauer and Lauer 2011).

Ambiguous Cultural Norms

A lack of clear social norms for roles of stepparents, as well as roles of grandparents, and a lack of institutionalized support for remarried couples contributes to greater stress and family dysfunction (Zarelli 2009). For example, the legal system provides ambiguous and inconsistent guidelines concerning the visitation rights of grandparents (especially parents of a noncustodial parent) and their access to their grandchildren (Hoffman 2013). Each state makes its own laws that generally say that grandparents can petition for visitation when it is in the best interests of the child; however, some states require grandparents to prove that. Additionally, in many instances, if grandparents see their grandchildren even once a year, the state may consider that they have visitation. There is also no consistent legal definition of the obligations and rights of stepparents toward stepchildren (Bryniczka 2013).

Ambiguity of cultural norms regarding remarriage is reflected in a study of children from stepfather families who were equally divided in opinion over whether the mother should give priority to her children or to both stepfather and the children (S. Moore and Cartwright 2005). Each blended family must work out a unique solution to many unclear situations and issues. For example, there are no clear norms or guidelines concerning questions such as the following:

- What do stepchildren call stepparents: "Mom-two," "Fred," "My dad's wife"? What do stepparents call stepchildren?

- What rights or obligations should there be to the family of an ex-spouse?

- What is the role of a stepparent?

- Should discipline be administered by the biological parent or both? What about when the stepparent is much more permissive or much more authoritarian than the biological parent?

- How are differing rules (such as curfew or television time) in two households managed for nonresidential children when they visit?

Carrying Expectations from One Marriage to Another

Remarried couples have many of the same expectations as first-married couples. But in addition, remarried couples usually have other expectations unique to their status as people who have been married more than once. One expectation is that being married to the second spouse will be similar in some ways to being married to the first one. However, these expectations may be not only unrealistic but also unfair to the second spouse. Spouses who expect the marital situation to be the same may continue old mistakes in the new relationship.

One potential predicament is rooted in pain experienced in the previous marriage. People remember all too well the problem behaviors of their former spouse, such as alcohol abuse, extramarital affairs, belittling comments, violent outbursts, rancorous arguments, irresponsibility, selfishness, and a lack of love and affection. As a result, these people enter a second marriage with a real fear that the troubles and hurts they experienced before will happen again. This may make them oversensitive to anything their new partner does or says that reminds them of the difficulties they had before. One man explained his feelings:

> My first wife hated sex and rejected me most of the time over the many years of our marriage. At first I was hypersensitive to anything that my second wife did which seemed to be rejection. Even when she was tired or sick, I was hurt. Actually, she's very affectionate, and loves to make love. I even had trouble accepting that. I couldn't believe that she really liked it. Gradually, though, I realized that she really wanted me, so that now I'm not upset by those rare occasions when she is not in the mood. (Counseling notes.)

In another example, a woman was sensitive to criticism because her first spouse had frequently berated her, especially in relation to her role as a mother. She became upset whenever her second spouse made observations or asked questions (such as "Have the kids brushed their teeth tonight?" or "Johnny needs a haircut soon") about the children. The last thing she wanted was similar treatment from this man. Many other examples could be given. In each case, the reaction of the remarried person is understandable, but it creates

Merging Families and Finances

When individuals remarry, they bring assets as well as children, financial obligations, values, and dreams for the future. Careful planning and effective communication are needed to merge the financial aspects of remarriage. Following are some considerations:

- If your future spouse is paying child support:
  - Child support payments usually continue.
  - Child support payments could increase.
  - Your fiancée's ex can ask for more child support as a result of *your* contributions to household income.
- If your future spouse is receiving child support payments:
  - Payments usually continue.
  - There is no guarantee the payments will stay the same.
  - An ex can petition to reduce his/her payments in certain circumstances.
- If your future spouse is receiving alimony:
  - Alimony may be reduced or stopped on remarriage.

- Check her/his divorce decree for details.
- A prenuptial agreement between you and your future spouse:
  - Details the assets and liabilities each brings to the remarriage.
  - Spells out the couple's agreement on the division of assets in the event of divorce.
- To provide for your children from a previous marriage:
  - Use life insurance or an irrevocable life insurance trust (children named as beneficiaries).
  - Name children as beneficiaries of your retirement plans/funds/accounts.
  - Leave a lump sum to your spouse and the remainder of your estate to your children.
  - Let your surviving spouse use your assets (house, bank accounts, etc.), with the remainder of the estate going to your children on her/his death (in other words, her/his children do not inherit your estate).

---

problems when it interferes with the new spousal relationship.

One of the most important steps to developing a successful remarriage is to heal from the pain of a previous divorce. This healing involves letting go of the negative emotions of resentment and hostility and then engaging in forgiveness (Rye and Moore 2015). Research indicates that forgiveness of a former spouse is associated with more positive mood and less depression (Bartlett et al. 2012; Rash, Matsuba, and Prkachin 2011).

Another obstacle in remarriage involves confusion about role expectations. This confusion arises because of the difficulty in sorting out what one's second spouse expects from what one's first spouse required. Both men and women in remarriages tend to base some of their expectations of spousal roles

on the role performance of former spouses, even if the first marriage was unhappy. This is unfair to the current spouse, who may not be at all like the former spouse. The key is to relate to one's spouse as a unique individual; as much as possible, avoid preconceived ideas about him or her.

Problems also arise when people want a new partner to play a role completely different from that played by the former spouse. This happens when a person has developed an intense dislike of things a former spouse did and, consequently, expects the second spouse to behave in a completely different manner. This can lead to some interesting behavior. Here is one such example:

Ann was first married to a husband who expected her to wait on him hand and foot. To

A couple's primary loyalty is to each other and secondarily to their children.

keep the peace, she did so for 25 years, even though she became more and more resentful of having to do so. Finally she could stand it no longer and got a divorce. She vowed that she never wanted anything to do with that type of man again.

Hank was first married to a wife who never assumed any responsibility for the house, the children, or for earning income. He did virtually everything for the whole family, because he couldn't stand a dirty house, unkempt children, and living in poverty. After 25 years he grew to resent it and divorced his wife. He vowed he would never marry that type of woman again.

Ann and Hank met and fell in love. Ann was very impressed that Hank was the kind of man who was very capable of taking care of himself. At last, she would be married to the kind of husband she had always wanted. Hank was delighted when he found out that Ann had cared for her husband and home for all those years. At last, he would have a wife who would help him.

But in the beginning, both Ann and Hank were very much disappointed. Hank became resentful because Ann asked him to do the same things he had resented doing for his first wife. Ann was disillusioned because she found out that Hank expected her to serve him just as she had done for her first husband. It took some time before they each understood the feelings and needs of the other and before they learned to compromise in meeting those needs. (Counseling notes.)

It can be unfair to expect a spouse to fulfill needs that were not met in a previous marriage, although a person naturally might want important needs met that were not fulfilled before. The key is *mutual* fulfillment, not a situation in which one person does all the giving and the other does all the receiving.

Finances

Financial arrangements can be particularly complicated for remarried couples. Many times, people enter a first marriage with few assets and debts, but by the time of a subsequent marriage, assets and debts have accumulated. These include homes, vehicles, insurance policies, retirement plans, boats, jewelry, credit cards, loans, investments, and personal property. An ex-spouse's name may be on the title or the loan agreement or as a beneficiary. A divorced father who remarries usually must pay child support. If he is also helping support his new wife's children, he carries a double financial burden, particularly if her ex-spouse does not keep up with child support payments. However, for a female-headed single-parent family, marriage is one of the fastest routes out of economic hardship. In general, women benefit more financially from remarriage than do men (Ozawa and Yoon 2002).

The traditional assumption has been that remarried couples will put all their monies and resources into "one pot"—to be used to pay household and family expenses. One benefit is that this may serve as a way of unifying the family. However, resentments can arise when the new wife finds herself writing checks to the ex-wife, as Ana Lopez explains:

> I was divorced and single for five and a half years. I had money then and didn't have to worry. When I married Joe, I handed my paycheck over to him, and all of a sudden, I had no money. We were living paycheck to paycheck, and that was a rude awakening for me. I also became bothered with our joint checking account because Joe was paying a tremendous amount of alimony and child support, and here I was, handing my check over to him. He was also paying for his ex's phone bills, her AAA card, and I didn't understand why. (C. Taylor and Taylor 2005)

C. Taylor and Taylor (2005) suggest several other approaches to managing finances in stepfamilies: (1) "Two pots." In this approach, everything stays separate, with him paying his own liabilities, child support, and alimony, as well as making his own investments and estate planning. She does the same. They decide who will be responsible for what part of their shared expenses; for example, he pays utilities while she buys food, and the mortgage is halved. (2) "Three pots." In this model, each member of the couple keeps an account ("his" and "hers"), plus they have a shared account ("ours") to cover shared expenditures. Each contributes to the ours pot—either equally or proportionally, depending on income, or in some other way that they regard as equitable. (3) "Merged pots." This model uses the three pots pattern as a way to start out, but adds a plan to merge the his and hers into the ours over time.

A financial commitment to a new spouse often comes slowly; and even more slowly, if at all, comes financial commitment to stepchildren. For example, compared to biologically intact families, stepparents are less likely to agree that parents should provide economic support as children make the transition to adulthood (college tuition, for example). However, stepparents perceived financial obligations as stronger when the couple have a child together in addition to children from prior relationships (Aquilino 2005). The challenge for each stepfamily is to build the interpersonal bonds, sense of group commitment, and economic system that meet both family and individual needs and that reflect family members' commitment to one another.

Relationships with the Ex-Spouse

In reality, although divorced people seldom have affectionate feelings toward a former spouse, they typically must develop a new relationship with the ex-spouse when children are involved (Deal 2006; Shafer 2003). This new relationship can be difficult, particularly in the early stages of divorce as ex-spouses deal with feelings of ambivalence, anger, attachment, and remorse, as well as sometimes fighting viciously and even reconciling passionately.

Buunk and Mutsaers (1999) examined how the nature of one's relationship with a former spouse is related to satisfaction in remarriage by focusing on three aspects of the relationship with the ex-spouse: attachment, hostility, and friendship. After 6 years of remarriage, on average, there was little continued attachment to or friendship with the ex-spouse, although there were still feelings of hostility, particularly when children were involved. In general, positive feelings toward the ex-spouse were rare. The relationship with the ex-spouse was more positive among more highly educated individuals and among those who did not have children from the former marriage. Continued attachment to the ex-spouse was especially problematic in relation to current marital satisfaction. Men who still felt attached to a former spouse reported that their current spouse had problems with the relationship with the ex-spouse. The more attached men still felt to the former spouse, the less happy the second marriage. In addition, the more women reported feelings of continued attachment to a former spouse, the less happy were their second marriages.

In general, relationships between ex-spouses seem to reach a low level of intensity after a number of years, with most remarried individuals not feeling a need to maintain a close relationship with a former spouse. This suggests that most individuals eventually get over the severe hostility characteristic of many relationships between ex-spouses during the initial stages of separation.

Family Relationships from a Previous Marriage

When parents divorce and remarry, new families are created, but previous family ties still remain. A divorce not only separates two individuals, but also can separate or strain a myriad of relationships that were once close and considered family. If the divorced

Humor

Humor has great value as a coping skill. Individuals with a good sense of humor are less likely to have negative emotions when reacting to stressful situations than are those who lack a sense of humor. Humor helps us cope with stress in the following ways:

- Generating laughter and relieving tension;
- Encouraging a more optimistic outlook;
- Helping keep our lives in balanced perspective (not taking ourselves too seriously or exaggerating the seriousness of a problem);
- Providing a sense of control as we choose to laugh or see humor in the midst of a stressful situation; or
- Reducing or minimizing negative emotions such as fear or anger (Frankel 2006; Kleinke 2002).

---

individuals have a hostile and conflicted relationship, family loyalty issues may prevent continued relationships between different sides of the family. Imagine the complexity of relationships stemming from ex-mothers-in-law, ex-brothers- and sisters-in-law, cousins, nieces, and nephews. In addition, many divorced people feel uncomfortable around their former in-laws and may not know the right term to attach to these people who were once considered family (Ahrons 2004).

The changing status of these relationships, as well as their possible termination, can be a painful process for both children and the individuals divorcing. It also can be an awkward process to figure out what role a previous family member plays now that the marriage that granted them family status and access to each other has ended. For example, is an ex-daughter-in-law invited to her ex-niece's wedding or notified of a death in the extended family? At times, ex-family members, who have shared decades of family history together, experience a complete disconnection with their previous family. This disconnect can be particularly painful for children, who may not understand the complexity of the situation.

Maintaining family ties can be critical for children to help them adjust to a new family system, particularly if children had a close family relationship before the divorce. When physical custody of children is shared, the relationship between children and extended family members on both sides of their family can generally be maintained more easily than if/when only one parent has physical custody.

If children live with only one parent and the other parent is not a central figure in their life, the extended family members of the noncustodial parent, such as grandparents, aunts, and uncles, can be denied access to, or at least discouraged from, maintaining a relationship with the children. For example, contact with grandparents is often diminished when the grandparents' son or daughter no longer has custody of their grandchildren (Westphal, Poortman, and Van der Lippe 2015). Some grandparents have sued their grandchildrens' custodial parent (typically their ex-daughter-in-law) over visitation rights. These lawsuits have raised the fundamental question of whether the government should intrude on the rights of parents to allow grandparents to visit with their grandchildren (Hoffman 2013). In a review of court cases involving grandparents' visitation rights, the courts did not assume that grandparent visitation automatically serves the best interests of the child. Justices in 50% of cases protected parental rights and did not allow grandparent visitation rights, compared to 24% of cases in which they awarded grandparents visitation with their grandchild (Henderson 2005).

Another issue in maintaining previous family relationships is related to proximity. It is not uncommon for people to move, particularly after a divorce and when a new family is being created. For example,

Matt and Linda divorced when their son, Sam, was about 9 years old. Matt and Sam had always been very close, with Matt taking a primary role in taking care of him. However, Linda was given primary physical custody and Matt had standard visitation. This hurt Matt considerably and he grieved the loss of time with his son, but they were still in the same community. Then Linda remarried and her new husband's work took him to Idaho—three states away. Matt's visitation time changed from every other weekend and split time at holidays to six weeks in the summer and some time at Christmas. The father–son relationship grew gradually more and more distant (emotionally).

One parent could live on the West Coast, whereas the other parent lives on the East Coast. Custody could be shared, with the child living with one parent during the school year and spending the summer months and some holidays with the other parent. In awarding visitation rights, the courts do not always consider how a child might feel about becoming part of a new family system and at the same time spending months at a time away from that family. In contrast, to maintain previous relationships when divorced parents do not live close, the child must spend time with the other side of his or her family.

The battle over visitation and custody can be stressful for a child, particularly if the child is young, does not understand the reasoning behind the visits, and/or is being shuffled back and forth over long distances. However, as stated earlier, losing family ties also can be stressful and have long-term consequences. Children can lose a sense of identity or a bond to the original family and at the same time fear being rejected or disliked in their new family (S. Thomas 2005). Maintaining a connection with previous family members, particularly after a stepfamily has been created, can be challenging.

Stepfamilies

Many children are growing up in stepfamilies today. About 9% of married couples and 11.5% of cohabiting households have a stepchild in their family (Teachman and Tedrow 2008). It is also estimated that 40% of all mothers and 30% of all children in America will live part of their lives in a remarried or recoupled, cohabiting household.

Couples who expect stepfamily relationships to be similar to those of primary families may be disappointed, surprised, and bewildered when they find differences. Expecting or insisting that a stepfamily

be like a traditional biological family can lead to new problems or exacerbate existing ones. It is helpful to recognize that building a sense of family takes time, that family boundaries must be flexible to accommodate existing ties to noncustodial parents and extended family, and that stepparents cannot replace biological parents and may need to develop a separate, nontraditional parenting role (Lofas 2013; D. Olson, DeFrain, and Skogrand 2014).

Disappointment may occur if stepparents have unrealistically high expectations of themselves and their new family. Especially when they are already parents, they may expect that they will be able to step right into the stepparent role. They may be shocked to discover that their stepchildren do not take to them the way they do to their biological parents. This may cause feelings of anxiety, anger, guilt, and low self-esteem. They may feel that there is something wrong with them, or they may blame the children. They must realize that it likely will take several years to develop close relationships.

Family boundary ambiguity is more common in the early stages of stepfamily development (Zarelli 2009). This is because an initial period of disequilibrium often is associated with divorce and remarriage, followed by the eventual restabilization of the new family system, which typically takes 2 to 3 years. However, some researchers have estimated that restabilization in stepfamilies may take as long as 5 to 7 years. One problem area stepfamilies face immediately is helping the children to deal with effects of the divorce of their biological parents, which frequently include academic, emotional, and behavioral issues. For example, research indicates that a significant proportion of children experience a decline in reading and math scores as well as an increase in behavioral and emotional problems after divorce. Problematic changes for children following divorce are more common than beneficial changes (Amato and Anthony 2014).

After stepfamilies have been together for 5 or more years, restabilization seems to have taken place, and it is then that we see more similarities than differences in the ways in which families function. Thus, in long-term stable stepfamilies, relationship patterns become more like those in nondivorced families (R. M. Ryan and Claessens 2012). This transition or restabilization is somewhat dependent on family history. Children whose parents had a highly conflictual marital relationship show a decrease in behavioral problems following divorce, whereas those from families with little conflict experience an increase in problems following divorce (Knox and Schacht 2016).

Parents and stepparents sometimes enter into their new family with a great deal of guilt and regret over their failed marriage. They feel sorry for their children, whom they have put through an upsetting experience. This has several effects. Usually, parents and stepparents tend to be overindulgent, are not as strict as they might otherwise be, and have more trouble guiding and controlling the children's behavior. Often, they try to buy the children's affection and cooperation. One stepfather reported,

> I would get angry at something my step-daughter did and feel guilty afterward, so I'd take her to the store and buy her a present. One day after a similar episode, she asked, "What are you going to buy me today?" I realized she had caught on very quickly and had learned how to use my guilt to her own advantage. (Counseling notes.)

Stepparents' roles are ill-defined and state laws give almost no recognition to the parental role of residential stepparents (Mason et al. 2002). Stepparents have no legal decision-making authority in their stepchildren's lives. Dependent benefits, including medical insurance and death benefits, sometimes exclude stepchildren, and in the event of death or divorce, there is no recognition of inheritance, visitation, or custody rights for stepparents, nor is there an obligation of child support or continuation of dependent benefits (Lofas 2013). In fact, residential stepparents generally have fewer rights than legal guardians or foster parents (Malia 2005).

Yet stepparents take on parenting tasks in a stepfamily and often are primary caregivers. Stepparents function like biological parents on caregiving tasks. For example, stepparents and biological parents put in a similar number of hours per week on parental tasks such as transporting children and helping with homework. They give advice, set and enforce rules, and contribute economically to the well-being of their stepchildren. The majority of stepparents believe it is false to state that stepparents do not have the full responsibility of being a parent (Mason et al. 2002).

Efforts to try to be parents may be rejected by older children. Stepparents cannot be mere friends; as responsible adults, they must make a contribution to the lives of stepchildren. Clinicians advise stepparents to focus initially on nurturing stepchildren and developing feelings of affection before attempting to discipline. Too often, stepparents do not spend enough time building trust and friendships before they start disciplining, which typically leads to resistance and negative reactions from stepchildren.

Stepparents must deal with children who have already been socialized by another set of parents. Stepparents may not agree with the way their stepchildren were brought up, but their suddenly stepping in and trying to change things is deeply resented. Stepparents may have to gradually introduce changes. Or they may need to accept the differences in the way that children are brought up and recognize that their way is not the only right way.

Stepparents expect gratitude for what they do, but they may get rejection and criticism instead. They take for granted the responsibility to support and care for their own biological children but feel they are being generous and helpful by offering the same support to stepchildren. Indeed, the move from a single-parent family to a stepfamily may result in improved financial resources and another adult to provide emotional support for the biological parent. However, a new stepparent may be viewed by a stepchild as an intruder in and a threat to an existing close relationship with the biological parent (Deal 2006), regardless of emotional or financial support. Stepchildren may take the emotional and financial support for granted and ask for more, offering little appreciation for what is done for them. One stepfather complained, "I don't expect the world, but it would help to have a little thanks once in a while." (In reality, both biological children and stepchildren tend to take help for granted.)

Stepparents must deal with a network of complex kinship relationships: with their own biological family members, with their stepchildren, with their ex-spouse's family members, and with their new spouse's family members. Instead of two major family groups, they have four family groups to contend with. There may be rivalry between the stepsiblings, and they may all be competing for the attention of the parents. However, for the sake of the children, stepparents must help children cope with the difficulty of the divorce and remarriage.

Research indicates that compared with first-time couples, stepfamily couples use less positive communication, are less negative, and withdraw from interaction more frequently. These communication patterns may reflect the challenge of negotiating parenting roles in stepfamilies (K. Halford, Nicholson, and Sanders 2007).

Family cohesion is lower in stepfamilies than in intact families. Stepfamilies also have less clear role expectations and are more flexible in response to change. This may be an adaptive approach that allows for more open family boundaries. Less closeness among family members and decreased bonding may facilitate adaptation to the unique challenges confronted by stepfamilies, such as living with different sets of parents and siblings at different times of the year.

Some of the differences in closeness between stepfamilies and first-marriage families have to do with biological relatedness. Both mothers and fathers have been found to be warmer with, more supportive of, and more involved with their biological children than with their stepchildren. Even when stepparents have a long period of time in which to become attached to their stepchildren, they remain more distant, are less warm and involved, and have less rapport with their stepchildren than parents do with their biological children in either first-marriage families or stepfamilies. In addition, children have more distant, less affectionate relationships with stepparents than with biological parents, even in long-established stepfamilies. This suggests that, although many stepparents and stepchildren have the opportunity to establish close relationships, bonding is more difficult between nonrelated parents and children. In general, research shows that being a stepparent is more difficult than raising one's own children, especially when the stepparent is a stepmother (Pasley and Moorefield 2004).

However, although it may take time to solve problems, stepfamily relationships can become a real source of joy and satisfaction. Skills training programs for parents and stepfamilies and remarriage education programs can help people who are remarrying prepare for all the new experiences they are about to encounter.

Stepfathers

Stepfathers in particular have a unique place in families because their relationship with their stepchildren is often contingent on their relationship with the stepchildren's birth mother (Marsiglio 2004). For example, because stepfathers have no legal relationship with stepchildren unless adoption occurs, a stepfather can spend years raising a stepchild as his own, only to have those ties cut off if the relationship to the stepchild's mother ends.

Marsiglio (2004) sought to uncover how men construct, negotiate, and assign meaning to their evolving identities and life circumstances as stepfathers. In his interviews with stepfathers, he found that most expressed a reasonably strong connection to their stepchildren and felt as though they were responsible for them in numerous ways, although not necessarily claiming the children as "their own." "Men may feel like a father because they change diapers, pack lunches, or get involved in carpooling kids to soccer practice, but they may feel awkward about disciplining children or balk at taking on formal or informal financial obligations for children who are not their own" (Marsiglio 2004, 29). The presence or absence of a biological father is an important variable in shaping stepfather identity, as well as the stepfather's commitment to family relationships with a romantic partner and her children. In most cases where the stepfather felt as though the stepchildren were his own, the biological father was only marginally involved in the child's life, if at all (Marsiglio 2004).

Stepfamily Turning Points

Several researchers have sought to discover how it is that people in stepfamilies come to build new family relationships—how they come to "feel like family." They have focused on the first 3 to 5 years and have determined specific turning points (events or relational incidents that move the stepfamily either toward feeling like family or away) and several pathways/trajectories of development (Baxter, Braithwaite, and Nicholson 1999; Nuru and Wang 2014; Papermow 2013; Vangelisti 2012).

Based on a developmental stage model, five pathways to feeling like a family have been described. The accelerated pattern is seen when the new stepfamily members move quickly and in a sustained manner toward higher levels of feeling like a family. In the prolonged pathway, the movement is also positive, but it is slower. In the stagnating pattern, levels of feeling like a family are low at the beginning and stay that way. The declining trajectory is seen when family feelings are high at the outset, but decline quickly, perhaps because expectations were unrealistic—that there would be "instant love," for example. Some members of stepfamilies feel as if they are on a rollercoaster because feelings of family swing from very high to suddenly very low; this is the high-amplitude turbulent pattern (Vangelisti 2012).

Turning points are events or relationship interactions that alter family members' sense of feeling more like a family. Turning points may be negative or positive in their impact. Quality time is one of the usually positive turning points. Events such as watching a football game or going shopping together promote a sense of family and consequently are perceived as positive by about two-thirds of people. Holidays and special events are viewed as positive by most, although one-third reported them as negative. Although family celebrations offer opportunities for emotional bonding and making memories, some people are stressed by conflicting obligations and others grieve the loss associated with memories of past celebrations (Nuru and Wang 2014).

Household composition is an area for numerous turning points; the structure of a blended family can be inconsistent and unstable, with children's visitation, multiple residences, and loss and gain of family members posing continuous challenges to family boundaries. Changes in the household and family composition are regarded as positive about 60% of the time (Nuru and Wang 2014). Children may welcome new siblings, for example: remarriage may help everyone feel more secure and stable. Relocation or a geographical move is regarded as positive about 60% of the time as well. Again, a new home in a new neighborhood or town may mark a fresh start as a new family.

In contrast, the conflict-related turning points were overwhelmingly (53%) perceived as negative events involving stepparent–stepchild and spousal relationships (Nuru and Wang 2014). However, although it might seem that family crises would be negative, a good number of stepfamilies report them as having a positive effect on family identity. These turning points represented times of need when the family came together and in some instances represented the first time a family member, especially a stepchild, recognized that other members of the new family cared about them personally.

Identifying these turning points helps to reveal the moments and experiences that are significant to stepfamilies in forming an identity and may help family members gain insight into the complex and sometimes confusing process of becoming a new family.

Stepparent–Stepchild Relationships

As stated earlier, biological parents see themselves as having higher-quality relationships with their children than stepparents report having with their stepchildren. Part of the problem of living in stepfamilies is that the roles of stepparents are not clearly defined. This is especially true early in remarriage when variations in role expectations and behaviors present challenges for stepparents in deciding what their roles are or should be in the lives of stepchildren (Pasley and Moorefield 2004; Weaver and Coleman 2005). In addition, many stepfamilies experience confusion about who is in and who is out of the family system (Stewart 2005a). For example, is a stepson, who is 21 and a college student—who only comes "home" for holidays—viewed as a stepchild or as a spouse's child?

In addition, negative stereotypes of stepparents increase the difficulty of functioning in a positive manner. For example, fairy tales and folklore present the stereotype of the cruel stepmother, a myth that is hard to overcome; media portrayals today still depict stepfamilies in negative ways (Leon and Angst 2005). The stepmother role may be more difficult than that of stepfather because the mother has more responsibilities for direct care of the children. Stepfathers appear to have more of an option to remain disengaged and participate less in child care than do biological fathers and stepmothers because most divorced custodial fathers expect the new stepmother to participate actively in housework and in child care (Hetherington and Kelly 2002; "Stepfamilies: what affects" 2013). In general, mothers in all families assume more responsibility for household tasks and child care than fathers do, but fathers participate more actively in the care of their own children than in the care of their stepchildren.

The age and gender of the children involved also affect the stepparenting relationship (Palsey and Moorefield 2004). In general, stepparents have more conflicts with adolescent stepchildren than

Stepfamilies in Cultural Context

There are many cultural differences in how step-families are perceived and how they function. As stated previously in the main text, culture shapes and instructs most family patterns. Berger (2000) examined the differences in stepfamilies in two different countries: the United States and Israel. He found that American stepfamilies see themselves as being more different from biological nuclear families, whereas Israeli stepfamilies see themselves as being more similar to nuclear families. American stepfamilies reported lower levels of functioning on psychological measures than did Israeli stepfamilies, and they were much more likely to view therapy as a means for working out problems in stepfamilies. Only a small minority of Israeli stepfamilies considered therapy an option for family problems.

Berger (2000) attributes these differences to a fundamental difference in culture: American culture places emphasis on individuality, personal freedom, and personal happiness; Israeli culture places more emphasis on collectivity, compliance with social norms, and strong social controls that regulate unconventional behavior. Interestingly, American stepfamilies were much more comfortable with being seen as different than were Israeli stepfamilies. The Israeli emphasis on conformity may stigmatize nonconventional family configurations and contribute to the tendency of stepfamilies in Israel to pass for nonstepfamilies. The American emphasis on personal happiness and satisfaction may contribute to reported lower levels of functioning because of the difficulty in meeting unrealistic personal expectations. For example, the belief that adjustment will occur quickly, love and caring will develop instantaneously, working hard prevents problems, and personal happiness will be met are unrealistic measures for success in stepfamilies. Consequently, American stepfamilies give themselves a lower rating, compared to Israeli stepfamilies, on levels of family satisfaction and personal satisfaction because of higher expectations for personal happiness, which have been shaped by culture.

with younger stepchildren because adolescents often react negatively to attempts by any adults to limit or control their behavior (Hetherington and Kelly 2002). Adolescents also face developmental issues such as egocentrism, self-consciousness, and an embarrassing awareness of mom or dad as sexual beings (Kail and Cavanaugh 2016).

Parenting a stepdaughter has been found to be more challenging than parenting a stepson. Typically, relationships between stepparents and step-daughters have more conflict and negative interactions than do relationships between stepparents and stepsons. It may be that girls tend to have close relationships with their biological mothers—thus making it harder for a stepmother or stepfather to be accepted into the picture ("Stepfamilies: what affects" 2013). Thus, parenting an adolescent stepdaughter may be most challenging.

Without question, the development of positive stepparent–stepchild relationships is one of the major tasks of remarried family life. Along with challenges and conflicts, the relationships also introduce positive life changes, new resources, and opportunities for new fulfilling family relations that contribute to the well-being of parents and children.

Child Well-Being in Stepfamilies

Research reports mixed findings regarding outcomes for children growing up in stepfamilies. According to some research that has compared the adjustment of children in stepfamilies with that of children in first-marriage families, children in stepfamilies tend to be less well adjusted, to exhibit more behavioral or emotional problems, to have poorer academic achievement, and to have lower social competence and social responsibility (Lofas 2013; Nicholson et al. 2008; D. Olson, DeFrain, and Skogrand 2014). However, many of the differences were small, and most stepchildren did not have psychological and behavioral difficulties or school-related problems (Pasley and Moorefield 2004). It is important to keep in mind that child adjustment and well-being in stepfamilies are related to a variety of factors.

Moving into a blended family presents challenges, stress, adjustments, and changes for children. Most children in remarried families have experienced the major family changes of (a) a divorce or separation, (b) a period of time in a single-parent family, and (c) a remarriage or repartnering. Divorce and separation are typically associated with an increase in conflict, anger, stress, and depression; these, in turn, are associated with children's internalizing and externalizing behaviors and an increase in children's behavioral problems (Ryan and Claessens 2012).

Frequently, children in remarriage situations express more negative behavioral outcomes because they are still dealing with the stress and challenges they experienced from the divorce/separation of parents and from the move to a single-parent family. When children can be helped to adjust to the divorce/separation transition more successfully, they are more likely to adjust to the remarriage successfully. Research also suggests that a harmonious remarriage may benefit children by helping them to recover from the stress, anxiety, and behavioral problems caused by the parental divorce/separation (Ryan and Claessens 2012). Research has shown that the younger the child at the time of remarriage, the more easily the child establishes an attachment to a new stepparent ("Stepfamilies: what affects" 2013), which helps in terms of adjustment and well-being. The remarriage transition appears to be more difficult for early adolescents than for younger children, especially those who have not experienced multiple family transitions before. Relationship problems between a biological custodial parent and a child are more common when the remarriage occurs when the child is an adolescent, even in parent–child relationships that previously had been relatively close and constructive.

As stated earlier, gender differences exist in terms of children's relationships with parents and stepparents. Boys, especially preadolescent boys, are more likely to accept and to adapt more quickly to a stepparent, whereas adolescent girls experience greater conflict and negativity with their stepparents. Girls in stepfamilies exhibit more defiant, aggressive, and disruptive behavior toward both biological mothers and stepfathers, and withdrawn, avoidant, noncommunicative behavior is more common between adolescent stepdaughters and stepfathers (Hetherington 1993; "Stepfamilies: what affects" 2013).

The number of transitions children experience also seems to affect adjustment. Typically, children entering stepfamilies have experienced many family transitions: conflict in the previous marriage, parental separation and divorce, possible cohabitation of the custodial biological parent and future stepparent or other partners before remarriage, and then the transition into a stepfamily. Some children also experience the remarriage of their noncustodial parent. Adolescents experiencing their custodial parent's remarriage usually encounter a number of concurrent life transitions, such as moving to a new home, starting a new school, or adjusting to a new sibling. Although many adolescents do not perceive these events as negative (Gonzales 2009), they are often difficult adjustments and have lasting effects. The cumulative impact of multiple transitions is evident: higher levels of negative emotional and behavioral outcomes are observed in children who experience the most family transitions (Ryan and Claessens 2012).

Another common explanation for why children in stepfamilies show more behavioral problems is related to a change in parenting styles. Research on parenting indicates the benefits to children's well-being of an authoritative parenting style (high levels of warmth and responsiveness, effective monitoring and control of children's behavior, enforcement of rules, and low levels of manipulation and conflict). In stepfamilies, such parenting-related processes often become disrupted, particularly during the period of adjustment to a remarriage. Many studies, in fact, find temporary increases in conflict and overall negativity between children and parents during the first year of adjustment to remarriage. Stepparents who do use authoritative parenting involving warmth and expectations for mature behavior experience less externalizing and internalizing behavior and greater social and academic competence in their stepchildren (Hetherington and Kelly 2002; "Stepfamilies: what affects" 2013).

Although children in stepfamilies may experience higher rates of negative outcomes than children in biological families, many children get along well with their stepparents. Communication with stepparents is an important predictor of well-being in children in stepfamilies (Golish 2003). In fact, most stepchildren view their stepparents positively, although usually not as positively as children view their biological parents.

Part of the problem of living in stepfamilies is that positive stepparenting roles are not clearly defined.

It is important to remember that, although stepchildren may show more behavioral problems, they are not necessarily suffering from a mental or behavioral disorder. Studies have found that 70% to 80% of children in stepfamilies function in the nonclinical range (not suffering from mental or behavioral disorders) and only 20% to 30% function in the clinical range (suffering from such disorders). In contrast, 85% to 90% of children in nondivorced families function in the nonclinical range. Although statistically the risk is double, most children in stepfamilies seem to function normally (Bray 1999). And although problems may reemerge or develop in late adolescence and adulthood, the percentage of children who experience severe, lasting problems is relatively small. Thus, most children in divorced families and stepfamilies do not develop behavioral problems, are resilient through all the transitions, and become competent and well-adjusted individuals (Knox and Schacht 2016). Also, many studies do not consider length of time in a family when comparing children of first-married families and stepfamilies. Studies often compare long-established nondivorced families to stepfamilies in early stages of family formation, with negative conclusions drawn about stepfamilies (Ryan and Claessens 2012).

Most family scholars who study divorce and remarriage today conclude that what happens inside a family is more important than family type or structure in influencing children's adjustment. Children appear to be at greater risk for behavioral problems when they grow up in highly conflictual first marriages, more so than in well-functioning, supportive single-parent or remarried families. Children, regardless of the family structure (nondivorced nuclear families, single-parent families, stepfamilies), exhibit greater well-being, achievement, socially responsible behavior, and social competence and fewer behavioral problems when they are raised in a loving, harmonious, supportive family environment (D. Olson, DeFrain, and Skogrand 2014).

Facilitating Bonds between Stepparents and Stepchildren

Most stepparents want to get along with their stepchildren, but, as stated previously, this relationship can be difficult and problematic. Recent research has examined the challenges faced by stepparents in developing bonds with stepchildren, and some common styles and strategies have emerged.

One study revealed three common patterns of behavior among stepparents in forming a relationship

Psychologically, if a biological parent is alive and showing interest in a child, the child will not want a new parent and will often resent any attempts to replace the biological parent.

with their stepchild: (1) nonseekers of affinity with children, (2) early affinity seekers, and (3) continuous affinity seekers (Ganong et al. 1999). Affinity-seeking strategies are intentional actions by people who are trying to get other people to like them or feel positive toward them. Nonseekers were not mean or neglectful, but they mainly interacted with the children to become closer to the parent, not to win the children's affection. They did little or nothing intentionally to get their stepchildren to like them and usually did not think a lot about this. Early seekers pursued a relationship with the children prior to living with them. Although they sought to bond with the children, they had other motivations, such as getting the children to respond to their discipline as they filled a new role of replacement parent. These stepparents stopped seeking affinity soon after they began living with the stepchildren. Continuous affinity seekers actively pursued the children's affection early in the relationship and continued to do so after the remarriage. They deliberately tried to get their stepchildren to like them and purposefully engaged in activities that stepchildren liked to do. Stepparents who were affinity seekers also described themselves as liking children in general. None of the nonseekers described themselves in this way. Stepparents who were continuous affinity seekers had the strongest bonds with their stepchildren because it was important to them to continue working on the relationship after becoming a stepfamily (Ganong et al. 1999).

Certain personality characteristics of both stepparents and stepchildren have been found to contribute to the development of a close relationship. Stepparents who are effective at establishing a close relationship with their stepchildren tend to be more laid back and less eager to establish control or fill a role as a disciplinarian ("Building a healthy" 2013; Deal 2006). Although they make attempts to become friends with their stepchildren, they have less need to be in control of the relationship and do not need to have a friendship develop immediately (Deal 2006). As for stepchildren, those who have something in common with their stepparent and those who want the stepparent to function as a parent experience a stronger bond with the stepparent. Children who are easy-going and well behaved tend to evoke good reactions from adults, thus making relationship formation easier ("Stepfamilies: what affects" 2013). Stepchildren who think the stepparent had something to do with their parents' separation

or who perceive unfriendly attitudes toward biological parents typically reject the stepparent's attempts at bonding ("Building a healthy" 2013; Deal 2006; Ganong et al. 1999).

Common activities stepparents use to get their stepchildren to like them include doing fun things as a family, going on family outings, playing games, nonverbally expressing feelings, spending money on things the stepchildren want, and spending time talking together. Although stepchildren may have fun doing things as a family, group activities do not necessarily offer many opportunities for stepparents and stepchildren to interact directly with each other. One-on-one activities, such as playing board games, going fishing, and having conversations between just the stepparent and stepchild appear to be the most effective means for bonding. Stepparents are wise to look for an interest the child has and express an interest in it themselves as a way of building a relationship ("Building a healthy" 2013; Deal 2006).

Indeed, as in all families, good communication in stepfamilies is critical in developing bonds among family members. Because of the large number of issues that must be managed in newly formed stepfamilies, communication is perhaps never more important than it is in the early years of the stepfamily. Unlike first marriages, where couples generally have the opportunity to work some issues out and establish patterns of relating before having children, stepfamilies often must deal with issues quickly and sometimes without time for careful deliberation and negotiation (Coleman, Ganong, and Fine 2004). It is important to remember that multiple transformations occur during the postdivorce years, and parents and grandparents must work on their new roles in the children's lives and be willing to revise (and continue working on) their new roles as children pass through various developmental stages (Wallerstein and Blakeslee 2003).

Coparents and Parenting Coalitions

One of the most difficult situations for the millions of postdivorce American parents is learning to raise children in two separate households (Wallerstein and Blakeslee 2003), often with the addition of new stepparents. Many develop effective and healthy coparenting relationships (T. Campbell 2005) by learning to cooperate and show respect for each other. One ideal for cooperative postdivorce parenting is coparenting by divorced parents; another is a parenting coalition when there are more than two parenting adults after remarriage. In **coparenting**, the two divorced parents cooperate rather than compete in the task of raising their children. In a **parenting coalition**, the biological parents (now divorced and remarried) plus the stepparents cooperate in rearing their own children and any stepchildren. The children have contact with both of their parents and with their stepparents.

There are a number of advantages to these kinds of cooperative parenting arrangements. Both the children's and the adults' needs can be met more adequately than if there is continued antagonism between adults. The children are not caught in a web of hostility; they are not made messengers between two households; and their fear of losing a parent is reduced. The power struggles between households are lessened as well. Not only is the children's self-esteem enhanced, making them easier to be with, but also the parents' responsibilities are lessened because the task of rearing the children is shared.

In a stepfamily, instead of obtaining one new brother or sister at a time, a child may get several at once. The child also may be confronted with the parent's having to share attention with stepsiblings.

When parents do not get along cooperatively or are hostile toward each other, they are often unaware of the pain they are causing their children. Studies repeatedly show that children adjust better to change and have better relationships with their parents when the family environment is harmonious. In particular, children exposed to parental conflict commonly experience distress and dysfunction (Garber 2004). However, despite evidence that a positive relationship is beneficial for children's adjustment and well-being, many ex-spouses, along with their new partners, do not get along well. When tensions are high between ex-spouses, it eventually can result in the nonresidential parent, particularly fathers, withdrawing and having limited or no contact with their children. In contrast to fathers, nonresidential mothers are almost twice as likely to remain in contact with their children following divorce, and stepmothers and biological mothers are more likely to get into competitive relationships that lead to loyalty conflicts in children. It is important to remember that mothers have been referred to as the gatekeepers to relationships of other people with their children. This is especially notable in children's relations with both noncustodial fathers and stepfathers.

Stepsibling Relationships

Sibling relationships in stepfamilies that are warm and supportive are associated with greater social competence and responsibility in children, whereas sibling rivalry and aggression are associated with antisocial behavior (Deal 2006; Golish 2003). The term **sibling rivalry** refers to the competition of brothers and sisters for the attention, approval, and affection of parents. The problem arises because of envy and fear that one brother or sister is receiving more physical or emotional care and benefits from parents.

Sibling rivalry is often exacerbated in a stepfamily. Instead of obtaining one new brother or sister, a child may get several all at once. And the stepsiblings may not be helpless infants, but children of similar or older ages who can be demanding of adult attention. From the child's point of view, a tendency to be jealous is understandable. The child may have become used to living with one parent and to having easy access to that parent for help, comfort, and advice. Then the child is confronted with that

Being a Stepmom

Anita has been a stepmother for 10 years to two teenage boys. The boys live with her and their father half of the week. She feels very connected to them and wants to be the best stepmother possible. She has no biological children of her own and feels she has the time and energy to devote to them and be involved in most aspects of their lives. She knows, however, that her commitment to her stepchildren, her involvement in their overall development, and her mere presence at some school and social functions creates tension between her and the boys' biological mother. For example, Anita helps the boys with homework and school projects and she maintains contact with the teachers about school performance and attends school meetings. She volunteers for the same things other parents volunteer for, such as field trips, room parent, class projects, and PTA committees. Although this attests to her commitment to being a parent to her stepchildren, the biological mother sees it as an "intrusion" of her space and a violation of appropriate boundaries.

Anita remarks, "I know if I had my own children, I would be a different stepmother, but in my heart I believe I am doing the right thing. While the mom may not like it and it creates tension between us, the boys are better off with a stepmother who cares and is committed. I think my family life and marriage also run smoother because I am involved. For example, I am constantly reminding the boys about what they need for school or sports so they are prepared. I organize and pay attention to the details of their lives which takes a lot of time and forethought. I knew there would be tension and adjustments in the beginning, I just never imagined it lasting so long."

parent's turning his or her attention to a new spouse and stepchildren. Children also may have to share living quarters—even their own bedroom, as well as bathrooms and playrooms. They may find their toys broken, their things messed up, their clothes borrowed, and so on. However, on average, relationships among stepsiblings are less contentious than those among biologically related siblings, particularly in adolescence. This may be because of ambiguity in the stepsibling role and the lack of connection and involvement among many stepsiblings. It also is possible that children can more easily understand that a different relationship exists with their siblings based on biological relatedness of parent and child (Hetherington and Stanley-Hagan 1999).

Learning to share with one another and to live with others who have not been part of one's immediate family is a broadening, enriching experience. It is easier to build positive relationships when the children are young. Generally, younger children are more trusting and accepting than older children and more flexible in making adjustments. Also, families with harmonious relationships between the spouses show less sibling rivalry than do families in which the marriage is troubled, indicating the effect of the total marriage on the children in the family.

About half of women who remarry will have a baby in their new families. The new baby can serve as a bond between the two groups of children. It gives them something in common and someone to care for besides themselves and can unite them around a mutual interest. However, the birth of a child involves considerable reorganization of parental responsibility and family life and thus also has the potential to negatively affect stepparents' relationships with stepchildren (Nuru and Wang 2014; Stewart 2005b). In her research, Stewart found that the addition of a half sibling is not particularly beneficial to stepchildren

coparenting Two divorced parents cooperate rather than compete in the task of raising their children.

parenting coalition The biological parents (now divorced and remarried) plus the stepparents cooperate in rearing their own children and any stepchildren.

sibling rivalry The competition of brothers and sisters for the attention, approval, and affection of parents.

Stepfamily Rights

As stated previously in the chapter, stepparents have no legal rights to their stepchildren if a legal adoption has not occurred. If the marriage ends, regardless of how many years they were the stepparent, they may have no custody rights, legal responsibility for child support, or visitation rights with the child. Basically, the relationship of the stepparent to the stepchild is legally terminated on the divorce from or death of the custodial parent.

The legal standing of stepchildren would be improved by adoption, but the stepparent can only adopt if the noncustodial natural parent has relinquished his or her parental rights. Even when noncustodial parents offer no child support and are absent from the child's life, they rarely are willing to give up parental rights. Mason (2003) believes that "federal and state policies affecting families and children, as well as policies governing private sector employee benefits, insurance and other critical areas of everyday life, may need to be adapted to address the concerns of modern stepfamilies" (97). The American Bar Association Family Law Section is working on legislative reforms regarding stepparents' legal rights to discipline, to provide child support, and to receive visitation and custody rights.

Questions to Consider

Should stepchildren receive the survivor and death benefits that a natural child would when a stepparent dies? Should this be based on the number of years a family relationship was established? Discuss.

How can a will protect the interests of a stepfamily given the fact that the stepchild has no inheritance rights if his or her stepparent dies?

What happens to the relationship between stepparent and stepchild in the case of a divorce? What responsibility, if any, does the stepparent have to the child?

Should the stepparent rights and responsibilities differ if the child has not resided with the stepparent (stepmom married to a noncustodial dad, for example)?

What policy should be in place for stepchildren who have been economically and emotionally dependent on a stepparent for many years?

and suggests that couples with children from prior relationships should not make the decision to reproduce to "cement" stepfamily bonds.

In summary, remarriage and the formation of stepfamilies are common today. After divorce, the majority of people do remarry and, although some may divorce again, many relationships are successful. When people remarry, they should be aware that the challenges of their new marriage may be complicated if either spouse has children from a previous marriage. However, most stepchildren eventually will adjust well to the new family structure. The likelihood of a positive relationship between stepparent and stepchild is greater if the stepparent retains an active interest in a friendship with the child. In general, when the children's needs are adequately addressed, the stepfamily can live in harmony.

Summary

1. Marrying more than once has become common. The majority of divorced people also have children; when they remarry, new stepfamilies are created.

2. Remarried families may have one or two remarried spouses, each with or without children. Family relationships and integration become complicated and difficult in reconstituted families.

3. The probability of divorce is slightly greater in remarriages than in first marriages, but successful remarrieds state that their new marriage is better than their first marriage. Overall, research indicates few differences in marital satisfaction between first marriages and remarriages.

4. Courtship and mate selection in remarriage differ from those in first marriage. The couple is older and most have children.

5. Individuals can prepare for remarriage by allowing time to work through divorce issues or grief, by getting to know each other's family and children, and by discussing practical matters such as money and discipline.

6. Remarried couples must deal with a number of issues and tasks. These fall into the following areas ("facets"): emotional, psychic, community, economic, parental, and legal.

7. Remarriage introduces some complexity not present in first marriage. The biggest challenge is children. Relationships with ex-spouses and stepsiblings also can pose problems.

8. Family boundaries defining who is part of the family and who is not typically are ambiguous in remarried families.

9. Cultural norms regarding remarriage are also ambiguous. The legal system has inconsistent guidelines with regard to the rights and obligations of stepparents.

10. Couples carry expectations from one marriage to another. One expectation is that a second spouse is going to be similar to the first spouse. One result is that people replicate the mistakes of their first marriage in remarriage or have apprehension that the problems and hurts they experienced before will happen again.

11. Another challenge may arise because of confusion about role expectations and enactment. A person may desire a spouse to play a role similar to or completely different from the one played by a former spouse.

12. Financial problems may emerge in remarriage because of the necessity of supporting both the new family and the children from the previous family.

13. Some remarrieds pool all of their resources in a "common pot," distributing them according to each family member's needs. Other remarrieds use a "two-pot" system in which each partner maintains an account for paying personal bills, such as his child support; household expenses are divided. In a "three-pot" arrangement, each partner maintains a personal account with some monies going into a shared account used to pay household expenses. Many experts recommend starting with a three-pot setup and eventually merging into one.

14. Individuals who divorce typically must develop a new relationship with the former spouse when children are involved. This new relationship is often difficult, particularly in the early stages of divorce. In general, relationships between ex-spouses seem to reach a low level of intensity after a number of years, with most remarried individuals not feeling a need to maintain a close relationship with the former spouse.

15. In successful remarriages, spouses give themselves time to get to know each other well, resist the many pressures to remarry before they are ready, discuss every aspect of their relationship before marriage, have learned from past mistakes, and put their marriage first.

16. When parents divorce and remarry, new families are created, but previous family ties still remain. The connection with previous family members can be a challenging situation for postdivorce families.

17. Many couples expect stepfamily relationships to be like those of primary families. Many are disappointed because they are not the same.

18. Part of the problem of living in a stepfamily is that positive roles of stepparents are not clearly defined.

19. Most family scholars who study divorce and remarriage today conclude that what happens inside a family is more important than family type or structure in influencing children's adjustment. Children, regardless of the family structure, exhibit greater well-being, higher achievement, more socially responsible

behavior and social competence, and fewer behavioral problems when they are raised in a loving, harmonious, supportive family environment.

20. Overall, the friendship style of stepparenting seems to be the most successful in facilitating bonding with stepchildren.

21. Coparenting by divorced parents involves cooperating in the task of raising the children. A parenting coalition involves the biological parents and the stepparents raising their own children and any stepchildren together. Coparenting and parenting coalitions are advantageous to children and parents alike.

22. Sibling rivalry refers to the competition of siblings for the attention, approval, and affection of parents. The situation is often exacerbated in the stepfamily.

23. Couples report that having a baby of their own improves stepsibling relationships, although it can also complicate sibling rivalry.

Key Terms

coparenting

parenting coalition

sibling rivalry

Questions for Thought

1. If you were divorced at age 30 with two school-age children in your custody, would you want to remarry? Why or why not? If you did remarry, what are some of the problems you would be most likely to encounter? If you did not remarry, what are some of the problems you would be most likely to encounter?

2. What do you believe would be the differences between being a parent and being a stepparent as far as relationships with children are concerned?

3. If you divorced, what sorts of things would you try to do to safeguard the best interests of your children?

4. If you divorced and wanted to remarry, what would you do to ensure that your remarriage was successful?

5. Should grandparents have visitation rights? Aunts and uncles? Under what circumstances?

6. Suggest some ways to handle "names" for stepparents—for young children, school-age children, teens, and adult children.

For Further Reading

Church, E. (2005). *Understanding stepmothers: Women share their struggles, successes and insights.* Toronto: HarperPerennial. A popular press book providing numerous insights into the challenges of being a stepmother.

The National Stepfamily Resource Center website, http://www.stepfamilies.info, has information about programs and services to stepfamilies as well as articles on a variety of subjects related to life in a blended family.

Philips, S. (2005). *Stepchildren speak.* Vancouver, WA: AYWN. Ten grown-up stepchildren teach us how to build healthy stepfamilies.

The Smart Stepfamilies organization's website offers seminars, webinars, therapy, and enrichment for stepfamilies, as well as articles on a variety of topics. http://www.smartstepfamilies.com.

Information on remarriage and living in a stepfamily is offered at the Stepfamily Foundation website. http://www.stepfamily.org.

Glossary

abortion: The expulsion of the fetus. Can be either spontaneous or induced.

abruptio placentae (placental abruption): The premature separation of the placenta from the uterine wall.

acquired immunodeficiency syndrome: A disease caused by the human immunodeficiency virus and characterized by irreversible damage to the body's immune system and, eventually, death.

affective sensitivity: Empathy, or the ability to identify with the feelings, thoughts, and attitudes of another person.

affinity: A relationship formed by marriage without ties of blood.

AIDS: See *acquired immunodeficiency syndrome.*

altruistic love: Unselfish concern for the welfare of another.

androgyny: A blending of male and female characteristics and roles; especially, a lack of gender typing with respect to roles.

Apgar scale: A widely used system to evaluate the physical condition of a newborn, named after the originator, Virginia Apgar.

artificial insemination/intrauterine insemination: Injection of sperm into the vagina, cervix, or uterus for the purpose of achieving conception.

autonomy: The assertion of independence and self-will.

avoidance: Method of dealing with conflict by avoiding the people, situations, and issues that stimulate it.

bag of water (amniotic sac): Sac containing the fluid in which the fetus is suspended.

bargaining: The process by which two parties decide what each will give and receive in arriving at a decision.

basal body temperature method: A method of fertility awareness based on the rise in basal body temperature that signals ovulation.

bilateral descent: Inheritance is passed through both the male and the female line.

binuclear family: An original family divided into two families by divorce.

birth rate: The number of live births per 1,000 population.

blended, or reconstituted, family: A family formed when a widowed or divorced person, with or without children, remarries another person who may or may not have been married before and who may or may not have children.

B-love: Term used by Maslow for Being-love, which is love for the very being and uniqueness of another person.

body language: Posture, facial expression, eye contact, tense muscles, blushing, panting, tears, sweating, shivering, increased pulse rate, thumping heart, and other bodily reactions that convey feelings and reactions.

bonding: Development of emotional attachment between the mother and newborn immediately after birth.

breech birth: When the buttocks or feet are the first part of the baby to pass through the vagina.

calendar method: A method of birth control whereby the couple has intercourse only during those times of the menstrual cycle when the woman is least likely to get pregnant.

castration: Removal of the testicles.

catharsis: Venting negative emotions to rid oneself of them so that they can be replaced by more positive ones.

cervical cap: A small, thimble-shape, rubber barrier that fits over the cervix and prevents sperm from entering the uterus.

cervical mucus method: A method of fertility awareness that uses changes in cervical mucus as indicators of ovulation.

cesarean section: Removal of the fetus by incising the abdominal and uterine walls.

child abuse: May include not only physical assaults on a child but also malnourishment, abandonment, neglect, emotional abuse, and sexual abuse.

chlamydia: Common bacterial sexually transmitted disease; women often show no symptoms; may lead to pelvic inflammatory disease if untreated; treated with antibiotics.

civil union: A legally recognized union similar to marriage.

climacteric: The transitional time when fertility ends for women (with menopause) and declines for men (as testosterone declines). Both men and women may experience depression, anxiety, and loss of bone density.

coercive power: The threat of physical force or other types of punishment to force compliance.

cognition: Literally, the act of knowing; the act of becoming acquainted with the world and the objects, people, and conditions in it.

cognitive developmental theory: A theory suggesting that gender roles and identities cannot be learned until children reach a certain stage of intellectual development.

cohabiting family: Two people of the opposite sex who are living together and sharing sexual expression and who are committed to their relationship without formal legal marriage.

combination pills: Oral contraceptives containing both estrogen and progestin.

common-law marriage: A marriage by mutual consent, without a license or ceremony, recognized as legal under certain conditions by some states.

communication: A message one person sends and another receives.

companionate love: A type of love characterized by warmth, affection, and commitment.

compatibility: The capability of living together in harmony.

conciliation counseling: Marriage counseling ordered by the court in which spouses try to decide whether they want to dissolve their marriage or agree to try to solve their problems.

conflict theory: A theory that family conflict is normal and that the task is not to eliminate conflict but to learn to control it so that it becomes constructive.

consanguinity: The state of being related by blood; having descended from a common ancestor.

conscious love: Rational, reasoning love.

constructive arguments: Arguments that stick with the issues, that attack the problem and not the other person, that employ rational methods, and that result in greater understanding, consensus, compromise, and closeness between two people.

consummate love: A term used by Sternberg to describe love as a combination of intimacy, passion, and commitment.

contraceptive patch: A patch applied weekly to the buttocks, abdomen, or upper torso that releases hormones to prevent pregnancy.

contraceptive sponge: A polyurethane foam disk that contains spermicide and is placed over the cervix to block and absorb semen.

coparenting: Two divorced parents cooperate rather than compete in the task of raising their children.

corporal punishment: Physical or bodily punishment with the intention of inflicting pain but not injury for the purpose of correction or control.

crisis: A drastic change in the course of events; a turning point that affects future events.

crisis overload: A series of crises occurring one after another until they become more than a person can handle.

cross-sectional study: A research design where individuals are selected at various stages of the life course and compared to one another for similarities or differences.

culture: The sum total of ways of living, including the values, beliefs, aesthetic standards, linguistic expressions, patterns of thinking, behavioral norms, and style of communication a group of people has developed to ensure its survival in a particular physical and human environment.

custody: A term that refers to both legal custody (the parent's right to make decisions regarding the welfare of the child) and physical custody (the parent's right to have the child living with him or her).

date rape: The forcing of involuntary sexual compliance on a person during a voluntary, prearranged date or after a couple meets informally in a social setting.

dating: A courting practice in which two people meet and participate in activities together to get to know each other.

dependent love: Love that one develops for someone who fulfills one's needs.

destructive arguments: Arguments that attack the other person rather than the problem; that increase resentment and hostility and undermine trust, friendship, and affectionate feelings; that result in greater alienation; and that do not solve the problem.

developmental tasks: Growth responsibilities that arise at various stages of life.

diaphragm: A thick, dome-shape, rubber latex cap that is stretched over a collapsible metal ring, designed to cover the cervical opening to prevent sperm from entering the uterus.

discipline: A means by which socialization takes place; the process of instruction in proper conduct or action.

D-love: Term used by Maslow for Deficiency-love, which develops when another person meets one's needs.

domestic partnership: A legal or personal relationship between two people who live together and share a common domestic life but are not joined by marriage or civil union.

dopamine: A neurotransmitter that functions in the parts of the brain that control emotions and bodily movement.

double-bind communication: Conflicting messages sent when verbal messages and body language do not agree.

dual-career family: A subtype of the dual-earner family in which there are two career-committed partners, both of whom are trying to fulfill professional roles that require continuous development as well as family roles.

dual-earner family: A family in which both spouses are in the paid labor force.

dyspareunia: Persistent pain during intercourse; may be experienced by both men and women; causes are largely physical, including infection, tight foreskin, or tumors.

ectopic pregnancy: Attachment and growth of the embryo in any location other than inside the uterus.

egalitarian marriage: A relationship of equality rather than strict role definition; the focus is on shared power and shared work.

ego resiliency: The generalized capacity for flexible and resourceful adaptation to stressors.

elder abuse: Includes physical abuse, sexual abuse, emotional and psychological abuse, neglect, abandonment, and financial or material exploitation of an elderly person.

emergency contraceptive pills: Oral contraceptives taken after intercourse to prevent unwanted pregnancy.

empathy: The ability to identify with the emotional state of another—to feel with him or her.

endogamy: Marriage within a particular group.

endorphins: Chemical neurotransmitters that have a sedative effect on the body and can give a sense of tranquility.

equity theory: A subcategory of exchange theory holding that people seek a fair and balanced exchange in which the partners can mutually give and take what is needed.

erectile disorder: A common sexual disorder involving the inability to attain or maintain an erection; causes may be psychological (depression or concern with performance) or physical (disease, medications, alcohol, for example).

erotic love: Sexual, sensuous love.

ethnicity: The way people define themselves as part of a group through similarities in an ancestry and cultural heritage.

evolutionary theories: Theories suggesting that genetic heritage is more important than social learning in the development of gender roles.

exchange theory: The theory that people choose relationships in which they can maximize their benefits and minimize their costs.

exogamy: Marriage outside of a particular group.

expert power: Power that is given because a person is considered superior in knowledge of a particular subject.

expressive role: The role of the family in meeting the emotional and social needs of family members.

extended family: An individual, possibly a partner, any children an individual might have, and other relatives who live in the household or nearby.

extradyadic involvement: Emotional or physical intimacy outside the dyadic, or couple, relationship.

familism: A social pattern in which the interests of the individual are subordinated to the values and demands of the family.

family: Any group of people united by ties of marriage, blood, or adoption or any sexually expressive relationship in which (1) the adults cooperate financially for their mutual support, (2) the people are committed to one another in an intimate interpersonal relationship, (3) the members see their individual identities as importantly attached to the group, and (4) the group has an identity of its own.

family developmental theory: A theory that divides the family life cycle into phases, or stages, over the life span and emphasizes the developmental tasks that need to be accomplished by family members at each stage as well as the importance of normative order.

family life cycle: The phases, or stages, of the family life span, each of which is characterized by changes in family structure, composition, and function.

family of origin: The family into which you are born and in which you are raised.

family of procreation: The family you establish if you have children of your own.

family planning: Having children by choice and not by chance; having the number of children wanted at the time planned.

family violence: Any rough or extended use of physical force or aggression or verbal abuse by one family member toward another.

feedback: Response to the message another has sent and disclosure of one's own feelings and ideas.

female condom: A polyurethane pouch inserted in the vagina to collect sperm, preventing fertilization.

femininity: Personality and behavioral characteristics of a female according to culturally defined standards of femaleness.

feminist theory: Theory (or perspective) that focuses on male dominance in families and society and examines how gender differences are related to power differentials between men and women.

feminization of poverty: The trend toward increasing proportions of women, regardless of ethnicity or age, living in poverty.

fertility rate: The number of children a woman is expected to have in her lifetime.

filtering process: A process by which mates are sorted by filtering out ineligibles according to various standards.

flextime: A company policy that allows employees to choose the most convenient hours for them to work during the day, selected from hours designated by the employer.

friendship love: A love based on common concerns and interests, companionship, and respect for the partner's personality and character.

gamete intrafallopian transfer: The process of inserting sperm cells and egg cells directly into the fallopian tube, where fertilization is expected to occur.

gaslighting: The process by which one person destroys the self-confidence, perception, and sense of reality of another person.

gay or lesbian family: Two people of the same sex who are living together and sharing sexual expression and commitment.

gender: Personality traits and behavior that characterize an individual as masculine or feminine.

gender identity: A person's personal, internal sense of maleness or femaleness, which is expressed in personality and behavior.

gender role: A person's outward expression of maleness or femaleness.

gender-role congruence: Agreement between partners' gender-role expectations and their performance.

gender schema theory: A theory suggesting that people have definite ideas about how males and females should look and behave, based on the framework of logic and ideas used to organize information and make sense of it.

gender stereotypes: Assumed differences, norms, attitudes, and expectations about men and women.

gonorrhea: Old sexually transmitted disease; women often show no symptoms; may lead to infertility in men and women; treated with antibiotics.

hepatitis: A liver infection caused by different viruses (A, B, C); all may be transmitted sexually as well as by other ways (sharing dirty needles, for example).

herpes: Widespread viral sexually transmitted disease characterized by painful blisters during outbreaks; medications reduce outbreaks but cannot cure herpes.

heterogamy: The selection of a partner who is different from oneself.

HIV: See *human immunodeficiency virus*.

homogamy: The selection of a partner who is similar to oneself.

hooking up: Engaging in sexual behavior—from kissing to having intercourse—without emotional involvement.

human chorionic gonadotropin: A hormone produced by the placenta that, if present in the mother's blood or urine, is an indication of pregnancy.

human immunodeficiency virus: A sexually transmitted disease caused by a virus that attacks the immune system, eventually resulting in AIDS; HIV is transmitted during sexual contact, in body fluids such as blood, semen, or breast milk; and prenatally.

human papillomavirus: Most common sexually transmitted disease; some strains of human papillomavirus cause genital warts; others cause cervical cancer.

hypergamous union: Marriage in which one spouse marries upward on the social ladder.

hypoactive sexual desire: Persistent or recurrent absence of sexual desire; described as *secondary hypoactive sexual desire* when the person has experienced sexual interest but loses it.

hypogamous union: Marriage in which one spouse marries downward on the social ladder.

ideal mate theory: A theory that people tend to marry someone who fulfills their fantasy of what an ideal mate should be like, based partly on early childhood experiences.

imaging: The process of "playacting" to present oneself in the best possible manner.

implant: A matchstick-size device that is placed under the skin and releases progestin.

implementation power: Power that sets decisions in motion.

incest: Sexual activity between two people who are closely related.

infertility: Failure to achieve a pregnancy after 1 year of frequent, unprotected sexual intercourse.

informational power: Power acquired because of extensive knowledge of a specific area.

instrumental role: The role of the family in meeting the needs of society or the physical needs of family members.

intergenerational stake: Family members' perceptions of closeness, especially as they relate to life course concerns that characterize each generation.

International Family Strengths Model: A model that proposes that all families—from around the world—have basic qualities that make them strong and that can be used to promote success in relationships.

interpersonal sources of conflict: Tensions that occur in the relationships between people.

intracytoplasmic sperm injection: The process of injecting a single sperm cell directly into a single egg cell to further enhance the possibility of fertilization.

intrauterine device: A device that is inserted into the uterus and worn there as a means of preventing pregnancy.

intrauterine system: A contraceptive device that is inserted into the uterus and releases small amounts of progestin continuously for up to 5 years.

in vitro fertilization: Removing egg cells from a woman, fertilizing with sperm in the laboratory, and then placing the fertilized egg in the uterus.

involuntary stable (permanent) singles: Never-marrieds and previously marrieds who wanted to marry, who have not found a mate, and who have more or less accepted being single.

involuntary temporary singles: Never-marrieds and previously marrieds who have been actively seeking a mate but have not found one.

joint legal custody: Custody shared by both parents, both of whom are responsible for childrearing and for making decisions regarding the child.

Kaplan sexual response model: Model of human sexual response cycle including the phases of sexual desire, vasocongestion, and reversal of vasocongestion.

labor: Rhythmic muscular contractions of the uterus that expel the baby.

Lamaze method: A popular childbirth training method in which the woman has control of the childbirth experience by getting in good physical shape, learning controlled breathing and muscle relaxation techniques, and receiving emotional support from her partner.

laparoscopy: Surgical procedure whereby a tubular instrument is passed through the abdominal wall.

legitimate power: Power that is bestowed by society on men and women as their right according to social prescription.

limerence: A term used by Tennov (1979) to describe the intense, wildly emotional highs and lows of being in love.

longitudinal study: A research design with repeated observations of the same individuals at various points in time.

machismo: Spanish for "manhood"; masculinity.

male condom: A latex sheath worn over the penis to prevent sperm from being ejaculated into the vagina; also prevents the spread of sexually transmitted disease.

marital adjustment: The process of modifying, adapting, and altering individual and couple patterns of behavior and interaction to achieve maximum satisfaction in the relationship.

marital adjustment tasks: Areas of concern in marriage in which adjustments must be made.

masculinity: Personality and behavioral characteristics of a male according to culturally defined standards of maleness.

Masters and Johnson sexual response model: Model of human sexual response cycle including the phases of excitement, plateau, orgasm, and resolution.

matriarchal family: A family in which the mother is head of the household, with authority over other family members.

matrilineal descent: Inheritance that is traced through the female line.

matrilocal residence: A residential pattern in which newlyweds reside with or near the woman's family.

mini-pill: An oral contraceptive containing progestin only.

Naegele's formula: A method of calculating the expected date of birth by subtracting 3 months from the first day of the last period and adding 7 days.

narcissistic love: Love of self; selfish, self-centered love.

needs theories: Theories of mate selection proposing that we select partners who will fulfill our own needs—both complementary and instrumental.

negative affect reciprocity: A pattern of communication in unhappy couples whereby partners respond negatively to each other's statements.

negative identification: The effort on the part of the child not to be like the parent.

neolocal residence: A residential pattern in which newlyweds leave their parents' homes and reside in a new location of their choice rather than with either family.

no-fault divorce: A legal approach that eliminates fault as a precondition for access to courts and recognizes the right of individuals to petition for divorce on the grounds of irretrievable breakdown of the marriage or irreconcilable differences.

noncontingent reinforcement: Unconditional approval of another person.

norepinephrine: A hormone secreted by the adrenal glands that has a stimulating effect on blood pressure and acts as a neurotransmitter.

norms: See *social norms*.

nuclear family: A father, a mother, and their children.

oral contraceptives: Birth control pills taken orally (by mouth).

orchestration power: The power to make the important decisions that determine family lifestyle.

orgasmic disorder: Personal distress caused by a persistent difficulty in, delay in, or absence of experiencing orgasm; causes may be physical or psychological.

oxytocin: A neurotransmitter that produces feelings of attachment and union with someone; a "cuddle chemical."

parental identification and modeling: The process by which the child adopts and internalizes parental values.

parent image theory: A theory of mate selection that a person is likely to marry someone resembling his or her parent of the opposite sex.

parenting coalition: The biological parents (now divorced and remarried) plus the stepparents cooperate in rearing their own children and any stepchildren.

patriarchal family: A family in which the father is head of the household, with authority over other family members.

patrilineal descent: Inheritance that is traced through the male line.

patrilocal residence: A residential pattern in which a newlywed couple resides with or near the man's family.

pediculosis: Body lice; transmitted by close body contact; cause severe itching.

personal sources of conflict: Those that originate within the individual when inner drives, instincts, and values pull against one another.

physical sources of conflict: Inner tensions having a physical origin, such as fatigue, hunger, or a headache.

placebo: A pill that has no pharmacological effect.

placenta previa: A complication of pregnancy in which the placenta grows partly or all the way over the opening to the cervix.

polyandrous family: A woman married to more than one man/husband.

polygamous family: A single family unit based on the marriage of one person to two or more mates.

polygynous family: A man married to more than one woman/wife.

positive identification: The attachment of a child to positive images of desired loving behavior.

positive signs: Signs of pregnancy detected by the physician that indicate positively that the woman is pregnant.

postparental years: The period between the last child leaving home and the parents' retirement; also called the empty-nest years.

post–traumatic stress disorder: Severe stress reactions that occur after a person has suffered a trauma.

power: In intimate relationships, the ability to influence one's partner to get what one wants.

power processes: The ways in which power is applied.

pregnancy-induced hypertension: A dangerous elevation of blood pressure; also called toxemia or preeclampsia.

premature ejaculation: Reaching orgasm too rapidly for his or his partner's enjoyment; very easily and successfully treated.

prepared childbirth: Physical, social, intellectual, and emotional preparation for the birth of a baby.

presumptive signs: Signs by which a woman presumes she is pregnant.

probable signs: Signs detected by the examining physician that indicate pregnancy is probable.

progestin injection: An injection of progestin to prevent pregnancy.

propinquity: In mate selection, the tendency to choose someone who is geographically near.

psychological game: A pattern of interaction that appears legitimate, but actually has an ulterior motive.

psychological power: The ability to bestow or withhold affection.

psychosocial task: The skills, knowledge, functions, and attitudes individuals need to acquire at different periods in their lives.

refractory period: A period of time following orgasm when men cannot be rearoused; stimulation of the penis is unpleasant and orgasm is not physiologically possible.

reliability: The degree to which a measurement technique produces similar outcomes when it is repeated.

Rh incompatibility: A condition in which the mother has Rh-negative blood and the fetus has Rh-positive blood.

rites of passage: Ceremonies by which people pass from one social status to another.

role ambiguity: The uncertainty felt when choosing a gender role.

roles: See *social roles*.

role strain: The stress of trying to meet the demands of many roles.

romantic love: A profoundly tender or passionate affection for another person, characterized by intense feelings and emotion.

rooming-in: Method of postpartum care in which the mother and father care for their newborn themselves in an area of the hospital assigned to them.

sandwich generation: Middle-age adults caught between caregiving for their children and for their elderly parents.

scapegoating: Blaming someone else for every bad thing that happens.

selfism: A personal value system that emphasizes that the way to find happiness is through self-gratification and narcissism.

sexual addiction: Compulsive sexual behavior that continues despite severe negative consequences.

sexuality: Everything about us that makes us male or female, including emotions, values, ethics, social relationships, and spiritual faith.

show: Blood-tinged mucus plug that is expelled from the cervix.

sibling rivalry: The competition of brothers and sisters for the attention, approval, and affection of parents.

single-parent family: A parent (who may or may not have been married) and one or more children.

situational or environmental sources of conflict: These include living conditions, societal pressures, cultural strains, and unexpected events.

socialization: The process by which people learn the ways of a given society or social group so that they can function within it.

social learning theory: A theory that suggests that children learn how to behave in relationships by modeling their parents' behaviors and attitudes.

social learning theory of gender identity: A theory emphasizing that boys develop "maleness" and girls develop "femaleness" through exposure to scores of influences—including parents, television, school, and peers—that teach them what it means to be a man or a woman in their culture.

social norms: Expectations for behavior as one performs social roles.

social roles: Culturally defined social positions such as mother, grandparent, supervisor, or student.

social structure/cultural theories: Theories suggesting that most of the differences between male and female gender roles are established because of the status, power, and division of labor in a given society.

sole legal custody: Situation in which the noncustodial parent forfeits the right to make decisions about the children's health, education, or religious training.

spermicides: Chemicals that are toxic to sperm and are used as a contraceptive in the form of foam, suppository, cream, jelly, or film.

spouse abuse: Physical or emotional mistreatment of one's spouse.

stepfamily: A remarried man and/or woman plus children from a former marriage.

sterilization: The process of rendering a person infertile by performing either a vasectomy in the male or a tubal ligation in the female.

structural-functional theory: A theory that emphasizes the function of the family as a social institution in meeting the needs of society.

structured separation: A time-limited approach in which partners terminate cohabitation, commit themselves to regularly scheduled therapy with a therapist, and agree to regular interpersonal contact—with a moratorium on a final decision either to reunite or to divorce.

surrogate mother: A woman who agrees to be impregnated (by artificial insemination or in vitro fertilization), to carry the fetus to term, and then to give the child to the couple, along with all parental rights.

symbolic interaction theory: A theory that describes the family as a unit of interacting personalities communicating through symbols.

symptothermal method: Combining several natural family planning methods (basal body temperature plus cervical mucus, for example) to achieve greater accuracy in pinpointing ovulation.

syphilis: Untreated syphilis proceeds through three stages; the last may result in paralysis, insanity, or death; treated with antibiotics; may be transmitted prenatally.

systems theory: A theory that emphasizes the interdependence of family members and how those members affect one another.

teratogens: Agents that disrupt prenatal development.

theory: A tentative explanation of facts and data that have been observed.

theory of primary interest and presumed competence: The theory that the person who is most interested in, most involved with, and best qualified to make a particular choice will be more likely to do so.

transgender people: People who feel their biological sex does not match their gender identity.

transsexual: A transgendered person who seeks to live as a member of the opposite sex with the help of hormones and surgery.

transverse birth: When the shoulder and arm of the baby are the first parts seen at the opening of the vagina.

tubal ligation: Female sterilization by severing and/or closing the fallopian tubes so that the ova cannot pass down the tube.

tubal pregnancy: A type of ectopic pregnancy in which attachment and growth of the embryo occur in the fallopian tube.

umbilical cord: The hollow cord connecting the circulation system of the fetus to the placenta.

unconditional positive regard: Acceptance of another person as he or she is.

vaginal ring: A flexible, transparent ring that is inserted into the vagina and releases a combination of estrogen and progestin continuously at a low dose for 1 month.

vaginismus: Painful, involuntary contractions of the vaginal muscles that make intercourse exceedingly difficult or impossible.

vaginitis: Any inflammation of the vagina; may be caused by microscopic parasites, fungal infection, or bacterial infection.

validity: The degree to which the instrument being used is measuring what it is intended to measure.

vasectomy: Male sterilization whereby the vasa deferentia are cut and tied to prevent the sperm from being ejaculated out of the penis.

vasocongestion: The buildup of blood in the pelvic area and penis.

vasopressin: A neurotransmitter that produces feelings of attachment and union with someone; a "cuddle chemical."

ventilation: The process of airing, or expressing, negative emotions and feelings.

voidable marriage: A marriage that can be set aside by annulment under certain prescribed legal circumstances.

void marriage: A marriage considered invalid in the first place because it was illegal.

voluntarily childless family: A couple who decide not to have children.

voluntary stable (permanent) singles: Never-marrieds and previously marrieds who choose to be single.

voluntary temporary singles: Never-marrieds and previously marrieds who are not opposed to the idea of marriage but are not currently seeking mates.

withdrawal: Withdrawal of the penis from the vagina prior to ejaculation; used as an attempt at birth control.

work–family spillover: The extent to which participation in one domain (e.g., work) impacts participation in another domain (e.g., family).

zygote: A fertilized egg cell.

zygote intrafallopian transfer: Removing egg cells from a woman, mixing with sperm in the laboratory, and placing the fertilized egg cells directly into the fallopian tube.

References

Abortion Law Homepage. (2000, April 10). Partial-birth abortion laws. Retrieved from http://members.aol.com/abtrbng/pbal.htm

Abram, K. M., Zwecker, N. A., Welty, L. J., Hershfield, J. A., Dulcan, M. K., and Teplin, L. A. (2015). Comorbidity and continuity of psychiatric disorders in youth after detention: A prospective longitudinal study. *JAMA Psychiatry, 72*(1), 84–93.

Acitelli, L. K. (2001). Maintaining and enhancing a relationship by attending to it. In J. H. Harvey and A. Wenzel (Eds.), *Close Relationships: Maintenance and Enhancement* (pp. 153–167). Mahwah, NJ: Erlbaum.

Ackard, D. M., and Neumark-Sztainer, D. (2002). Date violence and date rape among adolescents: Associations with disordered eating behaviors and psychological health. *Child Abuse and Neglect, 26*(5), 455–473.

Ackerman, R.A., Kashy, D.A., Donnellan, M.B., Neppl, T., Lorenz, F.D., and Conger, R.D. (2013). The interpersonal legacy of a positive family climate in adolescence. *Psychological Science, 24*(3), 243–250.

Adamcyzk-Robinette, S. L., Fletcher, A. C., and Wright, K. (2002). Understanding the authoritative parenting–early adolescent tobacco use link: The mediating role of peer tobacco use. *Journal of Youth and Adolescence, 31*(4), 311–318.

Administration on Aging. (2015). National Family Caregiver Support Program. OAA Title IIIE. http://www.aoa.acl.gov/AoA.

AFCARS. (2015). Adoption and Foster Care Analyses and Reporting System. U.S. Department of Health and Human Services. Administration for Children, Youth, and Families. http://www. acf.hhs.gov

Agocha, V., and Cooper, M. (1999). Risk perceptions and safer-sex intentions: Does a partner's physical attractiveness undermine the use of risk-relevant information? *Personality and Social Psychology Bulletin, 25*(6), 746–759.

Ahrons, C. (2004). *We're Still Family: What Grown Children Have to Say about Their Parents' Divorce.* New York: HarperCollins.

Ahrons, C. R., and Rodgers, R. (1987). *Divorced Families: A Multidisciplinary View.* New York: Norton.

Alayi, Z., AhmadiGatab, T., and Khamen, A. Z. (2011). Relation between communication skills and marital adaptability among university students. *Procedia—Social and Behavioral Sciences, 30*, 1959–1963.

Albada, K. F., Knapp, M. L., and Theune, K. E. (2002). Interaction appearance theory: Changing perceptions of physical attractiveness through social interaction. *Communication Theory, 12*, 8–40.

Aleccia. J. (2013, September 27). Two weeks after baby? More new moms cut maternity leave short. *Today Health.* Retrieved from http://www.today.com/health.

Al-Krenawi, A., and Graham, J. R. (1998). Divorce among Muslim Arab women in Israel. *Journal of Divorce and Remarriage, 29*, 103–119.

Allen, E. S., Rhoades, G. K., Stanley, S. M., Loew, B., and Markman, H. J. (2012). The effects of marriage education for Army couples with a history of infidelity. *Journal of Family Psychology, 26*(1), 26–35.

Allen, K. R., and Pickett, R. S. (1987). Forgotten streams in the family life course: Utilization of qualitative retrospective interviews in the analysis of lifelong single women's family careers. *Journal of Marriage and Family, 49*, 517–526.

Amato, P. R. (2000). Diversity within single parent families. In D. H. Demo and K. R. Allen (Eds.), *Handbook of Family Diversity* (pp. 149–172). London: Oxford University Press.

Amato, P. R. (2001). Children of divorce in the 1990s: An update of the Amato and Keith (1991) meta-analysis. *Journal of Family Psychology, 15*(3), 355–370.

Amato, P. R. (2005). The impact of family formation change on the cognitive, social, and emotional well-being of the next generation. *The Future of Children, 15*, 75–96.

Amato, P. R. (2010). Research on divorce: Continuing trends and new developments. *Journal of Marriage and Family, 72*, 650–666.

Amato, P. R., and Anthony, C. J. (2014). Estimating the effects of parental divorce and death with fixed effects models. *Journal of Marriage and Family, 76* (April), 370–376. doi:10.1111/jomf.12100.

Amato, P. R., and Booth, A. (2001) The legacy of parents' marital discord: Consequences for children's marital quality. *Journal of Personality and Social Psychology, 81*(4), 627–638.

Amato, P. R., Booth, A., Johnson, D. R., and Rogers, S. J. (2007). *Alone Together: How Marriage in America Is Changing.* Cambridge, MA: Harvard University Press.

Amato, P. R., and Cheadle, J. (2005). The long reach of divorce: Divorce and child well-being across three generations. *Journal of Marriage and Family, 67*(1), 191–206.

Amato, P. R., and DeBoer, D. D. (2001). The transmission of marital instability across generations: Relationship skills or commitment to marriage? *Journal of Marriage and Family, 63*(4), 1038–1051.

Amato, P. R., and Gilbreth, J. G. (1999). Nonresident father and children's well-being: A meta-analysis. *Journal of Marriage and Family, 61*, 557–573.

Amato, P. R., and Homann-Marriott, B. (2007). A comparison of high- and low-distress marriages that end in divorce. *Journal of Marriage and Family, 69*(3), 621–638.

Amato, P. R., and Previti, D. (2003). People's reasons for divorcing: Gender, social class, the life course, and adjustment. *Journal of Family Issues, 24*(5), 602–626.

Ambert, A. (1988). Relationships with former in-laws after divorce: A research note. *Journal of Marriage and Family, 50*, 679–686.

Ambert, A.M. (2009). *Divorce: Facts, Causes, and Consequences.* Ottawa, Canada: Vanier Institute of the Family.

American College of Obstetricians and Gynecologists. (2011/2012). Substance abuse reporting and pregnancy: The role of the obstetrician and gynecologist. American College of Obstetricians and Gynecologists (ACOG). Committee on Health Care for Underserved Women. January, 2011/Reaffirmed 2012. Retrieved from http://www.acog.org.

American Pregnancy Association. (2016). Gestational hypertension: Pregnancy induced hypertension. http://americanpregnancy.org

American Society for Aesthetic Plastic Surgery. (2005). Plastic surgery. Retrieved August 18, 2005, from http://www.plasticsurgery.org/news-room/index.cfm

Andersen, M. (2005). Thinking about women: A quarter century's view. *Gender and Society, 19*(4), 437–455.

Anderson, C., John, O.P., and Keltner, D. (2012). The personal sense of power. Journal of Personality, 80(2). DOI: 10.1111/j.1467-6494.211.00734x

Anderson, D., and Hamilton, M. (2005). Gender role stereotyping of parents in children's picture books: The invisible father. *Sex Roles, 52*(3–4), 145–151.

Anderson, E., Greene, S., Walker, L., Malerba, C., Forgatch, M., and DeGarmo, D. (2004). Ready to take a chance again: Transitions into dating among divorced parents. *Journal of Divorce and Remarriage, 40*(2–4), 61–75.

Anderson, J. Q., and Rainie, L. (2010). The future of social relations. *The Pew Center's Internet and American Life Project.* Retrieved from http://www.pewinternet.org.

Anderson, S. (2014). *The Journey from Abandonment to Healing.* New York: Berkley.

Anetzberger, G. J. (2005). Preface to the clinical management of elder abuse. *Clinical Gerontologist, 28* (1–2), xv–xvi.

Anisman, H., and Merali, Z. (1999). Understanding stress: Characteristics and caveats. *Alcohol Research and Health, 23*, 241–249.

Anjalin, U. (2015). A content analysis of gender stereotypes in contemporary teenage magazines. Master's Thesis, University of Tennessee. http://trace.tennessee.edu/utk-gradthes/3343

Antonucci, T. C., Lansford, J. E., Schaberg, L., Smith, J., Baltes, M., Akiyama, H., et al. (2001). Widowhood and illness: A comparison of social network characteristics in France, Germany, Japan, and the United States. *Psychology and Aging, 16*, 655–665.

APA Task Force on Mental Health and Abortion. (2008). *Executive Summary: Mental Health and Abortion.* Retrieved from http://www.apa.org.

Aquilino, W. S. (2005). Impact of family structure on parental attitudes toward the economic support of adult children over the transition to adulthood. *Journal of Family Issues, 26*(2), 143–167.

Arber, S. (2004). Gender, marital status, and aging: Linking material, health, and social resources. *Journal of Aging Studies, 18*, 91–108.

Archer, J. (2002). Sex differences in physically aggressive acts between heterosexual partners: A meta-analytic review. *Aggression and Violent Behavior, 7*, 313–351.

Archer, J. (2006). Cross-cultural differences in physical aggression between partners: A social-role analysis. *Personality and Social Psychology Review, 10*, 133–153.

Ariely, D., and Loewenstein, G. (2006). The heat of the moment: The effect of sexual arousal on sexual decision making. *Journal of Behavioral Decision Making, 19*, 87–98.

Arnett, J. J. (1998). Learning to stand alone: The contemporary American transition to adulthood in cultural and historical context. *Human Development, 41*, 295–315.

Arnett, J. J. (2000). Emerging adulthood. *American Psychologist, 55*, 469–480.

Arnett, J. J. (2003). Conceptions of the transition to adulthood among emerging adults in American ethnic groups. In J. Arnett and N. Galambos (Eds.), *New Directions for Child and Adolescent Development: Cultural Conceptions of the Transition to Adulthood* (pp. 63–75). Chichester, UK: Wiley.

Arnold, L., and Campbell, C. (2013). The high price of being single. *The Atlantic.* http://www.theatlantic.com

Aron, A., Fisher, H., Mashek, D., Strong, G., Li, H., and Brown, L. (2005). Reward, motivation and emotion systems associated with early-stage intense romantic love. *Journal of Neurophysiology, 94*(1), 327–337.

Aron, A., Norman, C. C., Aron, E. M., McKenna, C., and Heyman, R. E. (2000). Couples' shared participation in novel and arousing activities and experienced relational quality. *Journal of Personality and Social Psychology, 78,* 273–284.

Arp, D. H., Arp, C. S., Stanley, S. M., Markman, H. J., and Blumberg, S. L. (2000). *Fighting for Your Empty Nest Marriage: Reinventing Your Relationship When the Kids Leave Home.* San Francisco: Jossey–Bass/Pfeiffer.

Artis, J. E. (2007, February). Maternal cohabitation and child well-being among kindergarten children. *Journal of Marriage and Family, 69,* 222–236.

Asante, K. O., Osafo, J., and Nyamekye, G. K. (2014). An exploratory study of factors contributing to divorce among married couples Accra, Ghana: A qualitative approach. *Journal of Divorce and Remarriage, 55*(1), 16–32. doi:10.1080/10502556.2013.837715.

Askan, M., Noah, S. B. M., Hassan, S. A. Bt., and Baba, M. Bt. (2012). Comparison of the effects of communication and conflict resolution skills training on marital satisfaction. *International Journal of Psychological Studies, 4*(1), 182–195.

Austin, S. B., Haines, J., and Veugelers, P. J. (2009). Body satisfaction and body weight: Gender differences and sociodemographic determinants. *BMC Public Health, 9,* 313.

Aydt, H., and Corsaro, W. (2003). Difference in children's construction of gender across culture. *American Behavioral Scientist, 46*(10), 1306–1325.

Aylor, B., and Dainton, M. (2004). Biological sex and psychological gender as predictors of routine and strategic relational maintenance. *Sex Roles, 50*(9–10), 689–697.

Azemun, M., and Benito, L. (2014). Immigration reform 2014: A state and national perspective. *Social Policy, 44,* 3–8.

Baber, K. M., and Allen, K. R. (1992). *Women and Families: Feminist Reconstructions.* New York: Guilford Press.

Bachman, H. J., and Chase-Lansdale, P. L. (2005). Custodial grandmothers' physical, mental, and economic well-being: Comparisons of primary caregivers from low-income neighborhoods. *Family Relations, 54,* 475–487.

Bada, H. S., Das, A., Bauer, C. R., Shankaran, S., Lester, B., LaGasse, L., et al. (2007). Impact of prenatal cocaine exposure on child behavior problems through school age. *Pediatrics, 119,* 348–359.

Baghdjian, A. (2011). Rise in male eating disorders tip of iceberg. *Reuters,* July 13.

Baker, C. (2005). Images of women's sexuality in advertisements: A content analysis of black and white oriented women's and men's magazines. *Sex Roles, 52,* 13–27.

Balsam, K.F., Beauchaine, T.P., Rothblum., E.D., and Solomon, S.E. (2008). Three-year follow-up of same-sex couples who had civil unions in Vermont, same-sex couples not in civil unions and heterosexual married couples. *Developmental Psychology, 44,* 102–116. DOI:10.1037/0012-1649.44.1.102

Banks, R. R. (2011). *Is Marriage for White People? How the African American Marriage Decline Affects Everyone.* New York: Dutton.

Banschick, M. (2012). The high failure rate of second and third marriages. *Psychology Today.* Retrieved from https://psychologytoday.com.

Banschick, M. (2013). *The Intelligent Divorce.* Katonah, NY: Intelligent Divorce Press.

Baptist, J. A., Thompson, D. E., Norton, A. M., Hardy, N. R., and Link, C. D. (2012). The effects of the intergenerational transmission of family emotional processes in conflict styles: The moderating role of attachment. *The American Journal of Family Therapy, 40,* 56–73.

Barnes, S. L. (2001). Stressors and strengths: A theoretical and practical examination of nuclear, single-parent, and augmented African American families. *Families in Society, 82*(5), 449–460.

Barnes, T., and Eardley, I. (2007). Premature ejaculation. The scope of the problem. *Journal of Sex and Marital Therapy, 33,* 151–170.

Barnett, R. C. (2004). Women and multiple roles: Myths and reality. *Harvard Review of Psychiatry, 12,* 158–164.

Barnett, R. C., and Hyde J. S. (2001). Women, men, work, and family: An expansionist theory. *American Psychologist, 56*(10), 781–796.

Barnett, R. C., Kibria, N., Baruch, G. K., and Pleck, J. H. (1991). Adult daughter–parent relationships and their associations with daughters' subjective well-being and psychological distress. *Journal of Marriage and Family, 53,* 29–42.

Barnett, R. C., Marshall, N. L., and Pleck, J. H. (1992). Adult son–parent relationships and their associations with sons' psychological distress. *Journal of Family Issues, 13,* 505–525.

Barqawi, A., and Crawford, E. D. (2006). Testosterone replacement therapy and the risk of prostate cancer. Is there a link? *International Journal of Impotence Research, 18,* 323–328.

Barranti, C. C. R. (1985). The grandparent–grandchild relationship: Family resource in an era of voluntary bonds. *Family Relations, 34,* 343–352.

Barrett, A. (1999). Social support and life satisfaction among the never married. *Research on Aging, 21*(1), 46–72.

Barsky, J. L., Friedman, M. A., and Rosen, R. C. (2006). Sexual dysfunction and chronic illness: The role of flexibility in coping. *Journal of Sex and Marital Therapy, 32,* 235–253.

Dunn, M. S., Bartee, R. T., and Perko, M. A. (2003). Self-reported alcohol use and sexual behaviors of adolescents. *Psychological Reports, 92*, 339–348.

Durex.com. (2007). Sexual well-being global study 2007–2008. Retrieved from http://durex.com/cm/sexualwellbeing

Dush, C. M. K., and Taylor, M. G. (2012). Trajectories of marital conflict across the life course: Predictors and interactions with marital happiness trajectories. *Journal of Family Issues, 33*(3), 341–360.

Dutro, E., and Selland, M. (2012). "One like to read, but one know one'm not good at it": Children's perspectives on high-stakes testing in a poverty school. *Curriculum Inquiry, 42*(3), 340–367.

Dutton, D., and Aron, A. P. (1974). Some evidence of heightened sexual attraction under conditions of high anxiety. *Journal of Personal and Social Psychology, 30*, 510–517.

Duvall, E. M. (1954). *In-Laws: Pro and Con*. New York: Association Press.

Duvall, E. M. (1977). *Marriage and Family Development* (5th ed.). Philadelphia: Lippincott.

Dykeman, C., and Nelson, J. (1995). Building strong working alliances with American Indian families. *Social Work in Education, 17*(3), 148–159.

Eaton, A. A., and Rose, S. (2011). Has dating become more egalitarian? A 35-year review using Sex roles. *Sex Roles.* Retrieved from http://www.FIU.edu/eaton%20rose%202011.pdf

Ebrahimi, E., and Kimiaei, S. E. (2014). The study of the relationship among marital satisfaction, attachment styles, and communication patterns in divorcing couples. *Journal of Divorce and Remarriage, 55*, 451–463. doi:1080/10502556.2014.931759.

Eccles, J. (2007). Families, schools, and developing achievement-related motivation and engagement. In J. Grusec and P. Hastings (Eds.), *Handbook of Socialization* (pp. 665–691). New York: Guilford Press.

Edin, K., and Shaefer, L. (2015). $2.00 a day: Living on almost nothing in America. NY: Houghton Mifflin Harcourt.

Ehrensaft, M., Langhinrichsen-Rohling, J., Heyman, R., O'Leary, K., and Lawrence, E. (1999). Feeling controlled in marriage: A phenomenon specific to physically aggressive couples. *Journal of Family Psychology, 13*(1), 20–32.

Eisenberg, R. (2013). The U.S. faces a married couples' retirement crisis. http://www.forbes.com.

Elder, G. H., Jr., Eccles, J. S., Ardelt, M., and Lord, S. (1995). Inner-city parents under economic pressure: Perspectives on strategies of parenting. *Journal of Marriage and Family, 57*, 771–784.

El Issa, E. (2016). 2015 American household credit debt study. Nerd Wallet. https://www.nerdwallet.com

Elkind, D. (2001). *The Hurried Child: Growing Up too Fast too Soon* (3rd ed.). Cambridge, MA: Perseus.

Elliott, D. B., and Lewis, J. M. (2010). Embracing the institution of marriage: The characteristics of remarried Americans. Retrieved from http://www.census.gov/population/www/socdem/marr-div/Remarriage

Elliott, M. (2015). The problems with maternity leaves in America. Money and Career Cheat Sheet. http://www.cheatsheet.com

Ellis, R. R., and Simmons, T. (2014). Coresident grandparents and their grandchildren. Retrieved from http://www.census.gov.

El-Sheikh, M., and Elmore-Staton, L. (2004). The link between marital conflict and child adjustment: Parent–child conflict and perceived attachments as mediators, potentiators, and mitigators of risk. *Development and Psychopathology, 16*(3), 631–648.

Emery, R. E., Sbarra, D., and Grover, T. (2005). Divorce mediation: Research and reflections. *Family Court Review, 43*(1), 22–37.

Engel, G., Olson, K. R., and Patrick, C. (2002). The personality of love: Fundamental motives and traits related to components of love. *Personality and Individual Differences, 32*(5), 839–853.

Erikson, E. H. (1959). *Identity and the Life Cycle*. New York: International Universities Press.

Erkut, S., Fields, J., Sing, R., and Marx, F. (1996). Diversity in girls' experiences: Feeling good about who you are. In B. Leadbeater and N. Way (Eds.), *Urban Girls*. New York: New York University Press.

Esmaeili, N. S., Yaacob, S. N., Juhari, R., and Schoebi, D. (2015).Predictors of psychological distress among divorced women in Iran. *Journal of Divorce and Remarriage, 56*(3), 248–259. doi:10.1080/10502556.2015.1012700.

Evan B. Donaldson Adoption Institute. (2008). Adoption by lesbians and gays: A national survey of adoption policies, practices, and attitudes. Retrieved from http://www.adoptioninstitute.org.

Evans, G. W. (2004). The environment of childhood poverty. *American Psychologist, 59*(2), 77–92.

Evertsson, M., and Nermo, M. (2004). Dependence within families and the division of labor: Comparing Sweden and the United States. *Journal of Marriage and the Family, 66*, 1272–1286.

Exner-Cortens, D., Eckenrode, J., and Rothman, E. (2013). Longitudinal associations between teen dating violence victimization and adverse health outcomes. *Pediatrics, 131*(1), 71–78.

Fabes, R. A. (1994). Physiological, emotional, and behavioral correlates of gender segregation. *New Directions for Child Development, 65*, 19–34.

Fagan, P. F., Kidd, A. J., and Potrykus, H. (2011). Marriage and economic well-being: The economy of the family rises or falls with marriage. Marriage and Religion Institute. Retrieved from http://downloads.frc.org

Fair Market Rents. (2015). Fair market rents for select metropolitan areas, 2015. U.S. Department of Housing and Urban Development.

Families USA. (2016). $27,950: Federal Poverty Guidelines 2016. http://familiesusa

Family Business Institute. (2013). Managing the stress of running a family business. Retrieved from http://familybusinessinstitute.com.

Fauchier, A., and Margolin, G. (2004). Affection and conflict in marital and parent–child relationships. *Journal of Marital and Family Therapy, 30*(2), 197–211.

Federal Bureau of Investigation. (2014). *Crime in the United States.* U.S. Department of Justice.

Federal Reserve. (2015). Report on the economic well-being of U.S. households in 2014. Balance sheet of households and nonprofit organizations. *Federal Reserve Flow of Funds Report.* Retrieved from http://www.federalreserve.gov

Federal Reserve Bank of New York. (2015). Household debt continues upward climb while student loan delinquencies worsen. Retrieved from http://newyorkfed.org.

Federenko, I. S., and Wadhwa, P. D. (2004). Women's mental health during pregnancy influences fetal and infant developmental and health outcomes. *CNS Spectrums, 9*(3), 198–206.

Feeney, J. A. (1999). Issues of closeness and distance in dating relationships: Effects of sex and attachment style. *Journal of Social and Personal Relationships, 16*(5), 571–590.

Feeney, J. A. (2004). Transfer of attachment from parents to romantic partners: Effects of individual and relationship variables. *Journal of Family Studies, 10*(2), 220–238.

Feeney, J. A., and Noller, P. (2004). Attachment in sexuality in close relationships. In J. H. Harvey, A. Wentzel, and S. Sprecher (Eds.), *The Handbook of Sexuality in Close Relationships* (pp. 183–201). Mahwah, NJ: Erlbaum.

Feldman, R., Sussman, A. L., and Zigler, E. (2004). Parental leave and work adaptation at the transition to parenthood: Individual, marital, and social correlates. *Journal of Applied Developmental Psychology, 25*(4), 459–479.

Feldman, S. S., Mont-Reynaud, R., and Rosenthal, D. A. (1992). When East moves West: Acculturation of values of Chinese adolescents in the United States and Australia. *Journal of Research on Adolescence, 2,* 147–173.

Feldman, S. S., Wentzel, K. R., and Gehring, T. M. (1989). A comparison of the views of mothers, fathers, and preadolescents about family cohesion and power. *Journal of Family Psychology, 3,* 39–60.

Fernandez, M. (2013). Abortion restrictions become law in Texas, but opponents will press fight. Retrieved from http://www.nytimes.com/2013/07/19

Fiebert, M. S., Nugent, D., Hershberger, S. L., and Kasdan, M. (2004). Dating and commitment choices as a function of ethnicity among American college students in California. *Psychological Reports, 94*(3), 1293–1300.

Fields, J. (2004). America's families and living arrangements: 2003. *Current Population Reports,* P20–553. Washington, DC: U.S. Bureau of the Census.

Fifth and Pacific Companies. (2010). College dating violence and abuse poll. Conducted by Knowledge Networks. Retrieved from http://www.breakthecycle.org.

Filsinger, E. E., and Thoma, S. J. (1988). Behavioral antecedents of relationship stability and adjustment: A five-year longitudinal study. *Journal of Marriage and Family, 50,* 785–795.

Fincham, F. D., Beach, S. R., and Davila, J. (2007). Longitudinal relations between forgiveness and conflict resolution in marriage. *Journal of Family Psychology, 21,* 542–545.

Find Law. (2015). *Adoption.* Retrieved from http://findlaw.com

Find Law. (2016). *Marriage versus Cohabitation.* http://family.findlaw.com

Fine, M. A., McKenry, P. C., Donnelly, B. W., and Voydanoff, P. (1992). Perceived adjustment of parents and children: Variations by family structure, race, and gender. *Journal of Marriage and Family, 54,* 118–127.

Fingerman, K. L., Cheng, Y. P., Birditt, K., and Zarit, S. (2012). Only as happy as the least happy child: Multiple grown children's problems and successes and middle-aged parents' well-being. *The Journal of Gerontology: Series B, Psychological Sciences and Social Sciences, 67*(2), 184–193. doi:10.1093/geronb/gbr086.

Fingerman, K. L., Hay, E. L., and Birditt, K. S. (2004). The best of ties, the worst of ties: Close, problematic, and ambivalent social relationships. *Journal of Marriage and Family, 66,* 792–808.

Fingerman, K. L., and Pitzer, L. M. (2007). Socialization in old age. In P. D. Hastings and J. E. Grusee, (Eds.), *Handbook of Socialization* (pp. 232–255). New York: Guilford Press.

Finkel, E. J. (2008). Intimate partner violence perpetration: Insights from the science of self-regulation. In J. P. Forgas and J. Fitness (Eds.), *Social Relationships: Cognitive, Affective, and Motivational Processes* (pp. 271–288). New York: Psychology Press.

Finkel, E. J., Eastwick, P. W., Karney, B. R., Reis, H. T., and Sprecher, S. (2012). Online dating: A critical analysis from the perspective of psychological science. *Psychological Science in the Public Interest, 13*(1), 3–66.

Firestone, J., Harris, R., and Lambert, L. (1999). Gender role ideology and the gender based differences in earnings. *Journal of Family and Economic Issues, 20*(2), 191–215.

Fisch, H. (2009). How often should you be having sex? Retrieved from http://www.doctoroz.com.

Fish, M. (2004). Attachment in infancy and preschool in low socioeconomic status rural Appalachian children: Stability and change and relations to preschool and kindergarten competence. *Developmental Psychopathology, 16*, 293–312.

Fisher, H. (2009). *Why Him? Why Her?* New York: Holt.

Fisher, L. (2010). Chelsea Clinton's interfaith marriage challenge: Kids, holidays, soul-searching. Retrieved from http://abcnews.go.com.

Fitness, J., and Duffield, J. (2004). Emotion and communication in families. In A. L. Vangelisti (Ed.), *Handbook of Family Communication* (pp. 473–494). Mahwah, NJ: Erlbaum.

FOCCUS. (2016). http://www.foccusinc.com

Food and Drug Administration. (2014). FDA approves Gardasil 9 for prevention of certain cancers caused by five additional types of HPV. Retrieved from http://www.fda.gov/news

For Your Marriage. (2012). Newly Married. For Your Marriage. http://www.foryourmarriage.org/everymarriage

Foster, B.L. (2014). The night shift. *Psychology Today.* http://www.psychologytoday.com

Foster care alumni. (2009). Retrieved September 2009 from http://www.fostercarealumni.org.

Foster, S. E., Vaughan, R. D., Foster, W. H., and Califano, J. A., Jr. (2003). Alcohol consumption and expenditures for underage drinking and adult excessive drinking. *Journal of the American Medical Association, 289*(8), 989–995.

Fottrell, Q. (2015). Women are still doing the majority of housework. *Daily Worth.* http://www.daily-worth.com

Fowers, B. J., and Olson, D. H. (1986). Predicting marital success with PREPARE: A predictive validity study. *Journal of Marital and Family Therapy, 12*, 403–413.

Francome, C. (1992). Irish women who seek abortions in England. *Family Planning Perspectives, 24*, 265–268.

Frankel, V. (2006). *Man's Search for Meaning.* Boston: Beacon.

Frederick, D., Fessler, D., and Haselton, M. (2005). Do representations of male muscularity differ in men's and women's magazines? *Body Image, 2*, 81–86.

Frederick, D. A., Forbes, G. B., Grigorian, K. E., and Jarcho, J. M. (2007). Gender and ethnic differences in self-objectification and body satisfaction among 2,206 undergraduates. *Sex Roles, 57*, 317–327.

Fredriksen-Goldsen, K., and Farwell, N. (2004). Dual responsibilities among black, Hispanic, Asian, and white employed caregivers. *Journal of Gerontological Social Work, 43*(4), 25–44.

Freeman, J.G., King, M., Pickett, W., Craig, W., Elgar, F., Janssen,I., and Klinger, D. (2012). *The Health of Canada's Young People: A Mental Health Focus.* Public Health Agency of Canada. www.publichealth.gc.ca

Freud, S. (1953). *Three Essays on the Theory of Sexuality* (standard ed., Vol. 7). London: Hogarth.

Friedan, B. (1993). *The Fountain of Age.* New York: Simon & Schuster.

Friedman, J., Shapiro, I., and Greenstein, R. (2005). Recent tax and income trends among high-income tax payers. Center on Budget and Policy Priority. Retrieved September 8, 2005, from http://www.cbpp.org/4-13-05tax.htm.

Friedman, P. (2000, April). The earned income tax credit. *Welfare Information Network Issue Notes, 4*(4). Retrieved April 9, 2003, from http://www.welfareinfo.org.

Fromm, E. (1956). *The Art of Loving.* New York: Harper & Row.

Fruh, S. M., Fulkerson, J. A., Kendrick, L. A., and Clanton, C. C. (2011). The surprising benefits of the family meal. *The Journal for Nurse Practitioners, 7*(1), 18–22.

Fry, R. (2013). A rising share of young adults live in their parents' home. Pew Research Center. Retrieved from http://www.pewsocialtrends.org/2013/08/01.

Fryar, C. D., Hirsch, R., Porter, K. S., Kottiri, B., Brody, D., and Louis, T. (2007, June 28). Drug use and sexual behaviors reported by adults: United States, 1999–2002. Advanced data from Vital and Health Statistics, Centers for Disease Control and Prevention, 384. Retrieved from http://www.cdc.gov/nchs/data/ad/ad384.pdf.

Fuligni, A., Burton, L., Marshall, S., Perez-Febles, A., Yarrington, J., Kirsh, L., and Merriwether-DeVries, C. (1999). Attitudes toward family obligations among American adolescents with Asian, Latin American, and European backgrounds. *Child Development, 70*(4), 1030–1044.ental health perspective. Sage Publications. http://sgo.sagepub.com. DOI: 10.1177/2158244015623593

Fullchange, A., and Furlong, M.J. (2016). An exploration of effects of bullying victimization from a complete

Gable, S. L., Reis, H. T., Impett, E. A., and Asher, E. R. (2004). What do you do when things go right? The intrapersonal and interpersonal benefits of sharing positive events. *Journal of Personality and Social Psychology, 87*(2), 228–245.

Gagliardi, A. (2005). Postpartum depression. In C. B. Fisher and R. M. Lerner (Eds.), *Encyclopedia of Applied Developmental Science* (Vol. 2, pp. 867–870). Thousand Oaks, CA: Sage.

Galinsky, E. (1999). *Ask the Children: What America's Children Really Think about Working Parents.* New York: Morrow.

Galliher, R. V., Rostosky, S. S., Welsh, D. P., and Kawaguchi, M. C. (1999). Power and psychological well-being in late adolescent romantic relationships. *Sex Roles, 40,* 689–710.

Galvin, K. M., and Brommel, B. J. (1986). *Family Communication: Cohesion and Change* (2nd ed.). Glenview, IL: Scott, Foresman.

Gander, K. (2015). One chart which shows how many hours people actually want to work every day. *Independent.* http://www.independent.co.uk

Ganong, L. H., Coleman, M., Fine, M., and Martin, P. (1999). Stepparents' affinity-seeking and affinity-maintaining strategies with stepchildren. *Journal of Family Issues, 20*(3), 299–327.

Garber, B. (2004). Directed co-parenting intervention: Conducting child-centered interventions in parallel with highly conflicted co-parents. *Professional Psychology: Research and Practice, 35*(1), 55–64.

Garcia, E. C. (2001). Parenting in Mexican American families. In N. B. Webb (Ed.), *Culturally Diverse Parent–Child and Family Relationships: A Guide for Social Workers and Other Practitioners* (pp. 157–179). New York: Columbia University Press.

Garcia, F. D., and Thibaut, F. (2010). Sexual addictions. *The American Journal of Drug and Alcohol Abuse, 36,* 254–260.

Garcia, J.R., Reiber, C., Massey, S.G., and Merrwether, A.M. (2012). Sexual hookup culture: A review. *Review of General Psychology: A Journal of Division 1, of the American Psychological Association, 16*(2), 161–176. http://doi.org.1037/a0027911

Garner, D. M. (1997, January/February). Body image. *Psychology Today, 32–84.*

Garrett, M. T., and Wilbur, M. P. (1999). Does the worm live in the ground? Reflections on Native American spirituality. *Journal of Multicultural Counseling and Development, 27*(4), 193–206.

Garry, J. P., Morrissey, S. L., and Whetstone, L. M. (2003). Substance use and weight loss tactics among middle school youth. *International Journal of Eating Disorders, 33*(1), 55–63.

Gaudin, S. (2007). Cybercriminals playing mind games with users. Retrieved November 16, 2009, from http://www.networkcomputing.com.

Gaufberg, S.V.(2008). Abruptio placentae. Retrieved September 2009 from http://emedicine.com/article

Gauthier, Y., Fortin, G., and Jeliu, G. (2004). Clinical application of attachment theory in permanency planning for children in foster care: The importance of continuity of care. *Infant Mental Health Journal, 25*(4), 379–396.

Geller, P. A. (2004). Pregnancy as a stressful life event. *CNS Spectrums, 9*(3), 188–197.

Geller, P. A., Kerns, D., and Klier, C. M. (2004). Anxiety following miscarriage and the subsequent pregnancy: A review of the literature and future directions. *Journal of Psychosomatic Research, 56*(1), 35–45.

Gelles, R. J., and Cavanaugh, M. M. (2005). Violence, abuse, and neglect in families and intimate relationships. In P. C. McHenry and S. J. Price (Eds.), *Families and Change* (3rd ed.). Thousand Oaks, CA: Sage.

Gelman, S. A., Taylor, M. G., and Nguyen, S. P. (2004). Mother–child conversations about gender. *Monographs of the Society for Research in Child Development, 69*(1), vii–127.

Gershoff, E.T. (2016). Spanking and child development: We know enough to stop hitting our children. *Child Development Perspectives, 7*(3), 133–137.

Gershon, A., Gowen, L., Compian, L., and Hayward, C. (2004). Gender-stereotyped imagined dates and weight concerns in sixth-grade girls. *Sex Roles, 50*(7–8), 515–523.

Gerson, K., and Jacobs, J. A. (2007). The work–home crunch. In S. J. Ferguson (Ed.), *Shifting the Center.* New York: McGraw–Hill.

Gerstel, N. (1988). Divorce and kin ties: The importance of gender. *Journal of Marriage and Family, 50,* 209–219.

"Gestational hypertension (PIH)." (2014). Baby Center. Retrieved from http://www.babycenter.com.

Giarrusso, R., Stallings, M., and Bengtson, V. L. (1995). *The "Intergenerational Hypothesis" Revisited: Parent–Child Differences in Perceptions of Relationships 20 Years Later.* New York: Springer.

Gibbs, J. (1996). Health compromising behaviors in urban early adolescent females: Ethnic and socioeconomic variations. In B. Leadbeater and N. Way (Eds.), *Urban Girls.* New York: New York University Press.

Gigy, L., and Kelly, J. B. (1992). Reasons for divorce: Perspectives of divorcing men and women. *Journal of Divorce and Remarriage, 18,* 169–187.

Giles, J., and Heyman, G. (2005). Young children's beliefs about the relationship between gender and aggressive behavior. *Child Development, 76*(1), 107–121.

Gillespie, R. (2003). Understanding the gender identity of voluntarily childless women. *Gender and Society, 17*(1), 122–136.

Gillis, J. (2004). Marriages of the mind. *Journal of Marriage and Family, 66*(4), 988–991.

Gilman, J., Schneider, D., and Shulak, R. (2005). Children's ability to cope post-divorce: The effects of kids' turn intervention program on 7 to 9 year olds. *Journal of Divorce and Remarriage, 42*(3–4), 109–126.

Girl Guiding UK. (2009). Girls' attitude survey 2009. http://new.girlguiding.org/uk

Girl Guiding UK. (2015). Girls' attitude survey 2015. http://new.girlguiding.org.uk

Giugliano, J. R. (2012). Sex addiction as a mental health diagnosis: Coming together or coming apart? Sexologies. Retrieved from http://dx.doi.org

Glascock, J., and Preston-Schreck, C. (2004). Gender and racial stereotypes in daily newspaper comics: A time-honored tradition? *Sex Roles, 51*(7–8), 423–431.

Glass, J. (1992). Housewives and employed wives: Demographic and attitudinal change, 1972–1986. *Journal of Marriage and Family, 54*, 559–569.

Glenn, N. D., and Marquardt, E. (2001). *Hooking Up, Hanging Out, and Hoping for Mr. Right: College Women on Dating and Mating Today.* New York: Institute for American Values.

Glorieux, I., Minnen, J., and van Tienoven, T.P. (2011). Spouse "together time": Quality together time within the household. *Social Indicators Research, 101*, 281–287.

Glover, G. (2001). Parenting in Native American families. In N. B. Webb (Ed.), *Culturally Diverse Parent–Child and Family Relationships: A Guide for Social Workers and Other Practitioners.* New York: Columbia University Press.

Godeau, E., Gabhainn, S. N., Vignes, C., Ross, J., Boyce, W., and Todd, J. (2008). Contraceptive use by 15-year-old students at their last sexual intercourse. *Archives of Pediatric Medicine, 162*, 66–73.

Gold, L. (2009). *The Healthy Divorce.* Naperville, IL: Sphinx.

Goldberg, A. E., and Perry-Jenkins, M. (2004). Division of labor and working-class women's well-being across the transition to parenthood. *Journal of Family Psychology, 18*(1), 225–236.

Goldberg, S. B. (2003, Spring). For a woman to get that federal court nomination, does she have to be Scalia in a skirt? *Ms.,* pp. 42–46.

Goldstein, M. H., King, A. P., and West, M. J. (2003). Social interaction shapes babbling: Testing parallels between birdsong and speech. *Proceedings of the National Academy of Sciences USA, 100*(13), 8030–8035.

Gonzales, J. (2009). Prefamily counseling: Working with blended families. *Journal of Divorce and Remarriage, 50*, 148–157.

Gonzalez-Lopez, G. (2004). Fathering Latina sexualities: Mexican men and the virginity of their daughters. *Journal of Marriage and Family, 66*, 1118–1130.

Gonzalez-Mena, J. (1993). *Multicultural Issues in Child Care.* Mountain View, CA: Mayfield.

Good, G. E., and Mintz, L. B. (1990). Gender role conflict and depression in college men: Evidence for compounded risk. *Journal of Counseling and Development, 69*, 17–21.

Goodman, C. C., and Silverstein, M. (2006). Grandmothers raising grandchildren. *Journal of Family Issues, 27*, 1605–1626.

Goodman, C.K. (2011). Work stress can strain marriage. *Chicago Tribune*, June 3, 2011. http://articles.chicagotribune.com/2011.

Goodwin, M. H. (1998). Games of stance: Conflict and footing in hopscotch. In S. Hoyle and C. T. Adger (Eds.), *Kid's Talk: Strategic Language Use in Later Childhood* (pp. 23–46). New York: Oxford University Press.

Goodwin, M. H. (2001). Organizing participation in cross sex jump rope: Situating gender differences within longitudinal studies of activities. *Research on Language and Social Interaction, 34*, 75–106.

Gorchoff, S.M., John, O.P., and Helson, R. (2008). Contextualizing change in marital satisfaction during middle age: An 18-year longitudinal study. *Psychological Science, 19*(11), 1194–1200.

Gordis, E. B., Margolin, G., and John, R. S. (1997). Marital aggression, observed parental hostility, and child behavior during triadic family interaction. *Journal of Family Psychology, 11*, 76–89.

Gordon, K. C. (2012). Constraint vs dedication commitment: Have to versus want to. Retrieved from http://relationshiprx.utk.edu.

Gornick, J.C. (2004). Women's economic outcomes, gender inequality, and public policy: Findings from the Luxembourg Income Study. *Socio-Economic Review, 2*, 213–238.

Gostin, L. O., and DeAngelis, C. D. (2007). Mandatory HPV vaccination. *Journal of the American Medical Association, 297*, 1921–1923.

Gottfried, A. E., Gottfried, A. W., Killian, C., and Bathurst, K. (1999). Maternal and dual-earner employment. In M. Lamb (Ed.), *Parenting and Child Development in "Nontraditional" Families* (pp. 15–37). Mahwah, NJ: Erlbaum.

Gottlieb, L. (2006). How do I love thee? *The Atlantic Monthly,* (March), 58–70.

Gottman, J. M. (1994). *What Predicts Divorce? The Relationship between Marital Process and Marital Outcomes.* Hillsdale, NJ: Erlbaum.

Gottman, J. M. (1998). Psychology and the study of marital processes. *Annual Review of Psychology, 49,* 169–197.

Gottman, J. M. (2000a). Decade review: Observing marital interaction. *Journal of Marriage and Family, 62*(4), 927–947.

Gottman, J. M. (2000b). *Seven Principles of Marriage.* New York: Crown.

Gottman, J. M., Coan, J., Carrere, S., and Swanson, C. (1998). Predicting marital happiness and stability from newlywed interaction. *Journal of Marriage and Family, 60*(1), 5–22.

Gottman, J. M., and Levenson, R. W. (1988). The social psychophysiology of marriage. In P. Noller and M. A. Fitzpatrick (Eds.), *Perspective on Marital*

Interaction (pp. 182–200). Philadelphia: Multilingual Matters.

Gottman, J. M., and Levenson, R. W. (1992). Marital processes predictive of later dissolution: Behavior, physiology, and health. *Journal of Personality and Social Psychology, 63*, 221–233.

Gottman, J. M., and Levenson, R. W. (2000). The timing of divorce: Predicting when a couple will divorce over a 14-year period. *Journal of Marriage and Family, 62*, 737–745.

Gottman, J.M., and Silver, N. (2013). *What Makes Love Last?* New York: Simon and Schuster.

Gottman, J. M., and Silver, N. (2015). *The Seven Principles for Making Marriage Work.* New York: Harmony.

Gottman Institute. (2015). Couples therapy. Retrieved from http://www.gottman.com.

Government Mandated. (2013). Government mandated marriage promotion. Unmarried Equality. Retrieved from http://unmarried.org/government-mandated

Grabe, S., and Hyde, J.S. (2006). Ethnicity and body dissatisfaction among women in the United States: A meta-analysis. *Psychological Bulletin, 132*(4), 622–640.

Grady, D., Herrington, D., Bittner, V., and Blumenthal, R. (2002). Cardiovascular disease outcomes during 6.8 years of hormone therapy. *Journal of the American Medical Association, 288*(1), 49–57.

Grall, T.S. (2011). Custodial mothers and fathers and their child support: 2009. *Current Population Reports.* Retrieved from http://www.census.gov.

Grant-Vallone, E. J., and Donaldson, S. I. (2001). Consequences of work–family conflict on employee well-being over time. *Work and Stress, 15*(3), 214–226.

Graves, J. A. (2013). 6 things you need to know about the Family Medical Leave Act. *U.S. News and World Report.* Retrieved from http://money.usnews.com

Gray-Little, B., Baucom, D., and Hamby, S. (1996). Marital power, marital adjustment, and therapy outcome. *Journal of Family Psychology, 10*(3), 292–303.

Grce, M., and Davies, P. (2008). Human papillomavirus testing for primary cervical cancer screening. *Expert Review of Molecular Diagnostics, 8*, 599–605.

Green, M. C., and Sabini, J. (2006). Gender, socioeconomic status, age, and jealousy: Emotional responses to infidelity in a national sample. *Emotion, 6*, 330–334.

Green, R. J. (2004). Risk and resilience in lesbian and gay couples: Comment on Solomon, Rothblum, and Balsam. *Journal of Family Psychology, 18*(2), 290–292.

Greenberg, B. S., Eastin, M., Hofschire, L., Lachlan, K., and Brownell, K. (2003). How commercial television treats obesity and other body types. *American Journal of Public Health, 93*(8), 1342–1348.

Greenberg, P. (2005). The older American act: An overview. *National Council on Family Relations Report, 50*(3), F4–F5.

Greenblat, C. (1983). The salience of sexuality in the early years of marriage. *Journal of Marriage and Family, 45*(2), 289–299.

Greenstein, R. (2005). The earned income tax credit. Center on Budget and Policy Priority. Retrieved September 8, 2005, from http://www.cbpp.org.

Greenstein, T. N. (1996). Husbands' participation in domestic labor: Interactive effects of wives' and husbands' gender ideology. *Journal of Marriage and Family, 68*, 585–595.

Grenier, G., and Byers, E. (2001). Operationalizing premature or rapid ejaculation. *Journal of Sex Research, 38*(4), 369–378.

Gross, H., and Van Den Akker, O. (2004). Editorial: The importance of the postnatal period for mothers, fathers and infant behaviour. *Journal of Reproductive and Infant Psychology, 22*(1), 3–4.

Grossman, C. L. (2012). Only just begun to owe? *USA Today*, August 10, 2012, B 1–2.

Grote, N. K., Naylor, K., and Clark, M. S. (2002). Perceiving the division of family work to be unfair: Do social comparisons, enjoyment and competence matter? *Journal of Family Psychology, 16*(4), 510–522.

Grover, S., and Helliwell, J. F. (2014). How's life at home? New evidence on marriage and the set point for happiness. NBER Working Paper No. w20794. Retrieved from http://SSRN.com/abstract=2545179.

Grunbaum, J. A., Kann, L, and Kinchen, S. (2004). Youth risk behavioral surveillance—United States, 2003. *Morbidity and Mortality Weekly Report, 53*(ss02), 1–96.

Grunfeld, E., Coyle, D., Whelan, T., Clinch, J., Reyno, L., Earle, C., et al. (2004). Family caregiver burden: Results of a longitudinal study of breast cancer patients and their principal caregivers. *Canadian Medical Association Journal, 170*(2), 1795–1801.

Gunderson, J.G. (2009). Borderline personality disorder: Ontogeny of a diagnosis. *American Journal of Psychiatry, 166*, 530–539.

Gurmen, M.S. (2015). Extended family kinship following divorce: Investigating ongoing relationships, social support resource, and role in family therapy. Doctoral Dissertation. University of Connecticut. http://digitalcommons,uconn.edu

Gutmann, M. C. (1996). *The Meanings of Macho: Being a Man in Mexico City.* Berkeley: University of California Press.

Guttmacher Institute. (2012). Contraceptive use in the United States. Retrieved from http://www.guttmacher.org

Guzzo, K. B. (2009). Marital intentions and the stability of first cohabitations. *Journal of Family Issues, 30,* 179–205.

Ha, J-H., and Ingersol-Dayton, B. (2008). The effects of widowhood on intergenerational ambivalence. *Journal of Gerontology: Social Sciences, 63B*(1), 549–558.

Haase, C. M., Saslow, L. R., Bloch, L., Saturn, S. R., Casey, J., Seider, B. H., Lane, J., Coppola, G., and Levenson, R. W. (2013). The 5-HTTLPR polymorphism in the serotonin transporter gene moderates the association between emotional behavior and changes in marital satisfaction over time. *Emotion.* October 7, 2013.

Haddock, S. A., Ziemba, S. J., Schindler Zimmerman, T., and Current, L. R. (2001). Ten adaptive strategies for family and work balance: Advice from successful families. *Journal of Marital and Family Therapy, 27*(4), 445–458.

Halbreich, U. (2004). Prevalence of mood symptoms and depressions during pregnancy: Implications for clinical practice and research. *CNS Spectrums, 9*(3), 177–184.

Haley, J. (1982). Restoring law and order in the family. *Psychology Today, 16,* 61–69.

Halford, K., Nicholson, J., and Sanders, M. (2007). Couple communication in stepfamilies. *Family Process, 4,* 471–483.

Hall, R., and Greene, B. (2003). Contemporary African American families. In L. B. Silverstein and T. J. Goodrich (Eds.), *Feminist Family Therapy: Empowerment in Social Context* (pp. 107–120). Washington, DC: American Psychological Association.

Halpern, D. F., Benbow, C. P., Geary, D. C., Gur, R. C., Hyde, J. S., and Gernsbacher, M. A. (2007). The science of sex differences in science and mathematics. *Psychological Science in the Public Interest, 8,* 1–51.

Halpern-Meekin, S., Manning, W.D., Giordano, P.C., and Longmore, M.A. (2013). Relationship churning, physical violence, and verbal abuse in young adult relationships. *Journal of Marriage and Family, 75*(1), 2–12. DOI: 10.1111/j.1741-3737.2012.01029.x

Hamama, L. and Ronen-Shenhav, A. (2012). Self-control, social support, and aggression among adolescents in divorced and two-parent families. *Children and Youth Services Review, 34,* 1042–1049.

Hamer, J., and Marchioro, K. (2002). Becoming custodial dads; Exploring parenting among low-income and working-class African American fathers. *Journal of Marriage and Family, 64*(1), 116–129.

Hamilton, B.E., Martin, J.A., and Ventura, S.J. (2013). National Vital Statistics Report 62. National Center for Health Statistics, pp. 1–20.

Hamilton, B. E., Minino, A. M., Martin, J. A., Kochanek, K. D., Strobino, D. M., and Guyer, B. (2007). Annual summary of vital statistics, 2005. *Pediatrics, 119,* 345–360.

Hamner, T. J., and Turner, P. H. (2001). *Parenting in Contemporary Society.* Needham Heights, MA: Allyn & Bacon.

Haning, R. V., O'Keefe, S., Randall, E., Kommor, M., Baker, E., and Wilson, R. (2007). Intimacy, orgasm likelihood, and conflict predict sexual satisfaction in heterosexual male and female respondents. *Journal of Sex and Marital Therapy, 33,* 93–113.

Hans, J. D., and Fine, M. A. (2001). Children of divorce: Experiences of children whose parents attended a divorce education program. *Journal of Divorce and Remarriage, 36*(1/2), 1–26.

Hardey, M. (2004). Mediated relationships: Authenticity and the possibility of romance. *Information, Communication, and Society, 7*(2), 207–222.

Harding, A. (2009). Eating disorders may be rising among male athletes. *Reuters,* January 8.

Harper, G. W., Gannon, C., Watson, S. E., Catania, J. A., and Dolcini, M. (2004). The role of close friends in African American adolescents' dating and sexual behavior. *Journal of Sex Research, 41*(4), 351–362.

Harrar, S., and DeMaria, R. (2007). *The 7 Stages of Marriage.* Pleasantville, NY: The Reader's Digest Association.

Harriger, J. A., Calogero, R. M., Witherington, D. C., and Smith, J. E. (2010). Body size stereotyping and internalization of the thin-ideal in preschool-age girls. *Sex Roles, 63,* 609–620. doi:10.1007/s11199-010-9868-1.

Harris, P. S., Lampe, K., and Chaffin, B. (2004). Always green and full of sap: Facilitating wholeness in aging. *Journal of Religious Gerontology, 15*(1–2), 107–125.

Hartwell-Walker, M. (2015). Parent-child power struggles. Psychology Central. http://psychcentral.com/lib/parent-child-power-struggles/

Harvey, H., and Fine, M. (2004). *Children of Divorce: Stories of Loss and Growth.* Mahwah, NJ: Erlbaum.

Harvey, S. M., and Bird, S. T. (2004). What makes women feel powerful? An exploratory study of relationship power and sexual decision-making with African Americans at risk for HIV/STDs. *Women and Health, 39*(3), 1–18.

Harway, M. (2003). Assessment of domestic violence. In L. B. Silverstein and T. J. Goodrich (Eds.), *Feminist Family Therapy: Empowerment in Social Context* (pp. 319–332). Washington, DC: American Psychological Association.

Hatcher, R. A., Trussell, J., Nelson, A. L., Cates, W., Kowal, D., and Policar, M. S. (2011). *Contraceptive Technology* (20th ed.). New York: Ardent Media.

Hatcher, R. A., Zieman, M., Watt, A. P., Nelson, A., Darney, P. A., and Pluhar, E. (1999). *A Pocket Guide to Managing Contraception.* Tiger, GA: Bridging the Gap Foundation.

Hattery, A. J. (2001). Tag-team parenting: Costs and benefits of utilizing nonoverlapping shift work in families with young children. *Families in Society, 82*(4), 419–427.

Hawkins, A. J., Carroll, J. S., Doherty, W. J., and Willoughby, B. (2004). *Family Relations, 53*(5), 547–558.

Hawkins, A. J., Nock, S. L., Wilson, J. C., Sanchez, L., and Wright, J. D. (2002). Attitudes about covenant marriage and divorce: Policy implication from a three-state comparison. *Family Relations, 51*(2), 166–175.

Hazan, C., and Shaver, P. (1987). Romantic love conceptualized as an attachment process. *Journal of Personality and Social Psychology, 52*, 511–524.

Heaton, T. B. (2002). Factors contributing to increasing marital stability in the United States. *Journal of Family Issues, 23*, 392–409.

Hegewisch, A., and DuMonthier, A. (2016). The gender wage gap: Earning differences by race and ethnicity, 2015. Institute for Women's Policy Research. www.iwpr,org

Hegewisch, A., and Ellis, E. (2015). The gender wage gap by occupation, race, and ethnicity: 2014. Institute for Women's Policy Research. www.iwpr.org

Heiman, J. R. (2002). Sexual dysfunction: Overview of prevalence, etiological factors, and treatments. *Journal of Sex Research, 39*(1), 73–78.

Hellmuth, J. C., and McNulty, J. K. (2008). Neuroticism, marital violence, and the moderating role of stress and behavioral skills. *Journal of Personality and Social Psychology, 95*, 166–180.

Henderson, T. (2005). Grandparent visitation rights. *Journal of Family Issues, 26*(5), 638–664.

Henley, N., and Freeman, J. (1995). The sexual politics of interpersonal behavior. In J. Freeman (Ed.), *Women: A Feminist Perspective* (5th ed., pp. 79–91). Mountain View, CA: Mayfield.

Henline, B. H., Lamke, L. K., and Howard, M. D. (2007). Exploring perceptions of online infidelity. *Personal Relationships, 14*, 113–128.

Henricson, C., and Roker, D. (2001). Support for parents of adolescents: A review. *Journal of Adolescence, 23*, 763–783.

Herek, G. M. (2006). Legal recognition of same-sex relationships in the United States. *American Psychologist, 61*(6), 607–621.

Hess, A. and Stanton, G. T. (2012). The health benefits of marriage. Focus on the Family. Retrieved from http://focusonthefamily.org.

Hess, N. H., and Hagin, E. H. (2006). Sex differences in indirect aggression: Psychological evidence from young adults. *Evolution and Human Behavior, 27*, 231–245.

Hetherington, E. M. (1993). An overview of the Virginia longitudinal study of divorce and remarriage with a focus on early adolescence. *Journal of Family Psychology, 7*, 1–18.

Hetherington, E. M. (1999). Family functioning and the adjustment of adolescent siblings in diverse types of families. *Monographs of the Society for Research in Child Development, 64*(4), 1–25.

Hetherington, E. M., and Kelly, J. (2002). *For Better or Worse.* New York: Norton.

Hetherington, E. M., and Stanley-Hagan, M. M. (1999). Stepfamilies. In M. Lamb (Ed.), *Parenting and Child Development in "Nontraditional" Families* (pp. 137–159). Mahwah, NJ: Erlbaum.

Heyman, R. E., Sayers, S. L., and Bellack, A. S. (1994). Global marital satisfaction versus marital adjustment: An empirical comparison of three measures. *Journal of Family Psychology, 8*, 432–446.

Hickman, G. P., Bartholomae, S., and McKenry, P. C. (2000). Influence of partnering style on the adjustment and academic achievement of traditional college freshmen. *Journal of College Student Development, 41*(1), 41–54.

Higginbotham, B., Skogrand, L., and Torres, E. (2010). Stepfamily education: Perceived benefits for children. *Journal of Divorce and Remarriage, 51*, 36–49.

Hill, E. J. (2006). Researching the 60-hour dual-earner workweek. *American Behavioral Scientist, 49*, 1184–1203.

Hill, E. J., Hawkins, A. J., Ferris, M., and Weitzman, M. (2001). Finding an extra day a week: The positive influence of perceived job flexibility on work and family life balance. *Family Relations, 50*(1), 49–57.

Hiltz, S. R. (1978). Widowhood: A roleless role. *Marriage and Family Review, 1*, 1–10.

Hines, D.A., and Douglas, E.M. (2010a). A closer look at men who sustain intimate terrorism by women. *Partner Abuse, 1* (3), 286–313.

Hines, D. A., and Douglas, E. M. (2010b). Intimate terrorism by women towards men: Does it exist? *Journal of Aggression, Conflict, and Peace Research, 2* (3), 36–56.

Hines, D. A., and Douglas, E. M. (2011). Symptoms of post-traumatic stress disorder in men who sustain intimate partner violence: A study of help seeking and community samples. *Psychology of Men and Masculinity, 12*(2), 112–127.

Hines, M. (2004). *Brain Gender.* New York: Oxford University Press.

Hite, S. (1981). *The Hite Report: A Nationwide Study of Female Sexuality.* New York: Dell.

Hoffman, S. (2013). Grandparents' rights FAQ. Retrieved from http://www.grandparents.com/familyandrelationship/grandparents-rights/

Hogan, M. (2013). Love at any age. Retrieved from http://www.psychologytoday.com.

Holley, S. R., Sturm, V. E., and Levenson, R. W. (2010). Exploring the basis for gender differences in the demand–withdraw pattern. *Journal of Homosexuality, 57*(5), 666–684.

Hollon, S. D., DeRubeis, R. J., Fawcett, J., Amsterdam, J. D., Shelton, R. C., Zajecka, J., Young, P. R., and Gallop, R. (2014). Effect of cognitive therapy with antidepressant medications versus antidepressants alone on the rate of recovery in major depressive disorder: A randomized clinical trial. *JAMA Psychiatry, 71*(10), 1157–1164.

Holman, T. B., Larson, J., Stahmann, R., and Carroll, J. (2001). General principles, implications, and future directions. In T. B. Holman (Ed.), *Premarital Prediction of Marital Quality or Breakup* (pp. 191–222). New York: Kluwer Academic/Plenum.

Holmes, E. R., and Holmes, L. D. (1995). *Other Cultures, Elder Years.* Thousand Oaks, CA: Sage.

Holt, J. L. (2006, August). *Intimate Violence: The Effects of Family, Threatened Egotism, and Reciprocity.* Poster presented at the meeting of the American Psychological Association, New Orleans, LA.

Hoopes, D. S. (1979). Intercultural communication concepts and the psychology of intercultural experiences. In M. Pusch (Ed.), *Multicultural Education: A Cross-Cultural Training Approach* (pp. 3–33). La Grange Park, IL: Intercultural Press.

Hornberger, L. B., Zabriskie, R. B., and Freeman, P. (2010). Contributions of family leisure to family functioning among single-parent families. *Leisure Sciences, 32*(2), 143–161.

Horning, L. E., and Rouse, K. A. G. (2002). Resilience in preschoolers and toddlers from low-income families. *Early Childhood Education Journal, 29*(3), 155–159.

Hornor, G. (2005). Physical abuse: Recognition and reporting. *Journal of Pediatric Health Care, 19*, 4–11.

Howard, J. (1980). *Families.* New York: Berkeley.

Howe, G. W., Levy, M. L., and Caplan, R. D. (2004). Job loss and depressive symptoms in couples: Common stressors, stress transmission, or relationship disruption? *Journal of Family Psychology, 18*(4), 639–650.

Hudziak, J. J., and Rettew, D. C. (2009). Genetics of ADHD. In T.E. Brown (Ed.), *ADHD Co-morbidities: Handbook for ADHD Complications in Children and Adults* (pp. 23–26). Arlington, VA: American Psychiatric Publishing.

Hughes, B. (2010). Understanding sexual addiction in clinical practice. *Procedia Social and Behavioral Sciences, 5*, 915–919.

Hughes, F. M., Gordon, K. C., and Gaertner, L. (2004). Predicting spouses' perceptions of their parenting alliance. *Journal of Marriage and Family, 66*, 506–514.

Hughes, F. M., Stuart, G. L., Gordon, K. C., and Moore, T. M. (2007). Predicting the use of aggressive conflict tactics in a sample of women arrested for domestic violence. *Journal of Personal and Social Relationships, 24*, 155–176.

Hurlbert, D. F., and Apt, C. (1991). Sexual narcissism and the abusive male. *Journal of Sex and Marital Therapy, 17*, 279–292.

Huston, T. L., Caughlin, J. P., Houts, R. M., Smith, S. E., and George, L. J. (2001). The connubial crucible: Newlywed years as predictors of marital delight, distress, and divorce. *Journal of Personality and Social Psychology, 80*(2), 237–252.

Huston, T. L., and Holmes, E. K. (2004). Becoming parents. In A. L. Vanglelisti (Ed.), *Handbook of Family Communication* (pp. 105–133). Mahwah, NJ: Erlbaum.

Hyde, J., DeLamater, J., and Plant, E. (1996). Sexuality during pregnancy and the year postpartum. *Journal of Sex Research, 32*(2), 143–151.

Hyde, J. S., Essex, M. J., Clark, R., and Klein, M. H. (2001). Maternity leave, women's employment, and marital incompatibility. *Journal of Family Psychology, 15*(3), 476–491.

Hymowitz, K. (2013). Longer maternity leave not so great for women after all. *Time.* http://ideas.time.com

Igarashi, H., and Hooker, K., Coehlo, D.P., and Manoogian, M.M. (2013). "My nest is full": Intergenerational relationships at midlife. *Journal of Aging Studies, 27*(2), 102–112. DOI: 10.1016/j.jaging2012.12.004

Independent Drug Monitoring Unit. (2009). Retrieved from http://www.idmu.co.uk/sitemap.html.

Ingersoll-Dayton, B., and Neal, M. B. (1991). Grandparents in family therapy: The clinical research study. *Family Relations, 40*, 264–271.

Insel, P. M., and Roth, W. T. (2013). *Core Concepts in Health,* 13th Ed. New York: McGraw–Hill.

Institute for Women's Policy Research. (2009). The gender wage gap: 2009. Retrieved March 2010 from http://www.IWPR.org.

Internet Pornography by the Numbers. (2016). Webroot. http://www.webroot.com

Isay, J. (2008). *Walking on Eggshells: Navigating the Delicate Balance between Adult Children and Parents.* New York: Anchor Press.

Ishii-Kuntz, M. (1997). Chinese American families. In M. DeGenova (Ed.), *Families in Cultural Context* (pp. 109–130). Mountain View, CA: Mayfield.

Jackson, J., and Nelson, J. (2010). Health care reform bill summary: A look at what's in the bill. Retrieved from http://www.cbsnews.com.

Jackson, P. B. (2004). Role sequencing: Does order matter for mental health? *Journal of Health and Social Behavior, 45*, 132–154.

Jacobson, C. M., and Mufson, L. (2012). Interpersonal psychotherapy for depressed adolescents adapted for self-injury (IPT–ASI): Rationale, overview, and case summary. *American Journal of Psychotherapy, 66*(4), 349–374.

Jacoby, S. (1999). Great sex: What's age got to do with it? *Modern Maturity, 42*(5), 40–45, 91.

Jakubowski, S. F., Milne, E. P., Brunner, H., and Miller, R. B. (2004). A review of empirically supported marital enrichment programs. *Family Relations, 53,* 528–536.

James, R. K., and Gilliland, B. E. (2013). *Crises Intervention Strategies* (7th ed.). Belmont, CA: Brooks/Cole.

Jang, S. J., Zippay, A., and Park, R. (2012). Family roles as moderators of the relationship between schedule flexibility and stress. *Journal of Marriage and the Family, 74,* 897–912.

Jaques-Tiura, A. J., Abbey, A., Parkhill, M. R., and Zawacki, T. (2007). Why do some men misperceive women's sexual intentions more frequently than others do? An application of the Confluence Model. *Personality and Social Psychology Bulletin, 33,* 1467–1480.

Jasinski, J. L. (2004). Pregnancy and domestic violence: A review of the literature. *Trauma, Violence, and Abuse, 5*(1), 47–64.

Javors, I. R. (2004). Hip-hop culture: Images of gender and gender roles. *Annals of the American Psychotherapy Association, 7*(2), 42.

Jean-Gilles, M., and Crittenden, P. M. (1990). Maltreating families: A look at siblings. *Family Relations, 39,* 323–329.

Jedlicka, D. (1984). Indirect parental influences on mate choice: A test of the psychoanalytic theory. *Journal of Marriage and Family, 46,* 65–70.

Jeng, C.-J., Wang, L.-R., Chou, C.-S., Shen, J., and Tzeng, C.-R. (2006). Management and outcome of primary vaginismus. *Journal of Sex and Marital Therapy, 32,* 379–387.

Jenkins, J., Simpson, A., Dunn, J., Rasbash, J., and O'Connor, T. (2005). Mutual influence of marital conflict and children's behavior problems: Shared and nonshared family risks. *Child Development, 76*(1), 24–39.

Jensen, C. J., Ferrari, M., and Cavanaugh, J. C. (2004). Building on the benefits: Assessing satisfaction and well-being in elder care. *Aging International, 29,* 88–100.

Jha, P., Kumar, R., Vasa, P., Dhingra, N., Thiruchelvam, D., and Moineddin, R. (2006). Low male-to-female sex ratio of children born in India: National survey of 1.1 million households. *Lancet, 367*(9506), 211–218.

Jickling, M. (2005). Consumer bankruptcy and household debt. CRS Report for Congress. The Library of Congress. Retrieved September, 8, 2005, from http://www.bna.com/webwatch.bankruptcy

Johnson, E.M. (2015). More than 500,000 people homeless in the United States: Report. *Reuters.* http://www.reuters.com

Johnson, M. P. (2006). Violence and abuse in personal relationships: Conflict, terror, and resistance in intimate partnerships. In A. L. Vangelisti and D. Perlman (Eds.), *The Cambridge Handbook of Personal Relationships* (pp. 557–576). New York: Cambridge University Press.

Johnson, M. P., and Leone, J. M. (2005). The differential effects of intimate terrorism and situational couple violence. *Journal of Family Issues, 26,* 322–349.

Jordan, M. (2008, October1). Gardasil requirement for immigrants stirs backlash. *Wall Street Journal Online.* Retrieved November 5, 2008, from http://online.wsj.com/article/5B122282354408892791.html

Jose, A., O'Leary, K. D., and Moyer, A. (2010). Does premarital cohabitation predict subsequent marital stability and marital quality? *Journal of Marriage and the Family, 72,* 105–116.

Juby, C., and Rycraft, J. R. (2004). Family preservation strategies for families in poverty. *Families in Society, 85*(4), 581–587.

Juby, H., Le Bourdais, C., and Marcil-Gratton, N. (2005). Sharing roles, sharing custody? Couples' characteristics and children's living arrangements at separation. *Journal of Marriage and Family, 67*(1), 157–172.

Juergen, M. (2014). 9 harmful stereotypes we never realized our favorite Disney movies taught us. Retrieved from http://mic.com/articles.

Julian, P. W., McKenry, P. C., and McKelbey, M. W. (1994). Cultural variations in parenting. *Family Relations, 43,* 30–37.

Kagan, N., and Schneider, J. (1987). Toward the measurement of affective sensitivity. *Journal of Counseling and Development, 65,* 459–464.

Kahn, J. G., Brindis, C. D., and Glei, D. A. (1999). Pregnancies averted among U.S. teenagers by the use of contraceptives. *Family Planning Perspectives, 31*(1), 29–34.

Kail, R. V., and Cavanaugh, J. C. (2016). *Human Development: A Life-span View* (7th ed.). Belmont, CA: Wadsworth.

Kalmijn, M. (1999). Father involvement in childrearing and the perceived stability of marriage. *Journal of Marriage and Family, 61,* 409–421.

Kamo, Y. (2000). "He said, she said": Assessing discrepancies in husbands' and wives' reports on the division of household labor. *Social Science Research, 29,* 459–476.

Kanel, K. (2007). *A Guide to Crisis Intervention* (3rd ed.). Pacific Grove, CA: Brooks/Cole.

Kao, T.A., Guthrie, B., and Loveland-Cherry, C. (2007). An intergenerational approach to understanding Taiwanese American adolescent girls' and their mothers' perceptions about sexual health. *Journal of Family Nursing, 13,* 312–332.

Kapadia, F., Latka, M. H., Hudson, S. M., Golub, E. T., Campbell, J. V., Bailey, S., Frye, V., and Garfein, R. S. (2007). Correlates of consistent condom use with main partners by partnership patterns among young adult male drug users from five U.S. cities. *Drug and Alcohol Dependence.* 91S (2007), S56–S63. Retrieved from http://www.sciencedirect.com.

Kaperberg, A. (2014). Age at coresidence, premarital cohabitation, and marriage dissolution: 1985–2009. *Journal of Marriage and the Family,* 76, 352–369. doi:10.1111/jomf.12092.

Karasik, R. (2005). Aging: Everybody's doing it! *National Council on Family Relations Report,* 50(3), F1, F3.

Karavasilis, L., Doyle, A. B., and Markiewicz, D. (2003). Associations between parenting style and attachment to mother in middle childhood and adolescence. *International Journal of Behavioral Development,* 27(2), 153–164.

Karney, B. (2015). Remarriage in the United States: If at first they don't succeed, do most Americans "try, try again"? Council on Contemporary Families. Retrieved from https://contemporaryfamilies.org.

Karney, B.R., and Neff, L.A. (2013). Couples and stress: How demands outside a relationship affect intimacy within the relationship. In J.A. Simpson and L. Campbell, (Eds.), *The Oxford Handbook of Close Relationships,* (pp.664–684). New York: Oxford University Press.

Kaslow, F., and Kaslow, F. (2004). Death of one's partner: The anticipation and the reality. *Professional Psychology: Research and Practice,* 35(3), 227–233.

Kass, A. A., and Kass, L. (2000). *Wing to Wing, Oar to Oar: Readings on Courting and Marrying.* South Bend, IN: University of Notre Dame Press.

Kaukinen, C. (2004). Status compatibility, physical violence and emotional abuse in intimate relationships. *Journal of Marriage and Family,* 66, 452–471.

Kaura, S. A., and Lohman, B. J. (2007). Dating violence, victimization, relationship satisfaction, mental health problems, and acceptability of violence. *Journal of Family Violence,* 22, 367–381.

Kayser, K., and Rao, S.S. (2006). Process of disaffection in relationship breakdown. In M.A. Fine and J.H. Harvey, (Eds), *Handbook of Divorce and Relationship Dissolution,* (pp. 201–223). New York: Routledge.

Keen, C. (2006). Women more likely to be perpetrators of abuse as well as victims. University of Florida News. Retrieved from http://www.news.ufl.edu.

Keenan, J., Gallup, G., Goulet, N., and Kulkarni, M. (1997). Attributions of deception in human mating strategies. *Journal of Social Behavior and Personality,* 12(1), 45–52.

Keene, J., and Reynolds, J. (2005). The job costs of family demands: Gender differences in negative family-to-work spillover. *Journal of Family Issues,* 26(3), 275–299.

Keller, H., Lohaus, A., Kuensemueller, P., Abels, M., Yovsi, R., and Voelker, S. (2004). The bio-culture of parenting: Evidence from five cultural communities. *Parenting: Science and Practice,* 4(1), 25–50.

Kelly, G. F. (2013). *Sexuality Today* (11th ed.) New York: McGraw–Hill.

Kelly, J.B. (2007). Children's living arrangements following separation and divorce. Insights from empirical and clinical research. *Family Process,* 46, 35–52.

Kelly, J.B. (2010). Risk and resilience in children following separation and divorce. Presentation at the New York State Council on Divorce Mediation Pre-Conference. Saratoga Springs, NY. April 2010.

Kelley, M., and Tseng, H. (1992). Cultural differences in child rearing. *Journal of Cross Cultural Psychology,* 23(4), 444–455.

Kersten, K. K. (1990). The process of marital disaffection: Intervention at various stages. *Family Relations,* 39, 257–265.

Kertzner, R. M. (2004). Psychotherapy with lesbian and gay clients from an adult life course perspective. *Journal of Gay and Lesbian Social Services,* 16(2), 105–111.

Kickham, K., and Ford, D.A. (2009). Are state marriage initiatives having an effect? An initial exploration of the impact on divorce and childhood poverty rates. University of Central Oklahoma. *Public Administration Review,* 69(5), 846–854. doi:10.1111/1540.6210.2009.02034.x.

Kidjacked. (2016). Spanking laws by state. Kidjacked. http://www.kidjacked.com

Kiff, C.J., Lengua, L.J., and Zalewski, M. (2011). Nature and nurture: Parenting in the context of child temperament individual differences. *Clinical Child and Family Psychology Review,* 14, 251–301.

Kilborn, P. T. (2004, March 7). Alive, well, and on the prowl. *New York Times.* Retrieved from http://www.nytimes.com/2004/03/07

Kim, M. S., and Aune, K. S. (1998). The effects of psychological gender orientations on the perceived salience of conversational constraints. *Sex Roles,* 37, 935–953.

Kim, S. Y., Chen, Q., Li, J., Huang, X., and Moon, U. J. (2009). Parent–child acculturation, parenting, and adolescent depressive symptoms in Chinese immigrant families. *Journal of Family Psychology,* 23(3), 426–437. doi:10.1037/g0016019.

King, B. M. (2013). *Human Sexuality* (8th Ed). New York: Pearson.

King, V., and Heard, H. E. (1999). Nonresident father visitation, parental conflict, and mother's satisfaction: What's best for child well-being? *Journal of Marriage and Family,* 61, 385–396.

King, V., Silverstein, M., Elder, G., Bengtson, V., and Conger, R. (2003). Relations with grandparents. *Journal of Family Issues, 24*(8), 1044–1069.

King, V., and Sobolewski, J. M. (2006). Nonresident fathers' contribution to adolescent well-being. *Journal of Marriage and the Family, 68*(3), 537–557. doi:10.1111/i.1741-3737.2006.00274x.

Kingkade, T. (2015). Brown University shuts down date rape investigation after botched lab results. Retrieved from http://www.huffingtonpost.com.

Kinnison, J. (2014). *Bad Boyfriends: Using Attachment Theory to Avoid Mr. or Ms. Wrong and Make You A Better Partner.* Jeb Kinnison Publishing. http://www.jebkinnison.com

Klahr, A. M., Rueter, M. A., McGue, M., Iacono, W. G., and Burt, A. S. (2011). The relationship between parent–child conflict and adolescent antisocial behavior: Confirming shared environmental mediation. *Journal of Abnormal Child Psychology, 39,* 683–694.

Klaus, M., and Kennel, J. (1982). *Parent–Infant Bonding* (2nd ed.). St. Louis: Mosby.

Klebanov, P. K., Brooks-Gunn, J., and Duncan, G. J. (1994). Does neighborhood and family poverty affect mothers' parenting, mental health, and social support? *Journal of Marriage and Family, 56,* 441–455.

Klein, D. M., and White, J. M. (1996). *Family Theories: An Introduction.* Newbury Park, CA: Sage.

Kleinke, C. L. (2002). *Coping with Life Challenges.* Long Grove, IL: Waveland Press.

Kline, G. H., Stanley, S. M., Markman, H. J., Olmos-Gallo, P. A., St. Peters, M., et al. (2004, June). Timing is everything: Pre-engagement cohabitation and increased risk of poor marital outcomes. *Journal of Family Psychology, 18*(2), 311–318.

Klinenberg, E. (2012). One's a crowd. Retrieved from http://www.nytimes.com.

Klohnen, E. C., Vandewater, E. A., and Young, A. (1996). Negotiating the middle years: Ego-resiliency and successful midlife adjustment in women. *Psychology and Aging, 11,* 431–442.

Knegtering, H., Boks, M., Blijd, C., Castelein, S., van den Bosch, R. J., and Wiersma, D. (2006). A randomized open-label comparison of the impact of olanzapine versus risperidone on sexual functioning. *Journal of Sex and Marital Therapy, 32,* 315–326.

Knoester, C., and Booth, A. (2000). Barriers to divorce. *Journal of Family Issues, 21,* 78–99.

Knox, D., and Schacht, C. (2016). *Choices in Relationships: An Introduction to Marriage and the Family* (12th ed.). Belmont, CA: Wadsworth/Thompson Learning.

Knudson-Martin, C., and Mahoney, A.R. (2005). Moving beyond gender: Processes that create relationship equality. *Journal of Marital and Family Therapy, 31*(2), 235–258.

Koenig, L. J. (2006). *Happily married for life.* Life Journey Publishing.

Kosmin, B. A., Mayer, E., and Keysar, A. (2001). *American Religious Identification Survey.* New York: City University of New York, Graduate Center. Retrieved January 7, 2003, from http://www.gc.cuny.edu./studies/aris index.htm

Kosterman, R., Haggerty, K. P., Spoth, R., and Redmond, C. (2004). Unique influence of mothers and fathers on their children's antisocial behavior. *Journal of Marriage and Family, 66,* 762–778

Kposowa. A.J. (2003). Divorce and suicide risk. *Journal of Epidemiology and Community Health, 57,* 993. DOI: 10.1136/jech.57.12.993

Krafchick, J., Schindler Zimmerman, T., Haddock, S., and Banning, J. (2005). Best-selling books advising parents about gender: A feminist analysis. *Family Relations, 54*(1), 84–100.

Kreager, D. A., Cavanagh, S. E., Yen, J., and Yu, M. (2014). "Where have all the good men gone?" Gendered interactions in online dating. *Journal of Marriage and Family, 76*(2), 387–410.

Kreider, R. (2005). Number, timing, and duration of marriages and divorces: 2001. *Current Population Reports,* P70–97 Washington, DC: U.S. Bureau of the Census.

Kreider, R., and Fields, J. (2005). Living arrangements of children: 2001. *Current Population Reports,* P70–104. Washington, DC: U.S. Bureau of the Census.

Kreider, R. M. (2008). Improvements to demographic household data in the current population survey: 2007. Retrieved December 2009 from http://www.census.gov/population

Kreisman, J. J., and Straus, H. (2010). *I hate you—Don't leave me.* New York: Perigee.

Krishnamurti, T., and Loewenstein, G. (2008). *How Good Does Infidelity Feel: A Survey of Desire and Satisfaction with Primary and Secondary Partners.* Poster presented at the annual meeting of the Society for Personality and Social Psychology, Albuquerque, NM.

Kronenfeld, L.W., Reba-Harreleson, L., Holle. A.V., Reyes, M.L, and Bulik, C.M. (2010). Ethnic and racial differences in body size perception and satisfaction. *Body Image, 7*(2), 131—136. DOI: 10.1016/j.bodyim.2009.11.002

Kroska, A. (2004). Divisions of domestic work: Revising and expanding the theoretical explanations. *Journal of Family Issues, 25*(7), 900–932.

Krotz, J. L. (1999, July/August). Getting even. *Working Woman, 24*(7), 42–46.

Krueger, A. (2014). 9 reasons to love being single. Retrieved from http://www.forbes.com.

Kurtz, S. (2010). Adolescent boys' and girls' perceived body image and the influence of media: The impact of media literacy education on adolescents' body dissatisfaction. Carroll University.

Labbe, E., and Fobes, A. (2010). Evaluating the interplay between spirituality, personality, and stress. *Applied Psychophysiology and Biofeedback 35*(2), 141–146.

Lacy, K. K. (2002). Mature sexuality: Patient realities and provider challenges. *SIECUS Report, 30*(2), 22–30.

Laird, J. (1993). Lesbian and gay families. In R. Walsh and L. D. Wynne (Eds.), *Normal Family Processes* (pp. 282–328). New York: Guilford Press.

Lam, C. B., Solmeyer, A. R., and McHale, S. M. (2012). Sibling differences in parent–child conflict and risky behaviors: A three-wave longitudinal study. *Journal of Family Psychology, 26,* 521–531. doi:10.1r037/a0029083.

Lamanna, M.A., Riedmann, A., and Stewart, S. (2015). *Marriage, Families, and Relationships: Making Choices in a Diverse Society.* Belmont, CA: Wadsworth.

Lamaze International. (2013). History. Retrieved from http://www.lamaze.org.

Lambert, J., and Thomasson, G. (1997). Mormon American families. In M. K. DeGenova (Ed.), *Families in Cultural Context* (pp. 85–108). Mountain View, CA: Mayfield.

Lambert, N. M. (2011). Marriage in later life: A review of the research. National Healthy Marriage Resource Center. Brigham Young University.

Lambert, T. A., Kahn, A. S., and Apple, K. J. (2003). Pluralistic ignorance and hooking up. *Journal of Sex Research, 40,* 129–133.

Lansford, J. E., Malone, P. S., Castellino, D. R., Dodge, K. A., Pettit, G. S., and Bates, J. E. (2006). Trajectories of internalizing, externalizing, and grades for children who have and have not experienced their parents' divorce or separation. *Journal of Family Psychology, 20,* 292–301.

Larsen, A. S., and Olson, D. A. (1989). Predicting marital satisfaction using PREPARE: A replicator's study. *Journal of Marital and Family Therapy, 15,* 311–322.

Larson, J. H., Newell, K., Topham, G., and Nichols, S. (2002). A review of three comprehensive premarital assessment questionnaires. *Journal of Marital and Family Therapy, 28,* 233–239.

Lau, C.Q. (2012). The stability of same-sex cohabitation, different-sex cohabitation and marriage. *Journal of Marriage and Family, 74,* 973–988. DOI: 10.111/j.1741-3737.2012.01000.

Lauer, R., and Lauer, J. (2011). *Marriage and Family: The Quest for Intimacy.* New York: McGraw–Hill.

Laumann, E. O., Paik, A., Glasser, D. B., Kang, J., Wang, T., Levinson, B., et al. (2006). A cross cultural study of subjective sexual well-being among older women and men: Finding from the Global Study of Sexual Attitudes and Behaviors. *Archives of Sexual Behavior, 38,* 145–161.

Lavee, Y., McCubbin, H. I., and Patterson, J. M. (1985). The double ABCX model of family stress and adaptation: An empirical test by analysis of structural equations with latent variables. *Journal of Marriage and Family, 47,* 811–825.

Lavner, J., and Bradbury, T. (2012). Why do even satisfied newlyweds eventually go on to divorce? *Journal of Family Psychology, 26*(1), 1–10.

Lawford, C. K. (2014). *What Addicts Know.* Dallas, TX: BenBella Books.

Lawson, H. M., and Leck, K. (2006). Dynamics of Internet dating. *Social Science Computer Review, 24,* 189–208.

Lazarus, R. S., and Folkman, S. (1984). *Stress Appraisal and Coping.* New York: Springer.

Leaper, C., and Friedman, C. K. (2007). The socialization of gender. In J. E. Grusec and P. D. Davidson (Eds.), *Handbook of Socialization.* New York: Guilford Press.

Ledbetter, A.M., and Kuznekoff, J.H. (2012). More than a game: Friendship relational maintenance and attitudes toward X-box LIVE communication. *Communication Research, 39,* 269–290.

Lee, A.F. (2013). Statistics of children with special needs. *The inclusive church.* Retrieved from http://theinclusivechurch.wordpress.com

Lee, B.A., Tyler, K.A., and Wright, J.D. (2010). The new homelessness revisited. Sociology Department, Faculty Publications, Paper 127. http://digitalcommons.unl.edu/sociologyfacpub/127

Lee, T. (2012, August). More young adults living with parents. Retrieved from http://www.breitbart.com

Lee, Y., and Bhargava, V. (2004). Leisure time: Do married and single individuals spend it differently. *Family and Consumer Sciences Research Journal, 32*(3), 254–274.

Leggett, D. G., Roberts-Pittman, B., Byczek, S., and Morse, D. T. (2012). Cooperation, conflict, and marital satisfaction: Bridging theory, research, and practice. *Journal of Individual Psychiatry, 68*(2), 182.

Lehmiller, R., and Agnew, C. R. (2008). Commitment in age-gap heterosexual romantic relationships. *Psychology of Women Quarterly, 32,* 74–82.

Lei, X., Giles, J., Hu, Y., Park, A., Strauss, J., and Zhao, Y. (2012). Correlates of intergenerational non-time transfers: Evidence from CHARLS. In J.P. Smith and M.A. Majmunder, (Eds.), *Aging in Asia: Findings from New and Emerging Data Initiatives.* Washington DC: National Academic Press.

Leigh, G. K., Holman, T. B., and Burr, W. R. (1984). An empirical test of sequence in Murstein's SVR theory of mate selection. *Family Relations, 33,* 225–231.

Leitenberg, H., Gibson, L. E., and Novy, P. L. (2004). Individual differences among undergraduate women in methods of coping with stressful events: The impact of cumulative childhood stressors and abuse. *Child Abuse and Neglect, 28*(2), 181–192.

Leiter, V., Krauss, M., Anderson, B., and Wells, N. (2004). The consequences of caring: Effects of mothering a child with special needs. *Journal of Family Issues, 25*(3), 379–403.

Leon, K., and Angst, E. (2005). Portrayals of stepfamilies in film: Using media images in remarriage education. *Family Relations, 54*(1), 3–23.

Leondari, A., and Kiosseoglou, G. (2002). Parental, psychological control and attachment in late adolescents and young adults. *Psychological Reports, 90,* 1015–1030.

Leone, J. M., Johnson, M. P., Cohan, C. L., and Lloyd, S. E. (2004). Consequences of male partner violence for low-income minority women. *Journal of Marriage and Family, 66,* 472–490.

Leserman, J., and Drossman, D. A. (2007). Relationship of abuse history to functional gastrointestinal disorders and symptoms. *Trauma Violence Abuse, 8,* 331–343.

Leshner, A. I. (2000). *Anabolic Steroid Abuse* (NIH publication no. 00-3721). Washington, DC: U.S. Department of Health and Human Services, National Institutes of Health.

Levant, R. F. (2003). Treating male alexithymia. In L. B. Silverstein and T. J. Goodrich (Eds.), *Feminist Family Therapy: Empowerment in Social Context* (pp. 177–188). Washington, DC: American Psychological Association.

LeVay, S., Baldwin, J., and Baldwin, J. (2009). *Discovering Human Sexuality.* Sunderland, MA: Sinauer Associates.

Levesque, L. M., and Caron, S. L. (2004). Dating preferences of women born between 1945 and 1960. *Journal of Family Issues, 25*(6), 833–846.

Levinger, G. (1979). A social psychological perspective on marital dissolution. In G. Levinger and O. C. Moles (Eds.), *Divorce and Separation* (pp. 37–60). New York: Basic Books.

Lewis, J., Johnson-Reitz, L., and Wallerstein, J. (2004). Communication in divorced and single-parent families. In A. L. Vangelisti (Ed.), *Handbook of Family Communication* (pp. 197–214). Mahwah, NJ: Erlbaum.

Lewis, J.M., and Kreider, R.M. (2015). Remarriage in the United States. *American Community Survey Reports.* https://www.census.gov

Li, H. (2004). Barriers to unmet needs for supportive services: Experiences of Asian-American caregivers. *Journal of Cross-Cultural Gerontology, 19*(3), 241–260.

Li, N. P. (2008). Intelligent priorities: Adaptive long- and short-term mate preferences. In G. Gehr, and G. Miller (Eds.), *Mating Intelligence: Sex, Relationships, and the Mind's Reproductive System* (pp. 105–119). New York: Erlbaum.

Li, Y., Putallaz, M., and Su, Y. (2011). Interpersonal conflict styles and parenting behaviors: Associations with overt and relational aggression among Chinese children. *Merrill Palmer Quarterly, 57*(4). Article 4. Retrieved from http://digitalcommons.wayne.edu/mpq/vol57/iss4/4

Liang, J. (1982). Sex differences in life satisfaction among the elderly. *Journal of Gerontology, 37,* 100–108.

Lichter, D. T., and Qian, Z. (2008). Serial cohabitation and the marital life course. *Journal of Marriage and the Family, 70,* 861–878.

Lichter, E. L., and McCloskey, L. A. (2004). The effects of childhood exposure to marital violence on adolescent gender role beliefs and dating violence. *Psychology of Women Quarterly, 28*(4), 344–357.

Lilith Fund. (2015). FAQ: New abortion laws in Texas. Retrieved from http://www.lilithfund.org/new-laws.

Lin, C., and Liu, W. (1993). Intergenerational relationships among Chinese immigrant families from Taiwan. In H. McAdoo (Ed.), *Family Ethnicity: Strength in Diversity* (pp. 271–286). Newberg Park, CA: Sage.

Lin, I. (2000). Perceived fairness and compliance with child support obligations. *Journal of Marriage and Family, 62,* 388–398.

Linn, A. (2013). Why married people tend to be wealthier: It's complicated. *Today Money.* www.today.com

Lindner, K. (2004). Images of women in general interest and fashion magazine advertisements from 1955 to 2002. *Sex Roles, 51*(7–8), 409–421.

Lips, H. M. (1991). *Women, Men, and Power.* Mountain View, CA: Mayfield.

Lips, H. M. (1997). *Sex and Gender: An Introduction* (3rd ed.). Mountain View, CA: Mayfield.

Livingston, G. (2014). Four-in-ten couples are saying, "I do," again. Pew Research Center. Retrieved from https://www.pewsocialtrends.org/2014

Livingston, G. (2015). Childlessness falls, family size grows among highly educated women. Pew Research Center. http://www.pewsocialtrends.org

Livingston, G., and Cohn, D. (2010). Childlessness up among all women: Down among women with advanced degrees. Pew Social and Demographic Trends. Retrieved from http://www.pewsocialtrends.org/2010.

Living Wage Calculator. (2016). http://livingwage.mit.edu

Lofas, J. (2013). The dynamics of step. http://www.stepfamilies.org

Lonczak, H. S., Donovan, D. M., Fernandez, A., Marlatt, G. A., and Austin, L. (2007). Family structure and substance use among American Indian youth. *Families, Systems, and Health, 25,* 10–22.

London, K., Bruck, M., and Ceci, S. J. (2005). Disclosure of child sexual abuse: What does the research tell us about the ways that children tell? *Psychology, Public Policy, and Law, 11,* 194–226.

London, S. (2004). Current hormone therapy use linked to 30–100% rise in risk of breast cancer. *Perspectives in Sexual and Reproductive Health, 36*(1), 41–42.

Long, E. C., Angera, J. J., and Carter, S. J. (1999). Understanding the one you love; a longitudinal assessment of an empathy training program for couples in romantic relationships. *Family Relations, 48*(3), 235–242.

Longley, R. (2009). Should the US adopt a nationalized health care system? Retrieved May 2009 from http://usgovinfo.about.com/od/medicarehealthinsurance.

Loper, A.B., Carlson, L.W., Levitt, L., and Scheffel, K. (2009). Parenting stress, alliance, child contact, and adjustment of imprisoned mothers and fathers. *Journal of Offender Rehabilitation, 48*(6), 483–503.

Lowenstein, L. (2005). Causes and associated features of divorce as seen by recent research. *Journal of Divorce and Remarriage, 42*(3–4), 153–171.

Lucyck, K., Tildesley, E.A., Soenens, B., Andrews, J., Hampson, S.E., Peterson, M., and Duriez, B. (2011). Parenting and trajectories of children's maladaptive behaviors: A twelve year perspective community study. *Journal of Clinical Child and Adolescent Psychology, 40*(4), 468–478.

Luhby, T. (2015). Typical American family earned $53, 657 last year. *CNN Money.* http://money.cnn.com

Lutwak, N. (1985). Fear of intimacy among college women. *Adolescence, 77*, 15–20.

MacCallum, F., and Golombok, S. (2004). Children raised in fatherless families from infancy: A follow-up of children of lesbian and single heterosexual mothers at early adolescence. *Journal of Child Psychology and Psychiatry, 45*(8), 1407–1419.

MacDermid, S., Jurich, J., Myers-Walls, J., and Pelo, A. (1992). Feminist teaching: Effective education. *Family Relations, 41*(1), 31–38.

Mace, D., and Mace, V. (1974). *We Can Have Better Marriages If We Really Want Them.* Nashville: Abingdon.

Mace, D., and Mace, V. (1980). Enriching marriages: The foundation stone of family strength. In N. Stinnett et al. (Eds.), *Family Strengths: Positive Models for Family Life.* Lincoln: University of Nebraska Press.

MacGill, M. (2015). Oxytocin: What is it and what does it do? Medical News Today. http://www.medicalnewstoday.com

Mack-Canty, C., and Wright, S. (2004). Family values as practiced by feminist parents. *Journal of Family Issues, 25*(7), 851–880.

MacMillan, A. (2014). 7 ways being single affects your health. *Time.* http://time.com.

Mahin, A., Sidek, B., Mohd, N., Siti Aishah, Bt. H, and Maznah, Bt. B. (2012). Comparison of the effects of communication and conflict-resolution skills training on marital satisfaction. *International Journal of Psychological Studies, 4*(1), 182–195.

Maisel, N., Frederick, D. A., Usahacharoenporn, P., Holbert, S. A., and Lever, J. (2008). *When Partners Cheat: Using Interdependency Theory to Predict Infidelity.* Poster presented at the annual meeting of the Society for Personality and Social Psychology, Albuquerque, NM.

Major, V. S., Klein, K. J., and Ehrhart, M. G. (2002). Work time, work interference with family, and psychological distress. *Journal of Applied Psychology, 87*(3), 427–136.

Make the cover a sales tool. (1998, March 1). *Folio: The Magazine for Magazine Management.* Retrieved from http://www.foliomag.com/content/plus/1998/19980301.htm#3.

Malcolm, H. (2012). Get financially prepared before getting a divorce. *USA Today,* September 10.

Malia, S. E. (2005). Balancing family members' interests regarding stepparent rights and obligations: A social policy challenge. *Family Relations, 54*(2), 298–319.

Malkin, A. R., Wornian, K., and Chrisler, J. C. (1999). Woman and weight: Gendered messages on magazine covers. *Sex Roles, 40*(7/8), 647–655.

Manning, W. D. (2002). The implication of cohabitation for children's well-being. In A. Booth and A. C. Crouter (Eds.), *Just Living Together: Implications for Children, Families, and Public Policy.* Hillsdale, NJ: Erlbaum.

Manning, W.D., Fettro, M.N., and Lamidi, E. (2014). Child well-being in same-sex parent families: Review of research prepared for American Sociological Association. Amicus Brief. *Population Research Policy Review, 33*(4), 485–502.

Manning, W. D., Longmore, M. A., and Giordano, P. C. (2007, August). The changing institution of marriage: Adolescents' expectations to cohabit and marry. *Journal of Marriage and Family, 69*, 559–575.

Marazziti, D., and Canale, D. (2004). Hormonal changes when falling in love. *Psychoneuroendocrinology, 29*(7), 931–936.

Marchbanks, P. A., McDonald, J. A., Wilson, H. G., Folger, S. G., Mandel, M. G., Daling, J. R., et al. (2002). Oral contraceptives and the risk of breast cancer. *New England Journal of Medicine, 346*(26), 2025–2032.

March of Dimes. (2013). http://www.marchofdimes.org

Marcus, I. M. (1983). The need for flexibility in marriage. *Medical Aspects of Human Sexuality, 17*, 120–131.

Margolin, G., Gordis, E. B., and Oliver, P. H. (2004). Links between marital and parent–child interactions: Moderating role of husband to wife aggression. *Development and Psychopathology, 16*(3), 753–771.

Mark, K., Janssen, E., and Milhausen, R. (2011). Infidelity in heterosexual couples: Demographic, interpersonal and personality-related predictors of extradyadic sex. *Archives of Sexual Behavior.* Retrieved from http://www.newsinfo.iu.edu

Markey, C. N., Markey, P. M., and Birch, L. L. (2004). Understanding women's body satisfaction. *Sex Roles, 51*, 209–216.

Marks, L. (2012). Same-sex parenting and children's outcomes: A closer examination of the American Psychological Association's brief on lesbian and gay parenting. *Social Science Research, 41*, 735–751.

Marks, N. F., and Lambert, J. D. (1998). Marital status continuity and change among young and midlife adults. *Journal of Family Issues, 19*, 652–686.

Marshall, P. J., Weston, R., and Honeycutt, T. C. (2000). Does men's positivity moderate or mediate the effect of their abuse on women's relationship quality? *Journal of Social and Personal Relationships, 17*, 660–675.

Marshall, S. K., and Markstrom-Adams, C. (1995). Attitudes on interfaith dating among Jewish adolescents. *Journal of Family Issues, 16*, 787–811.

Marsiglio, W. (2004). When stepfathers claim stepchildren: A conceptual analysis. *Journal of Marriage and Family, 66*(1), 22–39.

Martin, J. A., Hamilton, B. E., Osterman, M. J. K., Curtin, S. C., and Mathews, T. J. (2015). Births: Final data for 2013. *National Vital Statistics Report, 64*. Retrieved from http://cdc.gov/nchs/nvsr64

Martin, J. A., Hamilton, B. E., Sutton, P. D., Ventura, S. J., Menacker, F., Kirmeyer, S., et al. (2007). Births: Final data for 2005. *National Vital Statistics Report, 56*. Hyattsville, MD: National Center for Health Statistics.

Martin, J. A., Hamilton, B. E., Ventura, S. J., Osterman, J. K., Wilson, E. C., and Mathews, T. J. (2012). Births: Final data for 2010. *National Vital Statistics Report, 61*. Retrieved from http://cdc.gov/nchs/data/nvsr61

Martin, J.B. (2010). The development of ideal body image perceptions in the United States. *Nutrition Today 45*, 98–111.

Martin, T. C., and Bumpass, L. L. (1989). Recent trends in marital disruption. *Demography, 26*, 37–51.

Martini, T., Root, C., and Jenkins, J. (2004). Low and middle income mothers' regulation of negative emotion: Effects of children's temperament and situational emotional response. *Social Development, 13*(4), 515–530.

Maserejian, N.N., Shifren, J., Parish, S.J., Segraves, R.T., Huang, L., and Rosen, R.C. (2012). Sexual arousal and lubrication problems in women with clinically diagnosed hypoactive sexual desire disorder: Preliminary findings from the hypoactive sexual desire disorder registry for women. *Journal of Sex and Marital Therapy, 38*(1), 41–62. DOI: 10.1080/0092623x.2011.569642.

Maslow, A. H. (1970). *Motivation and Personality* (2nd ed.). New York: Harper & Row.

Maslow, A. H. (2000). *Motivation and Personality* (3rd ed.) Upper Saddle River, NJ: Pearson.

Mason, M. A. (2003). The modern American stepfamily: Problems and possibilities. In M. A. Mason, A. Skolnick, and S. D. Sugarman (Eds.), *All Our Families* (pp. 96–116). New York: Oxford University Press.

Mason, M. A., Harrison-Jay, S., Svare, G. M., and Wolfinger, N. H. (2002). Stepparents: De facto parents or legal strangers? *Journal of Family Issues, 23*(4), 507–522.

Massoni, K. (2004). Modeling work: Occupational messages in *Seventeen* magazine. *Gender and Society, 18*(1), 47–65.

Mastekaasa, A. (1994). Psychological well-being and marital disillusion: Selection effects. *Journal of Family Issues, 15*, 208–228.

Masters, W. H., and Johnson, V. E. (1966). *Human Sexual Response.* Boston: Little, Brown.

Masters, W. H., Johnson, V. E., and Kolodny, R. C. (1995). *Human Sexuality* (5th ed.). Boston: Pearson.

Mathews, T. J., and Hamilton, B. E. (2014). First births to older women continue to rise. *NCHS Data brief 152.* Retrieved from http://www.cdc.gov.

Matos, K., and Galinsky, E. (2014). National study of employers. Families and Work Institute. http://www.familiesandwork.org

Matsunaga, M., and Imahori, T. T. (2009). Profiling family communication standards: A U.S.–Japan comparison. *Communication Research, 36* (1), 3–31.

Mausbach, B., Coon, D., Deep, C., Rabinowitz, Y., Wilson-Arias, E., Kraemer, H., et al. (2004). Ethnicity and time to institutionalization of dementia patients: A comparison of Latina and Caucasian female family care-givers. *Journal of the American Geriatrics Society, 52*(7), 1077–1084.

Maynard, F. (1974). Understanding the crises in men's lives. In C. E. Williams and J. F. Crosby (Eds.), *Choice and Challenge* (pp. 135–144). Dubuque, IA: Brown.

Mayo Clinic Staff (2011). http://www.mayoclinic.org

Mayo Clinic Staff. (2012). http://www.mayoclinic.org

Mayo Clinic Staff. (2013). http://www.mayoclinic.org

Mayo Clinic Staff (2014). http://www.mayoclinic.org

Mayo Clinic Staff (2015). http://www.mayoclinic.org

Mayo Clinic Staff (2016). http://www.mayoclinic.org

Mberengwa, L. R. (2007). Family strengths perspectives from Botswana. *Marriage and Family Review, 41*, 27–46.

McAdoo, H. P. (Ed) (2007). *Black Families* (4th ed.). Thousand Oaks, CA: Sage.

McAnulty, R. D., and Brineman, J. M. (2007). Infidelity in dating relationships. *Annual Review of Sex Research, 18* (1), 94–114.

McCabe, C. (2013). Forgiveness and coping with divorce. Unpublished manuscript, Skidmore College.

McCabe, E., and Conley, G. (2015). E-Cigarettes. Presentation at American Congress of Obstetricians and Gynecologists, San Francisco, May 2–6, 2015.

McCabe, M. P., and Ricciardelli, L. A. (2004). Body image dissatisfaction among males across the lifespan: A review of past literature. *Journal of Psychosomatic Research, 56*(6), 675–685.

McCarthy, G. (1999). Attachment style and adult love relationships and friendships: A study of a group of women at risk of experiencing relationship difficulties. *British Journal of Medical Psychology, 72,* 305–321.

McCarthy, G., and Taylor, A. (1999). Avoidant/ambivalent attachment style as a mediator between abusive childhood experiences and adult relationship difficulties. *Journal of Child Psychology and Psychiatry and Allied Discipline, 40,* 465–477.

McCarthy, J. (2015). Record-high 60% of Americans support same-sex marriage. Gallup. Retrieved from http://gallup.com.

McCormack, K. (2007). Careers: The goods on generation Y. *Business Week,* June 26.

McCreary, L. L., and Dancy, B. L. (2004). Dimensions of family functioning: Perspectives of low-income African American single-parent families. *Journal of Marriage and Family, 66*(3), 690–701.

McDaniel, A., and Coleman, M. (2003). Women's experiences of midlife divorce following long-term marriage. *Journal of Divorce and Remarriage, 38*(4), 103–128.

McGrath, A. (2012). The single life: Results from our survey. Retrieved from http://www.washingtonpost.com.

McGregor, J. (2014). The average work week is now 47 hours. *The Washington Post.* September 2, 2014. http://www.washingtonpost,com

McHugh, M. C., Livingston, N., and Frieze, I. H. (2008). Intimate partner violence: Perspectives on research and intervention. In F. L. Denmark and M. A. Paludi (Eds.), *Psychology of Women: A Handbook of Issues and Theories* (2nd ed., pp. 555–589). Westport, CT: Praeger.

McKee-Ryan, F., Song, Z., Wanberg, C. R., and Kinicki, A. J. (2005). Psychological and physical well-being during unemployment: A meta-analytic study. *Journal of Applied Psychology, 90*(1), 53–76.

McKittrick, D. (2010). The big question: After decades of controversy, could abortion become legal in Ireland? Retrieved from http://www.safeandlegal.blogspot

McLain, R. (2000). The Hopi way of life. Tour to Hopi Indian Reservation, 2nd Mesa near Tuba City, AZ.

McLoyd, V. C., and Wilson, L. (1992). Telling them like it is: The role of economic and environmental factors in single mothers' discussion with their children. *American Journal of Community Psychology, 20,* 419–444.

McNulty, J. K., Neff, L. A., and Karney, B. R. (2008). Beyond initial attraction: Physical attractiveness in newlywed marriage. *Journal of Family Psychology, 22*(1), 135–143.

Mead, M. (1950). *Sex and Temperament in Three Primitive Societies.* New York: Merton Books.

Media Smarts. (2015). Body image. Retrieved from http://mediasmarts.ca/body-image.

Michael, R. T., Gagnon, J. H., Laumann, E. O., and Kolata, G. (1994). *Sex in America.* Boston: Little, Brown.

Mikulincer, M., and Shaver, P. R. (2007a). A behavioral systems perspective on the psychodynamics of attachment and sexuality. In D. Diamond, S. J. Blatt, and J. D. Lichtenberg (Eds.), *Attachment and Sexuality* (pp. 51–78). New York: Analytic Press.

Mikulincer, M., and Shaver, P. R. (2007b). *Attachment in Adulthood: Structure, Dynamics, and Change.* New York: Guilford Press.

Milkie, M. A., Mattingly, M. J., Nomaguchi, K. M., Bianchi, S. M., and Robinson, J. P. (2004). The time squeeze: Parental statuses and feelings about time with children. *Journal of Marriage and Family, 66,* 739–761.

Miller, K. J., Gleaves, D. H., Hirsch, T. G., Green, B. A., Snow, A. C., and Corbett, C. C. (2000). Comparisons of body image dimensions by race/ethnicity and gender in a university population. *International Journal of Eating Disorders, 27*(3), 310–316.

Miller, M. C. (2012). The psychological impact of infertility and its treatment. *Healthy Lifestyle.* Retrieved from http://www.intelihealth.com.

Miller, R. B., Yorganson, J. B., Sandberg, J. G., and White, M. B. (2003). Problems that couples bring to therapy: A view across the family life cycle. *The American Journal of Family Therapy, 31,* 395–407.

Miller, R. S. (2015). *Intimate Relationships* (7th ed.). New York: McGraw–Hill.

Miller, R. S., and Perlman, D. (2009). *Intimate Relationships.* New York: McGraw–Hill.

Mills, M., Janiszewska, A., and Zabala, L. (2011). Sex differences in making first-time risky relationship initiatives. Poster presented at the Western Psychological Association Meeting. April. Also in The how and why of sex differences: Why don't women ask men out on first dates? Retrieved from http://www.psychologytoday.com.

Ming, C., Fincham, F.D., and Durtschi, J.A. (2011). The effect of parental divorce on young adults' romantic relationship dissolution: What makes a difference? *Personal Relationships, 18*(3), 410–426. DOI: 10.1111/j.1475-6811,2010.013-06.x

Mishel, L., Bernstein, J., and Boushey, H. (2003). *The State of Working America 2002–03.* Ithaca, NY: Cornell University Press.

Mishori, R., McClaskey, E.L., and Winkler-Prins, V.J. (2012). *Chlamydia trachomatis* infections: Screening, diagnosis, and management. *American Family Physician, 86,* 1127–1132.

Mitchell, J. (2013). About half of kids with single moms live in poverty. *Wall Street Journal.* Retrieved from http://wsj.com.

Mohney, G. (2014). First woman charged on controversial law that criminalizes drug use during pregnancy. *ABC News.* Retrieved from http://abcnews.go.com.

Mollborn, S., and Lovegrove, P.J. (2011). How teenage fathers matter for children: Evidence from the FCLS-B. *Journal of Family Issues, 32*(1), 3–30. DOI: 10.1177/0192513x10370110

Monte, L.M., and Ellis, R.R. (2014). Fertility of women in the United States: 2012. https://www.census.gov

Montgomery, M. J., and Sorell, G. T. (1997). Differences in love attitudes across family life stages. *Family Relations, 46,* 55–61.

Mookherjee, H. N. (1997). A comparative assessment of life satisfaction in the United States: 1978–1988. *Journal of Social Psychology, 132,* 407–409.

Moore, S., and Cartwright, C. (2005). Adolescents' and young adults' expectations of parental responsibilities. *Journal of Divorce and Remarriage, 43,* 111–130.

Moore, S., and Leung, C. (2002). Young people's romantic attachment styles and their associations with well-being. *Journal of Adolescence, 25,* 243–255.

Moore, T. M., Stuart, G. L., McNulty, J. K., Addis, M. E., Cordova, J. V., and Temple, J. R. (2008). Domains of masculine gender role stress and intimate partner violence in a clinical sample of violent men. *Psychology of Men and Masculinity, 9,* 82–89.

More than one in four Americans is obese. (2008, July). Retrieved January 5, 2009, from http://www.foxnews.com/health.

Morrill, M.I., Hines, D.A., Mahmood, S., and Cordova, J.V. (2010). Pathways between marriage and parenting for wives and husbands: The role of co-parenting. *Family Process, 49,* 59–73.

Morse, B. J. (1995). Beyond the Conflict Tactics Scale: Assessing gender differences in partner violence. *Violence and Victims, 10,* 251–272.

Mosher, W., Allen, J., and Manlove, J. (2005). Sexual behavior and selected health measures: Men and women 15–44 years of age, United States, 2002. Child Trends Data Bank. Retrieved October, 20, 2005, from http://www.childtrendsdatabank.org/indicators/95OralSex.cfm

Moss, B. F., and Schwebel, A. I. (1993). Marriage and romantic relationships. Defining intimacy in romantic relationships. *Family Relations, 42,* 31–37.

Muise, A., Impett, E. A., Kogan, A., and Desmarais, S. (2013). Keeping the spark alive: Being motivated to meet a partner's sexual needs sustains sexual desire in long-term romantic relationships. *Social Psychology and Personality Science, 4*(3), 267–273.

Mulryan, C. (2013). Syphilis: Recognizing the "great pretender." *Practice Nursing, 24*(5), 217–221.

Mupinga, E. E., Garrison, M. E. B., and Pierce, S. H. (2002). An exploratory study of the relationships between family functioning and parenting styles: The perceptions of mothers of young grade school children. *Family and Consumer Sciences Research Journal, 31*(1), 112–129.

Murdock, G. P. (1949). *Social Structure.* New York: Macmillan.

Musick, K., Brand, J. E., and Davis, D. (2012). Variations in the relationship between education and marriage: Marriage market mismatch? *Journal of Marriage and the Family, 74,* 53–69.

Myers, D. G. (2000). Hope and happiness. In J. E. Gillham (Ed.), *The Science of Optimism and Hope: Research Essays in Honor of Martin E. P. Seligman. Laws of Life Symposia Series* (pp. 323–336). Philadelphia: Templeton Foundation Press.

Myers, S. M. (2006). Religious homogamy and marital quality. *Journal of Marriage and Family, 68,* 292–304.

Nadeau, C., and Glasmeier, A.K. (2016). Minimum wage: Can an individual or a family live on it? *Living Wage Calculator.* http://livingwage.mit.edu

Nasuti, J. P., York, R., and Sandell, K. (2004). Comparison of role perceptions of white and African American foster parents. *Child Welfare, 83*(1), 49–68.

Natali, A., Mondaini, N., Lombardi, G., Del Popolo, G., and Rizzo, M. (2005). Heavy smoking is an important risk factor for erectile dysfunction in young men. *International Journal of Impotence Research, 17,* 227–230.

National Alliance to End Homelessness. (2014). The state of homelessness in America 2014. Retrieved from http://3cdn.net/naeh

National Association of Realtors. (2016). U.S. housing affordability, 1990–2015. http://www.realtor.org

National Center for Health Statistics. (2002). Marriage and divorce. Retrieved January 6, 2003, from http://www.cdc.gov/nchs/fastats/marriage.htm

National Center for Health Statistics. (2011). Retrieved from http://www.cdc.gov/nchs.

National Center for Health Statistics (2012). Retrieved from http://www.cdc.org/nchs.

National Center for Health Statistics. (2013a). Divorce rates by states. Retrieved from http://www.cdc.gov/nchs.

National Center for Health Statistics. (2013b). Marriage and divorce rates in the U.S. Retrieved from http://www.cdc.gov/nchs.

National Center for Health Statistics. (2013). Retrieved from http://www.cdc.gov/nchs.

National Center for Health Statistics (2015). National Health Interview Survey. http://www.cdc.gov/nchs

National Center on Elder Abuse. (2015). Elder Abuse. National Center on Elder Abuse. http://www.ncea.aoa.gov

National Coalition for the Homeless. (2001). Homeless Families with Children, 2001. Available from the National Coalition for the Homeless, 2201 P Street NW, Washington, DC 20037.

National Committee on Pay Equity. (2005). Top ten reasons for the wage gap in 2001. Retrieved September 8, 2005, from http://www.pay-equity.org/info-top10.html.

National Council on Alcoholism and Drug Dependency. (2016). The real story about alcohol and other drugs. National Council on Alcoholism and Drug Dependency. http://www.ncadd.org

National Low Income Housing Coalition. (2016). Out of reach: Rental housing at what cost? http://nlihc.org

National Post-Secondary Student Aid Survey. (2015). Trends in graduate student financing: Selected years, 1995–96 to 2011–2012. National Center for Educational Statistics. Retrieved from https://nces.ed.gov.

National Women's Health Information Center. (2008). Retrieved December 2008 from http://www.women'shealth.go

Nauraine, J. (2011). Dating relationships: When closeness is an elusive quest. Retrieved from http://www.examiner.com.

Neal, J., and Frick-Horbury, D. (2001). The effects of parenting styles and childhood attachment patterns on intimate relationships. *Journal of Instructional Psychology, 28*(3), 178–183.

Neborsky, R. J., and Bundy, C. (2013). Prediction of attachment status from observation of a clinical intensive psychotherapy interview. *American Journal of Psychotherapy, 67*(1), 47–71.

Neff, L.A., and Geers, A.L. (2013). Optimistic expectations in early marriage: A resource or vulnerability for adaptive relationship functioning? *Journal of Personality and Social Psychology, 105*, 38–60. DOI: 10.1037/a0032600.

Neff, L. A., and Karney, B. R. (2005). To know you is to love you: Implications of global adoration and specific accuracy for marital relationships. *Journal of Personality and Social Psychology, 88*(3), 480–497.

Neff, L.A. and Morgan, T.H. (2014). The rising expectations of marriage: What we do and do not know. *Psychological Inquiry, 25*, 95–100. DOI: 10.1080/1047840x/2014.878234.

Neimeyer, R. S., Prigerson, H. G., and Davis, B. (2002). Mourning and meaning. *American Behavioral Scientist, 46*(2), 235–251.

Nelson, L. J. (2003). Rites of passage in emerging adulthood: Perspectives of young Mormons. In J. Arnett and N. Galambos (Eds.), *New Directions for Child and Adolescent Development: Cultural Conceptions of the Transition to Adulthood* (no. 100, pp. 33–49). Chichester, UK: Wiley.

Nelson, L. J., Badger, S., and Wu, B. (2004). The influence of culture in emerging adulthood: Perspectives of Chinese college students. *International Journal of Behavioral Development, 28*(1), 26–36.

Nelson, M. B. (2002/2003, December/January). And now they tell us women don't really like sports? *Ms.*, pp. 32–36.

Neumark-Sztainer, D., Wall, M. W., and Fulkerson, J. A. (2012). Changes in the frequency of family meals from 1999 to 2010 in the homes of adolescents: Trends by socio-demographic characteristics. *Journal of Adolescent Health, 6*(4), 1–6.

Newacheck, P., McManus, M., Fox, H. B., Hung, Y., and Hafton, N. (2000). Access to health care for children with special needs. *Pediatrics, 105*, 760–766.

New York University and Capitol One. (2015). *Rent affordability in eleven major cities across the United States.* New York: New York University Press.

Nguyen, P. V. (2008). Perceptions of Vietnamese fathers' acculturation levels, parenting styles, and mental health outcomes in Vietnamese American adolescent immigrants. *Social Work, 53*(4), 337–346.

Nicholas, G., DeSilva, A., Prater, K., and Bronkosoki, E. (2009). Empathic family stress as a sign of family connectedness in Haitian immigrants. *Family Process, 48*(1), 135–150.

Nicholson, J.M., Sanders, M.R., Halford, W.K., Phillips, M., and Whitton, S.W. (2012). The prevention and treatment of children's adjustment problems in stepfamilies. In J. Pryor, (Ed.), *The International Handbook of Stepfamilies: Policy and Practice in Legal, Research, and Clinical Environments*, (pp. 485–521). DOI: 10.1002/978111826-9923.ch20.

Nielson, L. (2013). Parenting time and shared residential custody: Ten common myths. The Nebraska Lawyer. 5-8. http://www.acfc.org/acfc/assets

Nieto, S. (1996). *Affirming Diversity: The Sociopolitical Context of Multicultural Education* (2nd ed.). New York: Longman.

Nobles, W. (1988). African-American family life: An instrument of culture. In H. P. McAdoo (Ed.), *Black Families* (2nd ed., pp. 44–53). Newbury Park, CA: Sage.

NOFAS (2015). Website of the National Organization on Fetal Alcohol Syndrome. Retrieved from http://nofas.org.

NREPP. (2015). *Prevention and Relationship Enhancement Program (PREP)*. SAMHSA National Registry of Evidence-based Programs and Practices. Retrieved from http://www.samhsa.gov.

Null, G., and Ashley, N. (2012). Gardasil: Big pharma killing us softly. Retrieved from http://www.vactruth.com/2012/1/25

Nuru, A. K., and Wang, T. R. (2014). "She was stomping on everything that we used to think of as a family": Communication and turning points in cohabiting (step) families. *Journal of Divorce and Remarriage, 55*, 145–163. doi:10.1080/10502556.2013.871957.

Oates, M. R., Cox, J. L., Neema, S., Asten, P., Glangeaud-Freudenthal, N., Figueiredo, B., et al. (2004). Postnatal depression across countries and cultures: A qualitative study. *British Journal of Psychiatry, 184*(Suppl. 46), s10–s16.

Office of Family Assistance Administration for Children and Families. (2016). Temporary Assistance for Needy Families (TANF). U.S. Department of Health and Human Services.

Offman, A., and Matheson, K. (2004). The sexual self-perceptions of young women experiencing abuse in dating relationships. *Sex Roles, 51*(9–10), 551–560.

Ogunwole, S. (2006). We the people: American Indians and Alaska natives. *Report CEIVSR, 28.* Washington, DC: U.S. Bureau of the Census.

O'Hara, M., and Gorman, L. L. (2004). Can postpartum depression be predicted? *Primary Psychiatry, 11*(3), 42–47.

Okagaki, L., and Sternberg, R. J. (1993). Parental beliefs in children's school performance. *Child Development, 64*, 36–56.

O'Brien, S.A. (2015). 78 cents on the dollar: The facts about the gender wage gap. *CNN Money.* http://money.cnn.com

O'Leary, K. D., Barling, J., Arias, I., Rosenbaum, A., Malone, J., and Tyree, A. (1989). Prevalence and stability of physical aggression between spouses: A longitudinal analysis. *Journal of Consulting and Clinical Psychology, 57*, 263–268.

Olson, D. (2000). *Empowering Couples: Building on Your Strengths*. Minneapolis: Life Innovations.

Olson, D. (2009). Top strengths of happy versus unhappy step couples. Retrieved from http://www.successfulstepfamilies.com

Olson, D. H., DeFrain, J., and Skogrand, L. (2014). *Marriage and Families: Intimacy, Diversity, and Strengths* (8th ed.). New York: McGraw–Hill.

Olson, D. H., Larson, P. J., and Olson, A. K. (2009). PREPARE: ENRICH program customized version. Minneapolis, MN: Life Innovations.

Olson, D. H., and Olson, A. K. (1999). PREPARE/ENRICH program: Version 2000. In R. Berger and M. T. Hannah (Eds.), *Preventive Approaches in Couples' Therapy* (pp. 196–216). Philadelphia: Brunner/Mazel.

Oncale, R. M., and King, B. M. (2001). Comparison of men's and women's attempts to dissuade sexual partners from the couple using condoms. *Archives of Sexual Behavior, 30*, 379–391.

O'Neil, R., and Greenberger, E. (1994). Patterns of commitment to work and parenting: Implications for role strain. *Journal of Marriage and Family, 56*, 101–118.

Orbuch, T. L. (2012). Finding love again: 6 simple steps to a new and happy relationship. Naperville, IL: Sourcebooks.

Orth-Gomer, K. (2001). Women and heart disease: New evidence for psychosocial, behaviorial, and biological mediators of risk and prognosis. *International Journal of Behavioral Medicine, 8*(4), 251–269.

Osborne, C., Manning, W. D., and Smock, P. J. (2007, December). Married and cohabiting parents' relationship stability: A focus on race and ethnicity. *Journal of Marriage and Family, 69*, 1345–1366.

Oscharoff, A.C.S. (2011). Emotional exhaustion, work family conflict, and marital satisfaction among professional psychologists. Master's Thesis. Loyola University Chicago.

Osmond, M. W., and Thorne, B. (1993). Feminist theories: The social construction of gender in families and society. In P. G. Boss, W. J. Doherty, R. LaRossa, W. R. Schumm, and S. K. Steinmetz (Eds.), *Source of Family Theories and Methods* (pp. 591–622). New York: Plenum.

Ostovich, J. M., and Sabini, J. (2004). How are sociosexuality and sex drive, and lifetime number of sexual partners related? *Personality and Social Psychology Bulletin, 30*, 1255–1266.

O'Sullivan, M. (2008). Deception and self-deception as strategies in short- and long-term mating. In G. Gehr and G. Miller (Eds.), *Mating Intelligence: Sex, Relationships and the Mind's Reproductive System* (pp. 135–157). New York: Erlbaum.

Otnes, C. C., and Pleck, E. H. (2003). *Cinderella Dreams: The Allure of the Lavish Wedding.* Berkeley: University of California Press.

Oyserman, D., Radin, N., and Benn, R. (1993). Dynamics in a three-generational family: Teens, grandparents, and babies. *Developmental Psychology, 29*, 564–572.

Ozawa, M. N., and Yoon H. S. (2002). The economic benefit of remarriage: Gender and income class. *Journal of Divorce and Remarriage, 36*(3/4), 21–39.

Pacey, S. (2004). Couples and the first baby: Responding to new parents' sexual and relationship problems. *Sexual and Relationship Therapy, 19*(3), 223–246.

Padgett, P. M. (2007). Personal safety and sexual safety for women using online personal ads. *Sexuality Research & Social Policy, 4*, 27–37.

Painter, K. (2012). IUDs, implants are changing birth control. *USA Today*, October 30, 2012. Life 3D.

Palihapitiya, M., and Eisenkraft, K.O. (2014). Addressing parenting disputes between estranged parents through community mediation. Sage Publications. http://sgo.sagepub.com. DOI: http://dx,doi.org/10.1177/2158244014542085.

Palkovitz, R. (2002). *Involved Fathering and Men's Adult Development: Provisional Balances*. Mahwah, NJ: Erlbaum.

Pamensky, A. (2005). The purpose of marriage. Retrieved from http://www.aish.com.

Panchanadeswaran, S., Johnson, S., Go, V. K., Srikrishnan, A. K., Sivaram, S., Solomon, S., Bentley, M., and Celentano, D. (2007). Using the theory of gender and power to examine experiences of partner violence, sexual negotiation, and risk of HIV/AIDS among economically disadvantaged women in southern India. *Journal of Aggression, Maltreatment, and Trauma, 15* (3–4), 155–178.

Papalia, D. E., Olds, S. W., and Feldman, R. D. (2009). *Human Development* (11th ed.). New York: McGraw–Hill.

Papernow, P.L. (2013). *Surviving and Thriving in Stepfamily Relationships: What Works and What Doesn't*. New York: Routledge.

Papernow, P.L. (2015). Therapy with couples in stepfamilies. In A. Gurman. J. Lebow, and D. Snyder, (Eds.). *Clinical Handbook of Couple Therapy*, 5th ed, ,(pp.467–488). New York: Guilford.

Papp, L. M., Cummings, E., and Schermerhorn, A. C. (2004). Pathways among marital distress, parental symptomatology, and child adjustment. *Journal of Marriage and Family, 66*(2), 368–384.

Papp, P. (2003). Gender, marriage and depression. In L. B. Silverstein and T. J. Goodrich (Eds.), *Feminist Family Therapy: Empowerment in Social Context* (pp. 211–224). Washington, DC: American Psychological Association.

Paquette, D. (2015). The states where parents spend the most on child care. *The Washington Post*. http://www.washingtonpost

Parental leave. (2007). Wikipedia. Retrieved March 2009 from http://en.wikipedia.org/wiki/Parental_leave.

Park, B. (2013). How stereotypes shape women's identities and careers. Society for Personality and Social Psychology Annual Meeting. New Orleans. January 17–19, 2013.

Park, C. L. (2005). Religion as a meaning-making system. *Psychology of Religion Newsletter, 30*, 1–9.

Parke, M. (2003, May). Are married parents really better for children? What research says about the effects of family structure on child well-being. *Couples and Marriage Research and Policy Brief*. Washington, DC: Center for Law and Social Policy.

Parke, R. D. (2002). Fathers and families. In M. Bornstein (Ed.), *Handbook of Parenting*. Hillsdale, NJ: Erlbaum.

Parke, R. D., Coltrane, S., Duffy, S., Buriel, R., Dennis, J., Powers, J., et al. (2004). Economic stress, parenting, and child adjustment in Mexican American and European American families. *Child Development, 75*(6), 1632–1656.

Parke, R. D., and Gauvain, M. (2009). *Child Psychology: A Contemporary Viewpoint*. New York: McGraw–Hill.

Parker, K., and Patten, E. (2013). The sandwich generation: Rising financial burdens for middle-aged Americans. Pew Research Center. http://www.pewsocialtrends.org

Parker, L. (2003). Bring power from the margins to the center. In L. B. Silverstein and T. J. Goodrich (Eds.), *Feminist Family Therapy: Empowerment in Social Context* (pp. 225–238). Washington, DC: American Psychological Association.

Parrott, A. C. (2008). Recreational ecstasy/MDMA, the serotonin syndrome, and serotonergic neurotoxicity. *Pharmacology and Biochemical Behavior, 71*(4), 537–844.

Parry, D. C., and Shinew, K. J. (2004). The constraining impact of infertility on women's leisure lifestyles. *Leisure Sciences, 26*(3), 295–308.

Pasley, K., and Moorefield, B. (2004). Stepfamilies: Changes and challenges. In M. Coleman and L. Ganong (Eds.), *Handbook of Contemporary Families* (pp. 317–332). Thousand Oaks, CA: Sage.

Patrick, S. W., Dudley, J., Martin, P. R., Harrell, F. E., Warren, M. D., Hartmann, K. E., Ely, E. W., Grijala, C. G., and Cooper, W. O. (2015). Prescription opioid epidemic and infant outcomes. *Pediatrics, 135*(5), 842–850. doi:10.1542peds.2014-3299.

Patten, E. (2015). On equal-pay day, key facts about the gender pay gap. Pew Research Center. Retrieved from http://www.pewresearch.org

Patten, E. (2015). How American parents balance work and family life when both work. Pew Research Center. http://www.pewresearch.org

Paul, E. L., Wenzel, A., and Harvey, J. H. (2008). Hookups: A facilitator or a barrier to relationship initiation and intimacy development? In S. Sprecher, A. Wenzel, and J. H. Harvey (Eds.), *Handbook of Relationship Initiation* (pp. 375–390). Mahwah, NJ: Erlbaum.

Paul, P. (2005). *Pornified: How Pornography Is Transforming Our Lives, Our Relationships and Our Families*. New York: Times Books.

Paulson, A. (2010, Feb. 2). Abstinence-only study could alter sex-education landscape. *The Christian*

Science Monitor. Retrieved March 2010 from http://www.csmonitor.com

Payne, D., and Wermeling, L. (2009). Domestic violence and the female victim: The real reason women stay! *Journal of Multicultural, Gender, and Minority Studies, 3.*(1), 1–6.

Payne, K. (2015). The remarriage rate: Geographic variation, 2013. (FP–15–08). National Center for Family and Marriage Research. Retrieved from https://www.bgsu.edu/ncfm.

Pazol, K., Zane, S. B., Parker, W. B., Hall, L. R., Berg, C., and Cook, D. A. (2011). Abortion surveillance—U.S. 2008. *Surveillance Summaries, 60*(SS15), 1–41. November 25, 2011. Retrieved from http://www.cdc.gov.

Penn, C. D., Hernandez, S. L., and Bermudez, J. M. (1997). Using a cross-cultural perspective to understand infidelity in couples therapy. *The American Journal of Family Therapy, 25,* 169–185.

Pereira, S. M., Jeoffrey, M., and Power, C. (2014). Depressive symptoms and physical activity during three decades in adult life. *JAMA Psychiatry, 71*(12), 1373–1380.

Perelman, M. A. (2002). FSD Partner Issue: Expanding sex therapy with sildenafil. *Journal of Sex and Marital Therapy, 28*(5), 195–204.

Peretti, P. O., and Abplanalp, R. R. (2004). Chemistry in the college dating process: Structure and function. *Social Behavior and Personality, 32*(2), 147–154.

Perez, E. (2014). Majority of young Americans believe income gap is a major problem, parties divided on root cause. *News Release*, April 29, 2014. http://www.10p,harvard.edu

Perrewe, P. L., and Hochwarter, W. A. (2001). Can we really have it all? The attainment of work and family values. *Current Directions in Psychological Science, 10*(1), 29–33.

Peterson, G. W., Steinmetz, S. K., and Wilson, S. M. (2003). Cultural and cross-cultural perspectives on parent-youth relations. *Marriage and Family Review, 35,* 5–19.

Pew Research Center. (2006). Are we happy yet? Retrieved from http://pewresearch.org.

Pew Research Center. (2007). As marriage and parenthood drift apart, public is concerned about social impact. Retrieved from http://pewresearch.org/pubs/526.

Pew Research Center (2010). The decline of marriage and the rise of new families. Survey conducted in association with *Time.* Retrieved from http://www.pewsocialtrends.org.

Phlieger, J.C., Cook, E.C., Niccolai, L.M., and Connell, C.M. (2013). Racial/ethnic differences in patterns of sexual risk behavior and rates of sexually transmitted infections among female young adults. *American Journal of Public Health, 103*(5), 903–909. DOI: 10.2105/agph.2012.301005

Picchi, A. (2015). How much money do U.S. families need to get by? CBS Money Watch. www.cbsnews.com

Pictman, J. S., and Blanchard, D. (1996). The effects of work history and timing of marriage on the division of household labor: A life-force perspective. *Journal of Marriage and Family, 58,* 78–90.

Piercy, F. P., and Sprenkle, D. H. (1990). Marriage and family therapy: A decade review. *Journal of Marriage and Family, 52,* 1116–1126.

Pinhas, L., Toner, B. B., Ali, A., Garfinkel, P. E., and Stuckless, N. (1999). The effects of the ideal of female beauty on mood and body satisfaction. *International Journal of Eating Disorders, 25*(2), 223–226.

Pinto, K.M., and Coltrane, S. (2009). Divisions of labor in Mexican and Anglo families. *Sex Roles, 60,* 482—495.

Pipher, M. (1994). *Reviving Ophelia: Saving the Selves of Adolescent Girls.* New York: Ballantine Books.

Placental abruption. (2014). Mayo Clinic. Retrieved from http://www.mayoclinic.org.

Planned Parenthood. (2012). Birth control. Retrieved from http://www.plannedparenthood.org/health-topics/birth-control.

Poortman, A. (2005). How work affects divorce: The mediating role of financial and time pressures. *Journal of Family Issues, 26*(2), 168–195.

Portman, J. (2015). Florida State University hires first full-time Title IX director. *Tallahassee Democrat,* April 29, 2015.

Pope, G., Olivardia, R., Gruber, A., and Borowiecki, J. (1999). Evolving ideals of male body image as seen through action toys. *International Journal of Eating Disorders, 26*(1), 65–72.

Popenoe, D. (2007). The state of our unions: The future of marriage in America. Retrieved July 2009 from http://marriage.rutgers.edu/Publications/soou/textsoou2007.htm

Popenoe, D., and Whitehead, B. D. (2000). *Sex without Strings: Relationships without Rings.* Piscataway, NJ: The National Marriage Project, Rutgers.

Popenoe, D., and Whitehead, B. D. (2002). *Should We Live Together? What Young Adults Need to Know about Cohabitation before Marriage.* New Brunswick, NJ: Rutgers University Publications, National Marriage Project.

Population Reference Bureau. (2012). Cohabiting age group and other characteristics. U.S. Census Bureau. Washington, DC: U.S. Government Printing Office.

Porcerelli, J. H., Cogan, R., and Hibbard, S. (2004). Personality characteristics of partner violent men: A Q-sort approach. *Journal of Personality Disorders, 18*(2), 151–162.

Pratto, F. (1996). Sexual politics: The gender gap in the bedroom, the cupboard, and the cabinet. In D. M. Buss and N. M. Malamuth (Eds.), *Sex, Power, Conflict: Evolutionary and Feminist Perspectives.* New York: Oxford University Press.

Pregnancy and baby. (2015). Mental health problems and pregnancy. Retrieved from http://www.nhs.uk.

Pregnancy and miscarriage. (2014). *Health and Pregnancy.* Retrieved from http://www.webmed.com.

Preidt, R. (2015). More babies born to mothers ad dicted to pain medicines. *Medline Plus.* Retrieved from https://www.nim.nih.gov

Presser, H. B. (2000, February). Nonstandard work schedules and marital instability. *Journal of Marriage and Family, 62,* 93–110.

Previti, D., and Amato, P.R. (2003). Why stay married? Rewards, barriers, and marital stability. *Journal of Marriage and Family, 65*(3), 561–573. DOI:10.1111/j.1741-3737.2003.00561x.

Previti, D., and Amato, P.R. (2004). Is infidelity a cause or a consequence of poor marital quality? *Journal of Social and Personal Relationships, 21*(2), 217–230.

Price, C. (2001). Siblings are forever. Ohio State University Extension Senior Series. Retrieved October 5, 2005, from http://www.ohioline.osu.edu/ss-fact/0180.html

Price, C. A. (2013). Marriage after retirement. Senior Series. Ohio State University Extension. Retrieved from http://ohioline.osu.edu/ss-fact/0212.html

Pruett, M., Insabella, G., and Gustafson, K. (2005). The collaborative divorce project: A court-based intervention for separating parents with young children. *Family Court Review, 43*(1), 38–51.

Purnell, M., and Bagby, B. H. (1993). Grandparents' rights. Implications for family specialists. *Family Relations, 42,* 173–178.

Querido, J. G., Warner, T. D., and Eyberg, S. M. (2002). Parenting styles and child behavior in African American families of preschool children. *Journal of Clinical Child and Adolescent Psychology, 31*(2), 272–277.

Raley, E. K. (1995). Black–white differences in kin contact and exchange among never married adults. *Journal of Family Issues, 16,* 77–103.

Ramey, S. L. (2005). Human developmental science serving children and families: Contributions of the NICHD study of early child care. In NICHD Early Child Care Network (Eds.), *Child Care and Development.* New York: Guilford Press.

Randle, A. A., and Graham, C.A. (2011). A review of the evidence on the effects of intimate partner violence on men. *Psychology of Men and Masculinity, 12*(2), 97–111.

Randolph, M. E., and Reddy, D. M. (2006). Sexual functioning in women with chronic pelvic pain: The impact of depression, support, and abuse. *Journal of Sex Research, 43*(1), 38–45.

Rank, J. (2015). Fictive kinship. *Marriage and Family Encyclopedia.* Retrieved from http://family.jrank.org/page/630

Rankin-Esquer, L. A., Burnett, C. K., Baucom, D. H., and Epstein, M. (1997). Autonomy and relatedness in marital functioning. *Journal of Marital and Family Therapy, 23,* 175–190.

Rapini, M. J. (2012). Depression kills people and marriages. *The Houston Chronicle.* September 4.

Raschick, M., and Ingersoll-Dayton, B. (2004). The costs and rewards of caregiving among aging spouses and adult children. *Family Relations, 53*(3), 317–325.

Rash, J. A., Matsuba, M. K., and Prkachin, K. M. (2011). Gratitude and well- being: Who benefits the most from a gratitude intervention? *Applied Psychology: Health and Well-Being, 3*(3), 350–369.

Ratican, K. L. (1992). Sexual abuse survivors: Identifying symptoms and special treatment considerations. *Journal of Counseling and Development, 71,* 33–40.

Rauh, V. A., Whyatt, R. M., Garfinkel, R., Andrews, H., Hoepner, L., Reyes, A., et al. (2004). Developmental effects of exposure to environmental tobacco smoke and material hardship among inner-city children. *Neurotoxicology and Teratology, 26,* 373–385.

Ravitch, D. (2010). *The Death and Life of the Great American School System: How Testing and Choice Are Undermining Education.* New York: Basic Books.

Read, J. (2004). Sexual problems associated with infertility, pregnancy, and ageing. *British Medical Journal, 329*(7465), 559–561.

Read, J. G., and Bartkowski, J. P. (2000). To veil or not to veil? A case study of identity negotiation among Muslim women in Austin, Texas. *Gender and Society, 14*(3), 395–417.

Rector, R., and Marshall, J.A. (2013). The unfinished work of welfare reform. The Heritage Foundation. Retrieved from http://www.heritage.org.

Reed, J. M. (2006, December). Not crossing the "extra line": How cohabitors with children view their unions. *Journal of Marriage and Family, 68,* 1117–1131.

Reed, J. P. (1975). The current legal status of abortion. In J. G. Well (Ed.), *Current Issues in Marriage and the Family* (pp. 200–208). New York: Macmillan.

Regan, P. C., Durvasula, R., Howell, L., Ureno, O., and Rea, M. (2004). Gender, ethnicity, and the developmental timing of first sexual and romantic experiences. *Social Behavior and Personality, 32*(7), 667–676.

Regnerus, M. (2012). How different are the adult children of parents who have same-sex relationships? Findings from the new family structures study. *Social Science Research, 41,* 752–770.

Rehman, U. S., and Holtzworth-Munroe, A. (2007). A cross-cultural examination of the relation of marital communication behavior to marital satisfaction. *Journal of Family Psychology, 21,* 759–763.

Rehman, U. S., Holtzworth-Munroe, A., Herron, K., and Clements, K. (2009). "My way or no way": Anarchic power, relationship satisfaction, and male violence. *Personal Relationships, 16*(4), 475–488. doi:10.1111/j.1475-6811.2009.01235x.

Reich, R. (2015). The real reason for the growing gap between rich and poor. *Newsweek.* http://www.newsweek.com

Reifman, A., Villa, L. C., Amans, J. A., Rethinam, V., and Telesca, T. Y. (2001). Children of divorce in the 1990s: A meta-analysis. *Journal of Divorce and Remarriage, 36*(1/2), 27–36.

Reik, T. A. (1957). *Of Love and Lust.* New York: Straus & Cudahy.

Reiner, W. (2000, May 12). Cloacal exstrophy: A happenstance model for androgen imprinting. Presentation at the meeting of the Pediatric Endocrine Society. Boston.

Reiner, W. G., and Gearhart, J. P. (2004). Discordant sexual identity in some genetic males with cloacal exstrophy assigned to female at birth. *New England Journal of Medicine, 350*(4), 333–341.

Reiss, I. L. (1980). *Family Systems in America* (3rd ed.). New York: Holt, Rinehart & Winston.

Reiter, M., and Leonard, R. (2013). *Solve Your Money Troubles: Debt, Credit, and Bankruptcy.* (14th ed.). Berkeley: Nolo.

Rexroat, C., and Shehan, C. (1987). The family life cycle and spouses' time in housework. *Journal of Marriage and Family, 49,* 737–750.

Reynolds, J., Wetherell, M., and Taylor, S. (2007). Choice and chance: Negotiating agency in narratives of singleness. *Sociological Review, 55,* 331–351.

Rhee, N. (2012). Black and Latino retirement (in)securities. University of California Center for Labor Research and Education.

Rhoades, G. K., Kline, G. H., Stanley, S. M., and Markman, H. J. (2006, December). Pre-engagement cohabitation and gender asymmetry in marital commitment. *Journal of Family Psychology, 20*(4), 553–560.

Rhoades, G. K., Stanley, S. M., and Markman, H. J. (2012). The impact of the transition to cohabitation on relationship functioning: Cross-sectional and longitudinal findings. *Journal of Family Psychology, 26*(3), 348–358.

Richardson, R. (2004). Early adolescence talking points: Questions that middle school students want to ask their parents. *Family Relations, 53,* 87–94.

Rickert, V. I., Wiemann, C. M., Vaughan, R. D., and White, J. M. (2004). Rates and risk factors for sexual violence among an ethnically diverse sample of adolescents. *Archives of Pediatric and Adolescent Medicine, 158,* 1132–1139.

Ridley, C. A., Cate, R. M., Collins, D. M., Reesing, A. L., Lucero, A. A., Gilson, M. S., et al. (2006). The ebb and flow of marital lust: A relational approach. *Journal of Sex Research, 43,* 144–153.

Riggio, H. R. (2001). Relations between parental divorce and the quality of adult sibling relationships. *Journal of Divorce and Remarriage, 36*(1/2), 67–82.

Riggio, H. R., and Valenzuela, A. (2011). Paranoid thinking, quality of relationships with parents, and social outcomes among young adults. *Personal Relationships, 18,* 392–409.

Rini, C., Dunkel-Schetter, C., Wadhwa, R., and Sandman, C. (1999). Psychological adaptation and birth outcomes: The role of personal resources, stress, and sociocultural context in pregnancy. *Health Psychology, 18*(4), 333–345.

Roan, C. L., and Raley, R. K. (1996). Intergenerational coresidence and contact: A longitudinal analysis of adult children's response to their mother's widowhood. *Journal of Marriage and Family, 58,* 708–717.

Roberto, K. A., Teaster, P. B., and Duke, J. (2004). Older women who experience mistreatment: Circumstances and outcomes. *Journal of Women and Aging, 16,* 3–16.

Roberts, D. (2002). *Shattered Bonds: The Color of Child Welfare.* New York: Basic Books.

Robertson, K., and Murachver, T. (2007). It takes two to tangle: Gender symmetry in intimate partner violence. *Basic and Applied Social Psychology, 29,* 109–118.

Robinson, B. E., Flowers, C., and Carroll, J. (2001). Work stress and marriage: A theoretical model examining the relationship between workaholism and marital cohesion. *International Journal of Stress Management.* Special Issue: Workaholism in Organizations, 8(2), 165–175.

Robnett, B., and Feliciano, C. (2011). Patterns of racial–ethnic exclusion by internet daters. *Social Forces, 89,* 807–828.

Rockquemore, K. A., and Brunsma, D. L. (2002). *Beyond Black: Biracial identity in America.* Thousand Oaks, CA: Sage.

Rodgers, K. B., and Rose, H. A. (2002). Risk and resiliency factors among adolescents who experience marital transitions. *Journal of Marriage and Family, 64*(4), 1024–1037

Rodriguez, H. (2015). How STDs can affect your fertility. Natural Fertility. http://natural-fertility-info.com

Roe v. Wade, 410 U.S. 113 (1973).

.Rogers, S. J. (1996). Mothers' work hours and marital quality: Variations by family structure and family size. *Journal of Marriage and Family, 58,* 606–617.

Rogers, S. J. (2004). Dollars, dependency, and divorce: Four perspectives on the role of wives' income. *Journal of Marriage and Family, 66*(1), 59–74.

Rogler, L. H., and Procidano, M. E. (1989). Egalitarian spouse relations and wives' marital satisfaction in intergenerationally linked Puerto Rican families. *Journal of Marriage and Family, 51*, 37–39.

Rollie, S. S., and Duck, S. (2006). Divorce and dissolution of romantic relationships: Stage models and their limitations. Divorce in the context of being African-American. In M. A. Fine and J. H. Harvey (Eds.), *Handbook of Divorce and Relationship Dissolution* (pp. 223–240). Mahwah, NJ: Erlbaum.

Romano, L. (2013). Reasons for retirement. Retrieved from http://www.ehow.com.

Romo, H.D. (2002). Celebrating diversity to support student success. *SEDL Letter, 14*(2).

Rosen, T. (2014). *Recovery 2.0: Move beyond Addiction and Upgrade Your Life.* Carlsbad, CA: Hay House.

Rosenbloom, C. A., and Whittington, F. J. (1993). The effects of bereavement on eating behaviors and nutrient intakes in elderly widowed persons. *Journal of Gerontology, 48*, S223–S229.

Rosenfeld, M. J. (2010). Nontraditional families and progress through school. *Demography, 47* (3), 755–775.

Rosenfeld, M.J. (2014). Couple longevity in the era of same-sex marriage in the U.S. *Journal of Marriage and Family, 76*(5), 905–918. DOI: 10.1111/jomf.12141

Rosenfeld, M. J., and Thomas, R. J. (2012). Searching for a mate: The rise of the Internet as a social intermediary. *American Sociological Review, 77*(4), 523–547.

Ross, C.E., Mirowsky, J., and Goldstein, K. (1990). The impact of family on health: The decade in review. *Journal of Marriage and Family, 52*, 1059–1078.

Ross, L. E., Sellers, E. M., Evans, S. E., and Romach, M. K. (2004). Mood changes during pregnancy and the postpartum period: Development of a biopsychosocial model. *Acta Psychiatrica Scandinavica, 109*(6), 457–466.

Ross, L. T., and Wynne, S. (2010). Parental depression and divorce and children's well-being: The role of family unpredictability. *Journal of Child and Family Studies, 19*, 757–761.

Ross, M. E., and Aday, L. A. (2006). Stress and coping in African American grandparents who are raising their grandchildren. *Journal of Family Issues, 27*, 912–932.

Rowland, D. L., Incrocci, L., and Slob, A. K. (2005). Aging and sexual response in the laboratory in patients with erectile dysfunction. *Journal of Sex and Marital Therapy, 31*, 399–407.

Roy, L., and Sawyers, J. K. (1986). The double-bind: An empirical study of responses to inconsistent communications. *Journal of Marital and Family Therapy, 12*, 395–402.

Rubinstein, R. L., Alexander, B. B., Goodman, M., and Luborsky, M. (1991). Key relationships of never married, childless older women: A cultural analysis. *Journal of Gerontology, 5*, S270–S277.

Rudy, D., and Grusec, J. E. (2006). Authoritarian parenting in individualist and collectivist groups: Associations with maternal emotion and cognition and children's self esteem. *Journal of Family Psychology, 20*, 68–78.

Ruffieux, M., Nussbeck, F. W., and Bodenmann, G. (2014). Long-term prediction of relationship satisfaction and stability by stress, coping, communication, and well-being. *Journal of Divorce and Remarriage, 55*(6), 485–501.

Ruggiero, K. J., Smith, D. W., Hanson, R. F., Resnick, H. S., Saunders, B. E., Kilpatrick, D. G., et al. (2004). Is disclosure of childhood rape associated with mental health outcome? *Child Maltreatment: Journal of the American Professional Society on the Abuse of Children, 9*(1), 62–77.

Rupert, P., Stevanovic, P., Hartman, E., Bryant, F., and Miller, A. (2012). Predicting work–family conflict and life satisfaction among professional psychologists. *Professional Psychologists Research and Practice, 33* (4), 341–348.

Rusbult, E., Olsen, N., Davis, J. L., and Hannon, P. A. (2001). Commitment and relationship maintenance mechanisms. In J. H. Harvey and A. Wenzel (Eds.), *Close Relationships: Maintenance and Enhancement* (pp. 87–113). Mahwah, NJ: Erlbaum.

Ruthig, J. C., Trisko, J., and Stewart, T. L. (2012). The impact of spouse's health and well-being on own well-being: A dyadic study of older married couples. *Journal of Social and Clinical Psychology, 31*(5), 508–529.

Rx list. (2008). Retrieved September 2009 from http://www.rxlist.com/mifeprex-ru486-drug.htm.

Ryan, E. G. (2014). Date rape drug detecting nail polish will not possibly work. Retrieved from http://www.jezebel.com.

Ryan, R. M. and Claessens, A. (2012). Associations between family structure changes and children's behavior problems: The moderating effects of timing and marital birth. *Developmental Psychology,* doi:10.1037/a0029397.

Rye, M. S., and Moore, C. D. (2015). *The Divorce Recovery Workbook.* Oakland, CA: New Harbinger.

Sabattini, L., and Leaper, C. (2004). The relation between mothers' and fathers' parenting styles and their division of labor in the home: Young adults' retrospective reports. *Sex Roles, 50*(3–4), 217–225.

Sabini, J., and Green, M. C. (2004). Emotional responses to sexual and emotional infidelity:

Constants and differences across genders, samples, and methods. *Personality and Social Psychology Bulletin, 30*(11), 1375–1388.

Sachs-Ericsson, N., Blazer, D., Plant, E. A., and Arnow, B. (2005). Childhood sexual and physical abuse and the 1-year prevalence of medical problems in the National Comorbidity Survey. *Health Psychology, 24*(1), 32–40.

Sacks, V., Moore, K.A., Shaw, A., and Cooper, P.M. (2014). The Family environment and adolescent well-being. *Child Trends.* http://www.childtrends.org

Sahlstein, E. M., and Baxter, L. A. (2001). Improving commitment in close relationships: A relational dialectics perspective. In J. H. Harvey and A. Wenzel (Eds.), *Close Relationships: Maintenance and Enhancement* (pp. 115–132). Mahwah, NJ: Erlbaum.

Salles, J.M. (2014). The wealth gap between rich and poor is the widest ever recorded. Think Progress. http://thinkprogress.org.

Samenow, C.P. (2010). A biopsychosocial model of hypersexual disorder/sexual addiction. *Sexual Addiction and Compulsivity, 17,* 69–81.

Santrock, J.W. (2014). *Adolescence* (15th ed.). New York: McGraw-Hill.

Santrock, J. W. (2015). *Lifespan Development* (15th ed.). New York: McGraw–Hill.

Sarkisian, N., and Gerstel, N. (2004). Explaining the gender gap in help to parents: The importance of employment. *Journal of Marriage and Family, 66,* 431–451.

Sarvis, B., and Rodman, H. (1974). *The Abortion Controversy.* New York: Columbia University Press.

Sassler, S. (2004). The process of entering into cohabiting unions. *Journal of Marriage and Family, 66,* 491–505.

Sayer, L.C.. England, P., Allison, P., and Kangas, N. (2011). She left, he left: How employment and satisfaction affect men's and women's decisions to leave marriage. American Journal of Sociology, 116(6), 1982–2018.

Scarf, M. (2013). Remarriage: The first five years. *Psychology Today.* Retrieved from https://psychologytoday.com.

Schachner, D. A., and Shaver, P. R. (2004). Attachment dimensions and sexual motives. *Personal Relationships, 11*(2), 179–195.

Scharf, M., Shulman, S., and Avigad-Spitz, L. (2005). Sibling relationships in emerging adulthood and in adolescence. *Journal of Adolescent Research, 20*(1), 64–90.

Schindler, H. S., and Coley, R. L. (2012). Predicting marital separation: Do parent–child relationships matter? *Journal of Family Psychology, 26*(4), 499–508.

Schlenker, J. A., Caron, S. L., and Halteman, W. A. (1998). A feminist analysis of *Seventeen* magazine:

Content analysis from 1945–1995. *Sex Roles, 38*(1/2), 135–149.

Schmader, T., and Croft, A. (2013). How stereotypes shape women's identities and careers. Society for Personality and Social Psychology Annual Meeting. New Orleans. January 17–19.

Schrodt, P. (2009). Family strength and satisfaction as functions of family communication environments. *Communication Quarterly, 57*(2), 171–186.

Schubot, D. B. (2001). Date rape prevalence among female high school students in a rural Midwestern state during 1993, 1995, and 1997. *Journal of Interpersonal Violence, 16,* 291–296.

Schulte, B. (2014). Stress levels higher at home than work for those balancing career and family. *The Guardian.* http://www.theguardian.com

Schutzwohl, A. (2006). Sex differences in jealousy: Information search and cognitive preoccupation. *Personality and Individual Differences, 40,* 285–292.

Schutzwohl, A. (2008). Relief over the disconfirmation of the prospect of sexual and emotional infidelity. *Personality and Individual Differences, 44,* 666–676.

Schwartz, P. (2000). *Everything You Know about Love and Sex Is Wrong: Twenty-five Relationship Myths Redefined to Achieve Happiness and Fulfillment in Your Intimate Life.* New York: Penguin Putnam.

Schwartz, R., and Schwartz, L. J. (1980). *Becoming a Couple.* Englewood Cliffs, NJ: Prentice Hall.

Schwarz, J. E. (1998). The hidden side of the Clinton economy. *The Atlantic Monthly, 282*(4), pp. 18–21.

Scott-Sheldon, I. A., and Johnson, B. T. (2006). Eroticizing creates safer sex: A research synthesis. *Journal of Primary Prevention, 27,* 619–640.

Seay, N. (2014). Can opiates ruin your sex life? Recovery.org http://www.recovery.org

SECASA. (2015). The effects of childhood sexual abuse. Southeastern CASA. http://www.secasa.com.au

Seccombe, K., and Ishii-Kuntz, M. (1991). Perceptions of problems associated with aging: Comparisons among four older-age cohorts. *The Gerontologist, 31,* 527–533.

Secondi, G. (2002). Biased childhood sex ratios and the economic status of the family in rural China. *Journal of Comparative Studies, 33,* 215–235.

Seidman, S. N. (2006). Normative hypogonadism and depression: Does andropause exist? *International Journal of Impotence Research, 18,* 415–422.

Seidman, S. N., and Roose, S. P. (2006). The sexual effects of testosterone replacement in depressed men: Randomized, placebo-controlled clinical trial. *Journal of Sex and Marital Therapy, 32,* 267–273.

Seligson, H. (2012). The case for cohabitation. Retrieved from http://thedailybeast.com.

Serani, D. (2011). Acceptance and Commitment Therapy. *Psychology Today,* February 22, 2011. Retrieved from https://psychologytoday.com.

Sex after pregnancy: Set your own timetable. (2012). Mayo Clinic. Retrieved from http://www.mayo-clinic.org.

Shackelford, T. K., and Mouzos, J. (2005). Partner killing by men in cohabiting and marital relationships. *Journal of Interpersonal Violence, 20,* 1310–1324.

Shackelford, T. K., Voracek, M., Schmitt, D. P., Buss, D. M., Weekes-Schalford, V. A., and Michalski, R. L. (2004). Romantic jealousy in early adulthood and in later life. *Human Nature, 14*(3), 283–300.

Shafer, K. (2003). Difficult situation # 874: 10 respectful strategies to use with an unhealthy co-parent. Retrieved from http://www.smartstepfamilies.org

Shafer, K., Jensen, T. M., and Larsen, J. H. (2014). Relationship effort, satisfaction, and stability: Difference across union type. *Journal of Marriage and Family Therapy, 40*(2), 212–232.

Shapiro, A. (2004). Revisiting the generation gap: Exploring the relationships of parent/adult–child dyads. *International Journal of Aging and Human Development, 58*(2), 127–146.

Shapiro, A. D. (1996). Explaining psychological distress in a sample of remarried and divorced persons. *Journal of Family Issues, 17,* 186–203.

Shapiro, A. D., and Lambert, J. D. (1999). Longitudinal effects of divorce on the quality of father–child relationship and on father's psychological well-being. *Journal of Marriage and Family, 61,* 397–408.

Shaw, B. A., Krause, N., Chatters, L. M., Connell, C. M., and Ingersoll-Dayton, B. (2004). Emotional support from parents early in life, aging, and health. *Psychology and Aging, 19,* 4–12.

Shaw, E.K. (2008). Fictive kin and helping behavior: A social psychological exploration among Haitian immigrants, Christian fundamentalists, and gang members. *Sociation Today, 6*(2). Retrieved from http://www.ncsociology.org/sociationtoday.

Shaw, L.A. (2010). Divorce mediation outcome research: A meta-analysis. *Conflict Resolution Quarterly, 27*(4), 447–467. DOI: 10.1002/crq.2006.

Shea, A., Walsh, C., MacMillan, H., and Steiner, M. (2005). Child maltreatment and HPA axis dysregulation: Relationship to major depressive disorder and post traumatic stress disorder in females. *Psychoneuroendocrinology, 30,* 162–178.

Shea, D. L., Lubinski, D., and Benbow, C. P. (2001). Importance of assessing spatial ability in intellectually talented young adolescents: A 20-year longitudinal study. *Journal of Educational Psychology, 93,* 604–614.

Sherkat, D. E. (2004). Religious intermarriage in the United States: Trends, patterns, and predictors. *Social Science Research, 33*(4), 606–625.

Sherrard, J. (1980). *Mother/Warrior/Pilgrim: A Personal Chronicle.* New York: Andrews McMeel.

Shih, M., and Sanchez, D. T. (2005). Perspectives and research on the positive and negative implications of having multiple racial identities. *Psychological Bulletin, 131*(4), 569–591.

Shirley, C., and Wallace, M. (2004). Domestic work, family characteristics, and earning: Reexamining gender and class differences. *Sociological Quarterly, 45*(4), 663–690.

Siassi, S. (2015). *Forgiveness in Intimate Relationships.* New York: Karnac Books.

Siegel, J. M. (1995). Looking for Mr. Right? *Journal of Family Issues, 16,* 194–211.

Signorielli, N. (1998, February). Television and the perpetuation of gender-role stereotypes. *AAP News,* 7–10.

Silberstein, L. R., Striegel-Moore, R. H., Timko, C., and Rodin, J. (1988). Behavioral and psychological implications of body dissatisfaction: Do men and women differ? *Sex Roles, 19,* 219–232.

Sillars, A., Canary, D., and Tafoya, M. (2004). Communication, conflict, and the quality of family relationships. In A. L. Vangelisti (Ed.), *Handbook of Family Communication* (pp. 413–446). Mahwah, NJ: Erlbaum.

Silverberg, C. (2014). Sex and ecstasy. About Relationships. http://sexuality.about.com

Silverman, J. G., Raj, A., Mucci, L. A., and Hathaway, J. E. (2001). Dating violence against adolescent girls and associated substance use, unhealthy weight control, sexual risk behavior, pregnancy, and suicidality. *Journal of the American Medical Association, 286*(5), 572–579.

Silverstein, M., and Bengston, V. L. (1997). Intergenerational solidarity and the structure of adult child–parent relationships in American families. *American Journal of Sociology, 103,* 429–460.

Silverstein, M., Chen, X., and Heller, K. (1996). Too much of a good thing? Intergenerational social support and the psychological well-being of older parents. *Journal of Marriage and Family, 58,* 970–982.

Simeon, J. R., and Miller, R. S. (2005, January). *Relationship Functioning, Personalities, and Attention to Attractive Alternatives over Time.* Paper presented at the meeting of the Society for Personality and Social Psychology, New Orleans, LA.

Simpson, J. A., Collins, W. A., Tran, S., and Haydon, K. C. (2007). Attachment and the experience and expression of emotions in romantic relationships: A developmental perspective. *Journal of Personality and Social Psychology, 92,* 355–367.

Simpson, J. A., Ickes, W., and Orina, M. (2001). Empathic accuracy and preemptive relationship maintenance. In J. Harvey and A. Wenzel (Eds.), *Close Romantic Relationships: Maintenance and Enhancement* (pp. 27–46). Mahwah, NJ: Erlbaum.

Single-Payer Health Care. (2009). Retrieved May 2009 from http://en.wikipedia.org/wiki/Single-payer_health_care.

Singleton, A., and Maher, J. (2004). The "new man" is in the house: Young men, social change, and housework. *Journal of Men's Studies, 12*(3), 227–240.

Siordia, C. (2014). Married once, twice, and three or more times: Data from the American Community Survey. *Journal of Divorce and Remarriage, 55*(3), 206–215. doi:10.1080/10502556.2014.887377.

Skogrand L., Hatch, D., and Singh, A. (2008). Strong marriages in Latino culture. In R. Dalla, J. DeFrain, J. Johnston, and D. Abbott (Eds.), *Strengths and Challenges of New Immigrant Families: Implications for Research, Policy, Education, and Service.* Lanham, MD: Lexington Books.

Slack, K. S., Holl, J. L., McDaniel, M., Yoo, J., and Bolger, K. (2004). Understanding the risks of child neglect: An exploration of poverty and parenting characteristics. Child maltreatment. *Journal of the American Professional Society on the Abuse of Children, 9*(4), 395–408.

Slater, L. (2006, February). This thing called love. *National Geographic,* pp. 34–49.

Small, A., Teagno, L., and Selz, K. (1980). The relationship of sex role to physical and psychological health. *Journal of Youth and Adolescence, 9,* 305–314.

Smith, C. J., Noll, J. A., and Bryant, J. B. (1999). The effect of social context on gender self-concept. *Sex Roles, 40*(5/6), 499–512.

Smith, E. E. (2013). What's so good about being single? https://psychologytoday.com.

Smith, G., Mysak, K., and Michael, S. (2008). Sexual double standards and sexually transmitted illnesses: Social rejection and stigmatization of women. *Sex Roles, 58,* 391–401.

Smith, L. M., LaGasse, L. L., Derauf, C., Grant, P., Shah, R., Arria, A., et al. (2006). The infant development, environment, and lifestyle study: Effects of prenatal methamphetamine exposure, polydrug exposure, and poverty on intrauterine growth. *Pediatrics, 118,* 1149–1156.

Smith, M., and Segal, J. (2012). Domestic violence: Abuse. Retrieved from http://www.helpguide.org.

Smith, P., and Beaujot, R. (1999). Men's orientation toward marriage and family roles. *Journal of Comparative Family Studies,* 471–487.

Smith, T. W. (1994). *The Demography of Sexual Behavior.* Menlo Park, CA: Kaiser Family Foundation.

Smits, J., and Park, H. (2009). Five decades of educational assertive mating in 10 East Asian societies. *Social Forces, 88,* 227–255.

Society for Human Resource Management. (2005). Society for Human Resource Management benefit survey. Retrieved August 30, 2005, from http://www.shrm.com.

Solomon, S. E., Rothblum, E. D., and Balsam, K. F. (2004). Pioneers in partnership: Lesbian and gay male couples in civil unions compared with those not in civil unions and married heterosexual siblings. *Journal of Family Psychology, 18,* 275–286.

Somerville, C. (2012). Major breakthrough in hepatitis C vaccine development. Burnet Institute. Retrieved from http://www.burnet.edu

Sorensen, E., and Halpern, A. (1999). Single mothers and their child support receipt: How well is child support enforcement doing? Unpublished manuscript. Washington, DC: Urban Institute.

Sotile, W. M., and Sotile, M. O. (2004). Physicians' wives evaluate their marriages, their husbands, and life in medicine. *Bulletin of the Menninger Clinic, 68,* 39–59.

South, S. J. (1991). Sociodemographic differentials in mate selection preferences. *Journal of Marriage and Family, 53,* 928–940.

South, S. J. (1995). Do you need to shop around? *Journal of Family Issues, 16,* 432–449.

Spangler, A., and Payne, K. K. (2014). Marital duration at divorce, 2012. (FP-14-11). National Center for Family and Marriage Research. Retrieved from https://bgsu.edu/content/dam

Speroff, L., and Darney, P. D. (2005). *Clinical Guide for Contraception.* Philadelphia: Lippincott, Williams & Wilkins.

Spitze, G., Logan, J. R., Deane, G., and Zerger, S. (1994). Adult children's divorce and intergenerational relationships. *Journal of Marriage and Family, 56,* 279–293.

Sprecher, S., Schwartz, P., Harvey, J., and Hatfield, E. (2008). Thebusinessoflove.com: Relationship initiation at Internet matchmaking sites. In S. Sprecher, A. Wenzel, and J. Harvey (Eds.), *Handbook of Relationship Initiation* (pp. 249–265). New York: Psychology Press.

Stacey, D. (2009). Birth control pills. Retrieved August 2009 from http://www.About.com/Contraception.

Stafford, L., Kline, S. L., Rankin, C. T., and Stafford, L. (2004). Married individuals, cohabiters, and cohabiters who marry: A longitudinal study of relational and individual well-being. *Journal of Social and Personal Relationships, 21*(2), 231–248.

Stanley, S. M., and Markman, H. J. (1992). Assessing commitment in personal relationships. *Journal of Marriage and Family, 54,* 595–608.

Statistical Abstract of the United States. (2012). Retrieved from http://www.census.gov

Stein, P. (Ed.). (1981). *Single Life: Unmarried Adults in Social Context.* New York: St. Martin's Press.

Stepfamilies: What affects children's and adolescents' adjustment to stepfamilies? (2013) Retrieved from http://www.social.jrank.org

Stepfamily Foundation. (2016). Stepfamily statistics. http://www.stepfamily.org

Stern, R. (2007). *The Gaslight Effect*. New York: Morgan Road Books.

Sternberg, R. (1986). A triangular theory of love. *Psychological Review, 93*, 119–135.

Sternberg, R., and Barnes, M. (Eds.). (1988). *The Psychology of Love*. New Haven, CT: Yale University Press.

Sternberg, R. J. (1998). *Cupid's Arrow: The Course of Love through Time*. Cambridge, UK: Cambridge University Press.

Sternberg, R. J. (1999). *Love Is a Story: A New Theory of Relations*. New York: Oxford University Press.

Stets, J. E. (1990). Verbal and physical aggression in marriage. *Journal of Marriage and Family, 52*, 501–514.

Stevens, D., Kiger, G., and Riley, P. (2001, May). Working hard and hardly working: Domestic labor and marital satisfaction among dual-earner families. *Journal of Marriage and Family, 63*, 514–526.

Stewart, S. (2005a). Boundary ambiguity in stepfamilies. *Journal of Family Issues, 26*(7), 1002–1029.

Stewart, S. (2005b). How the birth of a child affects involvement with stepchildren. *Journal of Marriage and Family, 67*(2), 461–473.

Stier, H., Lewin-Epstein, N., and Braun, M. (2012). Work-family conflict in comparative perspective: The role of social policies. *Research in Social Stratification and Mobility, 30*, 265–279.

Stinnett, N., Hilliard, D., and Stinnett, N. (2000). *Magnificent Marriage*. Montgomery, AL: Pillar Press.

Stinnett, N., and Stinnett, N. (2005). *Loving and Caring— Always and Regardless*. Northport, AL: Family Vision Press.

Stinnett, N., and Stinnett, N. (2010). *Relationships in Marriage and the Family* (6th ed.). Boston: Pearson.

Stone, G. (2002). Nonresidential father postdivorce well-being: The role of social supports. *Journal of Divorce and Remarriage, 36*(3/4), 139–150.

Storaasli, R. D., and Markman, H. J. (1990). Relationship problems in the early stages of marriage. *Journal of Family Psychology, 4*, 80–98.

Storey, W. (2000). Children in married and common law relationships: Legal differences. *Parents News Magazine*.

Storksen, I., Roysamb, E., Holmen, T. L., and Tambs, K. (2006). Adolescent adjustment and well-being: Effects of parental divorce and distress. *Scandinavian Journal of Psychology, 47*, 75–84.

Story, L. B., and Bradbury, T. N. (2004). Understanding marriage and stress: Essential questions and challenges. *Clinical Psychology Review, 23*, 1139–1162.

Stosny, S. (2004). Compassion power: Helping families reach their core value. *Family Journal: Counseling and Therapy for Couples and Families, 12*(1), 58–63.

Straus, M. A. (2001). *Beating the Devil out of Them: Corporal Punishment in American Families and Its Effects on Children*. New Brunswick, NJ: Transaction.

Straus, M. A. (2006). Dominance and symmetry in partner violence by male and female university students in 32 countries. Paper presented at Trends in Intimate Violence Intervention Conference, New York University.

Straus, M. A., and Donnelly, D. (1993). Corporal punishment of teenage children in the United States. *Youth and Society, 24*, 419–442.

Straus, M. A., and Yodanis, C. L. (1996). Corporal punishment in adolescence and physical assaults on spouses in later life: What accounts for the link? *Journal of Marriage and Family, 58*, 825–841.

Strauss, N. (2005). *The Game*. New York: HarperCollins.

Strazdins, L., Clement, M. S., Korda, R. J., Broom, D. H., and D'Souza, R. M. (2006). Unsociable work? Nonstandard work schedules, family relationships, and children's well-being. *Journal of Marriage and Family, 68*, 394–410.

Stritof, S. (2015). Covenant marriage—Pros and cons. Retrieved from http://marriage.about.com/cs/covenantmarriage.

Stubben, J. D. (1998). Culturally competent substance abuse prevention research among rural Native American communities. *Rural Substance Abuse: State of Knowledge and Issues* (National Institute on Drug Abuse Research Monograph Series No. 168, pp. 459–483).

Stubben, J. D. (2001). Working with and conducting research among American Indian families. *American Behavioral Scientist, 44*(9), 1466–1481.

Student Debt Relief. (2015). Obama student loan forgiveness. Retrieved from http://www.studentdebt-relief.ua/forgiveness

Student monitor. (2008). What's in on college campuses. Retrieved from http://www.studentmonitor.com/whoismonitor.php#slideframe_9

Substance Abuse and Mental Health Services Administration. (2014). *Emergency room visits and substance abuse*. U.S. Department of Health and Human Services.

Sue, D. (1997). Counseling strategies for Chinese Americans. In C. C. Lee (Ed.), *Multicultural Issues in Counseling: New Approaches to Diversity* (2nd ed., pp. 173–187). Alexandria, VA: American Counseling Association.

Sugarman, S. D. (2003). Single-parent families. In M. A. Mason, A. Skolnick, and S. D. Sugarman (Eds.), *All Our Families* (pp. 14–39). New York: Oxford University Press.

Suitor, J. J. (1991). Marital quality and satisfaction with the division of household labor across the family life cycle. *Journal of Marriage and Family, 53,* 221–230.

Suldo, S. M., and Huebner, E. S. (2004). The role of life satisfaction in the relationship between authoritative parenting dimensions and adolescent problem behavior. *Social Indicators Research, 66*(1–2), 165–195.

Sullivan, B. (2010). The Internet's most successful scams. Retrieved April 2, 2010, from http://www.redtape.msnbc.com.

Swartz, J. (2004, March 9). Online porn often leads high-tech way. *USA Today.* Retrieved from http://www.USAToday.com/money/industries/technology/2004-03-09-onlineporn_x:htm.

Sweeney, M. M. (2002). Remarriage and the nature of divorce: Does it matter which spouse chose to leave? *Journal of Family Issues, 23*(3), 410–440.

Swinford, S. P., DeMaris, A., Cernkovich, S. A., and Giordano, P. C. (2000). Harsh physical discipline in childhood and violence in later romantic involvements: The mediating role of problem behaviors. *Journal of Marriage and Family, 62,* 508–519.

Swafford, M, and Jolley, L. (2012). Exploring the FCS role in promoting secure relationships in families. *Journal of Family and Consumer Sciences, 104*(4), 34–39.

SX 21(2016). Male orgasmic disorder. Sex in the 21st Century. http://sexualmed.org

Sykes, M. (2000). "Late-term" confusion, "partial-birth" lies. *Pro-Choice Views.* Retrieved from http://prochoice.about.com/newsissues/prochoice/library/bllatetermconfusion.htm.

Symptothermal method. (2008). Retrieved August 2009 from http://www.mayoclinic.com/health/symptothermal

Tafoya, M. A., and Spitzberg, B. H. (2007). The dark side of infidelity: Its nature, prevalence, and communicative functions. In B. H. Spitzberg and W. R. Cupach (Eds.), *The Dark Side of Interpersonal Communication* (2nd ed., pp. 201–242). Mahwah, NJ: Erlbaum.

Tasker, R. (2015). Does marriage counseling work? Guide Doc. Retrieved from http://www.guidedoc.com.

Taylor, C., and Taylor, G. (2005) Stepfamily finances: Money & stuff: Part 2. Retrieved from http://smart-stepfamilies.com.

Taylor, R. J., Chatters, L. M., and Mays, V. M. (1988). Parents, children, siblings, in-laws, and non-kin as sources of emergency assistance to Black Americans. *Family Relations, 37,* 298–304.

Taylor, R. L. (2002). Black American families. In *Minority Families in the United States: A Multicultural Perspective* (3rd ed., pp. 19–47). Upper Saddle River, NJ: Prentice Hall.

Teachman, J. D. (2002). Childhood living arrangements and the intergenerational transmission of divorce. *Journal of Marriage and Family, 64*(3), 717–729.

Teachman, J., and Tedrow, L. (2008). The demography of stepfamilies in the United States. In J. Pryor (Ed.), *The International Handbook of Stepfamilies: Policy and Practice in Legal, Research, and Clinical Environments,* (pp. 3–29). Hoboken, NJ: Wiley.

Ten Brummelhuis, L. L., Haar, J. M., and van der Lippe, T. (2010). Crossover of distress due to work and family demands in dual-earner couples: A dyadic analysis. *Work and Stress, 24*(4), 324–341.

Tennov, D. (1979). *Love and Limerence: The Experience of Being in Love.* New York: Stein & Day.

Tenore, J. L. (2000). Ectopic pregnancy. *American Family Physician, 61,* 1080–1088.

Thomas, A., and Speight, S. (1999). Racial identity and racial socialization attitudes of African American parents. *Journal of Black Psychology, 25*(2), 152–170.

Thomas, S. (2005). *Two Happy Homes.* Longmont, CO: Springboard.

Thomas, S. G. (2012). Divorce late in life: The gray divorce. Retrieved from http://online.wsj.com/news/articles/

Thompson, K. M., Wonderlich, S. A., Crosby, R. D., and Mitchell, J. E. (2001). Sexual violence and weight control techniques among adolescent girls. *International Journal of Eating Disorders, 29,* 166–176.

Thompson, L., and Walker, A. J. (1995). The place of feminism in family studies. *Journal of Marriage and Family, 57*(4), 847–865.

Thompson, R. A. (2006). The development of the person. In W. Damon and R. Lerner (Eds.), *Handbook of Child Psychology* (6th ed.). New York: Wiley.

Thornton, J., and Lasswell, M. (1997). *Chore Wars: How Households Can Share the Work and Keep the Peace.* Berkeley, CA: Conari Press.

Tichenor, V. J. (1999). Status and income as gendered resources: The case of marital power. *Journal of Marriage and Family, 61,* 638–650.

Tiefer, L. (2001). A new view of women's sexual problems: Why new? Why now? *Journal of Sex Research, 38*(2), 89–96.

Timmer, S., and Veroff, J. (2000). Family ties and the discontinuity of divorce in black and white newlywed couples. *Journal of Marriage and Family, 62,* 349–361.

Torpy, J.M., Lynm, M.A., and Golub, R.M. (2013). Gonorrhea. *Journal of the American Medical Association, 309,* 196. DOI: 10.1001/2012.jama.10802.

Tough, S., Newburn-Cook, C., Johnson, D. W., Svenson, L. W., Rose, S., and Belik, J. (2002). Delayed childrearing and its impact on population rate changes in lower birth weight, multiple birth, and preterm delivery. *Pediatrics, 109*(3), 399–403.

Tran, S., Simpson, J.A., and Fletcher, G.J.O. (2008). The role of ideal standards in relationship initiation processes. In S. Sprecher, A. Wenzel, and J. Harvey (Eds.), *Handbook of Relationship Initiation* (pp. 487–498). New York: Psychology Press.

Traub, A., and McElwee, S. (2015). Despite a raise, Walmart wages and schedules still aren't livable. Demos. http://www.demos.org

Trigg, B., Kerndt, P., and Aynalem, G. (2008). Sexually transmitted infections and pelvic inflammatory diseases in women. *Medical Clinics of North America, 92,* 1083 1113.

Trudel, G. (2002). Sexuality and marital life: Results of a survey. *Journal of Sex and Marital Therapy, 28,* 229–249.

Tschann, J. M., Johnston, J. R., and Wallerstein, J. S. (1989). Resources, stressors, and attachment as predictors of adult adjustment after divorce: A longitudinal study. *Journal of Marriage and Family, 51,* 1033–1046.

Tuan, M. (1999). Neither real Americans nor real Asians? Multigenerational Asian ethnics navigating the terrain of authenticity. *Qualitative Sociology, 22*(2), 105–125.

Tulandi, T. (2015). Ectopic pregnancy: Incidence, risk factors, and pathology. UpToDate. Retrieved from http://www.uptodate.com.

Turner, J., and Vasan, M. (2003). *Dating and Sexuality in America: A Reference Handbook.* Santa Barbara, CA: ABC-CLIO.

Turner, M. J., Young, C. R., and Black, K. I. (2006). Daughters-in-law and mothers-in-law seeking their place within the family. *Family Relations, 55,* 588–600.

Turner, S. L., Conkel, J. L., Reich, A. N., Trotter, M. J., and Siewart, J. J. (2006). Social skills efficacy and proactivity among Native American adolescents. *Professional School Counseling, 10*(2), 189–194.

Ubell, E. (1990, January 14). You don't have to be childless. *Parade Magazine,* pp. 14, 15.

Uhlenberg, P., and Hammill, B. G. (1998). Frequency of grandparent contact with grandchildren sets: Factors that make a difference. *The Gerontologist, 38,* 276–285.

Umberson, D., Pudrovska, T., and Reczek, C. (2010). Parenthood, childlessness, and well-being: A life-course perspective. *Journal of Marriage and the Family, 73*(3), 612–629.

Understanding Teen Dating Violence. (2016). Fact Sheet. National Center for Injury Prevention and Control. CDC. http://www.cdc.gov

Underwood, M. K., Beron, B. J., Gentsch, J. K., Galperin, M. B., and Rosser, S. D. (2008). Interparental conflict resolution strategies, parenting styles, and children's social and physical aggression with peers. *International Journal of Behavioral Development, 32,* 566–579.

UNICEF (2007). Equality in employment. *The State of the World's Children 2007.* pp. 37–49.

Uphold-Carrier, H., and Utz, R. (2012). Parental divorce among young and adult children: A long-term quantitative analysis of mental health and family solidarity. *Journal of Divorce and Remarriage, 53*(4), 247–266.

UPI (2008). 14% of U.S. kids with special needs. http://www.upi.com

Urbaniak, G. C., and Kilmann, P. R. (2003). Physical attractiveness and the "nice guy paradox": Do nice guys really finish last? *Sex Roles, 49,* 413–426.

U.S. Bureau of Economic Analysis. (2016). Economic status of families in the U.S. U.S. Department of Commerce.

U.S. Bureau of Justice Statistics. (2007). Intimate partner violence in the U.S. Bureau of Justice Statistics Website.

U.S. Bureau of Labor Statistics. (2005a). Consumer expenditures in 2003. U.S. Department of Labor. Retrieved September 5, 2005, from http://www.bls.gov/cex.

U.S. Bureau of Labor Statistics. (2005b). Women in the labor force: A databook. U.S. Department of Labor. Retrieved September 8, 2005, from http://www.bls.gov/cps.

U.S. Bureau of Labor Statistics. (2012). Unemployment. Retrieved from http://www.bls.gov.

U.S. Bureau of Labor Statistics. (2014). http://www.bls.gov

U.S. Bureau of Labor Statistics. (2015). http://www.bls.gov

U.S. Bureau of Labor Statistics. (2016). http://www.bls.gov

U.S. Bureau of the Census. (2002). *Statistical Abstract of the United States, 2002.* Washington, DC: U.S. Government Printing Office.

U.S. Bureau of the Census. (2005). *Statistical Abstract of the United States, 2004–2005.* Washington, DC: U.S. Government Printing Office.

U.S. Bureau of the Census. (2007). America's families and living arrangements: 2006. *Statistical Abstract of the United States.* Washington, DC: U.S. Government Printing Office.

U.S. Bureau of the Census. (2008a). America's families and living arrangements: 2007. *Current Population Reports,* P20–537 and earlier. Retrieved from http://www.census.gov.

U.S. Bureau of the Census. (2008b). *Statistical Abstract of the United States, 2008.* Washington, DC: U.S. Government Printing Office. Also available at http://www.census.gov.

U.S. Bureau of the Census. (2010). http://www.census.gov

U.S. Bureau of the Census. (2011). http://www.census.gov

U.S. Bureau of the Census. (2012). http://www.census.gov

U.S. Bureau of the Census. (2013). http://www.census.gov

U.S. Bureau of the Census. (2014). http://www.census.gov

U.S. Bureau of the Census. (2015). http://www.census.gov

U.S. Bureau of the Census. (2016). http://www.census.gov

U.S. Conference of Mayors. (2003). A status report on hunger and homelessness in America's cities: 2003. Available from the U.S. Conference of Mayors, 1620 Eye St. NW, 4th Floor, Washington, DC, 20006-4005.

U.S. Department of Agriculture. (2015). Center for Nutrition Policy and Promotion. Retrieved from http://www.cnpp.usda.gov/tools/crc

U.S. Department of Health and Human Services. (2012). Child maltreatment. Retrieved from http://www.acf.hhs.gov/programs/cb/publications/afcars/report9/indexz.htm

U.S. Department of Health and Human Services. (2014). Growing older in America: The health and retirement study. http://www.hhs.gov

U.S. Department of Health and Human Services. (2015). http://www.hhs.gov

U.S. Department of Labor (2007). Family and Medical Leave Act regulations: A report on the Department of Labor's request for information. Retrieved April 2009 from http://www.dol.gov/ES/WHD/FMLA2007Report/Chapter11.pdf

U.S. Department of Labor. (2014). Women of working age. http://www.aol.gov

Utz, R. L., Reidy, E. B., Carr, D., Nesse, R., and Wortman, C. (2004). The daily consequences of widowhood: The role of gender and intergenerational transfers on subsequent housework performance. *Journal of Family Issues, 25*(5), 683–712.

Vandell, D. L. (2004). Early child care: The known and unknown. *Merrill-Palmer Quarterly, 50,* 387–414.

Van den Hoonaard, D. K. (2001). *The Widowed Self: The Older Woman's Journey through Widowhood.* Waterloo, Canada: Wilfrid Laurier University Press.

Vangelisti, H. L. (2012). *The Routledge Handbook of Family Communication.* New York: Routledge.

van-Schaick, K., and Stolberg, A. L. (2001). The impact of paternal involvement and parental divorce on young adults' intimate relationships. *Journal of Divorce and Remarriage, 36*(1/2), 99–122.

Vaquera, E., and Kao, G. (2005). Private and public displays of affection among interracial and intra-racial adolescent couples. *Social Science Quarterly, 86*(2), 484–505.

Vaughn, R. P. (2010). Girls' and women's education within UNESCO and the World Bank: 1945–2000. *Compare, 40* (4), 405–423.

Venosa, E. (2015). Amphetamines and sex: Illicit drug use may cause erectile dysfunction and reduced sexual satisfaction in men. Medical Daily. http://www.medicaldaily.com

Vitaliano, P. P., Young, H. M., and Zhang, J. (2004). Is care-giving a risk factor for illness? *Current Directions in Psychological Science, 13*(1), 13–16.

Voigt, K., and Brown, S. (2013). International adoptions in decline as number of orphans grows. *CNN News.* Retrieved from http://www.cnn.com/2013/09/16

Voydanoff, P. (2002). Linkages between the work–family interface and work, family, and individual outcomes; An integrative model. *Journal of Family Issues, 23*(1), 138–164.

Voydanoff, P. (2004). The effects of work demands and resources on work-to-family conflict and facilitation. *Journal of Marriage and Family, 66,* 398–412.

Voydanoff, P., and Donnelly, B. W. (1999). Multiple roles and psychological distress: The intersection of the paid worker, spouse, and parent roles with the role of the adult child. *Journal of Marriage and Family, 61,* 725–738.

Vuong, Z. (2012). New vasectomy procedure available at Planned Parenthood. Retrieved from http://newsmedill.northwestern.edu

Waite, L. J., and Gallagher, M. (2000). *The Case for Marriage: Why Married People Are Happier, Healthier, and Better Off Financially.* New York: Doubleday.

Walker, A. J. (1985). Reconceptualizing family stress. *Journal of Marriage and Family,*

Wallerstein, J., and Blakeslee, S. (2003). *What about the Kids? Raising Your Children before, during, and after Divorce.* New York: Hyperion.

Wallerstein, J., and Lewis, J. (1998). The long-term impact of divorce on children: A first report from a 25-year study. *Family and Conciliation Courts Review Special Issue: A Commemoration of the Second World Congress on Family Law and the Rights of Children and Youth, 36*(3), 368–383.

Wallerstein, J., and Lewis, J. (2004). The unexpected legacy of divorce. *Psychoanalytic Psychology, 21*(3), 353–370.

Walsh, F. (2009). Spiritual resources in family adaptation to death and loss. In F. Walsh (Ed.), *Spiritual Resources in Family Therapy* (2nd ed., pp. 81–102). New York: Guilford Press.

Wampler, K. S., and Powell, G. S. (1982). The Barrett–Lennard Relationship Inventory as a measure of marital satisfaction. *Family Relations, 35,* 539–545.

Wandewater, E. A., and Lansford, J. E. (1998). Influences of family structure and parental conflict on children's well-being. *Family Relations, 47,* 323–330.

Wang, H., and Amato, P. R. (2000). Predictors of divorce adjustment: Stressors, resources, and definitions. *Journal of Marriage and Family, 62,* 655–668.

Wang, H., and Wellman, B. (2010). Social connectivity in America: Changes in adult friendship network size from 2002 to 2007. *American Behavioral Scientist, 53,* 1148–1169. DOI: 10.1177/0002764209356247.

Wang, W. (2012). The rise of intermarriage: Rates, characteristics vary by race and gender. Pew Research Center. Retrieved from http://pewsocialtrends.org.

Wang, W. (2015). Interracial marriage: Who is marrying out? Pew Research Center. http://www.pewresearch.org

Warbelow, K., and Bass, F. (2012). Young adults flock to parents' homes amid economy. Retrieved from http://bloomberg.com.

Ward, J. (1996). Raising resisters: The role of truth telling in the psychological development of African American girls. In B. Leadbeater and N. Way (Eds.), *Urban Girls.* New York: New York University Press.

Ward, L. M., and Friedman, K. (2006). Using TV as a guide: Associations between television viewing and adolescents' sexual attitudes and behavior. *Journal of Research on Adolescence, 16,* 133–156.

Ward, R. A., and Spitze, G. D. (2004). Marital implications of parent–adult child coresidence: A longitudinal view. *Journal of Gerontology, 59,* 2–8.

Warner, J. (2005). *Perfect Madness: Motherhood in the Age of Anxiety.* New York: Riverhead Books.

Waterman, A. S. (1993). Two conceptions of happiness: Constructs of personal expressiveness, eudaimonial, and hedonistic enjoyment. *Journal of Personality and Social Psychology, 64,* 678–691.

Watkins, K. J., and Baldo, T. D. (2004). The infertility experience: Biopsychosocial effects and suggestions for counselors. *Journal of Counseling and Development, 82,* 394–402.

Watson, D. (2013). Drastic growth in "extreme poverty" in U.S. Retrieved from http://www.wsws.org/en/articles/2013/08/19

Way, N. (1995). "Can't you see the courage, the strength that I have?" Listening to urban adolescent girls speak about their relationships. *Psychology of Women Quarterly, 19*(1), 107–128.

Weale, S. (2014). Culture, not curriculum, determines east Asian school success. *The Guardian.* http://www.theguardian.com

Weaver, S., and Coleman, M. (2005). A mothering but not a mother role: A grounded theory study of the non-residential stepmother role. *Journal of Social and Personal Relationships, 22*(4), 477–497.

Webb, N. B. (2004). The impact of traumatic stress and loss on children and families. In N. Boyd Webb (Ed.), *Mass Trauma and Violence: Helping Families and Children Cope* (pp. 3–22). New York: Guilford Press.

WebMD. (2012). Health A–Z. Retrieved from http://www.webmd.com.

WebMD. (2016), Birth Control. http://www.webmd.com/sex/birth-control

Weir, E. (2001). Drug-facilitated date rape. *Canadian Medical Association Journal, 165,*1.

Weishaus, S., and Field, D. (1988). A half century of marriage: Continuity or change? *Journal of Marriage and Family, 50,* 763–774.

Weisman, C. (2014). Covenant marriages—How some Christian couples make it a lot harder to divorce each other. http://www.alternet.org/belief.

Weston, F. (2009). Effects of divorce or parental separation on children. *British Journal of School Nursing, 4*(5), 237–243.

Westphal, S. K., Poortman, A-R., and Van der Lippe, T. (2015). What about the grandparents? Children's post-divorce residence arrangements and contact with grandparents. *Journal of Marriage and Family, 77*(2), 424–440. doi:10.1111/jomf.12173.

What are Mormon Women Like? (2016). The Church of Jesus Christ of Latter-Day Saints. https://www.mormon.org/faq/gender

Whipps, H. (2009). The 300-year history of Internet dating. http://www.livescience.com.

White, J. (2001). Sibling relationships over the life course: A panel analysis. *Journal of Marriage and Family, 63*(2), 555–568.

Whitehead, B., and Popenoe, D. (2005). The state of our unions. Retrieved October 10, 2005, from http://marriage.rutgers.edu/Publications/Print/Print-SOOU2005.htm

Whitton, S. W., Nicholson, J. M., and Markman, H. (2008). Research on intervention for stepfamily couples. In J. Pryor (Ed.), *The International Handbook of Stepfamilies: Policy and Practice in Legal, Research, and Clinical Environments,* (pp. 455–484). Hoboken, NJ: Wiley.

Whitton, S. W., Stanley, S. M., Markman, H. J., and Johnson, C. A. (2013). Attitudes toward divorce, commitment, and divorce proneness in first marriages and remarriages. *Journal of Marriage and the Family, 75*(2), 276–287.

Wigfield, A., Eccles, J., and Schiefele, U. (2006). Motivation. In W. Dannon and R. M. Lerner (Series Eds.) and N. Eisenberg (Vol. Ed.), *Handbook of Child Psychology* (Vol. 3, 6th ed., pp. 933–1022). New York: Wiley.

Wijckmans, B., and Van Babel, J. (2013). Divorce and adult children's perceptions of family obligations. *Journal of Comparative Studies, 44*(3), 291–310.

Wilhelm, A. (2012). Playing house: What living together can do to your relationship. Retrieved from http://northbynorthwestern.com.

Wilkie, J. R., Ferree, M. M., and Ratcliff, K. S. (1998). Gender and fairness: Marital satisfaction in two-earner couples. *Journal of Marriage and Family, 60,* 577–594.

Wilkinson, D. (1997). American families of African descent. In M. K. DeGenova (Ed.), *Families in Cultural Context.* Mountain View, CA: Mayfield.

Willetts, M. C., Sprecher, S., and Beck, F. D. (2004). Overview of sexual practices and attitudes within relational contexts. In J. H. Harvey, A. Wenzel, and S. Sprecher (Eds.), *The Handbook of Sexuality in Close Relationships* (pp. 57–85). Mahwah, NJ: Erlbaum.

Williams, J. (2000). *Unbending Gender: Why Family and Work Conflict and What to Do about It.* New York: Oxford University Press.

Williams, L. (2015). Communication training, marriage enrichment, and premarital counseling. In J. L. Wetchler and L. L. Hecker (Eds), *An Introduction to Marriage and Family Therapy* (2nd ed., pp. 401–430). New York: Routledge.

Williams, L., and Jurich, J. (1995). Predicting marital success after five years: Assessing the predictive validity of FOCCUS. *Journal of Marital and Family Therapy, 21,* 141–153.

Williams, M. (2013). How stereotypes shape women's identities and careers. Society for Personality and Social Psychology Annual Meeting. New Orleans. January 17–19, 2013.

Williams, S. L., and Frieze, I. H. (2005). Courtship behaviors, relationship violence, and breakup persistence in college men and women. *Psychology of Women Quarterly, 29,* 248–257.

Willson, A. E., Shuey, K. M., Elder, G. H., and Wickrama, K. A. S. (2006). Ambivalence in mother–adult child relations: A dyadic analysis. *Journal of Marriage and the Family, 65,* 1055–1072.

Wilmot, W. W., and Hocker, J. L. (2007). *Interpersonal conflict* (7th ed.). New York: McGraw–Hill.

Winch, R. F. (1958). *Mate Selection: A Study of Complementary Needs.* New York: Harper & Row.

Winch, R. F. (1967). Another look at the theory of complementary needs in mate selection. *Journal of Marriage and Family, 29,* 756–762.

Winch, R. F. (1971). *The Modern Family.* New York: Holt.

Wineberg, H. (1994). Marital reconciliation in the United States: Which couples are successful? *Journal of Marriage and Family, 56,* 80–88.

Winton, C. A. (1995). *Frameworks for Studying Families.* Guilford, CT: Dushkin.

Wisner, K., Perel, J., Peindl, K., and Hanusa, B. (2004). Timing of depression recurrence in the first year after birth. *Journal of Affective Disorders, 78*(3), 249–252.

Witt, J. L. (2010). The gendered division of labor in parental caretaking: Biology or socialization? *Journal of Women and Aging, 6,* 65–89.

Wolak, J., Finkelhor, D., and Mitchell, K. J. (2005). Child pornography possessors arrested in Internet-related crimes: Findings from the National Juvenile Online Victimization Study. Retrieved from http://www.missingkids.com/en_US/publications/NC144.pdf.

Wolchik, S. A., Sandler, I. N., Winslow, E., and Smith-Daniels, V. (2005). Programs for promoting parenting of residential parents: Moving from efficacy to effectiveness. *Family Court Review, 43*(1), 65–80.

Wolf-Smith, J. H., and LaRossa, R. (1992). After he hits her. *Family Relations, 41,* 324–329.

Wood, J. T. (2004). Monsters and victims: Male felons' accounts of intimate partner violence. *Journal of Social and Personal Relationships, 21,* 555–576.

Woolcott, R. (2014). How to treat vasectomy and vasectomy reversal. *Australian Doctor.* Retrieved from http://www.australiandoctor.com.au.

Worden, J. W. (2002). *Grief Counseling and Grief Therapy: A Handbook for the Mental Health Practitioner.* New York: Springer.

World Almanac. (2016). New York: Simon and Schuster.

World Bank. (2016). Fertility rate, total (births per woman). The World Bank. Retrieved from http://data.worldbank.org/indicators

World Population Clock. (2016). Worldometers. http://www.worldometers.info

Wright, J. W. (2009). *The New York Times Almanac.* New York: Penguin Books.

Wright, J. W. (2011). *The New York Times Almanac.* New York: Penguin Books.

Wu, S.-J. (2001). Parenting in Chinese American families. In N. B. Webb (Ed.), *Culturally Diverse Parent–Child and Family Relationships: A Guide for Social Workers and other Practitioners.* New York: Columbia University Press.

Xia, Z., Li, X., and Stanton, B. (2011). Perceptions of parent–adolescent communication within families: It is a matter of perspective. *Psychology, Health, and Medicine, 16*(1), 53–65.

Xiong, Z., Eliason, P., Detzner, D. F., and Cleveland, M. J. (2005). Southeast Asian immigrants' perceptions of good adolescents and good parents. *Journal of Psychology, 139,* 159–175.

Yamagata, S., et al. (2013). Bidirectional influences between maternal parenting and children's peer problems: A longitudinal monozygotic twin difference study. *Developmental Science, 16*(2), 249–259.

Yanowitz, K.L, and Weathers, K.J. (2004). Do boys and girls act differently in the classroom? A content analysis of student characters in educational psychology textbooks. *Sex Roles, 51*(1), 101–107.

Yarber, W. L., and Sayad, B. W. (2013). *Human Sexuality: Diversity in Contemporary America.* New York: McGraw–Hill.

Yarber, W.L., Sayad, B.W., and Strong, B. (2015). *Human Sexuality: Diversity in Contemporary America.* (9th ed.). New York: McGraw-Hill.

Yeo, S., Fetters, M., and Maeda, Y. (2000). Japanese couples' childbirth experiences in Michigan: Implications for care. *Birth, 27,* 191–198.

Young, S., and Wilson, J. (2014). Virus detected in baby "cured" of HIV. *CNN News.* July 10, 2014. Retrieved from http://www.cnn.com/2014/07/10

Young, S. L., and Metto, S. (Eds.). (2004). Factors that influence recipients' appraisals of hurtful communication. *Journal of Social and Personal Relationships, 21*(3), 291–303.

Zarelli, D. A. (2009). Role-governed behaviors in stepfathers in families with a child with chronic illness. *Journal of Pediatric Nursing, 24,* 90–100.

Zayas, V., and Shoda, Y. (2007). Predicting preferences for dating partners from past experiences of psychological abuse: Identifying the psychological ingredients of situations. *Personality and Social Psychology, 33,* 123–138.

Zhan, M., and Pandey, S. (2004). Postsecondary education and economic well-being of single mothers and single fathers. *Journal of Marriage and Family, 66*(3), 661–673.

Zilanawala, A., and Pilkauskas, N.V. (2010). Low-income mothers' material hardship and children's socioemotional well-being. Fragile Families Working Paper. WP 1102-FF. http://crew.princeton.edu/workingpapers

Zimmerman, K. (2005). Parenting again. Grandparents raising grandchildren. *National Council on Family Relations Report, 50*(3), F18–F19.

Zubkov, V. (2007). Russian families: Historical and contemporary perspectives on problems and strengths. *Marriage and Family Review, 4,* 361–392

Zuo, J. (1992). The reciprocal relationship between marital interaction and marital happiness: A three-way study. *Journal of Marriage and Family, 54,* 870–878.

Zuo, J., and Tang, S. (2000). Breadwinner status and gender ideologies of men and women regarding family roles. *Sociological Perspectives, 43*(1), 29–43.

Image Credits

Index

abortion
  gender selection, 304
  legal considerations, 301–2
  moral considerations, 302
  psychological considerations, 303
  social considerations, 302–3, 312
  spontaneous, 301, 310, 323–24
abortion pill. *See* Mifeprex
abruptio placentae (placental
    abruption), 324, 325
abstinence, as family planning
    method, 287–88
abstinence-only-until-marriage
    programs, 84
abuse. *See* family violence
acceptance and commitment
    therapy, 243
acculturation, 22–23, 346–47
acquired immune deficiency
    syndrome (AIDS), 277–78
action figures, 52, *53*
adaptability, flexibility, tolerance,
    marital success and, 160–62
addiction
  characteristics of, 405
  coping with, 406–8
  effects on family, 405–6
  overcoming, 406 – 408
  reasons for, 405
  sexual, 264–65
admiration and respect, marital
    success and, 152
adolescents
  body image, 89
  dating violence, 99–100
  divorce and, 447, 449–50
  as fathers, 347
  grandparents and, 381–82
  mothers as, 379
  parents relationships with, 344
  pregnancy of, 253
  sexual behavior, 76–77
  STDs, 254
  in stepfamilies, 469–70
adoption
  foreign, 309
  gay and lesbian parenting by,
    34, 173
  independent, 308

open, 308–9
as parenthood choice, 307–9
second-parent, 34
by singles, 80
by stepparent, 468, 476
Adoption and Safe Family Act, 419
Adoption Assistance and Child
    Welfare Act, 419
adult children, parents and, 187–88
  divorce and, 442
  elder care, 371–73
  in-laws, 373–77
  living together, 76, 76t, 77f, 375–77
  partner choice, disapproval of,
    366–67
  psychological issues, 371
adulthood, emerging, 370
advertisements, personal, 88
affairs, extramarital, 252–53, 263,
    392, 400–402, 429
affection
  as dating motive, 93
  marital success and, 134, 156–57
  sexual activity and, 113
  as strong family quality, 32
affective sensitivity, 161
affinity, 135
African Americans
  body image, 55
  child care arrangements, 355f
  collectivist family style, 181
  divorce rate, 426f, 446
  elder care, 373
  foster care, 309, 419
  gender roles, 55
  life expectancy, 18
  marital status, 68, 69f, 71
  mate selection by, 126
  media and, 55
  median income, 206t
  never-married, 69
  number of children, 13f
  percentage of population,
    20, 20f, 21
  poverty, 21, 71, 189, 214, 216
  prenatal care, 320
  remarriage by, 19, 456
  sexual behavior, 253
  single-parent family, 14, 23, 71, 81

age difference, in marriage,
    129–30
aggression, sexual, 99–101
AI. *See* artificial insemination
AIDS. *See* acquired immune
    deficiency syndrome
alcohol, 321–22
  as counterproductive coping
    strategy, 73
  sex and, 269–70
  use during pregnancy, 336
alcoholism, as family illness, 29
alprazolam. *See* Xanax
altruistic love, 111, 116–17
American Academy of Child and
    Adolescent Psychiatry, 17
American Academy of Pediatrics,
    17, 34
American Association for Single
    People, 68
American Association of Retired
    Persons, 150
American Bar Association Family
    Law Section, 476
American Psychological
    Association, 34
American Religious Identification
    Survey, 129
amniotic sac. *See* bag of water
amphetamines, 270
androgyny, 60–61
anger
  coping strategies, 442–43
  in marital disaffection
    process, 430
antidepressants, 270
Apgar scale, 331
appraisal, of situations, 149, 175
appreciation, as strong family
    quality, 32
approximation of ideals, for marital
    success evaluation, 146–47
Arab Muslim societies, divorce
    in, 437
Area Agencies on Aging, 190, 381
arguments
  constructive, 243–44, 395
  destructive, 395
arousal, sexual, 258

artificial insemination (AI), 306–7
Asian Americans. *See also* Chinese
    Americans
    divorce rate, 446
    elder care, 373
    ethnic identity and acculturation,
      22–23
    marital status, 68, 69f
    median income, 206t
    never-married, 69
    remarriage by, 456
    sexual behavior, 253
Asian/Pacific Islander Americans, 23
    percentage of population, 20, 20f
    poverty, 214
    single-parent family, 24
at-risk families, 360
attachment, of children to parents,
    351–53
attachment styles, 119–20
    dating, 98–99
    sexual relationships, 255
attachment theory, love and,
    119–20
attraction
    mate selection and, 123
    personality and social factors, 89
    physical attractiveness, 88–89, 123
    standards of, 89
    unconscious influences, 89
authoritative parenting, 358,
    359, 471
autonomy, 156–57, 343, 344, 353
avoidance of conflict, 393–94

bacterial vaginitis/vaginosis, 279
bag of water (amniotic sac),
    330, 331
bargaining, as power process,
    233–34
barrier methods, of contraception, 293
    cervical cap, 295
    condoms, 294
    contraceptive sponge, 295
    diaphragm, 295
basal body temperature contraceptive
    method, 298
Being-love (B-love), 115–16
Being-needs (B-needs), 115–16
bilateral descent, 9
Bing, Elisabeth, 329
binuclear family, 6, 7
biological theories of gender, 47
birth control. *See* contraception
birthing rooms, 328

birthrate
    fertility rate, 12, 12f, 13
    number of children per family by
      race, 13f
    unmarried women, 80
Black Americans. *See* African
    Americans
blame, as counterproductive coping
    strategy, 73
blended family, 5, 20, 160. *See also*
    stepfamilies
B-love. *See* Being-love
B-needs. *See* Being-needs
body dissatisfaction, 52, 89
body image
    attractiveness standards, 89
    ethnicity and, 55
    gender roles and, 51–53, 55
    media and, 42, 51, 52, 89
body language, 238, 239
bonding, 330–33
boomerang kids, 182
borderline personality disorder
    (BPD), 352–53
botho, 345
boundary maintenance, in
    remarriage, 460
BPD. *See* borderline personality
    disorder
brains, male and female differences, 47
breaking up, of relationship, 98, 99,
    101–5, 173
    cascade model for, 103
    exchange theory on, 102–3
    sequential process of, 103
breech birth, 328, 329
Bronfenbrenner, Uri, 356
budget, 213–14, 214f
Bureau of Economic Analysis, 213
Bureau of Justice Statistics, 99, 100
Bureau of Labor Statistics, 208

calendar method contraceptive
    method, 297–99, 299f
caregiving/caregivers, 180–81,
    380–81
cascade model for breaking up, 103
castration, 296
casual sex, 92, 113, 255, 272
catharsis, 394–95
Catholic Church, 129, 138
Centers for Disease Control and
    Prevention (CDC), 277
cervical cap contraceptive
    method, 295

cervical mucus contraceptive
    method, 298–99
cesarean section, 330
change-of-life period, 264
child abuse, 413
    corporal punishment, 345,
      359–61, 409
    definition, 409
    detecting, 415–16
    effects of, 414–15
    emotional abuse, 414
    neglect and, 414
    physical abuse, 414
    policy on, 419
    sexual abuse, 414, 416
    treatment, 415
Child and Youth Health, 76
childbirth
    cesarean section, 330
    delivery options, 328
    labor and delivery, 329–30
    Lamaze method of, 329
    postpartum period, 330–35
    prepared, 328–29
    return to work after, 333, 335
    sexual relations after, 335
child care
    by fathers, 201
    gender roles, 58–60
    by grandparents, 355, 379–80
    quality of, 355–56
    responsibilities of, 159
    for single parents, 81
    types of, 355, 355f
    by working parents, 200–203
child custody, 428, 436, 438
    adjustments with divorce, 440–41,
      444–45
    joint and sole legal custody, 445
    stepfamilies and, 466–69
child-free marriage choice, 311
child neglect, 414
children
    attachment to parents, 351–53
    behavioral problems, 471–72
    child-centered family, 9, 173
    cognitive and intellectual growth,
      349–50, 351
    conflict effects on, 389–90
    cost of raising, 207, 210f, 287
    differences in, 343–44, 347–48
    divorce and, 428, 447–49
    emotional needs, 350–55
    family structure and, 16
    father absence effect on, 82

children (*continued*)
grandparents and, 377–80
identification with parents, 344, 367, 368, 369
language development and education, 350
not living with married biological parents, 16
per family by race, 13f
poverty and, 215–16
power sources of, 231
reasons for having, 308
self-esteem building in, 345, 351–52, 354
social competence development in, 356, 359
socialization of, 27, 356, 357
special needs, 342, 348
in stepfamilies, 466, 469–72
stress and, 348–49
Children's Defense Fund, 215, 217
child support, 16, 438, 441, 442, 445–47, 451
Child Welfare Service, 419
Chinese Americans
cultural conflict and acculturation, 346
familism, 179
Chinese culture
adulthood markers, 370
familism, 179
preference for male children, 304
wedding ceremonies, 138
chlamydia, 271
Civil Rights Act, Title VII of, 209–10
civil union, 17, 173
clarity, in communication, 243
climacteric, 262–64
clonazepam. *See* Klonapin
closeness, in dating relationship, 97–99
Coalition of Marriage, Family, and Couples Education, 162
cocaine, 270
codependency, 406
coercive power, 231–32
cognition, 349–50, 351
cognitive developmental theory, 45
cohabitation, 11, 16f, 136
child-rearing and, 15–16
as family structure, 6, 7, 14–16
marriage and, 14–16, 70–71, 131–33
patterns of, 131–33
statistics on, 14–15, 15f
utilitarian arrangement, 132

cohabiting family, 6, 7, 14–16
coitus interruptus, 299–300
collectivistic care of elderly, 181
College Board, 207
combination pill oral contraceptive, 289
commitment
acceptance therapy, 243
of cohabitating couples, 15
constraint, 155
dating and, 91
love and, 118, 118f, 119, 259–60
marital success and, 154–56
as strong family quality, 32
common-law marriage, 135–36
common residence, in family, 25
communication
barriers to, 239–41, 240t
clarity in, 243
definition, 238, 239
gender differences, 240–41, 240t
improving skills, 241–44
language development in children, 350
marital satisfaction, 232, 237–44
marital success and, 151–52
power and, 230
self-disclosure in, 242–43
sexual relationships and, 260, 261
in stepfamilies, 457, 458, 462, 471, 473
as strong family quality, 32, 261
technology and, 239
verbal and nonverbal, 238–39
companionate love, 112, 113, 116, 119
companionship, 7–8
dating and, 92–93
of elderly, 185
marital success and, 152–54
compatibility, 125
individual traits and behavior for, 129
marital success and, 117–19
role concepts and, 130–31
components of love, 111, 113, 117–19
comprehensive sex education, 84
conciliation counseling, 434, 435
condoms, 269, 294–95
confidants, of never-married adults, 83
conflict
avoidance of, 393–94
children and, 389–90
constructive and destructive, 395
dealing with, 393–97, 397f

with in-laws, 374–75
interparent, 389–90
interpersonal sources of, 391–92
situational or environmental sources of, 389, 392–93
sources, 390–93
conflict resolution, 32, 232, 341, 395, 410, 444
conflict theory, 30, 31
consanguinity, 135
conscientiousness, love and, 119
conscious love, 112, 113
consensus, for compatibility, 129
constraint commitment, 155
constructed ties, 82
constructive arguments, 243–44, 395
consumerism, 344
Consumer Price Index (CPI), 206–7, 207t
consummate love, 119
contraception. *See also specific methods*
abstinence, 287–88
barrier methods, 293–95
calendar/rhythm methods, 297–99, 299f
ECP, 289–90
effectiveness ratings, 298t
hormonal control, 288–92
IUD, 293–94
method choice, 300–301, 300t
oral, 289–92
spermicide, 293
STDs and, 291
sterilization, 295–97
contraceptive patch, 292, 293
contraceptive sponge, 295
control, need for, 233
coparenting, 442, 473–74, 475
coping
with addiction, 406–8
with anger, 442–43
attachment related to, 352–53
attachment styles and sexual relationships, 255
with depression, 59
with economic distress, 404–5
humor as skill for, 133, 233, 465
importance of, 28
with infertility, 305
irrational appraisals replaced by rational appraisals, 175
meaning-making, 399
with need to control, 233
with own jealousy, 98
with parenting, 334
reframing, 376

with stress, 157–58
as strong family quality, 32
time pressure, 200
coresidence by parents and adult
children, 369, 376, 377
corporal punishment, 345,
359–61, 409
counseling
conciliation, 434, 435
marriage, 433–34, 435
premarital, 126, 137, 434
pre-remarriage, 459
counterproductive coping strategies, 73
couple attractiveness, 88–89
couple violence, 388, 409–11, 411t
courtship, 90, 458
covenant marriage, 164
CPI. See Consumer Price Index
credit card debt, 208, 211, 213
crises, family
addictions, 264–65, 405–8
death and grief, 417–18
definition, 397
economic distress, 403–5
infidelity, 96–97, 252–53, 263, 392,
400–402, 429
stages of family adjustment to,
397–99, 397f
violence and abuse, 359–61,
408–17, 419
crisis overload, 399
cross-sectional study, 33
cultural norms
of power, 228–29
remarriage ambiguous, 461
culture
acculturation, 346–47
communication barriers, 240
dating and, 89–90
definition, 20, 21
divorce and, 437
individualism versus familism, 179
markers of adulthood, 370
parenting and, 344–45
values, 370, 373
custody. See child custody
cybersex, 401

date rape, 100–103, 102f
date rape drugs, 101–2
dates, finding and meeting, 93–95
dating
attachment styles, 98–99
breaking up, 102–5, 173
closeness and distance in, 97–99
couple attractiveness, 88–89

culture and, 89–90
deception in, 96
definition, 89, 91
in early America, 90
finding and meeting dates, 93–95
gender roles in, 93, 95–96
hard-to-get tactic, 234
history of, 90–91
jealousy and, 96–97, 98
in late twentieth century, 91
marriage preparation from, 93
modern, 91–92
online, 94–95
partner selection, 93
problems in, 96–99
reasons for, 92–93
women's equality movement
and, 91, 95
dating services, 93
dating violence, 90–91
adolescents, 99–100
date rape, 101–3, 102f
gender differences, 99
psychological and emotional
effects of, 99–100
school, 100–101, 104
suicide and, 100
daughters, relationship with parents,
369, 370, 371, 372
death and grief, 417–18
debt
compulsive buying, 212
cost of living and, 211
credit abuse, 208, 211, 213
crisis spending, 211
for elderly, 213
student loan, 208–209
Deficiency-love (D-love), 115
Deficiency-needs (D-needs), 115
deliberate choice, as reason for
remaining single, 72
democratic family, 8–9
dependent love, 114–16, 117
Depo-Provera, 291
depression
coping with, 59
gender differences, 60, 69
marriage and, 60, 157
in parents, 371
postpartum, 333, 334, 335
desire, sexual, 257, 258
destructive arguments, 395
developmental process theories,
of mate selection, 122–26
developmental tasks, of elderly,
182–86

development theory, of family, 26–28
diaphragm contraceptive method, 295
discipline
corporal punishment, 345,
359–61, 409
definition, 356, 357
principles of, 357–58
stress of, 358
styles of, 359
discrimination
gays and lesbians, 173
by marital status, 79
dispositional optimism, 163
distance, in dating relationships,
97–99
divorce. See also marriage
adjustment to, 437, 449–50
adolescents and, 447, 449–50
alternatives to, 433–36
causes of, 429–30
child custody, 440–41, 444–45
children's reactions to, 447–49
child support, 16, 438, 441, 442,
445–47, 451
cohabitation and, 15, 133
cultural perspectives, 437
decision, 431–33
disaffection, 430–31
emotional trauma, 438–39
exchange theory and, 431–32
ex-spouse, relationship with,
442, 464
family life cycle and, 171, 172f, 187
financial issues, 441
geographic area, 426
grandparents role after, 379, 383
intergenerational transmission of,
426–28
kinship interaction, 442–43
in late adulthood, 187
loneliness after, 439–40
mediation and dispute resolution,
436–38
no-fault, 436–38
parental, 187, 426–28
parenting after, 428, 447, 449
personal experiences with,
420, 433
population of, 68f
poverty and, 426, 427f, 441, 451
presence of children and, 428
probability by social and
demographic factors,
424–29, 426f
rates, 19, 19f, 424
redivorce rates, 19

divorce (*continued*)
    remarriage and, 424, 439, 456–58
    single-mother family and, 451
    societal attitudes toward, 439
    spouses' perception of, 429–30
    three-factor theory of marital
      cohesion, 431–32
    visitation rights, 438, 440, 442,
      447, 466
    women and, 426, 428, 430, 438,
      439, 441
D-love. *See* Deficiency-love
D-needs. *See* Deficiency-needs
Doe v. Bolton, 301
domestic partnerships, 17, 173
dopamine, 112, 113
double-bind communication, 239
drugs. *See also* addiction
    as counterproductive coping
      strategy, 73
    date rape, 101–2
    sex and, 269–70
    use during pregnancy, 336
dual-career family, 205–6
dual-earner family, 196–97, 360
    family time in, 199
    positive benefits of, 198–99
    scaling back by, 202
durability, marital success and, 146
dyspareunia, 267

earned income tax credit (EITC), 221
eating, as counterproductive coping
    strategy, 73
e-cigarettes, during pregnancy, 322
economic cooperation, in family,
    25, 27
economic distress
    coping with, 404–5
    effects on individuals and family
      relationships, 403–5
    types of, 403
economic hardship, of singles, 74
ECPs. *See* emergency contraceptive
    pills
Ecstasy (MDMA), 101, 270
ectopic pregnancy, 324, 325
education, 84, 230
    equality in, 44, 53
    gender development influences
      from, 44
    median earnings by, 210*f*
    parents' influence on children's
      goals in, 350
    poverty influence on, 216–17
    premarital, 134, 136–37

educational homogamy, 126–27
educational level, mate selection
    and, 126–27
egalitarian family, 9
egalitarian marriage, 57
ego ideal, 89, 111
ego resiliency (ER), 180, 181
EITC. *See* earned income tax credit
elder abuse, 416–17
elderly
    care of, 180–81, 190, 371–73
    contributions to younger
      generations, 369
    debt for, 213
    developmental tasks of, 182–86
    gender roles of, 184
    loneliness of, 188–89
    marital satisfaction and, 183–85
    marital status, by age and gender,
      186, 186*t*
    sexuality and, 150, 261–64
embryos
    development, 326–27, 326*f*, 327*f*
    policy issues, 312–13
embryo transfer, 306, 307
emergency contraceptive pills
    (ECPs), 289–90
emotion, romantic love and, 111, 112
emotional abuse, 414
emotional infidelity, 96
emotional need
    of children, 350–55
    as infidelity reason, 400–401
emotional trauma, of divorce,
    438–39
emotional vulnerability, 255–56
empathy, 160, 242
employment
    gender and, 43, 49
    instability, 403
    marital status and, 79
    maternal, 204
    uncertainty, 403
endogamy, 124, 125
endorphins, 112, 113
engagement, 138
Equal Pay Act, 209–10
equity theory, 30, 31, 122
ER. *See* ego resiliency
erectile disorder, 267–69
Erikson, Erik, 351
erotic love, 113–14, 117
Essure contraceptive method, 297
ethnic identity, 20
    acculturation and, 22–23
ethnicity. *See* race and ethnicity

evolutionary theories of gender,
    46–47
exchange theory
    description, 30, 31
    divorce and, 431–32
    mate selection, 122
    relationship breakup, 102–3
exogamy, 125
expert power, 230, 231
expressive role, of family, 7
extended family, 5. *See also* in-laws
    and grandparents
extradyadic dating and sexual
    activity, 96, 97
extramarital affairs, 252–53, 263,
    392, 400–402, 429

Facilitating Open Couple
    Communication,
    Understanding, and Study
    (FOCCUS), 137
Fair Market Rent, 217–18
families, 311
    at-risk, 360
    blended, 5, 20, 460
    changes in philosophy and
      emphasis, 6–9
    child-centered, 9, 173
    cohabitating, 6, 7, 14–16
    conflict-resolution skills, 32, 232,
      341, 395, 410, 444
    conflict theory, 30, 31
    debt and, 208, 211–13
    definitions of, 4–5, 288
    dual-career, 205–6
    dual-earner, 196–99, 202, 360
    equity theory, 30, 31, 122
    ethnic and cultural diversity of,
      20–25
    exchange theory, 30, 31, 102–3,
      122, 431–32
    expressive role of, 7
    family development theory, 27–28
    family-friendly policies, 360
    forms of, 5–6
    gay and lesbian, 4, 6, 7, 16–17, 173
    gender roles in, 56–60
    happiness and wealth, 354
    identity development, 61
    from institution to
      companionship, 7–8
    interdependence between
      generations, 368–69
    intergenerational stake, 344, 345
    International Family Strengths
      Model, 28, 31–32

interparent conflict, 389–90
life expectancy increase, impact of, 18–19
matriarchal, 6, 7
nuclear, 5, 25–26
parent-child relationships, 342–47, 428–29
from patriarchal to democratic, 8–9
single-parent, 14, 16, 23–24, 71
size, 11–13, 13f
social learning theory, 30, 31
strengths of Russian, 97
strong, qualities of, 32–33, 35, 81, 152, 261, 288, 444
structural-functional theory, 25
study of, 32–33, 35
symbolic interaction theory, 28–29
systems theory, 29, 428
time together, 32, 81, 199–200
values, 343
working wives and mothers, 13
familism, 23, 179
Family and Medical Leave Act (FMLA), 202, 203
family background, mate selection and, 126–29
family boundary, 460–61, 466
family business, 377
family crises, 397–408, 397f
family development theory, 27–28
family-friendly policies, 360
family life cycle
    definition, 171
    divorce and, 171, 172f, 187
    early marriage adjustments, 174–77, 177t
    gay and lesbian families, 172–74
    intact family, 170f, 171
    late adulthood, 182–88
    love attitudes and, 120–21
    middle adulthood, 180–82
    parent-adult child relationships, 187–88
    parenthood adjustments, 177–78, 332–33
    postparental years, 181–82
    widowhood, 68, 188–89, 189t, 259, 456
family-of-origin, 5, 161, 227, 368
family of procreation, 5
family planning, 287–88. See also contraception
family relationships
    economic distress effect on, 403–5
    remarriage and, 464–66

family reunion, 375
family theories, 25–31
family violence
    child abuse, 359–61, 408–17, 419
    control chart, 414f
    definition, 408, 409
    elder abuse, 416–17
    factors related to, 410–11
    IT, 409, 410, 411
    SCV, 409–10, 411t
    spouse abuse, 388, 409–12
FAS. See fetal alcohol syndrome
FASDs. See fetal alcohol syndrome disorders
fatherhood
    family life cycle and, 178–79
    timing of, 287
fathers
    absence of, 82
    adolescent, 347
    child care, 201
    divorced, 440, 445, 450
    incest by, 416, 417
    non-father-friendly workplace, 440–41
    single, 80, 83
    stepfathers, 461, 468, 469, 471, 474
FDA. See Food and Drug Administration
fear-breeds-passion principle, 112
federal judges power, 245
feedback, 241, 243
feeding the weeds, 73
female condoms, 294–95
female orgasmic disorder, 266–67
female sterilization, 296–97
femininity
    cultural concepts of, 41
    race and, 54
    social expectations of, 41
    traits of, 48–49
feminism, 8
    marital delay and, 71–72
    parenting practices and, 343
feminist movement, dating and, 91, 95
feminist theory, 30–31
feminization of poverty, 218, 220
fertility awareness, 297–300
fertility rate, 12, 12f, 13
fetal alcohol syndrome (FAS), 321–22
fetal alcohol syndrome disorders (FASDs), 321
fetal period, of development, 327
fictive kinship, 378

field of eligibles, in mate selection, 122
filtering process, of mate selection, 125–26, 125f
financial issues. See also poverty
    budget, 213–14, 214f
    children expenses, 207, 210f, 287
    CPI and, 206–7, 207t
    divorce and, 441
    economic cooperation in families, 25, 27
    economic distress as a crisis, 403–5
    gas and residential heating oil, 209
    general debt, 208, 211–13
    health care costs, 207–8
    housing, 207
    management of finances, 213–14
    remarriage, 462, 463–64
    stagnant or declining incomes, 206
    student loan debt, 208–9
    unemployment, 208, 403
    widowhood, 189
flextime, 201, 202
FMLA. See Family and Medical Leave Act
FOCCUS. See Facilitating Open Couple Communication, Understanding, and Study
Food and Drug Administration (FDA), 275, 292
foreign adoption, 309
forgiveness, 159, 442, 444
foster care, 309–10, 419
foster parents, grandparents as, 381
The Fountain of Age (Friedan), 189
Four Horsemen of the Apocalypse, in unhappy marriages, 148
Frankl, Viktor, 399
Freud, Sigmund, 113, 114
friendship
    of elderly, 185
    in marriage, 153–54
    of never-married adults, 82–83
friendship love, 111, 116, 117
friends with benefits, 78
Fromm, Erich, 250
    altruistic love view, 117
fungal vaginitis/candidiasis, 279

gamete intrafallopian transfer (GIFT), 306
gamma-hydroxybutyric acid (GHB), 101
gaslighting, 236, 237

gays and lesbians
  civil unions and domestic
      partnerships, 17, 173
  discrimination, 173
  families, 4, 6, 7, 16–17, 173
  family life cycle, 172–74
  marriage, 16–17
  parenting, 17, 34
  parenting by adoption, 34, 173
  sexual behavior, 77–78
gender
  boundaries of, 50
  definition, 31, 40, 41
  environmental influences on,
      41–44
  median earnings by, 210f
  norms, power and, 229
  sex distinguished from, 40–41
  as social construct, 50
  workplace inequality, 56, 96
gender barriers, in communication,
      240–41, 240t
gender constancy, 45
gender differences, 162, 185
  in communication patterns,
      240–41, 240t
  in dating violence, 99
  depression and, 60, 69
  in sexual response, 252, 258–59
gender dysphoria, 40
gender identity
  definition, 40, 41
  development of, 47, 55
  dissatisfaction with, 51, 52
  social context and, 61
  theories of, 44–47
gender-role congruence, 57
gender roles
  androgyny, 60–61
  body image and, 51–53, 55
  class and, 54–56
  dating and, 93, 95–96
  definition, 40, 41
  in family, 56–60
  family authority, 186
  female, 41, 48–49
  housework and, 58–60, 184
  in marriage, 57, 130–31, 159
  masculine, 40–41, 56
  mate selection and, 130–31
  media and, 43–44
  parental identification and
      modeling, 41–42
  power and, 229
  race and, 19, 54–56

at retirement, 184
  role ambiguity, 56, 57
  role strain, 56, 57, 80–81
  school influences, 44
  societal expectations, 41
  theories of, 44–47
gender schema theory, 45–46
gender selection, abortion and, 304
gender stereotypes
  definition, 48
  in employment, 43
  femininity, 48–49
  masculinity, 48
  media and, 43
  onset of, 47, 55
  problems, 49, 51
gender wage gap, 209–11
genetic theories of gender, 47
geographic area, divorce and, 426
germinal period, of fetal
      development, 327
getting together, 91
GHB. See gamma-hydroxybutyric
      acid
GIFT. See gamete intrafallopian
      transfer
Global Study of Sexual Attitudes
      and Behaviors, 253
gonorrhea, 271–72
grandparents, 377
  adolescents and, 381–82
  child care by, 355, 379–80
  as foster parents, 381
  grandchildren and, 379–80
  modern, 378–79
  parenting by, 17–18, 18f, 380–81
  remarriage and, 379
  rights of, 383
  role after divorce, 379, 383
gray divorce, 187
grief, 417–18
guardianship, 381
Guttmacher Institute, on contraception
      use, 300–301, 300t

happiness
  family material wealth, 354
  marital, 147–51
  practices associated with, 123
hard-to-get tactic, in dating, 234
HCG. See human chorionic
      gonadotropin
health. See also mental health
  life satisfaction and, 180
  during pregnancy, 321

sexual behavior measure, 78–79
  of singles, 74–75
  work stress and, 197
health care
  costs of, 207–8
  nationalized/universal, 190–91
Health Care and Education
      Reconciliation Act (Obama
      Student Loan Forgiveness
      Program), 209
Hefner, Hugh, 250
hepatitis, 276–77
heroin, 270
herpes, 275–76, 276
heterogamy, 123–24, 125, 126, 128
Hispanics. See also Mexican
      Americans
  body image, 55
  child care arrangements, 355, 355f
  collectivistic family style, 181
  divorce rate, 19, 426f, 446
  elder care, 373
  fertility rate, 12
  foster care, 309
  gender roles, 19, 54
  machismo, 21, 54
  marital status, 68, 69f
  median income, 206t, 216
  never-married, 69
  number of children, 13f
  percentage of population,
      20, 20f, 21
  poverty, 189, 214
  prenatal care, 320
  remarriage by, 19, 456
  single-parent family, 14, 23
HIV. See human immunodeficiency
      virus
home birth, 328
homelessness, 212, 217–18
homogamy, 123–24, 125
  educational, 126–27
  religious, 128
honesty
  marital success and, 160
  in relationships, 96
hooking up, 92, 93
hormonal control contraception
  combination pills, 289
  contraceptive patch, 292
  ECPs, 288–89
  implants, 291
  IUS, 292
  mini-pill, 289
  oral contraceptives, 288

progestin injection, 291
vaginal ring, 291–92
hormone replacement therapy (HRT), 262–64
household labor, 58, 158–59, 201, 203
housework
gender roles and, 58–60, 184
parent-adult child coresidence and, 377
shared responsibility of, 58, 158–59, 201, 203
housing, cost of, 207
HPV. *See* human papillomavirus
HRT. *See* hormone replacement therapy
human chorionic gonadotropin (HCG), 318–19
human immunodeficiency virus (HIV), 277–78
human papillomavirus (HPV), 274–75, 291
humor, as coping skill, 133, 233, 465
hurried child syndrome, 348
hypergamous and hypogamous unions, 127
hypoactive sexual desire, 265–66

ideal mate theory, 121
identity, child's development of, 354–55
imaging, 96, 97
immigrant parents, 344, 346, 390
implant contraception, 291
implementation power, 232, 233
incest, 416, 417
income
distribution of selected household types, 219f
gender wage gap, 209–11
by race and Hispanic origin, 206t, 216
stagnant or declining, 206
independent adoption, 308
individualism *versus* familism, 179
individualistic care of elderly, 180–81
individual traits and behavior, for compatibility, 129
infertility
causes of, 254, 303–5
coping with, 305
defined, 303
experience of, 305
subjective well-being and, 305
treatment of, 305–6, 312

infidelity
in dating relationship, 96–97
emotional, 96
marital, 252–53, 263, 392, 400–402, 429
reasons for, 400–402
informational power, 231
in-laws
living with, 375–77
roots of conflict, 374–75
successful relationships, 373–74
insanity, marriage and, 135
insecurity, 352
instrumental role, of family, 7
intact family, 170f, 171
intellectual growth, of children, 349–50
intelligence, mate selection and, 126–27
interdependence, between generations, 368–69
interethnic marriages, 127–28, 128f
interfaith marriages, 128–29
intergenerational relationships, 369–70
intergenerational stake, 344, 345
intergenerational transmission, of divorce, 426–28
International Family Strengths Model, 28, 31–32
Internet dating, 94–95
Internet pornography, 280
interpersonal sources of conflict, 391–92
interracial marriage, 127–28, 128f
intimacy
as love component, 118, 119
sex and, 150–51, 259
sexual relationships and, 250
intimate terrorism (IT), 409, 410, 411
intrauterine device (IUD), 293–94
intrauterine insemination (IUI), 306
intrauterine system (IUS), 292, 293
in vitro fertilization (IVF), 306
involuntary stable (permanent) singles, 69, 69t, 70, 71
involuntary temporary singles, 69, 69t, 70, 71
irrational appraisals replaced by rational appraisals, 175
Islamic culture, 150
divorce and, 437
veils, 228
Israeli stepfamilies, 470
IT. *See* intimate terrorism

IUD. *See* intrauterine device
IUI. *See* intrauterine insemination
IUS. *See* intrauterine system
IVF. *See* in vitro fertilization

jealousy
in dating relationship, 96–97, 98
in early marriage years, 177t
power tactic, 235
joint legal custody, 445
Judaism, 138

Kaplan sexual response model, 257–58
Karmel, Marjorie, 329
ketamine, 101
kinship
divorce and, 442–43
fictive, 378
Klonapin (clonazepam), 101

labor, in childbirth, 329–30
Lamaze International, 329
Lamaze method, of childbirth, 329
language development, in children, 350
laparoscopy, 297
late adulthood
adjustments during, 182–88
developmental tasks, 182–86
divorce, 187
marital satisfaction, 186–87
parent-adult child relationships, 187–88
Latinos. *See* Hispanics
law, marriage and, 134–36
legitimate power, 226–27
levels of marital conflict model (LMCM), 396–97, 396t
life expectancy, 18–19
gray divorce and, 187
life satisfaction, 74, 180
liking, loving and, 116
limerence, 111
listening, 243, 244
living alone, 76, 77f
living arrangements, of singles, 77f
with parents, 76, 76t, 375–77
LMCM. *See* levels of marital conflict model
loneliness
after divorce, 439–40
of elderly, 188–89
of singles, 74
longitudinal study, 33

love. *See also* romantic love
altruistic, 111, 116–17
attachment and, 119–20
B-love, 115–16
change over time, 120–21
commitment, 118, 118f, 119,
259–60
companionate, 112, 113, 116, 119
components of, 111, 113, 117–19
conscious, 112, 113
consummate, 119
definition, 111
dependent, 114–16, 117
D-love, 115–16
erotic, 113–14, 117
friendship, 111, 116, 117
liking and, 116
narcissistic, 111
as need, 115–16, 115f, 121–22
sex confused with, 113–14,
164–65, 254
triangle of, 118f
love object, 113, 114

machismo, 21, 54
male condom, 294
male orgasmic disorder, 266–67
manipulation, sex and, 234–37, 256
Man's Search for Meaning (Frankl), 399
marijuana, 270
marital adjustment
definition, 174, 175
in early marriage, 174–77, 177t
during late adulthood, 182–88
in middle adulthood, 179–82
to parenthood, 177–80
tasks, 174–75, 176t
women's employment and, 204
marital delay, 70–72
marital disaffection process, 430–31
marital power patterns, 231–32
marital readiness, 134
marital rituals, 156
marital satisfaction
aging and, 183–85
communication and, 232, 237–44
coresidence with adult
children, 377
family life cycle and, 171–72,
186–87
happiness, 147–51
household labor division, 58
in late adulthood, 186–87
marital disaffection process,
430–31

marital success and, 157
newlywed years as predictor of, 163
parenting practices and, 320, 334
positive affect and, 428, 429
in remarriage, 457
sex and, 149–51
marital status
employment and income, effect
on, 79
of older Americans, by age and
gender, 186, 186t
of population 15 years and older, 11f
of population over 18, 68, 68f, 69f
by race and ethnicity, 68, 69f, 71
well-being and, 69, 74–75, 163
marital success
age at first marriage, 425
approximation of ideals, 146–47
characteristics of, 151–62
compatibility, 117–19
consensus, 129
coping with stress and, 157–58
criteria for evaluating, 146–47
durability and, 146
fulfillment of needs, 147
habits as obstacle to, 130–31
in-laws and, 373–74
personality traits, 123, 126, 129
predictors of, 162–63
religion and, 130, 154, 425
satisfaction and, 147
socioeconomic status and, 425–26
spirituality and, 130, 154, 425
time together and, 161, 241–42
values and, 154
marital success characteristics
adaptability, flexibility and
tolerance, 160–62
admiration and respect, 152
affection, 134, 156–57
commitment, 154–56
communication, 151–52
companionship, 152–54
coping with crises and stress,
157–58
empathy and sensitivity, 160
honesty, trust and fidelity, 160
responsibility, 158–59
spirituality and values, 154
unselfishness, 159–60
marital violence, 388, 409–11
marriage, 111–12. *See also* divorce;
weddings
adjustments in middle adulthood,
179–82

age at first, 10–11, 11f, 425
age differences, 129–30
arranged, 94
child-free, 311
circumstances for remaining
single, 72
cohabitation and, 14–16, 70–71,
131–33
common-law, 135–36
covenant, 164
dating as preparation for, 93
definition of, 9–10
depression and, 60, 157
family life cycle, 170f, 171–89,
172f, 177t, 332–33
fear of, 72
friendship in, 153–54
gays and lesbians, 16–17
gender roles in, 57, 130–31, 159
happiness, 147–51
health and, 74–75
hypergamous and hypogamous
union, 127
incentives, 140
insanity and, 135
interethnic, 127–28, 128f
interfaith, 128–29
interracial, 127–28, 128f
lack of opportunity for, 72
legal issues, 134–36
life expectancy and, 18–19
life satisfaction and, 74
mental health and, 60, 74,
75, 135
personal happiness and, 170
preparation for, 136–37
quality, premarital predictors of,
161–62
readiness, 134
same-sex, 10, 16, 17, 173
sex outside of marriage,
73–74, 84
success in, 146 – 47
transition to, 133–37
trial, 132
void and voidable, 136, 137
working women, 9, 13, 58, 198,
204, 228, 229
marriage counseling, 433–34, 435
marriage enrichment program, 434
marriage license, 135, 434
marriage mandate, 49, 56
marriage rates, 10, 10f
marriage reasons, race and ethnicity,
134, 134f

marriage success. *See* martial success and marital success characteristics

Married Women's Property Act, 8–9, *9*

martyr, playing, 235

masculinity
cultural concepts of, 41
definition, 11
gender roles, 40–41, 56
social expectations of, 41
traits of, 48

Maslow, Abraham, 115

Maslow's theory of love as need, 115–16, 115*f*, 121–22

Masters and Johnson sexual response model, 256–57

maternity leave, 202, 333, 360

mate selection
attraction and, 123
compatibility, 124
desired qualities in partner, 124–25, 124*f*
educational level and, 126–27
endogamy and exogamy, 124
family background factors in, 126–29
field of eligibles, 122
filtering process, 125–26, 125*f*
gender roles and, 130–31
homogamy and heterogamy, 123–24, 125, 126, 128
personal characteristics and, 129–31
propinquity, 122–23
regretting, 163–65
remarriage and, 458
socioeconomic class and, 126, 133, 146
theories, 121–26

mate selection theories
developmental process, 122–26
exchange, 122
needs, 121–22
psychodynamic, 121

matriarchal family, 6, 7

matrilineal descent, 8, 9

matrilocal residence, 8

MDMA. *See* Ecstasy

meaning-making coping, 399

media
body image and, 42, 51, 52, 89
gender roles and, 43–44
portrayal of women, 42, 51, 52, 89

mediation and dispute resolution, for divorce, 436–38

Medicaid, 215, 219

men, 47, 294, 304. *See also* fathers; masculinity
body image, 52
changing roles of, 56
depression, 60, 69
erectile disorder, 267–69
male climacteric, 262–63
male orgasmic disorder, 266–67
premature ejaculation, 269

menstruation, sex during, 251

mental health
marriage and, 60, 74, 75, 135
pregnancy and, 325–26

me-we pull, 97

Mexican Americans, 54
familism, 179
prenatal care, 320

middle adulthood
adjustments during, 179–82
caretaker role, 180–81
marital adjustments, 180–81
postparental years, 181–82

Mifeprex (abortion pill), 292

minimum wage, 215

mini-pill oral contraceptive, 289

miscarriage, 320, 323–24

Miss America contestants, *88*, 89

MIT Living Wage Calculator, 214*t*

modern
dating, 91–92
grandparents, 378–79

mother-daughter relationships, 369–70, 372

motherhood mandate, 49, 56

mothers. *See also* parenting
adolescent, 379
incest by, 416
single, 79–82, 451
stepmothers, 475
surrogate, 306–7
widowhood and, 369
working, 9, 13, 196–97

multiple partners, for sex, 251, 291

multiracial individuals, 128

Muslim culture. *See* Islamic culture

Naegele's formula, for pregnancy, 318, 319

narcissistic love, 111

NAS. *See* neonatal abstinence syndrome

National Association of Realtors, 207

National Center on Addiction and Substance Abuse, 61

National Center on Child Abuse and Neglect, 416

National Center on Elder Abuse, 416

National Coalition for the Homeless, 217

National Collegiate Athletic Association, 43

National Committee on Pay Equity, 211

National Family Caregiver Support Program, 372

National Health and Social Life Survey, 400

National Health Interview Survey, 89

National Institute of Child Health and Human Development (NICHD), 355

nationalized/universal health care, 190–91

National Low Income Housing Coalition, 218

National Opinion Research Center, 49

National Poverty Center report, 219

National Survey of Families and Households, 187, 376, 377

National Survey of Family Growth, 76

Native Americans
cultural conflict and acculturation, 346
fictive kinship, 378
percentage of population, 20, 20*f*
prenatal care, 320
single-parent family, 24

need
for control, 233
emotional, 350–55, 400–401
Maslow's theory of love as, 115–16, 115*f*, 121–22

needs fulfillment, marital success and, 147

negative affect reciprocity, 147

negative identification, 368, 369

neolocal residence, 9

neonatal abstinence syndrome (NAS), 322

never-married adult, 68*f*, 69, 69*t*, 70*f*, 74, 82–83

newborn
care of, 331
parent-infant bonding, 330–33
rooming-in with, 332, 333

newlywed years, as marital satisfaction predictor, 163

NICHD. *See* National Institute of Child Health and Human Development
Nineteenth Amendment, of Constitution, 8
no-fault divorce, 436–38
noncoital stimulation, 300
noncontingent reinforcement, 152, 153
non-father-friendly workplace, 440–41
nonmarital cohabitation. *See* cohabitation
norepinephrine, 112, 113
nuclear family, 5, 25–26
nutrition, during pregnancy, 321

Obama Student Loan Forgiveness Program. *See* Health Care and Education Reconciliation Act
Older Americans Act, 372
older individuals. *See* elderly
one-parent family. *See* single-parent family
open adoption, 308–9
openness, in relationships, 96
opiates, 270
opportunity lack, as reason for remaining single, 72
oral contraceptives, 289, 292
    advantages of, 290
    disadvantages of, 290–91
orchestration power, 232, 233
orgasm, 112, 259, 296, 300, 305
orgasmic disorder, 266–67
outercourse. *See* noncoital stimulation
oxytocin, 113, 254

parent-adult child relationships, 181–82, 187–88, 369, 371
parental divorce, 187, 426–28
parental identification and modeling for children, 344, 367, 368, 369
    of gender roles, 41–42
parent-child relationships, 342–47, 428–29
parenthood
    adjustments to, 177–80, 332–33
    decision to avoid, 311
    delayed, 310–11
    in family life cycle, 177–78, 332–33
    stress and, 177–78, 348–49
    timing of, 287

parent image theory, 121
parenting
    after divorce, 428, 447, 449
    authoritative, 358, 359, 471
    child care choices, 355–56, 355f
    cognitive and intellectual growth, fostering, 349–50, 351
    coparenting, 442, 473–74, 475
    coresidence with adult children, 369, 376, 377
    cultural differences, 344–45
    differences between parents, 342–43
    differences in children, 343–44, 347–48
    discipline, 356–61, 409
    economic pressure and, 403–5
    emotional needs, meeting child's, 350–55
    gay and lesbian, 17, 34
    gender role learning and, 41–42
    by grandparents, 17–18, 18f, 379–81
    interparent conflict, 389–90
    life circumstances and, 345, 347
    marital satisfaction and, 320, 334
    parent-child differences, 343–44
    philosophies of, 342–48
    socialization, 356, 357
    special needs children, 342, 348
    stress and children, 348–49
    in stepfamilies, 458, 466–68, 470, 471
    styles, 343, 352, 359
    value differences, 343
parenting alliance, 343
parenting coalition, 473–74, 475
partner choice, parental disapproval of, 366–67
passion
    as love component, 118, 119
    romantic love and, 111, 112
patriarchal family, 6, 7, 8–9
patrilineal descent, 8, 9
patrilocal residence, 8, 9
pediculosis, 279
pelvic inflammatory disease (PID), 271
Perfect Madness (Warner), 203
personal ads, 94–95
personal dedication, 155
personality
    attractiveness and, 89
    marital success, 123, 126, 129
    power and, 230

personality development, dating and, 93
Personal Responsibility, Work, and Family Promotion Act, 140, 190
personal sources, of conflict, 391
persuasion, 234
Pew Research Center, 124, 125, 134
    on sandwich generation, 181
physical abuse, 414
physical attractiveness, 88–89, 123
physical sources of conflict, 391
PID. *See* pelvic inflammatory disease
PIH. *See* pregnancy-induced hypertension
placebo, 289
placental abruption. *See* abruptio placentae
placenta previa, 324, 325
Playboy magazine, 89, 250
policy
    child abuse, 419
    covenant marriage, 164
    divorce and single-mother family, 451
    EITC, 221
    on elder care, 190
    embryos, 312–13
    family-friendly, 360
    family medical leave, 202, 203
    federal judges power, 245
    gay and lesbian parenting and adoption, 34
    grandparents rights, 383
    Internet pornography, 280
    marriage incentives, 140
    nationalized/universal health care, 190–91
    sex outside of marriage, 84
    stepfamily rights, 476
    substance abuse by pregnant women, 335
    Title IX, 62
polyandrous family, 7
polygamous family, 6, 7, 150
polygynous family, 6, 7, 150
pornography, 280
positive identification, 368, 369
positive signs, of pregnancy, 318, 319
postparental years, 181–82
postpartum depression, 333, 334, 335
postpartum period
    adjustments, 332–33
    bonding with baby, 330–33
    newborn and, 330–33

population of, 68
reasons for remaining single, 72
sexual behavior, 73–74, 84
social support of, 69, 75, 82–83
voluntary compared to involuntary, 69, 69t, 70, 71
situational couple violence (SCV), 409–10, 411t
situational or environmental sources of conflict, 389, 392–93
SNAP. *See* Supplemental Nutrition Assistance Program
social competence, development in children, 356, 359
social control theory, 227
social exchange theory. *See* exchange theory
social expectations
of femininity and masculinity, 41
power and, 226–27
socialization
of children, 27, 356, 357
dating as means of, 93
definition, 356, 357
social learning theory
description, 30, 31
of gender identity, 44–45
social norms, 356, 357
social roles, 356, 357
social structure/cultural theories of gender, 46, 47
social support, of singles, 69, 75, 82–83
societal expectations, in gender roles, 41
socioeconomic class, mate selection and, 126, 133, 146
socioeconomic status, divorce and, 425–26
sole legal custody, 445
sons, relationship with parents, 369, 371
spankings. *See* corporal punishment
special needs children, 342, 348
speed dating, 95
spermicides, 293
spirituality, marital success and, 130, 154, 425
spiritual well-being, as strong family quality, 32
spontaneous abortion, 301, 310, 323–24
sports, women's opportunities in, 43, 62
spouse abuse, 388, 409–12

SSI. *See* Supplemental Security Income
STDs. *See* sexually transmitted diseases
stepfamilies, 5, 16
adolescents in, 469–70
adoption in, 468, 476
bond development in, 472–73
children in, 466, 469–72
communication in, 457, 458, 462, 471, 473
couple happiness, 467–68
cultural context and, 470
cultural norm ambiguity, 461
developmental turning points, 468–69
legal rights, 476
maternal employment and, 204
parenting in, 458, 466–68, 470, 471
stepsibling relationships, 474–76
turning points, 468–69
stepfathers, 461, 468, 469, 471, 474
stepmothers, 475
stepsibling relationships, 474–76
sterilization, 295–97
steroids, use of, 52
stress
ability to deal with, 157
children and, 348–49
of discipline, 358
dual-career families and, 205
managing, 205
marital success and, 157
parent-adult child coresidence and, 377
parenthood and, 177–78, 348–49
time pressure, 199–200
work-family balance, 197–98
structural-functional theory, 25
structured separation, 434, 435
student loan debt, 208–9
suicide, dating violence and, 100
Supplemental Nutrition Assistance Program (SNAP), 215
Supplemental Security Income (SSI), 219
surrogate mother, 306–7
symbolic interaction theory, 28–29
symptothermal method contraceptive method, 299
syphilis, 273, *274*
systems theory, 29, 428

TANF. *See* Temporary Assistance to Needy Families
technology, communication and, 239
teens. *See* adolescents
television, gender stereotyping and, 43–44
Temporary Assistance to Needy Families (TANF), 215, 218–19
teratogen, 321
testosterone, 258, 263, 264, 266
theory, definition, 25. *See also specific theories*
theory of primary interest and presumed competence, 231
three-factor theory of marital cohesion, 431–32
time pressure, 199–200
time together, as strong family quality, 32, 81, 199–200
Title IX, 62
Title VII, of Civil Rights Act, 209–10
tobacco
as counterproductive coping strategy, 73
during pregnancy, 322
transgendered people, 40, 41
transsexuals, 40, 41
transverse birth, 328, 329
triangle of love, 118*f*
tribes, 366
trichomoniasis, 279
tubal ligation, 297
tubal pregnancy, 325

ultra-Orthodox community, divorce and, 437
ultrasound, 323
umbilical cord, 331
unconditional positive regard, 152, 153
unconscious influences, on attractiveness, 89
underemployment, 403
unemployment, 208, 403
universal health care, 190–91
unplanned pregnancy, 253
unselfishness, marital success and, 159–60
utilitarian arrangement, of cohabitation, 132

vaginal ring, 291–92
vaginal spermicides, 293
vaginismus, 266, 267

vaginitis, 279
validity, 33
values
    culture and, 370, 373
    marital success and, 154
    parenting, 343
vasectomy, 296
vasocongestion, 257
vasopressin, 112, 113
ventilation, 394–95
violence. *See* dating violence; family
    violence
violent resistance, 409
visitation rights, 438, 440, 442,
    447, 466
void and voidable marriage, 136, 137
voluntarily childless family, 5, 311
voluntary stable and temporary
    singles, 69, 69t, 70, 71

Warner, Judith, 203
wealth, happiness and, 354
wealth gap, 220
weddings
    Chinese ceremonies, 138
    cost of, 139
    as religious and civil rite, 138–39
weight issues, media and, 42, 51,
    52, 89
welfare, 218–20
well-being, of singles, 69, 74–75
Whites
    body image, 55
    child care arrangements, 355f
    divorce rate, 426f, 446
    elder care, 373
    fertility rate, 12
    foster care, 309
    gender roles, 55
    life expectancy, 18

marital status, 68, 69f
median income of, 206t
never-married, 69
number of children, 13f
percentage of population,
    20, 20f
poverty, 216
prenatal care, 320
remarriage by, 19, 456
single-parent families, 14
widowhood, 68, 369
    population, 68f, 188
    problems of, 188–89
    remarriage and, 456
    widows to widowers ratio,
        188, 189t
withdrawal contraceptive method,
    299–300
women. *See also* pregnancy
    as abusers, 412
    body image, 52
    brains, 47
    changing roles of, 56
    depression, 60
    divorced, 426, 428, 430, 438,
        439, 441
    female climacteric, 262
    female condoms, 294–95
    gender stereotypes, 41, 48–49
    Islamic, 228
    marital adjustment and
        employment, 204
    maternity leave, 202, 333, 360
    media weight-related messages,
        42, 51, 52, 89
    orgasmic disorder, 266–67
    percentage of births to
        unmarried, 14f
    single, 71–72, 79
    sports opportunities, 43, 62

sterilization, 296–97
    working, 9, 13, 58, 198, 204,
        228, 229
women's equality movement, dating
    and, 91, 95
work
    balancing with family, 197–98
    child care and, 200–203
    dual-career families, 205–06
    dual-earner families, 196–99
    flextime, 201, 202
    gender wage gap, 209–11
    housework and, 158–59, 201
    longer hours of, 197, 199
    marital adjustment, 204
    of mothers, 9, 13, 196–97
work-family spillover, 197
workforce
    marital status discrimination, 79
    retirement from, 183, 184, 185
    women in, 9, 13, 58, 198, 204,
        228, 229
workplace
    family-friendly policies, 360
    gender inequality in, 56, 96
    non-father-friendly, 440–41
World Population Clock, 287

Xanax (alprazolam), 101

young adults, living with parents,
    76, 76t, 375–77. *See also*
    coresidence

ZIFT. *See* zygote intrafallopian
    transfer
Zika virus, 322
zygote, 307, 327
zygote intrafallopian transfer
    (ZIFT), 306